D0780783

In loving memory of my mother,
Margaret Baran—
she gave me life;
and in honor of my wife,
Susan Baran—
she gave that life meaning.

From the Author

Dear Friends,

The media, like sports and politics, are what we talk about, argue over, dissect, and analyze. Those of us who teach media know that these conversations are essential to the functioning of a democratic society. We also know that what moves these conversations from simple chatting and griping to effective public discourse is media education. And regardless of what we might call the course—Introduction to Mass Communication, Introduction to Mass Media, Media and Society, or Media and Culture—media education has been part of the university for more than seven decades. From the outset, the course has fulfilled these goals:

Courtesy of Stanley Baran

- Increasing students' knowledge and understanding of the mass communication process and the mass media industries
- Increasing students' awareness of how they interact with those industries and their content to create meaning
- Helping students become more skilled and knowledgeable consumers of media content and therefore more ethical and confident participants in their worlds

We now call the fulfillment of these goals *media literacy.*

A Cultural Perspective

This text's cultural orientation toward mass communication places a great deal of responsibility on media consumers. In the past, people were considered either victims of media influence or impervious to it. The cultural orientation asserts that audience members are as much a part of the mass communication process as are the media technologies and industries. As important agents in the creation and maintenance of their own culture, audience members have a moral obligation not only to participate in the process of mass communication but also to participate critically as better consumers of mass media.

Enriching Students' Literacy

The focus of this book, from the start, has been on media literacy and culture, and those emphases have shaped its content and its various learning aids and pedagogical features. Every chapter's *Cultural Forum* box poses a critical thinking dilemma based on a current social problem and asks students to work through their solution. The *Using Media to Make a Difference* feature offers chapter-specific examples of how people in and outside the media industries have employed technology to meet important cultural and social needs. And each chapter ends with a *Media Literacy Challenge* that asks students to apply what they've learned to a contemporary media issue. Literacy, in this case media literacy, is about living in, interacting with, and making the most of the world that surrounds us. That belief is the central philosophy of this text.

My Thanks to You

Thank you for teaching mass communication. There are few college courses that will mean more to our students' lives now and after they graduate than this one. Thank you, too, for considering *Introduction to Mass Communication: Media Literacy and Culture* for use in your course. I have poured the last 50 years of my career into this text and what it has to say about mass communication and the world that our interaction with the media produces. Your interest in this text confirms my passion.

—**Stanley J. Baran**

Brief Contents

Contents

PART 2 MEDIA, MEDIA INDUSTRIES, AND MEDIA AUDIENCES 50

PART 3 STRATEGIC COMMUNICATION INDUSTRIES   262

Preface

Introduction to Mass Communication, 12e, focuses on literacy and culture, equipping students with essential skills in today's ever-changing media landscape. Along with the core content, students are supported by a suite of personalized study tools, customizable assessments, new scenario-driven activities, and writing tools in McGraw Hill Connect™.

Instructor's Guide to Connect for *Introduction to Mass Communication: Media Literacy and Culture*

McGraw Hill Connect offers full-semester access to comprehensive, reliable content and learning resources for the Communication course. **Connect's** deep integration with most learning management systems (LMSs), including Blackboard and Desire2Learn (D2L), offers single sign-on and deep gradebook synchronization. Data from Assignment Results reports synchronize directly with many LMSs, allowing scores to flow automatically from Connect into school-specific gradebooks, if required.

When you assign **Connect** you can be confident—and have data to demonstrate—that your students, however diverse, are acquiring the skills, principles, and critical processes that constitute effective communication. This leaves you to focus on your highest course expectations.

Connect offers on-demand, single sign-on access to students—wherever they are and whenever they have time. With a single, one-time registration, students receive access to McGraw Hill's trusted content. **Connect** seamlessly supports all major learning management systems with content, assignments, performance data, and SmartBook, the leading adaptive learning system. With these tools you can quickly make assignments, produce reports, focus discussions, intervene on problem topics, and help at-risk students—as you need to and when you need to.

A PERSONALIZED AND ADAPTIVE LEARNING EXPERIENCE WITH SMARTBOOK 2.0®. SmartBook 2.0 is the leading adaptive reading and study experience designed to change the way students read and master key course concepts. As a student engages with SmartBook 2.0, the program creates a personalized learning path by highlighting the most impactful concepts the student needs to learn at that moment in time.

READER/eBOOK. Alongside SmartBook 2.0, there is also Connect eBook for simple and easy access to reading materials on smartphones and tablets. Students can study on the go without an Internet connection, highlight important sections, take notes, search for materials quickly, and read in class. Offline reading is available by downloading the eBook app on smartphones and tablets, and any notes and highlights created by students will be synced between devices when they reconnect. Unlike SmartBook 2.0, there is no pre-highlighting, practice of key concepts, or reports on usage and performance.

A SUITE OF APPLICATION-BASED ACTIVITIES. New to this edition and positioned at the higher level of Bloom's taxonomy, McGraw Hill's Application-Based Activities are highly interactive, automatically graded, learn-by-doing assignments that provide students with a safe space to apply their knowledge and problem-solving skills. Topics include Media Freedom, Regulation, Ethics, and Media Literacy.

ACCESS TO JUST-IN-TIME GRAMMAR & WRITING REMEDIATION AND ORIGINAL-ITY DETECTOR. McGraw Hill's new Writing Assignment Plus tool delivers a learning experience that improves students' written communication skills and conceptual understanding with every assignment. Instructors can assign, monitor, and provide feedback on writing more efficiently and grade assignments more easily within McGraw Hill Connect.

INFORMED BY THE LATEST RESEARCH. The best insights from today's leading mass communication scholars infuse every lesson and are integrated throughout the text.

FRESH EXAMPLES ANCHORED IN THE REAL WORLD. Every chapter of *Introduction to Mass Communication: Media Literacy and Culture* opens with a vignette exploring media literacy situations in our everyday lives. Dozens of additional examples appear throughout the text. Whether students are reading the text, responding to question probes, or reviewing key concepts in a learning resource, their every instructional moment is rooted in the real world. McGraw Hill Education research shows that high-quality examples reinforce academic theory throughout the course. Relevant examples and practical scenarios—reflecting engagement with multiple forms of mass media—demonstrate how effective communication informs and enhances students' lives and media literacy skills.

BOXED FEATURES. Students must bring media literacy—the ability to critically comprehend and actively use mass media—to the mass communication process. This edition of *Introduction to Mass Communication: Media Literacy and Culture* includes a variety of boxed features to support student learning and enhance media literacy skills.

 Using Media to Make a Difference boxes highlight interesting examples of how media practitioners and audiences use the mass communication process to further important social, political, or cultural causes.

 Cultural Forum boxes highlight media-related cultural issues that are currently debated in the mass media to help students develop their moral reasoning and critical thinking skills.

 Media Literacy Challenge boxes build on ideas from each chapter's "Developing Media Literacy Skills" section and ask students to think critically about media content they encounter in their daily lives and actually use the skills they've learned.

Video Capture Powered by GoReact™

With just a smartphone, tablet, or webcam, students and instructors can capture video of presentations with ease. Video Capture Powered by GoReact, fully integrated in McGraw Hill's Connect platform, doesn't require any extra equipment or complicated training. All it takes is five minutes to set up and start recording! Create your own custom Video Capture assignment, including in-class and online speeches and presentations, self-review, and peer review. With our customizable rubrics, time-coded comments, and visual markers, students will see feedback at exactly the right moment, and in context, to help improve their speaking, presentation skills, and confidence!

- Time-coded feedback via text, video & audio
- Visual markers for short-hand, repetitive comments
- Customizable rubrics

Functionality List

- Asynchronous video
- Synchronous screen capture & video ("Live Event")
- Group assignment/presentation
- Presenter split screen for visual aids or presentation decks
- Customizable rubrics
- Self and peer review
- Time-coded feedback with text, video & audio
- Customizable in-line comment markers
- Rubric placement and comment box next to video for easier grading
- Mobile recording & uploading
- Improved accessibility
- Deep integration with most Learning Management Systems via McGraw Hill's Connect

Instructor Reports

Found in Connect, Instructor Reports allow instructors to quickly monitor learner activity, making it easy to identify which students are struggling and to provide immediate help to ensure performance improvement. The Instructor Reports also highlight the concepts and learning objectives that the class as a whole is having difficulty grasping. This essential information lets you know exactly which areas to target for review during limited class time.

Some key reports include:

Progress Overview report—View student progress for all chapters, including how long students have spent working, which chapters they have used outside of any that were assigned, and individual student progress.

Missed Questions report—Identify specific assessment items, organized by chapter, that are problematic for students.

Most Challenging Learning Objectives report—Identify the specific topic areas that are challenging for your students; these reports are organized by chapter and include specific page references. Use this information to tailor your lecture time and assignments to cover areas that require additional remediation and practice.

Metacognitive Skills report—View statistics showing how knowledgeable your students are about their own comprehension and learning.

Classroom Preparation Tools

Whether before, during, or after class, there is a suite of Baran tools designed to help instructors plan their lessons and to keep students building upon the foundations of the course.

POWERPOINT SLIDES. Accessible PowerPoint presentations for *Introduction to Mass Communication: Media Literacy and Culture* provide chapter highlights that help instructors create focused yet individualized lesson plans.

TEST BANK AND TEST BUILDER. The *Introduction to Mass Communication: Media Literacy and Culture* Test Bank is a treasury of more than 1,000 examination questions based on the most important mass communication concepts explored in the text. New to this edition and available within Connect, Test Builder is a cloud-based tool that enables instructors to format tests that can be printed and administered within a learning management system. Test Builder offers a modern, streamlined interface for easy content configuration that matches course needs without requiring a download. Test Builder enables instructors to:

- Access all test bank content
- Easily pinpoint the most relevant content through robust filtering options
- Manipulate the order of questions or scramble questions and answers
- Pin questions to a specific location within a test
- Determine the preferred treatment of algorithmic questions
- Choose the layout and spacing
- Add instructions and configure default settings

REMOTE PROCTORING. New remote proctoring and browser-locking capabilities are seamlessly integrated within Connect to offer more control over the integrity of online assessments. Instructors can enable security options that restrict browser activity, monitor student behavior, and verify the identity of each student. Instant and detailed reporting gives instructors an at-a-glance view of potential concerns, thereby avoiding personal bias and supporting evidence-based claims.

MEDIA LITERACY WORKSHEETS. Media literacy worksheets provide students with thought-provoking questions and exercises based on the most important concepts addressed in each chapter. Students are encouraged to examine their own experiences with media and form their own opinions.

INSTRUCTOR'S MANUAL. Written by the author, this comprehensive guide to teaching from *Introduction to Mass Communication* contains lecture suggestions and resources for each chapter.

CONTACT OUR CUSTOMER SUPPORT TEAM

McGraw Hill is dedicated to supporting instructors and students. To contact our customer support team, please call us at 800-331-5094 or visit us online at http://mpss.mhhe.com/contact.php

---

Changes to the New Edition: Highlights

The new edition maintains its commitment to enhancing students' critical thinking and media literacy skills. New and updated material in this edition reflects the latest developments in new digital technologies and highlights the most current research in the field.

Chapter 1 Mass Communication, Culture, and Media Literacy: Discussion of anti-Asian discrimination and the increase in media consumption during the pandemic.

Chapter 2 Convergence and the Reshaping of Mass Communication: Investigation of video streaming during the pandemic and the rise of user-generated content; examination of ghost papers and the value of enterprise reporting; discussion of the danger of meme wars.

Chapter 3 Books: Discussion of the popularity of anti-racist books in the wake of social justice protests; coverage of the troubling rise in American illiteracy; introduction of shopfiction (books as sales devices) and bibliotherapy (books as therapeutic devices).

Chapter 4 Newspapers: Discussion of the importance of engagement reporting, newspapers dropping their paywalls for coronavirus coverage, hyperlocal free weeklies, and online e-replica editions of papers' print versions.

Chapter 5 Magazines: Discussion of technologies like Google Lens connecting readers to wider arrays of content. For example during "Say Their Names" reporting and advances in magazines' use of artificial intelligence writing.

Chapter 6 Film: Examination of the importance of women to origins of movie making and a look at challenges to the theatrical window and movie theaters themselves because of the pandemic lockdown.

Chapter 7 Radio, Recording, and Popular Music: New Cultural Forum box on how streaming changes the nature of the music itself. Added discussions of the return of protest music, the popularity of deep catalog albums, and industry use of album equivalents as unit of sales measure.

Chapter 8 Television, Cable, and Mobile Video: Discussion of Peak TV, television's new Golden Age; total viewer impressions as an alternative to traditional ratings; the increase in long-tail viewing; and the rise of virtual multichannel video programming distributors (VMVPD).

Chapter 9 Video Games: Discussion of technological advances such as ray tracing and the growth of hyper-casual gaming.

Chapter 10 The Internet and Social Media: New Cultural Forum box debating high-speed Internet as a human right; an examination of fake news as disinformation rather than misinformation, producing truth decay, as well as the impact of social media on the insurrectionist attack on the U.S. Capitol; exploration of "finstas," fake Instagram accounts for the presentation of the real self; and discussion of several troubling new Internet phenomena, including facial recognition technology, the growth of surveillance capitalism, the rise of the "manosphere," and deep fakes.

Chapter 11 Public Relations: Examination of the troubling trends of mercenary science, "Black PR," and pink slime journalism; a detailed look at paid vs earned media; and a discussion of the relationship between the new Principles of Corporate Governance and the practice of public relations.

Chapter 12 Advertising: Expanded discussion of neuromarketing research and associative and demonstrative advertising; look at blinks and increased hypercommercialism.

Chapter 13 Theories and Effects of Mass Communication: Introduction and discussion of mediatization theory and its resulting media logic.

Chapter 14 Media Freedom, Regulation, and Ethics: Examination of informed consent and the ethics of privacy; discussion of the coverage of protests and the value of movement journalism; look at deplatforming as a response to harmful speech.

Chapter 15 Global Media: Discussion of the independence of the VOA and an examination of authoritarian governments' throttling of the Internet and its potential to create the splinternet.

Acknowledgments

A project of this magnitude requires the assistance of many people. For this latest edition, I benefited from several e-mails from readers—instructors and students—making suggestions and offering advice. This book is better for those exchanges. Rather than run the risk of failing to include one of these essential correspondents, I'll simply say, "Thanks. You know who you are."

Reviewers are an indispensable part of the creation of a good textbook. In preparing for the 12th edition, I was again impressed with the thoughtful comments made by my colleagues in the field. Although I didn't know them by name, I found myself in long-distance, anonymous debate with several superb thinkers, especially about some of the text's most important concepts. Their collective keen eye and questioning attitude sharpened each chapter to the benefit of both writer and reader. Now that I know who they are, I would like to thank the reviewers by name.

Mario Acerra, *Northampton Community College*

Alan Buck, *Meredith College*

Jill Gibson, *Amarillo College*

Carmen Brookins House, *Lincoln University*

Ron McBride, *Northwestern State University of Louisiana*

Travice Baldwin Obas, *Georgia Highlands College*

Martin Sommerness, *Northern Arizona University*

Michelle Steven, *St. Francis College*

Leesha Throner, *Cincinnati State Technical and Community College*

Bertena Varney, *Southcentral Kentucky Community and Technical College*

Chris Willis, *Chattanooga State Community College*

I would also like to thank the reviewers of the first 10 editions. **Tenth Edition Reviewers:** Shira Chess, The University of Georgia; Phillip Cunningham, Quinnipiac University; Robert F. Darden, Baylor University; Meredith Guthrie, University of Pittsburgh; Kelli Marshall, DePaul University; Elizabeth Behm-Morawitz, University of Missouri-Columbia; Pamela Hill Nettleton, Marquette University; Rick Stevens, University of Colorado Boulder; Matthew R. Turner, Radford University. **Ninth Edition Reviewers:** Cathy Ferrand Bullock, Utah State University; Alta Carroll, Worcester State University; Antoinette Countryman, McHenry County College; Adrienne E. Hacker Daniels, Illinois College; Lori Dann, Eastfield College; Jessica M. Farley, Delaware Technical Community College; Jeffrey Goldberg, Mass Bay Community College; Barbara J. Irwin, Canisius College; Christopher Leigh, University of Charleston; Katherine Lockwood, University of Tampa; Jodi Hallsten Lyczak, Illinois State University; Susan McGraw, Henry Ford College; Larry Moore, Auburn University at Montgomery; Travice Baldwin Obas, Georgia Highlands College-Cartersville; Luis Lopez-Preciado, Lasell College; Terri F. Reilly, Webster University; Joseph M. Sirianni, Niagara University; Sandra Luzzi Sneesby, Community College of Rhode Island; Martin D. Sommerness, Northern Arizona University; Pamela Stovall, University of New Mexico-Gallup; Joanne A. Williams, Olivet College; Joe Wisinski, University of Tampa; Robert Wuagneux, Castleton State College. **Eighth Edition Reviewers:** Lee Banville, University of Montana; Rick Bebout, West Virginia University; Bob Britten, West Virginia University; Cathy Bullock, Utah State University; James Burton, Salisbury University; Yolanda Cal, Loyola University-New Orleans; Nathan Claes, State University of New York-Buffalo; Helen Fallon, Point Park University; Ray Fanning, University of Montana; Richard Ganahl, Bloomsburg University; Paul Hillier, University of Tampa; Daekyung Kim, Idaho State University; Charles Marsh, University of Kansas-Lawrence; Susan McGraw, Henry Ford Community College; Bob Mendenhall,

Southwestern Adventist University; Bruce Mims, Southeast Missouri State University; Jensen Moore, West Virginia University; Timothy Pasch, University of North Dakota; Kenneth Ross, Eastern Connecticut State University; Siobhan Smith, University of Louisville; Jeff South, Virginia Commonwealth University; Richard Taflinger, Washington State University-Pullman; Clifford Vaughn, Belmont University; Kimberly Vaupel, Henry Ford Community College; Joe Wisinski, University of Tampa. **Seventh Edition Reviewers:** Kwasi Boateng, University of Arkansas at Little Rock; Mike Igoe, Buffalo State College; Joe Marre, Buffalo State College; Sonya Miller, University of North Carolina-Asheville; Yuri Obata, Indiana University-South Bend; Danny Shipka, Louisiana State University. **Sixth Edition Reviewers:** Chris Cakebread, Boston University; Cynthia Chris, College of Staten Island; Laurie Hayes Fluker, Texas State University; Jacob Podber, Southern Illinois University-Carbondale; Biswarup Sen, University of Oregon; Lisa A. Stephens, University of Buffalo; Denise Walters, Front Range Community College. **Fifth Edition Reviewers:** Jennifer Aubrey, University of Missouri; Michael Boyle, Wichita State University; Tim Coombs, Eastern Illinois University; Denise Danford, Delaware County Community College; Tim Edwards, University of Arkansas at Little Rock; Junhao Hong, State University of New York at Buffalo; Mark Kelly, University of Maine; Alyse Lancaster, University of Miami; Carol S. Lomick, University of Nebraska at Kearney; Susan Dawson-O'Brien, Rose State College; Alicia C. Shepard, University of Texas at Austin; Tamala Sheree Martin, Oklahoma State University; Stephen D. Perry, Illinois State University; Selene Phillips, University of Louisville. **Fourth Edition Reviewers:** Kristen Barton, Florida State University; Kenton Bird, University of Idaho; Katia G. Campbell, University of Colorado; Paul A. Creasman, Azusa Pacific University; Annette Johnson, Georgia State University; James Kelleher, New York University; Polly McLean, University of Colorado; Anthony A. Olorunnisola, Pennsylvania State University; Stephen D. Perry, Illinois State University; Michael Porter, University of Missouri; Stephen J. Resch, Indiana Wesleyan University; Christopher F. White, Sam Houston State University. **Third Edition Reviewers:** Roger Desmond, University of Hartford; Jules d'Hemecourt, Louisiana State University; Deborah A. Godwin-Starks, Indiana University-Purdue University Fort Wayne; Junhao Hong, State University of New York at Buffalo; Alyse Lancaster, University of Miami; Carol S. Lomicky, University of Nebraska at Kearney; Jenny L. Nelson, Ohio University; Enid Sefcovic, Florida Atlantic University; Kevin R. Slaugher, George Mason University; Terri Toles Patkin, Eastern Connecticut State University; David Whitt, Nebraska Wesleyan University; Gary J. Wingenbach, Texas A&M University. **Second Edition Reviewers:** Rob Bellamy, Duquesne University; Beth Grobman Burruss, DeAnza College; Stephen R. Curtis, Jr., East Connecticut State University; Lyombe Eko, University of Maine; Junhao Hong, State University of New York at Buffalo; Carol Liebler, Syracuse University; Robert Main, California State University, Chico; Stephen Perry, Illinois State University; Eric Pierson, University of San Diego; Ramona Rush, University of Kentucky; Tony Silvia, University of Rhode Island; and Richard Welch, Kennesaw State University. **First Edition Reviewers:** David Allen, Illinois State University; Sandra Braman, University of Alabama; Tom Grimes, Kansas State University; Kirk Hallahan, Colorado State University; Katharine Heintz-Knowles, University of Washington; Paul Husselbee, Ohio University; Seong Lee, Appalachian State University; Rebecca Ann Lind, University of Illinois at Chicago; Maclyn McClary, Humboldt State University; Guy Meiss, Central Michigan University; Debra Merskin, University of Oregon; Scott R. Olsen, Central Connecticut State University; Ted Pease, Utah State University; Linda Perry, *Florida Today* newspaper; Elizabeth Perse, University of Delaware; Tina Pieraccini, State University of New York-College at Oswego; Michael Porter, University of Missouri; Peter Pringle, University of Tennessee at Chattanooga; Neal Robison, Washington State University; Linda Steiner, Rutgers University; and Don Tomlinson, Texas A&M University.

The 12th edition was written with the usual great support (and patience) of my McGraw Hill Education team. The Internet may make producing a book more efficient, but it does have a big drawback—despite spending hundreds of hours "working together," I have yet to meet many of my teammates face-to-face. This, certainly, is my loss. Still, I have had few better colleagues than Sarah Remington and Thomas Finn. An author cannot surround himself with better people than those McGraw Hill Education has given me.

Finally, my most important inspiration throughout the writing of this book has been my family. My wife, Susan, is educated in media literacy and a strong disciple of spreading its lessons far and wide—which she does with zest. Her knowledge and assistance in my writing is invaluable; her love in my life is sustaining; her fire—for improved media literacy and for our marriage—is empowering. My children—Jordan and Matthew—simply by their existence require that I consider and reconsider what kind of world we will leave for them. I've written this text in the hope that it helps make the future for them and their friends better than it might otherwise have been.

S.J.B.

Cultural Forum Blue Column icon, Media Literacy Red Torch Icon, Using Media Green Gear icon, Developing Media book in starburst icon: ©McGraw Hill

Twelfth Edition

Introduction to
Mass Communication

MEDIA LITERACY AND CULTURE

Mass Communication, Culture, and Media Literacy

1

◀ We touch the world, and the world touches us, through mass communication.

Elnur/Shutterstock

Learning Objectives

Mass communication, mass media, and the culture that shape us (and that we shape) are inseparable. After studying this chapter, you should be able to

▶ Define *communication, mass communication, mass media,* and *culture.*

▶ Describe the relationships among communication, mass communication, culture, and those who live in the culture.

▶ Evaluate the impact of technology and economics on those relationships.

▶ List the components of media literacy.

▶ Identify key skills required for developing media literacy.

c 600 Wooden block printing press invented in China

c 1000 The Chinese develop movable clay type

c 1200 Simple movable metal printing press invented in Korea

1400

1446 Gutenberg printing press perfected

1456 ▶ First Gutenberg Bible printed

North Wind Picture Archives/Alamy Stock Photo

1800

1800s Availability of printed materials spreads knowledge that leads to the Industrial Revolution; the Industrial Revolution leads to the creation of the first mass audiences

1830s Publishers begin selling newspapers for a penny and profitting from ad sales, selling readers rather than papers

1900

1948 Harold Laswell defines communication in its simplest, linear form

1954 Osgood–Schramm model of communication and mass communication developed

1962 Marshall McLuhan publishes *The Gutenberg Galaxy* and argues the advent of print is the key to modern consciousness

1975 Carey's cultural definition of communication

Showtime Networks/Photofest

2000

2008 Art Silverblatt identifies elements of media literacy

2013 Term "binge viewing" enters mainstream use

2016 Annual global Internet traffic passed the zettabyte threshold

2017 ▶ First gender non-binary character on American TV appears in *Billions*

2020 ▶ Coronavirus in the US; anti-Asian discrimination rises; controversy over racist brand imagery

John Angelillo/UPI/Alamy Stock Photo

YOUR SMARTPHONE'S RADIO ALARM SINGS YOU AWAKE. It's Lil Naz X, the last few lyrics of "Old Town Road." The upbeat DJ shouts at you that it's 7:41 and you'd better get going. But before you do, she adds, listen to a few words from your friends at Best Buy electronics, home of fast, friendly, courteous service—"Expert Service. Unbeatable Price!"

Before you get up, though, you take a quick pass at Facebook and Instagram. But you have to get going now. In the living room, you find your roommate has left the television on. You stop for a moment and listen: Interest rates are rising, which may affect the availability of student loans; several states are considering providing free high-speed Internet to all students to improve their access to the digital world; a massive storm, not yet a hurricane, is working its way up the coast; and you deserve a break today at McDonald's. As you head toward the bathroom, your bare feet slip on some magazines littering the floor—*Wired, Fast Company, People.* You need to talk to your roommate about cleaning up!

After showering, you quickly pull on your Levi's, lace up your Nike cross-trainers, and throw on an Under Armour jacket. No time for breakfast; you grab a Nature Valley granola bar and your tablet and head for the bus stop. As the bus rolls up, you can't help but notice the giant ad on its side: another *Marvel* movie. Rejecting that as a film choice for the weekend, you sit down next to a teenager listening to music on his Beats headphones and playing *Words With Friends.* You fire up your tablet and busy yourself with a few quick TikTok videos, raucous Twitter celebrity feuds, and your favorite news app, scanning the lead stories and the local news, then checking out *Zits* and *Garfield.*

Hopping off the bus at the campus stop, you run into your friend Chris. You walk to class together, talking about last night's *Walking Dead* episode. It's not yet 9:00, and already you're involved in mass communication. In fact, like 80% of smartphone owners, you're involved with media first thing in the morning, checking your device even before brushing your teeth (Pinkham, 2020), or perhaps like two-thirds of all American adults, you've even slept with your technological best friend (Doby, 2020).

In this chapter, we define *communication, interpersonal communication, mass communication, media,* and *culture,* and explore the relationships among them and how they define us and our world. We investigate how communication works, how it changes when technology is introduced into the process, and how differing views of communication and mass communication can lead to different interpretations of their power. We also discuss the opportunities mass communication and culture offer us and the responsibilities that come with those opportunities. Always crucial, these issues are of particular importance now, when we find ourselves in a period of remarkable development in new communication technologies. This discussion inevitably leads to an examination of media literacy, its importance, and its practice.

What Is Mass Communication?

"Does a fish know it's wet?" influential cultural and media critic Marshall McLuhan would often ask. The answer, he would say, is "No." The fish's existence is so dominated by water that only when water is absent is the fish aware of its condition.

So it is with people and mass media. The media so fully saturate our everyday lives that we are often unconscious of their presence, not to mention their influence. Media inform us, entertain us, delight us, annoy us. They move our emotions, challenge our intellects, insult our intelligence. Media often reduce us to mere commodities for sale to the highest bidder. Media help define us; they shape our realities.

A fundamental theme of this book is that media do none of this alone. They do it *with* us as well as *to* us through mass communication, and they do it as a central—many critics and scholars say *the* central—cultural force in our society.

Communication Defined

In its simplest form, **communication** is the transmission of a message from a source to a receiver. For more than 70 years now, this view of communication has been identified with

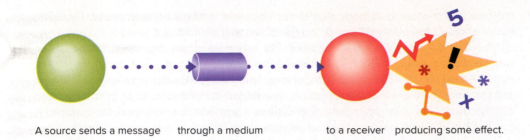

◀ **Figure 1.1** The Basic Communication Process.

A source sends a message   through a medium   to a receiver   producing some effect.

the writing of political scientist Harold Lasswell (1948). He said that a convenient way to describe communication is to answer these questions:

- *Who*?
- Says *what*?
- Through *which* channel?
- To *whom*?
- With *what effect*?

Expressed in terms of the basic elements of the communication process, communication occurs when a source sends a message through a medium to a receiver, producing some effect (Figure 1.1).

This idea is straightforward enough, but what if the source is a professor who insists on speaking in a technical language far beyond the receiving students' level of skill? Obviously, communication does not occur. Unlike mere message-sending, communication requires the response of others. Therefore, there must be a *sharing* (or correspondence) of meaning for communication to take place.

A second problem with this simple model is that it suggests that the receiver passively accepts the source's message. However, if our imaginary students do not comprehend the professor's words, they respond with "Huh?" or look confused or yawn. This response, or **feedback**, is also a message. The receivers (the students) now become a source, sending their own message to the source (the offending professor), who is now a receiver. Hence, communication is a *reciprocal* and *ongoing process* with all involved parties more or less engaged in creating shared meaning. Communication, then, is better defined as *the process of creating shared meaning*.

Communication researcher Wilbur Schramm, using ideas originally developed by psychologist Charles E. Osgood, developed a graphic way to represent the reciprocal nature of communication (Figure 1.2). This depiction of **interpersonal communication**—communication between two or a few people—shows that there is no clearly identifiable source or receiver. Rather, because communication is an ongoing and reciprocal process, all the participants, or "interpreters," are working to create meaning by **encoding** and **decoding** messages. A message is first *encoded*, that is, transformed into an understandable sign and symbol system. Speaking is encoding, as are writing, printing, and filming a television program. Once

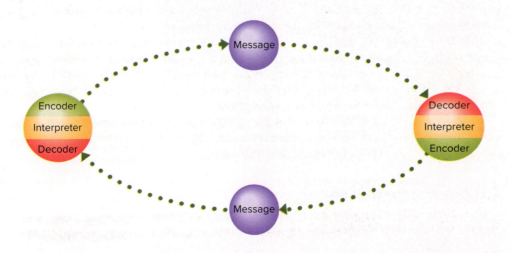

◀ **Figure 1.2** Osgood and Schramm's Model of Communication.
Source: Schramm, Wilbur Lang, The Process and Effects of Mass Communication. Champaign, IL: University of Illinois Press, 1954, 586.

received, the message is *decoded*; that is, the signs and symbols are interpreted. Decoding occurs through listening, reading, or watching that television show.

The Osgood–Schramm model demonstrates the ongoing and reciprocal nature of the communication process. There is, therefore, no source, no receiver, and no feedback. The reason is that, as communication is happening, both interpreters are simultaneously source and receiver. There is no feedback because all messages are presumed to be in reciprocation of other messages. Even when your friend starts a conversation with you, for example, it can be argued that it was your look of interest and willingness that communicated to her that she should speak. In this example, it is improper to label either you or your friend as the source—who really initiated this chat?—and, therefore, it is impossible to identify who is providing feedback to whom.

Not every model can show all aspects of a process as complex as communication. Missing from this representation is **noise**—anything that interferes with successful communication. Noise is more than screeching or loud music when you are trying to work online. Biases that lead to incorrect decoding, for example, are noise, as is a page torn out of a magazine article you want to read or that spiderweb crack in your smartphone's screen.

Encoded messages are carried by a **medium**, that is, the means of sending information. Sound waves are the medium that carries our voice to friends across the table; the telephone is the medium that carries our voice to friends across town. When the medium is a technology that carries messages to a large number of people—as the Internet carries text, sounds, and images and radio conveys the sound of news and music—we call it a **mass medium** (the plural of medium is *media*). The mass media we use regularly include radio, television, books, magazines, newspapers, movies, sound recordings, and computer networks. Each medium is the basis of a giant industry, but other related and supporting industries also serve them and us—advertising and public relations, for example. In our culture, we use the words *media* and *mass media* interchangeably to refer to the communication industries themselves. We say, "The media entertain" or "The mass media are too conservative (or too liberal)."

Mass Communication Defined

We speak, too, of mass communication. **Mass communication** is the process of creating shared meaning between the mass media and their audiences. Schramm recast his and Osgood's general model of communication to help us visualize the particular aspects of the mass communication process (Figure 1.3). This model and the original Osgood–Schramm model have much in common—interpreters, encoding, decoding, and messages—but it is their differences that are most significant for our understanding of how mass communication differs from other forms of communication. For example, whereas the original model

▶ **Figure 1.3** Schramm's Model of Mass Communication.

Source: Schramm, Wilbur Lang, The Process and Effects of Mass Communication. Champaign, IL: University of Illinois Press, 1954, 586.

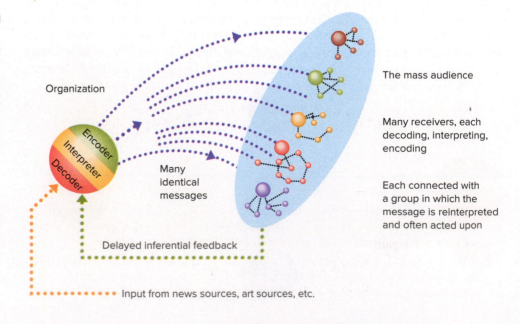

Organization

The mass audience

Many identical messages

Many receivers, each decoding, interpreting, encoding

Each connected with a group in which the message is reinterpreted and often acted upon

Delayed inferential feedback

Input from news sources, art sources, etc.

includes "message," the mass communication model offers "many identical messages." In addition, the mass communication model specifies "feedback," whereas the interpersonal communication model does not. When two or a few people communicate face-to-face, the participants can immediately and clearly recognize the feedback residing in the reciprocal messages (our boring professor can see and hear the students' disenchantment as they listen to the lecture). Things are not nearly as simple in mass communication.

In Schramm's mass communication model, feedback is represented by a dotted line labeled "delayed **inferential feedback**." This feedback is indirect rather than direct. Television executives, for example, must wait a day, at the very minimum, and sometimes a week or a month, to discover the ratings for new programs. Even then, the ratings measure only how many sets are tuned in, not whether people liked or disliked the programs. As a result, these executives can only infer what they must do to improve programming, hence the term *inferential feedback*. Mass communicators are also subject to additional feedback, usually in the form of criticism in other media, such as a television critic writing a column in a newspaper.

The differences between the individual elements of interpersonal and mass communication change the very nature of the communication process. How those alterations influence the message itself and how the likelihood of successfully sharing meaning differs are shown in Figure 1.4. For example, the immediacy and directness of feedback in interpersonal communication free communicators to gamble, to experiment with different approaches. Their knowledge of one another enables them to tailor their messages as narrowly as they wish. As a result, interpersonal communication is often personally relevant and possibly even adventurous and challenging. In contrast, the distance between participants in the mass communication process, imposed by the technology, creates a sort of "communication conservatism." Feedback comes too late to enable corrections or alterations in communication that fails. The sheer number of people in many mass communication audiences makes personalization and specificity difficult. As a result, mass communication tends to be more constrained, less free. This does not mean, however, that it is less potent than interpersonal communication in shaping our understanding of ourselves and our world.

Media theorist James W. Carey (1975) recognized this and offered a **cultural definition of communication** that has had a profound impact on the way communication scientists and others have viewed the relationship between communication and culture. Carey wrote, "Communication is a symbolic process whereby reality is produced, maintained, repaired and transformed" (p. 10).

Carey's (1989) definition asserts that communication and reality are linked. Communication is a process embedded in our everyday lives that informs the way we perceive, understand, and construct our view of reality and the world. Communication is the foundation of our culture. Its truest purpose is to maintain ever-evolving, "fragile" cultures; communication is that "sacred ceremony that draws persons together in fellowship and commonality" (p. 43).

What Is Culture?

Culture is the learned behavior of members of a given social group. Many writers and thinkers have offered interesting expansions of this definition. Here are four examples, all from anthropologists. These definitions highlight not only what culture *is* but also what culture *does*:

- Culture is the learned, socially acquired traditions and lifestyles of the members of a society, including their patterned, repetitive ways of thinking, feeling, and acting. (Harris, 1983, p. 5)
- Culture lends significance to human experience by selecting from and organizing it. It refers broadly to the forms through which people make sense of their lives, rather than more narrowly to the opera or art of museums. (Rosaldo, 1989, p. 26)
- Culture is the medium evolved by humans to survive. Nothing is free from cultural influences. It is the keystone in civilization's arch and is the medium through which all of life's events must flow. We are culture. (Hall, 1976, p. 14)
- Culture is an historically transmitted pattern of meanings embodied in symbolic forms by means of which [people] communicate, perpetuate, and develop their knowledge about and attitudes toward life. (Geertz, as cited in Taylor, 1991, p. 91)

	Interpersonal Communication You invite a friend to lunch.		**Mass Communication** Idiot Box Productions produces *The Walking Dead*.	
	Nature	Consequences	Nature	Consequences
Message	Highly flexible and alterable	You can change it in midstream. If feedback is negative, you can offer an alternative. Is feedback still negative? Take a whole new approach.	Identical, mechanically produced, simultaneously sent Inflexible, unalterable The completed *The Walking Dead* episode that is aired	Once production is completed, *The Walking Dead* cannot be changed. If a plotline or other communicative device isn't working with the audience, nothing can be done.
Interpreter A	One person—in this case, you	You know your mind. You can encode your own message to suit yourself, your values, and your likes and dislikes.	A large, hierarchically structured organization—in this case, Idiot Box Productions and the AMC television network	Who really is Interpreter A? Production's executives? The writers? The director? The actors? The network and its standards and practices people? The sponsors? All must agree, leaving little room for individual vision or experimentation.
Interpreter B	One or a few people, usually in direct contact with you and, to a greater or lesser degree, known to you—in this case, your friend	You can tailor your message specifically to Interpreter B. You can make relatively accurate judgments about B because of information present in the setting. Your friend is a vegetarian; you don't suggest a steak house.	A large, heterogeneous audience known to Interpreter A only in the most rudimentary way, little more than basic demographics—in this case, several million viewers of *The Walking Dead*	Communication cannot be tailored to the wants, needs, and tastes of all audience members or even those of all members of some subgroup. Some more or less generally acceptable standard is set.
Feedback	Immediate and direct yes or no response	You know how successful your message is immediately. You can adjust your communication on the spot to maximize its effectiveness.	Delayed and inferential Even overnight ratings are too late for this episode of *The Walking Dead*. Moreover, ratings are limited to telling the number of sets tuned in.	Even if the feedback is useful, it is too late to be of value for this episode. In addition, it doesn't suggest how to improve the communication effort.
Result	Flexible, personally relevant, possibly adventurous, challenging, or experimental		Constrained by virtually every aspect of the communication situation A level of communication most likely to meet the greatest number of viewers' needs A belief that experimentation is dangerous A belief that to challenge the audience is to risk failure	

▲ **Figure 1.4** Elements of Interpersonal Communication and Mass Communication Compared.
(photo left): Daniel Thistlewaite/Image Source; (photo right): Jace Downs/AMC/PictureLux/The Hollywood Archive/Alamy Stock Photo

Culture as Socially Constructed Shared Meaning

Virtually all definitions of culture recognize that culture is *learned*. Recall the opening vignette. Even if this scenario does not exactly match your early mornings, you probably recognize its elements. Moreover, all of us are familiar with most, if not every, cultural reference in it. *Transformers*, *The Walking Dead*, McDonald's, Under Armour, TikTok—all are points of reference, things that have some meaning for all of us. How did this come to be?

Creation and maintenance of a more or less common culture occur through communication, including mass communication. When we talk to our friends, when a parent raises a child, when religious leaders instruct their followers, when teachers teach, when grandparents pass on recipes, when politicians campaign, and when media professionals produce content that we read, listen to, or watch, meaning is being shared and culture is being constructed and maintained.

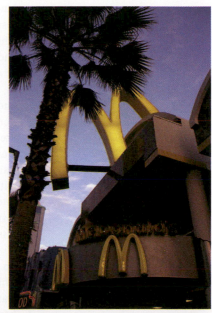

▲ These images have meaning for all of us—meaning that is socially constructed through communication in our culture. How many can you recognize? What specific meaning or meanings does each have for you? How did you develop each meaning? How closely do you think your meanings match those of your friends? Of your parents? What value is there—if any—in having shared meaning for these things in our everyday lives?

(top left) Fadziel Nor/Shutterstock; (top right) John Flournoy/McGraw Hill; (bottom left) Kevin Dietsch/UPI/Alamy Stock Photo; (bottom right) Rokas Tenys/Alamy Stock Photo

Functions and Effects of Culture

Culture serves a purpose. It helps us categorize and classify our experiences; it helps define us, our world, and our place in it. In doing so, culture can have a number of sometimes conflicting effects.

LIMITING AND LIBERATING EFFECTS OF CULTURE   A culture's learned traditions and values can be seen as patterned, repetitive ways of thinking, feeling, and acting. Culture limits our options and provides useful guidelines for behavior. For example, when conversing, you do not consciously consider, "Now, how far away should I stand? Am I too close?" You simply stand where you stand. After a hearty meal with a friend's family, you do not engage in mental self-debate, "Should I burp? Yes! No! Arghhhh. . . ." Culture provides information that helps us make meaningful distinctions about right and wrong, appropriate and inappropriate, good and bad, attractive and unattractive, and so on. How does it do this?

Obviously, it does so through communication. Through a lifetime of communication, we have learned just what our culture expects of us. The two examples given here are positive results of culture's limiting effects. But culture's limiting effects can be negative, such as when we are unwilling or unable to move past patterned, repetitive ways of thinking, feeling, and acting or when we entrust our "learning" to teachers whose interests are selfish, narrow, or otherwise inconsistent with our own.

US culture, for example, values thinness and beauty in women. How many women endure weeks of unhealthy diets and succumb to potentially dangerous surgical procedures in search of a body that for most is physically unattainable? How many women are judged by the men and other women around them for not conforming to our culture's standards of thinness and beauty? Why does an expression like "fat shaming" exist in our language? Why are 50% of preadolescent girls and 30% of preadolescent boys unhappy with their bodies (Muhlheim, 2020)? Why do over one-half of teenage girls and nearly one-third of teenage boys use unhealthy weight control behaviors like skipping meals, fasting, smoking cigarettes, vomiting, and taking laxatives (National Eating Disorders Association, 2020)?

Now consider how this situation may have come about. Our parents did not bounce us on their knees when we were babies, telling us that thin was good and heavy was bad. Think back, though, to the stories you were told and the television shows and movies you watched growing up. The heroines (or, more often, the beautiful love interests of the heroes) were invariably tall, beautiful, and thin. The bad guys were usually mean and fat. From Disney's depictions of Snow White, Cinderella, Belle, Jasmine, and Pocahontas to the impossible dimensions of most video-game and comic book heroines, the message is embedded in the conscious (and unconscious) mind of every girl and boy: You can't be too thin or too beautiful! As it is, 69% of women and 65% of girls cite constant pressure from advertising and media to reach unrealistic standards of beauty as a major factor fueling their anxiety about their appearance (Dove, 2020). And it does not help that these messages are routinely reinforced throughout the culture—for example, in the recent explosion of plastic surgery game apps that let kids give perfect nose jobs and face-lifts, all with brightly colored graphics (Yan, 2018); the popularity of Instagram's plastic surgery filters—a billion applications in 2019 alone, leading the company to ban them from its platform (Marikar, 2019); and the now-routine "sexy fill-in-the-blank" women's Halloween costumes (Lake, Macedo, & Riegle, 2019).

This message and millions of others come to us primarily through the media, and although the people who produce these media images are not necessarily selfish or mean, their motives are undeniably financial. Their contribution to our culture's repetitive ways of thinking, feeling, and acting is most certainly not primary among their concerns when preparing their communication.

Culture need not only limit. The fact that media representations of female beauty often meet with debate and disagreement points out that culture can be liberating as well. This is so because cultural values can be *contested.* In fact, today, we're just as likely to see strong, intelligent female characters who save the day, such as *Brave*'s Merida, *Mulan*'s Fa Mulan, *Cloudy with a Chance of Meatballs*'s Sam Sparks, and *Frozen*'s sisters, Anna and Elsa, as we are movie princesses who need to be saved by the hero.

▲ Culture can be contested. Actor Asia Kate Dillon plays Taylor Mason in the hit Showtime series *Billions*. They (Dillon's preferred self-referencing pronoun) identify as non-binary, in stark contrast to the actors typically chosen for prime roles on big-budget TV shows. Dillon's role on *Billions* is the first gender non-binary main character on North American television and challenges the culture's everyday assumption of what a TV star should be and look like, as you can clearly see when looking at the casts of other video fare such as those of *Riverdale*, *NCIS*, and *Chicago Fire*. *Showtime Networks/Photofest*

Especially in a pluralistic, democratic society such as ours, the **dominant culture** (or **mainstream culture**)—the one that seems to hold sway with the majority of people—is often openly challenged. People do meet, find attractive, like, and love people who do not fit the standard image of beauty. In addition, media sometimes present images that suggest different ideals of beauty and success. Actors Katy Mixon, Issa Rae, Dascha Polanco, and Mindy Kaling; singer/actor Beyoncé; and comedians Riki Lindhome and Amy Schumer all represent alternatives to our culture's idealized standards of beauty, and all have undeniable appeal (and power) on the big and small screens. Liberation from the limitations imposed by culture resides in our ability and willingness to learn and use *new* patterned, repetitive ways of thinking, feeling, and acting; to challenge existing patterns; and to create our own.

DEFINING, DIFFERENTIATING, DIVIDING, AND UNITING EFFECTS OF CULTURE Have you ever made the mistake of calling a dolphin, porpoise, or even a whale a fish? Maybe you have heard others do it. This error occurs because when we think of fish, we think "lives in the water" and "swims." Fish are defined by their "aquatic culture." Because water-residing, swimming dolphins, porpoises, and whales share that culture, we sometimes forget that they are mammals, not fish.

We, too, are defined by our culture. We are citizens of the United States; we are Americans. If we travel to other countries, we will hear ourselves labeled "American," and this label will conjure up stereotypes and expectations in the minds of those who use and hear it. The stereotype, whatever it may be, will probably fit us only incompletely, or perhaps hardly at all—perhaps we are dolphins in a sea full of fish. Nevertheless, being American defines us in innumerable important ways, both to others (more obviously) and to ourselves (less obviously).

▲ *Riverdale*, *NCIS*, and *Chicago Fire*—these three television programs are aimed at different audiences, yet in each, the characters share certain traits that mark them as attractive. Must people in real life look like these performers to be considered attractive? Successful? Good? The people shown are all slender, tall, and attractive. Yes, they are just make-believe television characters, but the producers of the shows on which they appear chose these people—as opposed to others—for a reason. What do you think it was? How well do you measure up to the cultural standard of beauty and attractiveness represented here? Do you ever wish that you could be just a bit more like these people? Why or why not?

(top) The CW Television Network/Photofest; (bottom left) Kevin Lynch/CBS/Getty Images; (bottom right) NBC/Photofest

Within this large, national culture, however, there are many smaller, **bounded cultures** (or **co-cultures**). For example, we speak comfortably of Italian neighborhoods, fraternity row, the South, and the suburbs. Because of our cultural understanding of these categories, each expression communicates something about our expectations of these places. We think we can predict with a good deal of certainty the types of restaurants and shops we will find in the

Italian neighborhood, even the kind of music we will hear escaping from open windows. We can predict the kinds of clothes and cars we will see on fraternity row, the likely behavior of shop clerks in the South, and the political orientation of the suburbs' residents. Moreover, the people within these cultures usually identify themselves as members of those bounded cultures. An individual may say, for example, "I'm Italian American" or "I'm a Southerner." These smaller cultures unite groups of people and enable them to see themselves as different from other groups around them. Thus, culture also serves to differentiate us from others.

In the United States, we generally consider this a good thing. We pride ourselves on our pluralism, on our diversity, and on the richness of the cultural heritages represented within our borders. We enjoy moving from one bounded culture to another or from a bounded culture to the dominant national culture and back again.

Problems arise, however, when differentiation leads to division. All Americans suffered the painful personal, financial, and physical effects of the coronavirus pandemic of 2020. But that ongoing tragedy was compounded for the millions of Asian Americans whose "Americanness" was challenged simply because of their perceived cultural connection to the people of Wuhan, China, where the disease originated. Before the virus struck the United States, anti-Asian hate crimes had been on a two-decade decline (Feinberg, 2020). But 4 months into the country's battle against the disease's physical and economic toll, the Asian Pacific Policy and Planning Council had received more than 1,800 reports of harassment or violence against Asian Americans in 45 states and Washington, D.C. (Kambhampaty, 2020), and by the end of that year, there were 2,808 *reported* "hate incidents" nationwide aimed at Asian Americans (Nakamura, 2021). Asian Americans' looks, names, and sometimes facility with a "strange-sounding" language somehow communicated otherness, not-American, to many of their fellow citizens. Just as culture is constructed and maintained through communication, it is also communication (or miscommunication) that turns differentiation into division.

Yet Americans of all colors, ethnicities, genders, nationalities, places of birth, economic strata, and intelligence levels often get along; in fact, we *can* communicate, *can* prosper, and *can* respect one another's differences. Culture can divide us, but culture also unites us. Our culture represents our collective experience. We converse easily with strangers because we share the same culture. We automatically know when a handshake is appropriate, use titles or first or last names appropriately, know how much to say, and know how much to leave unsaid. Through communication with people in our culture, we internalize cultural norms and values—those things that bind our many diverse bounded cultures into a functioning, cohesive society.

From this discussion comes the definition of culture on which the remainder of this book is based: Culture is the world made meaningful; it is socially constructed and maintained through communication. It limits as well as liberates us; it differentiates as well as unites us. It defines our realities and thereby shapes the ways we think, feel, and act.

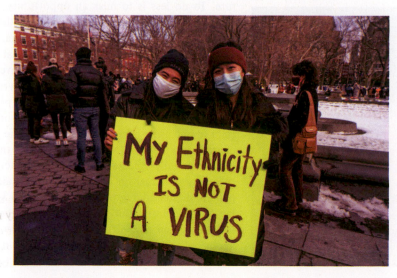

◀ There is nothing about these Asian American people that should "communicate otherness" in the United States, yet too many people cannot see beyond their own bounded cultures.
Ron Adar/Alamy Stock Photo

Mass Communication and Culture

Despite the fact that culture can limit and divide, it can also liberate and unite. As such, it offers us infinite opportunities to use communication for good—if we choose to do so. James Carey (1975) wrote:

> Because we have looked at each new advance in communication technology as opportunities for politics and economics, we have devoted them, almost exclusively, to government and trade. We have rarely seen them as opportunities to expand [our] powers to learn and exchange ideas and experience. (pp. 20–21)

Who are "we" in this quote? *We* are the people involved in creating and maintaining the culture that defines us. *We* are the people involved in mass media industries and the people who compose their audiences. Together we allow mass communication not only to occur but also to contribute to the creation and maintenance of culture.

Everyone involved has an obligation to participate responsibly. For people working in the media industries, this means professionally and ethically creating and transmitting content. For audience members, it means behaving as critical and thoughtful consumers of that content. Two ways to understand our opportunities and our responsibilities in the mass communication process are to view the mass media as our cultural storytellers and to conceptualize mass communication as a cultural forum.

Mass Media as Cultural Storytellers

A culture's values and beliefs reside in the stories it tells. Who are the good guys? Who are the bad guys? How many of your childhood heroines were even slightly overweight? How many good guys dressed in black? How many heroines lived happily ever after without marrying Prince Charming? Probably not very many. How many news accounts of demonstrations in our streets take the vantage point of the protesters? Again, probably not very many. Our stories help define our realities, shaping the ways we think, feel, and act. "Stories are sites of observations about self and society," explains media theorist Hanno Hardt (2007, p. 476). The media's stories—real, imaginary, an intentional or unintentional mixture of the two—become the material for our cultural conversations. Therefore, the "storytellers" have a responsibility to tell their stories in as professional and ethical way as possible.

At the same time, we, the audience for these stories, also have opportunities and responsibilities. We use these stories to learn about the world around us, to understand the values, the way things work, and how the pieces fit together. We have a responsibility to question the tellers and their stories, to interpret the stories in ways consistent with larger or more important cultural values and truths, to be thoughtful, and to reflect on the stories' meanings and what they say about us and our culture. To do less is to miss an opportunity to construct our own meaning and, thereby, culture.

For example, for 131 years, Aunt Jemima, a character from a 19th-century minstrel song that longed for the days before the Civil War ended slavery, was the name and face of a popular maple syrup, featured in its branding and advertising. The product's maker, Quaker Oats, knew something was not quite right about using a racial stereotype as the central character in the story of its brand, so over the years it occasionally updated her look, replacing the "Mammy" kerchief on her head with a plaid headband and later adding pearl earrings and a lace collar to her outfit. But in the wake of the video documentation of George Floyd's killing by Minneapolis police, America undertook a serious reconsideration of their nation's often racist past (and the

▼ For 131 years the central character in the Aunt Jemima maple syrup story was an unkind racial stereotype. The culture wanted a different take on its past; Aunt Jemima disappeared, but not before she became a central character in an important conversation about race and racism.

John Angelillo/UPI/Alamy Stock Photo

stories it told itself to gloss over many uncomfortable truths). Quaker Oats responded, deciding it was time to tell a different story with different characters, announcing in mid-2020 the aunt's retirement (Hsu, 2020). Mars Food quickly followed suit with its Uncle Ben's Rice (becoming Ben's Original Rice), and two other companies announced they would rethink the racist imagery central to their brands' stories: ConAgra Brands (Mrs. Butterworth's pancake syrup) and B&G Foods (Cream of Wheat porridge, dropping altogether the image of the grinning Black chef). The culture was tired of these ignorant stories and demanded something better (Cramer, 2020).

Mass Communication as Cultural Forum

Imagine a giant courtroom in which we discuss and debate our culture—what it is, and what we want it to be. What do we think about welfare? Single motherhood? Labor unions? Nursing homes? What is the meaning of "successful," "good," "loyal," "moral," "honest," "beautiful," or "patriotic"? We have cultural definitions or understandings of all these things and more. Where do they come from? How do they develop, take shape, and mature?

Mass communication has become a primary forum for the debate about our culture. Logically, then, the most powerful voices in the forum have the most power to shape our definitions and understandings. Where should that power reside—with the media industries or with their audiences? If you answer "media industries," you will want members of these industries to act professionally and ethically. If you answer "audiences," you will want individual audience members to be thoughtful and critical of the media messages they consume. The forum is only as good, fair, and honest as those who participate in it.

Scope and Nature of Mass Media

No matter how we choose to view the process of mass communication, it is impossible to deny that an enormous portion of our lives is spent interacting with mass media. We spend well over half our day, 13 hours and 35 minutes, interacting with media of some sort (Dolliver, 2020).

The average American adult watches 27 hours per week of traditional television; that is, in the home and including live, on-demand, and recorded viewing (Epstein, 2020). Watching online video adds another 100 minutes a day (Brooks, 2020). A large majority of TV viewers admit to **binge watching**, watching five or more episodes of a series in one sitting. As for 18- to 29-year-old bingers, 76% stay up all night to do so; 51% will watch an entire new season of a show within 24 hours of its release; 45% cancel social plans to binge; and 42% will watch at work to finish a series (Feldman, 2018). People watch more than 1 billion hours of video daily on YouTube alone; and there's plenty of material, as 500 hours of new content are uploaded to the site every minute (Chi, 2021).

Ninety-three percent of Americans will tune in to the radio every week, averaging 102 minutes a day (Watson, 2020), and Americans also stream over 1 trillion songs a year (Blake, 2020). We spend more than $11 billion a year at the movies, buying more than a billion-and-a-quarter tickets (McNary, 2020). If Facebook were a country, its 2.6 billion users would make it the largest in the world; 1.7 billion people log on daily (Noyes, 2020). Seventy-five percent of American households are home to at least one person who plays video games three or more hours a week, and 65% of American adults play video games (Entertainment Software Association, 2020).

More than 333 million North Americans, 90% of the population, use the Internet. Globally, 4.9 billion people go online, 63% of the world's population and a 1,271% increase since 2000 ("Internet Usage," 2021). One-third of American adults are online "almost constantly" (Perrin & Atske, 2021). In *one minute* of Internet time, users will send 210 million e-mails, download 26,000 apps, make 4.2 million Google searches, and send 15.2 million texts (Heitman, 2021). There's little doubt that we actively engage the media, but you can see in Figure 1.5 how Americans' typical levels of consumption rose dramatically when sheltering at home during the 2020 coronavirus pandemic. In fact, so reliant were we on the media to help us get through that difficult time, that 2 months into states' stay-at-home orders, nearly half of Americans "ran out" of things to watch, read, and listen to (Mandese, 2020).

Despite the pervasiveness of mass media in our lives, many of us are dissatisfied with or critical of the media industries' performance and much of the content provided. For example,

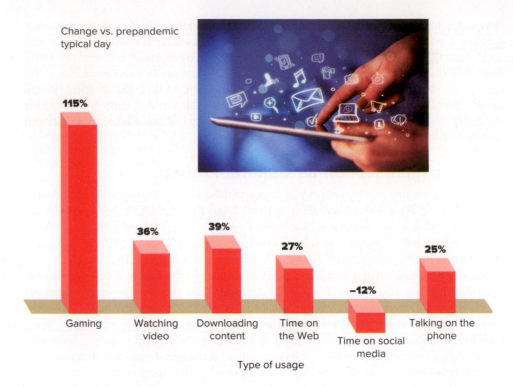

▶ **Figure 1.5** Increase in Media Usage over a Typical Pre-Pandemic Day.
Source: Waterman, 2020.
(tablet pc) ra2studio/Shutterstock

Change vs. prepandemic typical day

115%   36%   39%   27%   −12%   25%

Gaming   Watching video   Downloading content   Time on the Web   Time on social media   Talking on the phone

Type of usage

fewer than half of all Americans trust the traditional mass media, and only 27% trust social media as a source of information (Salmon, 2021); globally, only 14% of consumers trust advertising to help them gain information about a business (Stewart, 2020); 91% of Americans think advertising has become more intrusive in the past few years (Coppola, 2020), and even advertising professionals hate commercials: 27% block digital ads, 79% skip TV commercials on their DVRs, and 98% stream ad-free content (Whitman, 2018).

Our ambivalence—we criticize, yet we consume—comes in part from our uncertainties about the relationships among the elements of mass communication. What is the role of technology? What is the role of money? And what is *our* role in the mass communication process?

The Role of Technology

To some thinkers, it is machines and their development that drive economic and cultural change. This idea is referred to as **technological determinism**. Certainly, there can be no doubt that movable type contributed to the Protestant Reformation and the decline of the Catholic Church's power in Europe, or that television changed the way members of American families interact, or that social media have altered the nature of friendship. Those who believe in technological determinism would argue that these changes in the cultural landscape were the inevitable result of new technology.

But others see technology as more neutral and claim that the way people *use* technology is what gives it significance. This perspective accepts technology as one of many factors that shape economic and cultural change; technology's influence is ultimately determined by how much power it is given by the people and cultures that use it.

This disagreement about the power of technology is at the heart of the controversies that always seem to spring up with the introduction of new communication technologies. Are we more or less powerful given the range of media available to us in the digital age? If we are at the mercy of technology, the culture that surrounds us will not be of our making, and the best we can hope to do is make our way reasonably well in a world outside our control. But if these technologies are indeed neutral and their power resides in *how* we choose to use them, we can utilize them responsibly and thoughtfully to construct and maintain whatever kind of culture we want.

Technology does have an impact on communication. At the very least it changes the basic elements of communication (see Figure 1.4). But what technology does not do is relieve us of our obligation to use mass communication responsibly and wisely.

The Role of Money

Money, too, alters communication. It shifts the balance of power; it tends to make audiences products rather than consumers.

The first newspapers were financially supported by their readers; the money they paid for the paper covered its production and distribution. But in the 1830s, a new form of newspaper financing emerged. Publishers began selling their papers for a penny—much less than it cost to produce and distribute them. Because so many more papers were sold at this bargain price, publishers could "sell" advertising space based on their readership. However, what they were actually selling to advertisers was not space on the page—it was readers. How

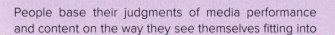

CULTURAL FORUM
Audience as Consumer or Audience as Product?

People base their judgments of media performance and content on the way they see themselves fitting into the economics of the media industry. Businesses operate to serve their consumers and make a profit. The consumer comes first, then, but who *is* the consumer in our mass media system? This is a much-debated issue among media practitioners and media critics. Consider the following models.

BUSINESS MODEL	PRODUCER	PRODUCT	CONSUMERS
Basic US Business Model	A manufacturer . . .	produces a product . . .	for consumers who choose to buy or not. The manufacturer must satisfy the consumer. Power resides with consumers.
Basic US Business Model for Cereal: Rice Krispies as Product, Public as Consumer	Kellogg's . . .	produces Rice Krispies . . .	for us, the consumers. If we buy Rice Krispies, Kellogg's makes a profit. Kellogg's must satisfy the consumer. Power resides with consumers.
Basic US Business Model for Television (A): Audience as Product, Advertisers as Consumer	NBC . . .	produces audiences (using its programming) . . .	for advertisers. If they buy NBC's audiences, NBC makes a profit from ad time. NBC must satisfy its consumers, the advertisers. Power resides with advertisers.
Basic US Business Model for Television (B): Programming as Product, Audience as Consumer	NBC . . .	produces (or distributes) programming . . .	for us, the audience. If we watch NBC's shows, NBC makes a profit from ad sales. NBC must satisfy its audience. Power resides with audiences.

Enter Your Voice

The first three models assume that the consumer *buys* the product; that is, the consumer is the one with the money and therefore the one who must be satisfied. The last model makes a different assumption. It sees the audience, even though it does not buy anything, as sufficiently important to NBC's profit-making ability to force NBC to consider the audience's interests above others' (even those of advertisers).

- Which model do you think best represents the economics of American mass media?
- Can you speculate on how the different models might influence the relationship between the media and their audiences?
- How might different models shape the kinds of content available to audiences?

much they could charge advertisers was directly related to how much product (how many readers) they could produce for them.

This new type of publication changed the nature of mass communication. The goal of the process was no longer for audience and media to create meaning together. Rather, it was to sell those readers to a third participant: advertisers.

Some observers think this was a devastatingly bad development, not only in the history of mass communication but also in the history of democracy. It robbed people of their voices, or at least made the voices of the advertisers more powerful. Others think it was a huge advance for both mass communication and democracy because it vastly expanded the media, broadening and deepening communication. Models showing these two different ways of viewing mass communication are presented in the box "Audience as Consumer or Audience as Product?" Which model makes more sense to you? Which do you think is more accurate? ABC journalist Ted Koppel once explained to *The Washington Post,* "[Television] is an industry. It's a business. We exist to make money. We exist to put commercials on the air. The programming that is put on between those commercials is simply the bait we put in the mousetrap" (in "Soundbites," 2005, p. 2). Do you think Koppel is unnecessarily cynical, or is he correct in his analysis of television?

The goals of media professionals will be questioned repeatedly throughout this book. For now, keep in mind that ours is a capitalist economic system and that media industries are businesses. Movie producers must sell tickets, book publishers must sell books, and even public broadcasters have bills to pay.

This does not mean, however, that the media are or must be slaves to profit. Our task is to understand the constraints placed on these industries by their economics and then demand that, within those limits, they perform ethically and responsibly. We can do this only by being thoughtful, critical consumers of the media.

Two Revolutions in Mass Communication

Culture and communication are inseparable, and mass communication, as we've seen, is a particularly powerful, pervasive, and complex form of communication. Our level of skill in the mass communication process is therefore of utmost importance. This skill is not necessarily a simple one to master (it is much more than booting up the computer, turning on the television, or flipping through the pages of your favorite magazine). But it is, indeed, a learnable skill, one that can be practiced. This skill is **media literacy**—the ability to effectively and efficiently comprehend and use any form of mediated communication. But let's start with the first mass medium, books, and the technology that enabled their spread, the printing press.

The Gutenberg Revolution

As it is impossible to overstate the importance of writing, so too is it impossible to overstate the significance of Johannes Gutenberg's development of movable metal type. Historian S. H. Steinberg (1959) wrote in *Five Hundred Years of Printing*:

Neither political, constitutional, ecclesiastical, and economic, nor sociological, philosophical, and literary movements can be fully understood without taking into account the influence the printing press has exerted upon them. (p. 11)

Marshall McLuhan expressed his admiration for Gutenberg's innovation by calling his 1962 book *The Gutenberg Galaxy.* In it, he argued that the advent of print is the key to our modern consciousness because **literacy**—the ability to effectively and efficiently comprehend and use written symbols—had existed since the development of the first alphabets more than 5,000 years ago, it was reserved for very few, the elites. Gutenberg's invention was world-changing because it opened literacy to all; that is, it allowed *mass* communication.

THE PRINTING PRESS Printing and the printing press existed long before Gutenberg perfected his process in or around 1446. The Chinese were using wooden block presses as early as 600 C.E. and an artisan named Bi Sheng developed movable clay type by 1000 C.E. (Marantz, 2019). A simple movable metal type was even in use in Korea in the 13th century. Gutenberg's printing press was a significant leap forward, however, for two important reasons.

Gutenberg was a goldsmith and a metallurgist. He hit on the idea of using metal type crafted from lead molds in place of type made from wood or clay. This was an important advance. Not only

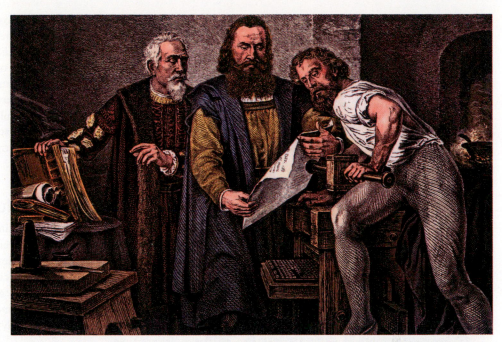

▲ Johannes Gutenberg takes the first proof from his printing press.
North Wind Picture Archives

was movable metal type durable enough to print page after page, but letters could be arranged and rearranged to make any message possible, and Gutenberg was able to produce virtually identical copies.

In addition, Gutenberg's advance over Korean metal mold printing was one of scope. The Korean press was used to produce books for a very small, royal readership. Gutenberg saw his invention as a way to produce many books for profit. He was, however, a poor businessman. He stressed quality over quantity, in part because of his reverence for the book he was printing, the Bible. He used the highest-quality paper and ink and turned out far fewer volumes than he otherwise could have.

Other printers, however, quickly saw the true economic potential of Gutenberg's invention. The first Gutenberg Bible appeared in 1456. By the end of that century, 44 years later, printing operations existed in 12 European countries, and the Continent was flooded with 20 million volumes of 7,000 titles in 35,000 different editions (Drucker, 1999).

THE IMPACT OF PRINT Although Gutenberg developed his printing press with a limited use in mind, printing Bibles, the cultural effects of mass printing have been profound.

Handwritten or hand-copied materials were expensive to produce, and the cost of an education, in time and money, had made reading an expensive luxury. However, with the spread of printing, written communication was available to a much larger portion of the population, and the need for literacy among the lower and middle classes grew. The ability to read became less of a luxury and more of a necessity; eventually literacy spread, as did education. Soldiers at the front needed to be able to read the emperor's orders. Butchers needed to understand the king's shopping list. So the demand for literacy expanded, and more (and more types of) people learned to read.

Tradespeople, soldiers, clergy, bakers, and musicians all now had business at the printer's shop. They talked. They learned of things, both in conversation and by reading printed material. As more people learned to read, new ideas germinated and spread, and cross-pollination of ideas occurred.

More material from various sources was published, and people were freer to read what they wanted when they wanted. Dominant authorities—the Crown and the Church—were now less able to control communication and, therefore, the people. New ideas about the world appeared; new understandings of the existing world flourished.

In addition, duplication permitted standardization and preservation. Myth and superstition began to make way for standard, verifiable bodies of knowledge. History, economics, physics, and chemistry all became part of the culture's intellectual life. Literate cultures were now on the road to modernization.

▲ This page from a Gutenberg Bible shows the exquisite care the printer used in creating his works. The artwork in the margins is hand painted, but the text is mechanically printed.

North Wind Picture Archives/Alamy Stock Photo

Printed materials were the first mass-produced product, speeding the development and entrenchment of capitalism. We live today in a world built on these changes. Use of the printing press helped fuel the establishment and growth of a large middle class. No longer must societies be composed of rulers and subjects; printing sped the rise of democracy. No longer were power and wealth solely functions of birth; power and wealth could now be created by the industrious. No longer was political discourse limited to accepting the dictates of Crown and Church; printing had given ordinary people a powerful voice.

The Industrial Revolution

By the mid-18th century, printing and its libraries of science and mathematics had become powerful engines driving the Industrial Revolution. Print was responsible for building and disseminating bodies of knowledge, leading to scientific and technological developments and the refinement of new machines. In addition, industrialization reduced the time necessary to complete work, and this created something previously unknown to most working people—leisure time.

Industrialization had another effect as well. As workers left their sunrise-to-sunset jobs in agriculture, the crafts, and trades to work in the newly industrialized factories, not only did they have more leisure time, but they also had more money to spend on their leisure. Farmers, fishermen, and tile makers had to put their profits back into their jobs. But factory workers took their money home; it was spendable. Combine leisure time and expendable cash with the spread of literacy, and the result is a large and growing audience for printed *information* and *entertainment*. By the mid-19th century, a mass audience and the means to reach it existed.

Media Literacy

Television influences our culture in innumerable ways. One of its effects, according to many people, is that it has encouraged violence in our society. For example, American television viewers overwhelmingly say there is too much violence on television. Yet, almost without exception, the local television news program that has the largest proportion of violence in its nightly newscast is the ratings leader. "If it bleeds, it leads" has become the motto for much of local television news. It leads because people watch.

So, although many of us are quick to condemn improper media performance or to identify and lament its harmful effects, we rarely question our own role in the mass communication process. We overlook it because we participate in mass communication naturally, almost without conscious effort. We possess high-level interpretive and comprehension skills that make even the most sophisticated television show, movie, or magazine story understandable and enjoyable. We are able, through a lifetime of interaction with the media, to *read media texts.*

Media literacy is a skill we take for granted, but like all skills, it can be improved. And if we consider how important the mass media are in creating and maintaining the culture that helps define us and our lives, it is a skill that *must* be improved.

Hunter College media professor Stuart Ewen (2000) emphasized this point in comparing media literacy with traditional literacy. "Historically," he wrote, "links between literacy and democracy are inseparable from the notion of an informed populace, conversant with the issues that touch upon their lives, enabled with tools that allow them to participate actively in public deliberation and social change" (p. 448). To Ewen, and others committed to media literacy, media literacy represents no less than the means to full participation in the culture.

Elements of Media Literacy

Media scholar Art Silverblatt (2008) identifies seven fundamental elements of media literacy. To these, we will add an eighth. Media literacy includes these characteristics:

1. *A critical thinking skill enabling audience members to develop independent judgments about media content.* Thinking critically about the content we consume is the very essence of media literacy. Why do we watch what we watch, read what we read, listen to what we listen to? Is that story you saw on Twitter real? If we cannot answer these questions, we have taken no responsibility for ourselves or our choices. As such, we have taken no responsibility for the outcome of those choices.

2. *An understanding of the process of mass communication.* If we know the components of the mass communication process and how they relate to one another, we can form expectations of how they can serve us. How do the various media industries operate? What are their obligations to us? What are the obligations of the audience? How do different media limit or enhance messages? Which forms of feedback are most effective, and why?

3. *An awareness of the impact of media on the individual and society.* Writing and the printing press helped change the world and the people in it. Mass media do the same. If we ignore the impact of media on our lives, we run the risk of being caught up and carried along by that change rather than controlling or leading it.

4. *Strategies for analyzing and discussing media messages.* To consume media messages thoughtfully, we need a foundation on which to base thought and reflection. If we make meaning, we must possess the tools with which to make it (for example, understanding the intent and impact of film and video conventions, such as camera angles and lighting, or the strategy behind the placement of images on a newspaper's website). Otherwise, meaning is made for us; the interpretation of media content will then rest with its creator, not with us.

5. *An understanding of media content as a text that provides insight into our culture and our lives.* How do we know a culture and its people, attitudes, values, concerns, and myths? We know them through communication. For modern cultures like ours, media messages increasingly dominate that communication, shaping our understanding of and insight into our culture.

6. *The ability to enjoy, understand, and appreciate media content.* Media literacy does not mean living the life of a grump, liking nothing in the media, or always being suspicious of harmful effects and cultural degradation. We take high school and college classes to enhance our understanding and appreciation of novels; we can do the same for media texts. Learning to enjoy, understand, and appreciate media content includes the ability to use **multiple points of access**—to approach media content from a variety of directions and derive from it many levels of meaning. Thus, we control meaning making for our own enjoyment or appreciation. For example, we can enjoy the hit show *The Handmaid's Tale* on Hulu as an action-laden adventure full of intrigue, danger, and romance, perfect for binge watching. But as TV buffs we might see it as a feminist manifesto, a story of an oppressed woman taking on a powerful man. Or we might read it as a cautionary tale for what might happen in America if women lose the right to control their bodies. Maybe it's a history lesson disguised as dystopian fiction, reminding us that women have always had to fight for their rightful place in society. Or maybe it's just a fun way to spend a cozy night, entertained by the same streaming video industry that so delights us with other prestige programming, such as *The Mandalorian*, *13 Reasons Why*, and *Fleabag*.

7. *Development of effective and responsible production skills.* Traditional literacy assumes that people who can read can also write. Media literacy also makes this assumption. Our definition of literacy (of either type) calls not only for effective and efficient comprehension of content but also for its effective and efficient *use*. Therefore, media-literate individuals should develop production skills that enable them to create useful media messages. If you have ever tried to make a narrative home video—one

that tells a story—you know that producing content is much more difficult than consuming it. If you have ever posted to Snapchat or Instagram or uploaded a video to TikTok, you are indeed a media content producer; why not be a good media content producer?

8. *An understanding of the ethical and moral obligations of media practitioners.* To make informed judgments about the performance of the media, we also must be aware of the competing pressures on practitioners as they do their jobs. We must understand the media's official and unofficial rules of operation. In other words, we must know, respectively, their legal and ethical obligations. Return, for a moment, to the question of televised violence. It is legal for a station to air graphic violence. But is it ethical? If it is unethical, what power, if any, do we have to demand its removal from our screens? Dilemmas such as this are discussed at length in Chapter 14.

▶ *Family Guy* has all the things you would expect from a television situation comedy—an inept dad, a precocious daughter, a slacker son, a loving wife, and zany situations. Yet it also offers an intellectual, philosopher dog and an evil-genius, scheming baby. Why do you think the producers have gone to the trouble to populate this show with the usual trappings of a sitcom but then add other, bizarre elements? And what's going on in *The Hand-maid's Tale*? Is it an action-laden adventure full of intrigue, danger, and romance? A feminist mani-festo? A history lesson disguised as dystopian fiction. Or maybe it's just a fun way to spend a cozy night binge watching.

(top) FOX Image Collection/Getty Images; (bottom) Calla Kessler for The Washington Post/Getty Images

Media Literacy Skills

Consuming media content is simple. Push a button and you have images on a television or music on your car radio. Come up with enough cash and you can see a movie or buy an e-book. Media-literate consumption, however, requires a number of specific skills.

1. *The ability and willingness to make an effort to understand content, to pay attention, and to filter out noise.* As we saw earlier, anything that interferes with successful communication is called noise, and much of the noise in the mass communication process results from our own consumption behavior. When we watch television, often we are also doing other things, such as eating, reading, or checking Instagram. We drive while we listen to the radio. We text while we read. Obviously, the quality of our meaning making is related to the effort we give it.

2. *An understanding of and* respect *for the power of media messages.* We are surrounded by mass media from the moment we are born. Just about every one of us can enjoy them. Their content is either free or relatively inexpensive. Much of the content is banal and a bit silly, so it is easy to dismiss media content as beneath serious consideration or too simple to have any influence. We also disregard media's power through the **third-person effect**—the common attitude that others are influenced by media messages but that we are not. That is, we are media literate enough to understand the influence of mass communication on the attitudes, behaviors, and values of others but not self-aware or honest enough to see its influence on our lives.

3. *The ability to distinguish emotional from reasoned reactions when responding to content and to act accordingly.* Media content is often designed to touch us at the emotional level. We enjoy losing ourselves in a good song or in a well-crafted movie or television show; this is among our great pleasures. But because we react emotionally to these messages does not mean they don't have serious meanings and implications for our lives. Television images, for example, are intentionally shot and broadcast for their emotional impact. Reacting emotionally is appropriate and proper. But then what? What do these images tell us about the larger issue at hand? We can use our feelings as a point of departure for meaning making. We can ask, "Why does this content make me feel this way?"

4. *The development of heightened expectations of media content.* We all use media to tune out, waste a little time, and provide background noise. When we decide to watch television, we are more likely to turn on the set and flip channels until we find something passable than we are to read the listings to find a specific program to view. When we search for online video, we often settle for the "10 most shared today," or we let Netflix's algorithm choose for us. When we expect little from the content before us, we tend to give meaning making little effort and attention.

5. *A knowledge of genre conventions and the ability to recognize when they are being mixed.* The term **genre** refers to the categories of expression within the different media, such as "evening news," "documentary," "horror movie," or "entertainment magazine." Each genre is characterized by certain distinctive, standardized style elements—the **conventions** of that genre. The conventions of the evening news, for example, include a short, upbeat introductory theme and one or two good-looking people sitting at a large, modern desk. When we hear and see these style elements, we expect the evening news. We can tell a documentary film from an entertainment movie by its more serious tone and a number of talking heads. We know by their appearance—the use of color, the types of images, and the amount of text on the cover—which magazines offer serious reading and which provide entertainment. Knowledge of these conventions is important because they cue or direct our meaning making.

6. *The ability to think critically about media messages, no matter how credible their sources.* It is crucial that media be credible in a democracy in which the people govern because the media are central to the governing process. This is why the news media are sometimes referred to as the fourth branch of government, complementing the executive, judicial, and legislative branches. This does not mean, however, that we should accept uncritically everything they report. But media-literate people know not to discount *all*

news media; they must be careful to avoid the **hostile media effect**, the idea that people see media coverage of important topics of interest as less sympathetic to their position, more sympathetic to the opposing position, and generally hostile to their point of view regardless of the quality of the coverage (Tsfati & Cohen, 2013). There are indeed very good media sources, just as there are those not deserving of our consideration. Media literacy, as you'll read throughout this text, helps us make that distinction. For example, the Internet has made possible the widespread of **fake news**, intentionally and verifiably false news stories designed to be spread and to deceive. Disguised to appear authentic, its real intention is to sow confusion and damage political discourse. Fake news is successful because its arresting headlines easily catch our attention and because **confirmation bias**, our tendency to accept information that confirms our beliefs and dismiss information that does not, encourages us to pass it on with little evaluation. How do we combat fake news?

- *First, vet the publisher's credibility.* Does the report meet traditional journalistic standards of evidence and corroboration? Has the author published anything else? What's the domain name? Check out the "About Us" page for indicators of bias.
- *Second, pay attention to quality and timeliness.* Is the story current, or is it recycled? Are there a lot of spelling errors, ALL CAPS, or dramatic punctuation???!!!
- *Third, check sources and citations.* How did you come upon the article? Who is or is not quoted? Is there supporting information on other sites? Can you perform reverse searches for sources and images?
- *Finally, ask a pro.* There are several good fact-checking sites such as FactCheck.org, International Fact-Checking Network, PolitiFact, and Snopes (Nagler, 2018).

7. *A knowledge of the internal language of various media and the ability to understand its effects, no matter how complex.* Just as each media genre has its own distinctive style and conventions, each medium also has its own specific internal language. This language is expressed in **production values**—the choice of lighting, editing, special effects, music, camera angle, location on the page, and size and placement of headlines. To be able to read a media text, you must understand its language. We learn the grammar of this language as early as childhood—for example, we know that when the television image goes "all woozy," the character is dreaming. Let's consider two versions of the same movie scene. In the first, a man is driving a car. Cut to a woman lying tied up on a railroad track. What is the relationship between the man and the woman? Where is he going? With no more information than these two shots, you know automatically that he cares for her and is on his way to save her. Now, here is the second version. The man is driving the car. Fade to black. Fade back up to the woman on the tracks. Now, what is the relationship between the man and the woman? Where is he going? It is less clear that these two people even have anything to do with each other. We construct completely different meanings from exactly the same two scenes because the punctuation (the quick cut/fade) differs. Media texts tend to be more complicated than these two scenes. The better we can handle their grammar, the more we can understand and appreciate texts. The more we understand texts, the more we can be equal partners with media professionals in meaning making.

▼ *The Daily Show with Trevor Noah* offers all the conventions we'd expect from the news—background digital graphics, an anchor behind his desk, and a well-known interviewee. But it also contains conventions we'd expect from a comedy program—a satirist as host and an unruly, loud audience. Why does this television show mix the conventions of these two very different genres? Does your knowledge of those conventions add to your enjoyment of this hit program?
Jason Kempin/Getty Images Entertainment/Getty Images

MEDIA LITERACY CHALLENGE
Recognizing Cultural Values

Media-literate people develop *an understanding of media content as a text that provides insight into our culture and our lives,* and they have *an awareness of the impact of media on the individual and society.* So, challenge your own media literacy skills. You can do this exercise with a parent or another person older than you, or you can speculate after using the Internet to view movies and television shows from 20 years ago. Compare your childhood heroes and heroines with those of someone older. What differences are there between the generations in what you consider heroic qualities? What are some similarities and differences between the heroic qualities you and people from an earlier generation identify? Are the good qualities of your personal heroes something you can find in today's movies or TV? If so, where on TV or in film can you find the qualities you consider heroic? Which cultural values, attitudes, and beliefs, if any, do you think have influenced how heroes and heroines have changed throughout the last few decades? How have the media helped establish the values you identify as important qualities in people?

Resources for Review and Discussion

REVIEW POINTS: TYING CONTENT TO LEARNING OBJECTIVES

▶ Define *communication, mass communication, mass media,* and *culture.*
- □ Communication is the process of creating shared meaning.
- □ Mass communication is the process of creating shared meaning between the mass media and their audiences.
- □ *Mass media* is the plural of *mass medium,* a technology that carries messages to a large number of people.
- □ Culture is the world made meaningful. It resides all around us; it is socially constructed and maintained through communication. It limits as well as liberates us; it differentiates as well as unites us. It defines our realities and shapes the ways we think, feel, and act.

▶ Describe the relationships among communication, mass communication, culture, and those who live in the culture.
- □ Mass media are our culture's dominant storytellers and the forum in which we debate cultural meaning.

▶ Evaluate the impact of technology and economics on those relationships.
- □ Technological determinism argues that technology is the predominant agent of social and cultural change. But it is not technology that drives culture; it is how people use technology.
- □ With technology, money, too, shapes mass communication. Audiences can be either the consumer or the product in our mass media system.

▶ List the components of media literacy.
- □ Media literacy, the ability to effectively and efficiently comprehend and use any form of mediated communication, consists of eight components:
  1. A critical thinking skill enabling the development of independent judgments about media content
  2. An understanding of the process of mass communication
  3. An awareness of the impact of the media on individuals and society
  4. Strategies for analyzing and discussing media messages
  5. An awareness of media content as a "text" providing insight into contemporary culture
  6. A cultivation of enhanced enjoyment, understanding, and appreciation of media content
  7. The development of effective and responsible production skills
  8. The development of an understanding of the ethical and moral obligations of media practitioners

▶ Identify key skills required for developing media literacy.
- □ Media skills include the following:
  - The ability and willingness to make an effort to understand content, to pay attention, and to filter out noise
  - An understanding of and respect for the power of media messages

- The ability to distinguish emotional from reasoned reactions when responding to content and to act accordingly
- The development of heightened expectations of media content

- A knowledge of genre conventions and the recognition of their mixing
- The ability to think critically about media messages
- A knowledge of the internal language of various media and the ability to understand its effects

KEY TERMS

communication, 4

feedback, 5

interpersonal communication, 5

encoding, 5

decoding, 5

noise, 6

medium (pl. media), 6

mass medium, 6

mass communication, 6

inferential feedback, 7

cultural definition of communication, 7

culture, 7

dominant culture (mainstream culture), 11

bounded culture (co-culture), 12

binge watching, 15

technological determinism, 16

media literacy, 18

literacy, 18

multiple points of access, 21

third-person effect, 23

genre, 23

conventions, 23

hostile media effect, 24

fake news, 24

confirmation bias, 24

production values, 24

QUESTIONS FOR REVIEW

1. What is culture? How does culture define people?
2. What is communication? What is mass communication?
3. What are encoding and decoding? How do they differ when technology enters the communication process?
4. What does it mean to say that communication is a reciprocal process?
5. What is James Carey's cultural definition of communication? How does it differ from other definitions of that process?
6. What do we mean by mass media as cultural storyteller?
7. What do we mean by mass communication as cultural forum?

8. What is media literacy? What are its components?
9. What are some specific media literacy skills?
10. What is the difference between genres and production conventions? What do these have to do with media literacy?

To maximize your study time, check out CONNECT to access the SmartBook study module for this chapter, watch videos, and explore other resources.

QUESTIONS FOR CRITICAL THINKING AND DISCUSSION

1. Who were your childhood heroes and heroines? Why did you choose them? What cultural lessons did you learn from them?
2. The arrival of the printing press dramatically changed history. Traditional seats of power lost influence, science flourished, and the seeds were planted for capitalism and the growth of a middle class. What effects has the Internet had on how you

live different aspects of your life? Will its ultimate impact be less than, equal to, or greater than the impact wrought by the printing press? Defend your answer.

3. How media literate do you think you are? What about those around you—your parents, for example, or your best friend? What are your weaknesses as a media-literate person?

REFERENCES

1. Blake, E. (2020, January 9). Music hit 1 trillion streams in 2019, but growth is slowing. *Rolling Stone*. Retrieved from https://www.rollingstone.com/pro/news/streams-music-2019-trillion-vinyl-935246/
2. Brooks, D. (2020, March 1). Video days. *New York Times Magazine*, pp. 7–10.
3. Carey, J. W. (1975). A cultural approach to communication. *Communication, 2*, 1–22.
4. Carey, J. W. (1989). *Communication as culture*. Boston: Unwin Hyman.
5. Chi, S. (2021, February 25). 50 YouTube stats every video marketer should know in 2021. *HubSpot*. Retrieved from https://blog.hubspot.com/marketing/youtube-stats
6. Coppola, J. (2020, January 23). *The psychology behind why people dislike ads (and how to make better ones)*. Retrieved from https://wistia.com/learn/marketing/the-psychology-behind-why-people-dislike-ads
7. Cramer, M. (2020, June 18). Uncle Ben's and Mrs. Butterworth's are feeling the heat. *New York Times*, p. B6.

8. Doby, J. (2020, February 25). About 66% of Americans sleep with their phone at night. *The Hype Magazine.* Retrieved from https://www.thehypemagazine.com/2020/02/about-66-of-americans-sleep-with-their-phone-at-night/

9. Dolliver, M. (2020, April). US time spent with media 2020. *eMarketer.* Retrieved from https://www.emarketer.com/content/us-time-spent-with-media-2020

10. Dove. (2020, May 20). Is your child's perception of beauty distorted by media influence? *Dove.com.* Retrieved from https://www.dove.com/us/en/dove-self-esteem-project/help-for-parents/media-and-celebrities/beauty-distorted-by-media.html

11. Drucker, P. E. (1999, October). Beyond the information revolution. *The Atlantic,* pp. 47–57.

12. Entertainment Software Association. (2020). *Essential facts about the computer and video game industry.* Retrieved from https://www.theesa.com/esa-research/2019-essential-facts-about-the-computer-and-video-game-industry/

13. Epstein, A. (2020, February 13). Streaming still has a long way to go before it catches regular old TV. *QZ.com.* Retrieved from https://qz.com/1801623/streaming-has-a-long-way-to-go-to-catch-regular-tv/

14. Ewen, S. (2000). Memoirs of a commodity fetishist. *Mass Communication and Society, 3,* 439–452.

15. Feinberg, A. (2020, April 13). Hate crimes against Asian Americans have been declining for years. Will the coronavirus change that? *Washington Post.* Retrieved from https://www.washingtonpost.com/politics/2020/04/13/hate-crimes-against-asian-americans-have-been-declining-years-will-coronavirus-change-that/

16. Feldman, S. (2018, November 7). Young adults keep pressing play. *Statista.* Retrieved from https://www.statista.com/chart/16023/binge-watching-young-adults/?utm_source=Statista+Global&utm_campaign=97bcb13bb6-All_InfographTicker_daily_COM_PM_KW462018__WED&utm_medium=email&utm_term=0_afecd219f5-97bcb13bb6-300053297

17. Hall, E. T. (1976). *Beyond culture.* New York: Doubleday.

18. Hardt, H. (2007, December). Constructing photography: Fiction as cultural evidence. *Critical Studies in Media Communication, 24,* 476–480.

19. Harris, M. (1983). *Cultural anthropology.* New York: Harper & Row.

20. Heitman, S. (2021, March 22). What happens in an Internet minute. *LocalIQ.* Retrieved from https://localiq.com/blog/what-happens-in-an-internet-minute-2021/

21. Hsu, T. (2020, June 18). Aunt Jemima to be renamed, after 131 Years. *New York Times,* p. B1.

22. "Internet Usage Statistics: The Internet Big Picture." (2021, January 27). *Internet World Stats.* Retrieved from https://www.internetworldstats.com/stats.htm

23. Kambhampaty, A. P. (2020, June 25). 'I will not stand silent.' 10 Asian Americans reflect on racism during the pandemic and the need for equality. *Time.* Retrieved from https://time.com/5858649/racism-coronavirus/

24. Lake, Z., Macedo, D., & Riegle, A. (2019, October 30). Sexy Mr. Rogers, Sexy Bob Ross and the evolution of the sexy Halloween costume. *ABC News.* Retrieved from https://abcnews.go.com/Business/sexy-mr-rogers-sexy-bob-ross-evolution-sexy/story?id=66643835

25. Lasswell, H. D. (1948). The structure and function of communication in society. In L. Bryson (Ed.), *The communication of ideas.* New York: Harper.

26. Mandese, J. (2020, April 28). Mindshare finds nearly half of Americans have "run out" of things to watch, read, listen to. *MediaPost.* Retrieved from https://www.mediapost.com/publications/article/350686/mindshare-finds-nearly-half-of-americans-have-run.html

27. Marantz, A. (2019). The more things change. *New Yorker,* pp. 69–74.

28. Marikar, S. (2019, November 3). How to be 'real' on Instagram. *New York Times,* p. SR3.

29. McLuhan, M. (1962). *The Gutenberg galaxy: The making of typographic man.* London: Routledge.

30. McNary, D. (2020, January 28). Domestic top 100 of 2019: Disney dominates down year. *Variety,* p. 20.

31. Muhlheim, L. (2020, March 25). The connection between body image and eating disorders. *Verywell Mind.* Retrieved from https://www.verywellmind.com/body-image-and-eating-disorders-4149424

32. Nagler, C. (2018). 4 tips for spotting a fake news story. *President and Fellows of Harvard College.* Retrieved from https://summer.harvard.edu/4-tips-for-spotting-a-fake-news-story/

33. Nakamura, D. (2021, February 22). Attacks on Asian Americans during pandemic renew criticism that U.S. undercounts hate crimes. *Washington Post.* Retrieved from https://www.washingtonpost.com/national-security/asian-american-hate-crimes/2021/02/21/c28a8e04-72d9-11eb-b8a9-b9467510f0fe_story.html

34. National Eating Disorders Association. (2018). Get the facts on eating disorders. *NEDA.org.* Retrieved from https://www.nationaleatingdisorders.org/blog/get-facts-eating-disorders-infographics

35. Noyes, D. (2020, May). The top 20 valuable Facebook statistics—updated May 2020. *Zephoria.* Retrieved from https://zephoria.com/top-15-valuable-facebook-statistics/

36. Perrin, A., & Atske, S. (2021, March 26). About three-in-ten U.S. adults say they are 'almost constantly' online. *Pew Research Center.* Retrieved from https://www.pewresearch.org/fact-tank/2021/03/26/about-three-in-ten-u-s-adults-say-they-are-almost-constantly-online/

37. Pinkham, R. (2020, May 29). 80% of smartphone users check their phones before brushing their teeth ... and other hot topics. *Constant Contact.* Retrieved from https://blogs.constantcontact.com/smartphone-usage-statistics/

38. Rosaldo, R. (1989). *Culture and truth: The remaking of social analysis.* Boston: Beacon Press.

39. Salmon, F. (2021, January 21). Media trust hits new low. *Axios.* Retrieved from https://www.axios.com/media-trust-crisis-2bf0ec1c-00c0-4901-9069-e26b21c283a9.html

40. Schramm, W. L. (1954). *The process and effects of mass communication*. Urbana: University of Illinois Press.

41. Silverblatt, A. (2008). *Media literacy* (3rd ed.). Westport, CT: Praeger.

42. "Soundbites." (2005, December). A better mousetrap. *Extra! Update*, p. 2.

43. Steinberg, S. H. (1959). *Five hundred years of printing*. London: Faber & Faber.

44. Stewart, R. (2020, May 15). Advertising and social media face fresh trust issues amid global crisis. *The Drum*. Retrieved from https://www.thedrum.com/news/2020/05/15/advertising-and-social-media-face-fresh-trust-issues-amid-global-crisis

45. Taylor, D. (1991). Transculturating transculturation. *Performing Arts Journal, 13,* 90–104.

46. Tsfati, Y., & J. Cohen. (2013). The third-person effect, trust in media, and hostile media perceptions. *International Encyclopedia of Media Studies: Media Effects/Media Psychology, 1,* 1–19.

47. Waterman, H. (2020, April 9). 4/9 update: How Americans are spending time in the new normal. *Telecom Ramblings*. Retrieved from https://newswire.telecomramblings.com/2020/04/4-9-update-how-americans-are-spending-time-in-the-new-normal/

48. Watson, A. (2020, February 26). Average daily time spent listening to the radio per adult in the United States from 1st quarter 2015 to 1st quarter 2019. *Statista*. Retrieved from https://www.statista.com/statistics/761889/daily-time-spent-radio/

49. Whitman, R. (2018, August 23). It turns out that advertisers hate ads too. *MediaPost*. Retrieved from https://www.mediapost.com/publications/article/324059/it-turns-out-that-advertisers-hate-ads-too.html

50. Yan, L. (2018, April 7). These plastic surgery apps are stirring up serious controversy. *Popular Mechanics*. Retrieved from https://www.popularmechanics.com/culture/a19709962/these-plastic-surgery-apps-are-stirring-up-serious-controversy/

Cultural Forum Blue Column icon, Media Literacy Red Torch Icon, Using Media Green Gear icon, Developing Media book in starburst icon: ©McGraw Hill

Convergence and the Reshaping of Mass Communication
2

◀ Netflix's *Unbreakable Kimmy Schmidt: Kimmy vs. The Reverend* lets viewers control the movie's narrative—a clear sign of significant change in how we interact with media.

PictureLux /The Hollywood Archive/ Alamy Stock Photo

Learning Objectives

The mass media system we have today has existed more or less as we know it since the 1830s. It is a system that has weathered repeated significant change with the coming of increasingly sophisticated technologies—the penny press newspaper was soon followed by mass-market books and mass-circulation magazines.

As the 1800s made way for the 1900s, these popular media were joined by motion pictures, radio, and sound recording. A few decades later came television, combining news and entertainment, moving images, and sound all in the home and all, ostensibly, for free. The traditional media found new functions and prospered side by side with television. Then came the Internet, the World Wide Web, and mobile technologies such as smartphones, tablets, and of course social media.

Now, because of these new technologies, all the media industries are facing profound alterations in how they are structured, how they do business, the nature of their content, and how they interact with and respond to their audiences. Naturally, as these changes unfold, the very nature of mass communication and our role in that process will evolve. After studying this chapter, you should be able to

▶ Summarize broad current trends in mass media, especially concentration of ownership and conglomeration, globalization, audience fragmentation, hypercommercialization, and convergence.

▶ Describe in broad terms how the mass communication process itself will evolve as the role of the audience in this new media environment is altered.

1830s Birth of the mass media system as we know it today

1945 Supreme Court Justice Hugo Black claims that a free press is a condition of a free society

1900

Interfoto/History/Alamy Stock Photo; CBS/Photofest

1950s ▶ Television displaces radio   1950

1967 Richard Dawkins introduces the term "meme"

1970 Postal Reorganization Act

1974 Internet emerges

1982 60% of journalists say they had compete freedom to choose their stories, as opposed to 34% 25 years later after explosion of concentration and conglomeration

1996 ▶ DVD introduced

Howard Kingsnorth/ Photodisc/Getty Images

fyv6561/Shutterstock

2004 ▶ Facebook debuts   2000

2012 ▶ Facebook buys Instagram

2014 Apple buys Beats Music; YouTube buys Twitch

2015 Actavision buys game company King Digital Entertainment; AT&T buys DirecTV

2016 Pepe the Frog becomes a hate symbol due to meme portrayals; news deserts proliferate

2018 State of New Jersey funds local journalism; Sirius XM buys Pandora

2019 Americans stream more than 1 trillion tunes for first time

2020 Coronavirus in US

2021 Warner Bros. releases all new films day-and-date

fyv6561/Shutterstock

"I DIDN'T LIKE THE ENDING."

"But you made it happen. The producers gave you a lot of choices. Make out or read the book? Walk 12 miles or wait 4,000 minutes for Uber? Eat the mushrooms and skip the banquet or eat the food and the women get harassed? The whole point of *Kimmy vs. The Reverend* is that it's interactive. You create your own movie through the choices you make. Netflix did this before; remember the *Black Mirror* episode *Bandersnatch*?"

"Yeah, but *Bandersnatch* was science fiction. It wasn't supposed to have a happy ending. I wanted *Kimmy* to have a happy ending."

"So you got the not-so-happy ending, but it was *your* ending."

"I don't get it. Maybe I should pay more attention!"

Like our disappointed viewer, we all will need to pay better attention to a mass communication process undergoing fundamental alteration, and that change goes far beyond interactive storylines. Well before the coronavirus shut down all US movie theaters, for example, producers were already streaming their films directly to fans. In 2018 Netflix gave the Sandra Bullock horror hit *Birdbox* **day-and-date release**, simultaneously streaming it on its pay service and screening it in theaters. Netflix's Spanish-language *Roma* had day-and-date release that same year, earning 10 Oscar nominations, including one for Best Picture and winning for Best International Feature Film.

So, already interested in direct-to-audience distribution, the big Hollywood studios jumped in full force when the pandemic struck. Disney rushed *Frozen 2*, scheduled for summer release, to its streaming service, and Universal's animated feature, *Trolls World Tour*, made $100 million in streaming rentals in 3 weeks, more than the original on which it was based earned in 5 months in theaters (Friedman, 2020b). Before the pandemic was fully controlled, even much-anticipated blockbusters like *Wonder Woman 1984* were enjoying Christmas Day, 2020, day-and-date release, and Warner Bros. decided to release every one of its 17 new 2021 movies day-and-date, including big-budget titles like *Dune*, *The Matrix 4*, and *The Suicide Squad* (Barnes & Sperling, 2020). Not to be outdone, Netflix debuted 71 feature films, some streaming only, some day-and-date, in 2021, more than one a week (Friedman, 2021).

There is indeed a seismic shift going on in the mass media—and therefore in mass communication—that dwarfs the changes to the media landscape wrought by television's assault on the preeminence of radio and movies in the 1950s and 1960s. Encouraged by the Internet, digitization, and mobility, producers are finding new ways to deliver new content to audiences. The media industries are in turmoil, and audience members, as they are confronted by a seemingly bewildering array of possibilities, are now coming to terms with these new media.

How will you listen to the radio—satellite radio, terrestrial radio, digital terrestrial radio, or streamed Internet radio? If it's streamed over the Internet, is it still "radio"? You may not hold the physical newspaper in your hands, but when you access a newspaper's story on its app (abbreviation for *application*; software for mobile digital devices), you're reading the newspaper. Or are you? What will you pay to stream movies, $20, or will you subscribe to Red Carpet Home Cinema and get immediate access to first-run movies not otherwise available for home viewing for $1,500 to $3,000 each? What about on-demand TV shows? Would you be willing to view the commercials they contain if you could pay a bit less per episode? Would you pay more or less for classic programming than for contemporary shows? On which platform (the means of delivering a specific piece of media content) might you most enjoy watching your movies? Would you be willing to pay more or less for different platforms? In theaters? On your tablet or phone? On a wide-screen home TV? Is there such a thing as the "moviegoing experience" anymore? These are precisely the kinds of questions that audiences will continue to answer in the next several years. Media-literate audiences will be better equipped to do so.

▲ *Trolls World Tour earned Universal Pictures $100 million in three weeks from 5 million streaming rentals.*

DreamWorks/Universal/Kobal/Shutterstock

Traditional Media Industries in Transition: The Bad News and the Good

The way we interact with the mass media is indeed changing. Although this shift is good news for media consumers, it has not necessarily been beneficial for the established media industries. Just how much pain has been produced by this "perfect storm" of rapid technological change and our shifting consumption behavior? Here are a few examples:

- Although Americans typically spend over $11 billion a year at the movies, they continue to buy fewer tickets per person every year than they did in the past. Only 14% of American adults go to the movies once a month or more ("Frequency," 2020).

- Sales in the US of physical and digital music albums continue to fall, declining 18.7% between 2018 and 2019; the sale of individual digital songs dropped 25% in that time (Nielsen Music, 2020).

- Fifteen years ago, the four major broadcast networks commanded over 60% of all television viewing. Today their share hovers around 30%. The top-rated program in 1980 was *Dallas*, viewed in more than 34% of all homes with a television. In 1990, it was *Cheers*, watched by 21% of all TV homes. Today a top-rated show, such as *NCIS,* will draw 5% ("Tops of," 2020).

- US sales of DVD and Blue-Ray discs continue to decline, dropping 22% between 2018 and 2019 (Schnieder, 2020).

- One in five American newspapers has closed since 2004 (Sullivan, 2020); circulation has fallen to its lowest level since 1940 (Grieco, 2020).

- The US magazine industry saw a 20% drop in revenues from 2019 to 2020 (Gingerich, 2020).

- Annual revenue for traditional AM/FM radio in the US has decreased every year since 2015 (Hissong, 2020).

The challenge facing the traditional media industries today is how to capture a mass audience now fragmented into millions of niches, that is, into increasingly smaller subaudiences now accustomed to interacting with them in a growing variety of ways. Yet there is some good news for the media industries in all this change. Despite the fact that we are indeed consuming media in new and different ways, our levels of consumption are at an all-time high.

We saw in Chapter 1 that Americans spend well over half of a full day engaged with media of some sort, a practice made possible in part by the comfort with **media multitasking**, engaging simultaneously with many different media. Those declining ratings for network television? Viewers returned in droves during 2020's coronavirus shelter-at-home. The four national networks (ABC, CBS, Fox, and NBC) saw a 20% increase in viewership. Ratings for their evening news programs jumped 42% over those of the same period the year before (Epstein, 2020). Time with television, already on the rise because of the many subscription video streaming services, such as HBO Now, Apple +, Amazon Prime, Netflix, Hulu, and scores more, boomed during the coronarivus quarantine. Viewers spend $16 billion a year on these services ("The Quarantine," 2020). Those declining disc sales? They have been more than made up by **electronic sell-through (EST)**, the buying and downloading of digital movies that annually brings studios $2.6 billion (Gingerich, 2020). Falling music sales? American music fans more than made up for that decline by streaming 1.15 trillion tunes in 2019 (the first time that the number exceeded 1 trillion; Nielsen Music, 2020); world-wide, 2020's 2.2 trillion music streams propelled the industry to over $20 billion in revenues ("Year End," 2021).

The sad state of the newspaper industry? Tumultuous times—both political and medical—have driven news readership to record levels. The *Wall Street Journal* has more than 2 million digital subscribers; the *New York Times* has more than 5.3 million total subscriptions across print and digital editions; papers across the country of all sizes are experiencing growing digital subscriptions, fewer cancellations, and increased page views and daily visits (Benton, 2020; Doctor, 2020). You can see the number of hours in a day a typical American adult spends with media in Figure 2.1.

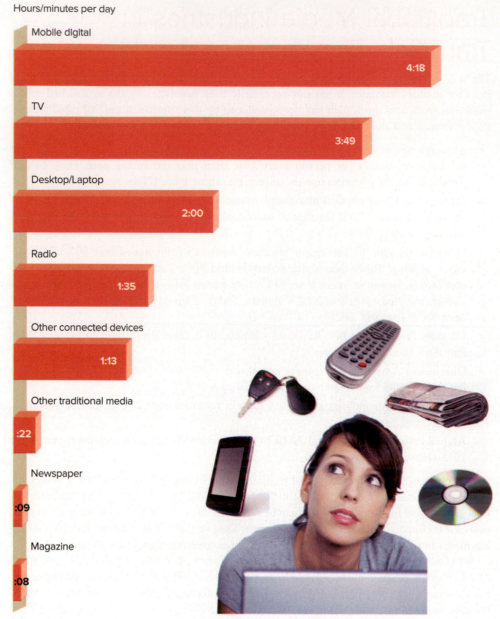

▶ **Figure 2.1** Average Daily Time US Adults Spend with Media, 2020 (in hours/minutes).
Source: Dolliver, 2020.

(Young woman using laptop) Photo-Alto/Matthieu Spohn/Getty Images; (Phone) Thomas Northcut/Photodisc/Getty Images; (Car key) Burazin/Photographer's Choice/Getty Images; (TV remote & CD disc) George Doyle & Ciaran Griffin/Getty Images; (Folded Newspaper) Fuse/Getty Images

Hours/minutes per day

Mobile digital — 4:18
TV — 3:49
Desktop/Laptop — 2:00
Radio — 1:35
Other connected devices — 1:13
Other traditional media — :22
Newspaper — :09
Magazine — :08

Total : 13:35

In fact, even before the coronavirus altered every aspect of our lives, we were watching more videos, listening to more music, reading more often, playing more video games, consuming more news, and accessing the Internet more often than ever before; we were simply doing it in new and different ways. For media industries, these facts offer good news—readers, viewers, and listeners are out there in ever-increasing numbers, and they value the mass communication experience. These data also offer good news for literate media consumers—their consumption choices will shape the media landscape to come and, inevitably, the mass communication process itself.

Changes in the Process of Mass Communication

Media industries face a number of challenges that promise to alter their relationship with their audiences. Concentration of media ownership and conglomeration can constrict the number and variety of voices available to audiences. Those audiences are becoming fragmented, potentially making it more difficult for media organizations to reach them. Globalization not only fragments the audience even more, but it can also make it less profitable for a media company to tailor its fare for its own homeland. Hypercommercialization might allow those companies to earn more income, but at what price to an audience awash in commercials? And fueling all this change is **convergence**—the erosion of traditional distinctions among media. As we've already seen, content typically associated with one medium is quite likely to be delivered by any number of other media; we, the **platform agnostic** audience members having no preference on which medium to consume content, seem quite content with that state of affairs.

Concentration of Ownership and Conglomeration

Ownership of media companies is increasingly concentrated in fewer and fewer hands. Through mergers, acquisitions, buyouts, and hostile takeovers, a very small number of large conglomerates is coming to own more and more of the world's media outlets. In the last few years, for example, telecommunication conglomerate AT&T acquired satellite TV provider DirecTV for $49 billion; cable company Charter Communications acquired Time Warner Cable for $57 billion; another telecom giant, Verizon, bought Yahoo! and its many Web brands (*TechCrunch, Huffington Post,* Flickr, and Tumblr, to name just a few) for nearly $5 billion; Viacom and CBS merged, creating a $28 billion-a-year company that marries Paramount Pictures and cable channels such as MTV, Nickelodeon, Comedy Central, and BET with the CBS broadcast network, cable channel Showtime, 28 owned-and-operated TV stations, streaming service Paramount+, and publisher Simon & Schuster; AT&T, the country's second-largest wireless carrier, paid $85 billion for the multinational media and entertainment conglomerate Time Warner and its holdings such as HBO, CNN, Bleacher Reports, DC Comics, and the Warner Bros. movie studio; and Disney bought 21st Century Fox for $71 billion, gaining movie studios Twentieth Century Fox, Fox Searchlight, Fox 2000, Twentieth Century Fox Television, the FX channels, and Fox 21. Media observer Ben Bagdikian reported that in 1997 the number of media corporations with "dominant power in society" was 10. Today five companies—Comcast, AT&T, Disney, ViacomCBS, and Sony—own the vast majority of "the most powerful companies in [our] lives, many of which don't offer products like cars and refrigerators, but rather services like cable TV and broadband Internet" (Franken, 2017, p. 342; Littleton & Low, 2019).

This **concentration of ownership** is more than an economic issue. It is a fundamental principle of our democracy that we have a right to information from a wide diversity of viewpoints so that we can make up our own minds. Democracy—rule by the people—requires an independent media. This is the crux of former associate justice of the Supreme Court Hugo Black's eloquent defense of a vibrant media in his 1945 *Associated Press et al. v. U.S.* decision: "The First Amendment rests on the assumption that the widest possible dissemination of information from diverse and antagonistic sources is essential to the welfare of the public, that a free press is a condition of a free society." Closely related to concentration is **conglomeration**, the increase in the ownership of media outlets by larger, nonmedia companies. The threat is clear, explained Vermont senator Bernie Sanders:

> What you've got today . . . is about a half a dozen major media conglomerates that own and control the distribution of the information that the American people receive. That is a massive concentration of control. And what is never discussed about this is, What is the goal of these major media conglomerates? Is it to educate the American people? Is it to give the five sides of the issue? No. Their function as major media conglomerates, owned by very large financial interests, is to make as much money as they possibly can. . . . This is a disaster for democracy. (in Smiley, 2016)

But the conflict of interest between profit and public service is only one presumed problem with conglomeration. Another is the dominance of a bottom-line mentality and its inevitable degradation of media content. *Variety*'s Peter Bart (2014) explains that the "corporate giants" who own media companies are in a "race for consolidation [that] continues to accelerate, burying movies, magazines, books, and music under still more layers of corporate number-crunchers." Wall Street, he argues, favors risk-free companies, whether they are media outlets or supermarkets (p. 28). Bart was speaking of media in general.

As for journalism, Senator Sanders explains that the news "portrays politics as entertainment, and largely ignores the major crises facing our communities. . .As a general rule of thumb, the more important the issue is to large numbers of working people, the less interesting it is to the corporate media" (in vanden Heuvel, 2019).

Conglomeration also renders investigative journalism unwelcome, as **enterprise reporting**, stories written not from press releases, but those journalists discover on their own. These potentially-controversial stories pose the risk of litigation, lost advertising dollars, and angering the powerful. NBC News producer Rich McHugh confirmed, "If you speak to any reporter who has chased down a story, whether it be for a month or two to seven months, everybody has a version of their story getting killed" (in Battaglio, 2019).

Local news, in particular, has been diminished by corporate demand for profit. Only 164 full-time newspaper journalists now report on the bills, debates, possible corruption, and politicians in the nation's 50 state capitals (Barber, 2014). Only 21 of 50 states currently have even one daily newspaper reporter assigned to Washington, DC, to cover Congress (Lu & Holcomb, 2016).

This produces **news deserts**, areas starved for news vital to their existences, currently affecting more than 1,300 communities. Two hundred counties have no newspaper at all (Brown, 2020) and 900 have lost all local news coverage (all media) since 2004 (Stites, 2018). Local media were "always the engines that powered much of American journalism, as great local reporting would bubble up to the national newspapers and television," write journalists Dan Rather and Elliot Kirschner (2018). They continue, "Local newspapers also provided a check on local and state governments, reporting on mayors, city councils, school boards, and statehouses. This is where much of the governing of the United States takes place, but a lot of it now occurs with little or no coverage."

A parallel product of concentrated ownership resides in **ghost papers**, once-prospering newspapers cut to bare bones in an effort to maximize profits, a state of affairs well-demonstrated by the *Ithaca Journal*. Located in upstate New York and one of the Gannett newspaper chain's 260 local papers, the daily has no locally based editor or publisher and only one reporter serving a town with 30,000 residents and another 30,000 students at Ithaca College. "Many" of Gannett's papers, admitted Amalie Nash, a company vice president, have 10 or fewer news staff, and "a lot" have five or fewer (in Edmonds, 2020). Newspaper industry researcher Penny Muse Abernathy has identified about 1,000 ghost papers across the country; they are, she says, "newspaper in name only, a newspaper that still has a nameplate, but its reporting abilities are drastically diminished (in Harris, 2020).

Both news deserts and ghost papers pose a problem for the culture because there is social scientific evidence that local newspapers, those "little machines that spit out healthier democracies," in the words of media writer Joshua Benton, "increase voter turnout, reduce government corruption, make cities financially healthier, make citizens more knowledgeable about politics and more likely to engage with local government, force local TV to raise its game, encourage split-ticket (and thus less uniformly partisan) voting, and make elected officials more responsive and efficient" (2019). You can read about recent efforts to overcome the problem of news deserts in the box titled "Should the Government Subsidize Local Journalism?"

There are, however, positive observations on concentration and conglomeration. Many industry professionals argue that concentration and conglomeration are not only inevitable but necessary in a telecommunications environment that is increasingly fragmented and internationalized; companies must maximize their number of outlets to reach as much of the divided and far-flung audience as possible. If they do not, they will become financially insecure, and that is an even greater threat to free and effective mediated communication because advertisers and other well-monied forces will have increased influence over them.

Another defense of concentration and conglomeration has to do with **economies of scale**; that is, bigger can in fact sometimes be better because the relative cost of an operation's output declines as the size of that endeavor grows. For example, the cost of collecting the news or producing a television program does not increase significantly when that news report or television program is distributed over 2 outlets, 20 outlets, or 100 outlets. The additional revenues from these other points of distribution can then be plowed back into even better news and programming. In the case of conglomeration, the parallel argument is that revenues from a conglomerate's nonmedia enterprises can be used to support quality work by its media companies.

The potential impact of this **oligopoly**—a concentration of media industries into an ever-smaller number of companies—on the mass communication process is enormous. What becomes of shared meaning when the people running communication companies are more committed to the financial demands of their corporate offices than they are to their audiences, who are supposedly their partners in the communication process? What becomes of

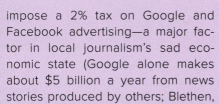

CULTURAL FORUM
Should the Government Subsidize Local Journalism?

Given the central role journalism plays in supporting democracy, it is no surprise that the United States has a long history of a government-supported press. Journalist Will Meyer (2018) quotes media scholars Robert McChesney and John Nichols to explain that historically there was little disagreement as to whether or not the press should be subsidized, but rather how much it should be: "While there were rollicking disagreements about the character and content of the post-colonial press in America, the one universally accepted the premise was that the government needed to heavily subsidize the creation and development of the press if the constitutional system were to succeed." As a result, from the 1790s on, news publications enjoyed a subsidy in the form of reduced postal fees, by as much as 90%. Post offices and roads were improved expressly to increase the spread of newspapers and pamphlets, and governments at all levels were legally required to post (and pay for) official notices in local publications.

It was in this tradition that, in July 2018, New Jersey governor Phil Murphy approved legislation dedicating $5 million to his state's efforts to revive, strengthen, and transform local media. It created a Civic Information Consortium that invests "in valuable local-news coverage in parts of the state that have become news deserts and will elevate the voices of people of color and others who have been systematically ignored by many media outlets" (Karr, 2020).

The philosophy behind government subsidy of news is that if journalism is indeed a public service, people should fund it through their taxes. This seemingly radical idea entered the cultural forum as the coronavirus, with shuttered local businesses no longer advertising and historic levels of unemployment leaving people unable to spend, "ravaged anew" an already weakened local news infrastructure (Tracy, 2020).

Several ideas for government support, old and new, were debated. Among them was the reinstatement of the low-cost postal subsidy, dramatically slashed by the Postal Reorganization Act of 1970. Another was to impose a 2% tax on Google and Facebook advertising—a major factor in local journalism's sad economic state (Google alone makes about $5 billion a year from news stories produced by others; Blethen, 2020). This revenue would be used to establish a Local Free Press Fund. Another was granting generous tax credits to companies that sell their newspapers to non-profit organizations or mission-oriented for-profit operations (Waldman, 2020). A bipartisan group of 250 congresspeople proposed directing the federal government to allocate a specific amount of the ad budgets of its many branches to local media (Eggerton, 2020). There were also conversations about creating **community information districts (CiDs)**, much like water districts and fire safety districts, paid for through taxes or annual fees (about $40 per household per year), and designed to provide support for local journalism services in the geographic areas (districts) that fund them. A July 2020 national poll found significant support for this particular solution, with 62% of Americans expressing support for CiDs (Kiefer, vGalperin, & Winter, 2020).

Enter Your Voice

- Americans rarely want more government, especially in matters of the press, and few are happy paying more taxes, so what do you think of the idea of the government using public money to subsidize local news?

- Do you agree with journalist Jeff Jarvis who argued, "I see danger everywhere if government funds or in any way approves or interferes with journalism and speech," he said. "To accept funding from government, no matter the alleged safeguards, puts us at risk of mortal conflict of interest. Whom do we serve then? Need I say it? Follow the money" (in Ingram, 2020)? But doesn't all financial support, for example, from advertisers, come with the potential for conflicts of interest?

- How do you imagine your community might benefit from local journalism subsidized by the people rather than advertiser-supported local journalism? How might the type of coverage differ?

▲ News deserts threaten the democratic functioning of the press and democracy itself.
Marc Turcan/Shutterstock

the process itself when media companies grow more removed from those with whom they communicate? And what becomes of the culture that is dependent on that process when concentration and conglomeration limit the diversity of perspective and information? Or are the critics making too much of the issue? Is this unnamed manager of newspaper chain 10/30 Communications correct when he says, "Many companies in our industry have wrongly divided their focus among many customer groups. We do not. Our customer is the advertiser. Readers are our customers' customers" (in Wemple, 2016)?

Globalization

Closely related to the concentration of media ownership is **globalization**. It is large, multinational conglomerates that are doing the lion's share of media acquisitions. The potential impact of globalization on the mass communication process speaks to the issue of diversity of expression. Will distant, anonymous, foreign corporations, each with vast holdings in a variety of nonmedia businesses, use their power to shape news and entertainment content to suit their own ends?

Here in America, the concern is that media companies, with an eye toward an expanding worldwide market for their fare, will tailor their content to the widest possible global audience, ignoring story and character in their television shows and movies in favor of car chases and explosions. Foreign audiences understand big-time action and adventure; nuance and subtlety don't translate as well. Abroad, the worry is that high-quality American media content will overwhelm local media industries and local cultures. As it is, almost every country in the world, including our friends in Canada, puts limits of some sort on the amount and type of US media content they allow across their borders.

There is, however, an alternative view to these concerns. Different people from different cultures can learn from one another through the exchange of their different media. Rather than fear the sharing of the stories we tell, we should embrace them. In addition, defenders of increased globalization point to the need to reach a fragmented and widespread audience—the same factor that fuels concentration—as encouraging this trend. They also cite the growing economic clout of emerging democracies (and the need to reach the people who live in them) and the increasing intertwining of the world's economies as additional reasons globalization is necessary for the economic survival of media businesses.

Audience Fragmentation

The nature of the other partner in the mass communication process is changing too. Individual segments of the audience are becoming more narrowly defined; the audience itself is less of a mass audience. This is **audience fragmentation**.

Before the advent of television, radio, and magazines were national media. Big national radio networks brought news and entertainment to the entire country. Magazines such as *Life*, *Look*, and the *Saturday Evening Post* once offered limited text and many pictures to a national audience. But television could do these things better: It was radio with pictures; it was magazines with motion. To survive, radio and magazines were forced to find new functions. No longer able to compete on a mass scale, these media targeted smaller audiences that were alike in some important characteristic and therefore more attractive to specific advertisers. So now we have magazines such as *Creative Scrapbooker* and *Brides*, and radio station formats such as Country, Urban, and Lithuanian. This phenomenon is known as **narrowcasting**, **niche marketing**, or **targeting**.

Technology has wrought the same effect on television. Before cable television, people could choose from among the three commercial broadcast networks—ABC, CBS, NBC—one noncommercial public broadcasting station, and, in larger markets, maybe an independent station or two. Now with cable, satellite, and Internet video streaming, people have literally millions of viewing options. The television audience has been fragmented. To attract advertisers, each channel now must find a more specific group of people to make up its viewership. For example, Nickelodeon targets kids, TV Land appeals to Baby Boomers, and HGTV seeks Millennial homeowners.

The new digital technologies promise even more audience fragmentation, almost to the point of audiences of one. For example, cable companies have the ability to send very specific commercials not only to specific neighborhoods but even to individual homes. Spotify inserts individually targeted commercials as listeners stream podcasts from its site, using a process called **streaming ad insertion** (Carman, 2020). And if you've ever used an Internet search engine, you know that the ads you see are specific to you based on the history of your overall Internet use. So, too, are the search results you're offered. **Zonecasting** technology allows radio stations to deliver different commercials to specific neighborhoods, and **location-based mobile advertising**, as you no doubt know well, lets marketers directly send ads targeted to you wherever you are in that moment.

But if these **addressable technologies**—technologies permitting the transmission of very specific content to equally specific audience members—are changing the nature of the mass media's audiences, then the mass communication process itself must also change. What will happen as smaller, more specific audiences become better known to their partners, the media companies, in the process of making meaning? What will happen to the national culture that binds us as we become increasingly fragmented into demographically targeted **taste publics**—groups of people bound by little more than an interest in a given form of media content? Will there be a narrowing of our collective cultural experience as media's storytelling function is disrupted because we are each listening to stories we individually preselect or that are preselected for us? "Maybe one day," wonders *Creativity* magazine editor Teressa Iezzi (2007), "you won't be able to say anything to anyone because a common language or the ability to grapple with or laugh at something outside of your comfort zone will have fallen away" (p. 11). National Public Radio's Michael Oreskes (2016) adds, "'Nichefication' may strengthen the business prospects of [individual media] companies, but it weakens their ability to serve the public." This is because *the public* is now *many publics* with many different interests in need of service.

There is an alternative view, however. Audiences may well be fragmenting, but the interactivity encouraged and facilitated by the digital media will reconnect and reconfigure us into more numerous, more robust, more varied communities. There is indeed a lot of conversation, curiosity, and sharing taking place on social networking sites such as Twitter and Instagram; yes, it can be small and juvenile, but very often it is passionate, informative, observant, clever, subversive, and maybe even community-building.

Hypercommercialism

The costs involved in acquiring numerous or large media outlets, domestic and international, and of reaching an increasingly fragmented audience must be recouped somehow. Selling more advertising on existing and new media and identifying additional ways to combine content and commercials are the two most common strategies. This leads to **hypercommercialism**. The rise in the number of commercial minutes in a typical television show is evident to most viewers, as nearly 20 of every 60 minutes of network and cable television time is devoted to nonprogramming content (Friedman, 2018). Hypercommercialization has hit the Internet as well, as you surely know as you try to separate the brand tweets from those of the real people you follow on Twitter and work to block the endless commercials on your Facebook news feed.

The sheer growth in the amount of advertising is one troublesome aspect of hypercommercialism. But for many observers, the increased mixing of commercial and noncommercial media content is even more troubling. Of course, not everyone has a problem with this practice. Angela Courtin, chief marketing officer of movie and television studio Relativity Media, explains, "We have come to an intersection of media and content where marketing is content and content is marketing" (in Downey, 2015).

But what do you think of these "intersections"? If you are a fan of the Hallmark Channel's holiday movies you may have learned how to set up a Balsam Hill synthetic Christmas tree, how to set its remote-control lights, and how to bake cookies with a foldaway Ninja Food oven. The three kids on *Young Sheldon* routinely enjoy Jimmy Dean breakfast sausage, Count Chocula cereal, Dairy Queen cookie dough Blizzards, and Red Vines licorice. Dunkin' drink cups are never far from the camera in *America's Got Talent,* and Lay's snacks appear in every episode of Snapchat's reality show *Endless.*

▲ Rarely off-screen, the real star of *America's Got Talent* was for several seasons Dunkin' Donuts. *NBC/Photofest*

But at least subscription streaming services are commercial-free, yes? No. Every single original program on Amazon Prime contains paid product placements; so does 91% of Hulu's original content and 74% of Netflix's (Weprin, 2018). For example, if you watch Netflix's *Stranger Things* you watch brands like the Chicago Cubs, BMX bikes, Coke, Swatch, Vuarnets, Nike, Chucks, Baskin-Robbins, Levis, Burger King, JC Penny, Orange Julius, and Gap.

The global product placement business is worth $20.5 billion a year, more than half, $11.6 billion, in the US alone (Friedman, 2020a). So ubiquitous has this **product placement**—the integration, for a fee, of specific branded products into media content—become that the Writers Guild of America demands additional compensation for writing what are, in effect, commercials.

The producers' response is that product placement is not a commercial; rather, it represents a new form of content, **brand entertainment**—when brands are, in fact, part of and essential to the program. Toyota, Kraft Foods, Chase credit cards, and Cigna insurance are recurring "characters" on *Top Chef*. Musical artists not only take payment to include brands in their songs, but some, for example, Mariah Carey, also now integrate brands into their CD booklets. Music channel Vevo retroactively inserts products into already existing music videos. Celebrities like Kylie Jenner and Ariana Grande (more than $1 million per post) and Cristiano Ronaldo and Selena Gomez (more than $900,000 per post) accept payments from brands to include their wares in their social media posts (Conklin, 2020). There are branded podcasts (for example Blue Apron's *Why We Eat What We Eat* and *The Sauce* from McDonald's), and many e-books come not only with products integrated into their storylines but also with links to the sponsors' websites.

Sometimes hypercommercialism involves direct payments of cash in exchange for exposure rather than "mere" branding. Many radio stations now accept payment from record promoters to play their songs, an activity once illegal and called **payola**. It is now quite acceptable as long as the "sponsorship" is acknowledged on the air.

Again, as with globalization and concentration, where critics see damage to the integrity of the media themselves and disservice to their audiences, defenders of hypercommercialism argue that it is simply the economic reality of today's media world.

Convergence: Erosion of Distinctions among Media

Movie studios make their titles available not only on DVD and EST but for handheld video-game systems as well. Cable's AMC runs a slate of **webisodes**, Web-only television shows, to accompany its hit series *The Walking Dead*. Satellite provider Dish Network offers interactive, TV remote–based play of classic video games. Magazines *Allure* and *Vanity Fair* maintain digital video channels and produce their own television shows. It may be a smartphone, but it's also a camera . . . sales of digital cameras have dropped 87% since 2010 (Richter, 2020). Video-game consoles don't just let players download movies and television shows, surf the Internet, check their social media accounts, and tune in to the Weather Channel and the BBC; they also offer streaming of tens of thousands of feature films. You can subscribe to *National Geographic* and play its issue-matched video game online or on a smartphone. There are tens of thousands of US commercial, noncommercial, and foreign radio stations delivering their broadcasts online.

You can read *The New York Times* or *Time* magazine and hundreds of other newspapers and magazines on a variety of screens. And what can "newspapers, magazines, and books," "radio and recordings," and "television and film" really mean (or more accurately, *really be*) now that we can access digital texts, audio, and moving images virtually anyplace, anytime via **Wi-Fi** (wireless Internet) and handheld devices? This erosion of distinctions among media is called *convergence*, and it has been fueled by three related phenomena that have overwhelmed the mass communication process all at once. First is the digitization of almost all content, making it possible to transmit and share information across all platforms. Second is the increasing data speed of both wired and wireless networks, making access to that digitized content fast, easy, and seamless. Third are the remarkably fast and ongoing advances in communication technology that make once-unimagined ideas quite possible.

The traditional lines between media are disappearing. Concentration is one reason for this convergence. If one company owns newspapers, an online service, television stations, book publishers, a magazine or two, and a film company, it has a strong incentive to get the greatest use from its content, whether news, education, or entertainment, by using as many channels of delivery as possible. The industry calls this **synergy**, and it is the driving force behind several recent mergers and acquisitions in the media and telecommunications industries. In 2012 Facebook bought photo-sharing platform Instagram for $1 billion specifically to gain access to its app-based mobile services and to make its Facebook offerings more visual, therefore increasing the site's value to advertisers. In 2018 radio giant Sirius XM spent $3.5 billion for music streaming company Pandora. In 2014 Apple, also deciding that the future of music was streaming, paid $3.2 billion for the headphone and music streaming company Beats Music. That same year YouTube, wanting to bring real-time video gameplay to its already massive array of channels, paid more than $1 billion for the game-streaming service Twitch. In 2015, Activision paid nearly $6 billion for King Digital Entertainment in order to move its console-bound games such as *Call of Duty* and *World of Warcraft* to more mobile platforms where King, with hits such as *Candy Crush*, was dominant.

A second reason for convergence is audience fragmentation. A mass communicator who finds it difficult to reach the whole audience can reach its component parts through various media. A third reason is the audience itself. We are increasingly platform agnostic, having no preference for where we access our media content. Will this expansion and blurring of traditional media channels confuse audience members, further tilting the balance of power in the mass communication process toward the media industries? Or will it give audiences more power—power to choose, power to reject, and power to combine information and entertainment in individual ways?

▲ Convergence killed the video store, victimized by video downloads, streaming, and online rentals—products of the convergence of movies, video, and the Internet. Convergence is strangling the bookstore as well, victimized by downloads and portable e-readers, smartphones, and tablets—products of the convergence of print, the Internet, and smartphones.
(DVD Express and Borders store): Susan Baran

The New Mass Communication Process

One essential element of media literacy is *having an understanding of the process of mass communication.* Understanding the process—how it functions, how its components relate to one another, how it limits or enhances messages, which forms of feedback are most effective, and why—permits us to form expectations of how the media industries and the process itself can serve us. However, throughout this chapter, we have seen that the process of mass communication is undergoing fundamental change. Media-literate individuals must understand why and how this evolution is occurring. We can do this by reconsidering its elements as described in Figure 1.4.

Interpreter A—The Content Producer

Traditionally, the content producer, the source, in the mass communication process is a large, hierarchically structured organization—for example, Pixar Studios, the *Philadelphia Inquirer,* or CBS Television. And as we saw, the typical consequence of this organizational structure is often scant room for individual vision or experimentation. But in the age of the Internet, with its proliferation of **blogs** (regularly updated online journals that comment on just about everything), newsletter platforms like Ghost and Substack, and social networking sites such as Facebook where users post all variety of free personal content, the distinction between content consumer and content provider disappears. Now, Interpreter A can be an independent musician self-releasing her music online, a lone blogger, a solitary online scrapbooker, or two pals who create digital videos.

Traditional media outlets routinely make use of people as sources who would have once been called amateurs. For example, Forbes.com publishes the work of 1,400 contributors. Advertisers now routinely use **user-generated content** in their commercials, for example, Starbuck's annual holiday #RedCup Contest and Calvin Klein's "I_____in #MyCalvins ads. Tens of millions of producers, big and small, distribute their video fare on the Internet. Much, if not many of the dramatic images from the 2020 protests following the killing of George Floyd, viewed by millions around the world, were produced by everyday people, true citizen journalists (Morrison & Estes, 2020). What are Snapchat's 360 million and Instagram's 1 billion monthly users who upload 3 billion and 400 million images a day, respectively, if not producers of a huge amount of sometimes very engaging content? And as you read in this chapter's opening, Netflix lets viewers choose the direction and outcome of the plots in some of its programming.

In the newly evolving model of mass communication, content providers are just as likely to be individuals who believe in something or who have something to say as they are big media companies in search of audiences and profits. Now sources themselves, they are *the people formerly known as the audience*, and it is not simply technological change that has given them voice; it is the reduction of the **cost of entry** for content production to nearly $0 that those digital technologies have wrought that has made them all creators. "Rates of authorship are increasing by historic orders of magnitude. Nearly universal authorship, like universal literacy before it, stands to reshape society by hastening the flow of information and making individuals more influential," wrote futurists Denis Pelli and Charles Bigelow (2009). "As readers, we consume. As authors, we create. Our society is changing from consumers to creators."

What are the likely consequences of this change? Will the proliferation of content sources help mitigate the effects of concentration and conglomeration in the traditional media industries? Will the cultural forum be less of a lecture and more of a conversation? Will new and different and challenging storytellers find an audience for their narratives? Does journalist William Greider (2005), speaking specifically of the news, overstate when he says, "The centralized institutions of press and broadcasting are being challenged and steadily eroded by widening circles of unlicensed 'news' agents—from talk-radio hosts to Internet bloggers and others—who compete with the official press to be believed. These interlopers speak in a different language and from many different angles of vision. Less authoritative, but more democratic" (p. 31)?

▼ Convergence and the low cost of entry have made us all authors.

Mother Goose and Grimm used with the permission of Grimmy, Inc. and the Cartoonist Group. All rights reserved.

The Message

The message in the traditional mass communication model is typically mechanically produced, simultaneously sent, inflexible, and unalterable. Once AMC airs tonight's episode of *The Walking Dead*, it has aired tonight's episode of *The Walking Dead*. The consequence? Audiences either like it or don't like it. The program either succeeds or fails.

But we've already seen that different commercial spots can be inserted into programs sent into specific homes. You can download only four tracks of an artist's latest CD, add three more from an earlier release, and listen to a completely unique, personally created album. Every music-streaming service now available allows you to create your own personalized "radio station" or playlist. **RSS**, or **really simple syndication**, feeds are aggregators that allow Web users to create their own content assembled from the Internet's limitless supply of material. Some of the most popular are Feedreader and NewsBlur. Users tell the aggregator what sites to collect, or their topics of interest, or even their favorite writers. As soon as any new content in their preselected categories appears online, it is automatically brought to their RSS file. Feedly, for example, is free and users can follow up to 100 sources, sort the sites into topical categories, watch YouTube videos, and read full-text articles.

As such, these aggregated "messages" are infinitely alterable, completely unique, and thoroughly idiosyncratic. Alternate-ending DVDs permitting viewers to "re-edit" an existing movie at home are old hat by now, but what do you think of director Steven Soderbergh's vision for a digital movie future? Some time ago he said that when theaters convert from film to digital projection, he would plan to exhibit multiple, different versions of the same film: "I think it would be very interesting to have a movie out in release and then, just a few weeks later say, 'Here's version 2.0, recut, rescored.' The other version is still out there—people can see either or both" (in Jardin, 2005, p. 257). Well, it's nearly 20 years later and digital projection is a reality, but alternate-ending movies haven't hit the big screen yet. Is it because the movie industry is content to stay with its mechanically produced, simultaneously sent, inflexible, unalterable films, or is it because *we* aren't ready for them yet?

What will be the impact on the mass communication process when content producers no longer have to amass as large an audience as possible with a single, simultaneously distributed piece of content? When a producer can sell very specific, very idiosyncratic, constantly changing content to very specific, very idiosyncratic, constantly changing consumers, will profitability and popularity no longer be so closely linked? What will "popular" and "profitable" messages really mean when audience members can create infinitely "alterable" messages? What will happen when the mass communication process, long dependent on **appointment consumption** (audiences consume content at a time predetermined by the producer and distributor; for example, a movie time at a theater, your favorite television show at 9:00 p.m. on Tuesdays, news at the top of the hour, your magazine in your mailbox on the third of the month), evolves more completely to **consumption on demand** (the ability to consume any content, anytime, anywhere)?

Feedback and Interpreter B—The Audience

In the traditional model of the mass communication process, feedback is inferential and delayed—what is a newspaper's circulation, what were this weekend's box office numbers for that movie, what are that program's ratings? Likewise, the audience is typically seen as large and heterogeneous, known to content producers and distributors in a relatively rudimentary way, little more than basic demographics.

But digital media have changed what content creators and distributors know about their audiences (Interpreter B) because they have changed how audiences talk back to those sources (feedback). Silicon Valley marketing consultant Richard Yanowitch explains, "The Internet is the most ubiquitous experimental lab in history, built on two-way, real-time interactions with millions of consumers whose individual consumption patterns can for the first time be infinitesimally measured, monitored, and molded." Adds Google advertising executive Tim Armstrong, "Traditionally, the focus has been on the outbound message. But we think the information coming back in is as important or more important than the messages going out" (both in Streisand & Newman, 2005, p. 60).

In today's mass communication, every visit to a specific Web address (and every click of a mouse once there), every download of a piece of content, and every product bought online provide feedback to someone. But it isn't just the Internet—every selection of a channel on cable or satellite; every rental or purchase by credit card of a video game or movie ticket; and every consumer product scanned at the checkout counter or purchased from an Internet-connected vending machine is recorded and stored in order to better identify us to Interpreter A, whomever that might be.

But this raises the question, Who is Interpreter A? It might be content providers who want to serve us more effectively because they know us so much more thoroughly than they once did when relying solely on demographics. Or it could be those who would make less honorable use of the feedback we so willingly provide—for example, identity thieves or a potential employer who would deny you a job because of your political or religious beliefs.

The Result

How will we use the new communication technologies? What will be our role in the new, emerging mass communication process? The world of content creators and distributors is now more democratic. Audiences, even though they may be fragmented into groups as small as one person or as large as 100 million, are better known to those who produce and distribute content, and they can talk back more directly and with more immediacy. Content, the message, is now more flexible, infinitely alterable, and unbound by time and space. Clearly, for content producers, there is more room for experimentation in content creation and consumption. There is less risk, and possibly even great reward, in challenging audiences. The evolving mass communication process promises not only efficiency but also great joy, boundless choice, and limitless access to information for all its partners. But the technologies that help provide these gifts are in fact double-edged swords: they cut both ways, good and bad. Media-literate people, because they understand the mass communication process in which they participate, are positioned to best decide how to benefit from the potential of those technologies and how to limit their peril.

DEVELOPING MEDIA LITERACY SKILLS
Making Our Way in the Meme Culture

At the end of his 1967 book *The Selfish Gene*, noted evolutionary biologist Richard Dawkins introduced the term *meme*. He likened memes to genes: "Memes propagate themselves in the meme pool by leaping from brain to brain via a process which, in the broad sense, can be called imitation" (in Staley, 2019, p. 14). He continued his analogy, arguing that, like genes, memes compete with each other for limited resources; memes compete for attention, because without attention they cease to be. And while he was speaking of any idea that spreads from person to person in a culture, he came to accept the Internet-based meaning of **meme**, an online idea or image that is repeatedly copied, manipulated, and shared.

For Professor Dawkins, memes are how ideas come into being, are propagated, and (if they survive) serve their host, the culture in which they flourish. But what of Internet memes specifically? Critics of meme culture argue that the ideas most likely to be spread—go viral—are the ones most guaranteed to attract attention. So we spend (or possibly waste) time on epic fail videos and funny cat pictures with oddly spelled slogans (the I Can Has Cheezburger Meme network has hundreds of millions of page and video views each month).

But maybe we aren't wasting time. Maybe we're building community by creating, viewing, and sharing ideas; on Instagram, for example, memes are 7 times more likely to be shared than non-meme content (Mezrahi, 2019). "Memes help people speak truths," writes technologist Jay Owens (2019). Memes are "iterative and quotable. That is how the meme functions, through reference to the original context and memes that have come before, coupled with creative remixing to speak to a particular audience, topic, or moment. Each new instance of a meme is thereby automatically familiar and recognizable."

Memes are unlike the traditional media that carry cultural ideas, bound as they are by economic and ethical considerations. As a result, argues tech writer Joan Donovan, as memes "are shared they shed the context of their creation, along with their authorship. Unmoored from the trappings of an author's reputation or intention, they become the collective property of the culture. As such, memes take on a life of their own, and no one has to answer for transgressive or hateful ideas" (2019). As such, hateful, racist, and misogynistic memes flourish on the Internet, often weaponized into **meme wars**, the use of images, slogans, and video for political purposes, typically employing disinformation and half-truths.

White supremacists utilize meme culture to spread their messages widely. For example, the so-called Boogaloo Bois, a dangerous far-Right militia intent on fomenting race war in America, are "loosely bound together by anti-government and pro-gun sentiment and memes . . . Like many other fringe groups, the Boogaloo's memes create a playful atmosphere that makes them approachable despite their extremism" (Ellis, 2020). Likewise, explained technology writer Abby Ohlheiser, in addition to pillaging and looting "the People's House," engaging in sedition, and brawling with police, killing one officer, the Donald Trump supporters, including a large Boogaloo Bois contingent, who invaded the US Capitol in January 2021 in an effort to block Congress from confirming Joe Biden's presidential win, were "having fun doing memes in the halls of American democracy" (2021).

Still, the most identifiable take-over of a meme by a hateful ideology involves Pepe the Frog. The Pepe the Frog cartoon, originally created in 2005 by artist Matt Furie and a hit meme subject on its own for years, was appropriated by white nationalists in 2016. Used in this racist manner, Pepe was declared a hate symbol by the Anti-Defamation League. Sufficiently dismayed by its vile use, Furie killed off Pepe in 2017, and then resurrected him in an attempt to regain control of his creation. He failed, as racists and anti-Semites continue to "own" Pepe (Rivera, 2020). The dark side of memes is that once they are in the culture, no one can control their use.

Memes survive because *we* spread them. They attract our attention, and we share them to attract the attention of others. But maybe this is how it should be in our new era of mass communication. We now have the opportunity to express ourselves, however seriously or frivolously, to offer our own point of view, however well-founded or off-the-wall, all without someone else vetting us. It makes us feel that what we have to say matters. This is the Internet's great gift to mass communication. But it is also its greatest challenge. What do we do with this immense freedom and the power it grants each of us?

As a media-literate individual, you understand and respect the power of media messages and you know that media content is a text providing insight into our culture and our lives. So the choice is yours: How will you use the Internet and social media? Memes are easy and fun; you are free to create and share them, to have a laugh, to skewer or honor. But the Internet and social media are also sites for more meaningful personal and cultural expression. You are free to undertake that more valuable, if a bit more difficult, work. What will you do? This question and some answers run throughout this text; the lessons you draw from what you read will be your own.

◀ Pepe the Frog: The meme that put a gentler face on the hate and ignorance of white supremacy.
CARLO ALLEGRI/REUTERS/Alamy Stock Photo

MEDIA LITERACY CHALLENGE
The Fraction of Selection

An important part of being media literate is *having critical thinking skills that enable you to develop independent judgments about media and media content.* Challenge your own skill by predicting which media will survive and which will disappear as a result of the dramatic technological, economic, and audience-preference turmoil currently shaking the traditional media industries. Which will change and how? The answers depend on you and your media choices. In 1954, when television was doing to movies, newspapers, magazines, and radio what the Internet and smartphones are doing to today's media, communication scholar Wilbur Schramm created the *fraction of selection* to answer the question "What determines which offerings of mass communication will be selected by a given individual?" It looks like this:

$$\frac{\text{Expectation of Reward}}{\text{Effort Required}}$$

It suggests that you weigh the level of reward you expect from a given medium or piece of content against how much effort—in the broadest sense—you make to secure that reward. Now, consider your own media consumption. For example, how do you typically watch movies: at the theater, streamed, downloaded, on disc, wait for them to come to cable? What "data" would go in your numerator? In your denominator? Create your personal formula for other media consumption as well. News on the Internet versus the newspaper? Popular music on commercial radio versus streamed from the Internet? Compare your outcomes with those of your friends. Based on your results, can you speculate on tomorrow's media winners and losers?

Resources for Review and Discussion

REVIEW POINTS: TYING CONTENT TO LEARNING OBJECTIVES

▶ **Summarize broad current trends in mass media, especially concentration of ownership and conglomeration, globalization, audience fragmentation, hypercommercialization, and convergence.**

- Encouraged by the Internet and other digital technologies, content producers are finding new ways to deliver content to audiences.
- All of the traditional media have begun to see either flattening or declines in audience, yet overall consumption of media is at all-time highs.
- Five trends are abetting this situation—convergence, audience fragmentation, concentration of ownership and conglomeration, globalization, and hypercommercialism.

- Convergence is fueled by three elements—digitization of nearly all information, high-speed connectivity, and advances in technology's speed, memory, and power.

▶ **Describe in broad terms how the mass communication process itself will evolve as the role of the audience in this new media environment is altered.**

- Content providers can now be lone individuals aided by low cost of entry.
- Messages can now be quite varied, idiosyncratic, and freed of the producers' time demands.
- Feedback can now be instantaneous and direct, and, as a result, audiences, very small or very large, can be quite well known to content producers and distributors.

KEY TERMS

day-and-date release, 32

media multitasking, 33

electronic sell-through (EST), 33

convergence, 35

platform agnostic, 35

concentration of ownership, 35

conglomeration, 35

enterprise reporting 36

news desert, 36

ghost papers 36

economies of scale, 36

community information district
  (CiD), 37

oligopoly, 37

globalization, 38

audience fragmentation, 38

narrowcasting, 38

niche marketing, 38

targeting, 38

zonecasting, 39

location-based mobile advertising, 39

streaming ad insertion, 39

addressable technologies, 39

taste publics, 39

hypercommercialism, 39

product placement, 40

brand entertainment, 40

payola, 40

webisode, 40

Wi-Fi, 40

synergy, 41

blog, 41

user-generated content, 42

cost of entry, 42

RSS (really simple syndication), 43

appointment consumption, 43

consumption on demand, 43

meme, 44

meme wars, 45

QUESTIONS FOR REVIEW

1. What is convergence?

2. What is media multitasking?

3. Differentiate between the concentration of media ownership and conglomeration.

4. What is globalization?

5. What is hypercommercialism?

6. What is audience fragmentation?

7. What are the two major concerns of globalization's critics?

8. What three elements are fueling today's rampant media convergence?

9. Differentiate among notions of content producers, audiences, messages, and feedback in the traditional view of the mass communication process and more contemporary understandings of these elements of the process.

10. What is the significance of low cost of entry?

To maximize your study time, check out CONNECT to access the SmartBook study module for this chapter, watch videos, and explore other resources.

QUESTIONS FOR CRITICAL THINKING AND DISCUSSION

1. Many industry insiders attribute the recent falloff in audiences for movies, recorded music, network television, DVD, radio, and newspapers to changes in technology; people are simply finding new ways to access content. And while this is certainly true to a degree, others say that in this age of concentrated and hypercommercialized media, audiences are simply being turned off by content that just isn't that compelling. Would you agree with the critics? Why or why not? Can you give examples from your own media consumption?

2. Critics of the concentration of media ownership and conglomeration argue that they are a threat to democracy.

What is the thrust of their concern? Do you share it? Why or why not?

3. A close reading of how the mass communication process is evolving has led some observers to argue that it is becoming less "mass" and more akin to interpersonal communication. Revisit Figure 1.4. From what you've read in this chapter and from your own media experience, can you make the argument that the "result" of the process has the potential to be more "flexible, personally relevant, possibly adventurous, challenging, or experimental"?

REFERENCES

1. *Associated Press et al. v. United States,* 326 U.S. 1, 89 L. Ed. 2013, 65 S. Ct. 1416 (1945).

2. Barber, G. (2014, July 10). Study: Statehouse press corps in decline. *National Public Radio*. Retrieved from http://www.npr.org/sections/itsallpolitics/2014/07/10/330456166/study-statehouse-press-corps-in-decline

3. Barnes, B., & Sperling, N. (2020, December 4). Warner Bros. will stream new movies. *New York Times*, p. B1.

4. Bart, P. (2014, August 19). Anti-Amazon rebels remind us bigger isn't always better. *Variety*, p. 28.

5. Battaglio, S. (2019, November 29). Why TV networks may be afraid of investigative stories. *Los Angeles Times*. Retrieved from https://www.latimes.com/entertainment-arts/business/story/2019-11-29/does-network-tv-news-still-want-to-be-in-the-investigative-reporting-business

6. Benton, J. (2020, February 10). The Wall Street Journal join the New York Times in the 2 million digital subscriber club. *NiemanLab*. Retrieved from https://www.niemanlab.org/2020/02/the-wall-street-journal-joins-the-new-york-times-in-the-2-million-digital-subscriber-club/

7. Benton, J. (2019, April 9). When local newspapers shrink, fewer people bother to run for mayor. *NiemanLab*. Retrieved from https://www.niemanlab.org/2019/04/when-local-newspapers-shrink-fewer-people-bother-to-run-for-mayor/

8. Blethen, F. (2020, May 18). In this moment of multiple crises, we need strong local journalism. *Washington Post*. Retrieved from https://www.washingtonpost.com/opinions/2020/05/18/this-moment-multiple-crises-we-need-strong-local-journalism/

9. Brown, J. (2020, January 1). Local newsrooms across the country are closing. Here's why that matters. *PBS*. Retrieved from https://www.pbs.org/newshour/show/local-newsrooms-across-the-country-are-closing-heres-why-that-matters

10. Carman, A. (2020, January 8). Spotify will use everything it knows about you to target podcast ads. *The Verge*. Retrieved from https://www.theverge.com/2020/1/8/21056336/spotify-streaming-ad-insertion-technology-ces-launch

11. Conklin, A. (2020, March 9). Top 5 highest paid social media influencers. *Fox Business*. Retrieved from https://www.foxbusiness.com/money/5-highest-paid-social-influencers

12. Doctor, K. (2020, March 27). Newsonomics: What was once unthinkable is quickly becoming reality in the destruction of local news. *NiemanLab*. Retrieved from https://www.nieman-lab.org/2020/03/newsonomics-what-was-once-unthinkable-is-quickly-becoming-reality-in-the-destruction-of-local-news/

13. Dolliver, M. (2020, April). US time spent with media 2020. *eMarketer*. Retrieved from https://www.emarketer.com/content/us-time-spent-with-media-2020

14. Donovan, J. (2019, October 24). How memes got weaponized: A short history. *MIT Technology Review*. Retrieved from https://www.technologyreview.com/2019/10/24/132228/political-war-memes-disinformation/

15. Downey, K. (2015, January 21). Product placement V2.0 is hot brand strategy. *TVNewscheck.com*. Retrieved from http://www.tvnewscheck.com/article/82404/product-placement-v20-is-hot-brand-strategy

16. Edmonds, R. (2020, June 10). At Gannett's Ithaca Journal, local news staffing is down to one reporter. *Poynter*. Retrieved from https://www.poynter.org/locally/2020/at-gannetts-ithaca-journal-local-news-staffing-is-down-to-one-reporter/

17. Eggerton, J. (2020, April 20). House majority favors fed ad dollars for local media. *Multichannel News*. Retrieved from https://www.multichannel.com/news/house-majority-favors-fed-ad-dollars-for-local-media

18. Ellis, E. G. (2020, June 18). The meme-fueled rise of a dangerous, far-right militia. *Wired*. Retrieved from https://www.wired.com/story/boogaloo-movement-protests/

19. Epstein, A. (2020, March 25). All broadcast TV needed to slow its ratings decline was a coronavirus pandemic. *Quartz*. Retrieved from https://qz.com/1824422/coronavirus-has-stopped-the-decline-of-broadcast-tv-ratings/

20. Franken, A. (2017). *Al Franken: Giant of the Senate*. New York: Twelve Books.

21. "Frequency of going to movie theaters to see a movie among adults in the United States as of June 2019." (2020). *Statista*. Retrieved from https://www.statista.com/statistics/264396/frequency-of-going-to-the-movies-in-the-us/

22. Friedman, W. (2021, January 15). Netflix leaps into big movie promotion, competitive with legacy film studios. *MediaPost*. Retrieved from https://www.mediapost.com/publications/article/359600/netflix-leaps-into-big-movie-promotion-competitiv.html

23. Friedman, W. (2020a, September 2). Growing U.S. product placement: How far can it go? *MediaPost*. Retrieved from https://www.mediapost.com/publications/article/355370/growing-us-product-placement-how-far-can-it-go.html?edition=119677

24. Friedman, W. (2020b, May 4). Should studios, movie theaters consider new TV deals? *MediaPost*. Retrieved from https://www.mediapost.com/publications/article/350933/should-studios-movie-theaters-consider-new-tv-dea.html

25. Friedman, W. (2018, May 16). 2 networks limit prime-time ad inventory. *MediaPost*. Retrieved from https://www.mediapost.com/publications/article/319292/2-networks-limit-prime-time-ad-inventory.html

26. Gingerich, J. (2020, May 29). Print ad spends to decline 20% in 2020. *O'Dwyers*. Retrieved from https://www.odwyerpr.com/story/public/14348/2020-05-29/print-ad-spends-decline-20-2020.html

27. Greider, W. (2005, November 21). All the king's media. *Nation*, pp. 30–32.

28. Grieco, E. (2020, February 14). Fast facts about the newspaper industry's financial struggles as McClatchy files for bankruptcy. *Pew Research Center*. Retrieved from https://www.pewresearch.org/fact-tank/2020/02/14/fast-facts-about-the-newspaper-industrys-financial-struggles/

29. Harris, L. (2020, August 19). The context for the crisis: A Q&A with Penny Abernathy. *Columbia Journalism Review*. Retrieved from https://www.cjr.org/business_of_news/the-context-for-the-crisis-a-qa-with-penny-abernathy.php

30. Hissong, S. (2020, April 21). In a crisis, radio should be bigger than ever—so why isn't it? *Rolling Stone*. Retrieved from https://www.rollingstone.com/pro/features/radio-coronavirus-crisis-985533/

31. Iezzi, T. (2007, January 29). A more-targeted world isn't necessarily a more civilized one. *Advertising Age*, p. 11.

32. Ingram, M. (2020, January 24). Government funding for journalism: necessary evil or just evil? *Columbia Journalism Review*. Retrieved from https://www.cjr.org/the_media_today/government-funding-journalism.php

33. Jardin, X. (2005, December). Thinking outside the box office. *Wired*, pp. 256–257.

34. Karr, T. (2020, January 16). New Jersey releases funds for innovative initiative to support civic-minded news and information across the state. *Freepress.net*. Retrieved from https://www.freepress.net/news/press-releases/new-jersey-releases-funds-innovative-initiative-support-civic-minded-news-and

35. Kiefer, P., Galperin, S., & Winter, E. (2020, July 27). Information districts are a popular way to expand funding for public media. *Data for Progress*. Retrieved from https://www.dataforprogress.org/blog/2020/7/27/information-districts-expand-public-media-funding

36. Littleton, C., & Low, E. (2019, December 17). Media space race. *Variety*, pp. 48–53.

37. Lu, K., & Holcomb, J. (2016, January 7). In 21 states, local newspapers lack a dedicated D.C. reporter covering Congress. *Pew Research Center*. Retrieved from http://www.pewresearch.org/fact-tank/2016/01/07/in-21-states-local-newspapers-lack-a-dedicated-reporter-keeping-tabs-on-congress/

38. Meyer, W. (2018, May 7). The American experiment was built on a government-supported press. *Columbia Journalism Review*. Retrieved from https://www.cjr.org/opinion/government-subsidy-facebook.php

39. Mezrahi, S. (2019, November 17). Tips from a memelord. *New York Times Magazine*, p. 87.

40. Morrison, S., & Estes, A. C. (2020, June 12). How protesters are turning the tables on police surveillance. *Vox*. Retrieved from https://www.vox.com/recode/2020/6/12/21284113/police-protests-surveillance-instagram-washington-dc

41. Nielsen Music. (2020). *Year-end music report: US 2019*. Retrieved from https://www.billboard.com/p/nielsen-music-mrc-datas-us-year-end-2019-report-us

42. Ohlheiser, A. (2021, January 8). Of course you could have seen this coming. *MIT Technology Review*. Retrieved from https://www.technologyreview.com/2021/01/08/1015890/trump-twitter-facebook-abuse-harassment-conspiracy/

43. Oreskes, M. (2016, November 2). Journalists can regain public's trust by reaffirming basic values. *Columbia Journalism Review*. Retrieved from http://www.cjr.org/first_person/trust_media_coverage.php

44. Pelli, D. G., & Bigelow, C. (2009, October 20). A writing revolution. *Seed Magazine*. Retrieved from http://seedmagazine.com/content/article/a_writing_revolution/

45. "The Quarantine Streaming Boom." (2020, April 22). *Variety*, p. 31.

46. Rather, D., & Kirschner, E. (2018, August 16). Why a free press matters. *Atlantic*. Retrieved from https://www.theatlantic.com/ideas/archive/2018/08/why-a-free-press-matters/567676/

47. Richter, F. (2020, February 7). Digital camera sales dropped 87% since 2010. *Statista*. Retrieved from https://www.statista.com/chart/5782/digital-camera-shipments/

48. Rivera, J. (2020, September 4). Pepe the Frog doc shows what happens when white nationalists steal your cartoon. *Vanity Fair*. Retrieved from https://www.vanityfair.com/hollywood/2020/09/pepe-the-frog-feels-good-man-documentary-white-nationlist

49. Rys, D. (2020, February 25). US Recorded Music Revenue Reaches $11.1 Billion in 2019, 79% From streaming: RIAA. *Billboard*. Retrieved from https://www.billboard.com/articles/business/8551881/riaa-music-industry-2019-revenue-streaming-vinyl-digital-physical

50. Schnieder, M. (2020, February 18). "Friends" gets old-school binge. *Variety*, p. 20.

51. Smiley, T. (2016, November 14). Interview with Senator Bernie Sanders. *PBS.org*. Retrieved from http://www.pbs.org/wnet/tavissmiley/interviews/senator-bernie-sanders-2/

52. Staley, W. (2019, January 20). Brain candy. *New York Times Magazine*, pp. 13–16.

53. Streisand, B., & Newman, R. J. (2005, November 14). The new media elites. *U.S. News & World Report*, pp. 54–63.

54. Stites, T. (2018, October 15). About 1,300 U.S. communities have totally lost news coverage, UNC news desert study finds. *Poynter Institute*. Retrieved from https://www.poynter.org/news/about-1300-us-communities-have-totally-lost-news-coverage-unc-news-desert-study-finds

55. Sullivan, M. (2020, February 15). The future of local newspapers just got bleaker. Here's why we can't let them die. *Washington Post*. Retrieved from https://www.washingtonpost.com/lifestyle/media/the-future-of-local-newspapers-just-got-bleaker-heres-why-we-cant-let-them-die/2020/02/14/a7089d16-4f39-11ea-9b5c-eac5b16dafaa_story.html

56. "Tops of 2020: Television." (2020, December 12). *A. C. Nielsen*. Retrieved from https://www.nielsen.com/us/en/insights/article/2020/tops-of-2020-television/

57. Tracy, M. (2020, April 13). News media outlets ravaged anew by the pandemic. *New York Times*, p. B6.

58. vanden Heuvel, K. (2019, August 20). Bernie Sanders has a smart critique of corporate media bias. *Washington Post*. Retrieved from https://www.washingtonpost.com/opinions/2019/08/20/bernie-sanders-has-smart-critique-corporate-media-bias/

59. Waldman, S. (2020, May 15). It's time to uproot American newspapers from hedge funds and replant them in more hospitable ground. *Poynter Institute*. Retrieved from https://www.poynter.org/business-work/2020/its-time-to-uproot-american-newspapers-from-hedge-funds-and-replant-them-into-more-hospitable-ground/

60. Wemple, E. (2016, October 17). Report: McNewspapers are gobbling up small-town America. *The Washington Post*. Retrieved from https://www.washingtonpost.com/blogs/erik-wemple/wp/2016/10/17/report-mcnewspapers-are-gobbling-up-small-town-america/?utm_term=.48c5710f0959

61. Weprin, A. (2018, January 30). No commercials? No problem. Brand integration thrives on streaming platforms. *MediaPost*. Retrieved from https://www.mediapost.com/publications/article/313665/no-commercials-no-problem-brand-integrations-thr.html

62. "Year End Report: U.S. 2020." (2021, January). *MRC Data*. Retrieved from https://www.musicbusinessworldwide.com/files/2021/01/MRC_Billboard_YEAR_END_2020_US-Final.pdf

Cultural Forum Blue Column icon, Media Literacy Red Torch Icon, Using Media Green Gear icon, Developing Media book in starburst icon: ©McGraw Hill

Racism &
Social Justice

Books

3

◀ As America was rocked by massive protests over police brutality in the summer of 2020, books on racism and social justice enriched a necessary cultural conversation and helped sow the seeds of change.

Pat Canova/Alamy Stock Photo

Learning Objectives

Books were the first mass medium and are, in many ways, the most personal. They inform and entertain. They are repositories of our pasts and agents of personal development and social change. Like all media, they mirror the culture. After studying this chapter, you should be able to

▶ Recognize the history and development of the publishing industry and the book itself as a medium.

▶ Describe the cultural value of books and the implications of censorship for democracy.

▶ Recall how the organizational and economic nature of the contemporary book industry shapes the content of books.

▶ Apply skills to be a more media-literate consumer of books, especially in considering their uniqueness in an increasingly mass-mediated, media-converged world.

1456 ▶ First Gutenberg Bible ·

1638 First printing press in the colonies

1644 ▶ *The Whole Booke of Psalms,* first book · · · · · printed in the colonies

1600

North Wind Picture Archives

1732 ▶ *Poor Richard's Almanack* · · · · · · · · · · · · ·

1765 Stamp Act

1774 Thomas Paine writes *Common Sense*

1700

~1800 Continuous roll paper

1807 John Wiley & Sons established

1811 Steam-powered printing press

1817 Harper Brothers established

1830 Improved pulp making

1852 Stowe's *Uncle Tom's Cabin*

1860 Dime novels appear

1861 US achieves highest literacy rate in the world

1884 Linotype machine

1885 Offset lithography

1800

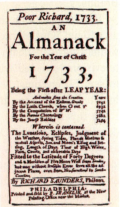

Universal History Archive/ UIG/Getty Images

Library of Congress Rare Books and Special Collections Division [BS1440 .B4 1640]

1926 Book of the Month Club begins

1935 Penguin Books (first paperbacks) established in London

1939 Pocket Books (paperbacks) established in the US

1953 ▶ Bradbury's *Fahrenheit 451* · · · · · · · · · · · ·

1960 Paperback sales surpass hardback sales for the first time

1995 Amazon.com goes online

1900

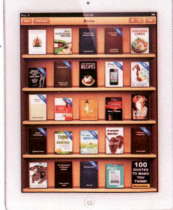

TCD/Prod.DB/Alamy Stock Photo

2000 First in-book paid product placement

2003 Project Gutenberg and *Search Inside the Book* debut

2007 Final *Harry Potter* book; Amazon's Kindle

2008 On-demand titles exceed number of traditional titles

2009 For first time, Amazon sells more e-books than hard-copy books in one day (Christmas Day) Little Free Libraries launched

2010 ▶ iPad

2011 E-books outsell all print books on Amazon

2017 Annual number of self-published books surpasses 1 million

2018 Audiobooks become publishing's fastest growing sector

2020 Coronavirus in the US; libraries become "second responders;" sales of books on racism soar; literacy declared a Constitutional right

2000

Oleksiy Maksymenko Photography/Alamy Stock Photo

YOU JUST WALKED INTO A ROOM WHERE YOUR FRIENDS ARE ENJOYING A MOVIE YOU'VE NEVER SEEN BEFORE. So there you are, watching an arresting scene from HBO's adaptation of Ray Bradbury's 1953 science fiction classic *Fahrenheit 451.*

At first, you can't make out what is happening. There are several people in a barn who seem to be talking to themselves. You recognize actor Michael B. Jordan from *Black Panther*, but the other performers are completely unfamiliar. You stay with the scene. It's dark, and there's a bird. A young man quietly recites some prose. Before you can figure out what it all means, the movie ends.

Moved by the film, the next day you download the e-book to your tablet, and you eventually discover that these people aren't just mumbling to themselves; they're memorizing books. In this near-future society, all books have been banned by the authorities, forcing book lovers into hiding. They hold the books in their heads because to hold them in their hands is a crime. If discovered with books, people are jailed and the books are set afire—*Fahrenheit 451* is the temperature at which book paper will burst into flames, according to Bradbury.

Bradbury's main character, Guy Montag, a firefighter who until this moment had been an official book burner himself, speaks a line that stays with you. After he watches an old woman burn to death with her forbidden volumes, he implores his ice-cold, drugged, and television-deadened wife to understand what he is only then realizing. He pleads with her to see: "There must be something in books, things we can't imagine, to make a woman stay in a burning house; there must be something there" (pp. 49–50).

In this chapter, we examine the history of books, especially in terms of their role in the development of the United States. We discuss the importance that has traditionally been ascribed to books, as well as the scope and nature of the book industry. We address the various factors that shape the contemporary economics and structures of the book industry, examining at some length the impact of convergence, concentration, and hypercommercialism on the book industry and its relationship with its readers. Finally, we discuss the media literacy issues inherent in the wild success of the *Harry Potter* books.

A Short History of Books

As detailed in Chapter 1, the use of Gutenberg's printing press spread rapidly throughout Europe in the last half of the 15th century. But the technological advances and the social, cultural, and economic conditions necessary for books to become a major mass medium were three centuries away. As a result, it was a printing press and a book industry much like those of Gutenberg's time that first came to the New World in the 17th century.

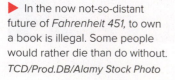

▶ In the now not-so-distant future of *Fahrenheit 451*, to own a book is illegal. Some people would rather die than do without. *TCD/Prod.DB/Alamy Stock Photo*

Books Come to Colonial North America

The earliest colonists came to America primarily for two reasons: to escape religious persecution and to find economic opportunities unavailable to them in Europe. So, most of the books they carried with them to the New World were religiously oriented. Moreover, they brought very few books at all. Better-educated, wealthier Europeans were secure at home. Those willing to make the dangerous journey tended to be poor, uneducated, and largely illiterate.

There were other reasons early settlers did not find books central to their lives. One was the simple fight for survival. In the brutal and hostile land to which they had come, leisure for reading books was a luxury for which they had little time. People worked from sunrise to sunset just to live. If there were to be reading, it would have to be at night, and it was folly to waste precious candles on something as unnecessary to survival as reading. In addition, books and reading were regarded as symbols of wealth and status and therefore not priorities for people who considered themselves to be pioneers, servants of the Lord, or anti-English colonists. The final reason the earliest settlers were not active readers was the lack of portability of books. Books were heavy, and few were carried across the ocean. Those volumes that did make it to North America were extremely expensive and not available to most people.

The first printing press arrived on North American shores in 1638, only 18 years after the Plymouth Rock landing. It was operated by a company called Cambridge Press. Printing was limited to religious and government documents. The first book printed in the colonies appeared in 1644—*The Whole Booke of Psalms*, sometimes referred to as the *Bay Psalm Book*. Among the very few secular titles were those printed by Benjamin Franklin 90 years later. *Poor Richard's Almanack*, which first appeared in 1732, sold 10,000 copies annually. The *Almanack* contained short stories, poetry, weather predictions, and other facts and figures useful to a population more in command of its environment than those first settlers. As the colonies grew in wealth and sophistication, leisure time increased, as did affluence and education. Franklin also published the first true novel printed in North America, *Pamela*, written by English author Samuel Richardson. Still, by and large, books were religiously oriented or pertained to official government activities such as tax rolls and the pronouncements of various commissions.

The primary reason for this lack of variety was the requirement that all printing be done with the permission of the colonial governors. Because these men were invariably loyal to King George II, secular printing and criticism of the British Crown or even of local authorities were never authorized, and publication of such writing meant jail. Many printers were imprisoned—including Franklin's brother James—for publishing what they believed to be the truth.

The printers went into open revolt against official control in March 1765 after passage of the Stamp Act. Designed by England to recoup money it spent waging the French and Indian War, the Stamp Act mandated that all printing—legal documents, books, magazines, and newspapers—be done on paper stamped with the government's seal. Its additional purpose was to control and limit expression in the increasingly restless colonies. This affront to their freedom, and the steep cost of the tax—sometimes doubling the price of a publication—was simply too much for the colonists. The printers used their presses to run accounts of antitax protests, demonstrations, riots, sermons, boycotts, and other antiauthority activities, further fueling revolutionary sympathies. In November 1765, when the tax was to take effect, the authorities were so cowed by the reaction of the colonists that they were unwilling to enforce it.

Anti-British sentiment reached its climax in the mid-1770s, and books were at its core. Short books, or pamphlets, motivated and coalesced political dissent. In 1774 England's right to govern the colonies was openly challenged by James Wilson's *Considerations on the Nature and Extent of the Legislative Authority of the British Parliament*, John Adams's *Novanglus Papers*, and Thomas Jefferson's *A Summary View of the Rights of British America*. Most famous of all was Thomas Paine's 47-page *Common Sense*. It sold 120,000 copies in the first three months after its release to a total population of 400,000 adults. Between 1776 and 1783, Paine also wrote a series of pamphlets called *The American Crisis*. *Common Sense* and *The American Crisis* made Paine the most widely read colonial author during the American Revolution.

THE EARLY BOOK INDUSTRY After the Revolutionary War, printing became even more central to political, intellectual, and cultural life in major cities like Boston, New York, and Philadelphia. To survive financially, printers also operated as booksellers, book publishers,

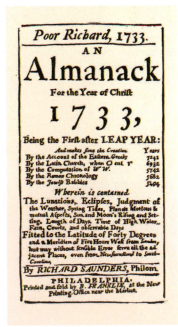

▲ First published in 1732, Benjamin Franklin's *Poor Richard's Almanack* offered readers a wealth of information for the upcoming year.

Universal History Archive/UIG/Getty Images

▲ British-born writer, patriot, and revolutionary leader Thomas Paine wrote *Common Sense* and *The American Crisis* to rally his colonial compatriots in their struggle against the British.
Library of Congress Prints & Photographs Division [LC-USZ62-46915]

and sometimes as postmasters who sold stationery and even groceries. A coffeehouse or tavern often was attached to the print shop. The era was alive with political change, and print shops and bookshops became clearinghouses for the collection, exchange, and dissemination of information.

The US newspaper industry grew rapidly from this mix, as detailed in Chapter 4. The book industry, however, was slower to develop. Books were still expensive, often costing the equivalent of a working person's weekly pay, and literacy remained a luxury. However, due in large measure to a movement begun before the Civil War, compulsory education had come to most states by 1900. This swelled the number of readers, which increased the demand for books. This increased demand, coupled with a number of important technological advances, brought the price of books within reach of most people. In 1861, the United States had the highest literacy rate of any country in the world (58%); and 40 years later at the start of the 20th century, nine out of every 10 US citizens could read.

THE FLOWERING OF THE NOVEL The 1800s saw a series of important refinements to the process of printing, most notably the **linotype** machine, a typewriter-like keyboard that allowed printers to set type mechanically rather than manually, and **offset lithography**, which permitted printing from photographic plates rather than from heavy, fragile metal casts. The combination of this technically improved, lower-cost printing (and therefore lower-cost publications) and widespread literacy produced the flowering of the novel in the 1800s. Major US book publishers Harper Brothers and John Wiley & Sons—both in business today—were established in New York in 1817 and 1807, respectively. And books such as Nathaniel Hawthorne's *The Scarlet Letter* (1850), Herman Melville's *Moby Dick* (1851), and Mark Twain's *Huckleberry Finn* (1884) were considered by many of their readers to be equal to or better than the works of famous European authors such as Jane Austen, the Brontës, and Charles Dickens.

The growing popularity of books was noticed by brothers Irwin and Erastus Beadle. In 1860, they began publishing novels that sold for 10 cents each. These **dime novels** were inexpensive, and because they concentrated on frontier and adventure stories, they attracted growing numbers of readers. Within 5 years of their start, Beadle & Company had produced over 4 million volumes of what were also sometimes called **pulp novels** (Tebbel, 1987). Advertising titles such as *Malaeska: Indian Wife of the White Hunter* with the slogan "Dollar Books for a Dime!" the Beadles democratized books and turned them into a mass medium.

THE COMING OF PAPERBACK BOOKS Dime novels were "paperback books" because they were produced with paper covers. However, publisher Allen Lane invented what we now recognize as the paperback in the midst of the Great Depression in London when he founded Penguin Books in 1935. Four years later, publisher Robert de Graff introduced the idea to the United States. His Pocket Books were small, inexpensive (25 cents) reissues of books that had already become successful as hardcovers. They were sold just about everywhere—newsstands, bookstores, train stations, shipping terminals, and drug and department stores. Within 8 weeks of their introduction, de Graff had sold 325,000 books (Menand, 2015). Soon, new and existing publishers joined the paperback boom, their popularity boosted by World War II soldiers' demand for "light, easily portable books" (Tompkins, 2020) and Fawcett Publication's decision in 1950 to start releasing paperback originals.

Traditionalists had some concern about the "cheapening of the book," but that was more than offset by the huge popularity of paperbacks and the willingness of publishers to take chances. For example, in the 1950s and 1960s, African American writers such as Richard Wright and Ralph Ellison were originally published in paperback, as were controversial works such as J. D. Salinger's *The Catcher in the Rye*. Eventually, paperback books became the norm, surpassing hardcover book sales for the first time in 1960. Today, the majority of all physical books sold in the United States are paperbacks, and bookstores generate half their revenue from these sales.

Books and Their Audiences

The book is the least "mass" of our mass media in audience reach and in the magnitude of the industry itself, and this fact shapes the nature of the relationship between medium and audience. Publishing houses, both large and small, produce narrowly or broadly aimed titles for readers, who buy and carry away individual units. This more direct relationship between publishers and readers renders books fundamentally different from other mass media. For example, because books are less dependent than other mass media on attracting the largest possible audience, books are more able and more likely to incubate new, challenging, or unpopular ideas.

As the medium least dependent on advertiser support, books can be aimed at extremely small groups of readers, challenging them and their imaginations in ways that many sponsors would find unacceptable in advertising-based mass media. Because books are produced and sold as individual units—as opposed to a single television program simultaneously distributed to millions of viewers or a single edition of a mass-circulation newspaper—more "voices" can enter and survive in the industry. This medium can sustain more voices in the cultural forum than can other traditional mass media. As former head of the New York Public Library Vartan Gregorian explained to journalist Bill Moyers (2007), when among books, "suddenly you feel humble. The whole world of humanity is in front of you. . . . Here it is, the human endeavor, human aspiration, human agony, human ecstasy, human bravura, human failures—all before you."

The Cultural Value of Books

The book industry is bound by many of the same financial and industrial pressures that constrain other media, but books, more than the others, are in a position to transcend those constraints. In *Fahrenheit 451,* Montag's boss, Captain Beatty, explains to Montag why all books must be burned: "Once books appealed to a few people, here, there, everywhere. They could afford to be different. The world was roomy. But then the world got full of eyes and elbows and mouths" (Bradbury, 1981, p. 53).

Bradbury's firefighters of the future destroy books precisely because they *are* different. It is their difference from other mass media that makes books unique in our culture. Although all media serve the following cultural functions to some degree (for example, people surf the Internet's self-help sites for personal development, and popular music is sometimes an agent of social change), books traditionally have been seen as a powerful cultural force for these reasons:

- *Books are agents of social and cultural change.* Free of the need to generate mass circulation for advertisers, offbeat, controversial, even revolutionary ideas can reach the public. For example, Andrew Macdonald's *Turner Diaries* is the ideological and how-to guide of the antigovernment militia movement in the United States. Nonetheless, this radical, revolutionary book is openly published, purchased, and discussed. When massive protests spread across the country in the wake of the summer, 2020, police killing of George Floyd, books on racism became staple reading for many Americans, helping sow the seeds of change. By the second week of the demonstrations seven of the 10 top best-selling books on Amazon and nine out of the top 10 at Barnes & Noble were about racism (Harris, 2020). (For a look at other culturally and politically important books, see the essay "Books That Changed American Life.")

- *Books are an important cultural repository.* Want to definitively win an argument? Look it up. We often turn to books for certainty and truth about the world in which we live and the ones about which we want to know. Which countries border Chile? Find the atlas. James Brown's sax player? Look in Bob Gulla's *Icons of R&B and Soul.* Books have been edited and fact-checked, unlike much of what you might find online, and they often contain information and detail that you might not know to search for.

- *Books are our windows to the past.* What was the United States like in the 19th century? Read Alexis de Tocqueville's *Democracy in America.* England in the early 1800s? Read Jane Austen's *Pride and Prejudice.* Written during the times they reflect, these books are more accurate representations than those available in the modern movie and television depictions.

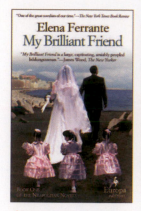

▲ Elena Ferrante's *My Brilliant Friend*, as well as the other books in her "Neapolitan Novels," and Suzanne Collins's *Hunger Games* trilogy are hugely popular sources of entertainment, escape, and personal reflection.
(left) Europa Editions; (right) Rune hellestad/Corbis/Getty Images

- *Books are important sources of personal development.* The obvious forms are self-help and personal improvement books. But books also speak to us more individually than advertiser-supported media because of their small, focused target markets. For example, *Our Bodies, Ourselves,* introduced by the Boston Women's Health Book Collective in the very earliest days of the modern feminist movement, is still published today. J. D. Salinger's *The Catcher in the Rye* was the literary anthem for the Baby Boomers in their teen years, as is William Gibson's *Neuromancer* for many Web pioneers. It is unlikely that any of these voices would have found their initial articulation in commercially sponsored media.

- *Books are wonderful sources of entertainment, escape, and personal enjoyment.* Suzanne Collins, John Grisham, Stephenie Meyer, and Stephen King all specialize in writing highly entertaining and imaginative novels. The enjoyment found in the works of writers Veronica Roth (the *Divergent* series), John Irving (*The World According to Garp*, *Hotel New Hampshire*), Paula Hawkins (*Girl on*

USING MEDIA TO MAKE A DIFFERENCE
Books That Changed American Life

Books have been central to many of the most important social and political movements in our nation's history. *Our Bodies, Ourselves*, a book for and about women, is credited with beginning the women's health movement. The profits this book generates—some 40 years after its first appearance—continue to support what has become a worldwide undertaking. This influential book, with more than 4 million copies sold in 18 different languages, was conceived of in 1969 when a group of women meeting on the issue of women's health came to the conclusion that most women were relatively ignorant about their bodies (and by extension, their sexuality) and that the male-dominated medical profession was not particularly receptive to their needs. So they gave themselves a "summer project" to write a book about women's health (Norsigian et al., 1999). In 2012, the Library of Congress designated that summer project one of 88 "books that shaped America."

But this is only one of many books that have had a profound effect on how Americans have come to live their lives. *Dr. Spock's Baby and Child Care* by Dr. Benjamin Spock was published in 1946. Selling more than 50 million copies in 42 languages, its opening line is "Trust yourself. You know more than you think you do." This then-revolutionary idea "was the first public acknowledgment of parents' unique knowledge of, and feelings for, their own babies," says psychologist Penelope Leach (in Stevens, 2012). It encouraged mothers and fathers to trust their own instincts, empowering them to parent with confidence and start to challenge established authority figures who long advocated keeping kids on strict schedules and carefully limiting affection.

Upton Sinclair's *The Jungle*, a fact-based work of fiction about America's meat industry, is "one of the most influential novels ever written. Published in 1906, it quickly became an international bestseller, inspiring sweeping and essential changes, including the passage of the Pure Food and Drug Act" (Andrew, 2018), that to this day continue to shape the safety regulations of our food as it is manufactured, shipped, and sold.

Silent Spring was released in 1962 as Rachel Carson's warning on the use of backyard pesticides such as DDT. "The number of books that have done as much good in the world can be counted on the arms of a starfish," writes *The New Yorker*'s Jill Lepore (2018, p. 64). We see its impact even today. *Silent Spring* launched the environmental movement; led to the passage of the Clean Air Act (1963), the Wilderness Act (1964), the National Environmental Policy Act (1969), the Clean Water Act, and the Endangered Species Act (both 1972); and led to the creation of the Environmental Protection Agency in 1970.

You might ask where is Elie Wiesel's *Night*, translated into English in 1960? It made the Holocaust feel real for millions of people who might have known it only from history books. Or *Fahrenheit 451*, significant enough to open this chapter? George Orwell's *1984*, again quite relevant in today's political climate? Harriet Beecher Stowe's *Uncle Tom's Cabin*, which awakened a still-young America to the horrors of slavery in 1852? Alex Haley's *Roots,* which reminded Americans of one of their country's most significant sins? Counterculture bible of the peace and love movement of the 1960s, Kahlil Gibran's *The Prophet*? There are scores more; you no doubt can offer a contender or two. But as a media-literate person, you might ask yourself if you could compile a similar list of TV shows or movies that have made the kind of difference wrought by these books.

a Train) is undeniable. "Books are "strange, magically potent talismans of safety, sanity, and order," explains writer Ptolemy Tompkins (2020, p. 18), and there is indeed research evidence that reading fiction, specifically novels, has powerful restorative powers, for example, in overcoming depression or loss. This use of reading for therapeutic effect is called **bibliotherapy** (Lindberg, 2020). Books' therapeutic potential may never have been more visible than during the 2020 coronavirus quarantine. Sales of print books were up over 6% from the same period the year before; demand was so high that printing companies were unable to turn out enough books to meet industry demand. "A book is the most uniquely, beautifully designed product to have with you in lockdown," explained Penguin Random House CEO Madeline McIntosh (in Alter, 2020a, p. B1).

- *The purchase and reading of a book is a much more individual, personal activity than consuming advertiser-supported (television, radio, newspapers, and magazines) or heavily promoted (popular music and movies) media.* As such, books tend to encourage personal reflection to a greater degree than these other media. We are part of the tribe, as media theorist Marshall McLuhan would say, when we consume other media. But we are alone when we read a book. "Books allow you to fully explore a topic and immerse yourself in a deeper way than most media today," explained Facebook founder Mark Zuckerberg on the launch of his book club, A Year of Books (in Widdicombe, 2015, p. 18).

- *Books are mirrors of culture.* Books, along with other mass media, reflect the culture that produces and consumes them.

- *Book readers are less likely to lose their jobs to robots.* Reading literature boosts human capital skills, says economist Morton Schapiro, and those "skills really pay off in the labor force. If you're worried about artificial intelligence, automation, robotics, outsourcing to cheaper providers in Hyderabad or other places, you'd better be able to understand people" (in Parramore, 2018). Book readers are soldiers in the resistance to the tech giant's takeover of humanity. "If the tech companies hope to absorb the totality of human existence," explains journalist Franklin Foer, "then reading on paper is one of the few slivers of life that they can't fully integrate" (in Kolbert, 2017, p. 45).

Libraries, Books, and Social Infrastructure

There is no better indicator of books' cultural value than people's widespread support for free and open access to public libraries. For example, when, in 2018, the Trump administration proposed to reduce funding for the Institute of Museum and Library Services, the federal agency charged with sustaining the nation's libraries, especially those in poorer rural and urban areas, the reaction was so swift and unfriendly that Congress actually voted to increase the Institute's budget (vanden Heuvel, 2018).

Supporters of libraries assert that libraries provide **social infrastructure**, physical spaces that shape the way people interact. Sociologist Eric Klineberg (2018) explained why libraries still matter:

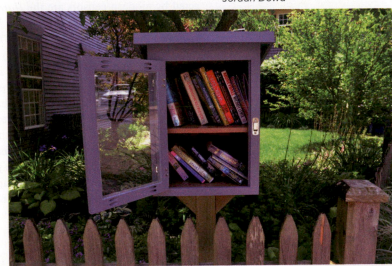

▼ 100,000 little libraries-on-a-stick dot the streets of 100 different countries.

Jordan Dowd

> Libraries are the kinds of places where people with different backgrounds, passions, and interests can take part in a living democratic culture. They are the kinds of places where the public, private, and philanthropic sectors can work together to reach for something higher than the bottom line. It's worth noting that "liber," the Latin root of the word "library," means both "book" and "free." Libraries stand for and exemplify something that needs defending: the public institutions that—even in an age of atomization, polarization, and inequality—serve as the bedrock of civil society. (p. SR6)

This reality is not lost on most Americans. Fifty-five percent of voters see the library as an essential local institution, and 53% see it as a source of community pride. Fifty-eight percent say public libraries advance education, and 51% believe libraries enhance the quality of life of their communities (OCLC, 2018). In fact, visiting the library is Americans' the most common communal cultural activity. Their annual average of 10.5 trips exceeds even the number of times they go to the movies and sporting events (McCarthy, 2020). Libraries' social infrastructure role was on vivid display during 2020's coronavirus pandemic, as they joined the ranks of "second responders," feeding the hungry, 3-D printing personal protection gear, providing 24-hour Wi-Fi hotspots, sheltering the homeless, offering emergency childcare, setting up curb-side book pick-up, and expanding availability to digital materials like e-books and online magazines (Fallows, 2020).

This libraries-build-community ethic spawned the Little Free Library movement in which individuals build small boxes and place them on posts on their lawns so that others can take and/or leave a book (originated in 2009, there are now 100,000 of these "libraries on a stick" in 100 different countries), and in some towns, even police cruisers have become bookmobiles, with which officers deliver a variety of titles to borrowers as they make their rounds ("The History," 2021).

Censorship

Because of their influence as cultural repositories and agents of social change, books have often been targeted for **censorship**. A book is censored when someone in authority limits publication of or access to it. Censorship can and does occur in many situations and in all media (more on this in Chapter 14). But because of the respect our culture traditionally holds for books, book banning takes on a particularly poisonous connotation in the United States.

Reacting to censorship presents a dilemma for book publishers. Publishers have an obligation to their owners and stockholders to make a profit. Yet, if responsible people in positions of authority deem a certain book unsuitable for readers, shouldn't publishers do the right thing for the larger society and comply with demands to cease its publication?

This was the argument presented by morals crusader Anthony Comstock in 1873 when he established the New York Society for the Suppression of Vice. It was the argument used in Berlin on the evening of May 10, 1933, when Nazi propaganda chief Joseph Goebbels put a torch to a bonfire that consumed 20,000 books. It was the argument made in 1953 when US senator Joseph McCarthy demanded the removal of more than 100 books from US diplomatic libraries because of their "procommunist" slant. (Among them was Thomas Paine's *Common Sense*.) It is the argument made today by people like the members of the Matanuska-Sustina Borough school board in Alaska who pulled *I Know Why the Caged Bird Sings* from the high school curriculum because it contained "sexually explicit material" and "anti-white messaging" (Taylor, 2020) and the parent group in Virginia's Loudoun County who unsuccessfully lobbied to banish *Hurricane Child* and *The Pants Project* from elementary school libraries because they featured LGBTQ characters (Nathanson, 2020).

According to the American Library Association Office of Intellectual Freedom and the American Civil Liberties Union, among the library and school books most frequently targeted by modern censors are the *Harry Potter* series, Mark Twain's *The Adventures of Huckleberry Finn*, Harper Lee's *To Kill a Mockingbird*, John Steinbeck's *Of Mice and Men*, the *Goosebumps* series, Alice Walker's *The Color Purple*, and children's favorite *In the Night Kitchen* by Maurice Sendak. You can see the 10 most frequently banned library books of 2020 in Figure 3.1. With how many are you familiar? Which ones have you read?

Book publishers can confront censorship by recognizing that their obligations to their industry and to themselves demand that they resist censorship. The publishing industry and the publisher's role in it are fundamental to the operation and maintenance of our democratic society. Rather than accepting the censor's argument that certain voices require silencing for the good of the culture, publishers in a democracy have an obligation to make the stronger argument that free speech be protected and encouraged. The short list of frequently censored titles in the previous paragraph should immediately make it evident why the power of ideas is worth fighting for. You can test your own willingness to censor in the box titled "Would You Ban Books by Nazis?"

1. *George* by Alex Gino (2015).
   Ages 8 to 12.
2. *Beyond Magenta: Transgender Teens Speak Out* by Susan Kuklin (2014).
   Ages 14 to 17.
3. *A Day in the Life of Marlon Bundo* by Jill Twiss, illustrated by EG Keller (2018).
   All ages.
4. *Sex Is a Funny Word* by Cory Silverberg, illustrated by Fiona Smyth (2015).
   Ages 7–10.
5. *Prince & Knight* by Daniel Haack, illustrated by Stevie Lewis (2018).
   Ages 4–8.
6. *I Am Jazz* by Jessica Herthel and Jazz Jennings, illustrated by Shelagh McNicholas (2014).
   Ages 4–8.
7. *The Handmaid's Tale* by Margaret Atwood (1985).
   Teens and up.
8. *Drama* written and illustrated by Raina Telgemeier (2012).
   Ages 10–14.
9. *Harry Potter series* by J. K. Rowling (began in 1997).
   Ages 9 and up.
10. *And Tango Makes Three* by Peter Parnell and Justin Richardson, illustrated by Henry Cole (2005).
    Ages 4–8.

▲ *The Handmaid's Tale* and *To Kill a Mockingbird* are two popular books that constantly raise censors' ire.
(left) Kathy deWitt/Alamy Stock Photo; (right) Thomas Cordy/Palm Beach Post/ZUMA Press/Alamy Stock Photo

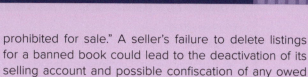

CULTURAL FORUM
Would You Ban Books by Nazis?

As 2016 began, a long-banned work showed up in German bookstores. Adolf Hitler's ultranationalist, racist, and anti-Semitic *Mein Kampf* reappeared after 70 years of censorship. Many Germans were appalled, arguing that the 1925 hate-filled tract, instrumental in the Nazi's rise to power, would further inflame the racist and xenophobic fervor that at the time of this new release seemed to be taking hold across Europe. Others were satisfied with the new version of the hateful book because, rather than a reissue of Hitler's original version, it was a heavily annotated edition, the culmination of 6 years of work by scholars from the Institute of Contemporary History in Munich. Their extensively researched rebuttal of the original's 600 pages of lies and half-truths swelled the reissue to 2,000 pages. "It would be simply irresponsible to let this racist work of inhumanity wander loose in the public domain without comment," wrote the Institute's director, Andreas Wirsching (in "Germany," 2016, p. 14).

Now consider this situation, one a bit closer to home. Amazon, the world's largest and most dominant bookseller (Shephard, 2020b), is "quietly canceling its Nazis." The online giant pulled from its list titles by David Duke, former leader of the Ku Klux Klan, and by George Lincoln Rockwell, founder of the American Nazi Party. Also banned are scores of anti-Semitic works like *Conspiracy of the Six-Pointed Star*, *The Ruling Elite: The Zionist Seizure of World Power*, and *A History of Central Banking and the Enslavement of Mankind*.

When Amazon drops a book it's as if it never existed, because not only does the company itself refuse to sell the book, but it refuses to honor sales from other sellers who provide much of its inventory. "Amazon reserves the right to determine whether content provides an acceptable experience," the company explained to one bookseller. . ."This product was identified as one that is prohibited for sale." A seller's failure to delete listings for a banned book could lead to the deactivation of its selling account and possible confiscation of any owed money.

The question that entered the cultural forum, therefore, is how far should a powerful—*the world's* most powerful—bookseller go in censoring disfavored expression? Deborah Caldwell-Stone, director of the American Library Association's Office for Intellectual Freedom, argued that Amazon has the same First Amendment right as any retailer, the "right to pick and choose the materials they offer. Despite its size, it does not have to sponsor speech it finds unacceptable."

"But," counter critics like Danny Caine, a bookstore owner and no fan of Nazi writing, "I still don't trust Amazon to be the arbiters of free speech. What if Amazon decided to pull books representing a less despicable political viewpoint? Or books critical of Amazon's practices?" (all quotes from Streitfeld, 2020, p. A15).

Enter Your Voice

- Did the Germans, in providing context and critique, offer a better solution to dealing with poisonous books than did Google, which simply banned them?

- Do you support the retailer's First Amendment right to deny expression to others, however odious? If so, what does this say about your commitment to free expression?

- There's an old expression in publishing, "There's no such thing as a little censorship." Do you agree? Why or why not?

Aliteracy as Self-Censorship

Censors ban and burn books because books are repositories of ideas, ideas that can be read and considered with limited outside influence or official supervision. But what kind of culture develops when, by our own refusal to read books, we figuratively save the censors the trouble of striking the match? First, there is the problem of **illiteracy**, the inability to read or write. A federal appeals court ruled in 2020 that literacy was a constitutional right, writing, "Effectively every interaction between a citizen and her government depends on literacy. Voting, taxes, the legal system, jury duty—all of these are predicated on the ability to read and comprehend written thoughts" (in Albanese, 2020). Nonetheless, today, 30 million adults in the United States cannot read or write, above a third-grade level (Editorial Team, 2020).

Then there is the issue of **aliteracy**, wherein people possess the ability to read but are unwilling to do so, which amounts to doing the censors' work for them. As Russian immigrant and writer Joseph Brodsky (1987) explained when accepting his Nobel Prize for Literature, "Since there are no laws that can protect us from ourselves, no criminal code is capable of preventing a true crime against literature; though we can condemn the material suppression

Demographics of US Adults Who Do Not Read Books

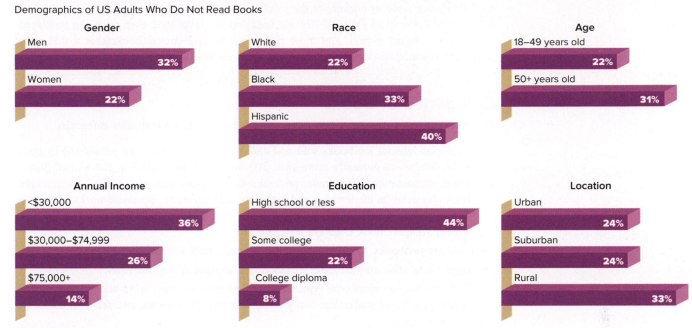

▲ **Figure 3.2** Percentage of American Adults Who Have Not Read a Book in the Last 12 Months. *Source: Perrin, 2019.*

of literature—the persecution of writers, acts of censorship, the burning of books—we are powerless when it comes to its worst violation: that of not reading the books. For that crime, a person pays with his whole life; if the offender is a nation, it pays with its history."

Only slightly more than half, 55%, of US adults has read a book in the past 12 months (Nawotka, 2020); the share of Americans who have not done so is higher today than it was a decade ago (Perrin, 2019). You can see the percentages of Americans who do not read by demographic in Figure 3.2. Do these data represent your reading habits? Do you agree with the argument that the lack of reading has consequences for our country, as well as for individuals?

And despite evidence that small children who are read to can recognize the letters of the alphabet, count to 20, write their own names, and read sooner than those who are not (National Education Association, 2019), a quarter of American kids from ages 0 to 8 are read to never or less often than once a week (Zickuhr & Rainie, 2014).

Declining reading rates are important far beyond issues of academic performance. Regardless of income, reading correlates closely with quality of social life, voting, political activism, participation in culture and fine arts, volunteerism, charity work, and exercise. National Endowment for the Arts chair Dana Gioia explained more than a decade ago after her organization's study of Americans' reading habits: "The habit of regular reading awakens something inside a person that makes him or her take their own life more seriously and at the same time develops the sense that other people's lives are real" (in Thompson, 2007, p. C1). Another well-qualified group of experts—your parents—endorses Gioia's argument. When asked to identify the skills "most important for children to get ahead in the world today," 86% identified reading, a score second only to that of communication's 90% (Clark, 2017).

Scope and Structure of the Book Industry

More than a million traditional and nontraditional (print-on-demand, self-published, and niche) titles are published in the United States each year. The American publishing industry annually sells over 1.8 billion print books ("Who We," 2021), producing about $15 billion in sales (Milliot, 2020b), and generating $26 billion in overall annual revenue (Milliot, 2020a).

And despite, or possibly because of the coronavirus lockdown, sales of print books increased 8.2% in 2020 over 2019 (Milliot, 2021b). Today, more books than ever are being published. More books are being read, and more people are writing books. Books that would never have been released through traditional publishers are now routinely published.

Categories of Books

The Association of American Publishers divides books into several sales categories:

- *Book club editions* are books sold and distributed (sometimes even published) by book clubs. There are currently more than 300 book club publishers in the United States. These organizations offer trade, professional, and more specialized titles—for example, books for aviation aficionados and expensive republications of classic works. The Book of the Month Club, started in 1926, is the best known; the Literary Guild and the Reader's Digest Book Club are also popular.

- *El-hi* are textbooks produced for elementary and high schools.

- *Higher education* are textbooks produced for colleges and universities.

- *Mass market paperbacks* are typically published only as paperbacks and are designed to appeal to a broad readership; many romance novels, diet books, and self-help books are in this category.

- *Professional books* are reference and educational volumes designed specifically for professionals such as doctors, engineers, lawyers, scientists, and managers.

- *Religious books* are volumes such as the Bible, the Koran, and the Śruti.

- *Standardized tests* are guide and practice books designed to prepare readers for various examinations such as the SAT or the bar exam.

- **Trade books** include not only fiction and most nonfiction but also cookbooks, biographies, art books, coffee-table books, and how-to books.

- *University press books* come from publishing houses associated with and often underwritten by universities. They typically publish serious nonfiction and scholarly books. The Oxford University Press and the University of California Press are two of the better-known university presses, and Cambridge University Press is the oldest publisher in the world.

Trends and Convergence in Book Publishing

Like all the media with which we are familiar, convergence is changing the nature of the book industry. In addition to convergence, contemporary publishing and its relationship with its readers are being reshaped by conglomeration, hypercommercialism and demand for profits, the growth of small presses, restructuring of retailing, and changes in readership.

Convergence

Convergence is altering almost all aspects of the book industry. Most obviously, the Internet is changing the way books are distributed and sold. But this digital technology, in the form of **e-publishing**, the publication of books initially or exclusively in a digital format, also offers a new way for writers' ideas to be published. In fact, many of today's "books" are no longer composed of paper pages snug between two covers. As former Random House editor Peter Osnos (2009) explained early in his industry's digital revolution, because books do not rely on advertising or subscribers, "[t]he main challenge is to manage inventory, making books available where, when, and how readers want them. And on that score, the advances in gadgetry and the changes in popular [reading] habits over the past decade...have produced a major advance" (p. 38). By gadgetry, Osnos means primarily e-books, print on demand (POD), and a host of electronic reading devices.

E-BOOKS In her mid-40s, Erika Mitchell, writing under the pen name E. L. James, was having some success publishing fan fiction based on the vampire novels *Twilight* as **e-books—** books downloaded in electronic form from the Internet to computers, e-readers, or mobile digital devices. This success brought her to the attention of traditional publisher Random House, and, working together, they turned her *50 Shades of Grey* trilogy into a series of best sellers and major motion pictures. In fact, those three titles are the last decade's top-3 selling books (Kelly, 2020). Romance writer Meredith Wild, who writes mainly after her children leave for school, has sold millions of self-published erotic novels on Amazon and other sites, and the success of her *Red Ledger* and *Book of Zeus* series brought her not only entry onto the *New York Times* and *USA Today* best-seller lists, but a multi-million dollar advance from traditional publisher Forever.

Established authors fare well, too: Stieg Larsson's best seller, *The Girl with the Dragon Tattoo*, and the other books in his trilogy, *The Girl Who Played with Fire* and *The Girl Who Kicked the Hornet's Nest*, have sold more digital than hard-copy editions, and big-name authors such as Stephen King now routinely write works primarily for e-publication.

Popular acceptance of e-books seemed in place by Christmas Day 2009, when Amazon reported that for the first time in its history, it sold more e-books than traditional paper books in a single day. Today, Americans read about 1.8 billion e-books a year, a number that has dropped in recent years (Milliot, 2020c). Industry experts explain the decrease in the growth of e-books to readers' digital fatigue, an explanation bolstered by data indicating that Americans' number-one favorite activity when unplugged from their digital devices is reading books in their paper version (Birth, 2016). You can see American readers' comfort with e-readers, by age in Figure 3.3.

▲ **Figure 3.3** Percentage of Americans Who Use and Prefer e-Readers, by Age.

Tanja Esser/Shutterstock

Source: Rae, 2020.

Still, e-publishing's greatest impact may be on new writers. In fact, the number of self-published titles has grown 156% since 2012 and in 2017 that number exceeded one million for the first time ("New Record," 2018). Why the growth? Because anyone with a computer and a story to tell can bypass the traditional book publishers, first-time authors or writers of small, niche books now have an outlet for their work. An additional advantage of e-publishing, especially for new or small-market authors, is that e-books can be published almost instantly. James Patterson has made enough money selling his books that he can wait the 1 to 2 years it typically takes for a traditional novel to be produced once it is in the publisher's hands. Rarely can new authors afford this luxury.

Another advantage is financial. Authors who distribute through e-publishers typically get royalties of 40% to 70%, compared to the 5% to 10% offered by traditional publishers. This lets aspiring writers offer their books for as little as 99 cents or $2.99, making those works more attractive to readers willing to take a low-cost chance to find something and someone new and interesting—earning writers even more sales. Authors who write for Amazon's e-reader Kindle, for example, earned more than $300 million in 2019 alone. More than a thousand of these Kindle Direct Publishing authors took in over $100,000 (Milliot, 2020c).

Still, traditional book publishers say their lower royalty rates are mandated by the expense of the services they provide, such as editorial assistance and marketing, not to mention the cost of production and distribution. The debate over self- versus traditional publishing is really a disagreement over the value of **disintermediation**, eliminating gatekeepers between artists and audiences. Eliminate the intermediaries and more original content of greater variety from fresher voices gets to more people. Keep the intermediaries and quality is ensured, and while an occasional interesting work or new voice might be missed, the industry's overall product remains superior. For books, disintermediation in the form of self-publication runs the gamut from completely self-published-and-promoted works to self-publishing with an assist, with digital publishers providing a full range of services—copyediting, securing and commissioning of artwork, cover design, promotion, and in some cases, distribution of traditional paper books to brick-and-mortar bookstores.

Print on demand (POD) is another form of e-publishing. Companies such as Xlibris, AuthorHouse, and iUniverse are POD publishers. They store works digitally and, once ordered, a book can be instantly printed, bound, and sent. Alternatively, once ordered, that book can be printed and bound at a bookstore that has the proper technology. The advantage for publisher and reader is financial. POD books require no warehouse for storage, there are no **remainders** (unsold books returned to publishers to be sold at great discount) to eat into profits, and the production costs, in both personnel and equipment, are tiny when compared to traditional publishing. These factors not only produce less expensive books for readers but also greatly expand the variety of books that can and will be published. And although a large publisher like Oxford University Press can produce thousands of volumes a year, smaller POD operations can make a profit on as few as 100 orders. Additionally, POD operations easily double as self-publishing houses, as do those listed just above. Large commercial publishers have also found a place for POD in their business, using the technology to rush hot, headline-inspired books to readers. In 2008, for the first time, American publishers released more POD titles than new and revised titles produced by traditional methods; in 2010 the ratio was more than three to one.

SMARTPHONES, TABLETS, E-READERS, AND AUDIOBOOKS Many booksellers and even publishing companies themselves offer e-books specifically for smartphones, tablets, and **e-readers**, digital devices with the appearance of traditional books that display content that is digitally stored and accessed. Although earlier attempts at producing e-readers had failed, the 2006 unveiling of the Sony Reader, dubbed the iBook, proved so successful that it was soon followed by several similar devices, such as Amazon's various Kindle models, Apple's iPad, and Barnes & Noble's Nook. (In 2014 Sony discontinued its e-reader technologies.) In addition, smartphone and tablet e-reader apps such as Libby, Bookari, and Scribd have also appeared. Today, the number of dedicated e-readers in use is in sharp decline; just under one in five American adults owns one (Haines, 2020), but because nearly 85% have smartphones and 53% have tablets, the large majority holds in its hands the ability to read digital books (Edison Research, 2020).

Nonetheless, readers have welcomed the devices and publishers have understandably responded, given the industry's belief that "any business that requires a truck these days, forget it" (Thompson, 2009). Hundreds of thousands of in- and out-of-print titles are available for **platform agnostic publishing**—digital and traditional paper books available for any and all reading devices. And those reading devices themselves will continue to evolve, with advances such as flexible screens so thin they can be rolled up and fully text-functional e-readers that let users copy and paste text to Word documents on their computers.

Book lovers have also flocked to **audiobooks**, the presentation, in sound, of a book's text, traditionally on tape or CD or, now most commonly, streamed or as a digital download. Nearly half of all Americans report having listened to audiobooks, and the medium has experienced nine straight years of double-digit revenue growth, reaching $1.3 billion in 2020 (Milliot, 2021a). The company Audible, with more than 440,000 titles, is the biggest "publisher" of audiobooks. Owned by Amazon, it offers monthly subscriptions rather than individual sales. Its ACX (Audiobook Creation Exchange) platform helps authors independently produce their own audiobooks. Other publishers (Scribd, for example) offer apps allowing "readers" to easily download new audio titles to their smartphones. One sign of audiobooks' vitality is that A-list authors, such as Michael Lewis (*Moneyball*, *The Blind Side*) and Jack Gantos (the *Joey Pigza* series), write new works specifically for audiobook release. Audiobooks are the fastest-growing sector of the publishing industry. As a result, all of the major publishers now have their own audio divisions.

The past decade has seen increasing efforts to digitize many of the world's books. Online bookseller Amazon has scanned every page of every in-print book it offers into its Search Inside the Book feature, and it has acquired its own POD service, CreateSpace, that instantly provides any book requested. Several nonprofit organizations are also making searchable and downloadable books available online. Project Gutenberg offers 62,000 noncopyrighted classics; the Internet Archive's Open Library has more than 4 million e-books for borrow; the Million Book Project also has 1 million government texts and older titles; and the International Children's Digital Library and the Rosetta Project make downloadable tens of thousands of current and antique children's books from around the world.

▲ Amazon's Kindle, Apple's iPad, and numerous other e-readers have transformed publishing and reading.
(left) Masterton/agefotostock/Newscom; (right) Oleksiy Maksymenko Photography/Alamy Stock Photo

Conglomeration

More than any other medium, the book industry into the 1970s and 1980s was dominated by relatively small operations. Publishing houses were traditionally staffed by fewer than 20 people, the large majority by fewer than 10. Today, however, although tens of thousands of businesses call themselves book publishers, only a very small percentage produces four or more titles a year. The industry is dominated now by the so-called Big 5 publishing houses—Penguin Random House (300 **imprints**, or individual book publishing companies), Hachette (23 imprints), HarperCollins (240 imprints), Macmillan (30 imprints), and Simon & Schuster (52 imprints)—and a few other large concerns, like Time Warner Publishing. Each of these giants was once, sometimes with another name, an independent book publisher. All are now part of large national or international corporate conglomerates. Penguin Random House and Simon & Schuster, both owned by German conglomerate Bertelsmann, together control more than a third of all US book sales (Mullin & Trachtenberg, 2020). These major publishers control more than 80% of all American book sales. Even e-publishing is dominated by the big companies, as all the major houses and booksellers maintain e-publishing units.

Opinion on the benefit of corporate ownership is divided. The positive view is that the rich parent company can infuse the imprint with necessary capital, enabling it to attract better authors or to take gambles on new writers that would, in the past, have been impossible. Another plus is that the corporate parent's other media holdings can be used to promote and repackage the books for greater profitability. Neither of these benefits is insignificant, argue many industry insiders, because book publishing is more like gambling than business. Literary agent Eric Simonoff says the industry is "unpredictable . . . the profit margins are so small, the cycles (from contract to publication) are so incredibly long" and there is an "almost total lack of market research" (quoted in Boss, 2007, p. B6). Fiction writer James Patterson, for example, suffered 12 rejections for *The Thomas Berryman Number* before Little, Brown accepted his first novel in 1976. Patterson has since rewarded his publisher with 114 *New York Times* best sellers (James Patterson, 2020). Even J. K. Rowling's first *Harry Potter* book was rejected 12 times before finding a publisher (Millington, 2018).

The negative view is that as publishing houses become just one in the parent company's long list of enterprises, product quality suffers as important editing and production steps are eliminated to maximize profits. Before conglomeration, publishing was often described as a **cottage industry**; that is, publishing houses were small operations, closely identified with their personnel—both their own small staffs and their authors. The cottage imagery, however, extends beyond smallness of size. There was a quaintness and charm associated with publishing houses—their attention to detail, their devotion to tradition, the care they gave to their façades (their reputations). "The act of publishing is essentially the act of making public one's own enthusiasm," reminisced Robert Gottlieb, longtime editor in chief at old-line houses Simon & Schuster and Knopf (in Menand, 2016, p. 80). The world of corporate conglomerates has little room for such niceties, as profit dominates all other considerations. More than 40 years ago, acclaimed novelist and editor E. L. Doctorow spoke about conglomeration in the book industry, testifying before Congress that the

> delicate balance of pressures within a publishing firm is upset by the conglomerate values. The need for greater and greater profits and the expectation of them overloads the scale in favor of commerce—depending on the particular house and its editorial resources, faster or more slowly: the crossword-puzzle books and cookbooks and sexual-position books and how-to books and movie-tie-in books and television-celebrity books gradually occupy more of the publishers' time and investment. (in The Editors, 2020)

Today he would see profits-over-quality at play in recent publishing practices such as the use of "big data" from online e-book readership not only to determine which books get published (Alter & Russell, 2016), but also to help shape characters and story lines in books as they are being written (Miller, 2014), as well as when fans read online manuscripts and then vote on which should be published (Alter, 2014).

Demand for Profits and Hypercommercialism

The threat from conglomeration resides in the parent company's overemphasis on the bottom line—that is, profitability at all costs. Unlike in the days when G. P. Putnam's sons and the Schuster family actually ran the houses that carried their names, critics fear that now little pride is taken in the content of books and that risk taking (tackling controversial issues, experimenting with new styles, finding and nurturing unknown authors) is becoming rarer and rarer. In industry parlance, the prevailing philosophy is "best sellers sell the best" (Alter, 2020a). "Given the choice between seeking out the new, the strange, and the shocking or hanging onto personalities and news hooks and follower counts, the Big Five opt for the latter," lament the Editors of culture journal *N+1* (2020).

As a result, writes Jason Epstein, founder of Anchor Books, his is an "increasingly distressed industry" mired in "severe structural problems." Among them are a retail bookselling system that favors "brand name" authors and "a bestseller-driven system of high royalty advances." He says that contemporary publishing is "overconcentrated," "undifferentiated," and "fatally rigid" (quoted in Feldman, 2001, p. 35). To Doctorow, Epstein, and other critics of conglomeration, the industry seems overwhelmed by a blockbuster mentality—lust for the biggest-selling authors and titles possible, sometimes with little consideration for literary merit. For example, Simon & Schuster recently formed a division, Keywords Press, to publish books written by Internet celebrities, signing YouTube stars Shane Dawson and Justine Ezarik, better known as iJustine. Tom Clancy received $45 million for two books from Penguin Putnam. James Patterson signed with Hachette for $150 million to write 11 adult and 6 young adult books in a three-year span. Michelle (for *Becoming*) and Barack Obama (for an eventual memoir) collected $65 million from Random House. Amy Schumer got $9 million for *The Girl with the Lower Back Tattoo* and Bruce Springsteen $10 million for his memoir, both from Simon & Schuster (Tanjeem, 2020).

As the resources and energies of publishing houses are committed to a small number of superstar writers and blockbuster books, smaller, more interesting, possibly more serious or important books do not get published. As one frustrated literacy agent explained, "This rarefied group now gets an outsize amount of the limited spoils: bigger advances, more of retailers' limited space, and more of publishers' time and attention," producing a "frustratingly circular" system (in Deahl, 2019).

If these types of books cannot get published, they may never be written. Will we be denied their ideas in the cultural forum? We will see, but as we read earlier in this chapter, it is converged technologies like POD and e-books that may well be the vehicles that ensure those ideas have access to the forum and us to them.

Publishers attempt to offset the large investments they do make through the sale of **subsidiary rights**, that is, the sale of the book, its contents, and even its characters to filmmakers, paperback publishers, book clubs, foreign publishers, and product producers like T-shirt, poster, coffee cup, and greeting card manufacturers. For example, based on the success of his first book, *Cold Mountain*, Charles Frazier's one-page proposal for his second novel earned his publisher $3 million for the film rights alone from Paramount Pictures. The industry itself estimates that many publishers would go out of business if it were not for the sale of these rights. Writers such as John Grisham (*The Client*) and Gay Talese (*Thy Neighbor's Wife*) can command several million dollars for the film rights to their books. In fact, demand for "prestige" content on the part of video streaming services, such as Hulu and Netflix, and other channels hoping to compete with them is fueling an "adaptation explosion." Where previously 95% of subsidy rights sales went to the film industry, television—broadcast, cable, and streaming—now buys the rights to more than 60% of books that make it to a screen (Bentley, 2018).

As greater and greater sums are tied up in blockbusters, and as subsidiary rights therefore grow in importance, the marketing, promotion, and public relations surrounding a book become crucial. This leads to the additional fear that only the most promotable books will be published—bookstores are flooded with celebrity cookbooks, celebrity picture books, unauthorized biographies of celebrities, and tell-all autobiographies from the children of celebrities.

In addition, **tie-in novels**—books based on popular television shows and movies—have become more common. *Bratva* is a novel using characters from the FX Network's hit series *Sons of Anarchy*. *Homeland*, *Fringe*, and *CSI* are other TV shows that have enjoyed novelization, as are *Murder She Wrote*, *Supernatural*, and *Beverly Hills 90210*.

Several other recent events suggest that the demand for profits is bringing even more hypercommercialism to the book business. One trend is the "Hollywoodization" of books. Potential synergies between books, television, and movies have spurred big media companies such as Viacom, Time Warner, and News Corp. to invest heavily in publishing, buying up houses big and small. Some movie studios are striking "exclusive" deals with publishers—for example, Walden Media teams with Penguin Young Readers, Focus Films with Random House, and Paramount with Simon & Schuster. In addition, ReganBooks (owned by HarperCollins, which, in turn, is owned by News Corp.) moved its offices from New York to Los Angeles to be in a better position to develop material that has both book and film potential. Several other major movie studios have set up operations in New York City to be closer to the source of books, magazine articles, and plays that they hope to turn into material for the big screen. Critics fear that only those books with the most synergistic potential will be signed and published. Advocates argue just the opposite—a

Actor, comic, and first-time author Amy Schumer landed a $9 million advance for her book *The Girl with the Lower Back Tattoo.*
Xavier Collin/Image Press Agency/Alamy Stock Photo

work that might have had limited profit potential as a "mere" book, and therefore gone unpublished, just might find a home across several mutually promoting platforms. They point to *Sideways*, a small-selling book that became a best-selling book after the movie it inspired became a hit.

Another trend that has created much angst among book traditionalists is the paid product placement. Movies and television have long accepted payments from product manufacturers to feature their brands in their content, but it was not until May 2000 that the first paid-for placement appeared in a fiction novel. Bill Fitzhugh's *Cross Dressing*, published by Avon, contains what are purchased commercials for Seagram liquor. As with other media that accept product placements, critics fear that content will be bent to satisfy sponsors rather than serve the quality of the work itself. Product placement in e-books has done little to allay those concerns. Embedded links in e-books can boost the potential value of a placement, making them attractive to sponsors. This has produced what the industry calls **shopfiction**, the embedding of links into traditional and e-books taking readers directly to paid sponsors' websites. Whenever a character's clothing or some other product is described, readers can click on a link in an e-book, or in a printed book scan a **QR code** (the small barcode with squares that direct mobile device users to a specific website), and be directed to a website where it can be purchased (Grady, 2019).

Growth of Small Presses

The overcommercialization of the book industry is mitigated somewhat by the rise in the number of smaller publishing houses. Today there are more than 80,000 book publishers in the United States, the vast majority being small presses. Although these smaller operations are large in number, they account for a very small proportion of books sold. They cannot compete in the blockbuster world. By definition *alternative*, they specialize in specific areas such as the environment, feminism, gay issues, and how-to. They can also publish writing otherwise uninteresting to bigger houses, such as poetry and literary commentary. Relying on specialization and narrowly targeted marketing, books such as women's study scholar Becca Anderson's *The Book of Awesome Women Writers*, published by Mango Publishing; Claudette McShane's *Warning! Dating May Be Hazardous to Your Health*, published by Mother Courage Press; and *Split Verse,* a book of poems about divorce published by Midmarch Arts, can not only earn healthy sales but also make a difference in their readers' lives.

And what may seem surprising is that it is the Internet, specifically Amazon, that is boosting the fortunes of these smaller houses. Because it compiles data on customer preferences (books bought, browsed, recommended to others, or wished for), it can make recommendations to potential buyers, and quite often those recommendations are from small publishers that the buyer might never have considered (or never have seen at a brick-and-mortar retailer). In other words, Amazon may help level the book industry playing field just a bit.

Restructuring of Book Retailing

There are approximately 20,000 bookstores in the United States, but the number is declining as small, independent operations find it increasingly difficult to compete with chains such as Barnes & Noble, Follett's, and Books-A-Million. Even giant chain store Borders (1,249 stores under its own name and Waldenbooks) was forced to file for bankruptcy in 2011 and gradually closed all its stores. The remaining chains and the independents must still contend with online retailers like Amazon; discount stores such as Target, Walmart, and Costco; the explosion of POD; and the migration of books from paper to the electronic screens of laptops, tablet computers, e-readers, and smartphones.

Where the big stores have prospered it is because their size enables them to purchase inventory in bulk cheaply and then offer discounts to readers. Because their locations attract shoppers, they can also profitably stock nonbook merchandise such as audiobooks, CDs and vinyl records, computer games, calendars, magazines, and greeting cards for the drop-in trade. But high-volume, high-traffic operations tend to deal in high-volume books. To book traditionalists, this only encourages the industry's blockbuster mentality. When the largest bookstores in the country order only the biggest sellers, the small books get lost. When floor space is given over to Garfield coffee mugs and pop star calendars, there is even less room for small but potentially interesting books. Although big bookselling chains have their critics, they also have their defenders. At least the big titles, calendars, and cheap prices get people into bookstores, the argument goes. Once folks begin reading, even if it is less sophisticated stuff, they might eventually move on to more sophisticated material.

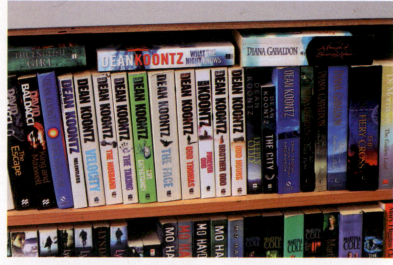

▲ Bookseller Amazon's signing of bestselling authors like Dean Koontz marks its entry into every aspect of the publishing industry, alarming its many critics.
Alisha Arif/Alamy Stock Photo

Independent bookstores are experiencing something of a renaissance. Today there are about 2,300 independent booksellers in the United States. And although this is a big decline from the 4,000 independent bookstores of the 1990s, the number of indies grew 49% between 2009 and 2019. Just as important, despite sales losses experienced by the big chains, independent bookstores saw their sales remain stable or even slightly increase over that time (Shephard, 2020a). They have accomplished this by using their small size and independence to their advantage, countering the chains and discount stores with expert, personalized service provided by a reading-loving staff, coffee and snack bars, cushioned chairs and sofas for slow browsing, intimate readings by favorite authors, and even neighborhood bookmobiles, book-filled vans that travel to readers. In fact, so successful have these strategies been that the big stores now are copying them. Barnes & Noble, for example, sponsors a program it calls Discover to promote notable first novels. Not only do these efforts emulate services more commonly associated with smaller independents, but they also help blunt some of the criticism suffered by the chains, specifically that they ignore new and smaller-selling books.

But the brick-and-mortar bookstore continues to face external pressure. The 2020 coronavirus shut-down is one example. Despite an overall increase in the sale of print books, bookstores suffered a 33% decline in sales, putting their renaissance to the test (Alter, 2020b). But their biggest threat continues to come from online retailers. Amazon is the best known of the online book sales services. It dominates book retailing, selling 45% of all new books sold every year and controlling 83% of all e-book sales (The Editors, 2020). This size gives Amazon outsized power in the book industry. Critics say Amazon is using its dominance of book retailing to extort high payments from the publishers, who have little choice but to sell their books on its site (a number of states have investigated the company for alleged abuse of its power; Weise & McCabe, 2020).

Further worrying its critics, Amazon has begun signing bestselling authors to produce books for its own Amazon Publishing imprints. The company, which already owns Kindle and Audible, giving it effective control over both the audio and e-book markets, also owns one of the world's most popular video streaming services, Amazon Prime. This puts it in a perfect position to offer big-name authors lucrative and unmatchable tie-in deals. Among its first two signing were Dean Koontz (30 paperback and hardcover bestsellers) and Patricia Cornwell (several bestsellers, including *Cause of Death*). Amazon now is involved in "every stage of the publishing process," warns critic Alex Shephard, "It is acquiring and publishing books, then marketing and selling them to customers. It is creating a marketplace that omits publishers altogether" (2020b).

DEVELOPING MEDIA LITERACY SKILLS
The Lessons of Harry Potter

J. K. Rowling's series of books about youthful British sorcerer Harry Potter offers several important media literacy lessons. For example, its huge appeal to young people can be used to examine one element of media literacy, understanding content as a text providing insight into our culture and lives. Just why have these books resonated so strongly with young readers? The controversy surrounding the numerous efforts to have the series banned from schools and libraries as antireligious and anti-Christian and its status as the "most challenged" (censored) children's literature in the United States call into play the particular media literacy skill of developing the ability and willingness to effectively and meaningfully understand content.

The publishing industry classifies the *Harry Potter* books as young adult fiction. But their phenomenal reception by readers of all ages suggests these works not only have broader appeal but are in themselves something very special. The initial US printing of a *Harry Potter* book is about 14 million copies—100 times that of a normal best seller. The seven *Harry Potter* books combined have sold more than 500 million copies worldwide, and two-thirds of all American children have read at least one *Harry Potter* book. The *Potter* series has been published in over 68 languages (including Greek, Latin, and "Americanized English") in more than 200 countries. *Potter* books occupy the top four spots on the all-time fastest-selling book list.

An important element of media literacy is the development of an awareness of the impact of media, and there is evidence that *Harry Potter* has helped create a new generation of readers. When the series first appeared, horror writer Stephen King wrote, "If these millions of readers are awakened to the wonders and rewards of fantasy at 11 or 12 . . . well, when they get to age 16 or so, there's this guy named King" (as quoted in Garchik, 2000, p. D10). Diane Roback, children's book editor at *Publishers Weekly,* cited "'the Harry Potter halo effect,' in which children come into stores and libraries asking for books that resemble the Rowling series" (*USA Today*, 2000, p. E4). When the final *Potter* book was released, a Scholastic Books survey of 500 *Harry Potter* readers aged 5 to 7 indicated that 51% said they did not read books for fun until they started reading the series. Three-quarters said reading the series had made them interested in reading other books (Rich, 2007).

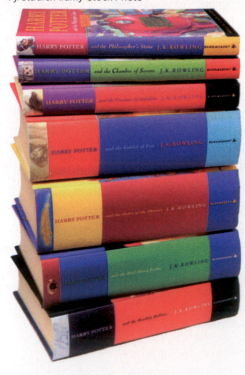

▼ Harry Potter, the wizard who launched a million readers and made them better people, too.
PjrStudio/Alamy Stock Photo

But the series has had another, arguably more important impact. There is a wealth of scholarly research on the link between reading literary fiction and developing empathy for others, for example, McCreary and Marchant's (2016) "Reading and Empathy" and Bal and Veltkamp's (2013) "How Does Fiction Reading Influence Empathy? An Experimental Investigation of the Role of Emotional Transportation." The logic behind these studies is that reading literary fiction engages us with the psychological, social, and cultural complexities of life by requiring us to become someone else, transporting ourselves not only into the situations of others but into their minds. Reading *Harry Potter*, then, should have a similar impact, especially as he "is continually in contact with stigmatized groups. The 'muggles' get no respect in the wizarding world as they lack any magical ability. The 'half-bloods,' or 'mud-bloods'—wizards and witches descended from only one magical parent—don't fare much better, while the Lord Voldemort character believes that power should only be held by 'pure-blood' wizards" (Stetka, 2014).

Loris Vezzali and her colleagues (2013) tested *Harry Potter*'s power to build empathy in an article titled "The Greatest Magic of Harry Potter: Reducing Prejudice" and discovered just what media-literate people who recognize the power of well-crafted media messages would expect. Readers who read parts of the book where Harry had to deal with prejudice showed more empathy toward immigrants, homosexuals, and refugees than did those who read neutral passages. In an interview with science writer Bret Stetka (2014), Professor Vezzali explained, "Unfortunately the news we read on a daily basis tells us we have so much work to do. But based on our work, fantasy books such as *Harry Potter* may be of great help to educators and parents in teaching tolerance."

MEDIA LITERACY CHALLENGE
Literacy: Limiting Access to Books in School

The *Harry Potter* books have been best sellers, but they have also been the frequent target of people who want to censor them from school libraries. You may never have read any of these works, but consider the possible reasons that parents might not want their children to read certain books without their knowledge, and then answer the following questions. To do so will call into play important components of media literacy: *the development of an understanding of the ethical and moral obligations of those who make (and dispense) media content* and *the awareness of media content as "texts" that provide insight into our culture.* Two media literacy skills are also involved: *the ability to distinguish emotional from reasoned reactions when responding to content* and *the ability to think critically about media messages.*

Your challenge is to answer these questions. Is it ever OK for groups outside the school (parents or concerned citizens, for example) to choose not to allow certain books in their schools? Why or why not? If you think it is appropriate to ask (or even insist) that movies, TV shows, video games, and recordings used in schools have warning labels or that parents who object to their children's exposure to that content be allowed to "opt out," would you hold books to those same controls? Should other in-school media be subject to greater control than books? Why or why not? Is it better to have children reading controversial books as long as it encourages them to read, or would it be better if those children were not reading at all? Which is the greater "evil"? You can approach this challenge as either an opportunity for personal reflection, committing your thoughts to paper, or you can set it up as a debate, for example, the No Limits versus the Some Limits versus the Strong Limits.

Resources for Review and Discussion

REVIEW POINTS: TYING CONTENT TO LEARNING OUTCOMES

▶ **Recognize the history and development of the publishing industry and the book itself as a medium.**
  - ☐ Although the first printing press came to the colonies in 1638, books were not central to early colonial life. However, books and pamphlets were at the heart of the colonists' revolt against England in the 1770s.
  - ☐ Developments in the 18th and 19th centuries, such as improvements in printing, the flowering of the American novel, and the introduction of dime novels, helped make books a mass medium.

▶ **Describe the cultural value of books and the implications of censorship for democracy.**
  - ☐ Books have cultural value because they are agents of social and cultural change; important cultural repositories; windows on the past; important sources of personal development; sources of entertainment, escape, and personal reflection;

mirrors of culture; and because the purchase and reading of a book is a much more individual, personal activity than consuming advertiser-supported or heavily promoted media. Widespread support for public libraries is evidence of people's recognition of books' cultural value.
  - ☐ Censorship, both formal and in the form of people's own aliteracy, threatens these values, as well as democracy itself.

▶ **Recall how the organizational and economic nature of the contemporary book industry shapes the content of books.**
  - ☐ Convergence is reshaping the book industry as well as the reading experience itself through advances such as e-publishing, POD, e-books, e-readers, smartphones and tablets, audiobooks, and several different efforts to digitize most of the world's books.
  - ☐ Conglomeration affects the publishing industry as it has all media, expressing itself through trends such as demand for profit and hypercommercialization.

□ Demand for profit and hypercommercialization manifest themselves in the increased importance placed on subsidiary rights, "Hollywoodization," and product placement.

□ Book retailing is undergoing change; chains and online sellers dominate the business but continue to be challenged by imaginative, high-quality independent booksellers.

▶ Apply skills to be a more media-literate consumer of books, especially in considering their uniqueness in an increasingly mass-mediated, media-converged world.

□ The wild success of the *Harry Potter* series holds several lessons for media-literate readers, not the least of which is that people value quality media content.

KEY TERMS

linotype, 54

offset lithography, 54

dime novels, 54

pulp novels, 54

bibliotherapy, 57

social infrastructure, 57

censorship, 58

illiteracy, 60

aliteracy, 60

trade books, 62

e-publishing, 62

e-book, 63

disintermediation, 64

print on demand (POD), 64

remainders, 64

e-reader, 64

platform agnostic publishing, 65

audiobook 65

imprint, 65

cottage industry, 66

subsidiary rights, 67

tie-in novels, 67

shopfiction, 68

quick response (QR) code, 68

QUESTIONS FOR REVIEW

1. What were the major developments in the modernization of the printing press?

2. Why were the early colonists not a book-reading population?

3. What was the Stamp Act? Why did colonial printers object to it?

4. What factors allowed the flowering of the American novel, as well as the expansion of the book industry, in the 1800s?

5. Name eight reasons books are an important cultural resource.

6. What is bibliotherapy?

7. What are the major categories of books?

8. What is the impact of conglomeration on the book industry?

9. What are the products of increasing hypercommercialism and demands for profit in the book industry?

10. What are e-books, e-readers, e-publishing, and audiobooks?

To maximize your study time, check out CONNECT to access the SmartBook study module for this chapter, watch videos, and explore other resources.

QUESTIONS FOR CRITICAL THINKING AND DISCUSSION

1. Do you envision books ever again having the power to move the nation as they did in revolutionary or antislavery times, and even a few decades ago? Why or why not?

2. Are you proud of your book-reading habits? Why or why not? For example, do you read for fun? How often do you read outside of required school material? When you do read, which genres do you prefer?

3. Under what circumstances is censorship permissible? Whom do you trust to make the right decision about what you should and should not read? If you were a librarian, under what circumstances would you pull a book off the shelves?

REFERENCES

1. Albanese, A. (2020, April 23). Federal appeals court declares literacy a constitutional right. *Publishers Weekly*. Retrieved from https://www.publishersweekly.com/pw/by-topic/industry-news/publisher-news/article/83143-federal-appeals-court-declares-literacy-a-constitutional-right.html

2. Alter, A. (2020a, September 20). Best sellers sell the best. *New York Times*, pp. B1, B8.

3. Alter, A. (2020b, May 20). Shutdown takes heavy toll on book sales, but hopeful signs emerge. *New York Times*, p. B5.

4. Alter, A. (2014, August 12). Publishers turn to the crowd to find the next best seller. *New York Times*, p. B1.

5. Alter, A., & Russell, K. (2016, March 15). Moneyball for book publishers: A detailed look at how we read. *New York Times*, p. B1.

6. Andrew, G. G. (2018, July 11). 32 books that changed the world. *BookBub*. Retrieved from https://www.bookbub.com/blog/2018/07/11/books-that-changed-the-world

7. Bal, P. M., & Veltkamp, V. (2013). How does fiction reading influence empathy? An experimental investigation of the role of emotional transportation. *PLoS One, 8*, e55341.

8. Bentley, J. (2018, November 6). Reading revolution roars onscreen. *Variety*, p. 143.

9. Birth, A. (2016, February 25). Unplugging: Majority of Americans try to disconnect from tech; 45% try weekly. *The Harris Poll*. Retrieved from http://www.theharrispoll.com/health-and-life/Unplugging-Americans-Disconnect-Tech.html

10. Boss, S. (2007, May 13). The greatest mystery: Making a best seller. *New York Times,* pp. B1–B6.

11. Bradbury, R. (1981). *Fahrenheit 451.* New York: Ballantine. (Originally published in 1953.)

12. Brodsky, J. (1987, December 8). *Nobel lecture.* Retrieved from http://www.nobelprize.org/nobel_prizes/literature/laureates/1987/brodsky-lecture.html

13. Charles, R. (2020, September 28). For Banned Books Week, I read the country's 10 most challenged books. The gay penguins did not corrupt me. *Washington Post*. Retrieved from https://www.washingtonpost.com/entertainment/books/banned-books-week-2020/2020/09/27/8e8a9320-fd12-11ea-b555-4d71a9254f4b_story.html

14. Clark, T. (2017, March 2). The most important skills kids need to succeed in life. *First Things First*. Retrieved from https://www.firstthingsfirst.org/2017/03/important-skills-kids-need-succeed-life/

15. Deahl, R. (2019, November 1). Is publishing too top-heavy? *Publishers Weekly*. Retrieved from https://www.publishersweekly.com/pw/by-topic/industry-news/publisher-news/article/81637-is-publishing-too-top-heavy.html

16. Edison Research. (2020). *The infinite dial 2020*. Retrieved from https://www.rab.com/whyradio/wrnew/wr-research/pdf/Infinite%20Dial%202020.pdf

17. Editorial Team. (2020). Crisis point: The state of literacy in America. *Resilient Educator*. Retrieved from https://resilienteducator.com/news/illiteracy-in-america/

18. The Editors. (2020, Winter). Smorgasbords don't have bottoms. *N+1*. Retrieved from https://nplusonemag.com/issue-36/the-intellectual-situation/smorgasbords-dont-have-bottoms/

19. Fallows, D. (2020, March 31). Public libraries' novel response to a novel virus. *Atlantic*. Retrieved from https://www.theatlantic.com/notes/2020/03/public-libraries-novel-response-to-a-novel-virus/609058/

20. Feldman, G. (2001, February 12). Publishers caught in a Web. *Nation*, pp. 35–36.

21. Garchik, L. (2000, July 25). Death and hobbies. *San Francisco Chronicle*, p. D10.

22. "Germany: How dangerous is Mein Kampf?" (2016, January 15). *The Week*, p. 14.

23. Grady, C. (2019, April 8). The unsuccessful history of product placement in books, from Bulgari to Sweet'N Low. *Vox*. Retrieved from https://www.vox.com/the-goods/2019/4/8/18250031/book-product-placement-bulgar-connection-click-fic-shopfiction

24. Haines, D. (2020, June 8). Kindle sales—The e-reader device is dying a rapid death. *Just Publishing Advice*. Retrieved from https://justpublishingadvice.com/the-e-reader-device-is-dying-a-rapid-death/

25. Harris, E. A. (2020, June 9). Books may sow seeds of change. *New York Times*, p. C1.

26. "The History of the Little Free Library." (2021). *Littlefreelibrary.org*. Retrieved from https://littlefreelibrary.org/ourhistory/

27. "James Patterson." (2020, March 19). *Biography*. Retrieved from https://www.biography.com/writer/james-patterson

28. Kelly, K. J. (2020, January 1). "Fifty Shades of Grey" was the dominant book of the decade. *New York Post*. Retrieved from https://nypost.com/2020/01/01/fifty-shades-of-grey-was-the-dominant-book-of-the-decade/

29. Klineberg, E. (2018, September 9). Why libraries still matter. *New York Times*, p. SR6.

30. Kolbert, E. (2017, August 28). The content of no content. *New Yorker*, pp. 42–45.

31. Lepore, J. (2018, March 26). The shorebird. *New Yorker*, pp. 64–66, 68–72.

32. Lindberg, S. (2020, January 3). Bibliotherapy: How stories can help guide the therapeutic process. *Very Well Mind*. Retrieved from https://www.verywellmind.com/what-is-bibliotherapy-4687157

33. McCarthy, J. (2020, January 24). In U.S., library visits outpaced trips to movies in 2019. *Gallup*. Retrieved from https://news.gallup.com/poll/284009/library-visits-outpaced-trips-movies-2019.aspx

34. McCreary, J. J., & Marchant, G. J. (2016). Reading and empathy. *Reading Psychology*. Retrieved from http://dx.doi.org/10.1080/02702711.2016.1245690

35. Menand, L. (2015, January 5). Pulp's big moment. *New Yorker*, pp. 62–69.

36. Menand, L. (2016, December 12). Banned books and blockbusters. *New Yorker*, pp. 78–85.

37. Miller, L. (2014, January 8). Big data's next frontier: Crowd-testing fiction. *Salon*. Retrieved from http://www.salon.com/2014/01/09/big_datas_next_frontier_crowd_testing_fiction/

38. Millington, A. (2018, July 30). J.K. Rowling's pitch for 'Harry Potter' was rejected 12 times — read the now-famous letter here. *Insider*. Retrieved from https://www.insider.com/revealed-jk-rowlings-original-pitch-for-harry-potter-2017-10

39. Milliot, J. (2021a, June 1). APA says audiobook sales rose 12% in 2020. *Publisher's Weekly*. Retrieved from https://www.publishersweekly.com/pw/by-topic/industry-news/audio-books/article/86531-apa-says-audiobook-sales-rose-12-in-2020.html#:~:text=The%20Audio%20Publishers%20Association's%20annual,profound%20shift%20in%20listening%20habits.

40. Milliot, J. (2021b, January 7). Print book sales rose 8.2% in 2020. *Publishers Weekly*. Retrieved from https://www.publishersweekly.com/pw/by-topic/industry-news/bookselling/article/85256-print-unit-sales-rose-8-2-in-2020.html

41. Milliot, J. (2020a, July 31). AAP pegs 2019 sales growth at 1.1%. *Publishers Weekly*. Retrieved from https://www.publishersweekly.com/pw/by-topic/industry-news/financial-reporting/article/83995-aap-pegs-2019-sales-growth-at-1-1.html

42. Milliot, J. (2020b, March 10). StatShot: Publishing sales rose 1.8% in 2019. *Publishers Weekly*. Retrieved from https://www.publishersweekly.com/pw/by-topic/industry-news/financial-reporting/article/82640-statshot-publishing-sales-rose-1-8-in-2019.html

43. Milliot, J. (2020c, January 30). KDP authors earned over $300 million through Kindle Unlimited. *Publishers Weekly*. Retrieved from https://www.publishersweekly.com/pw/by-topic/digital/content-and-e-books/article/82303-kdp-authors-earned-over-300-million-in-2019-amazon-says.html

44. Moyers, B. (2007, February 12). *Discovering what democracy means*. Retrieved from http://www.commondreams.org/views/2007/02/12/discovering-what-democracy-means

45. Mullin, B., & Trachtenberg, J. A. (2020, November 24). Random House parent near deal to buy Simon & Schuster from ViacomCBS. *Wall Street Journal*. Retrieved from https://www.wsj.com/articles/penguin-random-house-parent-near-deal-to-buy-simon-schuster-from-viacomcbs-11606268232

46. Nathanson, H. (2020, January 15). Some Northern Virginia parents wanted two books with LGBTQ characters removed from schools. Officials said no. *Washington Post*. Retrieved from https://www.washingtonpost.com/local/education/some-northern-virginia-parents-wanted-two-books-with-lgbtq-characters-removed-from-schools-officials-said-no/2020/01/15/06f8be0e-36df-11ea-bb7b-265f4554af6d_story.html

47. National Education Association. (2019). *Helping your child learn to read*. Retrieved from http://www.nea.org/home/59869.htm

48. Nawotka, E. (2020, March 13). NEA says 55% of Americans are readers. *Publishers Weekly*. Retrieved from https://www.publishersweekly.com/pw/by-topic/industry-news/publisher-news/article/82685-nea-says-55-of-americans-are-readers.html

49. "New Record: More than 1 million books self-published in 2017." (2018, October 10). *Bowker*. Retrieved from http://www.bowker.com/news/2018/New-Record-More-than-1-Million-Books-Self-Published-in-2017.html

50. Norsigian, J., et al. (1999). The Boston women's health book collective and *Our Bodies, Ourselves:* A brief history and reflection. *Journal of the American Medical Women's Association*. Retrieved from http://www.ourbodiesourselves.org

51. OCLC. (2018, March). *From awareness to funding: Summary report*. Retrieved from https://www.oclc.org/content/dam/oclc/reports/awareness-to-funding-2018/2018_From_Awareness_to_Funding_Report.pdf

52. Osnos, P. (2009, March/April). Rise of the reader. *Columbia Journalism Review*, pp. 38–39.

53. Parramore, L. S. (2018, February 22). Don't want a robot to replace you? Start reading literature. *Alternet*. Retrieved from https://www.alternet.org/culture/dont-want-robot-replace-you-start-reading-literature

54. Perrin, A. (2019, September 26). Who doesn't read books in America? *Pew Research Center*. Retrieved from https://www.pewresearch.org/fact-tank/2019/09/26/who-doesnt-read-books-in-america/

55. Rea, A. (2020, January 6). Reading through the ages: Generational reading survey. *Library Journal*. Retrieved from https://www.libraryjournal.com/?detailStory=Reading-Through-the-Ages-Generational-Reading-Survey

56. Rich, M. (2007, July 22). A magical spell on kids' reading habits? *Providence Journal*, p. J2.

57. Richter, F. (2020, June 16). The world's largest retailers. *Statista*. Retrieved from https://www.statista.com/chart/22016/top-10-global-retailers/

58. Rowe, A. (2019, June 25). 6 facts about the $26 billion that U.S. publishers earned in 2018. *Forbes*. Retrieved form https://www.forbes.com/sites/adamrowe1/2019/06/25/6-facts-about-the-26-billion-that-us-publishers-earned-in-2018/#a192dc77e61b

59. Shephard, A. (2020a, April 16). Is this the end of the indie bookstore? *New Republic*. Retrieved from https://newrepublic.com/article/157315/end-indie-bookstore

60. Shephard, A. (2020b, January 16). Can Amazon finally crack the bestseller code? *New Republic*. Retrieved from https://newrepublic.com/article/156228/can-amazon-finally-crack-bestseller-code

61. Stetka, B. (2014, September 9). Why everyone should read Harry Potter. *Scientific American*. Retrieved from https://www.scientificamerican.com/article/why-everyone-should-read-harry-potter/

62. Stevens, H. (2012, August 6). "Dr. Spock's Baby and Child Care" empowered, encouraged parents. *Chicago Tribune*. Retrieved from http://www.chicagotribune.com/lifestyles/books/sc-ent-0104-books-change-benjamin-spock-20120106-story.html

63. Stewart, D. (2020, February 25). Consumers are all ears for audiobooks, podcasts. *Deloitte*. Retrieved from https://deloitte.wsj.com/cmo/2020/02/25/consumers-are-all-ears-for-audio-books-podcasts/

64. Streitfeld, D. (2020, February 10). Amazon takes on Nazis, book by unsold book. *New York Times*, p. A15.

65. Tanjeem, N. (2020, February 24). 10 of the biggest book deals in history. *Book Riot*. Retrieved from https://bookriot.com/2020/02/24/biggest-book-deals/

66. Taylor, D. B. (2020, April 30). "Why the Caged Bird" falls silent: A school board is cutting classics. *New York Times*, p. A19.

67. Tebbel, J. (1987). *Between covers: The rise and transformation of American book publishing*. New York: Oxford University Press.

68. Tompkins, P. (2020, October 4). Dover paperbacks. *New York Times Magazine*, 18–19.

69. Thompson, B. (2007, November 19). A troubling case of readers' block. *Washington Post*, p. C1.

70. Thompson, B. (2009, June 1). At publishers' convention, is writing on the wall? *Washington Post.* Retrieved from http://www.washingtonpost.com/wp-dyn/content/article/2009/05/31/AR2009053102119.html

71. *USA Today.* (2000, July 9). The Potter phenomenon: It's just magic. *Honolulu Advertiser,* p. E4.

72. vanden Heuvel, K. (2018, September 18). Want to defend democracy? Start with your public library. *Washington Post.* Retrieved from https://www.washingtonpost.com/opinions/want-to-defend-democracy-start-with-your-public-library/2018/09/18/7addf05a-bab2-11e8-9812-a389be6690af_story.html?noredirect=on&utm_term=.f7f33ef21430

73. Vezzali, L., et al. (2013). The greatest magic of Harry Potter: Reducing prejudice. *Journal of Applied Social Psychology*, *45*, 105–121.

74. Weise, K., & McCabe, D. (2020, June 15). Amazon said to be under scrutiny in 2 states for abuse of power. *New York Times.* Retrieved from https://www.nytimes.com/2020/06/12/technology/state-inquiry-antitrust-amazon.html

75. Widdicombe, L. (2015, January 19). The Zuckerberg bump. *New Yorker,* pp. 18–19.

76. "Who We Are." (2021). *Association of American Publishers.* Retrieved from https://publishers.org/

77. Zickuhr, K., & Rainie, L. (2014, January 15). E-reading rises as device ownership jumps. *Pew Research Center*. Retrieved from http://www.pewinternet.org/2014/01/16/e-reading-rises-as-device-ownership-jumps/

Cultural Forum Blue Column icon, Media Literacy Red Torch Icon, Using Media Green Gear icon, Developing Media book in starburst icon: ©McGraw Hill

Newspapers 4

◀ Has reading the newspaper become old-fashioned?

Joseph McKeown/Picture Post/Hulton Archive/Getty Images

Learning Objectives

Newspapers were at the center of our nation's drive for independence and have a long history as the people's medium. The newspaper was also the first mass medium to rely on advertising for financial support, changing the relationship between audience and media from that time on. After studying this chapter, you should be able to

▶ Recognize the history and development of the newspaper industry and the newspaper itself as a medium.

▶ Identify how the organizational and economic nature of the contemporary newspaper industry shapes the content of newspapers.

▶ Describe the relationship between the newspaper and its readers.

▶ Recall changes in the newspaper industry brought about by converging technologies and how those alterations may affect the medium's traditional role in our democracy.

▶ Apply key newspaper-reading media literacy skills, especially in interpreting the relative placement of stories and use of photos.

100 B.C.E. ▶ Acta Diurna in Caesar's Rome

1600

1620 Corantos
~1625 Broadsides
1641 Diurnals
~1660 "Newspaper" enters the language
1665 *Oxford Gazette*
1690 ▶ *Publick Occurrences Both Foreign and Domestick*

1700

1704 *Boston News-Letter*
1721 *New-England Courant's* James Franklin jailed for "scandalous libels"
1729 ▶ Benjamin Franklin's *Pennsylvania Gazette*
1734 The Zenger Trial
1765 Stamp Act
1791 The First Amendment to the Constitution
1798 The Alien and Sedition Acts

1800

1827 The first African American newspaper, *Freedom's Journal*
1828 *Cherokee Phoenix*
1833 The penny press
1844 Introduction of the telegraph
1847 Frederick Douglass's *The North Star*
1856 The New York Associated Press
1883 Pulitzer's *New York World,* yellow journalism
1889 ▶ *The Wall Street Journal*

1900

1905 *Chicago Defender*
1907 United Press International
1908 *Christian Science Monitor*
1909 International News Service
1970 Newspaper Preservation Act
1982 *USA TODAY*

2000

2007 Murdoch buys *The Wall Street Journal*
2009 *Christian Science Monitor* ceases daily publication; *Rocky Mountain News* shuttered; Internet overtakes newspapers as news source
2012 Association of Alternative Newsweeklies becomes Association of Alternative Newsmedia
2016 Number of people employed in digital publishing passes number working at newspapers; Newspaper Association of America becomes the News Media Alliance and begins accepting digital-only news sites as members; American Society of News Editors sets membership dues by monthly web traffic; Facebook offers free online training for journalists
2018 ▶ Report for America; *Village Voice* shuttered
2019 *The North Star is* reborn online
2020 Coronavirus in the US; Google begins payment to high quality news outlets
2021 ▶ *The Village Voice returns*

Pixtal/age fotostock

Courtesy of John Frost Historical Newspapers

H.S. Photos/Alamy Stock Photo

Jill Braaten/McGraw Hill

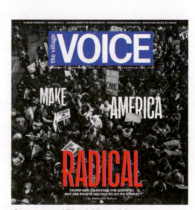
Courtesy of The Village Voice

"YOU GOT A JOB AS A NEWSPAPER REPORTER?"

"I told you that's what I wanted to be."

"And I told you that newspaper employment is down 60% since 1990, and it's gotten so bad that even the American Society of News Editors stopped reporting newsroom employment numbers."

"And I'll remind you again, journalism is not just a job, it's how people who do it fulfill their destiny. It's my destiny and I found a way to meet it."

"What, a low-paid internship somewhere?"

"Nope. You ever hear of AmeriCorps, where people get paid for public service work in education or helping the environment? There's a journalism equivalent, Report for America, funded by donors worried about what's happening to local papers. They're training me, placing me in an understaffed newsroom somewhere, and paying half my $45,000 annual salary. The local paper and local donors will make up the rest. There'll be 1,000 more like me in the next few years."

"Forty-five thousand dollars?"

"Yup, better than the median reporter's salary in a lot of big cities."

In this chapter, we examine the massive changes that have given birth to organizations like Report for America ("About," 2021) and what they mean for the relationship between the newspaper and its readers. And there is indeed much to say about a medium that has lost 52% of its employment, nearly 150,000 jobs, since 2009 (Johnson, 2020) and has suffered 300 newspaper closures in 2019 and 2020 alone (Dobbins, 2021), and yet whose major function, journalism, continues to attract a growing number of young people to its ranks (Orso, 2019).

We start with a look at the medium's roots, beginning with the first papers and following them from Europe to colonial America, where many of the traditions of today's free press were set. We study the cultural changes that led to the creation of the penny press and to competition between these mass circulation dailies that gave us "yellow journalism."

We then review the modern newspaper in terms of its size and scope. We discuss different types of newspapers and the importance of newspapers as an advertising medium. The wire and feature services, important providers of newspaper content, are also highlighted.

We then detail how the relationship between medium and audience is shifting as a result of the loss of competition within the industry, hypercommercialism in the guise of commercial pressure on papers' editorial content, the positive and negative impacts of new and converging technology, newspapers' gravitation to online formats, and changes in the nature of newspaper readership. Finally, we test our media literacy skills through a discussion of how to read the newspaper—for example, interpreting the relative positioning of stories.

A Short History of Newspapers

The opening vignette makes an important point about contemporary newspapers—they are in a state of **disruptive transition**—radical change brought about by the introduction of a new technology or product—but they are working hard and often successfully to secure new identities for themselves in an increasingly crowded media environment. As a medium and as an industry, newspapers are in the midst of a significant change in their role and operation. The changing relationship between newspapers and readers is part of this upheaval. Newspapers in paper form are still around, but they are increasingly likely to be read in digital form.

The Earliest Newspapers

In Caesar's time, Rome had a newspaper, the **Acta Diurna** (actions of the day). It was carved on a tablet and posted on a wall after each meeting of the senate. Its circulation was one, and there is no reliable measure of its total readership. However, it does show that people have always wanted to know what was happening and that others have helped them do so.

The newspapers we recognize today have their roots in 17th-century Europe. **Corantos**, one-page news sheets about specific events, were printed in English in Holland in 1620 and imported to England by British booksellers who were eager to satisfy public demand for information about the continental European happenings that eventually led to what we now call the Thirty Years' War.

Englishmen Nathaniel Butter, Thomas Archer, and Nicholas Bourne eventually began printing their own occasional news sheets, using the same title for consecutive editions. They stopped publishing in 1641, the same year that regular, daily accounts of local news started appearing in other news sheets. These true forerunners of our daily newspaper were called **diurnals**, but by the 1660s the word *newspaper* had entered the English language (Lepore, 2009).

Political power struggles in England at this time boosted the fledgling medium, as partisans on the side of the monarchy and those supporting Parliament published papers to bolster their positions. When the monarchy prevailed, it granted monopoly publication rights to the *Oxford Gazette*, the official voice of the Crown. Founded in 1665 and later renamed the *London Gazette*, this journal used a formula of foreign news, official information, royal proclamations, and local news that became the model for the first colonial newspapers.

COLONIAL NEWSPAPERS In the colonies, bookseller/print shops became the focal point for the exchange of news and information, which led to the beginning of the colonial newspaper. It was at these establishments that **broadsides** (sometimes referred to as **broadsheets**), single-sheet announcements or accounts of events imported from England, would be posted. In 1690, Boston bookseller and printer (and coffeehouse owner) Benjamin Harris printed his own broadside, *Publick Occurrences Both Forreign and Domestick*. Intended for continuous publication, the country's first paper lasted only one day; Harris had been critical of local and European dignitaries, and he had also failed to obtain a license.

More successful was Boston postmaster John Campbell, whose 1704 *Boston News-Letter* survived until the Revolution. The paper featured foreign news, reprints of articles from England, government announcements, and shipping news. It was dull and expensive. Nonetheless, it established the newspaper in the colonies.

The *Boston News-Letter* was able to survive in part because of government subsidies. With government support came government control, but the buildup to the Revolution helped establish the medium's independence. In 1721, Boston had three papers. James Franklin's *New-England Courant* was the only one publishing without authority. The *Courant* was popular and controversial, but when it criticized the Massachusetts governor, Franklin was jailed for printing "scandalous libels." When released, he returned to his old ways, earning himself and the *Courant* a publishing ban, which he circumvented by installing his younger brother Benjamin as nominal publisher. Benjamin Franklin soon moved to Philadelphia, and without his leadership, the *Courant* was out of business in 3 years. Its lasting legacy, however, was demonstrating that a newspaper with popular support could indeed challenge authority.

In Philadelphia, Benjamin Franklin established a print shop and later, in 1729, took over a failing newspaper, which he revived and renamed the *Pennsylvania Gazette*. By combining the income from his bookshop and printing business with that from his popular daily, Franklin could run the *Gazette* with significant independence. Even though he held the contract for Philadelphia's official printing, he was unafraid to criticize those in authority. In addition, he began to develop advertising support, which helped shield his newspaper from government control by decreasing its dependence on official printing contracts for survival. Benjamin Franklin demonstrated that financial independence could lead to editorial independence. It was not, however, a guarantee.

In 1734, *New York Weekly Journal* publisher John Peter Zenger was jailed for criticizing that colony's royal governor. The charge was seditious libel, and the verdict was based not on the truth or falsehood of the printed words but on whether

▲ The first daily newspaper to appear in the 13 colonies, *Publick Occurrences Both Forreign and Domestick* lasted all of one edition.

Courtesy of John Frost Historical Newspapers

▼ Benjamin Franklin published America's first political cartoon— "Join, or Die," a rallying call for the colonies—in his *Pennsylvania Gazette* in 1754.

H.S. Photos/Alamy Stock Photo

they had been printed. The criticisms had been published, so Zenger was clearly guilty. But his attorney, Andrew Hamilton, argued to the jury, "For the words themselves must be libelous, that is, false, scandalous and seditious, or else we are not guilty" (in Pusey, 2013). Zenger's peers agreed, and he was freed. The Zenger trial became a powerful symbol of colonial newspaper independence from the Crown.

NEWSPAPERS AFTER INDEPENDENCE After the Revolution, the new government of the United States had to determine for itself just how free a press it was willing to tolerate. When the first Congress convened under the new Constitution in 1790, the nation's founders debated, drafted, and adopted the first 10 amendments to the Constitution, called the **Bill of Rights**. The **First Amendment** reads:

> Congress shall make no law respecting an establishment of religion, or prohibiting the free exercise thereof; or abridging the freedom of speech, or of the press; or the right of the people peacefully to assemble, and to petition the Government for a redress of grievances.

But a mere 8 years later, fearful of the subversive activities of foreigners sympathetic to France, Congress passed a group of four laws known collectively as the **Alien and Sedition Acts**. The Sedition Acts made illegal writing, publishing, or printing "any false scandalous and malicious writing" about the president, Congress, or the federal government. So unpopular were these laws with a citizenry who had just waged a war of independence against similar limits on their freedom of expression that they were not renewed when Congress reconsidered them two years later in 1800. See Chapter 14 for more detail on the ongoing commitment to the First Amendment, freedom of the press, and open expression in the United States.

The Modern Newspaper Emerges

At the turn of the 19th century, New York City provided all the ingredients necessary for a new kind of audience for a new kind of newspaper and a new kind of journalism. The island city was densely populated, a center of culture, commerce, and politics, and especially because of the waves of immigrants that had come to its shores, demographically diverse. Add to this the growing literacy among working people, and conditions were ripe for the **penny press**, one-cent newspapers for everyone. Benjamin Day's September 3, 1833, issue of the *New York Sun* was the first of the penny papers. Day's innovation was to price his paper so inexpensively that it would attract a large readership, which could then be "sold" to advertisers. Day succeeded because he anticipated a new kind of reader. He filled the *Sun*'s pages with police and court reports, crime stories, entertainment news, and human interest stories. Because the paper lived up to its motto, "The Sun shines for all," there was little of the elite political and business information that had characterized earlier papers.

Soon there were penny papers in all the major cities. Among the most important was James Gordon Bennett's *New York Morning Herald*. Although more sensationalistic than the *Sun*, the *Herald* pioneered the correspondent system, placing reporters in Washington, DC, and other major American cities as well as abroad. Correspondents filed their stories by means of the telegraph, invented in 1844. Horace Greeley's *New York Tribune* was an important penny paper as well. Its nonsensationalistic, issues-oriented, and humanitarian reporting established the mass newspaper as a powerful medium of social action.

THE PEOPLE'S MEDIUM People typically excluded from the social, cultural, and political mainstream quickly saw the value of the mass newspaper. The first African American newspaper was *Freedom's Journal*, published initially in 1827 by John B. Russwurm and the Reverend Samuel Cornish. Others soon followed, but it was Frederick Douglass who made best use of the new mass circulation style in his newspaper *The Ram's Horn*, founded expressly to challenge the editorial policies of Benjamin Day's *Sun*. Although this particular effort failed, Douglass had established himself and the minority press as a viable voice for those otherwise silenced.

▼ Volume 1, Number 1 of Benjamin Day's *New York Sun*, the first of the penny papers. *North Wind Picture Archives*

Douglass's *The North Star*, founded in 1847 with the masthead slogan "Right is of no Sex—Truth is of no Color—God is the Father of us all, and we are all Brethren," was the most influential African American newspaper before the Civil War. And because its message is timeless, *The North Star* was reborn as an online newspaper in 2019.

The most influential African American newspaper after the Civil War, and the first to be a commercial success (its predecessors typically were subsidized by political and church groups), was the *Chicago Defender*. First published on May 5, 1905, by Robert Sengstacke Abbott, the *Defender* eventually earned a nationwide circulation of more than 230,000. After Abbott declared May 15, 1917, the date of "the Great Northern Drive," the *Defender*'s central editorial goal was to encourage southern African Americans to move north.

"I beg of you, my brothers, to leave that benighted land. You are free men. . . . Get out of the South," Abbott editorialized (in Fitzgerald, 1999, p. 18). The paper would regularly contrast horrific accounts of southern lynchings with northern African American success stories. Within two years of the start of the Great Drive, more than 500,000 former slaves and their families moved north. Within two more years, another 500,000 followed.

Native Americans found early voice in papers such as the *Cherokee Phoenix*, founded in 1828 in Georgia, and the *Cherokee Rose Bud*, which began operation 20 years later in Oklahoma. The rich tradition of the Native American newspaper is maintained today around the country in publications such as the Oglala Sioux *Lakota Country Times* and the Shoshone-Bannock *Sho-Ban News*, as well as on the World Wide Web. For example, the *Cherokee Observer*, the *Navajo Times*, and *Indian Country News* can all be found online.

Throughout this early period of the popularization of the newspaper, numerous foreign-language dailies also began operation, primarily in major cities in which immigrants tended to settle. By 1880, there were more than 800 foreign-language newspapers published across America in German, Polish, Italian, Spanish, and various Scandinavian languages (Sloan, Stovall, & Startt, 1993). As you'll see later in this chapter, the modern foreign language press remains an important part of the contemporary newspaper environment.

THE FIRST WIRE SERVICES In 1848, six large New York papers, including the *Sun*, the *Herald*, and the *Tribune*, decided to pool efforts and share expenses collecting news from foreign ships docking at the city's harbor. After determining rules of membership and other organizational issues, in 1856 the papers established the first news-gathering (and distribution) organization, the New York Associated Press. Other domestic **wire services**, originally named for their reliance on the telegraph but later renamed "news services," followed—the Associated Press in 1900, the United Press in 1907, and the International News Service in 1909.

This innovation, with its assignment of correspondents to both foreign and domestic bureaus, had a number of important implications. First, it greatly expanded the breadth and scope of coverage a newspaper could offer its readers. This was a boon to dailies wanting to attract as many readers as possible. Greater coverage of distant domestic news helped unite an expanding country while encouraging even more expansion. The United States was a nation of immigrants, and news from people's homelands drew more readers. As important, newspapers were able to reduce expenses (and increase profits) because they no longer needed to have their own reporters in all locations.

YELLOW JOURNALISM In 1883 Hungarian immigrant Joseph Pulitzer bought the troubled *New York World*. Adopting a populist approach to the news, he brought a crusading, activist style of coverage to numerous turn-of-the-century social problems—growing slums, labor tensions, and failing farms, to name a few. The audience for his "new journalism" was the "common man," and he succeeded in reaching readers with light, sensationalistic news coverage, extensive use of illustrations, and circulation-building stunts and promotions (for example, an around-the-world balloon flight). Ad revenues and circulation figures exploded.

Soon there were other new journalists. William Randolph Hearst applied Pulitzer's successful formula to his *San Francisco Examiner*, and then in 1895, he took on Pulitzer himself in New York by purchasing the failing *New York Morning Journal*. The competition between Hearst's *Morning Journal* and Pulitzer's *World* was so intense that it debased newspapers and journalism as a whole, which is somewhat ironic in that Pulitzer later founded the prize for excellence in journalism that still bears his name.

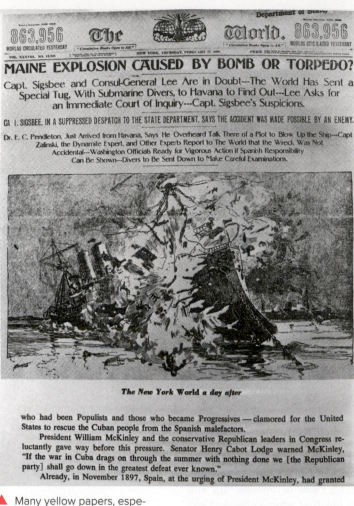

MAINE EXPLOSION CAUSED BY BOMB OR TORPEDO?

The New York World a day after

▲ Many yellow papers, especially those of Pulitzer and Hearst, used the sinking of the *Maine* as a call to war with Spain, hoping that war coverage would build circulation.

Bettmann/Getty Images

Drawing its name from the Yellow Kid, a popular cartoon character of the time, **yellow journalism** was a study in excess—sensational sex, crime, and disaster news; giant headlines; heavy use of illustrations; and reliance on cartoons and color. It was successful at first, and other papers around the country adopted all or part of its style. Although public reaction to the excesses of yellow journalism soon led to its decline, traces of its popular features remain. Large headlines, big front-page pictures, extensive use of photos and illustrations, and cartoons are characteristic even of today's best newspapers.

The years between the era of yellow journalism and the coming of television were a time of remarkable growth in the development of newspapers. From 1910 to the beginning of World War II, daily newspaper subscriptions doubled and ad revenues tripled. In 1910, there were 2,600 daily papers in the United States, more than at any time before or since. In 1923, the American Society of Newspaper Editors issued the "Canons of Journalism and Statement of Principles" in an effort to restore order and respectability after the yellow era. The opening sentence of the Canons was, "The right of a newspaper to attract and hold readers is restricted by nothing but considerations of public welfare." The wire services internationalized. United Press International started gathering news from Japan in 1909 and was covering South America and Europe by 1921. In response to the competition from radio and magazines for advertising dollars, newspapers began consolidating into **newspaper chains**—papers in different cities across the country owned by a single company. Hearst and Scripps were among the most powerful chains in the 1920s. For all practical purposes, the modern newspaper had now emerged. The next phase of the medium's life, as we'll soon see, begins with the coming of television.

Newspapers and Their Audiences

Six in 10 American adults read a daily paper every week, although not necessarily on printed paper (Mansi Media, 2019).

The industry that serves those readers looks quite different from the one that operated before television became a dominant medium. There are now fewer papers and different types of papers. They deliver the news on different platforms, and more newspapers are part of large chains.

The advent of television at the end of World War II coincided with several important social and cultural changes in the United States. Shorter work hours, more leisure, more expendable cash, movement to the suburbs, and women joining the workforce in greater numbers all served to alter the newspaper–reader relationship. Today, continuing a long and steady decline beginning in the 1970s, daily print newspaper circulation has reached its lowest point since 1940 (Grieco, 2020).

The number of daily newspapers also continues to fall. There were more than 1,600 in 1990; the current total is around 1,200. Big-name dailies such as the *Baltimore Examiner*, *New York Sun*, *Honolulu Advertiser*, *Albuquerque Tribune*, *Cincinnati Post*, *Kentucky Post*, and *Birmingham Post-Herald* have closed shop. Denver's 150-year-old *Rocky Mountain News* has folded, and the 146-year-old *Seattle Post-Intelligencer* converted to Web-only. In 2016, Pittsburgh had two daily print newspapers; in 2019, it had none (Conte, 2020). The 101-year-old *Christian Science Monitor* shut down its print operation to become an online daily and a weekend newsmagazine. One in five American newspapers has closed shop since 2004.

Circulation has suffered years of decline, and ad revenues are falling at a rapid pace, an ironic state of affairs as the local newspaper is not only Americans' most-trusted source for news, but the country's most prolific generators of journalism (Sullivan, 2020; Institute for Public Relations, 2019). Nonetheless, today's newspapers are buffeted by technological and economic change like no other traditional medium. You can see which news sources Americans use most in Figure 4.1. Note where print falls.

Scope and Structure of the Newspaper Industry

Today, there are roughly 7,000 newspapers operating in the United States. Of these, roughly 17% are dailies, and the rest are weeklies (75%) and semiweeklies (8%). They have a combined print circulation of nearly 100 million. **Pass-along readership**—readers who did not originally purchase the paper—brings 100 million people a day in touch with a daily and 200 million a week in touch with a weekly. But as we've seen, overall print circulation is falling despite a growing population. Therefore, to have success and to ensure their future, newspapers have had to adjust.

We've cited statistics about dailies and weeklies, but these categories actually include many different types of papers. Let's take a closer look at some of them.

▲ **Figure 4.1** Which News Sources Do Americans Use the Most?
Source: "What Americans," 2020.

National Daily Newspapers

We traditionally think of the newspaper as a local medium, our town's paper. But two national daily newspapers enjoy large circulations and significant social and political impact. The older and more respected is *The Wall Street Journal*, founded in 1889 by Charles Dow and Edward Jones. It has been ranked the most credible newspaper in every Pew Research newspaper study since 1985. Its focus is on the world of business, although its definition of business is broad. The *Journal* has a paid daily circulation, print and digital, of just short of 3 million, and an average household income of its readers of over $275,000 makes it a favorite for upscale advertisers. In 2007, it became part of Rupert Murdoch's News Corp. media empire.

The other national daily is *USA Today*. Founded in 1982, it calls itself "The Nation's Newspaper," and despite early derision from industry pros for its lack of depth and apparent dependence on style over substance, it has become a serious national newspaper with significant global influence. Today, the paper's daily circulation of over 4 million, including special branded editions and digital subscriptions, suggests that readers welcome its mix of short, lively, upbeat stories; full-color graphics; state-by-state news and sports briefs; and ample use of easy-to-read illustrated graphs and tables.

Large Metropolitan Dailies

To be a daily, a paper must be published at least five times a week. The circulation of big-city dailies has dropped over the past 30 years, and they continue to lose circulation at a rate approaching 10% a year. Many older, established papers, including the *Philadelphia Bulletin* and the *Washington Star*, have stilled their presses in recent years. When the *Chicago Daily News* closed its doors, it had the sixth-highest circulation in the country.

As big cities cease to be industrial centers, homes, jobs, and interests have turned away from downtown. Those large metropolitan dailies that are succeeding have used a number of strategies to cut costs and to attract and keep more suburban-oriented readers. Some publish **zoned editions**—suburban or regional versions of the paper—to attract readers and to combat competition for advertising dollars from the suburban papers. However, once-customary features such as these zoned editions (*Providence Journal*), stand-alone book review sections (*Chicago Tribune*, *Washington Post*), weekly magazines (*Los Angeles Times*), classified sections (*Cincinnati Enquirer, Boston Globe*), 7-days-a-week publishing (*New Orleans Times-Picayune*), and even daily home delivery (*Cleveland Plain Dealer*) are disappearing as papers big and small battle declining ad revenue and rising production and distribution costs.

The New York Times is a special large metropolitan daily. It is a paper local to New York, but the high quality of its reporting and commentary, the reach and depth of both its national and international news, and the solid reputations of its features (such as the weekly *Times Magazine* and the *Book Review*) make it the nation's newspaper of record. Its print circulation hovers around 830,000 a day, and its 6 million digital subscribers bring that number to more than seven million daily readers (Lee, 2020).

Suburban and Small-Town Dailies

As the United States has become a nation of suburb dwellers, so too has the newspaper been suburbanized. Starting in the 1980s, the number of suburban dailies greatly increased. Despite a stall in that growth because of the circulation and revenue woes plaguing the industry as a whole, one suburban daily, Long Island's *Newsday*, is the eighth-largest paper in the country, with a combined print and digital circulation of nearly 700,000.

Small-town dailies, other than their size, are similar to their suburban cousins if there is a nearby large metropolitan paper; for example, the small-town daily *Eagle-Tribune* publishes in the shadow of Boston's two big dailies. Its focus is the Merrimack River Valley region in Massachusetts and southern New Hampshire, 25 miles northwest of Boston, serving as the heart of that geographic community.

Weeklies and Semiweeklies

Many weeklies and semiweeklies have prospered because advertisers have followed them to the suburbs. Community reporting makes them valuable to those people who identify more with their immediate environment than they do with the neighboring big city. Suburban advertisers like the narrowly focused readership and more manageable advertising rates. Readers looking for national and international news have countless online sources for that information, but those looking for local and regional news as well as the "holy trinity" of local information—high school sports, obituaries, and the police blotter—do not. This thirst for local news and information has given birth to scores of **hyperlocal free weeklies**, most often online but frequently digital *and* print, across the country. They serve discrete neighborhoods, such as the *Queens Courier* and other Schneps Media outlets dedicated to New York's individual five boroughs, Long Island, and Westchester County (Blinder, 2020).

▼ High school sports, part of the "holy trinity" of local news buoying community papers' bottom lines.

Susan Baran

The Ethnic Press

Ethnic press refers to papers published for specific audiences based on their nationality, religion, or language. One hundred and thirty American cities are served by at least one Spanish-language publication. This number has remained constant for some time as publications backed by English-language papers, such as the *Dallas Morning News's Al Día* and the *Miami Herald's El Nuevo Herald*, join more traditional weekly and semiweekly independent Spanish-language papers, such as the nation's several *La Voz Hispana* papers. This stability is a result of three factors. First, the big dailies have realized, as have all media, that to be successful (and, in this case, to reverse ongoing declines in circulation), they must reach an increasingly fragmented audience. Second, at 18% of the population, self-described Hispanic or Latino people represent not only a sizable fragment of the overall audience but also America's fastest-growing minority group. Third, because the newspaper is the most local of the mass media and nonnative English speakers tend to identify closely with their immediate locales, Spanish-language papers—like most foreign-language newspapers—command a loyal readership, one attractive to advertisers who have relatively few other ways to reach this lucrative group of consumers holding $1.5 trillion in purchasing power (Vann, 2020).

African American papers, as they have for a century and a half, remain a vibrant part of this country's **ethnic press**. African Americans represent about 13% of the total population, but because English is their native language, African Americans typically read mainstream newspapers. In fact, after whites, they represent the second-largest group of newspaper readers in the country. Still, 200 dailies, weeklies, and semiweeklies aim specifically at African Americans, and papers such as the *Amsterdam News* in New York, the *Los Angeles Sentinel*, and the *Minnesota Spokesman-Recorder*, the second-oldest minority publication in America, specialize in urban-based journalism unlike that found in the traditional mainstream dailies.

▲ America's foreign-language readers are served by a robust ethnic press.
Susan Baran

A robust ethnic press exists beyond Spanish-language and African American newspapers. For example, New York City is home to foreign-language newspapers serving nationalities speaking 50 different languages—in the *B*s alone there are Bangladeshi, Bosnian, Brazilian, Bulgarian, and Byelorussian. The *I*s have Indian, Iranian, Irish, Israeli, and Italian. In addition, the United States is home to more than 200 other foreign-language papers.

The Alternative Press

Another type of newspaper, most commonly a weekly and available at no cost, is the **alternative press**. The offspring of the underground press of the 1960s antiwar, antiracism, prodrug culture, these papers have redefined themselves. The most successful among them—the *Chicago Reader*, the *Washington City Paper*, the *Miami New Times*, and the *Seattle Weekly*—succeed by attracting upwardly mobile young people and young professionals, not the disaffected counterculture readers who were their original audiences.

Their strategy of downplaying politics and emphasizing events listings, local arts advertising, and eccentric personal classified ads has permitted the country's 100 alternative weeklies to attract 25 million hard-copy and online readers a week. However, this figure masks the fact that the number of hard-copy readers is in decline because content once considered "alternative," and therefore, not suited for traditional newspapers, is quite at home on the Web. In response, most alternative papers have a Web presence, and there are now Web-only alternative "papers," which led the industry trade group, the Association of Alternative Newsweeklies, to change its name to the Association of Alternative Newsmedia.

▼ A pioneer in serving a fragmented audience, *The Village Voice* went online-only in 2017 and shut down completely in 2018. But America's first alternative weekly returned online and in quarterly print in 2021.
Courtesy of The Village Voice

The Newspaper as an Advertising Medium

The reason we have the number and variety of newspapers we do is that readers value them. When newspapers prosper financially, it is because advertisers recognize their worth as an ad medium. Nonetheless, the difficult truth for newspapers is that advertising revenues have fallen 62% between 2008 and 2018, to $14.3 billion (Adgate, 2020). Still, ad income, long the majority contributor to papers' bottom line, now makes up only about half of newspapers' overall revenue. Still, over $14 billion in annual ad sales suggests that advertisers find newspapers' readers an attractive audience. Why?

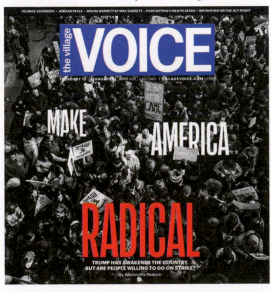

▲ Newspapers remain a powerful advertising platform because they are the most local mass medium and they continue to attract millions of print and online readers.

Gawrav Sinha/Getty Images

- The medium's reach. Two-thirds of all Americans read a print or online paper every month, and four out of 10 read one every day, or the equivalent of a daily Super Bowl broadcast.
- Newspapers are local. Supermarkets, car dealers, department stores, movie theaters, and other local merchants who want to announce a sale or offer a coupon automatically turn to the local paper. Eighty-two percent of American households make regular use of printed newspaper circulars (Mansi Media, 2019).
- Newspaper readers, regardless of the platform on which they read, are attractive to advertisers: their incomes, homeownership rates, education levels, and employment rates are above the national average.

The News and Feature Services

Much of the 35% of the newspaper that is not advertising space is filled with content provided not by the paper's own journalists, but by those working for independent news and feature services. News services, as we've already seen, collect news and distribute it to their subscribers. (They are no longer called "wire" services because they no longer use telephone wires. Today material is more likely to come by computer network or satellite.) Unlike the early days of the wire services, today's subscriber is three times more likely to be a broadcast outlet than a newspaper. These radio and television stations receive voice and video, as well as written copy. There are hundreds of news agencies. Agence France-Presse (AFP), the Associated Press (AP), and Reuters are well-known global operations, and there are nation-specific agencies, such as the Polish Press Agency, and topic-specific operations as well, for example the Catholic News Agency. Depending on the provider, subscribers receive a choice of material, for example, national and international news, state and regional news, sports, business news, farm and weather reports, and human interest and consumer material.

The feature services, called **feature syndicates**, do not gather and distribute news. Instead, they provide the work of columnists, essayists, cartoonists, and other creative individuals to their client publications. Among that material are opinion pieces, such as commentaries by Eugene Robinson or Dave Barry; horoscope, chess, and bridge columns; editorial cartoons, such as the work of Jim Morin and Mike Luckovich; and comics, the most common and popular form of syndicated material. Among the major syndicates, the best known are *The New York Times* Syndicate, King Features Syndicate, Newspaper Enterprise Association (NEA), *The Washington Post* News Service and Syndicate, and United Feature Syndicate.

Trends and Convergence in Newspaper Publishing

Loss of competition within the industry, hypercommercialism, convergence, and the evolution of newspaper readership are altering not only the nature of the medium but also its relationship with its audiences.

Loss of Competition

The newspaper industry has seen a dramatic decline in competition. This has taken two forms: loss of competing papers and concentration of ownership. In 1923, 502 American cities had two or more competing (having different ownership) dailies. Today, fewer than

12 cities have separate competing papers. With print circulation and advertising revenues continuing to fall for urban dailies, very few cities can support more than one paper, raising the issue of lack of editorial diversity. Cities with only one newspaper have only one newspaper editorial voice. This runs counter to two long-held American beliefs about the relationship between a free press and its readers:

- Truth flows from a multitude of tongues.
- The people are best served by a number of antagonistic voices.

These are the same values that fuel worry over concentration as well. What becomes of political, cultural, and social debate when there are neither multiple nor antagonistic (or at least different) voices? Media critic Robert McChesney (1997) offered this answer: "As ownership concentrated nationally in the form of chains, journalism came to reflect the partisan interests of owners and advertisers, rather than the diverse interests of any given community" (p. 13). Today, ownership of the nation's daily newspapers is concentrated among only 10 companies, controlling half (Abernathy, 2020). The 2020 merger of the country's two largest chains, Gannett and GateHouse Media, created a conglomerate, retaining the Gannett name, owning 613 daily, weekly, and community papers (Waldman, 2020).

▲ In 2019, after nearly 100 years of operation, the *Salt Lake Tribune* became one of the many papers across the country converting to non-profit ownership.
Sophia Eppolito/AP Images

Chains are not new. Hearst owned several big-city papers in the 1880s, but at that time most cities enjoyed significant competition between papers. Now that most communities have only one paper, nonlocal chain or conglomerate control of that voice is more problematic. Additional concern is raised about chain ownership when the chain is also a media conglomerate, owning several different types of media outlets, as well as other nonmedia companies. Will the different media holdings speak with one corporate voice? Will they speak objectively, and will they cover at all the doings of their nonmedia corporations?

Chains do have their supporters. Although some critics see big companies as more committed to profit and shareholder dividends, others see chains such as McClatchy, winner of numerous Pulitzer Prizes and other awards, as turning expanded economic and journalistic resources toward better service and journalism. (This legacy may be in jeopardy, as the chain declared bankruptcy in 2020 and operation of its papers taken over by hedge fund Chatham Asset Management; Robertson & Tracy, 2020.) Some critics see outside ownership as uncommitted to local communities and issues, but others see balance and objectivity (especially important in one-paper towns). Ultimately, we must recognize that not all chains operate alike. Some run their holdings as little more than profit centers; others see profit residing in exemplary service. Some groups require that all their papers toe the corporate line; others grant local autonomy.

Conglomeration: Hypercommercialism, Erosion of the Firewall, and Loss of Mission

As in other media, conglomeration has led to increased pressure on newspapers to turn a profit. This manifests itself in three distinct but related ways—hypercommercialism, erasure of the distinction between ads and news, and ultimately, loss of the journalistic mission itself.

Hypercommercialism takes many forms. For example, many papers, such as *USA Today*, *The New York Times*, the *Orange County Register,* and Michigan's *Oakland Press* and *Macomb Daily*, sell ad space on their front pages, once the exclusive province of news. Other papers, such as Rhode Island's *Providence Journal*, take this form of hypercommercialism halfway, affixing removable sticker ads to their front pages. Many papers now permit (and charge for) the placement of pet obituaries alongside those of deceased humans. The *Southeast Missourian* sells letters-to-the-editor placement to those who want to support political candidates.

A second problematic outcome of conglomeration, say critics, is that the quest for profits at all costs is eroding the *firewall*, the once inviolate barrier between newspapers' editorial and advertising missions. Although critics find the position of "advertorial editor" at the *Fairbanks Daily News-Miner*—whose salary is split equally between the newsroom and advertising department—strikingly inappropriate, most papers of all sizes face the same problem. "We're all salespeople now," said Mike Wilson, editor of the *Dallas Morning News* (in Parker, 2015).

Media industry reporter Greg Dool (2019) explains the shift from journalism toward sales, "Today's business climate requires editors to work side-by-side with ad sales teams (and their clients) in order to meet new and evolving demands from marketers and offset declines in traditional advertising." One particularly dramatic example of offsetting ad revenue declines is **sponsored content**, content paid for by an advertiser that adopts the appearance of traditional editorial material.

There are many names for the practice, including branded content, native advertising, brand journalism, and content marketing, but whatever the label, the strategy of permitting advertisers to pay for or even create articles that look like traditional editorial content is common as newspapers try to find new sources of income. Sometimes the material is written by the paper's journalists; other times it is provided by the sponsor or its advertising agency. In either case, the story typically looks in tone and design like content usually found on the paper's site or in its pages. All papers of size now engage in the practice. *The Wall Street Journal*, for example, maintains in-house teams to create sponsored content, the Custom Studios, staffed with experienced editors, journalists, and designers. *The New York Times* has a 100-person Brand Studio in its ad department; and the *Guardian* boasts a 62-person content studio, dubbed Labs. Sponsored content, while now common in all ad-supported media, remains controversial, as you'll read in Chapter 5. But for now, the question remains, "How can advertising intentionally designed to look like a newspaper's editorial content serve any purpose other than to diminish people's faith in its real journalism?"

Newspapers will die, say conglomeration's critics, because they will have abandoned their traditional democratic mission, a failure all the more tragic because despite falling circulation, more newspapers might have remained financially healthy had they invested rather than cut when times were good. In the era of record revenues and record profits, papers were laying off staff, closing state and regional bureaus, hiring younger and less experienced reporters, and shrinking their **newsholes**—the amount of space given to news. Newspaper owners were so focused on profit margins that the editors who worked for them were distracted from finding and running great stories, a problem magnified by the entry of hedge funds, big-money investment companies seeking maximum short-term profits for their investors, into the newspaper business. These hedge funds now own seven of the 10 largest newspaper chains and 55% of the country's daily newspaper circulation (Waldman, 2020). Some buy struggling papers, strengthen them, and sell them for a profit.

However, *vulture funds*, another kind of hedge fund, buy troubled papers, cut their staffs to the bone to maximize short-term profit, and sell off the remaining pieces of the business (for example, printing presses, delivery trucks, and buildings) when profits start to wane because of reduced news coverage. For example, After Alden Global Capitol acquired the *Monterey Herald*, wrote one of its reporters, Julie Reynolds, "Layoffs and attrition accelerated at breakneck speed. Instead of a story a day, reporters scrambled to crank out two or three because there were fewer and fewer of us. The office supplies vanished, and we had to buy our own pens, calendars, and manila folders. Then the hot water in the bathrooms was turned off. The gutters were never repaired, and staff creatively arranged house plants to try to soak up the leaks." Newspaper analyst Ken Doctor was not surprised: "The impact is obvious. . .It's the bankers who are deciding what will be defined as news, and who and how many people will be employed to report it" (both in Pompeo, 2020).

Are there alternatives to chain and hedge and vulture fund ownership of papers? One is converting to nonprofit status. The *Philadelphia Inquirer*, for example, is owned by the Philadelphia Foundation. The *Salt Lake City Tribune* and the *Tampa Bay Times* have followed a similar path, and the 14 New Jersey weeklies once owned by the New Jersey Hills

Media Group now operate as nonprofit newspapers under the auspices of the Corporation for New Jersey Local Media. Another option, although somewhat controversial given concerns over undue owner influence, is billionaire ownership as exists with the *Washington Post* (Jeff Bezos), *Boston Globe* (John Henry), and the *Los Angeles Times* (Patrick Soon-Shiong). Some papers, for example, the *Dallas Morning News*, are experimenting with memberships, in this case granting special benefits to "premium subscribers." You can read about another means of maintaining quality journalism in the box entitled "Nonprofit Newsrooms Fill the Void in Journalism."

Convergence with the Internet

Why so much talk about money? You and the new digital technologies are why. You are increasingly moving your media consumption online. The Internet has devastated newspapers' advertising income. For example, as much as 39% of all Google search results come from news publishers' original content, earning the company $5 billion a year from others' journalism. Along with Facebook, the two digital giants alone take in 60% of all online advertising dollars in the US, often using news outlets' work to drive those dollars away from those very same news outlets (Blethen, 2020; Ridings, 2020). In recognition of the damage it is inflicting on journalism, however, Google announced in mid-2020 that it would begin paying "high quality" news sites for their work (Bender, 2020).

The Internet has also proven extremely financially damaging in its attack on newspapers' classified advertising business. Before the Internet, classified advertising was the exclusive domain of local newspapers.

Today, the Internet overwhelms newspapers' one-time dominance through commercial online classified advertising sites (for example, eBay, Cars.com, and Zillow), advertisers connecting directly with customers on their own sites, and communitarian-minded (that is, free community-based) sites. Craigslist, for example, originating in San Francisco in 1995, is now in more than 700 cities across 70 different countries. Very quickly the site became a force, costing local papers more than $5 billion in classified ad revenue from 2000 to 2007 alone (Seamans & Zhu, 2013).

Advertising losses are most striking in employment and auto sales classifieds. To counter career sites like Monster.com, about one-third of the newspapers across the country created their own national service, CareerBuilder, which rivals Monster's number of listings but not income. Dozens more work with competitor-turned-partner Monster.com. To counter online auto sales classified sites, as well as real estate and general merchandise sites, virtually every newspaper in the country now maintains its own online classified pages. These efforts, however, have done little to save newspapers' one-time classified dominance.

The problem of the loss of classified ad income is magnified by the exodus of young people, that highly desirable demographic, from print to electronic news sources. Only 6% of the country's 18 to 29 year olds read the hard-copy paper daily, favoring every other platform, even podcasts, for their daily news consumption (Watson, 2020). In the late 1970s, 33% of 10th graders read a newspaper almost every day; today the number is 2% ("Teens Today," 2018).

Not only does the Internet provide readers with more information and more depth, and with greater speed, than the traditional newspaper, but they empower readers to control and interact with the news, in essence becoming their own editors in chief. As a result, the traditional newspaper is reinventing itself by converging with these very same technologies. And 2016 seems to have been a watershed year in papers' convergence with the Internet as, among other things, the number of people employed in digital publishing exceeded the number working at newspapers for the first time in history (Sass, 2016); the Newspaper Association of America dropped "paper" from its name, becoming the News Media Alliance, and began accepting digital-only news sites as members (Edmonds, 2016); the American Society of News Editors announced that it would estimate a newspaper's size not by circulation but by monthly Internet traffic when setting membership dues (Mullin, 2016b); and Facebook began offering free online training for journalists (Albeanu, 2016).

Still, the marriage of newspapers to the Internet has not yet proved financially successful for the older medium. And in this there resides a damaging irony for the newspaper industry. "The amount of time Americans spend with journalists' work and their

USING MEDIA TO MAKE A DIFFERENCE
Nonprofit Newsrooms Fill the Void in Journalism

As newspapers close shop, journalism suffers. "You know who loves this new day of the lack of journalism? Politicians. Businessmen. Nobody's watching them anymore," warns Russ Kendall, a veteran newspaper journalist now self-employed as a pizza maker. "I have a deep fear about what is happening to journalism. No one else is going to do what we do," added another former longtime journalist forced into retirement (Maharidge, 2016, pp. 22–23).

What is it that journalists do that no one else will? They do time-consuming and labor-intensive reporting. They go out and talk to people. They constantly dig for sources and leads; they read documents; they search for facts and information; they ferret out and tell the untold stories. They know the beats they cover; they strive for objectivity, and they have editors who check their facts and guard against unwarranted assumptions and conscious or unconscious bias. Journalists are the people's eyes, ears, and voices. And their numbers are dwindling, as you read in this chapter's opening vignette.

In that conversation between two friends, we saw one solution to the problem of the disappearing of journalism, Report for America, which trains, places, and subsidizes the salaries of journalists. There is another approach that is making a difference: nonprofit newsrooms staffed by veteran and newly minted professional journalists alike. Some are funded by foundations. Between 2009 and 2016, foundations gave $1.1 billion to American journalism projects (Nelson & Ferrucci, 2020), and in 2019, the Knight Foundation alone committed $300 million over 5 years to "build the future of local news" (Posner, 2020). Some receive voluntary payments from their for-profit media partners. For example, nonprofit ProPublica and the *New York Daily News* combined on an investigative series on noise abatement in New York City, and commercial TV station WGRZ in Buffalo funds the local nonprofit *Investigative Post* to produce five stories a month.

And while some nonprofit newsrooms are small and serve local communities and local media, many maintain partnerships with major national media. *The New York Times* uses the work of nonprofit newsrooms in Chicago, San Francisco, and other locations to strengthen its reporting in those locales. In addition to the *Times*, major media outlets, such as *60 Minutes*, National Public Radio, *Salon*, *USA Today*, NBC-owned television stations, the *Los Angeles Times*, *Bloomberg Businessweek*, and *The Washington Post,* make regular use of several nonprofits' investigative reporting on controversial and expensive investigations into issues such as natural gas drilling, abuse of federal money, and the failure of many of the nation's coroner and medical examiner offices.

Have nonprofit newsrooms made a difference? "We see a lot of legacy publications doing the formulaic press conference stuff—whereas the [nonprofit] publishers have never felt an obligation to do everything, because they couldn't," answers Matt DeRienzo, executive director of Local Independent Online News Publishers. "What they are doing, in many cases, is more enterprising, more investigative stuff. They step off the hamster wheel and get to what's really at the heart of community. . . . We never want to be the sixth person at a press conference, and we never will be" (in Mullin, 2016a).

ProPublica offers an example of this "more enterprising, more investigative stuff." The foundation-supported nonprofit uses **engagement reporting**, calling on citizens using online call-outs, flyers in community centers, and even announcements in traditional media to solicit tips, find sources, and identify under-reported stories, typically those ad-supported news outlets often ignore. Its reporting has uncovered "hot" topics like age discrimination at IBM, hospitals abusing life-support systems, and incompetence in the manufacture of coronavirus testing tubes problems (Scire, 2020).

If you're interested in a nonprofit journalism outfit in your area or one covering an issue of particular significance to you, the Institute for Nonprofit News maintains a list of more than 285 nonprofit newsrooms at https://inn.org/members/.

willingness to pay for it have both spiked, higher than at any point since Election 2016, maybe before," wrote journalism analyst Ken Doctor in 2020 at a time of medical, racial, and political turmoil in America. "But the business that has supported these journalists—shakily, on wobbly wheels—now finds the near future almost impossible to navigate. . .The increases in reader revenue are outmatched by the declines in advertising." The problem, in other words, is replacing *analog dollars* with *digital dimes*. That is, despite heavy traffic on newspaper websites—eight in 10 adults who go online will visit a newspaper website—online readers simply are not worth as much as print readers. Still, there are encouraging signs.

There are tens of thousands of online newspapers for every state in the union and most foreign countries. These papers have adopted a variety of strategies to become "relevant on the Internet." The *Arkansas Democrat-Gazette*, for example, offers subscribers free iPads (and personal training sessions). *The Washington Post* joined with *Newsweek* magazine, cable television channel MSNBC, and television network NBC to share content among all the parties' websites and to encourage users to link to their respective sites. Others (for example, *The Boston Globe*, the *Miami Herald*, and *The Kansas City Star*) have adopted just the opposite approach, focusing on their strength as local media by offering websites specific to their newspapers. Each offers not only what readers might expect to find in these sites' parent newspapers but also significant additional information on how to make the most of the cities they represent. These sites are as much city guides as they are local newspapers.

The local element offers several advantages. Local searchable and archival classified ads offer greater efficiency than do the big national classified ad websites such as Monster.com and Cars.com. No other medium can offer news on crime, housing, neighborhood politics, zoning, school lunch menus, marriage licenses, and bankruptcies—all searchable by street or zip code. Local newspapers can use their websites to develop their own linked secondary sites, thus providing impressive detail on local industry. For example, the *San Jose Mercury News*'s SiliconValley.com focuses on the digital industries. Several McClatchy papers offer SportsPass, a subscription service offering unlimited access to their sports reporting. Another localizing strategy is for online newspapers to build and maintain message boards and chat groups on their sites that deal with important issues. One more bow to the power of the Web—and users' demands for interactivity—is that most newspapers have begun their own blog sites, inviting readers and journalists to talk to one another.

Despite all this innovation and the readership it generates, papers still face two lingering questions about their online success. The first, as we've seen, is how they will earn more income from their Web operations. Internet users have come to expect free content, and for years newspapers were happy to provide their product at no cost, simply to establish their presence online. Unfortunately, they now find that people are unwilling to pay for what the papers themselves have been giving away for free online. So, newspapers have to fix their business models.

Among those "fixes" are newspapers that rely on advertising for their online revenue. Many continue to provide free access, hoping to attract more readers and, therefore, more advertising revenue. Some newspapers even offer free online classifieds to draw people to their sites (and to their paid advertisers). The vast majority of newspapers, recognizing that the Internet surpassed print papers as readers' source of news in 2009 (Mindlin, 2009), offer online subscriptions, averaging about $10 a month (although industry research suggests that $3.99 a week is the optimal subscription price; Williams, 2019).

Most are also experimenting with variations of a **paywall**, that is, making all or some of their content available only to those visitors willing to pay. Some have strict paywalls: readers gain access only by paying for it. *The Wall Street Journal* and *The Newport Daily News* employ this method. Others, *The New York Times* and *The Washington Post*, for example, offer a *metered system,* sometimes called a leaky paywall—print subscribers get all online content for free, but nonsubscribers are limited to a specified number of free stories before they have to pay. Paywalls, however, are flexible. Many papers, big and small, dropped paywalls on their 2020 coronavirus reporting, giving access to all who were interested (McBride & Edmonds, 2020). **Micropayments**, small individual payments (for example, 19 or 25 cents) per story provided by an aggregator such as Blendle, have been successful in Europe and have had limited success in the United States (Thorpe, 2020).

This digital readership raises the second question faced by online newspapers: How will circulation be measured? In fact, if visitors to a newspaper's website are added to its hard-copy readership, newspapers are more popular than ever; that is, they are drawing readers in

▼ *Boston.com* represents one paper's online strategy. The *Boston Globe* uses its site to focus on more local news and sports.
NetPhotos3/Alamy Stock Photo

larger numbers than ever before. Therefore, if many online papers continue to rely on a free-to-the-user, ad-supported model to boost their "circulation," how do they quantify that readership for advertisers, both print and online?

Industry insiders have called for a new metric to more accurately describe a paper's true reach, especially as ad rates are determined by how many **impressions**—the number of times an online ad is seen—an individual article can generate. "Circulation," they say, should be replaced by **integrated audience reach**, the total number of readers of the print edition plus those unduplicated Web readers who access the paper only online or via a mobile device. This is not insignificant given the heavy traffic enjoyed by newspaper websites. For example, the *Washington Post* has a million unique monthly visitors and the *New York Times* reaches more than 90 million and has 3.4 million digital-news-only subscribers (Benton, 2020). But there is the danger that new metrics might encourage newspapers to chase **click bait**, articles with catchy headlines designed to gain impressions rather than make an impression. You can learn more about this potential problem in the box titled "Attracting Readers with Click Bait."

Smartphones, Tablets, and e-Readers

One in five American adults owns an e-reader (Haines, 2020); 53% own a tablet and 85% have a smartphone (Edison Research, 2020). Data such as these have added to the newspaper industry's optimism about its digital future, especially because more than eight in 10 US adults get at least some of their news online (Shearer, 2021). Moreover, Facebook is "a regular source of news" for 36% of Americans and Twitter serves the same role for another 15% (Shearer & Mitchell, 2021). Social media as sources of news are of great interest to newspapers because they are especially attractive to young readers who seem to have abandoned print, as you'll soon read. Additional good news resides in the fact that fully 20% of American adults not only already pay for an online news subscription, one-third have multiple subscriptions, and 88% say they will continue to pay for online news (Fletcher, 2020). You can see their motivations in Figure 4.2.

Access to newspapers on tablets and smartphones has been further encouraged by apps and digital services designed specifically to link mobile readers with the news. With Apple News, for example, readers can select topics and publications and have stories instantly delivered without having to move from app to app. Facebook News uses live journalists

▶ **Figure 4.2** Reasons Americans Pay for Online News Subscriptions.
Source: Fletcher, 2020.
(photo) Maskot/Getty Images

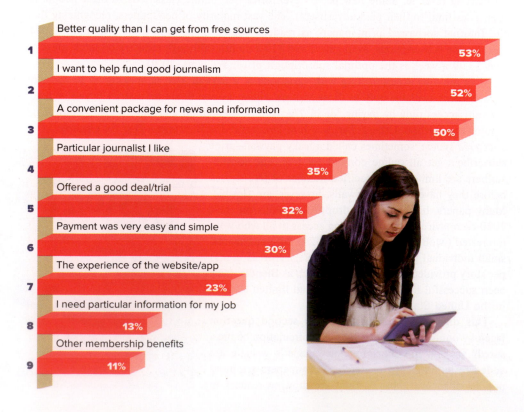

Better quality than I can get from free sources
1   53%

I want to help fund good journalism
2   52%

A convenient package for news and information
3   50%

Particular journalist I like
4   35%

Offered a good deal/trial
5   32%

Payment was very easy and simple
6   30%

The experience of the website/app
7   23%

I need particular information for my job
8   13%

Other membership benefits
9   11%

CULTURAL FORUM
Attracting Readers with Click Bait

Newspaper readers are moving to the Web, but the industry is still struggling to find a way to better monetize that digital migration to make up for the massive loss of print advertising revenue. A question now in the cultural forum is how far should newspapers go to bring even more readers, especially demographically prized young adults, to their sites? With hard-copy newspapers, the solution to the problem of attracting readers was easy: In addition to news, offer sports, entertainment news, weather, comics, horoscopes, and lifestyle reporting—something for everyone. Readers who came for one or more of those features (a) bought the paper and saw the ads (good for business) and (b) might come across some hard news and opinions of interest as they flipped through the pages in search of their desired content (good for developing an informed public). This model worked well for nearly two centuries. It didn't matter why people bought the paper; even if they bought it only for the sports section, they still bought the whole package. And that's how advertising rates were set—how many people bought the whole package.

But the Internet is different. People link directly to the stories that interest them. They can access *only* the results of last night's game, *only* the news of the layoffs at the fire department, or *only* accounts of the state representative's conflict of business interests. With the Internet, ad rates are determined by how many impressions specific articles can generate, so reporters researching and writing engaging stories to attract more readership to their work, whatever the topic, should be good news for journalism. But critics inside and outside the industry complain that isn't what's happening. Because an impression brings in anywhere from a fraction-of-a-cent to a few pennies, a journalist has to amass a lot of them and therefore may be incentivized to write more sensational stories.

Because of real-time analytics, newspapers now know more about their readers than ever before, allowing them to track how many people read each article, how long they stay on a page, and how they found the story. Knowing what gets read and what doesn't has produced a major transformation in newspaper journalism. Journalist Danielle Ryan (2017) is critical of that transformation: "Quantity and speed [become] vastly superior in importance to quality and factual accuracy. . . . The quality journalism that does appear in the midst of it all is fumbling to grab our attention through a mountain of far more appealing trash: listicles, quizzes, stenography masquerading as reporting, opinion masquerading as 'explainer' pieces, propaganda, conspiracy, fake news and cute cat videos." Headlines like "An Orphaned Boy Moved into His Grandparents' Home. The Homeowners Association Wants to Kick Him Out" and "Officials Said He Died in a Fall. Then His Wife Admitted to Poisoning His Water with Eye Drops" (both from Nolan, 2020) sit side-by-side with accounts of Supreme Court decisions and coronavirus death counts, potentially granting them equal importance.

"To be clear, there is nothing wrong with this," argues *Columbia Journalism Review* public editor Hamilton Nolan (2020). "Every for-profit news operation must, to some extent, subsidize important work with fluff, because fluff tends to attract readers much more reliably than important work." Not only does that pay the bills, he contends, but "the serious stuff gains at least the possibility of ambient readership from the clickbait traffic."

Enter Your Voice

The newspaper—and the news—have always lived a dual life, simultaneously a commodity *and* a public good.

- Knowing that the vast majority of this country's professionally reported serious news comes from newspapers, does the reliance on Web metrics and the rush toward judging the value of news reports based on the quantity of clicks trouble you?

- Will it mean more quickly written and less-researched news and more lists of best places to eat, feel-good stories, and articles with more conjecture than facts?

- Is this a fair (and necessary) price to pay to ensure that newspapers survive? Or because there's nothing that says articles that attract clicks must be shallow, might it even be a benefit to newspapers, as they can better understand their readers and give them news that *they* value?

and algorithms to personalize story selection. Scroll is a monthly subscription service that collates a selection of stories from a wide variety of news outlets and delivers them, without ads, to people's digital devices. And subscription news site aggregator Scroll joined existing digital news delivery options, such as Blendle, an app that sells individual articles aggregated from a variety of news sources.

▲ Young readers have abandoned print, but their consumption of news has simply moved online.

Peathegee Inc LLC/Blend Images

A Changing Readership

As has always been the case, newspapers must adapt to the ever-evolving culture of the "next" generation. It just so happens today's "next" generation are digital natives, born and raised in a digitized world. This digital revolution has changed the way we engage with content in unprecedented ways, especially the way young people engage with content. Look at Figure 4.3. Note how poorly print readership fares with younger news consumers. But how far should papers go to attract and keep younger readers, even if it is to their digital rather than the printed version of the paper?

What happens to journalistic integrity, what happens to the traditional role of newspapers in our democracy when front pages are forced to compete with an endless stream of social media gossip? What happens to depth, detail, and precision as stories get shorter and snappier to engage young readers whose attention is pulled in 15 different directions at once in any given moment? What happens to depth, detail, and precision as stories get shorter and snappier? And this is happening, as many major news organizations now require that their reporters keep their stories between 300 and 500 words, allowing only 700 words for the top two stories they're covering (Farhi, 2014), and that's when they aren't writing click bait.

What kind of culture develops on a diet of **soft news** (sensational stories that do not serve the democratic function of journalism) rather than **hard news** (stories that help citizens make intelligent decisions and keep up with important issues of the day)? Molly Ivins offered a pessimistic answer. The late columnist suggested that newspapers aren't dying; they're committing suicide. "This is the most remarkable business plan," she told *Editor & Publisher.*

Percentage of Americans Who Often Get Their News from Each Medium, by Age, 2021

Legend:
- Smartphone, Computer, Tablet
- Television
- Radio
- Print

18–29 years old: 71%, 16%, 7%, 3%
30–49 years old: 67%, 25%, 15%, 4%
50–64 years old: 52%, 54%, 20%, 11%
65+ years old: 48%, 68%, 11%, 25%

▲ **Figure 4.3** Percentage of Americans Who Often Get Their News from Each Medium, by Age.
Source: Roper, 2021. (photo): AfricaImages/Getty Images

"Newspaper owners look at one another and say, 'Our rate of return is slipping a bit; let's solve the problem by making our product smaller and less helpful and less interesting'" (in Timberg, 2015, p. 177).

The "softening" of newspapers raises a potential media literacy issue. The media-literate person has an obligation to be aware of the impact newspapers have on individuals and society and to understand how the text of newspapers offers insight into contemporary culture. We might ask ourselves, Are we getting what we asked for? What do we as a people and as individuals want from our newspaper? Do we understand the role newspapers play in our democratic process? Are we fully aware of how newspapers help shape our understanding of ourselves and our world?

In a 1787 letter, Thomas Jefferson wrote to a colleague, "Were it left to me to decide whether we should have a government without newspapers or newspapers without government, I should not hesitate to prefer the latter." Would he write that about today's newspaper, a newspaper increasingly designed to meet the wants, needs, and interests of younger, occasional newspaper readers or those who do not read at all?

There is another view, however—that there is no problem here at all. Ever since the days of the penny press, newspapers have been dominated by soft news. All we are seeing today is an extension of what has always been. Moreover, nonreaders are simply going elsewhere for the hard news and information that were once the sole province of newspapers. They're going online, to television, and to specifically targeted sources, including magazines and newsletters.

DEVELOPING MEDIA LITERACY SKILLS

Interpreting Relative Placement of Stories

Newspapers tell readers what is significant and meaningful through their placement of stories in and on their pages. Within a paper's sections (for example, front, leisure, sports, and business), readers almost invariably read pages in order (that is, page 1, then page 2, and so on). Recognizing this, papers place the stories they think are most important on the earliest pages. Newspaper jargon for this phenomenon has even entered our everyday language: "front-page news" means the same thing in the living room as in the pressroom.

The placement of stories on a page is also important (see Figure 4.4). English readers read from top to bottom and from left to right. Stories that the newspaper staff deems important tend to be placed above the fold and toward the left of the page. This is an important aspect of the power of newspapers to influence public opinion and of media literacy. Relative story placement is a factor in **agenda setting**—the way newspapers and other media influence not only what we think but also what we think about.

A media-literate newspaper reader should be able to make judgments about other layout decisions. The use of photos suggests the importance the editors assign to a story, as do the size and wording of headlines, the employment of *jumps* (continuations to other pages), and placement of a story in a given section. A report of a person's death on the front page, as opposed to the international section or in the obituaries, carries a different meaning, as does an analysis of an issue placed on the front page as opposed to the editorial page.

Moreover, this "grammar" holds for online newspapers as well, especially when, like the *Arkansas Democrat-Gazette* and the *Tampa Bay Times*, they offer a replica of the paper, an **e-replica edition**. Most newspapers, however, provide a digital "close version" of their front page that is not an exact

▼ **Figure 4.4** Placement of Stories on a Typical Front Page. *spxChrome/Getty Images*

The Daily Mass Communicator

1 — Most important story (Especially if accompanied by a photo)

2 — Next most important story (Importance can be boosted with a photo)

3 — Not quite as important but too significant for the inside pages; can be used for attention-grabbing soft news

4 — Least important front-page story; can be used for a report that accompanies one of the above-the-fold stories

replica but still maintains the traditional values of left-to-right and above-and-below-the-fold. And as you might imagine, others, the *Atlanta Journal-Constitution* and *Providence Journal* for example, take advantage of the Web's ease of navigation and present a "front page" that offers a wide array of headlines and images that link to stories throughout the edition, freeing readers to make their own determination of what is newsworthy.

MEDIA LITERACY CHALLENGE
Reading the Newspaper: Hard Copy vs. Online vs. Mobile

Two elements of media literacy are *critical thinking skills enabling the development of independent judgments about media content* and *strategies for analyzing and discussing media messages.* Both are involved in this challenge.

Find the online version of a newspaper with which you are familiar, its app-enabled version for your smartphone or tablet, and its dead-tree version, all from the same day. Compare the three. What content is common to all three? What content exists online or on mobile technology that is unavailable in the printed newspaper?

How would you characterize the online-specific content? The mobile-specific content? That is, are there specific types of content that seem to appear online and on mobile devices as opposed to appearing in the hard-copy version? Can you speculate why this might be?

How similar or different are the advertisers in the two electronic versions from those in the printed version? Do the online and mobile versions have different advertisers? Can you speculate why the similarities and differences you found exist? Describe your experience reading the online and mobile newspapers. What did you like about it? What did you dislike? Do the same for the printed version. Despite the demographic trends that might suggest otherwise, do you think you could ever become a regular reader of the hard-copy newspaper? Why or why not?

Resources for Review and Discussion

REVIEW POINTS: TYING CONTENT TO LEARNING OUTCOMES

▶ **Recognize the history and development of the newspaper industry and the newspaper itself as a medium.**

- ☐ Newspapers have been a part of public life since Roman times, prospering in Europe, and coming to the colonies in the 1690s.
- ☐ The newspaper was at the heart of the American Revolution, and, as such, protection for the press was enshrined in the First Amendment.
- ☐ The penny press brought the paper to millions of "regular people," and the newspaper quickly became the people's medium.

▶ **Identify how the organizational and economic nature of the contemporary newspaper industry shapes the content of newspapers.**

- ☐ There are several types of newspapers, including national dailies; large metropolitan dailies; suburban and small-town dailies; weeklies and semiweeklies; and ethnic and alternative papers.

- ☐ Despite falling hard-copy readership, newspapers remain an attractive advertising medium.
- ☐ The number of daily newspapers is in decline, and there are very few cities with competing papers. Chain ownership has become common.
- ☐ Conglomeration is fueling hypercommercialism, erosion of the firewall between the business and editorial sides of the newspaper, and the loss of the newspaper's traditional journalistic mission.

▶ **Describe the relationship between the newspaper and its readers.**

- ☐ Newspaper readership is changing—it is getting older, as young people abandon the paper for the Internet and social media. How newspapers respond will define their future.
- ☐ Localism, that is, providing coverage of material otherwise difficult to find on the Internet, has proven successful for many papers.

▶ Recall changes in the newspaper industry brought about by converging technologies and how those alterations may affect the medium's traditional role in our democracy.

  ☐ Newspapers have converged with the Internet. Although most people read news online, still unanswered are questions of how to charge for content and how to measure readership.

  ☐ The industry has found new optimism in the success of their mobile—smartphone, tablet, and e-reader—offerings.

▶ Apply key newspaper-reading media literacy skills, especially in interpreting the relative placement of stories and use of photos.

  ☐ Where content appears—factors such as what page a story is on, where on the page it appears, and the presence of accompanying photos—offers significant insight into the importance a paper places on that content.

  ☐ This relative placement of stories has an influence on what readers come to see as the important news of the day.

KEY TERMS

disruptive transition, 78

Acta Diurna, 78

corantos, 78

diurnals, 79

broadsides (broadsheets), 79

Bill of Rights, 80

First Amendment, 80

Alien and Sedition Acts, 80

penny press, 80

wire services, 81

yellow journalism, 82

newspaper chains, 82

pass-along readership, 83

zoned editions, 83

hyperlocal free weeklies, 84

ethnic press, 85

alternative press, 85

feature syndicates, 86

sponsored content, 88

newshole, 88

engagement reporting, 90

paywall, 91

micropayments, 91

impressions, 92

integrated audience reach, 92

click bait, 92

soft news, 94

hard news, 94

agenda setting, 95

e-replica edition, 95

QUESTIONS FOR REVIEW

1. What are Acta Diurna, corantos, diurnals, and broadsheets?

2. What is the significance of *Publick Occurrences Both Forreign and Domestick*, the *Boston News-Letter*, the *New-England Courant*, the *Pennsylvania Gazette*, and the *New York Weekly Journal*?

3. What factors led to the development of the penny press? To yellow journalism?

4. What are the similarities and differences between wire services (or news services) and feature syndicates?

5. When did newspaper chains begin? Can you characterize them as they exist today?

6. What are the different types of newspapers?

7. Why is the newspaper an attractive medium for advertisers?

8. How has convergence affected newspapers' performance?

9. What is the firewall? Why is it important?

10. How do online papers succeed?

To maximize your study time, check out CONNECT to access the SmartBook study module for this chapter, watch videos, and explore other resources.

QUESTIONS FOR CRITICAL THINKING AND DISCUSSION

1. Talk to your parents (or other adults if your parents aren't available) about what the paper meant to them before news migrated to the Web. How valuable did they find it and why? Have they abandoned print in favor of the Internet, and if so, why? If they are from a city that no longer has a good newspaper, how have they filled the void?

2. When you go online for news, what kinds of stories most attract you? Do you look for detail and depth, or do you chase click bait? Why? Does it have anything to do with what you have come to expect from online content? Explain your answers.

3. Compare your local paper and an alternative weekly. Choose different sections, such as front page, editorials, and classified ads, if any. How are they similar; how are they different? Which one, if any, speaks to you and why?

REFERENCES

1. Abernathy, P. M. (2020). Bigger and bigger they grow. *University of North Carolina Hussman School of Journalism and Media*. Retrieved from https://www.usnewsdeserts.com/reports/expanding-news-desert/loss-of-local-news/bigger-and-bigger-they-grow/

2. "About Us." (2021). *Report for America*. Retrieved from https://www.reportforamerica.org/about-us/

3. Adgate, B. (2020, April 13). Newspaper revenue drops as local news interest rises amid coronavirus. *Forbes*. Retrieved from

https://www.forbes.com/sites/bradadgate/2020/04/13/newspapers-are-struggling-with-coronavirus/#3912632e39ef

4. Albeanu, C. (2016, October 25). Facebook launches free online training for journalists. *Journalism.com*. Retrieved from https://www.journalism.co.uk/news/facebook-launches-free-online-training-for-journalists/s2/a686060/

5. Bender, B. (2020, June 25). A new licensing program to support the news industry. *Google*. Retrieved from https://www.blog.google/outreach-initiatives/google-news-initiative/licensing-program-support-news-industry-/?utm_source=CJR+Daily+News&utm_campaign=3c80fac650-EMAIL_CAMPAIGN_2018_10_31_05_02_COPY_01&utm_medium=email&utm_term=0_9c93f57676-3c80fac650-174360297&mc_cid=3c80fac650&mc_eid=33aeafd5ea

6. Blethen, F. (2020, May 18). In this moment of multiple crises, we need strong local journalism. *Washington Post*. Retrieved from https://www.washingtonpost.com/opinions/2020/05/18/this-moment-multiple-crises-we-need-strong-local-journalism/

7. Blinder, M. (2020, December 1). Schneps Media is rocking New York with hyperlocal free weeklies. *Editor & Publisher*. Retrieved from https://www.editorandpublisher.com/stories/schneps-media-is-rocking-new-york-with-hyperlocal-free-weeklies,181061

8. Conte, A. (2020, January 1). On media: 2019 marks the end of metro daily newspapers. *Next Pittsburgh*. Retrieved from https://nextpittsburgh.com/features/on-media-2019-marks-the-end-of-metro-daily-newspapers/

9. Doctor, K. (2020, March 27). Newsonomics: What was once unthinkable is quickly becoming reality in the destruction of local news. *Nieman Lab*. Retrieved from https://www.nieman-lab.org/2020/03/newsonomics-what-was-once-unthinkable-is-quickly-becoming-reality-in-the-destruction-of-local-news/

10. Dobbins, J. (2021, January 2). The 'news desert' is growing. So is a tiny upstart. *New York Times*, p. A10.

11. Dool, G. (2019, July 18). Separation of church and state is (mostly) dead in media, execs say. *Folio*. Retrieved from https://www.foliomag.com/separation-church-state-mostly-dead-media-execs-say/

12. Douglass, Frederick. (1847, December 3). *The North Star*.

13. Dumenco, S. (2008, June 23). Th-th-th-that's all, folks! No more talk of media end-times. *Advertising Age*, p. 48.

14. Edison Research. (2020. *The infinite dial 2020*. Retrieved from https://www.rab.com/whyradio/wrnew/wr-research/pdf/Infinite%20Dial%202020.pdf

15. Edmonds, R. (2016, June 10). NAA is getting ready to accept digital-only sites as members. *Poynter Institute*. Retrieved from http://www.poynter.org/2016/naa-is-getting-ready-to-accept-digital-only-sites-as-members/415989/

16. Farhi, P. (2014, May 12). New Associated Press guidelines: Keep it brief. *Washington Post*. Retrieved from http://www.washingtonpost.com/lifestyle/style/new-ap-guidelines-keep-it-brief/2014/05/12/f220f902-d9ff-11e3-bda1-9b46b2066796_story.html

17. Fitzgerald, M. (1999, October 30). Robert Sengstake Abbott. *Editor & Publisher*, p. 18.

18. Fletcher, R. (2020). How and why people are paying for online news. *Reuters/University of Oxford*. Retrieved from http://www.digitalnewsreport.org/survey/2020/how-and-why-people-are-paying-for-online-news/

19. Grieco, E. (2020, February 14). Fast facts about the newspaper industry's financial struggles as McClatchy files for bankruptcy. *Pew Research Center*. Retrieved from https://www.pewresearch.org/fact-tank/2020/02/14/fast-facts-about-the-newspaper-industrys-financial-struggles/

20. Haines, D. (2020, June 8). Kindle sales—The e-reader device is dying a rapid death. *Just Publishing Advice*. Retrieved from https://justpublishingadvice.com/the-e-reader-device-is-dying-a-rapid-death/

21. Institute for Public Relations. (2019). 2019 *IPR disinformation in society report*. Retrieved from https://instituteforpr.org/wp-content/uploads/2019-IPR-Disinformation-Study.pdf

22. Johnson, B. (2020, January 3). Internet media employment has tripled over the past decade. *AdAge*. Retrieved from https://adage.com/article/year-end-lists-2019/internet-media-employment-has-tripled-over-past-decade/2221941

23. Lee, E. (2020, November 6). New York Times amasses over 7 million subscribers. *New York Times*, p. B6.

24. Lepore, J. (2009, January 26). Back issues. *New Yorker*, pp. 68–73.

25. Maharidge, D. (2016, March 21). Written off. *Nation*, pp. 20–25.

26. Mansi Media. (2019). Newspaper data. *Pennsylvania NewsMedia Association*. Retrieved from https://mansimedia.com/expertise/newspaper-data/

27. McBride, K., & Edmonds, R. (2020, March 23). Do news sites have an ethical duty to remove paywalls on coronavirus coverage. *Poynter*. Retrieved from https://www.poynter.org/ethics-trust/2020/do-news-sites-have-an-ethical-duty-to-remove-paywalls-on-coronavirus-coverage/

28. McChesney, R. W. (1997). *Corporate media and the threat to democracy*. New York: Seven Stories Press.

29. Mindlin, A. (2009, January 5). Web passes papers as news source. *New York Times*, p. B3.

30. Mullin, B. (2016a, August 15). As legacy news organizations cut back, local sites are cropping up to fill the void. *Poynter Institute*. Retrieved from http://www.poynter.org/2016/as-legacy-news-organizations-cut-back-local-sites-are-cropping-up-to-fill-the-void/426361/

31. Mullin, B. (2016b, October 4). American Society of News Editors undergoes digital revamp. *Poynter Institute*. Retrieved from http://www.poynter.org/2016/american-society-of-news-editors-undergoes-digital-revamp/433269/

32. Nelson, J., & Ferrucci, P. (2020, January 13). "When money is offered, we listen": foundation funding and nonprofit journalism. *Columbia Journalism Review*. Retrieved from https://www.cjr.org/tow_center/journalism-foundations-advertisers-conditions.php

33. Nolan, H. (2020). How the *Washington Post* pulled off the hardest trick in journalism. *Columbia Journalism Review*. Retrieved from https://www.cjr.org/public_editor/washington-post-fluff-news.php

34. Orso, A. (2019, April 1). In the age of "enemy of the people" rhetoric, do young people still want to be journalists? *Philadelphia Inquirer*. Retrieved from https://www.inquirer.com/news/journalism-young-people-donald-trump-fake-news-temple-penn-state-enemy-of-the-people-central-conestoga-20190401.html

35. Parker, R. (2015, July 23). *Dallas Morning News* editor: "We are all salespeople now." *Columbia Journalism Review*. Retrieved from http://www.cjr.org/united_states_project/dallas_morning_news_mike_wilson.php

36. Pompeo, J. (2020, February 5). The hedge fund vampire that bleeds newspapers dry now has the *Chicago Tribune* by the throat. *Vanity Fair*. Retrieved from https://www.vanityfair.com/news/2020/02/hedge-fund-vampire-alden-global-capital-that-bleeds-newspapers-dry-has-chicago-tribune-by-the-throat

37. Posner, M. (2020, January 26). How business leaders can help rescue dying local news. *Forbes*. Retrieved from https://www.forbes.com/sites/michaelposner/2020/01/26/how-business-leaders-can-help-rescue-dying-local-news/#5ae62d3154c3

38. Pusey, A. (2013, August 1). August 4, 1735: John Peter Zenger acquitted. *ABA Journal*. Retrieved from http://www.abajournal.com/magazine/article/august_4_1735_john_peter_zenger_acquitted

39. Ridings, D. (2020, June 5). Make Facebook and Google pay for local news, just like you. *Bowman County Pioneer*. Retrieved from https://www.bowmanextra.com/opinion/make-facebook-and-google-pay-for-local-news-just-like-you/article_4cd5d686-a6e3-11ea-9547-fb1271f949d5.html

40. Robertson, K., & Tracy, M. (2020, February 14). Bankruptcy plan is to put lender in publisher's seat. *New York Times*, p. B1.

41. Roper, W. (2021, January 13). Smart devices dominate news. *Statista*. Retrieved from https://www.statista.com/chart/23909/how-americans-view-news/

42. Ryan, D. (2017, January 22). Clickbait culture and groupthink mentality have led to the collapse of journalism—and the rise of Donald Trump. *Salon*. Retrieved from http://www.salon.com/2017/01/22/clickbait-culture-and-groupthink-mentality-have-led-to-the-collapse-of-journalism-and-the-rise-of-donald-trump/

43. Sass, E. (2016, May 5). Digital publishing headcount passes newspapers. *MediaPost*. Retrieved from http://www.mediapost.com/publications/article/275191/digital-publishing-headcount-passes-newspapers.html

44. Shearer, E. (2021, January 12). More than eight-in-ten Americans get news from digital devices. *Pew Research Center*. Retrieved from https://www.pewresearch.org/fact-tank/2021/01/12/more-than-eight-in-ten-americans-get-news-from-digital-devices/

45. Shearer, E., & Mitchell, A. (2021, January 12). News use across social media platforms in 2020. *Pew Research Center*. Retrieved from https://www.journalism.org/2021/01/12/news-use-across-social-media-platforms-in-2020/

46. Scire, S. (2020, March 5). How engagement reporting is helping ProPublica journalists find their next big story. *NiemanLab*. Retrieved from https://www.niemanlab.org/2020/03/how-engagement-reporting-is-helping-propublica-journalists-find-their-next-big-story/

47. Seamans, R., & Zhu, F. (2013, May 28). Responses to entry in multi-sided markets: The impact of Craigslist on local newspapers. *NET Institute Working Paper no. 10–11*. Retrieved from http://www.gc.cuny.edu/CUNY_GC/media/CUNY-Graduate-Center/PDF/Programs/Economics/Course%20Schedules/Seminar%20Sp.2013/seamans_zhu_craigslist(1).pdf

48. Sloan, W., Stovall, J., & Startt, J. (1993). *Media in America: A history*. Scottsdale, AZ: Publishing Horizons.

49. Sullivan, M. (2020, February 15). The future of local newspapers just got bleaker. Here's why we can't let them die. *Washington Post*. Retrieved from https://www.washingtonpost.com/lifestyle/media/the-future-of-local-newspapers-just-got-bleaker-heres-why-we-cant-let-them-die/2020/02/14/a7089d16-4f39-11ea-9b5c-eac5b16dafaa_story.html

50. "Teens today spend more time on digital media, less time reading." (2018, August 20). American Psychological Association. Retrieved from http://www.apa.org/news/press/releases/2018/08/teenagers-read-book.aspx

51. Thorpe, E. K. (2020, January 30). Why micropayments aren't dead...yet. *WNIP Publishing*. Retrieved from https://whatsnewinpublishing.com/why-micropayments-arent-dead-yet/

52. Timberg, S. (2015). *Culture crash*. New Haven: Yale University Press.

53. Vann, L. (2020, January 30). 2020 will be the year of the Hispanic....... *Hispanic Online Marketing*. Retrieved from https://www.hispaniconlinemarketing.com/2020/01/2020-will-be-the-year-of-the-hispanic/

54. Waldman, S. (2020, May 15). It's time to uproot American newspapers from hedge funds and replant them in more hospitable ground. *Poynter*. Retrieved from https://www.poynter.org/business-work/2020/its-time-to-uproot-american-newspapers-from-hedge-funds-and-replant-them-into-more-hospitable-ground/

55. "What Americans Think of the News—and What That Means for Democracy." (2020, February 28). *Rand Corporation*. Retrieved from https://www.rand.org/blog/articles/2020/04/what-americans-think-of-the-news--and-what-that-means.html

56. Williams, R. (2019, November 1). Is $3.99 a week the best subscription price for newspapers? *MediaPost*. Retrieved from https://www.mediapost.com/publications/article/342745/is-399-a-week-the-best-subscription-price-for-ne.html?edition=115922

Cultural Forum Blue Column icon, Media Literacy Red Torch Icon, Using Media Green Gear icon, Developing Media book in starburst icon: ©McGraw Hill

Magazines

5

◀ Magazines survive, even prosper, by meeting the highly specialized interests of their readers.

Niloo/Shutterstock

Learning Objectives

Magazines were once a truly national mass medium. But changes in American society and the economics of mass media altered their nature. They are the medium that first made specialization a virtue, and they prosper today by speaking to ever-more-narrowly defined groups of readers. After studying this chapter, you should be able to

▶ Recognize the history and development of the magazine industry and the magazine itself as a medium.

▶ Identify how the organizational and economic nature of the contemporary magazine industry shapes the content of magazines.

▶ Describe the relationship between magazines and their readers.

▶ Explain the convergence of magazines with the Internet and mobile technologies.

▶ Apply key media literacy skills to magazine reading.

1729 Ben Franklin's *Pennsylvania Gazette*

1741 ▶ *American Magazine, or a Monthly View of the Political State of the British Colonies* and *General Magazine and Historical Chronicle, for All the British Plantations in America,* the first American magazines

1741–1794 45 new American magazines appear

1821 *Saturday Evening Post*

1800

Library of Congress,
[LC-USZC4-5309]

1850 ▶ *Harper's*

1850

1857 *Atlantic Monthly*

1879 Postal Act

Everett Historical/
Shutterstock

1910 *Crisis*

1900

1914 Audit Bureau of Circulations founded

1922 *Reader's Digest*

1923 ▶ *Time*

1925 *New Yorker*

1936 *Consumers Union Reports*

1939 NBC unveils TV at World's Fair

John Frost Newspapers/
Alamy Stock Photo

1956 *Collier's* closes

1950

1969 *Saturday Evening Post* closes

1971 ▶ *Look* closes; *Ms.* magazine

1972 *Life* closes

1994 *Salon* goes online; QR code invented

1996 *Slate* goes *online*

Apic/Hulton Archive/
Getty Images

2010 Magazine Publishers of America becomes Association of Magazine Media

2000

2012 Audit Bureau of Circulations renamed Alliance for Audited Media

2013 The *Atlantic's* Scientology controversy

2014 ▶ *Ladies' HomeJournal* ceases print publication

2016 *Prevention* goes ad-free

2017 Getty Images bans altered photos; #MeToo

2018 Kavanaugh Supreme Court nomination controversy

2019 *Redbook* halts print publication; *Seventeen* and *Glamour* become "digital first"

2020 Coronavirus in the US; half of all major titles reduce print frequency; "Say Their Names"; website MSN replaces journalists with AI

Andrew Burton/Getty Images News/Getty Images

ALTHOUGH YOU'D HEARD THE RUMORS AND THOUGHT YOU WERE READY FOR WHAT MIGHT COME, YOU ARE STILL IN SHOCK AFTER LEAVING THE MEETING WITH YOUR MANAGER. When you started at *More* you thought you'd made it. Twenty years in business and a million subscribers. Stories for smart, professional women, and none of that Photoshop stuff. But now it's gone, closed. Your manager would like you to move to a new magazine. It's *Eat This, Not That!,* based on an advice column from *Men's Health* magazine that became a book series. It features articles on topics such as nutrition-wise recipes and how to make good decisions when eating at fancy restaurants.

But you're thinking this really isn't up your alley; you're a general-interest sort of person. Recipes and nutrition seem, well, narrow. Maybe you'll leave the magazine business altogether. The handwriting seems to be on the wall. More than half of all major titles reduced their print frequency in 2020 (Williams, 2020). *Redbook*, with 2 million subscribers and publishing since 1903, ended its life as a print publication in 2019. That same year saw the last of 64-year-old *Mad Magazine* and 85-year-old *Brides,* and *Seventeen* and *Glamour* became "digital first," printing stand-alone issues tied to special issues and events. *Jet,* the 63-year-old "bible" of African American readers, closed in 2014; so did *Ladies' Home Journal* after 130 years and with more than 3 million subscribers. But maybe the handwriting isn't so clear; there are quite a few new magazines hitting the stands—at least 139 in 2019 alone and another 60 in pandemic-plagued 2020 (Association of Magazine Media, 2020; Meek, 2020).

Perhaps you can stay in magazines but move to the digital side. There are a lot of new digital-only publications starting up: *Podster* has been a hit with podcasters, and *SeniorsSkiing* is doing well with aging Baby Boomers. Maybe the Web *is* the way to go. But even there the evidence is inconclusive. The first Web-only magazines, *Slate* and *Salon,* are profitable, and there has indeed been a lot of exciting activity—*Vice* has a huge online presence, *Allure* and *Vanity Fair* launched digital video channels to enrich their online presence, and traditional books such as *The Atlantic* and *Esquire* publish weekly digital mini-mags exclusively for mobile devices. Big magazine companies such as Time Inc., Forbes, Condé Nast, and Hearst have even dropped the title "publisher" from their organizational charts, replaced by "chief business officer" and "chief industry officer." Although online magazines seem promising, they have yet to replace their lost print ad revenues with money from their digital operations (much like the situation with newspapers). So maybe you'll just stay with what you love. *Eat This, Not That!* it is!

In this chapter, we examine the dynamics of the contemporary magazine industry—print and online—and its audiences. We study the medium's beginnings in the colonies, its pre–Civil War expansion, and its explosive growth between the Civil War and World War I. This was the era of the great mass circulation magazines, and it was also the time of the powerful writers known as muckrakers.

Influenced by television and by the social and cultural changes that followed World War II, the magazine took on a new, more narrowly focused nature, which provided the industry with a growing readership and increased profits. We detail the various categories of magazines, discuss circulation research, and look at the ways the industry protects itself from competition from other media and how advertisers influence editorial decisions. The influence of convergence runs through all these issues. Finally, we investigate some of the editorial decisions that should be of particular interest to media-literate magazine consumers.

▼ After 130 years in business and with more than 3 million subscribers, *Ladies' Home Journal* closed shop in 2014.

Andrew Burton/Getty Images News/ Getty Images

A Short History of Magazines

Magazines, the word shares etymological roots with "storehouse" (Heller, 2021), were a favorite medium of the British elite by the mid-1700s, and two prominent colonial printers hoped to duplicate that success in the New World. In 1741 in Philadelphia, Andrew Bradford published *The American Magazine, or a Monthly View of the Political State of the British Colonies*, followed by Benjamin Franklin's *General Magazine and Historical Chronicle, for All the British Plantations in America*. Composed largely of reprinted British material, these publications were expensive and aimed at the small number of literate colonists. Without an organized postal system, distribution was difficult, and neither magazine was successful. *American Magazine* produced three issues; *General Magazine* produced six. Yet between 1741 and 1794, 45 new magazines appeared, although no more than three were publishing at the same time. Entrepreneurial printers hoped to attract educated, cultured, moneyed gentlemen by copying the successful London magazines. Even after the Revolutionary War, American magazines remained clones of their British forerunners.

The Early Magazine Industry

In 1821, *The Saturday Evening Post* appeared. Starting in 1729 as Ben Franklin's *Pennsylvania Gazette*, it was to continue for the next 148 years. Among other successful early magazines were *Harper's* (1850) and *Atlantic Monthly* (1857). Cheaper printing and growing literacy fueled the expansion of the magazine as they had for the book (see Chapter 3 for more on books). However, an additional factor in the success of early magazines was the spread of social movements such as abolitionism and labor reform. These issues provided compelling content, and a boom in magazine publishing began. In 1825, there were 100 magazines in operation; 25 years later, there were 600. Because magazine articles increasingly focused on matters of importance to American readers, publications such as the *United States Literary Gazette* and *American Boy* began to look less like London publications and more like a new and unique product.

Journalism historians John Tebbel and Mary Ellen Zuckerman (1991) called this "the time of significant beginnings" (p. 13); it was during this time that the magazine developed many of the characteristics we associate with it today. Magazines and the people who staffed them began to clearly differentiate themselves from other publishing endeavors, such as books and newspapers. The concept of specialist writers took hold, and their numbers rose. In addition, numerous and detailed illustrations began to fill the pages of magazines.

Still, these early magazines were aimed at a literate elite interested in short stories, poetry, social commentary, and essays. The magazine did not become a true national mass medium until after the Civil War.

The Mass Circulation Era

The modern era of magazines can be divided into two parts: the mass circulation era and the era of specialization, each characterized by a different relationship between medium and audience.

Popular mass circulation magazines began to prosper in the post–Civil War years. In 1865 there were 700 magazines publishing; by 1870 there were 1,200, and by 1885 there were 3,300. Crucial to this expansion was the women's magazine. Suffrage—women's right to vote—was the social movement that occupied its pages, but a good deal of content could also be described as how-to for homemakers. Advertisers, too, were eager to appear in the new women's magazines, hawking their

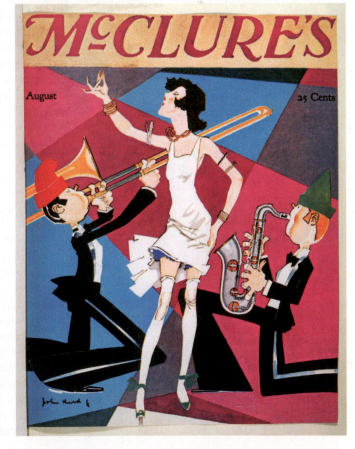

▼ This *McClure's* cover captures the spirit of the Roaring Twenties as well as the excitement of the burgeoning magazine industry. *JT Vintage/Glasshouse Images/ Alamy Stock Photo*

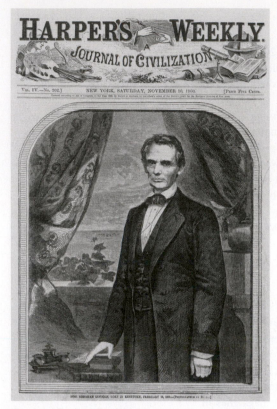

▲ Much respected today, *Harper's* gave early voice to the muck-rakers and other serious observers of politics and society.
Everett Historical/Shutterstock

▼ The first issue of *Time*.
John Frost Newspapers/Alamy Stock Photo

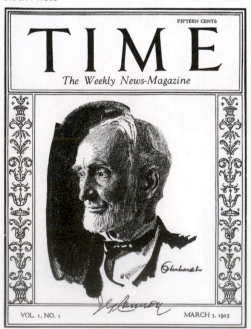

brand-name products. First published at this time were several magazines still familiar today, such as *Good Housekeeping*.

There were several reasons for this phenomenal growth. As with books, widespread literacy was one reason. Two other reasons were the Postal Act of 1879, which permitted mailing magazines at cheaper, second-class postage rates, and the spread of the railroad, which carried people and publications westward from the East Coast. A fourth reason was the reduction in cost. As long as magazines sold for 35 cents—a lot of money for the time—they were read largely by the upper class. However, a circulation war erupted between giants *McClure's*, *Munsey's Magazine*, and *The Saturday Evening Post*. Soon they, as well as *Ladies' Home Journal*, *McCall's*, *Woman's Home Companion*, *Collier's*, and *Cosmopolitan*, were selling for as little as 10 and 15 cents, which brought them within reach of many working people.

This 1870s price war was made possible by the newfound ability of magazines to attract growing amounts of advertising. Social and demographic changes in the post–Civil War era—urbanization, industrialization, the spread of roads and railroads, and development of consumer brands and brand names—produced an explosion in the number of advertising agencies (see Chapter 12). These agencies needed to place their messages somewhere. Magazines were the perfect outlet because they were read by a large, national audience. As a result, circulation—rather than reputation, as had been the case before—became the most important factor in setting advertising rates. Magazines kept cover prices low to ensure the large readerships coveted by advertisers. The fifth reason for the enormous growth in the number of magazines was industrialization, which provided people with leisure time to read and more personal income to spend.

Magazines were truly America's first national mass medium. Unlike newspapers, they were national in distribution and scope of coverage, and unlike books, they were inexpensive and meant for a large, general audience. Like books, they served as an important force in social change, especially in the **muckraking** era of the first decades of the 20th century. Theodore Roosevelt coined this label as an insult, but the muckrakers wore it proudly, using the pages of *The Nation*, *Harper's Weekly*, *The Arena*, and even mass circulation publications such as *McClure's* and *Collier's* to agitate for change. Their targets were the powerful. Their beneficiaries were the poor. You can read more about magazines' continuing political and social influence in the essay "Magazines and #MeToo."

The mass circulation magazine grew with the nation, affirming "the progress and promise of American life," in the 1913 words of the first issue of the modern *Vanity Fair* (Chayka, 2019, p. 48). From the start, there were general interest magazines such as *The Saturday Evening Post*, women's magazines such as *Good Housekeeping*, pictorial magazines such as *Life* and *Look*, and digests such as *Reader's Digest*, which was first published in 1922 and offered condensed and tightly edited articles for people on the go in the Roaring Twenties. What these magazines all had in common were the size and breadth of readership. They were mass market, mass circulation publications, both national and affordable. As such, magazines helped unify the nation. They were the country's dominant advertising medium, the primary source for nationally distributed news, and the preeminent provider of photojournalism.

Between 1900 and 1945, the number of families who subscribed to one or more magazines grew from 200,000 to more than 32 million. New and important magazines continued to appear throughout these decades. For example, African American intellectual W. E. B. DuBois founded and edited *The Crisis* in 1910 as the voice of the National Association for the Advancement of Colored People (NAACP). *Time* was first published in 1923. Its brief review of the week's news was immediately popular (it was originally only 28 pages long), and it made a profit within a year. *The New Yorker*, "the world's best magazine," debuted in 1925.

CULTURAL FORUM

Magazines and #MeToo

In its October 23, 2017, issue, *The New Yorker* broke the story of powerful Hollywood producer Harvey Weinstein's years of sexual harassment, assault, and even rape against several women. Scores of other victims immediately came forward. One, actor Alyssa Milano, took to Twitter to post "#MeToo," a phrase (and sentiment) coined in 2006 by social activist and community organizer Tarana Burke. Weinstein was fired and arrested (he was convicted of rape in the third degree in February, 2020), the magazine won a Pulitzer Prize for the article, millions more women posted #MeToo, and a movement was born.

A month later, on November 29, *Variety* published an account of multiple sexual harassment complaints against the *Today Show*'s long-time host, Matt Lauer. His network, NBC, fired him that same day. The mistreatment of women in the United States (currently ranked 53rd in the world in gender equality; Zahidi, 2020) was now firmly in the cultural forum, where it should have been all along, thanks to several brave women and magazines. "Virtually overnight," wrote *Washington Post* commentator Eugene Robinson (2017), "the paradigm for thinking about and dealing with sexual harassment has changed. A kind of Judgment Day has arrived for men who thought they had gotten away with their misdeeds." Dozens of influential film and TV executives, high-profile politicians, well-known entertainers, respected journalists—men long comfortable abusing women—quickly became unemployed and were publicly shamed.

But magazines weren't done. *Time* named those who came forward with their stories of abuse, "the Silence Breakers," its 2017 Persons of the Year (Zacharek, Dockterman, & Edwards, 2017). Then, in August, 2018, the *New Yorker* detailed several charges of sexual harassment, abuse, and intimidation against CBS's chair and CEO Les Moonves. He, too, was immediately fired. And magazines still weren't done. In the midst of the contentious Brett Kavanaugh Supreme Court confirmation hearings three months later, *The New Yorker*, in its September 23 issue, published an account of a new accusation against the nominee. Its cover for October 8, 2018, 2 days after Judge Kavanaugh was elevated to the highest court in the country despite those credible allegations of sexual misconduct, was an image of a woman silenced, a hand across her mouth.

Where magazines had helped thrust the issue of women's mistreatment into the cultural forum, magazines themselves soon became part of the #MeToo conversation. When Walmart announced it would pull *Cosmopolitan* from the checkout lines in its 5,000 stores "in response to #MeToo," the magazine's defenders protested. Business journalist Kate Taylor (2018) agrees that *Cosmopolitan* has not always represented women realistically or inclusively; however, she adds, "There can and should be discussions about how *Cosmopolitan* helps and hurts women. But to blame a publication primarily aimed at and created by women for the systematic harassment and assault many women endure—often at the hands of men—is an embarrassing repurposing of the #MeToo movement." Moreover, along with stories of the ilk of "20 Ways to Turn Him On," *Cosmo* has a long tradition of offering serious writing on women's political and social issues, including #MeToo.

Enter Your Voice

- Can you reconcile magazines' contribution to women's rights and welfare with their sometimes narrow and stereotypical representation of those very same people? This is a paragraph of placeholder text. It is only here to help show the layout of the page and how the text will flow. Replace this placeholder text with your own meaningful content.
- Should there be a greater emphasis on increasing the number of female journalists among their ranks, as there is among Bloomberg publications; using more women as sources for stories; and even forbidding their reporters from appearing on panels that do not have gender diversity (Guaglione, 2018)?
- Can you speculate on how magazines, dependent on the good will of advertisers and readers alike, might be able to contribute to the cultural forum in these increasingly politically divisive times?

▲ In 2017 the *New Yorker* broke the story of movie producer Harvey Weinstein's years of sexual harassment, assault, and rape, kickstarting the #MeToo movement.
Sundry Photography/Shutterstock

The Era of Specialization

In 1956 *Collier's* declared bankruptcy and became the first of the big mass circulation magazines to cease publication. But its fate, as well as that of other mass circulation magazines, had actually been sealed in the late 1940s and 1950s following the end of World War II. Profound alterations in the nation's culture—and, in particular, the advent of television—changed the relationship between magazines and their audience. No matter how large their circulation, magazines could not match the reach of television. Magazines did not have moving pictures or visual and oral storytelling. Nor could magazines match television's timeliness. Magazines were weekly, whereas television was continuous. Nor could they match television's novelty. In the beginning, *everything* on television was of interest to viewers. As a result, magazines began to lose advertisers to television.

▶ A change in people's tastes in magazines reflects some of the ways the world changed after World War II. *Vogue's* America replaced that of *Look*.
(left) Nathaniel Noir/Alamy Stock Photo; (right) Apic/Hulton Archive/ Getty Images

▶ A wide array of specialized magazines exists for all lifestyles and interests. Here are some of the 7,200 special interest consumer magazines available to American readers.
Susan Baran

The audience changed as well. As we've seen, World War II changed the nature of American life. The new, mobile, product-consuming public was less interested in the traditional Norman Rockwell world of *The Saturday Evening Post* (closed in 1969) and more in tune with the slick, hip world of narrower interest publications such as *GQ* and *Esquire*, which spoke to them about their new and exciting lives. And because World War II had further urbanized and industrialized America, people—including millions of women who had entered the workforce—had more leisure and more money to spend. They could spend both on a wider array of personal interests *and* on magazines that catered to those interests. Where there were once *Look* (closed in 1971) and *The Saturday Evening Post*, there were now *Flyfishing*, *Surfer*, *Creative Scrapbooker*, and *Easyriders*. The industry had hit on the secret of success: specialization and a lifestyle orientation. All media have moved in this direction in their efforts to attract an increasingly fragmented audience, but it was the magazine industry that began the trend.

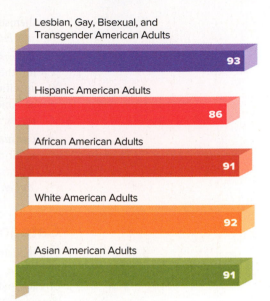

▲ **Figure 5.1** Percentage of Population that Regularly Reads Magazines, 2020.

Source: Association of Magazine Media. 2020. Magazine Media Factbook 2020.

Magazines and Their Audiences

Exactly who is the audience for magazines? Industry research indicates that it is large–across print, digital, and video platforms, America's 229 million magazine readers interact with magazines 1.7 billion times a month across print and digital media. And it is a demographically attractive audience. Ninety-one percent of American adults consume magazines either in print or digital form, a proportion that grows to 95% when considering only people younger than 25. They read on average 7.3 print magazines a month. It is a diverse audience, as these data remain near constant across all ethnicities, as you can see in Figure 5.1. Additionally, magazines tend to have an educated and affluent audience, as they are the preferred medium among households with a net worth over $250,000 (all data from Association of Magazine Media, 2020).

How readers use magazines also makes them an attractive advertising medium. Magazines sell themselves to potential advertisers based not only on the number and demographic desirability of their readers but also on readers' engagement with and affinity for magazine advertising. **Engagement** refers to the depth of the relationship between readers and the magazine advertising they see. People choose to read specific magazines for specific reasons. They have an existing interest that brings them to a particular publication. As a result, the magazine and its ads speak to them.

In addition, as opposed to many other media (radio and television, for example), readers' commitment to the magazine, and by extension its sponsors, is manifested in cash; that is, they pay to access that advertising. The success of publications such as *Wine Spectator*, *Cigar Aficionado*, *Whisky Advocate*, and *Scrap & Stamp Arts Magazine* rests heavily on readers' passion for their content, both editorial and commercial. **Affinity**, how much readers enjoy magazine advertising, is demonstrated by industry research showing that readers say not only that they trust magazine advertising more than Internet and television advertising but also that they value it as a way to learn about new products. It touches them deeply, gets them to try new things, inspires them to buy things, gives them something to talk about, and brings to mind things they enjoy (all data from Association of Magazine Media, 2020).

Scope and Structure of the Magazine Industry

In 1950, there were 6,950 magazines in operation. The number now exceeds 20,000, some 7,200 of which are general-interest consumer magazines. Of these, 800 produce about 75% of the industry's gross revenues. Contemporary magazines are typically divided into three broad types:

- *Trade, professional,* and *business magazines* carry stories, features, and ads aimed at people in specific professions and are distributed either by the professional organizations themselves *(American Medical News)* or by third-party companies such as DTN *(Progressive Farmer)*.

- *Industrial, company,* and *sponsored magazines* are produced by companies specifically for their own employees, customers, and stockholders, or by clubs and associations specifically for their members. *Boy's Life,* for example, is the magazine of the Boy Scouts of America. *VIA* is the travel magazine for AAA auto club members in eight Western states.

- *Consumer magazines* are sold by subscription and at newsstands, bookstores, and other retail outlets, including supermarkets, garden shops, and computer stores. *Sunset* and *Wired* fit in this category, as do *Road & Track, Us Weekly, TV Guide,* and *The New Yorker.*

Categories of Consumer Magazines

The industry typically categorizes consumer magazines in terms of their targeted audiences. Of course, the wants, needs, interests, and wishes of those readers determine the content of each publication. Although these categories are neither exclusive (where does *Chicago Business* fit?) nor exhaustive (what do we do with *Hot Rod* and *National Geographic*?), they are at least indicative of the cascade of options. Here is a short list of common consumer magazine categories, along with examples of each type.

Alternative magazines: *Mother Jones,* the *Utne Reader*

Business/money magazines: *Money, Black Enterprise*

Celebrity and entertainment magazines: *People, Entertainment Weekly*

Children's magazines: *Highlights, Ranger Rick*

Computer magazines: *Wired, PC World*

Ethnic magazines: *Hispanic, Ebony*

Family magazines: *Fatherhood, Parenting*

Fashion magazines: *Bazaar, Elle*

General-interest magazines: *Reader's Digest, The Week*

Geographic magazines: *Texas Monthly, Bay Living*

Gray magazines: *AARP The Magazine*

Literary magazines: *The Atlantic, Harper's*

Men's magazines: *GQ, Men's Fitness, Details*

Newsmagazines: *Time, U.S. News & World Report*

Political opinion magazines: *The Nation, National Review*

Sports magazines: *Shooting Times, Sports Illustrated*

Sunday newspaper magazines: *Parade, The New York Times Magazine*

Women's magazines: *Working Mother, Good Housekeeping, Ms.*

Youth magazines: *Seventeen, Tiger Beat*

Magazine Advertising

Magazine specialization exists and succeeds because the demographically similar readership of individual publications is attractive to advertisers. Marketers want to target ads for their products and services to those most likely to respond to them, so the typical editorial-to-advertising-page ratio is 54% to 46%. Despite revenue declines over the last few years (a drop of 9.7% from 2019 to 2020), this remains a lucrative situation for the magazine industry ($10.9 billion in ad revenue in 2020, roughly half of all income). Magazines command 4% of all the dollars spent on major media advertising in this country (Liesse, 2020). And of particular importance to marketers, the return on advertising dollars spent is higher for magazines than for any other medium (Association of Magazine Media, 2020). The brands that buy the most magazine advertising are shown in Figure 5.2.

◀ **Figure 5.2** Top 10 Magazine
Advertisers, 2019.
*Source: "Biggest U.S. spenders by
medium," 2019.*
(photo): Creative Crop/Digital Vision/Getty Images

Rank	Brand	Amount Spent (in millions)
1	L'Oréal	$690
2	Procter & Gamble Co.	$444
3	Kraft Heinz Co.	$315
4	LVMH Moët Hennessy Louis Vuitton	$211
5	Johnson & Johnson	$202
6	Nestlé	$199
7	Pfizer	$197
8	Berkshire Hathaway	$191
9	Unilever	$164
10	Kellogg Co.	$163

Magazines are often further specialized through **split runs**, special versions of a given issue in which editorial content and ads vary according to some specific demographic or regional grouping. *People,* for example, will sell A-B splits in which every other copy of the national edition will carry a different cover, regional splits by state and by major metropolitan area, and splits targeting the top 10 and top 20 largest metropolitan areas.

Magazines work to make themselves attractive to advertisers in other ways, especially as the industry, like all traditional media, deals with tough economic conditions. One strategy is *single-sponsor magazines*—having only one advertiser throughout an entire issue. Venerable titles such as *The New Yorker* (Target stores) and *Time* (Kraft foods) occasionally employ this tactic. Another strategy is to make *accountability guarantees. The Week,* for example, promises that independent testing will demonstrate that its readers recall, to an agreed-upon level, a sponsor's ad; if they do not, the advertiser will receive free ad pages until recall reaches that benchmark. Many of the large publishers—Meredith, Hearst, Condé Nast, and Time Inc., for example—also offer similar guarantees. (For a look at a magazine with no advertising at all, see the essay "No Ads? No Problem: *Consumer Reports.*")

▼ Like many national magazines, *The Week* offers accountability guarantees.
Tony Farrugia/Alamy Stock Photo

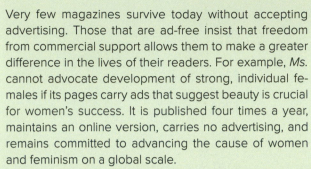

USING MEDIA TO MAKE A DIFFERENCE
No Ads? No Problem: *Consumer Reports*

Very few magazines survive today without accepting advertising. Those that are ad-free insist that freedom from commercial support allows them to make a greater difference in the lives of their readers. For example, *Ms.* cannot advocate development of strong, individual females if its pages carry ads that suggest beauty is crucial for women's success. It is published four times a year, maintains an online version, carries no advertising, and remains committed to advancing the cause of women and feminism on a global scale.

In 2016, *Prevention* decided to go ad-free in order to return "to its historical position as an authoritative, impartial voice in the health and wellness community" (Dool, 2016). And there is *Kazoo*, aimed at girls aged 5 to 12. The quarterly is not only ad-free, it's print-only. Featuring contributors like Ruth Bader Ginsburg, Jane Goodall, and Ellen DeGeneres, in 2019 it became the first children's magazine ever to win a National Magazine Award for General Excellence (Dool, 2019).

But it is *Consumer Reports* that makes the no-advertising case most strongly—it must be absolutely free of outside influence if its articles about consumer products are to maintain their well-earned reputation for fairness and objectivity. As its editors explain on the magazine's website, their mission is to test products and services and inform and protect consumers, all the while remaining independent and impartial. To do this, the magazine accepts no outside advertising, nor does it accept free products for its testing. Its only agenda is the interests of consumers. So protective is the magazine of that independence that it refuses to let its ratings be used in any advertising of the products and services it evaluates, even those that it judges superior. It can earn as much as $300,000 per advertised endorsement but refuses.

Consumer Reports, first published in 1936 as *Consumer Union Reports* and boasting an initial circulation of 400, charges for access to its Web version. Its 3.2 million online subscribers pay the same rate as its 3.8 million print readers. Nonetheless, its online readership is among the highest of the world's online magazines, and its print circulation is higher than that of all but a few major magazines, exceeding that of titles like *Good Housekeeping*, *Sports Illustrated*, and *People*.

The online version does offer a good deal of free information, especially when evaluated products may cause health and safety problems. Also occasionally available for free is special content, such as an ongoing series of media literacy videos examining the persuasive appeals used in consumer drug advertising. But subscribers have access to much more. For example, there are videos of front and side impact tests on just about every vehicle sold in this country. The *Consumer Reports* website maintains a searchable archive of all tests and their results as well as up-to-the-minute evaluations of new products.

Because the electronic version has no paper, printing, trucking, or mailing expenses, it actually makes more money than its print sibling. To increase profits on its print version, *Consumer Reports* is produced on less expensive paper rather than the glossy stock used by most magazines, and as a nonprofit group, it pays lower postage rates than other consumer magazines.

Another magazine that eschews advertising because it sees it as inimical to its larger mission of making a difference with its particular category of reader is *Adbusters*. Founded in 1992, *Adbusters* boasts a worldwide print circulation of 120,000 and won the *Utne Reader* Award for General Excellence three times in its first six years of operation. It aims to help stem the erosion of the world's physical and cultural environments by what it views as greed and commercial forces. Its online version allows users to download spoofs of popular ad campaigns and other anticonsumerism spots for use as banner ads on their own sites.

Types of Circulation

Magazines price advertising space in their pages based on **circulation**, the total number of issues of a magazine that are sold. These sales can be either subscription or single-copy sales. For the industry as a whole, about 92% of all sales are subscription. Some magazines, however—*Woman's Day*, *TV Guide*, and *Women's World*, for example—rely heavily on single-copy sales. Subscriptions have the advantage of an ensured ongoing readership, but they are sold below the cover price and have the additional burden of postage included in their cost to the publisher. Single-copy sales are less reliable, but to advertisers, they are sometimes a better barometer of a publication's value to its readers. Single-copy readers must consciously choose to pick up an issue, and they pay full price for it. It was just such a demonstration of reader enthusiasm that convinced Meredith to return *Coastal Living* to subscription sales in 2019 after having shifted it to newsstand-only a year earlier. Nonetheless, newsstand sales overall have shown declines for several years now.

A third form of circulation, **controlled circulation**, refers to providing a magazine at no cost to readers who meet some specific set of advertiser-attractive criteria. Free airline and hotel magazines fit this category. Although they provide no subscription or single-sales revenue, these magazines are an attractive, relatively low-cost advertising vehicle for companies seeking narrowly defined, captive audiences. United Airlines's *Hemispheres*, for example, has 158 million annual readers with a median household net worth of just over half a million dollars, the highest of any American print magazine. They're well educated, too, as 91% have a college education (*Hemispheres*, 2020). These "custom publishing" magazines are discussed in more detail later in this chapter.

Measuring Circulation

Regardless of how circulation occurs, it is monitored through research. The Audit Bureau of Circulations (ABC) was established in 1914 to provide reliability to a booming magazine industry playing loose with self-announced circulation figures. In 2012, recognizing that "circulation" should include digital editions and apps, the ABC became platform agnostic and renamed itself the Alliance for Audited Media (AAM). The AAM provides reliable circulation figures as well as important population and demographic data.

▲ Controlled circulation magazines such as United Airlines's *Hemispheres* take advantage of readers' captivity, offering them high-quality travel-oriented fare. They offer advertisers access to a well-educated, affluent readership.

Marco Arguello/Courtesy of Hemispheres Magazine

Circulation data are often augmented by measures of *pass-along readership,* which refers to readers who neither subscribe nor buy single copies but who borrow a magazine or read one in places like a doctor's office or library. For example, *The Costco Connection*, free to the big box retailer's "executive members" and available to others for a $120 annual subscription, has a monthly circulation of 14.3 million copies. But with its pass-along readership, it reaches nearly 26 million people a month (Meyersohn, 2020).

"Readership" has traditionally included subscribers, pass-along readership, and newsstand sales for each issue. This traditional model of measurement, however, is under increasing attack. As advertisers demand more precise assessments of accountability and return on their investment, new metrics beyond circulation and readership are being demanded by professionals inside and outside the industry (see Chapter 12).

Timeliness is one issue. Monthly and weekly magazines can, at best, offer data on how many issues they've shipped, but advertisers must typically wait for days after a particular issue is released for actual readership numbers, and even longer than that for additional pass-along readership. It can take as long as 10 or more days for a magazine to reach 100% of its total readership.

Others argue that it is one thing for magazine publishers to boast of engagement and affinity, but how are they measured? As a result, the advertising and magazine industries are investing in new measurement protocols. For example, in 2014, the Association of Magazine Media introduced Magazine Media 360°, a metric combining magazines' print audience, unique visitors to their Web and mobile sites, and unique video views of magazines' video channels (if any). This number is published monthly in addition to a second report that tracks magazines' presence on social media. You can see the Total 360° monthly audience for several popular titles in Figure 5.3. Note the huge jump in readership–in the tens of millions–when "readership" includes print and digital editions plus Internet, mobile, and video interactions. Nonetheless, for now, "mere" circulation remains the primary basis for setting magazine ad rates.

▶ **Figure 5.3** Top-Performing Total 360° Audience Magazines, in Thousands (000), December, 2020.

Source: Alliance for Audited Media, 2021.

(photo): *Image Source/Photodisc/ Getty Images*

Magazine

People
1. 88,045 / 27,472

Allrecipes
2. 75,075 / 8,896

Good Housekeeping
3. 64,986 / 13,229

WebMD
4. 51,656 / 6,612

Taste of Home
5. 43,318 / 10,274

Cosmopolitan
6. 34,084 / 10,283

Sports Illustrated
7. 31,322 / 12,189

■ Total 360° Audience

■ Print + Digital Editions

Several magazines, most prominently *Time*, offer advertisers the option of choosing between *total audience* and paid circulation when setting advertising rates. Total audience combines print and digital readership. An advertiser may be willing to pay more for those who buy subscriptions, assuming greater commitment to the magazine and its advertisers; another may prefer paying for as many readers as possible, paying a bit less for online readers. In *Time*'s case, for example, the paid circulation number of just over 3 million becomes a total audience of nearly six times that size.

Trends and Convergence in Magazine Publishing

The magazine industry's embrace of *total audience* rather than *readership* when discussing its reach makes it clear that the forces that are reshaping all the mass media are having an impact on magazines. Although the industry was slow to evolve—"We survivors danced on the edge of the volcano, unwilling to admit that anything had changed," in the words of long-time *Gourmet* editor Ruth Reichl (in Chayka, 2019, p. 50)—the industry changed how it did business, especially to compete with television and the Internet in the race for advertising dollars. Convergence, too, has its impact.

Online Magazines

Online magazines have emerged, made possible by the convergence of magazines and the Internet. Rare is the magazine that does not produce a digital version, and almost all that do offer additional content and a variety of interactive features not available to readers of their hard-copy versions. Different publications opt for different payment models, but most provide online-only content for free and charge nonsubscribers for access to print magazine content that appears online. This strategy encourages readers who might otherwise go completely digital (and drop print) to renew their subscriptions. This is important to publishers and their advertisers because ads in hard-copy magazines are more effective and therefore more valuable: Print magazine advertising produces greater increases in brand awareness, brand favorability, and purchase intent than online magazine advertising (Association of Magazine Media, 2020).

In the early 2000s, both *Salon* and *Slate* wanted to do magazine journalism—a mix of breaking news, cultural criticism, political and social commentary, and interviews—at the Internet's speed with the Internet's interactivity and instant feedback. Although both pioneers regularly draw sizable audiences—*Salon* and *Slate* each have 10 million unique monthly readers worldwide—it took them both more than a decade to become profitable. One reason is that, as opposed to sites produced by paper magazines, purely online magazines must generate original content, an expensive undertaking, yet they compete online for readers and advertisers as equals with those subsidized by paper magazines. In addition, these sites must compete with all other websites on the Internet. They are but one of an infinite number of choices for potential readers, and they do not enjoy the security of an audience loyal to a parent publication.

Smartphones, Tablets, and e-Readers

As with books and newspapers, mobile digital media are reshaping the relationship between magazines and their readers. In 2012, a group of major publishers came together to create Next Issue, a digital newsstand for magazines and newspapers. Bought by Apple, it's now know as Apple News+. For a relatively low monthly fee, readers gain full access to more than 200 publications, and in 2020, the company bundled Apple News+ with Apple TV+ and Apple Music in an attempt to attract an even larger audience for its services. There are a number of other digital subscription services operating as well. Magzter offers subscriptions to 8,000 titles; Zinio provides access to more than 6,000 magazines. Amazon Prime, through a feature called Prime Reading, gives its members access to a number of high-profile magazines. Mobile Web readership on both websites and apps now accounts for 36% of all magazine issues read, greatly exceeding desktop and laptop's 10% (Association of Magazine Media, 2020).

Magazines also thrive on social media. The number of followers and likes for magazines on Facebook, Twitter, Instagram, and Pinterest exceeded 1.1 billion in the first quarter of 2019 alone. Facebook accounts for the largest share of magazines' social media activity, accounting for nearly half of the active audience. Instagram is second but is the fastest growing of the three, and Twitter is a close third (Association of Magazine Media, 2020).

And interestingly, smartphones and tablets now make hard-copy magazines more attractive to readers and advertisers now that quick response (QR) codes, invented in 1994, appear on virtually all consumer magazines. When readers use their smartphones to capture the image of these square barcodes containing smaller squares and rectangles inside, they are instantly directed to a publisher's or marketer's website, increasing engagement. About a third of American smartphone users routinely utilize QR codes, and the number of individual interactions has shown a steady increase, growing 36% between 2018 and 2019 alone (Blue Bite, 2020), contributing to the magazine industry's economic stability.

To enhance the reading experience, some magazines (*Cosmopolitan*, for example) have taken QR a step further, combining it with **augmented reality (AR)**, technology that lets users point phones at a magazine page and be instantly linked to websites containing information about whatever is on that page superimposed over the screen image. In one example, users can snap a photo of a QR code, which takes them to a Macy's department store website where they can, in AR, try-on outfits and test their new look. *InStyle* uses AR to give readers virtual make-overs for beauty product advertisers.

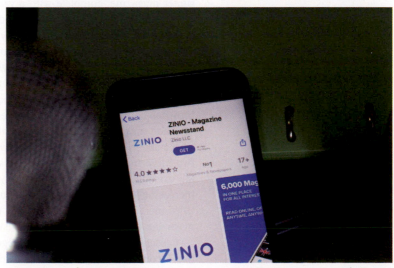

▼ Zinio is among several apps that bring millions of on-the-go readers to magazine websites. *Postmodern Studio/Shutterstock*

▲ Quick response codes have reached near ubiquity in the magazine industry.

leungchopan/YAY Media AS/Alamy Stock Photo

But magazines are also making dramatic editorial as well as advertising use of AR to meet their audiences' information needs. For example, in March, 2020, the *New York Times Magazine* encouraged readers to scan pages in its annual "25 Songs That Matter Right Now" edition using the Google Lens app. They would then hear the track and learn additional information about the song and its artist. The *New Yorker*, in the wake of the George Floyd murder, encouraged readers to "Say Their Name" by pointing Google Lens at its June 22, 2020, cover (a painting by Kadir Nelson) to access a "closer read" of the lives and deaths of the people referenced in the painting, scores of African Americans killed by the police (Dumenco, 2020).

Even easier to use than QR codes and AR scanning are **near-field communication (NFC) chips**, tags embedded in magazines that connect readers to advertisers' digital content when they simply hold their smartphones near an ad; there is no need to have the correct app or to take a picture of a code.

Custom Magazines

Another trend finds its roots in the magazine industry's response to an increasingly crowded media environment. **Custom publishing** is the creation of magazines specifically designed for an individual company seeking to reach a very narrowly defined audience, such as favored customers or likely users or buyers. If you've ever stayed at an Airbnb home-sharing location, for example, you might well have come across *Airbnb Magazine*, distributed for free to member hosts. *WebMD*, the medical information website, distributes for free to 85% of all American doctors' offices a magazine of the same name. Its monthly print circulation of 1.4 million is read by more than 10 million people; its print and online editions reach one in four American adults every month (WebMD, 2020). Forty-one percent of business-to-customer marketers use custom print magazines, as do 36% of business-to-business marketers (Spaight, 2016). Naturally, such specifically targeted magazines take advantage of readers' engagement with and affinity for magazine advertising.

There are two broad categories of custom publishing. First, a **brand magazine** is a consumer magazine, complete with a variety of general interest articles and features, published by a retail or other business for readers with demographic characteristics similar to those of consumers with whom it typically does business. These publications carry ad pages not only for the products of their parent business but for others as well. Outdoor goods company REI's quarterly *Uncommon Path* has a monthly circulation of 700,000, making it the largest outdoor magazine in the country. Energy drink maker Red Bull publishes *Red Bulletin*; Kraft has been publishing *Food & Family* for more than 20 years; Staples's *Worklife* provides conversation starters and resources for professionals. A small but growing number of brand magazines (for example, Enterprise Car Rental's *Pursuits with Enterprise* and active wear maker Outdoor Voices' *The Recreationalist*) are digital-only. Brand magazines recognize two important contemporary realities of today's media environment: (a) The cost of retaining existing customers is significantly lower than that of recruiting new ones, and (b) in an increasingly hypercommercialized and cluttered mass media system, advertisers who want to connect with their customers can rely on the engagement and affinity inherent in a good magazine to overcome growing consumer cynicism and suspicion.

Closely related is the second category, the **magalogue**, a designer catalog produced to look like a consumer magazine. Abercrombie & Fitch, J.Crew, Harry Rosen, Saks Fifth Avenue, Net-A-Porter, Asos, Frank & Oak, Bergdorf Goodman, Uniqlo, and Diesel all produce catalogs in which models wear for-sale designer clothes. Designers, photographers, writers, and editors from major fashion magazines typically contribute to these publications, and they are occasionally available for sale at newsstands (for example, Net-A-Porter's *Porter*).

Meeting the Competition

As we've seen, the move toward specialization in magazines was forced by the emergence of television as a mass audience, national advertising medium. But television again—specifically cable television—eventually came to challenge the preeminence of magazines as a specialized advertising medium. Advertiser-supported cable channels prosper using precisely the same strategy as maga-

▲ There are 46 local-language editions of *Elle* in 60 countries across the globe.
JOEL SAGET/AFP/Getty Images

zines—they deliver to advertisers a relatively large number of consumers who have some important demographic trait in common. Similar competition also comes from specialized online content providers, such as ESPN's several sports-oriented sites and the Discovery Channel Online. And of course, there is competition from the ultimate specialized advertising medium, the Internet itself. Magazines are well positioned to fend off these challenges for several reasons.

First is internationalization, which expands a magazine's reach, making it possible for magazines to attract additional ad revenues for content that, essentially, has already been produced. Internationalization can happen in one of several ways. Some magazines, *Time* and *Monthly Review,* for example, produce one or more foreign editions in English. Others enter cooperative agreements with overseas companies to produce native-language versions of essentially American magazines. For example, Hearst and the British company ITP cooperate to publish British and Middle Eastern editions of *Esquire*, two of the 18 international versions of the men's magazine. ITP and Hearst also team up on the Dubai version of the fashion magazine *Harper's Bazaar* and 75 other titles in the Middle East and India. Often, American publishers prepare special content for foreign-language editions. *Elle* has 46 local-language versions of its magazine, including countries like Argentina, Serbia, Poland, Thailand, and Turkey. *Vogue* offers 19 in locales such as China, Greece, and Portugal. *Cosmopolitan* has 64 international editions in 35 languages in 100 countries. The internationalization of magazines will no doubt increase as conglomeration and globalization continue to have an impact on the magazine industry as they have on other media businesses.

Second is technology. The Internet now allows instant distribution of copy from the editor's desk to printing plants around the world. The result is incredibly quick delivery to subscribers and sales outlets, which makes production and distribution of even more narrowly targeted split runs more cost-effective. More controversial, however, is a different technology, **artificial intelligence (AI)**, the use of machine learning, to write "original" articles. Given the necessary information and a deep machine-learned familiarity with a magazine's style, artificial intelligence can produce seemingly human-authored pieces. Publications can produce most or all their routine copy such as reviews and calendars, if not more original work, quite inexpensively. For example, in mid-2020 Microsoft replaced its human journalists at its British MSN website with AI software to write news reports (Waterson, 2020), and although not yet in wider use, there is already at least one completely AI-written magazine, *Montag.*

Third is the sale of subscriber lists and a magazine's own direct marketing of products. Advertisers buy space in specialized magazines to reach a specific type of reader. Most magazines are more than happy to sell those readers' names and addresses to those same advertisers, as well as to others who want to contact readers with direct mail pitches. Many magazines use their own subscriber lists and Web visitors' details for the same purpose, marketing products and programs of interest to their particular readership.

▲ Many magazines license their names—and reputations—to generate revenue. The Good Housekeeping Seal of Approval, initiated in 1909, is one of the better-known examples.
Susan Watts/New York Daily News/ Getty Images

Increasingly, this is accomplished through *paid memberships*. *Fortune* has a 3-tiered membership that, at the highest level, offers quarterly investment guides, a weekly research newsletter, a video channel packed with exclusive interviews with executives and instructional content, and monthly conference calls hosted by the magazine's CEO. Members of *The Atlantic*'s program The Masthead have access to members-only forums where they can interact with the magazine's editors. There is increased reliance on licensing the magazine's good name (its brand) as well. The *Good Housekeeping* seal of approval and the *Playboy* bunny logo are already familiar, but other trusted titles such as *Better Homes & Gardens*, *Shape*, *Popular Science*, and *Variety* have begun partnering with related businesses in licensing deals that account for 20% to 30% of publications' revenues. In 2018 alone, Meredith generated $22.8 billion in licensing fees from its stable of magazines (Smith, 2018).

Some magazines meet television's challenge by becoming television themselves. Fox Television Studios, for example, produces Web-based programs based on Hearst publications *CosmoGIRL!* and *Popular Mechanics*. *Allure*, and *Maxim* maintain video channels; *Teen Vogue* alone has five. *Vice*, which began in 1994 as the 16-page free publication *Voice of Montreal*, has an Emmy Award–winning news show on HBO and more than 50 video series across the Internet. Condé Nast has long had interests in film and video. Its Condé Nast Entertainment division produces big-budget movies (*No Exit*; *Argo*; *Eat, Pray, Love*) and several scripted and reality TV shows for a number of networks. It maintains five publication-specific studios (*GQ*, *New Yorker*, *Vanity Fair*, *Vogue*, and *Wired*). Mansueto Ventures, publishers of *Fast Company* and *Inc.*, produces several YouTube series, including *You Have to See This* and *Day in the Life*, which follows entrepreneurs.

Advertiser Influence over Magazine Content

Sometimes controversial is the influence that some advertisers attempt to exert over content. This influence is always there, at least implicitly. A magazine editor must satisfy advertisers as well as readers. One common way advertisers' interests shape content is in the placement of ads. Airline ads are moved away from stories about plane crashes. Cigarette ads rarely appear near articles on lung cancer. In fact, it is an accepted industry practice for a magazine to provide advertisers with a heads-up, alerting them that soon-to-be-published content may prove uncomfortable for their businesses. Advertisers can then request a move of their ad, or pull it and wait to run it in the next issue. Magazines, too, often entice advertisers with promises of placement of their ads adjacent to relevant articles.

But **complementary copy**—content that reinforces the advertiser's message, or at least does not negate it—is problematic when creating such copy becomes a major influence in a publication's editorial decision making. This happens in a number of ways. Editors sometimes engage in self-censorship, making decisions about how stories are written and which stories appear based on the fear that specific advertisers will be offended. Some magazines, *Architectural Digest*, for example, identify companies by name in their picture caption copy only if they are advertisers, and Lexus asks the magazines it advertises in to use its automobiles in photos in editorial content. These concessions may be necessary today because the very competitive media environment puts additional pressure on magazines to bow to advertisers' demands. However, many critics inside and outside the industry see these moves as an unfortunate

◀ Complementing this ad through placement near this story troubles few people, but some industry insiders see it as further breaching of the advertiser/editorial divide.

(left) Image Source/Getty Images; (right) Courtesy of The Advertising Archives

crumbling of the wall between advertising demands and editorial judgment. Others are not so concerned. Says one magazine editor, "As long as it's interesting to the reader, who cares? This ivory-tower approach that edit[orial] is so untouchable, and what they're doing is so wonderful and can't be tainted by the stink of advertising just makes me sick" (in Ives, 2008).

Another once-controversial and now far more common practice is sponsored content, articles paid for by advertisers. Sponsored content first caused controversy in early 2013, when the online edition of *The Atlantic* ran a long, laudatory article on the Church of Scientology. But it was quickly discovered that the piece was actually a paid placement written not by *Atlantic* journalists but by the Church of Scientology itself. A massive uproar ensued inside and outside the industry. But since that time, the practice has become not only commonplace across all media but also essential to many magazines' survival. Three-quarters of online publishers in the United States now offer sponsored content, sometimes called native advertising. And despite some continuing unease over the practice, most industry people have come to terms with what is an $85 billion annual global market (Pollitt, 2020). Still, to many the practice is inherently deceptive, otherwise why would it, in the words of the Native Advertising Institute itself, adopt "the form, feel and function of the content of the media on which it appears?" (in Scott, 2020).

The Federal Trade Commission agrees, writing, "Regardless of the medium in which an advertising or promotional message is disseminated, deception occurs when consumers acting reasonably under the circumstances are misled about its nature or source, and such misleading impression is likely to affect their decisions or conduct regarding the advertised product or the advertising" (in Scott, 2020). As such it now polices sponsored content, demanding clear identification. Among the allowable labels are "Ad," "Advertisement," "Paid Advertisement," "Sponsored Advertising Content," or some near variation. Prohibited are less definitive markers such as "Promoted" or "Promoted Stories" because they imply that the material is endorsed by the publisher.

DEVELOPING MEDIA LITERACY SKILLS
Recognizing the Power of Graphics

Detecting the use of and determining the informational value of complementary copy and sponsored content is only one reason media literacy is important when reading magazines. Another necessary media literacy skill is the ability to understand how graphics and other artwork provide the background for interpreting stories. Some notable incidents suggest why.

Kerry Washington, African American actor and star of the television series *Scandal*, appeared on an April 2016 cover of *Adweek*. Her skin had been lightened and her nose Photoshopped to appear smaller. *Adweek* denied it had made anything other than "minimal adjustments," but Ms. Washington and her fans felt otherwise. For them, this was especially disconcerting because it had happened to the star just a year earlier when *InStyle* lightened her skin to the point that she appeared to be Caucasian. Then, just a few weeks after the *Adweek* incident, *People*, in declaring tennis champion Serena Williams "one of the world's most beautiful people," published a photo of Ms. Williams that had been altered to slim her waist (Sass, 2016). A media-literate reader might ask, "Why isn't one of the world's most beautiful people beautiful enough?"

The subjects of magazines' digital alterations have weighed in on their own photographs' "improvements." Singer/actor Lady Gaga framed her objection to *Glamour's* touchup in media literacy terms: "I felt my skin looked too perfect. I felt my hair looked too soft. . . . I do not look like this when I wake up in the morning. . . . What I want to see is the change on your covers. . . . When the covers change, that's when culture changes" (Calkins, 2016). Actor Emily Ratajkowski took to Instagram to call out *Madame Figaro* magazine for changing her lips and breasts: "Everyone is uniquely beautiful in their own ways. We all have insecurities about the things that make us different from a typical ideal of beauty. I, like so many of us, try every day to work past those insecurities" (Ledbetter, 2017).

The American Medical Association found this common practice of altering images so harmful that at its 2011 annual meeting it voted to encourage magazine industry efforts to discontinue its use. The AMA board argued not only that altered images of women's bodies create unrealistic expectations in young people, but also that decades of social science research tie these unrealistic media images to eating disorders and other childhood and adolescent health problems.

Some, but not all, in the magazine industry have responded. *Seventeen*, acknowledging a teen-driven online movement to publish more unretouched photos, committed itself to a "Body Peace Treaty" in which it promised to never again change girls' body or face shapes and to begin including in its pages only images of girls and models who appear healthy. *Vogue* instituted its "Health Initiative," stating it would ban from its pages all models under 16 years old and super-skinny models who appear to have an eating disorder. And in 2017, Getty Images, the world's largest provider of stock photos, announced that it would no longer sell altered images.

An additional media literacy issue here has to do with maintaining the confidence of audience members. As digital altering of images becomes more widespread—and its occurrence better known—will readers come to question the veracity of even unaltered images and the truthfulness of the stories that employ them? Photojournalist Stanley Greene warns that altered images take the industry "down a dark road. . .We are the messengers, we are the seekers of the truths, we must be the ones that show the light in the darkest corners of the world. When viewers can no longer trust the picture or the photographer taking it, we are nothing but tricksters" (in Alexander, 2014).

What do you think? Did you see any of these images? Did you know they had been altered? If you did, would that have changed your interpretation of the stories they represented? Does the fact that major media outlets sometimes alter the images they present to you lead you to question their overall integrity? Do you believe that media outlets that use altered images have an obligation to inform readers and viewers of their decision to restructure reality? How does it feel to know that almost all of the images that we see in our daily newspapers and newsmagazines today are altered in some way?

▼ After she was dramatically Photoshopped for a *Glamour* cover, Lady Gaga had a message for the magazine industry: "When the covers change, that's when culture changes."

Larry Busacca/Getty Images Entertainment/Getty Images

MEDIA LITERACY CHALLENGE
Identifying Digital Alteration

Media-literate magazine readers are *critical thinkers who make independent judgments about content.* They *think critically about media messages,* and they *have heightened expectations of the content they read.* You'll have to use all these skills to complete this challenge.

In print or online, choose your favorite magazine and find all the content, both editorial and advertising, that shows images of people. Identify the images that appear to have been digitally enhanced or changed. Critics and proponents alike acknowledge that just about every image appearing in a consumer magazine has been altered. How many did you find? What were your clues? How do you feel about the practice, and do you think the magazine had the right to make these alterations? What do your answers say about your understanding and respect for the power of media messages, your expectations of magazine content, and your ability to think critically about the messages in magazines? You may want to meet this challenge individually, using your favorite publication, or make it a competition. You can have different people examining the same magazine to see who can find the greatest number of alterations, or you can have teams compete against one another looking at an array of titles.

Resources for Review and Discussion

REVIEW POINTS: TYING CONTENT TO LEARNING OUTCOMES

▶ **Recognize the history and development of the magazine industry and the magazine itself as a medium.**
- ☐ Magazines, a favorite of 18th-century British elite, made an easy transition to colonial America.
- ☐ Mass circulation magazines prospered in the post–Civil War years because of increased literacy, improved transportation, reduced postal costs, and lower cover prices.
- ☐ Magazines' large readership and financial health empowered the muckrakers to challenge society's powerful people and institutions.

▶ **Identify how the organizational and economic nature of the contemporary magazine industry shapes the content of magazines.**
- ☐ Television changed magazines from mass circulation to specialized media; as a result, they are attractive to advertisers because of their demographic specificity, reader engagement, and reader affinity for the advertising they carry.
- ☐ The three broad categories of magazines are trade, professional, and business; industrial, company, and sponsored; and consumer magazines.
- ☐ Magazine circulation comes in the form of subscription, single-copy sales, and controlled circulation. Advertiser demands for better measures of readership and accountability have rendered circulation an outmoded metric.

▶ **Describe the relationship between magazines and their readers.**
- ☐ Custom publishing, in the form of brand magazines and magalogues, is one way that magazines stand out in a cluttered media environment.
- ☐ Magazines further meet competition from other media, especially cable television, through internationalization, technology-driven improvements in distribution, the sale of subscriber lists, their own direct marketing efforts, and licensing.

▶ **Explain the convergence of magazines with the Internet and mobile technologies.**
- ☐ Virtually all print magazines have online equivalents, although they employ different financial models.
- ☐ Readers are overwhelmingly positive about electronic magazines.
- ☐ Readers are equally enthusiastic about accessing magazines from mobile devices.

▶ **Apply key media literacy skills to magazine reading.**
- ☐ A number of industry revenue-enhancing practices pose different challenges to media-literate readers:
  - ▪ Sponsored content is paid-for material that takes on the look and feel of the surrounding editorial content.
  - ▪ Complementary copy is editorial content that reinforces an advertiser's message.
  - ▪ Heavy reliance on digitally altered graphics is regularly employed in both advertising and editorial content and is highly controversial.

KEY TERMS

muckraking, 104

engagement, 107

affinity, 107

split runs, 109

circulation, 110

controlled circulation, 111

augmented reality (AR), 113

near-field communication (NFC)
   chips, 114

custom publishing, 114

brand magazine, 114

magalogue, 114

artificial intelligence (AI), 115

complementary copy, 116

QUESTIONS FOR REVIEW

1. How would you characterize the content of the first US magazines?

2. What factors fueled the expansion of the magazine industry at the beginning of the 20th century?

3. What factors led to the demise of the mass circulation era and the development of the era of specialization?

4. What are the three broad types of magazines?

5. Why do advertisers favor specialization in magazines?

6. What are engagement and affinity? Why are they important to advertisers?

7. In what different ways do magazines internationalize their publications?

8. Why is the magazine industry optimistic about the effects of new mobile technologies on its relationship with readers?

9. What are the arguments for and against the routine use of sponsored content?

10. What is a complementary copy? Why does it trouble critics?

To maximize your study time, check out CONNECT to access the SmartBook study module for this chapter, watch videos, and explore other resources.

QUESTIONS FOR CRITICAL THINKING AND DISCUSSION

1. Can you think of any contemporary crusading magazine or muckraking writers? Compared with those of the era of the muckrakers, they are certainly less visible. Why is this the case?

2. Which magazines do you read? Draw a demographic profile of yourself based only on the magazines you regularly read.

3. Are you troubled by the practice of altering photographs? Can you think of times when it might be more appropriate than others?

REFERENCES

1. Alexander, S. (2014, November 10). Retouching photos, processing the news. *Popular Photography*. Retrieved from https://www.popphoto.com/american-photo/processing-news-retouching-photojournalism/

2. Alliance for Audited Media. (2021, January). Magazine media 360° - December 2020. Retrieved from https://f.hubspotusercontent10.net/hubfs/1932461/MM360/MM360-Report-December2020. pdf?__hstc=&__hssc=&hsCtaTracking=69784d2e-e7d2-487f-912b-a00e0bd2f890%7C8736d100-da32-405c-b184-b8cd2db00f97

3. Association of Magazine Media (2020). *Magazine media factbook*. Retrieved from https://www.magazine.org/Magazine/Research_and_Resources_Pages/MPA_Factbook.aspx

4. "Biggest U.S. Spenders by Medium." (2019, June 24). *Ad Age* (insert), pp. 24–25.

5. Blue Bite. (2020, March 23). The state of QR in 2020. *Medium*. Retrieved from https://medium.com/@BlueBite/the-state-of-qr-in-2020-f40c6d85d9de#:~:text=QR%20Code%20Usage%20Statistics%20in%202020&text=The%2026%25%20growth%20in%20the,number%20of%20interactions%20per%20object.

6. Calkins, I. (2016, April 11). 13 times celebrities called out magazines over retouching. *Cosmopolitan*. Retrieved from https://www.cosmopolitan.com/entertainment/news/a56561/celebrities-respond-retouching-magazine-covers-criticism/

7. Chayka, K. (2019, November). Into the gloss. *New Republic*, pp. 46–51.

8. Dool, G. (2019, April 9). Ad-free, print-only and profitable, Kazoo is pushing girls to think bigger. *Folio*. Retrieved from https://www.foliomag.com/kazoo-magazine-girls-think-bigger/

9. Dool, G. (2016, February 1). Prevention announces plans to go advertising-free with print edition. *Folio*. Retrieved from http://www.foliomag.com/prevention-launches-ad-free-print-edition/

10. Dumenco, S. (2020, June 15). "Say Their Names": See the annotated, interactive version of the New Yorker's George Floyd cover. *Ad Age*. Retrieved from https://adage.com/article/media/say-their-names-see-annotated-interactive-version-new-yorkers-george-floyd-cover/2262131

11. Guaglione, S. (2018, October 4). Bloomberg pushes initiative to increase women sources. *MediaPost*. Retrieved from

https://www.mediapost.com/publications/article/326035/bloomberg-pushes-initiative-to-increase-women-sour.html

12. Heller, N. (2021, February 16). What are magazines good for? *New Yorker*. Retrieved from https://www.newyorker.com/culture/cultural-comment/what-are-magazines-good-for

13. *Hemispheres*. (2020). *Hemispheres* media kit 2020. *United Airlines*. Retrieved from https://view.publitas.com/ink/hemispheres-media-kit/page/1

14. Ives, N. (2008, November 17). As ASME fortifies ad/edit divide, some mags flout it. *Advertising Age*, p. 3.

15. Ledbetter, E. (2017, September 18). Emily Ratajkowski calls out magazine for Photoshopping her breasts and lips. *Huffington Post*. Retrieved from https://www.huffingtonpost.com.au/2017/09/18/emily-ratajkowski-calls-out-magazine-for-photoshopping-her-breasts-and-lips_a_23213986/

16. Liesse, J. (2020, January 27). Analysts predict global ad spending to grow despite uncertainty. *Ad Age*, p. 23.

17. Martin, C. (2018, September 23). "Cosmo" taps augmented reality for virtual try-ons. *MediaPost*. Retrieved from https://www.mediapost.com/publications/article/325453/cosmo-taps-augmented-reality-for-virtual-try-ons.html

18. Meek, A. (2020, December 30). Stop saying print journalism is dead. 60 magazines launched during this crazy year. *Forbes*. Retrieved from https://www.forbes.com/sites/andymeek/2021/12/30/stop-saying-print-journalism-is-dead-60-magazines-launched-during-this-crazy-year/?sh=f93987616d57

19. Meyersohn, N. (2020, February 24). The Costco Connection is America's fourth biggest magazine. *CNN*. Retrieved from https://www.cnn.com/2020/02/24/business/costco-connection-magazine-retail/index.html

20. Pollitt, C. (2020, June 6). The ultimate list of sponsored content marketplaces for marketers. *Relevance*. Retrieved from https://www.relevance.com/the-ultimate-list-of-sponsored-content-marketplaces-for-marketers/

21. Robinson, E. (2017, November 23). Congress must investigate Trump's alleged sexual misconduct. *Washington Post*. Retrieved from https://www.washingtonpost.com/opinions/its-time-for-congress-to-investigate-trumps-alleged-sexual-misconduct/2017/11/23/4354aef4-cfc0-11e7-81bc-c55a220c-8cbe_story.html?utm_term=. ef1b66b9a2c7

22. Sass, E. (2016, April 29). Fans slam "People" for Photoshopping Serena. *MediaPost*. Retrieved from http://www.mediapost.com/publications/article/274644/fans-slam-people-for-photoshopping-serena.html

23. Scott, S. (2020, February 4). The blurring boundaries between native ads and editorial. *The Drum*. Retrieved from https://www.thedrum.com/opinion/2020/02/04/the-blurring-boundaries-between-native-ads-and-editorial

24. Smith, S. (2018, May 1). Once a side gig, licensing has become a crucial revenue source for publishers. *Folio*. Retrieved from https://www.foliomag.com/publishers-bullish-on-licensing/

25. Spaight, S. (2016, July 29). High-quality branded print magazines among the most effective content marketing tactics. *GS Design*. Retrieved from https://www.gsdesign.com/blog/high-quality-branded-print-magazines-among-most-effective-content-marketing-tactics

26. Taylor, K. (2018, March 28). Walmart is pulling Cosmopolitan from checkout lines in response to #MeToo—but it's an embarrassing perversion of the movement. *Business Insider*. Retrieved from https://www.businessinsider.com/walmart-pulls-cosmopolitan-in-response-to-metoo-2018-3

27. Tebbel, J., & Zuckerman, M. E. (1991). *The magazine in America 1741–1990*. New York: Oxford University Press.

28. Waterson, J. (2020, May 30). Microsoft sacks journalists to replace them with robots. *Guardian*. Retrieved from https://www.theguardian.com/technology/2020/may/30/microsoft-sacks-journalists-to-replace-them-with-robots

29. WebMD (2020). *Media kit*. Retrieved from https://mediakit.webmd.com/files/WebMD_Media_Kit.pdf

30. Williams, R. (2020, December 15). Study: Hearst makes biggest cuts in print frequency. *Media Post*. Retrieved from https://www.mediapost.com/publications/article/358657/study-hearst-makes-biggest-cuts-in-print-frequenc.html

31. Zacharek, S., Dockterman, E., & Edwards, H. S. (2017, December 18). "The silence breakers." *Time*, pp. 34–70.

32. Zahidi, S. (2020). Global gender gap report 2020. *World Economic Forum*. Retrieved from http://www3.weforum.org/docs/WEF_GGGR_2020.pdf

Cultural Forum Blue Column icon, Media Literacy Red Torch Icon, Using Media Green Gear icon, Developing Media book in starburst icon: ©McGraw Hill

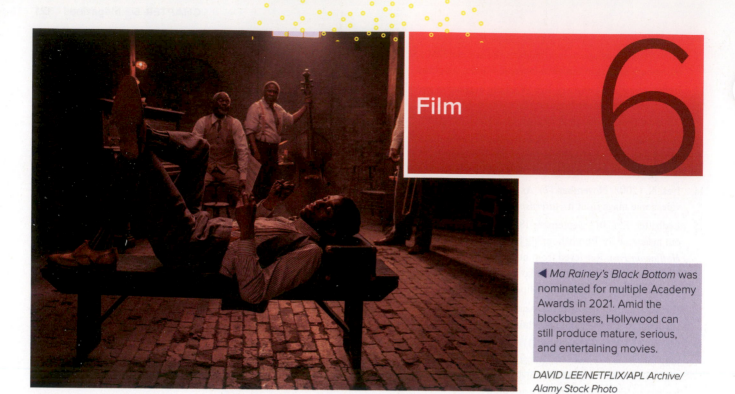

Film

6

◀ *Ma Rainey's Black Bottom* was nominated for multiple Academy Awards in 2021. Amid the blockbusters, Hollywood can still produce mature, serious, and entertaining movies.

DAVID LEE/NETFLIX/APL Archive/ Alamy Stock Photo

Learning Objectives

The movies are our dream factories; they are bigger than life. With books, they are the only mass medium not primarily dependent on advertising for their financial support. That means they must satisfy you, because you buy the tickets. As such, the relationship between medium and audience is different from those that exist with other media. After studying this chapter, you should be able to

▶ Recognize the history and development of the film industry and film itself as a medium.

▶ Describe the cultural value of film and the implications of the blockbuster mentality for film as an important artistic and cultural medium.

▶ Summarize the three components of the film industry—production, distribution, and exhibition.

▶ Explain how the organizational and economic nature of the contemporary film industry shapes the content of films.

▶ Describe the promise and peril of convergence and the new digital technologies to film as we know it.

▶ Recall that production is becoming more expensive and, simultaneously, less expensive.

▶ Apply film-watching media literacy skills, especially in interpreting merchandise tie-ins and product placements.

1720s Early efforts using chemical salts to capture temporary photographic images

1793 ▶ Niépce begins experimenting with methods to set optical images ·····

1816 Niépce develops photography

1839 ▶ Daguerreotype introduced; Talbot's ····· calotype (paper film)

1800

Pixtal/age fotostock

1877 ▶ Muybridge takes race photos ·····

1887 Goodwin's celluloid roll film

1888 Dickson produces kinetograph

1889 Eastman's easy-to-use camera

1891 Edison's kinetoscope

1895 Lumière brothers debut cinématographe

1896 Edison unveils Edison Vitascope

1850

George Eastman House/Getty Images

1902 Méliès's *A Trip to the Moon*

1903 Porter's *The Great Train Robbery* (montage)

1908 Motion Picture Patents Company founded

1915 Lincoln Motion Picture Company; Griffith's *The Birth of a Nation*

1922 Hays office opens

1926 Sound comes to film

1934 Motion Picture Production Code issued

1939 Television unveiled at World's Fair

1947 HUAC convenes

1948 Paramount Decision; Cable TV introduced

1900

Library of Congress, [LC-USZ62-45683]

1969 ▶ Indie film *Easy Rider* ·····

1976 VCR introduced

1996 ▶ DVD introduced ·····

1950

Courtesy of Everett Collection

2007 *Purple Violets* released directly to iTunes

2009 *Avatar*

2012 For first time, more money spent on online movies than on DVD

2014 Toy manufacturer Hasbro opens Allspark studios; major studios commit to all-digital movie distribution

2015 Netflix and Amazon begin production of feature films

2016 Mobile is top platform for watching Internet video

2017 Apple begins feature film production; *Manchester by the Sea* from Amazon is first movie from a streaming service nominated for an Academy Award

2018 *Unsane* shot entirely on iPhone; Mattel Films founded

2020 Coronavirus in the US; in-theater exhibition comes to a complete halt; Universal announces direct-to-viewer distribution; Paramount Decision reversed; Netflix buys Los Angeles theater

2021 Warner Bros. releases all new films day-and-date; Amazon buys MGM

2000

Howard Kingsnorth/Photodisc/ Getty Images

PARIS IS COLD AND DAMP ON THIS DECEMBER NIGHT, THREE DAYS AFTER CHRISTMAS IN 1895. But you bundle up and make your way to the Grand Café in the heart of the city. You've heard that brothers Auguste and Louis Lumière will be displaying their new invention that somehow makes pictures move. Your curiosity is piqued.

Tables and chairs are set up in a basement room of the café, and a white bedsheet is draped above its stage. The Lumières appear to polite applause. They announce the program: *La Sortie des usines Lumière (Quitting Time at the Lumière Factory)*; *Le Repas de bébé*, featuring a Lumière child eating; *L'Arroseur arrosé*, about a practical-joking boy and his victim, the gardener; and finally *L'Arrivée d'un train en gare*, the arrival of a train at a station.

The lights go out. Somewhere behind you, someone starts the machine. There is some brief flickering on the suspended sheet and then . . . you are completely awestruck. There before you—bigger than life-size—photographs are really moving. You see places you know to be miles away. You spy on the secret world of a prankster boy, remembering your own childhood. But the last film is the most impressive. As the giant locomotive chugs toward the audience, you and most of those around you are convinced you are about to be crushed. There is panic. People are ducking under their chairs, screaming. Death is imminent!

The first paying audience in the history of motion pictures has just had a lesson in movie watching.

The Lumière brothers were excellent mechanics, and their father owned a factory that made photographic plates. Their first films were little more than what we would now consider black-and-white home movies. As you can tell from their titles, they were simple stories. There was no editing; the camera was simply turned on, then turned off. There were no fades, wipes, or flashbacks, no computer graphics, no dialogue, and no music; yet much of the audience was terrified by the oncoming cinematic locomotive. And while this story may be the stuff of legends—film historians disagree—it has been around a long time because it reminds us that not only were the first audiences illiterate in the language of film, but also just how far we've come since the medium's earliest days.

We begin our study of the medium that Louis Lumière himself predicted would be "an invention without a future" (in Dargis & Scott, 2019, p. AR59), from its entrepreneurial beginnings, through the introduction of its narrative and visual language, to its establishment as a large, studio-run industry. We detail Hollywood's relationship with its early audiences and changes in the structure and content of films resulting from the introduction of television. We then look at contemporary movie production, distribution, and exhibition systems and how convergence is altering all three; the influence of the major studios; and the economic pressures on them in an increasingly multimedia environment. We examine the special place movies hold for us and how young audiences and the films that target them may affect our culture. Recognizing the use of product placement in movies is the basis for improving our media literacy skill.

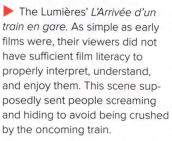

▶ The Lumières' *L'Arrivée d'un train en gare*. As simple as early films were, their viewers did not have sufficient film literacy to properly interpret, understand, and enjoy them. This scene supposedly sent people screaming and hiding to avoid being crushed by the oncoming train.
Collection Christophel/Alamy Stock Photo

A Short History of the Movies

We are no longer illiterate in the grammar of film, nor are movies as simple as the early Lumière offerings. Consider the sophistication necessary for filmmakers to produce a magical horror movie such as *Gretel & Hansel* (2020) and the skill required for audiences to read the unannounced jumbled time frames and fantasy sequences of *Rocket Man* (2019). How we arrived at this contemporary medium–audience relationship is a wonderful story.

Early newspapers were developed by businesspeople and patriots for a small, politically involved elite that could read, but the early movie industry was built largely by entrepreneurs who wanted to make money entertaining everyone. Unlike television, whose birth and growth were predetermined and guided by the already well-established radio industry, there were no precedents, no rules, and no expectations for movies.

Return to the opening vignette. The audience for the first Lumière movies did not "speak film." Think of it as being stranded in a foreign country with no knowledge of the language and cultural conventions. You would have to make your way, with each new experience helping you better understand the next. First, you'd learn some simple words and basic customs. Eventually, you'd be able to better understand the language and people. In other words, you'd become increasingly literate in that culture. Beginning with that Paris premiere, people had to become film literate. They had to develop an understanding of cinematic alterations in time and place. They had to learn how images and sound combined to create meaning. But unlike visiting another culture, there was no existing cinematic culture. Movie creators and their audiences had to develop and understand the culture together.

The Early Entrepreneurs

In 1873, former California governor Leland Stanford needed help winning a bet he had made with a friend. Convinced that a horse in full gallop had all four feet off the ground, he had to prove it. He turned to well-known photographer Eadweard Muybridge, who worked on the problem for 4 years before finding a solution. In 1877, Muybridge arranged a series of still cameras along a stretch of racetrack. As the horse sprinted by, each camera took its picture. The resulting photographs won Stanford his bet, but more importantly, they sparked an idea in their photographer. Muybridge was intrigued by the appearance of motion created when photos are viewed sequentially. He began taking pictures of numerous kinds of human

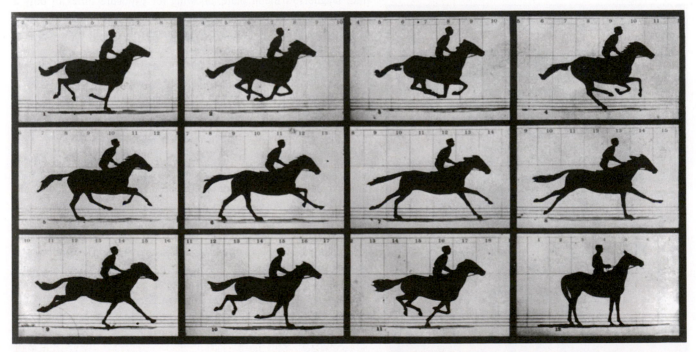

▲ Muybridge's horse pictures. When these plates were placed sequentially and rotated, they produced the appearance of motion.
Library of Congress, [LC-USZ62-45683]

and animal action. To display his work, Muybridge invented the **zoopraxiscope**, a machine for projecting slides onto a distant surface.

When people watched the rapidly projected sequential slides, they saw the pictures as if they were in motion. This perception is the result of a physiological phenomenon known as **persistence of vision**, in which the images our eyes gather are retained in the brain for about 1/24 of a second. Therefore, if photographic frames are moved at 24 frames a second, people perceive them as actually in motion absent any flicker or other interruption.

Muybridge eventually met the prolific inventor Thomas Edison in 1888. Edison quickly saw the scientific and economic potential of the zoopraxiscope and set his top scientist, William Dickson, to the task of developing a better projector. But Dickson correctly saw the need to develop a better system of *filming*. Dickson combined Hannibal Goodwin's newly invented celluloid roll film with George Eastman's easy-to-use Kodak camera to make a motion picture camera that took 40 photographs a second. He used his **kinetograph** to film all types of theatrical performances, some by unknowns and others by famous entertainers such as Annie Oakley and Buffalo Bill Cody. Of course, none of this would have been possible had it not been for photography itself.

THE DEVELOPMENT OF PHOTOGRAPHY The process of photography was first developed by French inventor Joseph Nicéphore Niépce around 1816. Although there had been much experimentation in the realm of image making at the time, Niépce was the first person to make practical use of a camera and film, but his color photographs of natural objects would last only a short time.

Niépce's success, however, attracted the attention of countryman Louis Daguerre, who joined with him to perfect the process. Niépce died before the 1839 introduction of the **daguerreotype**, a process of recording images on polished metal plates, usually copper, covered with a thin layer of silver iodide emulsion. When light reflected from an object passed through a lens and struck the emulsion, the emulsion would etch the image on the plate. The plate was then washed with a cleaning solvent, leaving a positive or replica image.

In the same year as the first public display of the daguerreotype, British inventor William Henry Fox Talbot introduced a paper film process. This process was more important to the development of photography than the metal film system, but the daguerreotype received widespread attention and acclaim and made the public enthusiastic about photography.

The **calotype** (Talbot's system) used translucent paper, what we now call the negative, from which several prints could be made. In addition, his film was much more sensitive than Daguerre's metal plate, allowing for exposure times of only a few seconds as opposed to the daguerreotype's 30 minutes. Until calotype, virtually all daguerreotype images were still lives and portraits, a necessity with long exposure times.

The final steps in the development of the photographic process necessary for true motion pictures were taken, as we've just seen, by Goodwin in 1887 and Eastman in 1889 and were adapted to motion pictures by Edison scientist Dickson.

THOMAS EDISON Edison built the first motion picture studio near his laboratory in New Jersey. He called it Black Maria, the common name at that time for a police paddy wagon. It had an open roof and revolved to follow the sun so the performers being filmed would always be illuminated.

The completed films were not projected. Instead, they were run through a **kinetoscope**, a sort of peep show device. Often they were accompanied by music provided by another Edison invention, the phonograph. Patented in 1891 and commercially available 3 years later, the kinetoscope quickly became a popular feature in penny arcades, vaudeville halls, and big-city Kinetoscope parlors. This marked the beginning of commercial motion picture exhibition.

THE LUMIÈRE BROTHERS The Lumière brothers made the next advance. Their initial screenings demonstrated that people would sit

▼ Typical of daguerreotypes, this plate captures a portrait. The method's long exposure time made all but the most stationary subjects impossible to photograph. *George Eastman House/Getty Images*

in a darkened room to watch motion pictures projected on a screen. The brothers from Lyon envisioned great wealth in their ability to increase the number of people who could simultaneously watch a movie. In 1895, they patented their **cinématographe**, a device that both photographed and projected action. Within weeks of their Christmastime showing, long lines of enthusiastic moviegoers were waiting for their makeshift theater to open. Edison recognized the advantage of the cinématographe over his kinetoscope, so he acquired the patent for an advanced projector developed by US inventor Thomas Armat. On April 23, 1896, the Edison Vitascope premiered in New York City, and the American movie business was born.

The Coming of Narrative

The Edison and Lumière movies were typically only a few minutes long and showed little more than filmed reproductions of reality—celebrities, weight lifters, jugglers, and babies. They were shot in fixed frame (the camera did not move), and there was no editing. For the earliest audiences, this was enough. But soon the novelty wore thin. People wanted more for their money. French filmmaker Georges Méliès, a magician and caricaturist before he became a filmmaker, began making narrative motion pictures, that is, movies that told a story. At the end of the 1890s, he was shooting and exhibiting one-scene, one-shot movies, but soon he began making stories based on sequential shots in different places. He simply took one shot, stopped the camera, moved it, took another shot, and so on. Méliès is often called the "first artist of the cinema" because he brought narrative to the medium in the form of imaginative tales such as *A Trip to the Moon* (1902). This fantastic tale came to America in 1903, and US moviemakers were quick not only to borrow the idea of using film to tell stories but also to improve on it.

Edwin S. Porter, an Edison Company camera operator, saw that film could be an even better storyteller with more artistic use of camera placement and editing. His 12-minute *The Great Train Robbery* (1903) was the first movie to use editing, intercutting of scenes, and a mobile camera to tell a relatively sophisticated tale. It was also the first Western. This new narrative form using **montage**—tying together two separate but related shots in such a way that they take on a new, unified meaning—was an instant hit with audiences.

◄ Scene from *A Trip to the Moon*. Narrative came to the movies through the inventive imagination of Georges Méliès.
Star Film/Edison Manufacturing Company/Photofest

Almost immediately hundreds of **nickelodeons**, some having as many as 100 seats, were opened in converted stores, banks, and halls across the United States. The price of admission was one nickel, hence the name. By 1905 cities such as New York were opening a new nickelodeon every day. From 1907 to 1908, the first year in which there were more narrative than documentary films, the number of nickelodeons in the United States increased tenfold. With so many exhibition halls in so many towns serving such an extremely enthusiastic public, many movies were needed. To create more films, hundreds of new **factory studios**, or production companies, were started.

Because so many movies needed to be made and rushed to the nickelodeons, people working in the industry had to learn and perform virtually all aspects of production. There was precious little time for, or profitability in, the kind of specialization that marks contemporary filmmaking. Writer, actor, and camera operator D. W. Griffith perfected his craft in this environment. He was quickly recognized as a brilliant director. He introduced innovations such as scheduled rehearsals before final shooting and production based on close adherence to a shooting script. He lavished attention on otherwise ignored aspects of a film's look—costume and lighting—and used close-ups and other dramatic camera angles to transmit emotion.

All his skill came together in 1915 with the release of *The Birth of a Nation*. Whereas Porter had used montage to tell a story, Griffith used it to create passion, move emotions, and heighten suspense. The most influential silent film ever made, this 3-hour epic was 6 weeks in rehearsal and 9 weeks in shooting, cost $125,000 to produce (making it the most expensive movie made to that date), was distributed to theaters complete with an orchestral music score, had a cast of thousands of humans and animals, and had an admission price well above the usual 5 cents—$3. It was the most popular and profitable movie made and remained so until 1939, when it was surpassed by *Gone with the Wind*.

With other Griffith masterpieces, *Intolerance* (1916) and *Broken Blossoms* (1919), *The Birth of a Nation* set new standards for the American film. They took movies out of the nickelodeons and made them big business. At the same time, however, *The Birth of a Nation* represented the basest aspects of US culture because it included an ugly, racist portrayal of African Americans and a sympathetic treatment of the Ku Klux Klan. The film inspired protests in front of theaters across the country and criticism in some newspapers and magazines, and it led African Americans to fight back with their own films (see the essay "African American Response to D. W. Griffith: The Lincoln and Micheaux Film Companies"). Nevertheless, *The Birth of a Nation* found acceptance by the vast majority of people.

▶ Scene from *The Great Train Robbery*. Porter's masterpiece introduced audiences to editing, intercutting of scenes, moving cameras, and the Western.
Edison/Kobal/Shutterstock

◀ The Ku Klux Klan was the collective hero in D. W. Griffith's *The Birth of a Nation*. This cinematic masterpiece and groundbreaking film employed production techniques never before used; however, its racist theme mars its legacy.

Courtesy of Everett Collection

The Big Studios

In 1908, Thomas Edison, foreseeing the huge amounts of money that could be made from movies, founded the Motion Picture Patents Company (MPPC), often simply called the Trust. This group of 10 companies under Edison's control, holding the patents to virtually all existing filmmaking and exhibition equipment, ran the production and distribution of film in the United States with an iron fist. Anyone who wanted to make or exhibit a movie needed Trust permission, typically not forthcoming. In addition, the MPPC had rules about the look of the movies it would permit: They must be one reel, approximately 12 minutes long, and must adopt a "stage perspective"; that is, the actors must fill the frame as if they were in a stage play.

Many independent film companies sprang up in defiance of the Trust, including Griffith's in 1913. To avoid MPPC scrutiny and reprisal, these companies moved as far away as they could, to California. This westward migration had other benefits. Better weather meant longer shooting seasons. Free of MPPC interference, people like Griffith who wanted to explore the potential of films longer than 12 minutes and with imaginative use of the camera were free to do so.

Another benefit of this new freedom were opportunities for women filmmakers. "The industry—new, ad hoc, making up its own rules as it went along—had not yet locked in a strict division of labor by gender," writes film essayist Margaret Talbot. "Women came to Los Angeles from all over the country, impelled not so much by dreams of stardom as by the prospect of interesting work in a freewheeling enterprise that valued them. 'Of all the different industries that have offered opportunities to women,' the screenwriter Clara Beranger told an interviewer in 1919, 'none have given them the chance that motion pictures have.'" Women played "an outsized role in the origins of moviemaking," but as movie making became bigger and consolidated around a few giant studios, opportunities for newcomers and outsiders, especially women, rapidly diminished (2019, p. 69).

The new studio system, with its more elaborate films and big-name stars, controlled the movie industry from California. Thomas H. Ince (maker of the William S. Hart Westerns), Griffith, and comedy genius Mack Sennett formed the Triangle Company. Adolph Zukor's Famous Players in Famous Plays—formed when Zukor was denied MPPC permission to

USING MEDIA TO MAKE A DIFFERENCE
African American Response to D. W. Griffith: The Lincoln and Micheaux Film Companies

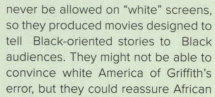

The African American community did not sit passively in the wake of D. W. Griffith's 1915 cinematic but hateful wonder, *The Birth of a Nation*. (It's original subtitle was "The former enemies of North and South are united again in common defense of their Aryan birthright.") The NAACP fought the film in court and on the picket line, largely unsuccessfully. But other African Americans decided to use film to combat *Birth*. The first was Emmett J. Scott, a quiet, scholarly man. He sought money from the country's Black middle class to produce a short film showing the achievements of African Americans. His intention was to attach his film, *Lincoln's Dream*, as a prologue to screenings of the Griffith film. Together with screenwriter Elaine Sterne, Scott eventually expanded the project into a feature-length movie. He approached Universal Studios with his film but was rejected.

With independent backing from both Black and white investors, the film was released in 1918. Produced by an inexperienced cast and crew working on a production beset by bad weather and technical difficulties, the retitled *The Birth of a Race* filled 12 reels of film and ran more than three hours. Its publicity hailed it as "The Greatest and Most Daring of Photoplays . . . The Story of Sin . . . A Master Picture Conceived in the Spirit of Truth and Dedicated to All the Races of the World" (Bogle, 1989, p. 103). It was an artistic and commercial failure. Scott, however, had inspired others.

Even before *The Birth of a Race* was completed, the Lincoln Motion Picture Company was incorporated, in Nebraska in 1916 and in California in 1917, by brothers Noble and George Johnson. Their tack differed from Scott's. They understood that their "black" films would never be allowed on "white" screens, so they produced movies designed to tell Black-oriented stories to Black audiences. They might not be able to convince white America of Griffith's error, but they could reassure African Americans that their views could find expression. Lincoln's first movie was *The Realization of a Negro's Ambition,* and it told the story of Black American achievements. The Johnson brothers turned US racism to their advantage. Legal segregation in the South and de facto segregation in the North had led to an explosion of Black theaters. These movie houses needed content. Lincoln helped provide it by producing 10 three-reelers between 1916 and 1920.

Another notable film company soon began operation, hoping to challenge, at least in Black theaters, Griffith's portrayals. Oscar Micheaux founded the Micheaux Film and Book Company in 1918 in Chicago and soon produced *The Homesteader*, an eight-reel film based on the autobiographical novel he'd written three years earlier. It was the story of a successful Black homestead rancher in South Dakota. But Micheaux was not content to boost Black self-esteem. Producing the first feature film and the first all-sound movie to employ Black talent in front of and behind the camera (Gray, 2020), he was determined to make "racial photoplays depicting racial life" (as quoted in Sampson, 1977, p. 42). In 1920, he released *Within Our Gates*, a drama about the southern lynching of a Black man. Censored and denied a screening in dozens of cities both North and South, Micheaux was undeterred, even taking on interracial marriage in his 1923 *The House Behind the Cedars*.

These early film pioneers used their medium to make a difference. They challenged the interpretation of history being circulated by the most popular movie in the world, and they provided encouragement and entertainment to the African American community.

distribute one of his films—joined with several other independents and a distribution company to become Paramount. Other independents joined to create the Fox Film Company (soon called 20th Century Fox) and Universal. Although films were still silent, by the mid-1920s, there were more than 20,000 movie theaters in the United States—many of them **movie palaces**, elaborately decorated, opulent, architecturally stunning theaters—and more than 350,000 people were making their living in film production. More than 1,240,000 feet of film were shot each year in Hollywood, and annual domestic US box office receipts exceeded $750 million.

The industry prospered not just because of its artistry, drive, and innovation but because it used these to meet the needs of a growing audience. At the beginning of the 20th century, generous immigration rules, combined with political and social unrest abroad, encouraged a flood of European immigrants who congregated in US cities where the jobs were and where people like themselves who spoke their language lived. American farmers, largely illiterate, also swarmed to the cities as years of drought and farm failure left them without home or hope. Jobs in the big mills and factories, although unpleasant, were plentiful. These new city dwellers had money and the need for leisure activities. Movies were a nickel, required no ability to read or to understand English, and offered glamorous stars and wonderful stories from faraway places.

Foreign political unrest proved to be a boon to the infant US movie business in another way as well. In 1914 and 1915, when the California studios were remaking the industry in their own grand image, war raged in Europe. European moviemaking, most significantly the influential French, German, and Russian cinema, came to a halt. European demand for movies, however, did not. American movies, produced in huge numbers for the hungry home audience, were ideal for overseas distribution. Because so few in the domestic audience could read English, few printed titles were used in the then-silent movies. Therefore, little had to be changed to satisfy foreign moviegoers. Film was indeed a universal language, but more important, the American film industry had firmly established itself as the world leader, all within 20 years of the Lumière's brothers' first screening.

Change Comes to Hollywood

As was the case with newspapers and magazines, the advent of television significantly altered the movie–audience relationship. But the nature of that relationship had already been shaped and reshaped in the three decades between the coming of sound to film and the coming of television.

THE TALKIES The first sound film was one of three films produced by Warner Bros. It may have been *Don Juan* (1926), starring John Barrymore, distributed with synchronized music and sound effects. Or perhaps it was Warner's more famous *The Jazz Singer* (1927), starring Al Jolson, which had several sound and speaking scenes (354 words in all) but was largely silent. Or it may have been the 1928 all-sound *Lights of New York*. Historians disagree because they cannot decide what constitutes a sound film.

There is no confusion, however, about the impact of sound on the movies and their audiences. First, sound made possible new genres—musicals, for example. Second, as actors now had to really act, performance aesthetics improved. Third, sound made film production a much more complicated and expensive proposition. As a result, many smaller filmmakers closed shop, solidifying the hold of the big studios over the industry. In 1933, 60% of all US films came from Hollywood's eight largest studios. By 1940, they were producing 76% of all US movies and collecting 86% of the total box office. As for the audience, in 1926, the year of *Don Juan*'s release, 50 million people went to the movies each week. In 1929, at the onset of the Great Depression, the number had risen to 80 million. By 1930, when sound was firmly entrenched, the number of weekly moviegoers had risen to 90 million (Mast & Kawin, 1996).

SCANDAL The popularity of talkies, and of movies in general, inevitably raised questions about their impact on the culture. In 1896, well before sound, *The Kiss* had generated a great moral outcry. Its stars, John C. Rice and May Irwin, were also the leads in the popular Broadway play *The Widow Jones*, which closed with a climactic kiss. The Edison Company asked Rice and Irwin to re-create the kiss for the big screen. Newspapers and politicians were bombarded with complaints from the offended. Kissing in the theater (for sophisticated elites) was one thing; in movies (for everyday people) it was quite another! The then-newborn industry responded to this and other calls for censorship with various forms of self-regulation and internal codes. But in the early 1920s, more Hollywood scandals forced a more direct response.

In 1920, "America's Sweetheart" Mary Pickford obtained a questionable Nevada divorce from her husband and immediately married the movies' other darling, Douglas Fairbanks, himself newly divorced. In 1920 and 1921, comedian Fatty Arbuckle was involved in legal problems with the police on two coasts. The first was apparently hushed up after a $100,000 gift was made to a Massachusetts district attorney, but the second involved a charge of manslaughter at a San Francisco hotel party thrown by the actor. Although he was acquitted in his third trial (the first two ended in hung juries) and the cause of the woman's death was never fully determined, the stain on Arbuckle and the industry remained. The cry for government intervention was raised. State legislatures introduced more than 100 separate pieces of legislation to censor or otherwise control movies and their content.

▲ Women were at the center of the emerging movie industry. Marion Fairfax, in addition to writing numerous successful silent film scripts, founded her own production company.
Historic Collection/Alamy Stock Photo

Hollywood responded in 1922 by creating the Motion Picture Producers and Distributors of America (MPPDA) and appointing Will H. Hays—chair of the Republican Party, a Presbyterian church elder, and a former postmaster general—president. The Hays Office, as it became known, undertook a vast effort to improve the image of the movies. Stressing the importance of movies to national life and as an educational medium, Hays promised better movies and founded a committee on public relations that included many civic and religious leaders. Eventually, in 1934, the Motion Picture Production Code (MPPC) was released. The code forbade the use of profanity, limited bedroom scenes to married couples (although they could not be shown in bed together), required that skimpy outfits be replaced by more complete costumes, delineated the length of screen kisses, ruled out scenes that ridiculed public officials or religious leaders, and outlawed a series of words from "God" to "nuts," all enforced by a $25,000 fine and the demand that scripts be submitted in advance for approval, a form of pre-censorship (Denby, 2016).

NEW GENRES, NEW PROBLEMS

By 1932, weekly movie attendance had dropped to 60 million. The Great Depression was having its effect. Yet the industry was able to weather the crisis for two reasons. The first was its creativity. New genres held people's interest. Feature documentaries such as *The Plow That Broke the Plains* (1936) spoke to audience needs to understand a world in seeming disorder. Musicals such as *42nd Street* (1933) and screwball comedies like *Bringing Up Baby* (1938) provided easy escapism. Gangster movies like *Little Caesar* (1930) reflected the grimy reality of Depression city streets and daily newspaper headlines. Horror films such as *Frankenstein* (1931) articulated audience feelings of alienation and powerlessness in a seemingly uncontrollable time. Socially conscious comedies like *Mr. Deeds Goes to Town* (1936) reminded moviegoers that good could still prevail, and the **double feature** with a **B-movie**—typically a less expensive movie—was a welcome relief to penny-pinching working people.

The second reason the movie business survived the Depression was because of its size and power, both residing in a system of operation called **vertical integration**. Using this system, studios produced their own films, distributed them through their own outlets, and exhibited them in their own theaters. In effect, the big studios controlled a movie from shooting to screening, guaranteeing distribution and an audience regardless of quality.

When the 1930s ended, weekly attendance was again over 80 million, and Hollywood was churning out 500 pictures a year. Moviegoing had become a central family and community activity for most people. Yet the end of that decade also brought bad news for the studios. In 1938, the Justice Department challenged vertical integration, suing the big five studios—Warner Bros., MGM, Paramount, RKO, and 20th Century Fox—for restraint of trade; that is, they accused the studios of illegal monopolistic practices. The case would take 10 years to decide, but the movie industry, basking in the middle of its golden age, was under attack. Its fate was sealed in 1939 when the Radio Corporation of America (RCA) made the first public broadcast of television from atop the Empire State Building. The impact of these two events was profound, and the medium would have to develop a new relationship with its audience to survive.

TELEVISION When World War II began, the government took control of all patents for the newly developing technology of television as well as of the materials necessary for its production. The diffusion of the medium to the public was therefore halted, but its technological improvement was not. In addition, the radio networks and advertising agencies, recognizing that the war would eventually end and that their futures were in television, were preparing for that day. When the war did end, the movie industry found itself competing not with a fledgling medium but with a technologically and economically sophisticated one. The number of homes with television sets grew from 10,000 in 1946 to more than 54 million in 1960 and movie attendance was fully 25% lower than that of even the worst Depression years. Where Americans spent 12.3% of their recreational budget on the movies in 1950, in 1965 they spent only 3.3% (Menard, 2021).

▼ Screwball comedies such as *Bringing Up Baby* helped Americans escape the misery of the Great Depression.

20th Century Fox Film Corp./ Courtesy Everett Collection

THE PARAMOUNT DECISION In 1948, 10 years after the case had begun, the Supreme Court issued its Paramount Decision, effectively destroying the studios' hold over moviemaking. Vertical integration was ruled illegal, as was **block booking**, the practice of requiring exhibitors to rent groups of movies, often inferior, to secure a better one. The studios were forced to sell off their exhibition businesses (the theaters). Before the Paramount Decision, the five major studios owned 75% of the first-run movie houses in the United States; after it, they owned none. Not only did they no longer have guaranteed exhibition, but other filmmakers now had access to the theaters, producing even greater competition for the dwindling number of movie patrons. In 2020, after nearly 8 decades, a federal court reversed the ruling in recognition of the scores of distribution channels available to moviemakers.

RED SCARE The US response to its postwar position as world leader was fear. So concerned were some members of Congress that communism would steal the people's rights that Congress decided to steal them first. The Hollywood chapter of the virulent anticommunism movement we now call McCarthyism (after the Republican senator from Wisconsin, Joseph McCarthy, its most rabid and public champion) was led by the House Un-American Activities Committee (HUAC) and its chair, J. Parnell Thomas (later imprisoned for padding his congressional payroll). First convened in 1947, HUAC's goal was to rid Hollywood of communist influence. The fear was that communist, socialist, and leftist propaganda was being secretly inserted into entertainment films by "Reds," "fellow travelers," and "pinkos." Rather than defend its First Amendment rights, the film industry abandoned those who were even mildly critical of the "Red Scare," jettisoning much of its best talent at a time when it could least afford to do so. In the fight against television, movies became increasingly tame for fear of being too controversial.

The industry was hurt not only by its cowardice but also by its shortsightedness. Hungry for content, the television industry asked Hollywood to sell its old features for broadcast. The studios responded by imposing on themselves the rule that no films could be sold to television and no working film star could appear on "the box." When it could have helped shape early television viewer tastes and expectations of the new medium, Hollywood was absent. It lifted its ban in 1958.

FIGHTING BACK The industry worked mightily to recapture audiences from television using both technical and content innovations. Some of these innovations remain today and serve the medium and its audiences well. These include more attention to special effects, greater dependence on and improvements in color, and CinemaScope (projecting on a large screen two and one-half times wider than it is tall). Among the forgettable technological innovations were primitive 3D and smellovision (wafting odors throughout the theater).

Innovation in content included spectaculars with which the small screen could not compete. *The Ten Commandments* (1956), *Ben Hur* (1959), *El Cid* (1960), and *Spartacus* (1960) filled the screen with many thousands of extras and lavish settings. Now that television was

◀ Warren Beatty is gunned down in the climax of the 1967 hit movie *Bonnie and Clyde.*
Warner Brothers/Seven Arts/ Photofest

catering to the mass audience, movies were free to present challenging fare for more sophisticated audiences. The "message movie" charted social trends, especially alienation of youth (*Blackboard Jungle*, 1955; *Rebel Without a Cause*, 1955) and prejudice (*12 Angry Men*, 1957; *Imitation of Life*, 1959; *To Kill a Mockingbird*, 1962). Changing values toward sex were examined (*Midnight Cowboy*, 1969; *Bob and Carol and Ted and Alice*, 1969), as was the new youth culture's rejection of middle-class values (*The Graduate*, 1967; *Goodbye Columbus*, 1969) and its revulsion/attraction to violence (*Bonnie and Clyde*, 1967). The movies as an industry had changed, which caused the films themselves to become a medium of social commentary and cultural impact.

Movies and Their Audiences

We talk of Hollywood as the "dream factory," the makers of "movie magic." We want our lives and loves to be "just like in the movies." The movies are "larger than life," and movie stars are much more glamorous than television stars. The movies, in other words, hold a very special place in our culture. Movies, like books, are a culturally special medium, an important medium. In this sense, the movie–audience relationship has more in common with that of books than with that of commercial television. Just as people buy books, they buy movie tickets. Because the audience, rather than advertisers, is in fact the true consumer, power rests with the audience in film more than it does in television.

Despite changing moviegoer demographics, the major studios continue to create movies as if youngsters and young adults make up the largest portion of the movie audience. There is no question that as age increases, the likelihood of going to the movies decreases (Watson, 2020), but that fact hides an ongoing and significant fall-off in movie attendance by young people. Although 18 to 24 year olds are still the largest single-age segment of moviegoers, people under 24 represent only a third of all moviegoers in the United States and Canada (Barnes, 2020). The reality is that a majority of all movie tickets sold are bought by people 25 and older.

Nonetheless, despite the fact that many in the industry are indeed producing fare for this more mature audience, major studios' attention and the bulk of their resources continue to be directed at a young audience. As you'll soon read, the reasons are potential income from licensing and product tie-ins (kids love toys, games, and fast food) and overseas ticket sales (audiences don't have to speak English to enjoy superheroes and big explosions). This explains why so many of today's movies and franchises are aimed at youngsters in the form of cartoons (the *Despicable Me* and *Minion* films) and films based on other media such as comic books (*The Avengers* and *Spider-Man* films), popular toys (the *Transformers* franchise), young adult novels (*A Wrinkle in Time* and *Artemis Fowl*), television shows (*The Loud House Movie* and *Baywatch*), and video games (*Assassin's Creed* and *Resident Evil*).

Look at the top 20 worldwide box office hits of all time in Figure 6.1, every one of which has earned more than a billion dollars. With the exception of *Titanic* (1997), a special-effects showcase itself, all are fantastic adventure films that appeal to younger audiences. The question asked by serious observers of the relationship between film and culture is whether the medium is increasingly dominated by the wants, tastes, and needs of what amounts to an audience of children. What becomes of film as an important medium, one with something to say, one that challenges people?

What becomes of film as an important medium, say Hollywood's defenders, is completely dependent on us, the audience; we get the movies we deserve because we tell the studios what we want by how we spend our money. In 2019 American audiences spent $858 million on *Avengers: Endgame*. Globally, the super hero movie passed the $2 billion mark in just 11 days. That same year moviegoers bought just under $2 billion in tickets on *The Lion King* ($544 million of that in the United States). Box office results like these certainly say something about what audiences want. Industry defenders further argue that films aimed at young people aren't necessarily movies with nothing to say. *Never Rarely Sometimes Always* (2020) and *Plan B* (2021) are "teen films" offering important insight into American society and youth culture, as well as into the topics they explicitly examine, namely, teen abortion and barriers to reproductive health care, especially for young women of color, respectively. In addition, despite Hollywood's infatuation with younger moviegoers,

Movie rank and box office revenues (in millions of dollars)

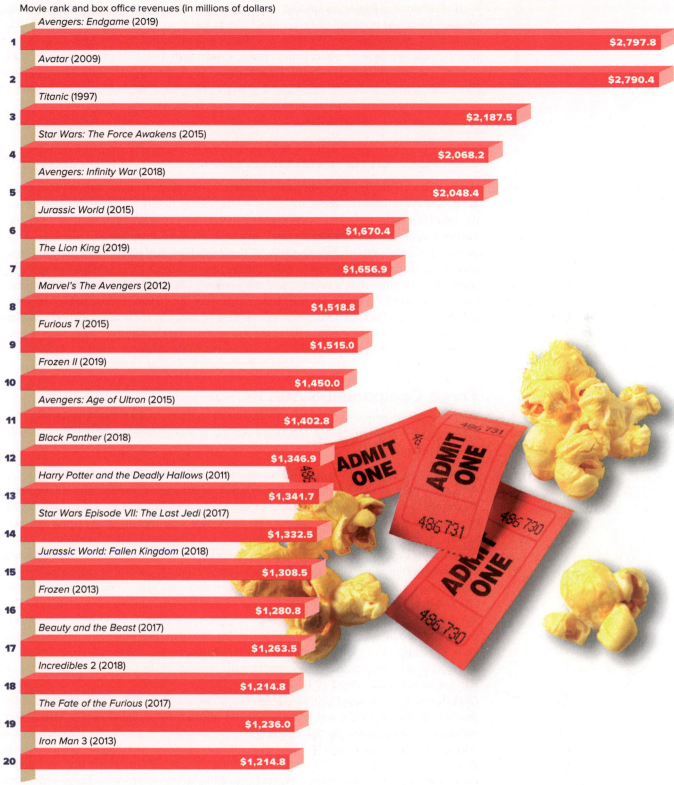

Rank	Movie	Revenue
1	*Avengers: Endgame* (2019)	$2,797.8
2	*Avatar* (2009)	$2,790.4
3	*Titanic* (1997)	$2,187.5
4	*Star Wars: The Force Awakens* (2015)	$2,068.2
5	*Avengers: Infinity War* (2018)	$2,048.4
6	*Jurassic World* (2015)	$1,670.4
7	*The Lion King* (2019)	$1,656.9
8	*Marvel's The Avengers* (2012)	$1,518.8
9	*Furious 7* (2015)	$1,515.0
10	*Frozen II* (2019)	$1,450.0
11	*Avengers: Age of Ultron* (2015)	$1,402.8
12	*Black Panther* (2018)	$1,346.9
13	*Harry Potter and the Deadly Hallows* (2011)	$1,341.7
14	*Star Wars Episode VII: The Last Jedi* (2017)	$1,332.5
15	*Jurassic World: Fallen Kingdom* (2018)	$1,308.5
16	*Frozen* (2013)	$1,280.8
17	*Beauty and the Beast* (2017)	$1,263.5
18	*Incredibles 2* (2018)	$1,214.8
19	*The Fate of the Furious* (2017)	$1,236.0
20	*Iron Man 3* (2013)	$1,214.8

▲ **Figure 6.1** Top 20 All-Time Worldwide Box Office Hits (in millions).

Source: "Top Lifetime Grosses." (2021).

(photo): Tony Cordoza/Alamy Stock Photo

it still produces scores of movies of merit for a wider audience–*12 Years a Slave* (2013), *The Assistant* (2020), *The Imitation Game* (2015), and *First Cow* (2020), for example. All eight Best Picture Academy Award nominees in 2021 were grown-up, important movies that had much to say about us as a people and as a culture: *The Father, Judas and the Black Messiah, Mank, Minari, Nomadland, Promising Young Woman, Sound of Metal,* and *The Trial of the Chicago 7.*

If Hollywood is fixated on kid and teen movies, why does it give us such treasures? True, Michael Eisner, as president of Paramount Pictures and then CEO of Disney, famously once wrote in an internal memo, "We have no obligation to make history. We have no obligation to make art. We have no obligation to make a statement. Our only obligation is to make money" (as quoted in Pulizzi, 2020). Nevertheless, the movie industry continues to produce films that indeed make history, art, and a statement while they make money. It does so because we buy tickets to those movies.

Scope and Nature of the Film Industry

Hollywood's record year of 1946 saw the sale of more than 4 billion tickets. Today, pandemic-free Americans buy about 1.2 billion movie theater tickets each year. In 2019, domestic box-office revenue was $11.4 billion, and 29 movies exceeded $100 million. Fifty-eight movies topped that amount worldwide; 2 of those—*Avengers: Endgame* and *The Lion King*—were billion-dollar movies. As impressive as these numbers may seem, movie industry insiders feel concern. On a per-capita basis, before the pandemic US moviegoing was at its lowest level in more than a century, and the average number of tickets bought by moviegoers was the lowest (3.5 tickets a year) it has been since 2002 (Ball, 2020). Today, about half of all Americans, 46%, go to the movies one time or less a year (Watson, 2019). The question the movie industry is asking about the future, then, one you can try to answer yourself after reading the essay, is "Will We Continue to Go to the Movies?"

Three Component Systems

There are three component systems in the movie industry—production, distribution, and exhibition. Each is undergoing significant change in the contemporary digital, converged media environment.

PRODUCTION Production is the making of movies. Between 700 and 800 feature-length films are produced annually in the United States, a large increase over the early 1980s, when, for example, in 1985, 288 features were produced. As we'll see later in this chapter, significant revenues from electronic sell-through (EST) are one reason for the increase, as is growing conglomerate ownership that demands more product for more markets.

Since the days of the Lumière brothers, movies have been shot on film. Today, almost none are, as film making has shifted to digital production. A handful of big-budget movies, titles requiring a specific look or feel, will shoot on film each year, for example, the Western *The Hateful Eight* (2015), fifties-style musical *West Side Story* (2021), retro super-hero flick *Wonder Woman 1984* (2020), and James Bond-style spy thriller *Tenet* (2020). Nonetheless, film shooting has become so unusual that major providers like Fugifilm and Kodak have ceased production of motion picture stock (Sax, 2016).

Another influence of technology can be seen in most of the top-grossing movies of the last few years. *Jurassic World* (2015), *Star Wars: The Force Awakens* (2015), *Captain America: Civil War* (2016), *Deadpool* (2016), *Spider-Man: Homecoming* (2017), *Black Panther* (2018), *Avengers: Endgame* (2019), and *Dune* (2020) are all marvels of digital effects. Digital filmmaking has made grand special effects not only possible but expected. Stunning special effects, of which *Titanic* (1997) and *Avatar* are fine examples, can make a good movie an excellent one. The downside of computer-generated special effects is that they can greatly increase production costs. *Avatar* cost more than $300 million to produce; *Avengers: Endgame* between $350 and $400 million. The *average* cost of producing and marketing a Hollywood feature is $100 million (Mueller, 2020), a figure inflated, in large part, by the demands of audience-expected digital spectacle.

Many observers see this increase in production costs as a major reason Hollywood studios are less willing to take creative chances in a big-budget film. However, lack of significant box-office growth, especially in summer blockbuster season, is one indication that moviegoers may be experiencing *special-effects fatigue*. "Today's computer-crazy visual-effects industry . . . has sucked the soul out of commercial cinema by churning out visuals like so much sausage,

CULTURAL FORUM
Will We Continue to Go to the Movies?

The data tell a troubling tale. The $11.4 billion box-office take of 2019 was a 4% decrease from the previous year, and the 1.24 billion tickets sold were among the smallest number in 25 years (McNary, 2020). In fact, in the wake of the 2020 coronavirus shutdown of America's movie houses, which produced an 80% decline in annual box office (Hoffman, 2021), 70% of the public said that, in the future, they would rather watch a first-run movie at home than in a theater (Vary, 2020). Even the Academy of Motion Pictures Arts and Sciences publicly expressed concern that moviegoers will "kick the habit," if they already hadn't (Cieply, 2020). So an issue often discussed in the cultural forum is, "Will people keep going to the movies?" As you might imagine, there is no shortage of answers.

1. *The last several years have seen too many bad movies.* Only big-budget sequels and higher-priced tickets for 3D movies saved box-office totals from decline. These made up for flops like *Maleficent: Mistress of Evil* (2019), *Call of the Wild* (2020), and *Dolittle* (2020).

2. Not unrelated, *fewer good movies* mean that not as many people are making it to the theater in the first place, denying them the opportunity to see trailers for and get excited about other films.

3. If there are good films, people go to the movies; if not, they go less frequently and they tend to forget about the movies as an option when looking for entertainment. Movie industry people call this *out of sight, out of mind*.

4. But what faces fans when they do arrive at the movies? A very *expensive* outing. The average ticket price has increased at twice the rate of inflation over the last several years, to $12.10. Add to this the cost of the overpriced Goobers, popcorn, and soda and the gas to get there, and "catching a flick" for a family of four comes to $152 per outing . . . quite expensive at a time when the at-home cost for two hours of on-demand movie viewing has dropped to nearly zero (Sharma, 2020).

5. And what happens when people get to their seats? The distinct likelihood of *noisy and possibly rude neighbors*, cell phone users, loud talkers, crying babies, and quite possibly antsy children.

6. But surely once the house goes dark, all is well. Well, no. People who have just paid handsomely to be at the movies are then faced with *full-length commercials before the trailers*. Almost every theater in America screens these commercials. And although a majority of Americans dislike them ("3 in 4," 2018), advertisers spend $1.2 billion dollars a year to buy them (Guttman, 2019). It's the movies; not TV!

7. Speaking of TV, this is, in fact, the industry's greatest fear: *new digital technologies*, especially wired homes, video on demand, high-definition smart TVs, and streaming services.

8. People's reliance on sophisticated in-home technologies poses an additional threat to the film industry because it presages a *generational shift away from movies*. It is precisely those young people who will be tomorrow's seat-fillers who are abandoning the theater experience with the least regret.

Enter Your Voice

- Do you go to the movies as much as you did when you were younger? If not, why not?
- If you remain a regular moviegoer, why? What makes the movie going experience worth the effort?
- When the 2020 coronavirus pandemic forced every movie house in the country to close, 37% of moviegoers said they planned to attend less often once the theaters reopened; 10% said they'd never go again (Vary, 2020). But director J. J. Abrams said people would indeed come back, sensing "a pent-up, desperate need to see each other—to socialize and have communal experiences" (in Barnes, 2020, p. BU7). What about you? Did the pandemic change your movie habits? Did you stay away or go back when theaters reopened?

taking us on an endless journey of dinosaur attacks, superhero mashups, and cities laid to waste that all blends together in viewers' minds," laments film critic Drew Turney (2018, p. 117).

But another technology, **cloud computing**, is helping moderate production costs. Cloud computing is the storage of system-operating software, including sophisticated and expensive digital and special-effects programs, on off-site, third-party servers hosted on the Internet that offer on-demand, for-lease access. Access to the cloud frees moviemakers, particularly smaller independent producers, from financial and technical limitations that might otherwise have stymied their productions.

DISTRIBUTION   Distribution was once as simple as making prints of films and shipping them to theaters. Now it means supplying these movies to television networks, cable and satellite networks, makers of DVDs, and Internet streaming companies. In all, a distributor must be able to offer a single movie in hundreds of different digital formats worldwide to accommodate the specific needs of the many digital retailers it must serve. The sheer scope of the distribution business ensures that large companies (most typically the big studios themselves) will dominate. In addition to making copies and guaranteeing their delivery, distributors now finance production and take responsibility for advertising and promotion and for setting and adjusting release dates.

The advertising and promotion budget for a Hollywood feature usually equals 50% of the production costs. Sometimes, the ratio of promotion to production costs is even higher. *Avengers: Endgame* may have cost upwards of $400 million to produce, but its studio, Disney, spent another $150 million in marketing and promotion, bringing the total to over half a billion dollars, the most expensive movie ever made (Mullaney, 2019). So spending almost as much to market a film as to make it is now standard practice, and the investment is seen as worthwhile, if not necessary. In fact, so important has promotion become to the financial success of a movie that studios such as Universal and MGM include their advertising and marketing people in the **green light process**, that is, the decision to make a picture in the first place. These promotion professionals can say yes or no to a film's production, and they must also declare how much money and effort they will put behind the film if they do vote yes.

Another important factor in a film's promotion and eventual financial success is the distributor's decision to release it to a certain number of screens. One strategy, called the **platform rollout**, is to open a movie on a few screens and hope that critical response, film festival success, and good word-of-mouth reviews from those who do see it will propel it to success. Naturally, the advantage of this approach for the distributor is that it can greatly reduce the cost of promotion. 20th Century Fox opened *The Post* on nine screens just before Christmas Day, 2017. It went into wide release—2,819 screens—3 weeks later after strong word of mouth and several film festival awards. It earned its producers more than $180 million on a production budget of $50 million ("The Post," 2018). Films likely to suffer at the hands of critics or from poor word of mouth—for example, *Underwater* (2020; 2,791 US screens) and *Pan* (2015; 11,000 screens globally)—typically open in thousands of theaters simultaneously. However, it is not uncommon for a potential hit to open on many screens, as *Avatar* did in 2009—on more than 18,300 worldwide—and as did *Avengers: Endgame,* which opened on 4,662 American screens in 2019.

EXHIBITION   There are currently 41,000 movie screens in the United States spread over 6,000 sites. The three largest American movie chains are AMC Entertainment (8,200 screens), Regal Cinemas (7,307 screens), and Cinemark USA (4,499 screens). These three

▲ Critics assailed *Titanic* for its weak storyline and two-dimensional characters, but the real stars of the world's first billion-dollar box-office hit were the special effects. Grand special effects, however, are no guarantee of success. Special-effects-laden *Cats* was an all-time box-office stinker, costing $200 million to make and promote but earning only $75 million worldwide in 2019, while 2009's *Paranormal Activity*, devoid of technical wizardry and made in seven days for $45,000, earned $170 million in global box office that year.
(left) 20th Century Fox/Courtesy Everett Collection; (middle) UNIVERSAL/WORKING TITLE FILMS/AMBLIN ENTERTAINMENT/APL Archive/Alamy Stock Photo; (right) Moviestore collection Ltd/Alamy Stock Photo

▲ Critically acclaimed *The Post* opened on nine US screens; critically panned *Underwater* opened on 2,791. Can you guess why?

(left) Ysanne Slide/Moviestore collection Ltd/Alamy Stock Photo; (right) BFA/Alamy Stock Photo

control half of all the country's screens and sell nearly 80% of all tickets. AMC and Cinemark have significant overseas presences, and AMC (Chinese) and Regal (British) have foreign ownership.

It is no surprise to any moviegoer that exhibitors make much of their money on concession sales of items that typically have an 80% profit margin, accounting for 40% of a theater's profits. This is the reason that matinees and budget nights are attractive promotions for theaters. A low-priced ticket pays dividends in overpriced popcorn and Dots. It's also the reason that 60% of moviegoers sneak contraband food into the theater (Friedman, 2014). Profits from concessions are also why many exhibitors present more than movies to keep seats filled and concessions flowing. Most theaters routinely schedule stand-up comedians, the NFL and NBA in 3D, live opera performances, big-name musical concerts, classic TV show marathons, and audience-participative screenings sometimes enhanced by airline-like dual pod seating, play areas, wine bars, restaurants and cafés, reserved seating, concierge desks, reclining leather seats, old-fashioned uniformed ushers, and touchpad gourmet-food ordering. Because 50% of America's movie seats typically go empty on the weekend, 75% on weekdays (Ebiri, 2020), exhibitors are engaging in a variety of other audience-friendly maneuvers, for example, loyalty programs, expanded ticket discounts, and subscription offers.

The Studios

Studios are at the heart of the movie business, and it's the studios that come to mind when we talk about Hollywood. There are major studios, corporate independents, and independent studios. The majors, who finance their films primarily through the profits of their own business, include Warner Bros., Columbia, Paramount, 20th Century Fox (owned by Disney), Universal, MGM/UA, and Disney. The **corporate independent studios** (so named because they produce movies that have the look and feel of independent films) include Sony Pictures Classics, New Line Cinema (Warner), Searchlight (Disney), and Focus Features (Universal). These companies are in fact specialty or niche divisions of the majors, designed to produce more sophisticated—but less costly—fare to (1) gain prestige for their parent studios and (2) earn significant cable, EST, and DVD income after their critically lauded and good word-of-mouth runs in the theaters. Focus Features, for example, is responsible for 2005 Best Picture Oscar winner *Brokeback Mountain* and 2018 nominee *Darkest Hour*; Searchlight is home to four recent Best Picture winners—*Slumdog Millionaire* (2008), *12 Years a Slave* (2013), *Birdman* (2014), and *The Shape of Water* (2018); New Line Cinema released the three *Lord of the Rings* films and all the *Rush Hour* movies; and Sony Pictures Classics brought to the screen Best Picture nominees *An Education* (2009), *Whiplash* (2014) and *Call Me By Your Name* (2017).

Despite the majors' and their specialty houses' big names and notoriety, they produce only about one-fifth of each year's feature films. The remainder come from independent studios, companies that raise money outside the studio system to produce their films. Lionsgate and Weinstein Company (renamed Lantern Entertainment in 2018) are two of the few remaining true independents in Hollywood, producing films like *Silver Linings Playbook*, *The Hateful Eight*, *The Imitation Game*, and the *Halloween* movies (Lantern Entertainment), as well as *The Hunger Games* trilogy, the *Twilight Saga*, the *Saw* and Tyler Perry movies, and the *Divergent* series (Lionsgate). Five of 2019's highest domestic grossing movies were from Lionsgate: *John Wick...Parabellum*, *Knives Out*, *Tyler Perry's Family Funeral*, *Scary Stories to Tell in the Dark*, and *Midway*. But countless other independents continue to churn out films, often with the hope of winning a distribution deal with one of the Hollywood studios. For example, *Paranormal Activity* was distributed by Paramount, which paid $300,000 for the rights; 2005 Oscar winner for Best Picture, *Crash*, from Stratus Films, was distributed by Lionsgate; and the 2004–2005 $100 million box-office hit *Million Dollar Baby*, from independent Lakeshore, was distributed by Warner Bros.

Independent films tend to have smaller budgets. Often this leads to much more imaginative filmmaking and more risk-taking than the big studios are willing to undertake. The 1969 independent film *Easy Rider*, which cost $370,000 to produce and made over $60 million in ticket sales, began the modern independent film boom. *My Big Fat Greek Wedding* (2002) cost $5 million to make and earned over $300 million in global box-office receipts. Some independent films with which you might be familiar are *Magic Mike* (2012), *Concrete Cowboy* (2020), Oscar winners for Best Screenplay *Pulp Fiction* (1994) and *The Pianist* (2002), 2015 Best Picture nominees *Brooklyn* and *Room*, *Boyhood* (2014), *Us* (2019), and Best Picture Oscar winners *Moonlight* (2017), *The Hurt Locker* (2009), and *Parasite* (2019).

A greater number of independents is now reaching audiences because of several factors, including a dramatic drop in what it costs to shoot and edit a movie on digital equipment (2018's hit horror movie *Unsane* from big-name director Steven Soderbergh was shot on three iPhones) and a drop in the cost of promoting a movie because of social media and websites such as YouTube. This low-cost-of-entry/reasonable-chance-of-success state of affairs has seen entry into the indie movie market from an increasingly wider array of sources. For example, *The Canyons* (2013) starring Lindsay Lohan; Zach Braff's *Wish I Was Here* (2014); Spike Lee's *Da Sweet Blood of Jesus* (2014); and the *Veronica Mars* movie (2013) are all independent films that were financed through online crowdfunding on Kickstarter, as was 2015's *Kung Fury*. Biographical portrait of Vincent van Gogh, *Loving Vincent* (2017), another Kickstarter flick starring big names such as Saoirse Ronan *(Lady Bird, Brooklyn)* and Chris O'Dowd *(Bridesmaids, The Cloverfield Paradox)*, won several national and international film awards.

Another factor is filmmakers' ability to distribute a movie using the Internet, either independently—using a platform dedicated specifically to that purpose such as MUBI—or through large-scale established operations such as Netflix and iTunes, as did the producers of *Snowpiercer* (2014) and *The Florida Project* (2017). In 2015, Netflix began producing features and Amazon announced plans to produce 12 films a year, screen them in theaters for a month or two, and then make them available to its Amazon Prime subscribers. Two years later, its *Manchester by the Sea* was the first movie from a streaming service to ever be nominated for an Academy Award. These "new indies" were joined in 2017 by Apple, which began producing feature-length movies for distribution on its Apple Music and Apple TV+ streaming services.

This perfect case study on the disruption wrought by convergence is not necessarily a welcomed development in filmland. If almost all production is digital, and virtually all distribution is digital, and digital video companies produce and distribute their works that sometimes debut in theaters, sometimes online, sometimes day-and-date, and sometimes in their own theaters (Netflix bought the legendary movie house Grauman's Egyptian in Los Angeles in 2020), what, ask many industry people, actually constitutes a "movie"? In fact, complaints about Netflix in particular forced industry-essential film festival Cannes to establish "theatrical distribution in France" as a requirement for entry into its legendary film competition, and for the American Academy Awards, at least a 1-week run in one of a handful of designated cities is required for Oscar eligibility (Alter, 2020).

◀ Indie movie *Parasite* not only won the Oscar for Best Picture in 2020, it had a global box office take of over $258 million. *NEON/MOVIESTORE COLLECTION LTD/Alamy Stock Photo*

◀ The smash success of *Easy Rider* (1969) ushered in the indie film boom. *Courtesy of Everett Collection*

Trends and Convergence in Moviemaking

Flat box office, increased production costs largely brought about by digital special-effects wizardry, and the "corporatization" of the independent film are only a few of the trends reshaping the film industry. There are several others, however, including some that many critics see as contributors to Hollywood's changing future.

Conglomeration and the Blockbuster Mentality

Other than MGM (itself bought by Amazon in 2021 for $8.45 billion), each of the majors is part of a large conglomerate. Paramount is owned by Viacom; Warner Bros. is part of the huge AT&T family of holdings; Disney is part of the giant conglomerate formed in the 1996 Disney/Capital Cities/ABC union; and Universal was bought by NBC's parent company, General Electric, in 2004 and later by cable TV giant Comcast in 2013. In 2018, Disney bought 20th Century Fox for $71 billion. According to many critics, this concentration of ownership forces the industry into a **blockbuster mentality**—filmmaking characterized by reduced risk-taking and more formulaic movies. Business concerns are said to dominate artistic considerations as accountants and financiers control more decisions once made by creative people.

"The most ominous change," in movie making, says Academy Award winning director Martin Scorsese, "has happened stealthily and under cover of night: the gradual but steady elimination of risk. Many films today are perfect products manufactured for immediate consumption. Many of them are well made by teams of talented individuals. All the same, they lack something essential to cinema: the unifying vision of an individual artist. Because, of course, the individual artist is the riskiest factor of all" (2019, p. A27).

One of the surest ways to limit risk is green-lighting **concept films**—movies that can be described in one line. *Godzilla* is about a giant, rogue monster. *Jurassic Park* is about giant, rogue dinosaurs. *Transformers* is about good giant alien robots who fight bad giant alien robots. International ownership and international distribution contribute to this phenomenon. High-concept films that depend little on characterization, plot development, and dialogue are easier to sell to foreign exhibitors than are more sophisticated films. *Fantastic Four* and other Marvel Comics heroes play well everywhere. Big-name stars also have international appeal. That's why they can command huge salaries. The importance of foreign distribution cannot be overstated.

Very few features make a profit on American box office. Much of their eventual profit comes from overseas sales. For example, 2016's *The Gods of Egypt* earned $31 million in US box office and another $113 million abroad; 2019's *Ralph Broke the Internet* took home $23 million domestically but $132 million globally. And it's not just domestic disappointments that do well overseas. The top-2 money makers of 2019, *Avengers: Endgame* ($858 million at home; $1.9 billion globally) and *The Lion King* ($543 million at home and $1.1 billion globally) both doubled their domestic take. Overseas box office accounts for about 70% of a studio movie's total ticket sales, and every one of the all-time top 20 Hollywood box office champions made more money abroad than it did domestically.

Critics contend that the blockbuster mentality has created an overreliance on a specific form of concept movie, the **IP-based movie**, productions based on intellectual property (IP)—that is, already existing stories, products, imaginary worlds, or characters that have a built-in fan base. We see this dependence-on-the-familiar play out in the abundance of sequels, remakes, and franchises that make their way to the big screen and in the scores of television, comic book, and video-game remakes that do so, as well.

SEQUELS, REMAKES, AND FRANCHISES How many *Batmans* have there been? *Jurassic Parks*? *American Pies* and *Terminators*? *Godzilla* flattened cities in 1954 and 1998, as well as in 2014 and 2019; we've shared excellent adventures with *Bill & Ted* in 1989, 1991, and 2020; people spotted the *Invisible Man* in 1933 and came out to see him again in 2021. Hollywood is making increasing use of **franchise films**, movies that are produced with the full intention of producing several sequels. Classic film franchises such as *James Bond* (beginning in 1962) and *Star Wars* (beginning in 1977) continue to churn out sequels over several decades with new casts, and many film franchises based on book series such as *Harry Potter* (beginning in 2001) are begun before all of the books are even written. Seventeen of the domestic top-20 grossing movies of 2019 (14 of the top-20 globally) were continuations of familiar franchises, giving credence to the old industry saying, "Nobody ever got fired for green-lighting a sequel."

But there are those who bristle at what is lost because of that timidity. Director Scorsese is one. "What's not there" he wrote, "is revelation, mystery or genuine emotional danger. Nothing is at risk. The pictures are made to satisfy a specific set of demands, and they are designed as variations on a finite number of themes . . . Everything in them is officially sanctioned because it can't really be any other way. That's the nature of modern film franchises: market-researched, audience-tested, vetted, modified, re-vetted and re-modified until they're ready for consumption" (2019, p. A27).

TELEVISION, COMIC BOOK, AND VIDEO-GAME REMAKES Teens and preteens make up a large proportion of the movie audience, and as a result many movies are adaptations

▲ *West Side Story* danced across movie screens in 1961 and again in 2021.
(left) SNAP/Entertainment Pictures/Alamy Stock Photo; (right) Twentieth Century Studios/Entertainment Pictures/Alamy Stock Photo

of television shows, comic books, and video games. In recent years *Bob's Burgers*, *Bewitched*, *Baywatch, Get Smart, Sex and the City, The Simpsons, 21 Jump Street*, and *Star Trek* have moved from small to big screens. *The 6 Million Dollar Man* made it to the movies, too, but with an upgrade to the *Six Billion Dollar Man*. *The Addams Family*, *Aquaman, Richie Rich, Spider-Man, Batman*, and *Superman* have traveled from the comics, through television, to the silver screen. *Sin City, Iron Man, Guardians of the Galaxy*, *Captain America, The Avengers, X-Men, Road to Perdition, 300, Men in Black, Fantastic Four*, and *The Hulk* have moved from comic books and graphic novels to movies. *Assassin's Creed, Resident Evil*, and *Mortal Kombat* went from Xbox to box office. In addition to their established IP appeal, another reason for the preponderance of TV, comic book, and video-game remakes may well be that these titles are especially attractive to studios because of their built-in merchandise tie-in appeal. For example, *Toy Story 3* (2018) made $1 billion at the global box office but $10 billion at toy stores and fast-food restaurants (Shelton, 2020).

MERCHANDISE TIE-INS Another byproduct of blockbuster thinking is merchandise tie-ins. Films are sometimes produced as much for their ability to generate a market for nonfilm products as for their intrinsic value as movies. Hit 2012 kids' film *The Lorax* had more than 70 "product partners." *Star Wars: The Force Awakens* made $2 billion at the box office and nearly $6 billion more in merchandise sales. The Harry Potter films have earned nearly $8 billion in ticket sales but over $25 billion in merchandise fees (Shelton, 2020). In one year, 2019, one studio alone, Disney, collected $57.4 billion in licensing fees (Richter, 2021). And as almost all of us know, it is nearly impossible to buy a meal at McDonald's, Burger King, or Taco Bell without being offered a movie tie-in product. Studios often believe it is riskier to make a $7 million film with no merchandising potential than a $250 million movie with greater merchandising appeal.

PRODUCT PLACEMENT Many movies are serving double duty as commercials. We'll discuss this $20 billion a year global phenomenon in detail later in the chapter as a media literacy issue.

AUDIENCE RESEARCH Because the blockbuster mentality encourages "cover-my-rear" thinking, before a movie is released, sometimes even before it is made, its script, concept, plot, and characters are subjected to market testing. Often multiple endings are produced and tested with sample audiences by companies such as National Research Group and Marketcast. Sometimes wholesale changes are made. For example, Sony spent $6 million reshooting scenes for its 2017 *The Dark Tower* after test audiences rated the film poorly. In 2020 Disney delayed the release and reshot *Woman in the Window* to make clearer its central mystery after test audiences were confused by the original version.

Filmmakers are divided over the value of testing. "For every film that has been reportedly 'saved' through extensive test screenings," writes film critic Rich Haridy, "you could find another to show that they're a complete waste of time" (2017). Testing convinced Disney that *Avengers: Endgame*'s 3-hour run-time was fine with audiences, but testing also produced data indicating that *Fight Club* (1999) would be "the flop of the century"; it made more than $100 million at the box office and has become a cult favorite, earning even more on cable, DVD, video-on-demand (VOD), and EST.

If testing is so unreliable, ask film purists, what is to become of the filmmaker's genius? What separates these market-tested films from any other commodity? *New York Times* film critic Brooks Barnes explains the dilemma facing blockbuster-driven Hollywood: "Forget zombies," he wrote. "The data crunchers are invading Hollywood. . . . As the stakes of making movies become ever higher, Hollywood leans ever harder on research to minimize guesswork." Research also serves as a "duck-and-cover technique—for when the inevitable argument of 'I am not going to take the blame if this movie doesn't work' comes up" (Barnes, 2013, p. A1). In other words, Hollywood can stand only so much creative freedom when a $400 million **tentpole** (an expensive blockbuster around which a studio plans its other releases) is in the works.

Convergence Reshapes the Movie Business

So intertwined are today's movie and television industries that it is often meaningless to discuss them separately. As much as 70% of the production undertaken by the seven largest studios is for smaller screens, and the percentage of their revenues from that source ranges between 35% and 45% (Dawson, 2016). But the growing relationship between **theatrical films**—those produced originally for theater exhibition—and television is the result of technological changes in the latter. The convergence of film with satellite, cable, VOD, pay-per-view, DVD, and Internet streaming has provided immense distribution and exhibition opportunities for the movies. For example, in 1947 box-office receipts accounted for 95% of the studios' film revenues. Now they make up just 20%. Today's distributors make three times as much from domestic home entertainment (DVD, network and cable television, EST, and streaming) as they do from rentals to movie theaters.

Although still lucrative, DVD sales are a declining source of studio income (Arnold, 2020). In 2012, for the first time, Americans spent more money downloading and streaming movies than they did buying discs, a trend that has since accelerated. This is because there is nothing to physically manufacture and ship for digital distribution of movies, so studio profit margins are much higher than can be realized with DVDs. Where a solid box-office performer—*The Hangover* (2009), for example—could once sell 10 million discs in its first six months of release, today's movies are far more likely to be downloaded for a few dollars on VOD, bought on EST, or streamed from a subscription service rather than purchased as a disc for $15.

The convenience of digital movies has encouraged this digital distribution and exhibition. In 2014 Paramount announced that it would no longer release movies on film in the United States, with the other majors quickly following suit (Scott & Dargis, 2014). As a result, almost all American movie screens have been converted to digital exhibition. Digital exhibition's savings in money and labor to both exhibitor and distributor are dramatic. Rather than making several thousand film prints to be physically transported to individual theaters in metal cans, the electronic distribution of digital movies costs under $100 per screen for the entire process (Stewart & Cohen, 2013).

Although once slowed by fears of piracy, the online distribution of feature films to homes is now routine. An American home with Internet and cable access has tens of thousands of full-length movies and television shows to choose from at any given moment. Netflix, which originally delivered DVDs to people's homes by mail, has discontinued that service in every country other than the United States, where it still services 2 million subscribers. Now focusing on streaming, it operates in 190 countries, bringing its subscriber total to 167 million, with 65 million in the United States alone (Moody, 2020).

Netflix is not the only source for streamed movies; Internet giants Google Play, Amazon Prime, Apple TV+, Disney+, and the Comcast cable operation are only a few of the more than 270 online video streaming services available to American audiences, offering everything from classic and niche films to the latest box-office hits (Barnes, 2019). In addition, and as you read in Chapter 2, there are multiple companies offering day-and-date digital home delivery of feature films.

But it was Universal's announcement in the midst of the 2020 coronavirus closure of the world's movie houses that put the threat of digital distribution to the future of in-theater exhibition into stark relief. When the Comcast cable company-owned studio announced it would begin releasing its movies directly to consumers for $20 each, it not only ignited an exhibitor boycott of any future releases, it forced the industry as a whole to reconsider the long-standing 90-day **theatrical window**–the time from when a movie is first released to theaters until it can be sold directly to retailers and the public. Not only do newcomers like Netflix and Amazon Prime ignore that tradition, but what, other than protecting exhibitor profits, studios asked, was sacred about 90 days, especially when those studios retained 80% of all digital rental and purchase fees compared to 50% of box office sales (Friedman, 2020)?

Finally, direct-to-home digital distribution of movies may be even more robust than described here because of new technologies that free downloads from the computer screen. For example, Netflix, LG Electronics, Amazon, and TiVo all sell devices that allow downloads directly to TV set-top boxes, avoiding the computer altogether; and with Apple Airplay, you can even send content from your iPhone or iPad to play through on a smart TV. See Chapter 10 for more about Internet distribution of film and video content.

Digital production has had an additional effect beyond encouraging digital distribution and exhibition. The surprise 1999 hit *The Blair Witch Project* is considered the start of the growing **microcinema** movement through which filmmakers using digital video cameras and desktop digital editing programs are finding audiences, both in theaters and online, for their low-budget (sometimes as little as $10,000) features. The 2009 success of *Paranormal Activity* reinforced interest in microcinema, interest that has been buoyed by the willingness of A-list talent to get involved with these "small" pictures; for example, Rashida Jones (*Parks and Recreation*), Andy Samberg (*Saturday Night Live*), and Elijah Wood (*The Lord of the Rings*) teamed up on *Celeste and Jesse Forever* (2012), and 2016's *Brother Nature* starred Bill Pullman (*Independence Day*) and Rita Wilson (*Mama Mia! Here We Go Again*).

Smartphones, Tablets, and Social Networking Sites

As they have with all media, smartphones, tablets, and social media are reshaping the relationship between audiences and the movies. Although director David Lynch is skeptical of small-screen viewing, stating, "If you're playing the movie on a telephone, you will never in a trillion years experience the film" (in Kenny, 2016, p. AR16), people are indeed starting to warm to movies on their mobile devices. In late 2016, for the first time, mobile devices accounted for more than 50% of all Internet video views, with half of all that consumption longer than 5 minutes (Ooyala, 2016).

Exhibitors are also benefiting from mobile technology. There are ticket-buying apps such as Fandango (embedded in Facebook and Snapchat feeds and serving 26,000 screens) and those of virtually all the major theater chains. Fandango's instant ratings feature, however, can kill a movie if ticket buyers alert their friends to a stinker, and coupled with its online movie-rating site Rotten Tomatoes, it has become a significant force in shaping fans' movie habits. Another app, Atom, offers more than movie times and ticket buying. It provides recommendations based not only on previous theater visits but also on the commentary on linked social network accounts; group discounts for linked purchases, which can be charged to individuals; exclusive merchandise sales to featured movies; concession preorders; and **dynamic pricing**, selling seats at varying prices depending on availability and demand.

Major and independent studios are also making use of social networking for the promotion of their films. Fans not only can visit the Miramax, Paramount, Universal Studios,

Warner Bros., Lionsgate, and Focus Features official pages on Facebook, but they can also use the sites' many features to "like" and share quotations, clips, trailers, and other features of the movies they enjoy with their friends. This use of social networking taps into an audience that is comfortable with the Internet and is more likely to stream movies through their smartphones and tablets with apps such as Netflix and Hulu.

Of course, with everyone linked by social media, reaction time is instantaneous, so if fans think a movie is a bomb, it will surely be. The industry sees this migration of movies to mobile screens as a mixed blessing. Yes, studios and distributors have many more ways to get content to audiences, but as fans (especially young people already comfortable with relatively small, mobile screens) increasingly watch movies in places other than theaters, what happens to what we have called "the movies" for more than a century?

DEVELOPING MEDIA LITERACY SKILLS
Recognizing Product Placements

Transformers (the toy) may be the stars of several movies by that name, but they share screen time with General Motors cars, apparently the only brand-name vehicles in Los Angeles or whatever other city needs saving. The 9 nominees for the 2020 Academy Award Best Picture collectively had placements for 350 brands across 135 different types of products. Together, they took in $166 million in product placement advertising. *Ford vs. Ferrari* made $55.8 million from 145 brands; *The Irishman* $34.7 million from 62; and *Once Upon a Time in Hollywood* made $31.3 million from 87 different sponsors ("Product Placement," 2020).

The practice of placing brand-name products in movies is not new. The 1920's Buster Keaton silent feature *Garage* had one of the first placements (Red Crown Gasoline); Hollywood's first Best Picture Oscar winner *Wings* featured Hershey chocolate bars; and in 1951 Katherine Hepburn famously dumped Gordon's gin into the river from *The African Queen* (Smith, 2020).

But in today's movie industry, product placement has expanded into a business in its own right. About 100 product placement agencies are operating in Hollywood, and there's even an industry association, the Entertainment Resources and Marketing Association (ERMA). The attraction of product placements for sponsors is obvious. For one flat fee paid up front, a product that appears in a movie is in actuality a commercial that lives forever—first on the big screen, then on purchased and rented discs, downloads, and streaming, and then on television and cable. That commercial is also likely to have worldwide distribution.

Many people in and outside the movie industry see product placement as inherently deceptive. "Why not identify the ads for what they are?" From a media literacy standpoint, the issue is the degree to which artistic decisions are being placed second to obligations to sponsors. Scripts are altered and camera angles are chosen to accommodate paid-for placements. For example, laundry detergent Tide replaced Britain's Daz in the script of *The Theory of Everything* (2014) because it was more familiar to American audiences. Apple refuses to allow cinema bad guys to use iPhones (Sharf, 2020). These may seem like a small concessions, but what of the many other small and large ones of which the audience is unaware? Media critic Emily Nussbaum (2015) sees the problem as even deeper than altered scripts; she sees betrayal:

> There is no art form that doesn't run a three-legged race with the sponsors that support its production, and the weaker an industry gets . . . the more ethical resistance flags. But readers [of novels] would be grossed out to hear that [autobiographical novelist] Karl Ove Knausgaard had accepted a bribe to put the Talking Heads into his childhood memories. They'd be angry if Stephen Sondheim slipped a Dewar's jingle into [his musical] *Company*. That's not priggishness or élitism. It's a belief that art is powerful, that storytelling is real, that when we immerse ourselves in that way it's a vulnerable act of trust. (p. 99)

But, argue defenders of the practice, there is no betrayal; products are part of everything we do in everyday life. All the products around us have brand names. Isn't it a lie to suggest that the things we come into constant contact with don't have logos?

Knowing how media content is funded and how that financial support shapes content is an important aspect of understanding the mass communication process. Therefore, an awareness of the efforts of the movie industry to maximize income from its films is central to good film literacy.

Does it trouble you that content is altered, even if sometimes only minimally, to allow for these brand identifications? To what extent would script alterations have to occur to accommodate paid-for messages before you find them intrusive? Do you think it is fair or honest for a moviemaker who promises you film content in exchange for your money to turn you into what amounts to a television viewer by advertising sponsors' products?

Literate film consumers may answer these questions differently, especially as individuals hold cinema in varying degrees of esteem—but they should answer them. And what do you make of the recent Hollywood product placement trend, **branding films**, the sponsor-financing of movies to advance a manufacturer's product line. Unilever (Dove soap) co-financed *The Women* (2008), and Chrysler underwrote *Blue Valentine* (2010). Marriott underwrote *Two Bellmen* (2015) and its two sequels (2016 and 2017). *Uncle Drew* (2018) is a feature-length movie/commercial financed by soda maker Pepsi based on a character in its TV commercials, an elderly, out-of-shape basketball fan, played in the ad and in the movie by real professional basketball player Kyrie Irving.

And in a marriage of branded films with IP themes, makers of copyrighted and trademarked materials now produce films featuring those things, such as *The Lego Movies* and *The Teenage Mutant Ninja Turtle Movies*. Hasbro, the world's second-largest toy maker, was once content to co-finance a picture a year based on its popular board games such as Candy Land and Monopoly. Then, in 2014, it announced it would begin producing movies in its own studio, Allspark Pictures. *My Little Pony* and *Jem and the Holograms* were its first two releases. Mattel Toys did the same in 2018, founding Mattel Films, to bring properties like Barbie, Hot Wheels, American Girl, and Thomas & Friends to the big screen. The goal, said company CEO Ynon Kreiz, was to "to shift the company away from manufacturing toys and toward managing and monetizing its brands" (in Forbes, 2018).

A media-literate movie fan, maybe one who was a child at one point in life, might ask not only when did movies become brands, but when did toys become brands to be managed and monetized?

◀ Even product placement is unnecessary when the brand is the star of the movie. Here's Mattel's Barbie headlining *Rock 'N Roll Royals*.
Atlaspix/Alamy Stock Photo

MEDIA LITERACY CHALLENGE
Product Placement in Movies

Choose two films. Try for variation, for example, a big-budget blockbuster and a romantic comedy of your choice. List every example of product placement that you can find. In which instances do you believe the film's content was altered, however minimally, to accommodate the placement? Product placement proponents argue that this is a small price to pay for the "reality" that using real brands brings to a film. Do you agree or disagree? Explain your answer in terms of your *expectations of movies' content* and your *ability to recognize when advertising and movie genre conventions are being mixed*. Tackle this one individually, committing your findings to writing, or make it a challenge against one or more classmates.

Resources for Review and Discussion

REVIEW POINTS: TYING CONTENT TO LEARNING OUTCOMES

▶ **Recognize the history and development of the film industry and film itself as a medium.**
- Film's beginnings reside in the efforts of entrepreneurs such as Eadweard Muybridge and inventors like Thomas Edison and William Dickson.
- Photography, an essential precursor to movies, was developed by Hannibal Goodwin, George Eastman, Joseph Nicéphore Niépce, Louis Daguerre, and William Henry Fox Talbot.
- Edison and the Lumière brothers began commercial motion picture exhibition, little more than representations of everyday life. George Méliès added narrative, Edwin S. Porter added montage, and D. W. Griffith developed the full-length feature film.
- Movies became big business at the turn of the 20th century, one dominated by big studios, but change soon came in the form of talkies, scandal, control, and new genres to fend off the impacts of the Great Depression.

▶ **Describe the cultural value of film and the implications of the blockbuster mentality for film as an important artistic and cultural medium.**
- Conglomeration and concentration affect the movie industry, leading to an overreliance on blockbuster films for its success.
- Debate exists over whether film can survive as an important medium if it continues to give its youth-dominated audience what it wants.
- The annual roster of adult, important movies suggests that film can give all audiences what they want.

▶ **Summarize the three components of the film industry—production, distribution, and exhibition.**
- Production is the making of movies, almost universally using digital technology.

- Distribution is supplying movies to television and cable networks, DVD makers, Internet streaming and downloading services, and even to individual viewers.
- Exhibition is showing movies in a theater, almost universally using digital technologies.

▶ **Explain how the organizational and economic nature of the contemporary film industry shapes the content of its films.**
- Studios are at the heart of the movie business and are increasingly in control of the three component systems.
- There are major, corporate independent, and independent studios.

▶ **Describe the promise and peril of convergence and the new digital technologies to film as we know it.**
- Convergence is reshaping the industry, promising to alter its structure and economics, especially as new distribution models fueled by the Internet and related mobile technologies become even more common than they are now.

▶ **Recall that production is becoming more expensive and, simultaneously, less expensive.**
- Distribution is becoming more complex, getting more movies to more people over more platforms.
- Exhibition is increasingly out-of-theater and mobile, but is it still "the movies"?

▶ **Apply film-watching media literacy skills, especially in interpreting merchandise tie-ins and product placements.**
- The financial benefits of merchandise tie-ins and product licensing are factors in the industry's overreliance on big-budget, youth-oriented movies (and the relative scarcity of more mature films).
- The inclusion of product placements in films can shape their scripts and production practices, either for better or worse.

KEY TERMS

zoopraxiscope, 126

persistence of vision, 126

kinetograph, 126

daguerreotype, 126

calotype, 126

kinetoscope, 126

cinématographe, 127

montage, 127

nickelodeons, 128

factory studios, 128

movie palaces, 130

double feature, 132

B-movie, 132

vertical integration, 132

block booking, 133

cloud computing, 137

green light process, 138

platform rollout, 138

corporate independent
   studios, 139

blockbuster mentality, 142

concept films, 142

IP-based movie, 142

franchise films, 142

tentpole, 144

theatrical films, 144

theatrical window, 145

microcinema, 145

dynamic pricing, 145

branding films, 147

QUESTIONS FOR REVIEW

1. What are the kinetograph, kinetoscope, cinématographe, daguerreotype, calotype, and nickelodeon?

2. What were Méliès's, Porter's, and Griffith's contributions to film as a narrative medium?

3. What was the Motion Picture Patents Company, and how did it influence the content and development of the movie industry?

4. What societal, technical, and artistic factors shaped the development of movies before World War II?

5. What are the three component systems of the movie industry?

6. What are major and corporate independent studios? What is an independent?

7. What are concept films? IP-based movies? Product tie-ins? Product placement?

8. What is platform rollout? When and why is it used?

9. How are digitization and convergence reshaping exhibition? Distribution? Production?

10. What is dynamic pricing? What digital technology makes it possible?

To maximize your study time, check out CONNECT to access the SmartBook study module for this chapter, watch videos, and explore other resources.

QUESTIONS FOR CRITICAL THINKING AND DISCUSSION

1. What do you think of the impact of the blockbuster mentality on movies? Should profit always be the determining factor in producing movie content? Why or why not?

2. Are you a fan of independent movies? When you are watching a movie, how can you tell that it's an independent? If you are an indie fan, do you welcome the microcinema movement? Why or why not?

3. Most industry watchers see the new distribution model promised by digitization of the three component systems as inevitably changing the economics of Hollywood. Some, though, think it will produce better movies. Do you agree or disagree? Why?

REFERENCES

1. Alter, R. (2020, April 28). Academy changes mind, says streaming movies can win Oscars. *New York*. Retrieved from https://www.vulture.com/2020/04/oscars-2021-eligibility-streaming-movies.html

2. Arnold, T. (2020, January 13). U.S. home entertainment market topped $25 billion in 2019, with 63% coming from streaming. *Variety*. Retrieved from https://variety.com/2020/digital/news/2019-us-home-entertainment-market-25-billion-1203463878/

3. Ball, M. (2020, February 7). Hollywood box office booms even as Americans stay home and chill. *Bloomberg*. Retrieved from https://www.bloomberg.com/news/articles/2020-02-07/hollywood-box-office-numbers-surge-even-as-americans-stay-home

4. Barnes, B. (2020, November 29). Hollywood's end, the sequel. Now streaming. *New York Times*, pp. BU6–7.

5. Barnes, B. (2019, December 1). The streaming era has finally arrived. Everything is about to change. *New York Times*, pp. F3–F4.

6. Barnes, B. (2013, May 6). Solving equation of a hit film script, with data. *New York Times*. Retrieved from https://www.nytimes.com/2013/05/06/business/media/solving-equation-of-a-hit-film-script-with-data.html

7. Bogle, D. (1989). *Toms, coons, mulattos, mammies, & bucks: An interpretive history of blacks in American films*. New York: Continuum.

8. Cieply, M. (2020, July 26). Even the Academy quietly warns: Moviegoers may break the habit. *Deadline*. Retrieved from https://deadline.com/2020/07/even-academy-warns-moviegoers-may-break-habit-1202995049/

9. Dargis, M., & Scott, A. O. (2019, September 15). Some thumbs up. Some thumbs down. Finger-wagging, too. *New York Times*, p. AR59.

10. Dawson, J. (2016, October 25). Studios turn up the TV. *Variety*, p. 23.

11. Denby, D. (2016, May 2). Sex and sexier. *New Yorker*, pp. 66–72.

12. Ebiri, B. (2020, May 26). What will make Americans feel comfortable going out to the movies again? *New York*. Retrieved from https://www.vulture.com/2020/05/movie-theaters-coronavirus.html

13. Friedman, W. (2014, January 10). TV may benefit from decline in moviegoing. *MediaPost*. Retrieved from http://www.mediapost.com/publications/article/217075/tv-may-benefit-from-decline-in-moviegoing.html

14. Forbes, T. (2018, September 7). Brenner to head Mattel Films, giving Barbie a Hollywood presence. *MediaPost*. Retrieved from https://www.mediapost.com/publications/article/324799/brenner-to-head-mattel-films-giving-barbie-a-holl.html

15. Friedman, W. (2020, May 4). Should studios, movie theaters consider new TV deals? *MediaPost*. Retrieved from https://www.mediapost.com/publications/article/350933/should-studios-movie-theaters-consider-new-tv-dea.html

16. Gray, T. (2020, October 21). The trailblazer. *Variety*, p. 33.

17. Guttman, A. (2019, December 12). Cinema advertising spending in North America 2002-2022. *Statista*. Retrieved from https://www.statista.com/statistics/882016/cinema-advertising-expenditure-in-north-america/

18. Haridy, R. (2017, July 31). Watching the watchers: The high-tech tools behind Hollywood test screenings. *New Atlas*. Retrieved from https://newatlas.com/neuroscience-watching-movies/50686/

19. Hoffman, J. (2021, January 2). 2020: A box office bust. *Vanity Fair*. Retrieved from https://www.vanityfair.com/hollywood/2021/01/2020-a-box-office-bust#:~:text=According%20to%20The%20Hollywood%20Reporter,is%20estimated%20at%20%242.3%20billion.

20. Kenny, G. (2016, November 13). Why Netflix is letting movie lovers down. *New York Times*, p. AR16.

21. Mast, G., & Kawin, B. F. (1996). *A short history of the movies.* Boston: Allyn & Bacon.

22. McNary, D. (2020, January 28). Domestic top 100: Disney dominates a down year. *Variety*, p. 20.

23. Menard, L. (2021, February 8). Now do it as you. *New Yorker*, pp. 59–64.

24. Moody, J. (2020, June 16). Netflix subscribers and revenue by country. *Comparitech*. Retrieved from https://www.comparitech.com/tv-streaming/netflix-subscribers/

25. Mueller, A. (2020, April 28). Why movies cost so much to make. *Investopedia*. Retrieved from https://www.investopedia.com/financial-edge/0611/why-movies-cost-so-much-to-make.aspx

26. Mullaney, J. (2019, May 11). How much did it cost to make "Avengers: Endgame"? *Cheatsheet*. Retrieved from https://www.cheatsheet.com/entertainment/avengers-endgame-production-cost.html/#:~:text=The%20movie%20cost%20%24350%20million%20to%20make

27. Nussbaum, E. (2015, October 12). The price is right. *New Yorker*, pp. 95–99.

28. Ooyala. (2016, December). Cord cutters on the march. Retrieved from http://go.ooyala.com/wf-video-index-q3-2016

29. "The Post." (2018, October 14). *Box Office Mojo*. Retrieved from https://www.boxofficemojo.com/movies/?id=untitledstevenspielberg.htm

30. "Product placement in 2020 Oscars Best Picture nominees–92nd Academy Awards." (2020, January 22). *Concave Brand Tracking*. Retrieved from https://concavebt.com/product-placement-2020-oscars-best-picture-nominees-92nd-academy-award/

31. Pulizzi, J. (2020, January 16). Do we have to create art? *Joepulizzi.com*. Retrieved from https://www.joepulizzi.com/news/do-we-have-to-create-art/

32. Richter, F. (2021, September 28). Licensed merch: Disney the clear number 1. *Statista*. Retrieved from https://www.statista.com/chart/11509/top-10-merchandise-licensors/

33. Sampson, H. T. (1977). *Blacks in black and white: A source book on black films.* Metuchen, NJ: Scarecrow Press.

34. Sax, D. (2016, Fall/Winter). The real revenge. *Columbia Journalism Review*, pp. 36–38.

35. Sharf, Z. (2020, February 2020). Rian Johnson reveals Apple won't allow bad guys in movies to use iPhones. *Salon*. Retrieved from https://www.salon.com/2020/02/27/rian-johnson-reveals-apple-wont-allow-bad-guys-in-movies-to-use-iphones_partner/

36. Scorsese, M. (2019, November 5). I said Marvel Movies aren't cinema. Let me explain. *New York Times*, p. A27.

37. Scott, A. O., and Dargis, M. (2014, May 4). Memo to Hollywood. *The New York Times*, pp. 23, 34.

38. Sharma, N. (2020, May 11). How much it does cost to watch a movie in theaters 2020. *Storyfi*. Retrieved from https://www.storefyi.com/blogs/blog/movie-watching-cost-2019

39. Shelton, J. (2020, April 21). Movies that made more money on merchandising than at the box office. *Ranker*. Retrieved from https://www.ranker.com/list/movies-that-made-money-merchandising/jacob-shelton

40. Smith, K. (2020, February 8). 5 times product placement improved the films it was in (& 5 times it was just distracting). *Screen Rant*. Retrieved from https://screenrant.com/product-placement-improved-films-distracting/

41. Stewart, A., & Cohen, D. S. (2013, April 16). The end. *Variety*, pp. 40–47.

42. Talbot, M. (2019, November 4). Out of frame. *New Yorker*, pp. 69–73.

43. "3 in 4 people feel they're seeing more ads now. How to break through the clutter?" (2018, February 7). *Marketing Charts*. Retrieved from https://www.marketingcharts.com/advertising-trends-82144

44. "Top Lifetime Grosses." (2021, June 10). *Box Office Mojo*. Retrieved from https://www.boxofficemojo.com/chart/top_lifetime_gross/?area=XWW

45. Turney, D. (2018, September 20). Volume threatens perception of VFX. *Variety*, pp. 117–118.

46. Vary, A. B. (2020, May 20). Fear factor goes viral. *Variety*, pp. 15–16.

47. Watson, A. (2020, April 24). U.S. frequent moviegoers 2017-2019, by age group. *Statista*. Retrieved from https://www.statista.com/statistics/251466/us-movie-theater-audience-by-age/

48. Watson, A. (2019, August 27). Frequency of going to the movies in the U.S. 2019. *Statista*. Retrieved from https://www.statista.com/statistics/264396/frequency-of-going-to-the-movies-in-the-us/

Cultural Forum Blue Column icon, Media Literacy Red Torch Icon, Using Media Green Gear icon, Developing Media book in starburst icon: ©McGraw Hill

7 Radio, Recording, and Popular Music

◀ Thirty dollars to download a beat; $20 in studio time; uploaded to TikTok, then a deal with a major label. Lil Nas X's *Old Town Road* was 2019's most consumed song, streamed 2.5 billion times.

Mario Anzuoni/REUTERS/Alamy Stock Photo

Learning Objectives

Radio was the first electronic mass medium, and it was the first national broadcast medium. It produced the networks, program genres, and stars that made television an instant success. But for many years radio and records were young people's media; they gave voice to a generation. As such, they may be our most personally significant mass media. After studying this chapter, you should be able to

▶ Recognize the history and development of the radio and sound recording industries and radio and sound recording themselves as media.

▶ Describe the importance of early financing and regulatory decisions regarding radio and how they have shaped the nature of contemporary broadcasting.

▶ Explain how the organizational and economic natures of the contemporary radio and sound recording industries shape the content of both media.

▶ Identify new and converging radio and recording technologies and their potential impact on music, the industries themselves, and listeners.

▶ Apply key music-listening media literacy skills, especially in assessing the benefits and drawbacks of algorithm-based music consumption.

1844 Samuel Morse's telegraph

1860 Scott's phonautograph

1876 Alexander Graham Bell's telephone

1877 ▶ Edison patents "talking machine" • • • • • • • • • • • • •

1896 Marconi sends wireless signal over 2 miles

1899 Marconi sends wireless signal across the English Channel

Mooziic/Alamy Stock Photo

~1900 Tesla and Marconi file radio patents

1903 ▶ Marconi sends first wireless signal across the Atlantic • • • • • • • • • • • • • • •

1905 Columbia Phonograph Company develops two-sided disc

1906 Fessenden makes first public broadcast of voice and music; DeForest invents audion tube

1910 Wireless Ship Act of 1910

1912 Radio Act of 1912

1916 Sarnoff sends Radio Music Box Memo

1919 Radio Corporation of America formed

1920 KDKA goes on air

1922 First radio commercial

1900

Comstock Images/Alamy Stock Photo

1926 NBC, first radio network

1927 Radio Act; Federal Radio Commission

1934 Communications Act; Federal Communications Commission

1939 Television introduced at World's Fair; FM goes on air

1946 GIs return from Germany with tape recorder

1947 Columbia Records introduces 33⅓ rpm disc

1949 ▶ Development of the DJ • • • • • • • • • • • • • •

1925

H. ARMSTRONG ROBERTS/ ClassicStock/Alamy Stock Photo

1951 Car radios exceed home sets

Mid-50s Network affiliation halved

1955 ▶ DJ Freed brings R&B to New York • • • • • • • • •

Late-50s National billings drop nearly 80%

1950

Edd Westmacott/Alamy Stock Photo

1983 ▶ CD introduced • • • • • • • •

1987 MP3 developed

1996 Telecommunications Act

1975

2001 Satellite radio begins

2002 Terrestrial digital radio

2003 ▶ iTunes • • • • • • • • • • •

2005 *MGM v. Grokster* P2P decision

2011 Digital music sales surpass physical sales

2014 Apple retires the iPod; Patreon founded

2015 Catalog sales outpace new releases for first time

2017 Physical music sales surpass digital music sales; Kickstarter funds 25,000th music project

2018 Apple Podcast's 50 billionth podcast; Denmark declares stream ripping illegal

2019 *Billboard* counts video streams in music chart rankings

2020 Coronavirus in the US; British Parliament investigates streaming royalty payments

2000

Digital Vision/Photodisc/Getty Images

Jill Braaten/McGraw Hill

"CAN WE LISTEN TO THE RADIO?"

"We are listening to the radio."

"I mean something other than this."

"You want music?"

"Yes, please, anything but public radio. Too much talk."

"OK. Here."

"What! That's the classical music station!"

"What's wrong with that?"

"Nothing . . . much."

"What's that supposed to mean, 'Nothing . . . much'?"

"Nothing . . . much. Let me choose."

"OK. You find a station."

"Fine. Here."

"What's that?"

"It's the New Hot One. All the hits all the time."

"That's not music!"

"You sound like my parents."

"I don't mean the stuff they play isn't music. I mean the DJ is just yammering away."

"Hang on. A song is coming up. Anyway, this is funny stuff."

"I don't find jokes about wheelchair races funny."

"It's all in fun."

"Fun for whom?"

"What's *your* problem today?"

"Nothing, I just don't find that kind of stuff funny. Here, I'll find something."

"What's that?"

"The jazz station."

"Give me a break. How about Sports Talk?"

"Nah. How about All News?"

"No way. How about the All Talk station?"

"Why? You need another fix of insulting chatter?"

"How about silence?"

"Yeah, how about it?"

In this chapter, we study the technical and social beginnings of both radio and sound recording. We revisit the coming of broadcasting and see how the growth of radio's regulatory, economic, and organizational structures led to the medium's golden age.

The chapter covers how television changed radio and produced the medium with which we are now familiar, the one that generated this friendly dispute. We review the scope and nature of contemporary radio, especially its local, fragmented, specialized, personal, and mobile nature. We examine how these characteristics serve advertisers and listeners. The chapter then explores the relationship between radio, the modern recording industry, popular music, and the way new and converging technologies serve and challenge all three. The convenience of algorithm-based music preference—and what that means for the music we hear—inspires our discussion of media literacy.

A Short History of Radio and Sound Recording

The particular stations you and your friend disagree about may be different than those in our opening vignette, but almost all of us have been through a similar conversation. Radio, the seemingly ubiquitous medium, matters to us. Because we often listen to it alone, it is personal. Radio is also mobile. It travels with us in the car, and we take it everywhere with our smartphones. Radio is specific as well. Stations aim their content at very narrowly defined audiences. These are characteristics of contemporary radio, but radio once occupied a very different place in our culture. Let's see how it all began.

Early Radio

Because both applied for patents within months of one another in the late 1890s, there remains disagreement over who "invented" radio, eastern European immigrant Nikola Tesla or Guglielmo Marconi, son of a wealthy Italian businessman and his Irish wife. Marconi, however, is considered the "Father of Radio" because not only was he among the first to send signals through the air, but he was also adroit at gaining maximum publicity for his every success. His improvements over earlier experimental designs allowed him to send and receive telegraph code over distances as great as two miles by 1896.

His native Italy was not interested in his invention, so he used his mother's contacts in Great Britain to find support and financing there. England, with a global empire and the world's largest navy and merchant fleets, was naturally interested in long-distance wireless communication. With the financial and technical help of the British, Marconi successfully transmitted wireless signals across the English Channel in 1899 and across the Atlantic in 1901. Wireless was now a reality. Marconi was satisfied with his advance, but other scientists saw the transmission of voices by wireless as the next hurdle, a challenge that was soon surmounted.

In 1903 Reginald Fessenden, a Canadian, invented the **liquid barretter**, the first audio device permitting the reception of wireless voice transmissions. His 1906 Christmas Eve broadcast from Brant Rock, a small New England coastal village, was the first public broadcast of voices and music. His listeners were in ships at sea and a few newspaper offices equipped to receive the transmission.

Later that same year American Lee DeForest invented the **audion tube**, a vacuum tube that improved and amplified wireless signals. Now the reliable transmission of clear voices and music was a reality. DeForest's second important contribution was that he saw radio as a means of *broadcasting*. The early pioneers, Marconi included, had viewed radio as a device for point-to-point communication—for example, from ship to ship or ship to shore. But in the 1907 prospectus for his radio company, DeForest wrote, "It will soon be possible to distribute grand opera music from transmitters placed on the stage of the Metropolitan Opera House by a Radio Telephone station on the roof to almost any dwelling in Greater New York and vicinity. . . . The same applies to large cities. Church music, lectures, etc., can be spread abroad by the Radio Telephone" (as quoted in Adams, 1996, pp. 104–106).

Soon, countless "broadcasters" went on the air. Some were giant corporations looking to dominate the medium for profit; some were hobbyists and hams playing with the medium for sheer joy. There were so many "stations" that havoc reigned. Yet the promise of radio was such that the medium continued to mature until World War I, when the US government ordered "the immediate closing of all stations for radio communications, both transmitting and receiving" (Greb & Adams, 2003, p. 109).

Early Sound Recording

The late 1800s have long been considered the beginning of sound recording. However, the 2008 discovery in a Paris archive of a

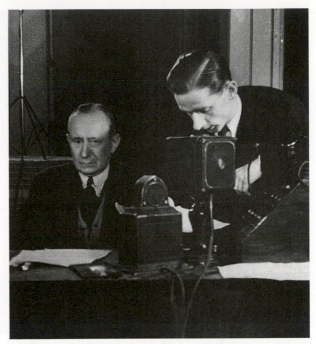

▲ Guglielmo Marconi (seated).
AP image

▼ Lee DeForest.
Library of Congress Prints & Photographs Division [LC-USZ62-54114]

▶ In 1887 Emile Berliner developed the flat disc gramophone and a sophisticated microphone, both important to the widespread public acceptance of sound recordings for the home. Nipper, the trademark dog for RCA Victor, is on the scene even today.
Mooziic/Alamy Stock Photo

10-second recording by an obscure French tinkerer, Edouard-Leon Scott de Martinville, has some audio historians rethinking recording's roots. Scott recorded a folk song on a device he called a phonautograph in 1860, and he always thought that Thomas Edison had stolen credit that should have been his ("Edison Not," 2008). Nonetheless, in 1877 prolific inventor Edison patented his "talking machine," a device for replicating sound that used a hand-cranked grooved cylinder and a needle. The mechanical movement caused by the needle passing along the groove of the rotating cylinder and hitting bumps was converted into electrical energy that activated a diaphragm in a loudspeaker and produced sound. The drawback was that only one "recording" could be made of any given sound; the cylinder could not be duplicated.

In 1887 that problem was solved by German immigrant Emile Berliner, whose gramophone used a flat, rotating, wax-coated disc that could easily be copied or pressed from a metal master. Two equally important Berliner contributions were the development of a sophisticated microphone and later (through his company RCA Victor Records) the import from Europe of recordings by famous opera stars. Now people had not only a reasonably priced record player but records to play on it as well. The next advance was the introduction of the two-sided disc by the Columbia Phonograph Company in 1905. Soon there were hundreds of phonograph or gramophone companies, and the device, by either name, was a standard feature in American homes by 1920. More than 2 million machines and 107 million recordings were sold in 1919 alone. Public acceptance of the new medium was enhanced even more by the development of electromagnetic recording in 1924 by Joseph P. Maxwell at Bell Laboratory.

The parallel development and diffusion of radio and sound recording are significant. For the first time in history, radio allowed people to hear the words and music of others who were not in their presence. On recordings, they could hear words and music that may have been created days, months, or even years before. And the technology changed not only music, but also people's relationship with it: individual pieces of music became shorter to fit onto records; on-demand listening, rather than attending scheduled performances, became the norm; listening alone rather than in groups became common; people began defining themselves by their favored genre of music; and despite the fears of the new technology's critics, rather than people giving up making their own music, there was a burst of interest in playing music as listeners were inspired by what they were hearing (Thompson, 2016).

The Coming of Broadcasting

The idea of broadcasting—that is, transmitting voices and music at great distances to a large number of people—predated the development of radio. Alexander Graham Bell's telephone company had a subscription music service in major cities in the late 1800s, delivering music to homes and businesses by telephone wires. A front-page story in an 1877 edition of the *New York Daily Graphic* suggested the possibilities of broadcasting to its readers. The public anticipated and, after DeForest's much publicized successes, was eager for music and voices at home.

Russian immigrant David Sarnoff, then an employee of the company American Marconi, recognized this desire and in 1916 sent his superiors what has become famously known as the "Radio Music Box Memo." In this memo, Sarnoff wrote of

> a plan of development which would make radio a "household utility" in the same sense as the piano or phonograph. The idea is to bring music into the house by wireless. . . . The receiver can be designed in the form of a simple "Radio Music Box" and arranged for several different wavelengths, which should be changeable with the throwing of a single switch or pressing of a single button. (Sterling & Kitross, 1990, p. 43)

The introduction of broadcasting to a mass audience was delayed in the first two decades of the 20th century by patent fights and lawsuits. Yet when World War I ended, an enthusiastic audience awaited what had become a much-improved medium.

In a series of developments that would be duplicated for television at the time of World War II, radio was transformed from an exciting technological idea into an entertainment and commercial giant. To aid the war effort, the government took over the patents relating to radio and continued to improve radio for military use. Thus, refinement and development of the technical aspects of radio continued throughout the war. Then, when the war ended in 1919, the patents were returned to their owners—and the bickering was renewed.

▲ This cover of an 1877 newspaper proved prophetic in its image of speakers' ability to "broadcast" their words.

Collection of the New-York Historical Society, USA/Bridgeman Images

Concerned that the medium would be wasted and fearful that a foreign company (British Marconi) would control this vital resource, the US government forced the combatants to merge. American Marconi, General Electric, American Telephone & Telegraph, and Westinghouse (in 1921)—each in control of a vital piece of technology—joined to create the Radio Corporation of America (RCA). RCA was a government-sanctioned monopoly, but its creation avoided direct government control of the new medium. Twenty-eight-year-old David Sarnoff, author of the Radio Music Box Memo, was made RCA's commercial manager. The way for the medium's popular growth was paved; its success was guaranteed by a public that, because of the phonograph, was already attuned to music in the home and, thanks to the just-concluded war, was awakening to the need for instant, wide-ranging news and information.

On September 30, 1920, a Westinghouse executive, impressed with press accounts of the number of listeners who were picking up broadcasts from the garage radio station of company engineer Frank Conrad, asked him to move his operation to the Westinghouse factory and expand its power. Conrad did so, and on October 27, 1920, experimental station 8XK in Pittsburgh, Pennsylvania, received a license from the Department of Commerce to broadcast. On November 2, this station, renamed KDKA, made the first commercial radio broadcast, announcing the results of the presidential election that sent Warren G. Harding to the White House. By mid-1922, there were nearly 1 million radios in American homes, up from 50,000 just a year before (Tillinghast, 2000, p. 41).

The Coming of Regulation

As the RCA agreements demonstrated, the government had a keen interest in the development, operation, and diffusion of radio. At first, government interest focused on point-to-point communication. In 1910 Congress passed the Wireless Ship Act, requiring that all ships using American ports and carrying more than 50 passengers have a working wireless and operator. Of course, the wireless industry did not object, as the legislation boosted sales. However, after the *Titanic* struck an iceberg in the North Atlantic in 1912 and it was learned that hundreds of lives were

▲ The wireless-telegraphy room of the *Titanic*. Despite the heroic efforts of wireless operator Jack Philips, hundreds of people died needlessly in the sinking of that great ocean liner because ships in its vicinity did not monitor their receivers.

Universal History Archive/UIG/Getty Images

lost needlessly because other ships in the area had left their radios unattended, Congress passed the Radio Act of 1912, which not only strengthened rules regarding shipboard wireless but also required that wireless operators be licensed by the Secretary of Commerce and Labor.

The Radio Act of 1912 established spheres of authority for both federal and state governments, provided for distributing and revoking licenses, fined violators, and assigned frequencies for station operation. The government was in the business of regulating what was to become broadcasting, a development that angered many operators. They successfully challenged the 1912 act in court, and eventually President Calvin Coolidge ordered the cessation of government regulation of radio despite his belief that chaos would descend on the medium.

He proved prophetic. The industry's years of flouting the 1912 act had led it to the brink of disaster. Radio sales and profits dropped dramatically. Listeners were tired of the chaos. Stations arbitrarily changed frequencies, power, and hours of operation, and there was constant interference between stations, often intentional. Radio industry leaders petitioned Commerce Commissioner Herbert Hoover and, according to historian Erik Barnouw—who titled his 1966 book on radio's early days *A Tower in Babel*—"encouraged firmness" in government efforts to regulate and control the competitors. The government's response was the Radio Act of 1927. Order was restored and the industry prospered, but the broadcasters had made an important concession to secure this saving intervention. The 1927 act authorized them to *use* the airwaves, which belonged to the public, but not to *own* them. Broadcasters were thus simply the caretakers of the airwaves, a national resource.

The act further stated that when a license was awarded, the standard of evaluation would be the public interest, convenience, or necessity. The Federal Radio Commission (FRC) was established to administer the provisions of the act. This **trustee model** of regulation is based on two premises (Bittner, 1994). The first is **spectrum scarcity**. Because broadcast spectrum space is limited and not everyone who wants to broadcast can, those who are granted licenses to serve a local area must accept regulation. The second reason for regulation revolves around the issue of influence. Broadcasting reaches virtually everyone in society. By definition, this renders radio powerful.

The Communications Act of 1934 replaced the 1927 legislation. The FRC gave way to the Federal Communications Commission (FCC), and its regulatory authority, which continues today, was cemented.

Advertising and the Networks

While the regulatory structure of the medium was evolving, so were its financial bases. The formation of RCA had ensured that radio would be a commercial, profit-based medium. The industry initially supported itself through the sale of receivers. The problem was that once everybody had a radio, people would stop buying them. The solution was advertising. On August 22, 1922, New York station WEAF accepted the first radio commercial, a 10-minute spot for Long Island brownstone apartments. The cost of the ad was $50.

The sale of advertising led to the establishment of national radio **networks**. Groups of stations, or **affiliates**, all broadcasting identical content from a single distributor, could deliver larger audiences, realizing greater advertising revenues, which would allow them to hire bigger stars and produce better programming, which would attract larger audiences, which could be sold for even greater fees to advertisers.

RCA set up a 24-station network, the National Broadcasting Company (NBC), in 1926. A year later it bought AT&T's stations and launched a second network, NBC Blue (the original NBC was renamed NBC Red). The Columbia Broadcasting System (CBS) was also founded in 1927, but it struggled until 26-year-old millionaire cigar maker William S. Paley bought it in 1928, making it a worthy competitor to NBC. The fourth network, Mutual, was established in 1934 largely on the strength of its hit Western *The Lone Ranger*. Four midwestern and eastern stations came together to sell advertising on it and other shows; soon Mutual had 60 affiliates. Mutual differed from the other major national networks in that it did not own and operate its own flagship stations (called **O&Os**, for owned and operated).

By 1938 the four national networks had affiliated virtually all the large US stations and the majority of smaller operations as well. These corporations grew so powerful that in 1943 the government forced NBC to divest itself of one of its networks. It sold NBC Blue to Life Saver candy-maker Edward Noble, who renamed it the American Broadcasting Company (ABC).

The fundamental basis of broadcasting (radio and later television) in the United States was now set:

- Broadcasters were private, commercially owned enterprises rather than government operations.
- Governmental regulation was based on the public interest.
- Stations were licensed to serve specific localities, but national networks programmed the most lucrative hours with the largest audiences.
- Entertainment and information (news, weather, and sports) were the basic broadcast content.
- Advertising formed the basis of financial support for broadcasting.

The Golden Age

The networks ushered in radio's golden age. Although the 1929–1939 Great Depression damaged the phonograph industry, it helped boost the radio industry. Phonographs and records cost money, but once a family bought a radio, a whole world of entertainment and information was at its disposal, free of charge. The number of homes with radios grew from 12 million in 1930 to 30 million in 1940, and half of them had not one but two receivers. Ad revenues rose from $40 million to $155 million over the same period. The four national networks broadcast 156 combined hours of network-originated programming a week. New genres became fixtures during this period: comedy (*The Jack Benny Show*, *Fibber McGee and Molly*), audience participation (*Professor Quiz*, *Truth or Consequences*), children's shows (*Little Orphan Annie*, *The Lone Ranger*), soap operas (*Oxydol's Own Ma Perkins*, *The Guiding Light*), and drama (Orson Welles's *The Mercury Theatre on the Air*). News, too, became a radio staple.

◀ George Burns and Gracie Allen were CBS comedy stars during radio's golden age. They were among the many radio performers to move easily and successfully to television.
Bettmann/Getty Images

▲ Family radio time disappeared with the coming of television.

George Marks/Retrofile RF/Getty Images

RADIO AND SOUND RECORDING IN WORLD WAR II The golden age of radio shone even more brightly as the United States entered World War II in 1941. Radio was used to sell war bonds, and much content was aimed at boosting the nation's morale. The war increased the desire for news, especially from abroad. The conflict also caused a paper shortage, reducing advertising space in newspapers. No new stations were licensed during the war years, so the 950 existing broadcasters reaped all the broadcast advertising revenues, as well as additional ad revenues that otherwise would have gone to newspapers.

Sound recording benefited from the war as well. Prior to World War II, recording in the United States was done either directly to master metal discs or on wire recorders, literally magnetic recording on metal wire. But GIs brought a new technology back from occupied Germany, a tape recorder that used an easily handled paper tape on a reel.

Then, in 1947, Columbia Records introduced a new 33⅓ rpm (rotations-per-minute) long-playing plastic record. A big advance over the previous standard of 78 rpm, it was more durable than the older shellac discs and played for 23 rather than 3⅓ minutes. Columbia offered the technology free to all other record companies. RCA refused the offer, introducing its own 45 rpm disc in 1948. It played for only 3⅓ minutes and had a huge center hole requiring a special adapter.

Still, RCA persisted in its marketing, causing a speed war that was settled in 1950 when the two giants compromised on 33⅓ as the standard for classical music and 45 as the standard for pop. And it was the 45, the single (played on cheap plastic record players that cost around $13; Menard, 2015), that sustained the music business until the mid-1960s, when the Beatles not only ushered in the "British invasion" of rock 'n' roll but also transformed popular music into a 33⅓ album-dominant cultural force, shaping today's popular music and helping reinvent radio.

TELEVISION ARRIVES When the war ended and radio licenses were granted again, the number of stations grew rapidly to 2,000. Annual ad revenues reached $454 million in 1950. Then came television. Network affiliation dropped from 97% in 1945 to 50% by the mid-1950s, as stations "went local" in the face of television's national dominance. National radio advertising income dipped to $35 million in 1960, the year that television found its way into 90% of American homes. If radio were to survive, it would have to find new functions.

Radio and Its Audiences

Radio more than survived; it prospered by changing the nature of its relationship with its audiences. The easiest way to understand this is to see pretelevision radio as network television is today—nationally oriented, broadcasting an array of recognizable entertainment program formats, populated by well-known stars and personalities, and consumed primarily in the home, typically with people sitting around the set. Posttelevision radio is local, fragmented, specialized, personal, and mobile. Whereas pretelevision radio was characterized by the big national networks, today's radio is dominated by formats, a particular sound characteristic of a local station.

Who are the people who make up radio's audience? In an average week, approximately 248 million people, 92% of all Americans 12 and over, will listen to the radio, making it the American mass medium with the greatest degree of audience reach. However, broadcast radio's audience size has shown almost no growth over the last few years, and time spent listening has fallen, dropping by an average of about 1 minute a day. Most troubling to radio professionals, though, is that time listening among young people is in decline (Radio Advertising Bureau, 2020).

The industry itself attributes this situation to dissatisfaction with unimaginative programming, hypercommercialization—on average between 12 and 16 minutes of commercials an hour—and the availability of online music sources and mobile technologies such as tablets and smartphones. Broadcast veteran Bob Lefsetz (2013) explains, "If you don't think new [digital] services will kill [commercial] radio, you must like inane commercials, you must like me-too music, you must think airplay on one of these outlets will sell millions of albums, but that almost never happens anymore" (p. 30). As it is, over 80% of Americans now listen to radio on digital devices (Kelly, 2019), and as you can see in Figure 7.1, radio's reach is lowest for younger adults.

▲ **Figure 7.1** Radio's Weekly Reach by Age (% of US Population). *Source: Kelly, 2019.* *(photo): Stockbyte/PunchStock/ Getty Images*

Scope and Nature of the Radio Industry

There are 15,478 full-power broadcast radio stations operating in the United States today: 4,580 commercial AM stations, 6,726 commercial FM stations, and 4,172 noncommercial FM stations. These are joined on the dial by 2,159 **low power FM (LPFM)** stations. There are more than two radios for every person in the United States. Despite remaining people's primary means of consuming audio content, radio has seen recent annual highs in ad sales of more $17 billion drop to around $15 billion (Andrews, 2019), and with the coronavirus's damage to local business—the medium's primary ad buyer—annual revenue has declined to just over $11 billion (Radio Ink, 2020).

FM, AM, and Noncommercial Radio

Although FMs constitute 60% of all commercial stations (to AMs' 40%), as much as 85% of all listening is on FM. In fact, from 2015 to 2020, while the numbers of commercial, noncommercial, and LPFM stations all either held steady or increased, the number of AM stations actually decreased (Federal Communications Commission, 2020). This has to do with the technology behind each. The FM (frequency modulation) signal is wider, allowing the broadcast not only of stereo (sound perceived from multiple channels, for example, bass and drums from the left speaker and guitars and vocals from the right) but also of better fidelity to the original sound than the narrower AM (amplitude modulation) signal. As a result, people attracted to music gravitate toward FM. People favoring news, sports, and information tend to find themselves listening to the AM dial. AM signals travel farther than FM signals, making them perfect for rural parts of the country. Rural areas tend to be less heavily populated, so most AM stations serve fewer listeners.

Many of today's FM stations are noncommercial—that is, they accept no advertising. When the national frequency allocation plan was established during the deliberations leading to the 1934 Communications Act, commercial radio broadcasters persuaded Congress that they alone could be trusted to develop this valuable medium. They promised to make time available for religious, children's, and other educational programming. Despite the fact that 40% of existing stations at the time were noncommercial, operated by churches, local governments, universities, and radio clubs (Zuckerman, 2019), no frequencies were set aside for noncommercial radio to fulfill these functions.

In 1945, at the insistence of critics who contended that the commercial broadcasters were not fulfilling their promise, the FCC set aside all FM frequencies between 88.1 and 91.9 megahertz for noncommercial radio. Today these noncommercial stations not only provide local service, but many also offer national network quality programming through affiliation with National Public Radio (NPR) and Public Radio International (PRI) or through a number of smaller national networks, such as Pacifica Network. Bucking the trend in most other media, public stations are strengthening their local journalism and, as such, show stronger audience growth than other types of stations (Jensen, 2020).

Radio Is Local

No longer able to compete with television for the national audience in the 1950s, radio began to attract a local audience. Because it costs much more to run a local television station than a local radio station, radio advertising rates tend to be as much as three times lower than television's to reach an equivalent-size audience. Local advertisers can afford radio more easily than they can television, which increases the local flavor of radio. And radio can be localized even more narrowly than by city or town, as you'll soon read.

Radio Is Fragmented

Radio stations are widely distributed throughout the United States. Virtually every town—even those with only a few hundred residents—has at least one station. The number of stations licensed in an area is a function of both population and proximity to other towns. Small towns may have only one AM or FM station, and a big city can have as many as 40 stations. This fragmentation—many stations serving many areas—makes possible contemporary radio's most important characteristic: its ability to specialize.

Radio Is Specialized

When radio became a local medium, it could no longer program the expensive, star-filled genres of its golden age. The problem now was how to program a station with interesting content and do so economically. A disc jockey (DJ) playing records was the best solution. Stations soon learned that a highly specialized, specific audience of particular interest to certain advertisers could be attracted with specific types of music. **Format** radio was born. Of course, choosing a specific format means accepting that many potential listeners will not tune in, but in format radio, the size of the audience is secondary to its composition.

American radio is home to about 60 different formats, from the most common, which include country, top 40, album-oriented rock, and all talk, to the somewhat uncommon, for example, world ethnic. Many stations, especially those in rural areas, offer **secondary services** (additional, nonprimary formats). For example, a country station may broadcast a religious format for 10 hours on Saturday and Sunday. In addition, radio's specialization permits an infinite variety of formats, for example, one or more stations in almost every city in America will switch to the Seasonal/Holiday format sometime between Thanksgiving and New Years Day. Figure 7.2 shows radio's top formats.

▼ The DJ and playlist have come to personify modern commercial radio since the 1950s.
H. ARMSTRONG ROBERTS/Classic-Stock/Alamy Stock Photo

Format radio offers stations many advantages beyond low-cost operations and specialized audiences that appeal to advertisers. Faced with falling listenership or loss of advertising, a station can simply change DJs and music. Neither television nor the print media have this content flexibility. When confronted with competition from a station with a similar format, a station can further narrow its audience by specializing its formula even more.

Music format radio requires a disc jockey. Someone has to play the music and provide the talk. The modern DJ is the invention of Todd Storz, who bought KOWH in Omaha, Nebraska, in 1949. He turned the radio personality/music formula on its head. Before Storz, radio announcers would talk most of the time and occasionally play music to rest their voices. Storz wanted more music, less talk. He thought radio should sound like a jukebox—the same few songs people wanted to hear played over and over again. His top-40 format, which demanded strict adherence to a **playlist** (a predetermined sequence of selected songs) of popular music for young people, up-tempo pacing, and catchy production gimmicks, became the standard for the posttelevision popular music station. Gordon McClendon of KLIF in Dallas refined the top-40 format and developed others, such as "beautiful music," and is therefore often considered, along with Storz, one of the two pioneers of format radio.

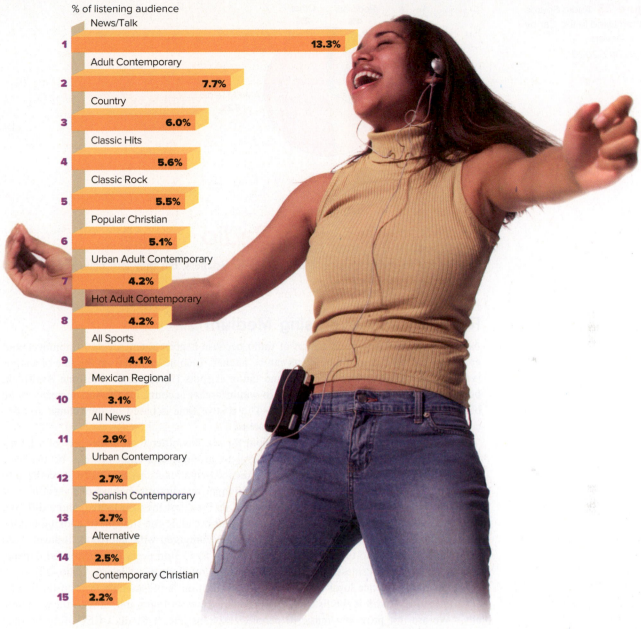

% of listening audience

	Format	%
1	News/Talk	13.3%
2	Adult Contemporary	7.7%
3	Country	6.0%
4	Classic Hits	5.6%
5	Classic Rock	5.5%
6	Popular Christian	5.1%
7	Urban Adult Contemporary	4.2%
8	Hot Adult Contemporary	4.2%
9	All Sports	4.1%
10	Mexican Regional	3.1%
11	All News	2.9%
12	Urban Contemporary	2.7%
13	Spanish Contemporary	2.7%
14	Alternative	2.5%
15	Contemporary Christian	2.2%

▲ **Figure 7.2** Top 15 Radio Formats, 2020.
Source: Katz Radio Group, 2020.
(photo): Photodisc/Rubberball/Getty Image

Radio Is Personal

With the advent of television, the relationship of radio with its audience changed. Whereas families had previously gathered around the radio to listen together, people now typically listen to the radio alone. We select personally pleasing formats, and we listen as an adjunct to other personally important activities.

Radio Is Mobile

The mobility of radio accounts in large part for its personal nature. We can listen anywhere at any time. We listen at work, while exercising, or while sitting in the sun. By 1947, the combined sale of car and alarm clock radios exceeded that of traditional living-room receivers, and in 1951, the annual production of car radios exceeded that of home receivers for the first time. Today, the majority, nearly three-quarters of all traditional radio listening occurs away from home. In fact, most listening occurs in the car, with 52% of daily listeners most often tuning in in the car (Richter, 2020), as you can see in Figure 7.3.

▶ **Figure 7.3** Audio Source
Most Often Used in the Car by
American Drivers.
Source: Richter, 2020.

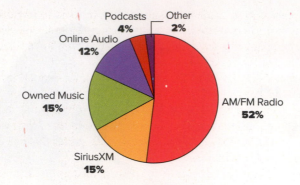

The Business of Radio

The distinctive characteristics of radio serve its listeners, but they also make radio a profitable business.

Radio as an Advertising Medium

Advertisers enjoy the specialization of radio because it gives them access to homogeneous groups of listeners to whom products can be pitched. Income earned from the sale of airtime is called **billings**. Local commercials and national spots (for example, Prestone Antifreeze buys time on several thousand stations in winter areas) account for the vast majority of all billings; network time makes up the rest. The cost of time is based on the **ratings**, the percentage of the total available audience reached.

Radio is an attractive advertising medium for reasons other than its delivery of a homogeneous audience. Radio ads are inexpensive to produce and therefore can be changed, updated, and specialized to meet specific audience demands. Ads can also be specialized to different times of the day. For example, a hamburger restaurant may have one version of its commercial for the morning audience, in which its breakfast menu is touted, and a different version for the evening audience driving home and dreading the thought of cooking dinner. Radio time is inexpensive to buy, especially when compared with television. Industry data show that buying radio time delivers a return of up to $23 on every dollar invested depending on the type of business advertised, in this case, retail stores (Nielsen Audio, 2020).

Finally, an audience loyal to a specific format station is presumably loyal to those who advertise on it. Radio is the listeners' friend; it travels with them and talks to them personally. "We are not providing music to people," explains iHeart Media's CEO Bob Pittman. "We are providing companionship to people. If you go into this thinking our job is to put music on, you'll miss the point" (in Andrews, 2019).

Deregulation and Ownership

The business of radio is being altered by deregulation and changes in ownership rules. To ensure that there were many different perspectives in the cultural forum, the FCC had long limited the number of radio stations one person or company could own to one AM and one FM locally and seven AMs and seven FMs nationally. These numbers were revised upward in the late 1980s, and controls were almost totally eliminated by the Telecommunications Act of 1996. Now, due to this **deregulation**, there are no national ownership limits, and one person or company can own as many as eight stations in one area, depending on the size of the market. This situation has allowed **duopoly**—one person or company owning and managing multiple radio stations in a single market—to explode.

Since the passage of the 1996 act, more than 10,000 radio stations have been sold, and there are now 1,100 fewer station owners, a 30% decline. The vast majority of these sales have been to already-large radio groups such as iHeart Media (850 stations in 153 markets), Cumulus (446 in 87 markets), and Entercom (235 in 48 markets). As a result, in 25 of the 50 largest radio markets, three companies claim 80% of all listeners. In over 40 cities, one-third of the radio stations are owned by a single company, leading insiders to identify the industry's two biggest problems not as competition from new digital technologies, but first as "control of the industry in the hands of a few giants" and a close second as "decline of local radio with its deep communities ties" (Editors, 2015).

The concern over these issues runs deep. Local public affairs shows now make up less than one-half of 1% of all commercial broadcast time in the United States. "There is a crisis," said FCC commissioner Michael Copps (2011), "when more than one-third of our commercial broadcasters offer little to no news whatsoever to their communities of license. America's news and information resources keep shrinking and hundreds of stories that could inform our citizens go untold and, indeed, undiscovered."

As for the music, a few years ago, when Clear Channel (now iHeart Media) and Cumulus collectively laid off hundreds of DJs in a move toward automated (no live DJ) and nationally syndicated programming, veteran Los Angeles rock DJ Jim Ladd said, "It's really bad news. It was people in my profession that first played Tom Petty, first played the Doors. But the people programming stations now are not music people—they're business people" (in Knopper, 2011, p. 19). It's important to note that Entercom stations, unlike those of the other giants, are locally programmed.

LPFM, 10- to 100-watt nonprofit community radio stations with a reach of only a few miles, are one response to "the homogenization of the FM band." As a result of the Local Community Radio Act of 2010, which enjoyed wide bipartisan support in Congress, 2,159 LPFM stations, serving all 50 states, now offer opportunities for additional radio voices to serve their local listenerships. The FCC encourages the growth of LPFM with regular online webinars explaining the application process to potential operators of this local medium designed to expand the number of community voices, promote media diversity, and enhance local radio programming. For example, the Pascua Yaqui Tribe in Arizona operates low-power KPTY; Seattle's KBFG broadcasts *Tristan's Bedtime Radio Hour*, hosted by 5-year-old Tristan; and KSFL of Portland, Oregon, features music from local bands.

Scope and Nature of the Recording Industry

When the DJs and top-40 format saved radio in the 1950s, they also changed for all time popular music and, by extension, the recording industry. Disc jockeys were color-deaf in their selection of records. They introduced record buyers to rhythm 'n' blues in the music of African American artists such as Chuck Berry and Little Richard. Until the mid-1950s, the works of these performers had to be **covered**—rerecorded by white artists such as Perry Como—before it was aired. Teens loved the new sound, however, and it became the foundation of their own subculture, as well as the basis for the explosion in recorded music. See the essay "Rock 'n' Roll, Radio, and Race Relations" for more on rock's roots.

Today more than 5,000 American companies annually release around 100,000 new albums, or more precisely **album equivalents**, a more contemporary and precise measurement that equals the purchase of one album (10 cuts), including streaming, downloads, and traditional album sales, on thousands of different labels. In 2020 American music buyers *purchased* 980.7 million (with an *m*) pieces of music in both digital (27%) and physical (73%) formats, but *streamed* 872.6 billion (with a *b*) more, producing domestic industry revenues in excess of $12 billion. Globally, there were 2.2 trillion (with a *t*) music streams, a 22.6% increase over the previous year, producing revenues of more than $20 billion ("Year End," 2021; RIAA, 2020).

▼ Little Richard was one of the early rock 'n' roll artists to make a lie of what American teens' dominant culture had to say about race and the inadequacies of African Americans.

Edd Westmacott/Alamy Stock Photo

USING MEDIA TO MAKE A DIFFERENCE
Rock 'n' Roll, Radio, and Race Relations

After World War II, African Americans in the United States refused to remain invisible. Having fought in segregated units in Europe and proven their willingness to fight and die for freedom abroad, they openly demanded freedom at home. President Harry Truman, recognizing the absurdity of racial separation in the self-proclaimed "greatest democracy on earth," desegregated the armed forces by executive order in 1948.

These early stirrings of equality led to a sense among African Americans that anything was possible, and that feeling seeped into their music. What had been called cat, sepia, or race music took on a new tone. While this new sound borrowed from traditional Black music—gospel, blues, and laments over slavery and racial injustice—it was different, much different. Music historian Ed Ward said that this bolder, more aggressive music "spoke to a shared experience, not just to black (usually rural black) life," and it would become the "truly biracial popular music in this country" (Ward, Stokes, & Tucker, 1986, p. 83).

Hundreds of small independent record companies sprang up to produce this newly labeled rhythm 'n' blues (R&B), which focused on Americans' shared experiences with topics that were part of life for people of all colors, such as sex and alcohol. With its earthy lyrics and thumping dance beat, R&B very quickly found an audience in the 1950s, one composed largely of urban Blacks (growing in number as African Americans increasingly migrated north) and white teenagers.

The major record companies took notice, and rather than sign already successful R&B artists, they had their white artists cover the Blacks hits. The Penguins's "Earth Angel" was covered by the reassuringly named Crew Cuts, who also covered the Chords's "Sh-Boom." Chuck Berry's "Maybellene" was covered by both the Johnny Long and Ralph Marterie orchestras. Even Bill Haley and the Comets's youth anthem "Shake, Rattle and Roll" was a cover of a Joe Turner tune.

However, these covers actually served to introduce even more white teens to the new music, and these kids demanded the original versions. This did not escape the attention of Sam Phillips, who in 1952 founded Sun Records in an effort to bring Black music to white teens. "If I could find a white man who had the Negro sound, I could make a billion dollars," he is reported to have mused (in Menard, 2015, p. 83). In 1954 he found that man: Elvis Presley, whose breakout hit, Hound Dog, was a cover of R&B singer Big Mama Thornton's 1953 song.

The situation also caught the attention of Cleveland DJ Alan Freed, whose nationally distributed radio (and later television) show featured Black R&B tunes, never covers. Freed began calling the music he played rock 'n' roll (to signify that it was Black and white youth music), and by 1955, when Freed took his show to New York, the cover business was dead. Black performers were recording and releasing their own music to a national audience, and people of all colors were tuning in.

Now that the kids had a music of their own, and now that a growing number of radio stations were willing to program it, a youth culture began to develop, one that was antagonistic toward their parents' culture. The music was central to this antagonism, not only because it was gritty and real but also because it exposed the hypocrisy of adult culture.

For young people of the mid-1950s and 1960s, the music of Little Richard, Fats Domino, Ray Charles, and Chuck Berry made a lie of all that their parents, teachers, and government leaders had said about race, the inferiority of African Americans, and African Americans' satisfaction with the status quo.

Ralph Bass, a producer for independent R&B label Chess Records, described the evolution to historian David Szatmary from his experience touring with R&B groups in the early 1950s:

> They didn't let whites into the clubs. Then they got "white spectator tickets" for the worst corner of the joint. They had to keep the white kids out, so they'd have white nights sometimes, or they'd put a rope across the middle of the floor. The blacks on one side, the whites on the other, digging how the blacks were dancing and copying them. Then, hell, the rope would come down, and they'd all be dancing together. Salt and pepper all mixed together. (Szatmary, 2000, p. 21)

Popular music did not end racism, but it made a difference, one that would eventually make it possible for Americans who wanted to do so to free themselves of racism's ugly hold. Rock and R&B (and the radio stations that played them) would again nudge the nation toward its better tendencies during the antiwar and civil rights movements of the late 1960s. And popular music was there again in 2020, during the "nationwide awakening to civil rights" following the killing of George Floyd. It was then that millions of Americans, "searching for music that speaks to the current moment," turned to artists like Childish Gambino ("This is America") and Kendrick Lamar ("All Right") to help articulate their anger at what they saw as their nation's failure to live its ideals (Stevens, 2020a).

The Major Recording Companies

Three major recording companies control most of the global recorded music market. Two (Sony and Universal) control nearly three-quarters of the world's $20 billion global music sales. Two of the three are foreign-owned:

- Sony, controlling about 30% of the world music market, is a Japanese-owned corporate group. Its labels include Columbia, Epic, RCA, and Arista.
- New York–based Warner Music Group, controlling about 20%, is owned by billionaire Len Blavatnik's Access Industries and several private investors. Its labels include Atlantic, Elektra, and Warner Bros.
- Universal Music Group, controlling about 40%, is owned by French conglomerate Vivendi Universal and controls labels such as EMI, MCA, Capitol, and Def Jam Records (Duncan, 2020).

Critics have long voiced concern over conglomeration in the music business, a concern that centers on the traditional cultural value of music, especially for young people. Multibillion-dollar conglomerates typically are not rebellious in their cultural tastes, nor are they usually willing to take risks on new ideas. These duties have fallen primarily to the independent labels, companies such as Real World Records and Epitaph. Still, problems with the music industry–audience relationship remain.

Cultural homogenization is the worrisome outcome of virtually all the world's influential recording being controlled by a few profit-oriented giants. If bands or artists cannot immediately deliver the goods, they aren't signed. So derivative artists and manufactured groups dominate—for example, JoJo Siwa and One Direction. Moreover, popular music is increasingly the product not of individual genius or artistry but of **mathematical songwriting**, songs written specifically to be commercial hits. They are "written to track, which means a producer makes a beat. Then a songwriter listens to it and attempts to generate words that fit that beat, sometimes singing nonsense until the language begins to take shape. It's more about how lyrics sound than what they mean. This has become a bedrock part of the industry" (Lansky, 2015/2016, p. 124).

Although a few artists like David Bowie were experimenting with it in the 1990s (Deahl, 2019), there is growing concern over **AI (artificial intelligence) songwriting**, composition of music and lyrics by computers. Programmed to "think" and act like a human, an AI machine "learns" to take actions that have the best chance of achieving a specific goal, in this case, writing hit songs. The music industry estimates that in the next 10 years, 20% to 30% of the top-40 singles will be written partially or totally by machine-learning software. It's no different than using any other technology, for example, synthesizers and drum machines, argue AI supporters. Music was once written with quill and parchment, they say, but now composers use computers.

However, its critics argue that it will produce just more of the same, killing creativity and artistry in songwriting. They point to one of AI's most common functions, analyzing libraries of songs and industry sales figures to predict (and write) songs that have the best chance of being hits (Reilly, 2018). A hit song is also as likely to come from a "songwriting camp," where groups of songwriters and musicians convene to construct hits. Hits like Drake's *Nice for What* had 16 writers and Cardi B's *Be Careful* had 17. "Looking at the charts, nine times out of ten, pretty much everything is co-written," explains BMI vice president Samantha Cox. "There's at least three to four to five writers on every song that's out there right now" (Knopper, 2018).

The *dominance of profit over artistry* worries many music fans. When a major label must spend millions to sign a bankable artist, such as Jay Z ($150 million), Bruce Springsteen ($150 million), or Adele ($130 million), it typically pares lesser-known, potentially more innovative artists from its roster. The chase for profit has also produced an increase in the number of product placements in songs (Sánchez-Olmos & Castelló-Martínez, 2020) and the use of computer algorithms to determine which songs are sufficiently similar to existing hits to even warrant recording (Timberg, 2015). "Just as major movie studios tend to finance only films with strong projected box-office returns, major record labels prefer to avoid risk, especially in an era when digital streaming has slashed profit margins. Executives mine social-media data to identify the next viral sensation, or pair unknown acts with established producers and songwriters to manufacture hits," explains music critic Matthew Trammell (2017, p. 45).

▶ **Figure 7.4** The Top 10 Best-Selling Albums and Artists of All Time, US Sales Only.

Source: Recording Industry Association of America, 2021.

(photo): P. Ughetto/ PhotoAlto

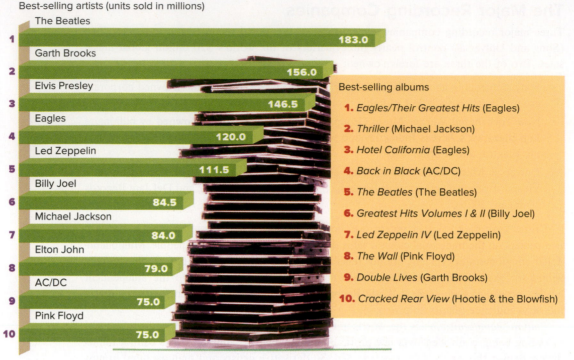

Best-selling artists (units sold in millions)

Rank	Artist	Units
1	The Beatles	183.0
2	Garth Brooks	156.0
3	Elvis Presley	146.5
4	Eagles	120.0
5	Led Zeppelin	111.5
6	Billy Joel	84.5
7	Michael Jackson	84.0
8	Elton John	79.0
9	AC/DC	75.0
10	Pink Floyd	75.0

Best-selling albums

1. *Eagles/Their Greatest Hits* (Eagles)
2. *Thriller* (Michael Jackson)
3. *Hotel California* (Eagles)
4. *Back in Black* (AC/DC)
5. *The Beatles* (The Beatles)
6. *Greatest Hits Volumes I & II* (Billy Joel)
7. *Led Zeppelin IV* (Led Zeppelin)
8. *The Wall* (Pink Floyd)
9. *Double Lives* (Garth Brooks)
10. *Cracked Rear View* (Hootie & the Blowfish)

Critics and industry people alike see these practices as problems for the industry, as well as for the music and its listeners. As the industry relies more heavily on superficial, disposable pop stars, it tells people that the music is superficial and disposable. As they increasingly rely on the same big stars, there is little new music for fans to discover and buy. What helps the industry prosper is continued strength in sales of **catalog albums**, albums more than 18 months old, and **deep catalog albums**, music more than 3 years old. In fact, catalog albums outsold new releases for the first time in 2015 (Singleton, 2016), and continue to out-perform new releases even in today's world of streaming music dominance, with catalog and deep catalog accounting for 63% of all recorded music consumption in 2020 ("Year End Report," 2021). But new releases cannot become catalog albums unless the artists and their music are worthy of fans' devotion and money. Look at the names of the best-selling albums and artists in Figure 7.4. How many current artists and albums do you think will ever join these ranks? Critics of the ascendance of profits over artistry argue that the industry simply lacks the patience to develop new sounds and careers.

Promotion overshadows the music, say the critics. If groups or artists don't come across well on television or are otherwise a challenge to promote (for example, they do not fit an easily recognizable niche), they aren't signed. Again, the solution is to create marketable artists from scratch. Promoting tours is also an issue. If bands or artists do not have corporate sponsorship for their tours, there is no tour. If musicians do not tour, they cannot create an enthusiastic fan base. But if they do not have an enthusiastic fan base, they cannot attract the corporate sponsorship necessary to mount a tour. In 1982, the top 1% of artists earned 26% of all touring income; today they command 60% (Krueger, 2019).

This makes radio even more important for the introduction of new artists and forms of music, but radio, too, is increasingly driven by profit-maximizing format narrowing and is therefore dependent on the major labels' definition of playable artists. As a result, when the Internet began to undermine a complacent industry's long-profitable business model, it was ill prepared to meet the challenges that came its way. Radio veteran Lefsetz (2015) comments again, "Music has become a second-class citizen because it's got no self-respect. . . . The enemy is not the techies, but those who make the music and promote it—who have no conviction and can't say no to a payday. We judge everything by money, and however much we've got is never enough" (p. 26).

Trends and Convergence in Radio and Sound Recording

Emerging and changing technologies have affected the production and distribution aspects of both radio and sound recording.

The Impact of Television

We have seen how television fundamentally altered radio's structure and relationship with its audiences. Television, specifically the cable channel MTV, changed the recording industry, too. MTV's introduction in 1981 helped pull the industry out of its disastrous 1979 slump, but at a price. First, the look of concerts has changed. No longer is it sufficient to pack an artist or group into a hall or stadium with a few thousand screaming fans. Now a concert must be an extravagant multimedia event approximating the sophistication of a music video. For example, U2's 360 Degrees tour needed 120 trucks to move its stage, screen, lights, 250 speakers, and other equipment from venue to venue. Beyoncé's Formation tour of Europe used 7 Boeing 747 cargo planes to transport all its necessary stage equipment (Iyengar, 2018). This means that fewer acts take to the road, changing the relationship between musicians and fans.

Second, the radio–recording industry relationship has changed. Even as MTV began to program fewer and fewer music videos, record companies grew even more reliant on television to introduce new music. For example, labels now time record releases and promotions to artists' television appearances, and new and old tunes alike find heavy play on television shows. Contestants on *The Voice* and *American Idol*, and before they left the air, the casts of *Glee* and *Nashville*, sold tens of millions of songs, and newer programs such as *Zoey's Extraordinary Playlist*, *High Fidelity*, and James Cordon's *Carpool Karaoke* now introduce or reintroduce and music to fans, producing sales and streams.

And if television has become the new radio, so has the Internet. YouTube, the world's largest source of streaming music, accounting for 47% of all on-demand play time globally (Dayen, 2021), served as the career launchpad for pop star Justin Bieber, who in 2007 used a series of homemade videos of his 12-year-old self singing in the mirror and around his hometown to catch the eye of the star-hungry record industry, as it did for 16-year-old New Zealander Lorde. Her success as a self-release, free-download Internet music star led Universal to commercially distribute her work, making both the song "Royals" and the artist global smash hits. Universal has since established Awesomeness Music, a label and YouTube channel specifically designed to record and promote YouTube talent such as Cimorelli, singing sisters from California whose channel has more than 5.4 million subscribers. In 2019, *Billboard* announced it would begin counting video plays from YouTube, Apple, and other video streaming sites in its top-music charts.

▼ TV is the new radio. TV shows such as *Zoey's Extraordinary Playlist* (pictured here) and Hulu's *High Fidelity* introduce and eventually sell music, sometimes new, sometimes old, to their fans.
TCD/Prod.DB/Alamy Stock Photo

Satellite and Cable

The convergence of radio and satellite has aided the rebirth of the radio networks. Music and other forms of radio content can be distributed quite inexpensively to thousands of stations. As a result, one "network" can provide very different services to its very different affiliates. Sports broadcaster ESPN, for example, maintains its own radio network, and Westwood One distributes the Rick Dees Weekly Top 40 to 200 of its 8,000 affiliates. In addition, Westwood One, through its **syndication** operations, delivers thousands of varied network and program syndication services to almost every commercial station in the country. The low cost of producing radio programming, however, makes the

establishment of other, even more specialized networks possible. Satellites and fiber-optic Internet make access to syndicated content and formats affordable for many stations. Syndicators can deliver news, top-10 shows, and other content to stations on a market-by-market basis. They can also provide entire formats, requiring local stations, if they wish, to do little more than insert commercials into what sounds to listeners to be a local broadcast.

Satellite has another application as well. Many listeners now receive "radio" through their cable televisions in the form of satellite-delivered services such as DMX (Digital Music Express) and Music Choice. Direct satellite home, office, and automobile delivery of audio by **digital audio radio service (DARS)** brings Sirius XM Radio to nearly 35 million American subscribers by offering hundreds of commercial channels—primarily talk, sports, and traffic—and commercial-free channels—primarily music. Those numbers will likely continue to grow because the company has arrangements with every major carmaker in the country to offer its receivers as a factory-installed option. DARS has proven to be so sufficiently inexpensive, reliable, and technologically sophisticated that Norway ceased all terrestrial broadcasting in 2017, making DARS its standard radio-delivery technology. Several other European countries are considering the same move.

Terrestrial Digital Radio

Since late 2002, thousands of radio stations have begun broadcasting **terrestrial** (land-based) **digital radio**. Relying on digital compression technology called **in-band-on-channel (IBOC)**, terrestrial digital radio allows broadcasters to transmit not only their usual analog signal but one or more digital signals using their existing spectrum space. And although IBOC also improves sound fidelity, making possible high-definition radio, many stations using the technology see its greatest value in pay services—for example, subscription data delivery. IBOC has yet to completely replace analog radio, as many stations today continue to air both digital and analog services.

Web Radio and Podcasting

Radio's convergence with digital technologies is nowhere more pronounced and potentially profound than in **Web radio**, the delivery of "radio" directly to individual listeners over the Internet, and in **podcasting**, streaming or downloading of audio files recorded and stored on distant servers.

First, we'll discuss Web radio. Tens of thousands of "radio stations" exist on the Web in one of two forms: radio simulcasts and bitcasters. *Radio simulcasts* are traditional, over-the-air stations transmitting their signals online. Some simply re-create their original broadcasts, but more often, the simulcast includes additional information, such as song lyrics or artists' biographical information and concert dates. **Bitcasters**, Web-only radio stations, can be accessed only online. There are narrowly targeted bitcasts, such as *NTS.live*, which is based in London and plays underground music, and allworship.com, a Christian station webcasting from Birmingham, Alabama. But the most dramatic evidence of the popularity of bitcasting exists in the success of the scores of **streaming** services that allow the simultaneous downloading and accessing of music.

The most successful streaming services, such as Apple Music, Spotify, and Pandora, are platform agnostic, available on virtually every new digital device—not only the obvious ones such as smartphones, televisions, and car radios, but also the less obvious devices, for example, Wi-Fi-enabled refrigerators (see the discussion of the Internet of Things in Chapter 10). Typically, listeners can pay a subscription fee to hear commercial-free music, or they can tune in for free and hear demographic- and taste-specific commercials.

Pandora accomplishes this ad specificity by coupling it with its Music Genome Project. After listeners tell Pandora what artists they like, the Genome Project, according to the company, "will quickly scan its entire world of analyzed music, almost a century of popular recordings—new and old, well known and completely obscure—to find songs with interesting musical similarities to your choice." Listeners can create up to 100 unique "stations," personally refining them even more if they wish, and at any time, they can purchase the tune they are hearing with a simple click.

In 2010 streaming accounted for 10% of music revenues. Today, despite falling *sales* of music in physical and digital formats, industry income is at its highest level in more than a decade, more than $12.2 billion in 2020 in the United States alone, attributed primarily to growth in paid music subscriptions services. Streaming now accounts for 83% of industry revenues (Smith, 2021). You can see how streaming dominates the way Americans access their recorded music in Figure 7.5.

Podcasts are also streamed, but because they are often posted online, they do not necessarily require streaming software. They can be downloaded, either on demand or automatically (typically by subscription). There are over 2 million US podcasts in operation, triple the number available in 2018 (Sisario, 2021).

Today, 104 million Americans listen to at least one podcast every month (Sisario, 2021), a number that is likely to grow with the development of app-based podcast services such as CastBox and Stitcher and as smartphones and Bluetooth-enabled cars become even more ubiquitous. Podcast listeners tend to be younger, better educated, and more affluent than the general American population, and they are comfortable with advertising (over a billion dollars a year's worth for the first time in 2021 and likely to top $1.6 billion by 2024; "Podcast," 2021), ensuring the financial future of the form.

2020 number of units and change from 2019

+17%
872.6 billion — Streams

-7.4%
680 million — Physical album sales

-22.3%
233.8 million — Digital song sales

34.4 million -12.5% — Digital album sales

27.5 million +46.2% — Vinyl album sales

▲ **Figure 7.5** How Americans Access Recorded Music by Format, 2020.
Source: "Year End Report: U.S. 2020," 2021.
(photo): Dean Drobot/Shutterstock

Smartphones, Tablets, and Social Networking Sites

One of radio's distinguishing characteristics, as we've seen, is its portability. Smartphones and tablets reinforce that benefit. For example, more than half of all streaming music listening is mobile, and there are scores of free iPhone and Android music apps. The average American streams more than 15 hours a week of audio on a mobile device (Edison Research, 2020).

Much smartphone and tablet listening occurs via social networking sites that play a much more important role in connecting fans to musical artists and their work. Artists themselves are using the Internet in general for their own production, promotion, and distribution, bypassing radio and the recording companies altogether. The most-streamed song of 2019, *Old Town Road*, is one dramatic example. Rap musician Lil Naz X leased its beat from online sample market BeatStars for $30, spent $20 on 30 minutes in an Atlanta recording studio, and uploaded the results to music-centric TikTok. The results: 2.5 billion audio and video streams, the sale of 1.4 million tracks, and a major label contract from Universal (Herman, 2020). Billie Eilish and Maia, who performs as Mxmtoon, are two other young artists among many who have used social media to create their own sounds, maintain artistic and financial control of their careers, and reach tens of millions of fans.

Musicians create their own sites and connect with sites designed specifically to feature new artists, such as Bandzoogle, TuneCore, and SoundCloud, that allow fans to hear (and in some cases, even download) new tunes for free; buy music downloads, CDs, and merchandise; get concert information and tickets; and chat with artists and other fans. Rapper Rico Nasty began posting to SoundCloud when she was 17, and by 23 she was with major label Atlantic Records. Others build their own YouTube channels to connect directly with listeners and use crowdfunding sites such as Kickstarter to finance production and distribution of their art (in 2017 Kickstarter funded its 25,000th music project; Neuman, 2017). More than 200,000 musicians are on Patreon, where 4 million fans (patrons) subscribe to artists and fund them on a recurring basis, not for individual, one-time projects, as on Kickstarter. Since its founding in 2013, Patreon has delivered over a billion dollars in revenues to artists (McCarthy, 2020).

▲ Erykah Badu is only one of the many top-tier music stars to take to Internet streaming to connect with fans.

Ricky Fitchett/ZUMA Wire/Alamy Stock Photo

On Facebook, musicians communicate directly with listeners on fan pages, create and manage their own profiles, offer music apps, and showcase performance events. They use Twitter to reach fans with news and other short notes of interest to keep them involved and encourage retweets to grow the size of their listening community. Instagram, especially since the 2020 introduction of short-video site Reels, and Snapchat serve much the same function but with the benefit of photos and video. TikTok, specializing in short-form mobile videos, is "turning unknowns into stars and obscure songs into hits" (Pippenger, 2020). The company maintains an artist-relations team that contacts successful viral musicians and schools them in how to maximize their TikTok reach, backing their commitment with $200 million in support for American artists who show promise (Bloomberg News, 2020).

Established stars take advantage of TikTok's popularity (80 million subscribers, 60% between the ages of 16 and 24; Doyle, 2020). Before completing what was to become "Toosie Slide," Drake asked TikTok celebrity hip-hop dancer Toosie to create a 15-second dance to the tune's chorus. The video quickly amassed 3 billion views and the song shot to the top spot on Billboard's single's chart (Curto, 2020).

On live-streaming app Periscope, artists can create live audio and video content and broadcast it from their mobile devices anywhere, anytime. And like any other social networking site, Periscope connects fans with one another through sharing and live discussions. Given all this activity, it is not surprising that when the 2020 coronavirus pandemic shut down public performances, artists "moved their gigs online." Celebrity acts like Lizzo, John Legend, and Brandi Carlile performed live concerts, streaming from their homes across a number of sites. Elton John performed from his driveway; Paul McCarthy crooned into his iPhone; and Erykah Badu created her own live stream company to deliver a series of interactive Quarantine Concerts (Stevens, 2020b; Aswad, 2020).

The Convergence of the Internet and the Recording Industry

In the 1970s, the basis of the recording industry changed from analog to **digital recording**. That is, sound went from being preserved as waves, whether physically on a disc or tape, to conversion into 1s and 0s logged in millisecond intervals in a computerized translation process. When replayed at the proper speed, the resulting sound was not only continuous but pristine—no hum, no hiss. The CD, or compact disc, was introduced in 1983 using digital coding on a 4.7-inch disc read by a laser beam. In 1986 "Brothers in Arms" by Dire Straits became the first million-selling CD. In 1988 the sale of CDs surpassed that of vinyl discs for the first time; by 1999 they accounted for 88% of industry revenues; today, CDs account for only 5.5% of that income (RIAA, 2020; Perry, 2016).

Convergence with computers and the Internet offers other challenges and opportunities to the recording industry. The way the recording industry operates has been dramatically altered by the Internet. Traditionally, a record company signed an artist, produced the artist's music, and promoted the artist and music through a variety of outlets but primarily through the distribution of music to radio stations. Then listeners, learning about the artist and music through radio, went to a record store and bought the music. But this has changed. Music fans now have access to more music from a greater variety of artists than ever before because of the Internet.

The Internet music revolution began with the development of **MP3**, compression software that shrinks audio files to less than a tenth of their original size. But rather than embrace MP3, the Recording Industry Association of America (RIAA), representing all of the United States' major labels, responded to the advance by developing their own "secure" Internet technology, but by the time it was available for release it was too late: MP3, driven by its availability and ease of use, had become the technology of choice for music fans already unhappy with the high cost of CDs and the necessity of paying for tracks they didn't want in order to get the ones they did. Today, the CD is going the way of the audiotape and 8-track cartridge. It has been replaced first by the download, and then by streamed music. Downloading occurs in two forms: industry-approved and **P2P** (peer-to-peer).

Streaming and Downloading

In the early days of Internet music, illegal file sharing proved the popularity of downloading music from the Internet. The major labels combined to offer "approved" music download sites. None did well. They offered downloads by subscription—that is, a certain number of downloads per month for a set fee. In addition, they placed encrypted messages in the tunes that limited how long the song would be playable and where the download could be used and copied. As a result, illegal file sharing continued.

It was Apple's 2003 introduction of its iPod and iTunes Music Store that suggested a better strategy. Although Apple ceased production of the iPod in 2014—largely due to the ubiquity of a far more versatile mobile music device, the smartphone—it had taught fans that they could easily buy and own albums and individual songs for as little as 99 cents.

Though the buying of digital downloads has been in steady decline for years (down 12.5% for albums and 22.3% for singles, 2019 to 2020; "Year End Report," 2021), there are still hundreds of legally licensed sites selling tens of millions of different music tracks. Digital download sales surpassed physical sales for the first time in 2011, but today, revenues from the sale of physical products—CDs and vinyl records—actually exceed those from the sale of downloads (RIAA, 2020). What the download did to the CD, streaming has done to the download; and while streaming has been a boon for the recording industry itself, it may not have served musicians and music as well, as you can see in the essay "Streaming Saved the Music Industry, But What Did It Do to the Music?"

Streaming may have diminished sales of downloads, but it is influencing the music business in another important way. The ease and inexpensiveness of listening to streamed music has dramatically reduced music **piracy**, the illegal recording and sale of copyrighted material and high-quality recordings (Smith, 2020b). Nonetheless, the industry claims that piracy still costs it billions of dollars. Sites such as Gnutella and Freenet use P2P technologies—that is, peer-to-peer software that permits direct Internet-based communication or collaboration between two or more personal computers while bypassing centralized servers. P2P allows users to visit a constantly and infinitely changing network of machines through which file sharing can occur. The record companies (and movie studios) challenged P2P by suing the makers of its software. In 2005's *MGM v. Grokster*, the Supreme Court unanimously supported industry arguments that P2P software, because it "encouraged" copyright infringement, rendered its makers liable for that illegal act.

The industry's current challenge, then, is **BitTorrent**, file-sharing software that allows anonymous users to create "swarms" of data as they simultaneously download and upload "bits" of a given piece of content from countless untraceable servers. And while these P2P sharing sites account for the large majority of music theft, their share, once as high as 99%, is being eroded by another form of piracy, **stream ripping**—downloading streamed media to a file on a personal device to be accessed locally—from sites such as YouTube and music streaming sites. The federal government estimates that about 17 million Americans now engage in stream ripping (Danaher, Smith, & Telang, 2020), most commonly from sites like FLVTO.biz and Yout.com.

▼ Among streaming's big winners is Ed Sheeran, who earned $10.1 million in one year from the streaming of a single song.

Matt Jelonek/WireImage/Getty images

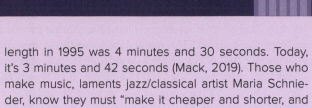

CULTURAL FORUM

Streaming Saved the Music Industry, But What Did It Do to the Music?

Streaming has brought the recording industry from near collapse to revenue heights it hasn't seen in years. Some individual artists are also doing quite well, as might be expected when 1% of artists account for 90% of all music streams (Smith, 2020a). For example, in 2019, the Ed Sheeran song, "Shape of You," earned the singer over $10.1 million from 2,307,000,000 Spotify streams (Earth, 2020). However, most musicians won't generate that many streams in their entire careers—the top one-tenth-of-one percent of musical artists account for half of all streams (Krueger, 2019)—and very few will earn any "real" money—82% of artists who stream their music earn less than $270 a year (King, 2020). This isn't surprising given streaming royalty rates, for example Pandora's $0.00203 and YouTube's $0.00022 per stream (Dayen, 2021).

Nonetheless, the money is good for the industry and good for some big-name talent. But, ask streaming's critics, what about the music itself? The question they inserted into the cultural forum, then, is, "Has streaming's dominance in the economy of the recording industry changed the music?"

First, there is the issue of streaming rather than buying (owning) music. Music distributor Jimmy Johnson says, "Digital music is like grains of sand or something at the beach . . . And there's no reason to think that any of those grains of sand is any better than any of the others. You would never build a shelf to store your grains of sand" (in Hann, 2019). He questions the value of the music. If the music is not something a listener has to commit to, how good does it have to be? Music writer Liz Pelly answers: "It has to be just good enough so you don't turn it off. This background experience, where music isn't really as intentional of a thing, and it's more music that people could just stream for hours and really not think about" (in Mejía, 2019).

The resulting music, contend critics, becomes increasingly predictable and the songs much shorter. It does not pay, literally, to scare off listeners with new or challenging music because the services require a song to be streamed for at least 30 seconds for it to qualify for its fraction-of a-penny payment. The average song length in 1995 was 4 minutes and 30 seconds. Today, it's 3 minutes and 42 seconds (Mack, 2019). Those who make music, laments jazz/classical artist Maria Schnieder, know they must "make it cheaper and shorter, and make more. It's antithetical to artistry. It's the death of creative music" (in Dayen, 2021).

Then there is the sound itself. It just isn't very good. Music critic David Samuels explains, "The compressed, hollow sound of free streaming music was a big step down from the CD. 'Huge step down from vinyl,' [Legendary rock n' roller Neil] Young said. Each step eliminated levels of sonic detail and shading by squeezing down the amount of information contained in the package in which music was delivered. Or, as Young told me, you are left with '5 percent of the original music for your listening enjoyment'" (2019, p. 41).

This flattening of the sound may explain why many music fans, in an attempt to enrich the sound, insert digital-to-analog converters between their music sources and their speakers or headphones, and why there has been a revival of interest in buying vinyl records, now accounting for 4.5% of the industry's revenues (RIAA, 2020).

Enter Your Voice

- Why is there any issue at all? After all, artists who can attract the most fans make the most money. Isn't that how it's supposed to be?

- Why does music have to be new or challenging? Isn't it enough that people like what they hear?

- Music has always been shaped by technology. The 45 rpm record was perfect for short, danceable rock 'n' roll tunes, and as you read, rock changed when the Beatles shifted the form from 45s to 33⅓ rpm albums. Isn't streaming's distinct sound good enough? After all, 1.1 trillion streams in a single year certainly suggest that fans are fine with it.

The major recording labels have joined forces to challenge the legality of the practice, suing with little success sites such as FLVTO.biz and 2conv.com, sites based in Russia that together receive hundreds of millions of visits a year (Sanchez, 2019). In 2018, a Danish court ruled the activity illegal, making Denmark the first country to move against that form of digital theft. No matter what model of music production and distribution eventually results from this technological and financial tumult, serious questions about the Internet's impact on **copyright** (protecting content creators' financial interest in their product) will remain. See Chapter 14 for more on copyright.

DEVELOPING MEDIA LITERACY SKILLS

You Are What You Listen To

There is scientific evidence that the music you listen to is a reflection of who you are. Psychologist Adrian North's research shows, for example, that jazz fans generally have high self-esteem and are creative, outgoing, and at ease; rap fans have high self-esteem and are outgoing; and rock and heavy metal fans often have low self-esteem, are creative, not hardworking, and at ease. As Professor North explains, "People do actually define themselves through music and relate to other people through it" (in Collingwood, 2016). But what if you are choosing your music not because it reflects who you are, but because it's all you know? Keeping in mind that an important element of media literacy is an understanding that media content is a text that provides insight into culture and our lives, how would you answer novelist Nick Hornby's question, "If you own all the music ever recorded in the entire history of the world [because of streaming], then who are you?" (in Thompson, 2016, p. 35).

So why do you listen to the music you do? At a time when almost every song ever recorded is equally accessible, are you making a personally meaningful decision on your choices of this particular form of media content? Maybe not. This is the age of *music by algorithms*, writes popular culture critic Scott Timberg (2016), "Algorithms—whether driving your streaming playlists, your Amazon recommendations, or suggestions on iTunes—are about driving you closer and closer to what you already know. And instead of taking you toward what you want to listen to, they direct you toward slight variations of what you're already consuming." This is not how we are supposed to find music (or ourselves, argues Radiohead's Thom Yorke. "'If you like this, you'll love this' or 'share this' is commodifying a deeply personal human experience between people," he said, "That experience is why music matters" (in Marchese, 2019, p. 14).

So how will you ever find that new sound, the one that reflects the true or maybe evolving you? If you are what you listen to, are you content with streamers' data-driven version of you, especially given their algorithms' "embedded bias" against gender and racial diversity (Antal, 2021; Tett, 2021)? Remember the lesson from this chapter's discussion of race and rock 'n' roll—music can be a powerful force of community and social change. But if music is just another highly-researched, technology-delivered commodity, how can it become important to you and for you?

Media-literate music fans understand that they don't know what they don't know. If you've never heard klezmer, how do you know you don't like it? You might "hate" jazz, but does that mean you hate Arturo Sandoval, Miles Davis, Duke Ellington, or Diana Krall? How can you say you dislike jazz, or country, pop, or classical, if you've never exposed yourself to their many forms? Media literacy means making personally meaningful use of media content. Relying on a distant algorithm's trillions of pieces of data to dictate that use diminishes not only music's social and cultural function but music's entertainment value as well. So, what will you listen to next?

◀ Radiohead frontman Thom Yorke says choosing your music is too personal to be left to streaming algorithms.
Rmv/Shutterstock

MEDIA LITERACY CHALLENGE
Finding New Music

Here are a few musical forms that you might be unfamiliar with: Americana, bluegrass, gospel, neoclassical, alternative country, electronic, ambient, chillwave, techno, Latin rap, indie electronic, Afro beat, bebop, post-punk, and ska. There are literally hundreds more, as a quick Internet search will demonstrate. Challenge yourself to find a genre you've never listened to before and explore it—listen not to just one tune, but five. Now discuss with a friend or your class what you heard. Did you like it? Why or why not? Were you inspired to further investigate this form or another form of music? Why or why not? Now do a little experiment. Find these tunes on Spotify, Pandora, or another streaming site. Listen to five or more in a given genre. Leave that site for a while and then go back. Does the site "recognize" the new musical you? If so, who does it think you are? You're media literate, so you know that music *provides context and insight into who you are.* Having these *heightened expectations of music,* will you continue to experiment with new forms? Why or why not?

Resources for Review and Discussion

REVIEW POINTS: TYING CONTENT TO LEARNING OUTCOMES

▶ **Recognize the history and development of the radio and sound recording industries and radio and sound recording themselves as media.**

- ☐ Guglielmo Marconi's radio allowed long-distance wireless communication; Reginald Fessenden's liquid barretter made possible the transmission of voices; Lee DeForest's audion tube permitted the reliable transmission of voices and music broadcasting.

- ☐ Thomas Edison possibly developed the first sound-recording device, a fact now in debate; Emile Berliner's gramophone improved on it as it permitted multiple copies to be made from a master recording.

▶ **Describe the importance of early financing and regulatory decisions regarding radio and how they have shaped the nature of contemporary broadcasting.**

- ☐ The Radio Acts of 1910, 1912, and 1927 and the Communications Act of 1934 eventually resulted in the FCC and the trustee model of broadcast regulation.

- ☐ Advertising and the network structure of broadcasting came to radio in the 1920s, producing the medium's golden age, one drawn to a close by the coming of television.

▶ **Explain how the organizational and economic natures of the contemporary radio and sound recording industries shape the content of both media.**

- ☐ Radio stations are classified as commercial and non-commercial, AM, FM, and low-power FM.

- ☐ Radio is local, fragmented, specialized, personal, and mobile.

- ☐ Deregulation has allowed concentration of ownership of radio into the hands of a relatively small number of companies.

- ☐ Three major recording companies control nearly three-quarters of the world's recorded music market.

▶ **Identify new and converging radio and recording technologies and their potential impact on music, the industries themselves, and listeners.**

- ☐ Convergence has come to radio in the form of satellite and cable delivery of radio, terrestrial digital radio, Web radio, podcasting, and music streaming from a number of different types of sites.

- ☐ Digital technology, in the form of Internet creation, promotion, and distribution of music, legal and illegal downloading from the Internet, and smartphone streaming, has reshaped the nature of the recording industry.

- ☐ Personal technologies such as smartphones and tablets reinforce radio's mobility and expand its audience.

▶ **Apply key radio-listening media literacy skills, especially in assessing the benefits and drawbacks of algorithm-based music consumption.**

- ☐ Streaming services offer you what they think you want to hear based on mountains of data about your listening habits and the music you favor. But how do you find new, interesting, or different music? What becomes of music as a personally and culturally important medium when your listening is data-driven?

KEY TERMS

QUESTIONS FOR REVIEW

1. What were the contributions made to radio by Guglielmo Marconi, Nikola Tesla, Reginald Fessenden, and Lee DeForest?

2. How do the Radio Acts of 1910, 1912, and 1927 relate to the Communications Act of 1934?

3. What were the five defining characteristics of the American broadcasting system just before it entered the golden age of radio?

4. How did World War II and the introduction of television change radio and recorded music?

5. What does it mean to say that radio is local, fragmented, specialized, personal, and mobile?

6. What are catalog and deep catalog albums?

7. How have cable and satellite affected the radio and recording industries? Computers and digitization?

8. Is the size of radio's audience in ascendance or in decline? Why?

9. What is streaming audio?

10. What is P2P technology? Stream ripping?

To maximize your study time, check out CONNECT to access the SmartBook study module for this chapter, watch videos, and explore other resources.

QUESTIONS FOR CRITICAL THINKING AND DISCUSSION

1. Have you ever illegally downloaded music? If you have never done so, what keeps you from engaging in the quite common practice? If you have, do you consider it stealing? If you don't see it as stealing, why not? But if you do consider it theft, how do you justify your action?

2. What do you think of the argument that control of the recording industry by a few multinational conglomerates inevitably leads to cultural homogenization and the ascendance of profit over music?

3. How much regulation do you believe is necessary in American broadcasting? If the airwaves belong to the people, how can we best ensure that license holders perform their public service functions?

REFERENCES

1. Adams, M. (1996). The race for radiotelephone: 1900–1920. *AWA Review, 10*, 78–119.

2. Andrews, J. (2019, August 9). Would you care if music disappeared from FM radio? You may only have a decade to save it. *CNBC*. Retrieved from https://www.cnbc.com/2019/08/09/would-you-care-if-music-disappeared-from-fm-radio.html

3. Antal, D. (2021, February 25). The racist music algorithm. *Data & Lyrics*. Retrieved from https://dataandlyrics.com/post/2020-10-30-racist-algorithm/

4. Aswad, J. (2020, April 22). Full stream ahead. *Variety*, p. 18.

5. Barnouw, E. (1966). *A tower in Babel: A history of broadcasting in the United States to 1933.* New York: Oxford University Press.

6. Bittner, J. R. (1994). *Law and regulation of electronic media.* Englewood Cliffs, NJ: Prentice Hall.

7. Bloomberg News. (2020, July 23). TikTok starts $200 million fund to help U.S. starts make careers. *Ad Age*. Retrieved from https://adage.com/article/news/tiktok-starts-200-million-fund-help-us-stars-make-careers/2269796

8. Collingwood, J. (2016, December 14). Preferred music style is tied to personality. *Psych Central*. Retrieved from http://psychcentral.com/lib/preferred-music-style-is-tied-to-personality/

9. Copps, M. J. (2011, June 9). Statement of Commissioner Michael J. Copps on release of FCC staff report "The Technology and Information Needs of Communities." *Federal Communications Commission*. Retrieved from https://www.fcc.gov/document/commissioner-copps-statement-release-staff-report

10. Curto, J. (2020, April 13). Drake's "Toosie Slide" TikTok scheme pays off, gives him another No. 1 debut. *New York Magazine*. Retrieved from https://www.vulture.com/2020/04/drakes-toosie-slide-tiktok-billboard-chart.html

11. Danaher, B., Smith, M. D., & Telang, R. (2020, March 20). Piracy landscape study. *U.S. Patent and Trademark Office*. Retrieved from https://www.uspto.gov/sites/default/files/documents/USPTO-Piracy%20Landscape-03-20-2020nr.pdf

12. Dayen, D. (2021, March 22). Islands in the stream. *American Prospect*. Retrieved from https://prospect.org/power/islands-in-the-stream-spotify-youtube-music-monopoly/

13. Deahl, D. (2019, August 31). How AI-generated music is changing the way hits are made. *The Verge*. Retrieved from https://www.theverge.com/2018/8/31/17777008/artificial-intelligence-taryn-southern-amper-music

14. Doyle, B. (2020, July 13). TikTok statistics—updated July 2020. *Walleroo Media*. Retrieved from https://wallaroomedia.com/blog/social-media/tiktok-statistics/#:~:text=U.S.%20Audience%20%E2%80%93%20As%20we%20mentioned,between%20the%20ages%2025%2D44.

15. Duncan, L. (2020, April 13). *Music Industry How To*. Retrieved from https://www.musicindustryhowto.com/best-major-record-labels/

16. Earth, M. (2020, January 15). Ed Sheeran's Spotify earnings revealed in study. *East Anglian Times*. Retrieved from https://www.eadt.co.uk/news/ed-sheeran-shape-of-you-spotify-rankings-1-6467968

17. "Edison not 'the father of sound'?" (2008, March 28). *Providence Journal*, p. A5.

18. Edison Research. (2020). *The infinite dial 2020*. Retrieved from https://www.rab.com/whyradio/wrnew/wr-research/pdf/Infinite%20Dial%202020.pdf

19. Editors of Media Life. (2015, September 17). Radio's big problem: Big radio. *Media Life*. Retrieved from http://www.medialifemagazine.com/radios-big-problem-big-radio/

20. Federal Communications Commission. (2020, April 6). *Broadcast station totals as of March 31, 2020*. Retrieved from https://docs.fcc.gov/public/attachments/DOC-363515A1.pdf

21. Greb, G., & Adams, M. (2003). *Charles Herrold, inventor of radio broadcasting*. Jefferson, NC: McFarland & Company.

22. Guttmann, A. (2019, December 10). Advertising spending in the United States in 2019 and 2023, by medium. *Statista*. Retrieved from https://www.statista.com/statistics/191926/us-ad-spending-by-medium-in-2009/

23. Hann, M. (2019, May 2). How Spotify's algorithms are ruining music. *Financial Times*. Retrieved from https://www.ft.com/content/dca07c32-6844-11e9-b809-6f0d2f5705f6

24. "How Much Do Music Streaming Services Pay Musicians?" (2020, January 16). *Ditto*. Retrieved from https://www.dittomusic.com/blog/how-much-do-music-streaming-services-pay-musicians

25. Iyengar, R. (2018, March 12). The logistics behind concert tours. *Medium*. Retrieved from https://medium.com/speedbox-is-typing/the-logistics-behind-concert-tours-7656f488b6c8

26. Jensen, E. (2020, March 6). Working together to alleviate "news deserts." *NPR*. Retrieved from https://www.npr.org/sections/publiceditor/2020/03/06/812096584/working-together-to-alleviate-news-deserts

27. Katz Radio Group. (2020, March). *Radio remains resilient*. Retrieved from https://www.rab.com/whyradio/wrnew/wr-research/pdf/Radio's%20Resilience_April%202020.pdf

28. Kelly, B. (2019, June). Audio Today 2019. *A. C. Nielsen*. Retrieved from https://www.nielsen.com/wp-content/uploads/sites/3/2019/06/audio-today-2019.pdf

29. King, A. (2020, December 9). 82% of musicians earn less than $270 a year from Spotify and other music streaming music platforms, study finds. *Digital Music News*. Retrieved from https://www.digitalmusicnews.com/2020/12/09/uk-musicians-music-streaming/

30. Knopper, S. (2018, August 5). The assembly line. *New York Magazine*. Retrieved from http://www.vulture.com/2018/08/the-songwriting-camps-where-pops-biggest-hits-get-crafted.html

31. Knopper, S. (2011, November 24). Rock radio takes another hit. *Rolling Stone*, p. 19.

32. Krueger, A. B. (2019, June 2). The economics of Rihanna's superstardom. *New York Times*, p. SR7.

33. Lansky, S. (2015/2016, December 28–January 4). Adele is music's past, present, and future. *Time*, pp. 120–126.

34. Lefsetz, B. (2015, January 28). True art must be about the band, not the brand. *Variety*, p. 26.

35. Lefsetz, B. (2013, June 21). Radio digs its own grave as cultural currents shift. *Variety*, p. 30.

36. Mack, Z. (2019, May 28). How streaming affects the lengths of songs. *The Verge*. Retrieved from https://www.theverge.com/2019/5/28/18642978/music-streaming-spotify-song-length-distribution-production-switched-on-pop-vergecast-interview

37. Marchese, D. (2019, November 13). How Thom Yorke learned to stop worrying and (mostly) love rock stardom. *New York Times Magazine*, pp. 13–15.

38. McCarthy, J. (2020, April 15). Amid swell of support, Patreon explains why it is now a "lifeline for creators." *The Drum*. Retrieved from https://www.thedrum.com/news/2020/04/15/amid-swell-support-patreon-explains-why-it-now-lifeline-creators

39. Mejía, P. (2019, July 22). The success of streaming has been great for some, but is there a better way? *NPR*. Retrieved from https://www.npr.org/2019/07/22/743775196/the-success-of-streaming-has-been-great-for-some-but-is-there-a-better-way

40. Menard, L. (2015, November 16). The elvic oracle. *The New Yorker*, pp. 80–88.

41. Neuman, M. (2017, April 21). A melodious milestone: 25,000 funded music projects. *Kickstarter*. Retrieved from https://www.kickstarter.com/blog/a-melodious-milestone-25000-funded-music-projects

42. Nielsen Audio. (2020). Radio–streaming–podcast–measurement. *A.C. Nielsen*. Retrieved from https://www.nielsen.com/us/en/solutions/capabilities/audio/

43. Perry, M. J. (2016, September 15). Recorded music sales by format from 1973–2015, and what that might tell us about the

limitations of GDP accounting. *AE Ideas*. Retrieved from https://www.aei.org/publication/annual-recorded-music-sales-by-format-from-1973-2015-and-what-that-tells-us-about-the-limitations-of-gdp-accounting/

44. Pippenger, M. (2020, April 15). TikTok Is the new MTV, and it's time we all get on board. *Popsugar*. Retrieved from https://www.popsugar.co.uk/entertainment/why-tiktok-is-new-mtv-47394949

45. "Podcast Ad Spending in the U.S. 2019-2024." (2021, February 11). *Statista*. https://www.statista.com/statistics/610071/podcast-ad-spending-us/

46. Radio Advertising Bureau. (2020). *Matter of fact*. Retrieved from https://www.rab.com/whyradio.cfm#facts

47. Radio Ink. (2020, April 28). *Coronavirus wipes out $17 billion in local advertising*. Retrieved from https://radioink.com/2020/04/28/coronavirus-wipes-out-17-billion-in-local-advertising/

48. Recording Industry Association of America. (2021). Gold & platinum. Retrieved from https://www.riaa.com/gold-platinum/

49. RIAA. (2020). U.S. sales database. Retrieved from https://www.riaa.com/u-s-sales-database/

50. Reilly, D. (2018, October 25). A.I. songwriting has arrived. Don't panic. *Fortune*. Retrieved from http://fortune.com/2018/10/25/artificial-intelligence-music

51. Richter, F. (2020, February 14). Radio still rules the road. *Statista*. Retrieved from https://www.statista.com/chart/4638/radio-still-rules-the-road/#:~:text=According%20to%20Edison%20Research%2C%2052,streaming%20service%20or%20online%20radio.

52. Samuels, D. (2019, August 25). Sound and fury. *New York Times Magazine*, pp. 36–41, 60–61.

53. Sanchez, D. (2019, May 6). The RIAA battles to keep its lawsuit against FLVTO.biz out of Russia. *Digital Music News*. Retrieved from https://www.digitalmusicnews.com/2019/05/06/riaa-v-flvto-response/

54. Sánchez-Olmos, C., & Castelló-Martínez, A. (2020). Brand placement in music videos: Artists, brands and products appearances in the Billboard Hot 100 from 2003 to 2016. *Journal of Promotion Management*. DOI: 10.1080/10496491.2020.1745986

55. Singleton, M. (2016, January 22). Old albums outsold new releases for the first time ever. *The Verge*. Retrieved from http://www.theverge.com/2016/1/22/10816404/2015-album-sales-trends-vinyl-catalog-streaming

56. Sisario, B. (2021, February 28). The state of the podcast. *New York Times*, pp. AR10–11.

57. Smith, D. (2021, February 26). The 2020 U.S. recorded music industry numbers are in—and streaming racked up more than $10 billion in revenues. *Digital Music News*. https://www.digitalmusicnews.com/2021/02/26/recorded-music-industry-growth/

58. Smith, D. (2020a, September 10). 1% of artists generate 90% of all music streams, latest data shows. *Digital Music News*. Retrieved from https://www.digitalmusicnews.com/2020/09/10/music-streams-data/

59. Smith, D. (2020b, June 24). Another study shows music piracy is sharply declining. *Digital Music News*. Retrieved from https://www.digitalmusicnews.com/2020/06/24/danish-piracy-rates-increasing-among-youth/#:~:text=Music%20piracy%2C%20for%20its%20part,%2Dstreaming%20services%20in%20Europe.

60. Sterling, C. H., & Kitross, J. M. (1990). *Stay tuned: A concise history of American broadcasting*. Belmont, CA: Wadsworth.

61. Stevens, A. D. (2020a, July 4). Protest music has come "roaring back to life" when we need it most. *Salon*. Retrieved from https://www.salon.com/2020/07/04/protest-music-songs-childish-gambino-kendrick-lamar/

62. Stevens, A. D. (2020b, April 19). How musicians are moving their gigs online during quarantine. *Salon*. Retrieved from https://www.salon.com/2020/04/19/musicians-virtual-concerts-gigs-teaching-classes-quarantine/

63. Szatmary, D. P. (2000). *Rockin' in time: A social history of rock-and-roll* (4th ed.). Upper Saddle River, NJ: Prentice-Hall.

64. Tett, G. (2021, April 7). Not OK, computer: music streaming's diversity problem. *Financial Times*. Retrieved from https://www.ft.com/content/fa53b5d6-0e79-4740-87ee-daaf8fc12212

65. Thompson, C. (2016, January/February). Rocking the house. *Smithsonian*, pp. 35–41.

66. Tillinghast, C. H. (2000). *American broadcast regulation and the First Amendment: Another look*. Ames: Iowa State University Press.

67. Timberg, S. (2016, June 10). Spotify is making you boring: When algorithms shape music taste, human curiosity loses. *Salon*. Retrieved from http://www.salon.com/2016/06/10/spotify_is_making_you_boring_when_algorithms_shape_music_taste_human_curiosity_loses/

68. Timberg, S. (2015, May 6). Radio is killing the guitar solo—and we'll lose more than our air-guitar skills when it's gone. *Salon*. retrieved from http://www.salon.com/2015/05/06/radio_is_killing_the_guitar_solo_%E2%80%94%C2%A0and_well_lose_more_than_our_air_guitar_skills_when_its_gone/

69. Trammell, M. (2017, May 15). Track record. *New Yorker*, pp. 44–51.

70. Ward, E., Stokes, G., & Tucker, K. (1986). *Rock of Ages: The Rolling Stone history of rock & roll*. New York: Rolling Stone Press.

71. "Year End Report: U.S. 2020." (2021, January). *MRC Data*. Retrieved from https://www.musicbusinessworldwide.com/files/2021/01/MRC_Billboard_YEAR_END_2020_US-Final.pdf

72. Zuckerman, E. (2019, November 27). Building a more honest Internet. *Columbia Journalism Review*. Retrieved from https://www.cjr.org/special_report/building-honest-internet-public-interest.php#:~:text=By%20Ethan%20Zuckerman&text=Over%20the%20course%20of,for%20better%20and%20for%20worse.

Cultural Forum Blue Column icon, Media Literacy Red Torch Icon, Using Media Green Gear icon, Developing Media book in starburst icon: ©McGraw Hill

Television, Cable, and Mobile Video

8

◀ YouTube cult favorite, *Hot Ones: The Game Show*, where contestants challenge celebrities to see who can eat the hottest sauces, made the jump from Web to cable television.

Daniel DeSlover/ZUMA Wire/Alamy Stock Photo

Learning Objectives

No one is neutral about television. We either love it or hate it. Many of us do both. This is because it is our most ubiquitous and socially and culturally powerful mass medium. Several recent and converging technologies promise to make it even more so. After studying this chapter, you should be able to

▶ Recognize the history and development of the television and cable television industries and television itself as a medium.

▶ Describe how the organizational and economic nature of the contemporary television and cable industries shapes the content of television.

▶ Explain the relationship between television in all its forms and its viewers.

▶ Identify new and converging video technologies and their potential impact on the television industry and its audience.

▶ Describe the digital and mobile television revolution.

▶ Apply key television-viewing media literacy skills to satirical news.

1884 ▶ Nipkow invents his disc

Bettmann/Getty Images

1900

1923 ▶ Zworykin demonstrates electronic iconoscope tube

Bettmann/Getty Images

1925

1927 Farnsworth demonstrates electronically scanned television images

1928 ▶ Baird transmits mechanical video image across Atlantic

1939 Sarnoff introduces regular television broadcasting at World's Fair

1941 First two commercial stations approved

PA Images/Alamy Stock Photo

1950

1950 *Red Channels*; Nielsen ratings

1951 US wired coast-to-coast; ▶ *I Love Lucy*

1954 Army–McCarthy Hearings telecast

1959 Quiz show scandal

1962 All-channel legislation

1963 FCC begins regulation of cable

1975

1975 HBO begins national distribution

1976 VCR introduced

1996 DVD introduced; Telecommunications Act

1998 First digital TV broadcast

1999 ▶ DVR introduced

Zealot/Shutterstock

(TV): Interfoto/History/ Alamy Stock Photo; (image on the screen): CBS/Photofest

2000

2002 FCC mandates digital receivers by 2007

2005 Networks begin selling program downloads

2009 All TV stations are digital

2010 Mobile digital television

2011 ▶ Netflix, Hulu, and YouTube begin original programming

2012 Online movie transactions exceed discs

2015 HBO, Nickelodeon, and others begin OTT streaming

2016 *Sesame Street* moves to HBO; VCR declared dead; video streaming revenues exceed DVD revenues for first time

2017 Nielsen's Total Content Ratings

2018 Netflix earns more Emmy nominations than any other channel; major networks combine to develop new standardized audience metric

2019 Streaming subscriptions surpass cable subscriptions

2020 Coronavirus in US

2021 January 6 attack on Capitol building livestreamed by congresspeople

Juan Carlos Baena/Alamy Stock Photo

"WHAT'S WITH THE CAMERA AND LIGHTS? YOUR PHONE'S NOT GOOD ENOUGH FOR MAKING VIDEOS ANYMORE?"

"Not for what I'm doing. I'm going to be a TV star."

"A TV star?"

"Well, first a YouTube star, then a TV star, and maybe then the movies, like Roman Atwood."

"Who?"

"Roman Atwood. He has more than 15 million subscribers to his YouTube pranks channel."

"Wait, is this the guy who tricked his girlfriend into thinking that one of their kids was killed in an accident? That's some prank."

"For real. It got him a movie deal from Lionsgate. And I bet you never heard of Ryan Kaji either. He's 8 years old and he makes over $26 million a year showing off toys for his 23 million YouTube subscribers. He now has a show on Nickelodeon. You ever watch *Hot Ones: The Game Show*?"

"Where celebrities embarrass themselves eating super-hot wings and things?"

"Right. Started on YouTube, became a cult favorite, now it's on cable's TruTV. Me? I'm using YouTube's Creator Hub to help me get started and make my mark. YouTube even has YouTube Spaces where people like me can go to produce their shows and maybe even get funding for good ideas. Then they help you get bigger. They have an originals division that connects its stars with big-time movie and TV producers."

"OK. So what are you going to do for your show? I imagine those folks who made it had some sort of idea, right?"

"I haven't figured that out yet. But I have a camera and lights. Action's sure to follow!"

Our aspiring star doesn't even have to work this hard to make the big time. Being "interesting" on social media may be enough, as casting agents "trawl through Instagram around the clock for people who pique their curiosity" (Marsh, 2018). Regardless of whether our wannabe will ever benefit from all this activity, there is indeed massive change roiling contemporary television and video. Social networking sites now produce original video: Facebook spends $2 billion a year on original programming for Facebook Watch; Instagram launched a video service, IGTV; and Snapchat has Snap Originals.

On the subscription streaming TV side of this new video environment, Netflix now spends upwards of $15 billion a year on original programming and is likely to boost that to $26 billion in 2028 ("Netflix Projected," 2020). Online retailer Amazon spends over $7 billion a year on original content for Amazon Prime. Its *Fleabag* won the 2019 Emmy for Outstanding Comedy Series a year after its *The Marvelous Mrs. Maisel* won 2018's. Hulu Plus streams existing and original shows such as *The Handmaid's Tale*, which in 2017 became the first streaming series to win the Emmy for Outstanding Drama series. Department store Walmart has a video streaming channel, Vudu, as do old-line broadcast networks CBS (Paramount+) and NBC (Peacock), offering programs, such as *Star Trek: Discovery*, *The Good Fight*, and *Brave New World* that are unavailable to their broadcast and cable audiences.

Viewers have enthusiastically taken to this new form of television—streaming accounts for one-fifth of all US television watching (Ha, 2020). In fact, during 2020's COVID-19 lock-down, global demand was such that governments around the world asked the major streaming companies to reduce the quality of their video to preserve Internet **bandwidth**, a channel's information-carrying capacity, for other use ("The Quarantine," 2020).

Yes, television is changing, and this chapter details that change, from early experiments with mechanical scanning to the electronic marvel that sits in our homes to the mobile screens we carry in our pockets. We trace the rapid transformation of television into a mature medium after World War II and examine how the medium, the entire television industry in fact, was altered by the emergence and success of cable television. And significant change is once again remaking what we currently know as television . . . and what we once knew as the audience. We are all now TV executives, choosing

▼ Amazon Prime's streaming hit *Fleabag* won television's Emmy Award for Outstanding Comedy Series in 2019.

TCD/Prod.DB/Alamy Stock Photo

our programs and *our* schedules, no longer limited by what some distant network television executives think is the schedule that best serves their advertisers' needs.

The remarkable reach of television—in all its forms—accounts for its attractiveness as an advertising medium. We discuss this reach, and we explore the structure, programming, and economics of the television and cable industries. We consider new technologies, their convergence with television, and how they promise to change the interaction between the medium and its audiences. Finally, we discuss media literacy in terms of the role of satirical television news in the cultural forum.

A Short History of Television

Television has changed the way teachers teach, governments govern, and religious leaders lead, and shaped how we organize the furniture in our homes. Television has changed the nature, operation, and relationship to their audiences of books, magazines, movies, and radio. Television even shapes how we think of the Internet. Will the Web's potential drown in television-level hypercommercialism? Do online news services deliver faster, better, and more accurate information than television? Even the computer screens we use look like television screens; we participate in online video conferencing, play new and improved online video games, and of course, stream hours and hours of video. Already the majority of all traffic that crosses the Internet, by 2022, online video will make up more than 82% of all consumer Internet traffic, 15 times higher than it was in 2017 (Cisco, 2020). Before we delve deeper into the nature of this powerful medium and its relationship with its audience, let's examine how television developed as it did.

Mechanical and Electronic Scanning

In 1884, Paul Nipkow, a Russian scientist living in Berlin, developed the first workable device for generating electrical signals suitable for the transmission of a scene that people could see. His **Nipkow disc** consisted of a rotating scanning disc spinning in front of a photoelectric cell. It produced 4,000 **pixels** (picture dots) per second, producing a picture composed of 18 parallel lines. Although his mechanical system proved too limiting, Nipkow demonstrated the possibility of using a scanning system to divide a scene into an orderly pattern of transmittable picture elements that could be recomposed as a visual image. British inventor John Logie Baird was able to transmit moving images using a mechanical disc as early as 1925, and in 1928 he successfully sent a television picture from London to Hartsdale, New York.

Electronic scanning came either from another Russian or from a US farm boy; historians disagree. Vladimir Zworykin, a Russian immigrant living near Pittsburgh and working for Westinghouse, demonstrated his **iconoscope tube**, the first practical television camera tube, in 1923. In 1929, David Sarnoff lured him to RCA to head its electronics research lab, and it was there that Zworykin developed the **kinescope**, an improved picture tube. At the same time, young Philo Farnsworth had moved from Idaho to San Francisco to perfect an electronic television system, the design for which he had shown his high school science teacher when he was 15 years old. In 1927, at the age of 20, he made his first public demonstration—film clips of a prize fight, movie scenes, and other graphic images. The "Boy Wonder" and Zworykin's RCA spent the next decade fighting fierce patent battles in court. In 1939, RCA capitulated, agreeing to pay Farnsworth royalties for the use of his patents.

In April of that year, at the World's Fair in New York, RCA made the first true public demonstration of television in the form of regularly scheduled 2-hour NBC broadcasts. These black-and-white telecasts consisted of cooking demonstrations, singers, jugglers, comedians, puppets—just about anything that could fit in a hot, brightly lit studio and demonstrate motion. People could buy television sets at the RCA Pavilion at prices ranging from $200 for the 5-inch screen to $600 for the deluxe 12-inch-screen model. The FCC granted construction permits to the first two commercial stations in 1941, and then World War II intervened. But as was the case with radio during World War I, technical development and improvement of the new medium continued.

▶ A Nipkow disc.
Bettmann/Getty Images

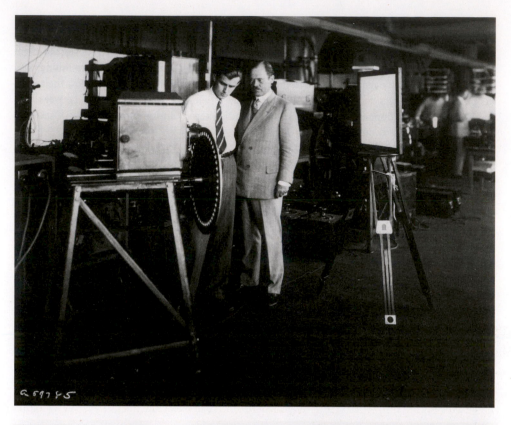

▶ Philo Farnsworth and Vladimir Zworykin, pioneers in the development of television.
(both): Bettmann/Getty Images

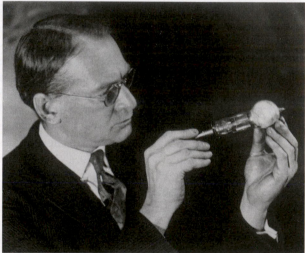

The 1950s

In 1952, 108 stations were broadcasting to 17 million television homes. By the end of the decade, there were 559 stations, and nearly 90% of US households had televisions. In the 1950s, more television sets were sold in the United States (70 million) than there were children born (40.5 million) (Kuralt, 1977). The technical standards were fixed, stations proliferated and flourished, the public tuned in, and advertisers were enthusiastic. The content and character of the medium were set in this decade as well:

- Carried over from the radio networks, television genres included variety shows, situation comedies, dramas (including Westerns and cop shows), soap operas, and quiz shows.
- Two new formats appeared: feature films and talk shows. Talk shows were instrumental in introducing radio personalities to the television audience, which could see its favorites for the first time.

- Television news and documentary remade broadcast journalism as a powerful force in its own right, led by CBS's Edward R. Murrow (*See It Now*, 1951) and NBC's David Brinkley and Chet Huntley. Huntley and Brinkley's 1956 coverage of the major political conventions gave audiences an early glimpse of the power of television to cover news and history in the making. This was reinforced over the next two decades by the medium's nation-galvanizing coverage of the assassination and funeral of President John F. Kennedy in 1963 and the 1973 Senate Watergate hearings, as well as by the journalism of CBS's Walter Cronkite throughout that time.

- AT&T completed its national **coaxial cable** and **microwave relay** network for the distribution of television programming in the summer of 1951. The entire United States was now within the reach of the major television networks, and they came to dominate the medium.

Four other events from the 1950s would permanently shape, even today, how television operates: the quiz show scandal, the appearance of *I Love Lucy*, McCarthyism, and the establishment of the ratings system. Another, in 1948, would permanently *reshape* the television industry. That development, as you'll soon see, was cable television.

THE QUIZ SHOW SCANDAL AND CHANGES IN SPONSORSHIP Throughout the 1950s, the networks served primarily as time brokers, offering airtime and distribution (their affiliates) and accepting payment for access to both. Except for their own news and sports coverage, the networks relied on outside agencies to provide programs. An advertising agency, for example, would hire a production company to produce a program for its client. That client would then be the show's sponsor—*The Kraft Television Theatre* and *Westinghouse Studio One* are two examples. The agency would then pay a network to air the program over its national collection of stations. This system had enriched the networks during the heyday of radio, and they saw no reason to change.

But in 1959, a quiz show scandal (enveloping independently produced, single-advertiser-sponsored programs) changed the way the networks did business. When it was discovered that popular shows like *The $64,000 Question* had been fixed by advertisers and producers to ensure desired outcomes, the networks, mindful of their reputations, were determined to take control of their schedules. They, themselves, began commissioning or buying the entertainment fare that filled their broadcast days and nights. Now, rather than selling blocks of time to ad agencies and sponsors, the networks paid for the content they aired through **spot commercial sales** (selling individual 60-second spots on a given program to a wide variety of advertisers).

As a result, the content of television was altered. Some critics argue that this change to spot sales put an end to the golden age of television. When sponsors agreed to attach their names to programs, *Alcoa Presents* or the *Texaco Star Theater*, for example, they had an incentive to demand high-quality programming. Spot sales, with network salespeople offering small bits of time to a number of different sponsors, reduced the demand for quality. Because individual sponsors were not identified with a given show, they had no stake in how well it was made—only in how many viewers it attracted. Spot sales also reduced the willingness of the networks to try innovative or different types of content. Familiarity and predictability attracted more viewers and, therefore, more advertisers.

There is a counterargument, however. Once the financial well-being of the networks became dependent on the programming they aired, the networks themselves became more concerned with program quality, lifting television from its dull infancy (remembered now as the golden age only by those small, early audiences committed to serious character-driven televised drama). Different historians and critics offer arguments for both views.

I LOVE LUCY **AND MORE CHANGES** In 1951, CBS asked Lucille Ball to move her hit radio program, *My Favorite Husband*, to television. Lucy was willing but wanted her real-life husband, Desi Arnaz, to play the part of her on-air spouse. The network refused (some historians say the network objected to the prime-time presentation of an interracial marriage—Desi Arnaz was Cuban—but CBS denies this). But Lucy made additional demands. Television programming at the time was broadcast live: Images were typically captured by three large television cameras, with a director in a booth choosing among the three available images. Lucy wanted

▶ Running from 1947 until 1958, NBC's *Kraft Television Theatre* aired some of the golden age's most respected live anthology dramas. *Top*, Richard Kiley and Everett Sloane; *left*, Ossie Davis; *right*, Walter Matthau and Nancy Walker.

(all): Courtesy Everett Collection

her program produced in the same manner—in front of a live audience with three simultaneously running cameras—but these cameras would be *film* cameras. Editors could then review the three sets of film and edit them together to give the best combination of action and reaction shots. Lucy also wanted the production to take place in Hollywood, the nation's film capital, instead of New York, the television center at the time. CBS was uncertain about this departure from how television was typically produced and refused these requests as well.

Lucy and Desi borrowed the necessary money and produced *I Love Lucy* on their own, selling the broadcast rights to CBS. In doing so, the woman now best remembered as "that zany redhead" transformed the business and look of television:

- Filmed reruns were now possible, something that had been impossible with live television, and this, in turn, created the off-network syndication industry.
- The television industry moved from New York, with its stage drama orientation, to Hollywood, with its entertainment film mind-set. More action and more flash came to the screen.

- Weekly series could now be produced relatively quickly and inexpensively. A 39-week series could be completed in 20 or 24 weeks, saving money on actors, crew, equipment, and facilities. In addition, the same stock shots—for example, certain exterior views—could be used in different episodes.

MCCARTHYISM: THE GROWING POWER OF TELEVISION The Red Scare that cowed the movie business also touched television, aided by the publication in 1950 of *Red Channels: The Report of Communist Influence in Radio and Television*, the work of three former FBI agents operating a company called American Business Consultants. Its 200 pages detailed the alleged pro-Communist sympathies of 151 broadcast personalities, including Orson Welles and journalist Howard K. Smith. Advertisers were encouraged to avoid buying time from broadcasters who employed these "Red sympathizers." Like the movie studios, the television industry caved in. The networks employed security checkers to look into people's backgrounds, refused to hire suspect talent, and demanded loyalty oaths from performers. In its infancy, television had taken the safe path. Many gifted artists were denied not only a paycheck but also the opportunity to shape the medium's content.

Ironically, it was this same Red Scare that allowed television to demonstrate its enormous power as a vehicle of democracy and freedom. Joseph McCarthy, the Republican junior senator from Wisconsin whose tactics gave this era its name, was seen by millions of viewers as his investigation of Reds in the US Army was broadcast by all the networks for 36 days in 1954. Daytime ratings increased 50% (Sterling & Kittross, 1990). At the same time, Edward R. Murrow used his *See It Now*, a documentary series broadcast by CBS, to expose the senator's lies and hypocrisy. As a consequence of the two broadcasts, McCarthy was ruined; he was censured by his Senate colleagues and later died a lonely alcoholic's death. Television had given the people eyes and ears—and power—where before they had little. The Army–McCarthy Hearings and Murrow's challenge to McCarthyism are still regarded as two of television's finest moments.

▲ *I Love Lucy* was significant for far more than its comedy. Thanks to Lucille Ball's shrewd business sense, it became the foundation for the huge off-network syndicated television industry. *(TV): Interfoto/History/Alamy Stock Photo; (image on the screen): CBS/Photofest*

◄ Wisconsin's Republican junior senator, Joseph McCarthy, claimed that the army was rife with Communists, Reds, and "fellow travelers." Network TV coverage of the his erratic behavior helped bring the despot into disrepute. *Everett Collection Historical/Alamy Stock Photo*

The Coming of Cable

In 1948 in Mahanoy City, Pennsylvania, appliance sales representative John Walson was having trouble selling televisions. The Pocono Mountains sat between his town and Philadelphia's three new stations; no receivable channels meant no TV sales. But Walson was also a powerline worker, so he convinced his bosses to let him run a wire to his store from a tower he erected on New Boston Mountain. As more and more people became aware of his system, he began wiring the homes of customers who bought his sets. In June of that year, Walson had 727 subscribers for his **community antenna television (CATV)** system (Chin, 1978). Although no one calls it CATV anymore, cable television was born.

The cable Walson used was a twin-lead wire, much like the cord that connects a lamp to an outlet. To attract even more subscribers, he had to offer improved picture quality. He accomplished this by using *coaxial cable* and self-manufactured boosters (or amplifiers). Coaxial cable—copper-clad aluminum wire encased in plastic foam insulation, covered by an aluminum outer conductor, and then sheathed in plastic—had more bandwidth than did twin-lead wire. As a result, it allowed more of the original signal to pass and even permitted Walson to carry a greater number of channels.

With expanded bandwidth and new, powerful signal boosters developed by Milton Jerrold Shapp, who would later become Pennsylvania's governor, these systems began experimenting with the **importation of distant signals**, using wires not only to provide improved reception but also to offer a wider variety of programming. They began delivering independent stations from as far away as New York to fill their then-amazing 7 to 10 channels. By 1962, 800 systems were providing cable television to more than 850,000 homes.

The industry today is composed of over 5,000 individual cable systems delivering video to 51 million households, high-speed Internet to 68 million, and digital telephone to 30 million (Internet & Television Association, 2020).

THE NIELSEN RATINGS The concept of measuring audience was carried over from radio to television, but the ratings as we know them today are far more sophisticated (see Chapter 7 for more on ratings). The A. C. Nielsen Company began in 1923 as a product-testing company but soon branched into market research. In 1936, Nielsen started reporting radio ratings and was doing the same for television by 1950.

To produce the ratings today, Nielsen selects 41,000 households, about 100,000 people, thought to be representative of the entire US viewing audience. To record data on what people in those TV households are watching, Nielsen employs the **Global Television Audience Metering (GTAM) meter**, which actively (requiring viewer input) and passively (automatically reading digital codes embedded in video content) measures viewing as people, with increasing mobility, consume video on a growing array of technologies. The data are then sent to Nielsen via the Internet, and the company determines the programs watched, who watched them, and the amount of time each viewer spent with them. But the same convergence that required the development of the GTAM meter is upsetting the business of audience measurement in many ways. In fact, many television and advertising people see the ratings as useless, a relic from an earlier time. "We are piloting interplanetary travel with a tachometer and a speedometer and a steering wheel that only moves 30 degrees in either direction," explains Jonathan Steuer, chief research officer for Omnicom Media Group, "which isn't really helpful" (in Steinberg, 2019, p. 24).

To present a fuller picture of a show's total audience by accounting for multiplatform and **nonlinear TV** viewing (people watching on their own schedules), the four major broadcast networks demanded a new rating that measured a program's true performance. Nielsen responded with several fixes, including its **C3 and C7 ratings**, counting audiences across several screens—TV (original airing plus DVR), Internet, and mobile video. The "3" and the "7" represent the viewing of the commercials (the "C") that appear in a specific program within 3 or 7 days of its premiere telecast. With C7, for example, a program like the Paramount Network's *Yellowstone* enjoys a "lift" of 215%; the viewership of ABC's *Emergence* grows 192% ("Tops of," 2020). This is extremely important to the networks as half to three-quarters of all commercial TV viewing is time-shifted (Lukovitz, 2020a).

Facing pressure from competitor ComScore, which can measure viewing across all screens (stationary and mobile) from more than 10 million homes, and heeding broadcasters' demand for more accurate measurement of **long-tail viewing** (TV program viewership over

▲ John Walson.
The Barco Library, The Cable Center, Denver, CO.

time, across multiple platforms, and on-demand), Nielsen rolled out its Total Content Ratings in 2017. The new measure captures all viewing across all possible devices, including traditional TV; video-on-demand; DVR playback; Internet-connected devices such as Roku, Xbox, and Apple TV; smartphones; desktop computers; laptops; and tablets.

Nonetheless, even after Nielsen announced in 2020 that it would include out-of-home viewing in its measurement, there remains great dissatisfaction with the company's ratings, leading many networks to augment them with their own measure they say better reflects today's video environment, **total viewer impressions**, the actual number of people watching rather than a percentage of possible viewers who tune in, counting all the ways a show is consumed: long-tail viewing, out-of-home, broadcasters' own websites, posted to social media, re-shown on YouTube, and so on. NBCUniversal, Hearst, and several other major station groups and networks have moved to the new measure. Some networks have gone as far as to drop Nielsen altogether, most notably cable channel CNBC. Still, as it has been from the earliest days of television, "the Nielsens" remain the *coin of the realm*, that is, they are, despite their limitations, the agreed-upon currency on which the vast majority of television advertising sales are based.

Another important measure of television's audience is its **share**, which is a direct reflection of a particular show's competitive performance. Share doesn't measure viewers as a percentage of *all* television households (as do the ratings). Instead, the share measures a program audience as a percentage of the *television sets in use* at the time it airs. It tells us what proportion of the *actual* audience a program attracts, indicating how well a particular program is doing on its given night, in its time slot, and against its competition. For example, game show *Wheel of Fortune* normally gets a rating of around 5—poor by prime-time standards—but because it airs when fewer homes are tuned in, its share of 50 (50% of the homes with sets in use) is quite spectacular. You can see how ratings and shares are computed in Figure 8.1.

Ratings and shares can be computed using these formulas:

$$\text{Rating} = \frac{\text{Households tuned in to a given program}}{\text{All households with television}}$$

$$\text{Share} = \frac{\text{Households tuned in to a given program}}{\text{All households tuned in to television at that time}}$$

Here's an example. Your talk show is aired in a market that has 1 million television households; 400,000 are tuned in to you. Therefore,

$$\frac{400,000}{1,000,000} = 0.40, \text{ or a rating of 40.}$$

At the time your show airs, however, there are only 800,000 households using television. Therefore, your share of the available audience is

$$\text{Share} = \frac{400,000}{800,000} = 0.50, \text{ or a share of 50.}$$

If you can explain why a specific program's share is always higher than its rating, then you understand the difference between the two.

▲ **Figure 8.1** Computing Ratings and Shares.

Television and Its Audiences

The 1960s saw some refinement in the technical structure of television, which influenced its organization and audience. In 1962, Congress passed **all-channel legislation**, which required that all sets imported into or manufactured in the United States be equipped with both VHF and UHF receivers. This had little immediate impact; US viewers were now hooked on the three national networks and their VHF affiliates. Still, UHF independents and educational stations were able to at least attract some semblance of an audience. The UHF independents would have to wait for the coming of cable to give them clout. Now that the educational stations were attracting more viewers, they began to look less educational in the strictest sense of the word and began programming more entertaining cultural fare (see the essay "The Creation of *Sesame Street*"). The Public Broadcasting Act of 1967 united the educational stations into an important network, the Public Broadcasting Service (PBS), which today has 350 member stations.

The 1960s also witnessed the immense social and political power of the new medium to force profound alterations in the country's consciousness and behavior. Particularly influential were the Nixon–Kennedy campaign debates of 1960, broadcasts of the aftermath of Kennedy's assassination and funeral in 1963, the 1969 transmission of Neil Armstrong's walk on the moon, and the use of television at the end of the decade by civil rights and anti–Vietnam War leaders.

The 1960s also gave rise to a descriptive expression sometimes used today when television is discussed. Speaking to the 1961 convention of the National Association of Broadcasters, John F. Kennedy's new FCC chair, Newton Minow, invited broadcasters to

sit down in front of your television set when your station goes on the air and stay there without a book, magazine, newspaper, profit and loss sheet, or ratings book to distract you, and keep your eyes glued to that set until the station signs off. I can assure you that you will observe a **vast wasteland**.

USING MEDIA TO MAKE A DIFFERENCE
The Creation of *Sesame Street*

In 1968, a public affairs program producer for Channel 13 in New York City identified a number of related problems that she believed could be addressed by a well-conceived, well-produced television show.

Joan Ganz Cooney saw that 80% of 3- and 4-year-olds and 25% of 5-year-olds in the United States did not attend any form of preschool. Children from financially disadvantaged homes were far less likely to attend preschool at these ages than their better-off peers. Children in these age groups who did go to preschool received little academic instruction; preschool was the equivalent of organized recess. Large numbers of US children, then, entered first grade with no formal schooling, even though education experts had long argued that preschool years were crucial in children's intellectual and academic development. In addition, the disparity in academic preparedness between poor and other children was a national disgrace.

What did these children do instead of going to preschool? Cooney knew that they watched television. But she also knew that "existing shows for 3- through 5-year-old children . . . did not have education as a primary goal" (Ball & Bogatz, 1970, p. 2). Her idea was to use an interesting, exciting, visually and aurally stimulating television show as an explicitly educational tool "to promote the intellectual and cultural growth of preschoolers, particularly disadvantaged preschoolers," and to "teach children how to think as well as what to think" (Cook et al., 1975, p. 7).

Cooney established a nonprofit organization, the Children's Television Workshop (CTW), and sought funding for her program. Several federal agencies, primarily the Office of Education, a number of private foundations including Carnegie and Ford, and public broadcasters, contributed $13.7 million for CTW's first four years.

After much research into producing a quality children's television show and studying the best instructional methods for teaching preschool audiences (it is the most-researched television show of all time; Lepore, 2020), CTW unveiled *Sesame Street* during the 1969 television season. It was an instant hit with children and parents. *The New Republic* said, "Judged by the standards of most other programs for preschoolers, it is imaginative, tasteful, and witty" (cited in Sedulus, 1970). Originally scheduled for 1 hour a day during the school week, within months of its debut *Sesame Street* was being programmed twice a day on many public television stations, and many ran the entire week's schedule on Saturdays and Sundays. Today, more than 50 years after its debut, *Sesame Street* airs 35 new episodes a year, and in 2016 it made HBO (including its streaming service) its new home network. Episodes run on HBO for nine months before being aired on free public television.

Did Cooney and her show make a difference? Several national studies demonstrated that academic performance in early grades was directly and strongly correlated with regular viewing of *Sesame Street.* The commercial networks began to introduce educational fare into their Saturday morning schedules. ABC's *Grammar Rock, America Rock* (on US history), and *Multiplication Rock* were critical and educational successes, and much of the programming on today's kids' channels, such as Nickelodeon, trace their pacing and production techniques to the show, winner of 228 Emmy Awards.

And *Sesame Street* continues to make a difference by never shying from topics, difficult as they might be for kids, tackling issues like death, autism, divorce, the trauma of the 9/11 terrorist attacks, and incarceration. During the 2020 coronavirus pandemic, *Sesame Street* even took on the virus, teaming with CNN for *The ABCs of COVID-19* to answer questions for both parents and kids, and with scores of networks and streaming services, for *Sesame Street: Elmo's Playdate,* showing the furry red monster, housebound like millions of other children, teleconferencing with his pals (Buckman, 2020).

Whether or not one agrees with Minow's assessment of television, then or now, there is no doubt that audiences continue to watch:

- There are just over 120 million television households in the United States, 96% of all US homes (Television Advertising Bureau, 2020).
- The average American adult watches television 27 hours a week (Epstein, 2020).
- Television reaches more adults each day than any other medium, and those people spend more time with television than with any other medium. Moreover, it tops all other media in building product awareness, interest, and intention to purchase (Television Advertising Bureau, 2020).

- Eighty-eight percent of American adults admit that they have lost sleep because they were binge watching a television series (Watson, 2020).

There can be no doubt, either, that television is successful as an advertising medium:

- Total annual billings for television are around $68.2 billion, 27.8% of all US ad spending ("Total U.S.," 2020).
- The average 30-second prime-time network television spot cost well over $100,000. A spot on *Sunday Night Football* gets $783,718; spots on *This Is Us* cost $476,352; 30 seconds on *The Voice* run $254,224 (Poggi, 2020).
- Prime ad time on the February 2021 Buccaneers–Chiefs Super Bowl broadcast cost $5.6 million for 30 seconds, or approximately $186,666 per second, and that does not include the cost of the commercials' production, typically more than $1 million per spot (Taylor, 2021).

Scope and Nature of the Broadcast Television Industry

Today, as it has been from the beginning, the business of broadcast television is dominated by a few centralized production, distribution, and decision-making organizations. These networks link affiliates for the purpose of delivering and selling viewers to advertisers. The large majority of the 1,372 commercial stations in the United States are affiliated with a national broadcasting network. ABC, NBC, CBS, and Fox each have over 200 affiliates, and these traditional outlets remain the four most-viewed television networks across the broadcast and cable dial. About 200 more stations are affiliated with the CW Network, jointly owned by CBS and Warner Bros., and there are two national Spanish-language networks, Telemundo (94 stations) and Univision (61). Although cable has introduced us to dozens of popular cable networks—ESPN, MTV, Comedy Central, and A&E, to name a few—for decades most programs that came to mind when we thought of television were either conceived, approved, funded, produced, or distributed by the broadcast networks. Although, as you read at this chapter's outset, that's quickly changing. More on that soon.

Local affiliates carry network programs (they **clear time**). Until quite recently, affiliates received direct payment for carrying a show, called compensation, and the right to keep all income from the sale of local commercials on that program. But loss of network audience and the rise of cable have altered this arrangement. Now networks receive **reverse compensation**, a fee paid by the local station for the right to be that network's affiliate. It is typically based on the amount of money the local cable operation pays to the station to carry its signal, called **retransmission fees**.

The Networks and Program Content

Networks control what appears on the vast majority of local television stations, but they also control what appears on non-network television, that is, when affiliates program their own content. In addition, they influence what appears on independent stations and on cable channels. This non-network material not only tends to be network-*type* programming but most often is programming that originally aired on the networks themselves (called **off-network** programs).

Why do network and network-type content dominate television? *Availability* is one factor. There is 75 years' worth of already successful network content available for airing on local stations. A second factor is that the *production and distribution* mechanisms that have long served the broadcast networks are well established and serve the newer outlets just as well as they did NBC, CBS, and ABC. The final reason is us, the audience. The formats we are most comfortable with—our television tastes and expectations—have been and continue to be developed on the networks.

How a Program Reaches the Screen, Traditionally and Otherwise

The national broadcast and cable networks look at about 4,000 proposals a year for new television series. Many, if not most, are submitted at the networks' invitation or instigation. Of the 4,000, about 60 to 70 will be filmed as **pilots**, or trial programs, at a cost of $5 million for a 60-minute show and $3 million for a 30-minute show (Friedman, 2019). Perhaps 20 to 30 of these will reach our screens. The broadcast and cable networks spend over $500 million a season to suffer this process. For this reason, they prefer to see ideas from producers with established track records and demonstrated financial and organizational stability—for example, Dick Wolf is the source of 9 *Law & Order* and 3 *Chicago* dramas, plus 36 other prime-time series aired in recent years. Jerry Bruckheimer, of the several titles in the *CSI* series, accounts for more than 25 more.

First premium cable and then, even more profoundly, the streaming services have dramatically altered how programs make it to our TV sets. This is largely due to the amount of money they are willing to spend on production (for example, $15 million an episode for HBO Max's *Game of Thrones* and $35.8 million per episode for Amazon Prime's *Lord of the Rings*; Friedman, 2021) and the creative freedom they promise.

The way to traditionally get a program on TV differs somewhat for those who have been asked to submit an idea and for producers who bring their concepts to the broadcast and cable networks. First, a producer has an *idea*, or a network has an idea and asks a proven producer to propose a show based on it, possibly offering a *straight-to-series commitment* to keep the show away from a competing channel, as was the case with NBC's *Young Rock* and ABC's *The Big Sky*. An independent producer, however, must *shop* the idea to one of the networks; naturally, an invited or locked-down producer submits the proposal to only one network. In either case, if the network is persuaded, it *buys the option* and asks for a written *outline* in which the original idea is refined. If still interested, the network will order a full *script*.

If the network approves that script, it will order the production of a pilot. Pilots are then subjected to rigorous testing by the networks' own and independent audience research organizations. Based on this research, networks will often demand changes, such as writing out characters who tested poorly or beefing up storylines that test audiences particularly liked.

If the network is still interested—that is, if it believes that the show will be a hit—it orders a set number of episodes and schedules the show. Of course, those with straight-to-series deals suffer no such indignities, as they are ordered in full without requiring a pilot episode. Upsetting the traditional model even more, streaming services have begun to offer successful producers *lockdown deals*, cash upfront to bind them to their platform. For example, Netflix signed *Game of Thrones* creators David Benioff and Dan Weiss to a $200 million multi-year deal to jump from HBO (Goldberg, 2019); Amazon made a similar pact with international movie star and lead actor on ABC's *Quantico*, Priyanka Chopra Jonas (Malkin, 2020).

The streaming services and premium cable channels invest in expensive programming to better attract paying subscribers and because it has an endless shelf life: their programming knows no "new season"; it's always available, year-after-year, to be discovered by existing and new viewers alike. Additionally, they make their content available for their subscribers all over the world—Netflix is in 190 countries, and HBO is in 50.

However, network television program producers participate in this expensive enterprise for a different reason: they can make large amounts of money in syndication, the sale of their programs to stations on a market-by-market basis. Even though the networks control the process from idea to scheduling and decide how long a show stays in their lineups, producers continue to own the rights to their programs. Once enough episodes have been made (generally about 88, which is the product of four years on a network), producers can sell the syndicated package to the highest bidder in each of the 210 US television markets, to the ad-supported cable channels, and overseas, keeping all the revenues for themselves.

This is the legacy of Lucille Ball's business genius (CBS still earns about $15 million a year from *I Love Lucy* syndication). The price of a syndicated program depends on the market size, the level of competition between the stations in the market, and the age and popularity of the program itself. The station buys the right to a specified number of plays, or airings. After that, the rights return to the producer to be sold again and again. A program that has survived at least four years on one of the networks has proven its popularity, has attracted a following, and has accumulated enough individual episodes so that local stations can offer weeks of daily scheduling without too many repeats. In a word, it is a moneymaker. Paramount has already earned more than $2 billion from its syndication of *Frasier*, and Warner Bros. has collected more than $5.8 million an episode from its original syndication of *Friends*, and that does not include income from the series's move to streamer HBO Max and money made from its position as the top-selling DVD television-show collection (Schneider, 2020).

So attractive is syndication's income potential, especially when coupled with the promise of profits from digital downloads, the sale of DVD collections, and pick up by streaming services, that the networks themselves have become their own producers (and therefore syndicators). In fact, the major broadcast networks now produce the vast majority of all the prime-time programming on their own and the top 20 cable networks.

It is important to note that there is another form of syndicated programming. **First-run syndication** is programming produced specifically for sale into syndication on a market-by-market basis. It is attractive to producers because they don't have to run the gauntlet of the network programming process, and they keep 100% of the income. Game and talk shows, long staples of the business, have been joined by court shows, such as *Judge Judy,* distributed daily to hundreds of stations. They are inexpensive to make, inexpensive to distribute, and easily **stripped** (broadcast at the same time five evenings a week). They allow an inexhaustible number of episodes with no repeats and are easy to promote.

Despite the fact that the most-watched programs in history were all aired by the traditional television networks (Figure 8.2), the process by which programs now come to our screens clearly has changed. And of course, all this change is the product of the introduction of new technologies—cable, VCR, DVD, digital video recorders, satellite, the Internet and digitization, and smartphones—that have upset the long-standing relationship between medium and audience. Convergence is also reshaping that relationship.

Top 10 Most-Watched Nonsports Television Broadcasts

Rank

Rank	Program	Rating/Share
1	*M*A*S*H* (final episode), 1983	60.2/77
2	*Dallas* ("Who Shot JR?"), 1980	53.3/76
3	*Roots* (Part VIII), 1977	51.1/71
4	*Gone with the Wind* (Part 1), 1976	47.7/65
5	*Gone with the Wind* (Part 2), 1976	47.4/64
6	*Bob Hope Christmas Show*, 1970	46.6/64
7	*The Day After* (movie), 1983	46.0/62
8	*The Fugitive* (last episode), 1967	45.9/72
9	*Roots* (Part VI), 1977	45.9/66
10	*Roots* (Part V), 1977	45.7/71

Rating/**Share**

CBS
ABC
NBC

▲ **Figure 8.2** Top 10 Most-Watched Nonsports Television Broadcasts.
Source: Television Advertising Bureau, 2020.

◀ Two of syndication's biggest winners, *Frasier* and *Friends*.
(left) AF archive/Alamy Stock Photo; (right) WARNER BROS/Allstar Picture Library/Alamy Stock Photo

Cable and Satellite Television

John Walson's brainchild reshaped the face of modern television. During cable's infancy, many over-the-air broadcasters saw it as something of a friend. It extended their reach, boosting both audience size and profits. Then, in November 1972, Sterling Manhattan Cable launched a new channel called Home Box Office. Only a handful of homes caught the debut of what we now call HBO, but broadcasters' mild concern over this development turned to outright antagonism toward cable in 1975, when new HBO owner Time Inc. began distributing the movie channel by satellite. Now **premium cable** was eating into the broadcasters' audience by offering high-quality, nationally produced and distributed content. The public enthusiastically embraced cable, which, coupled with the widespread diffusion of **fiber optic** cable (the transmission of signals by light beam over glass, permitting the delivery of hundreds of channels), brought the medium to maturity.

Programming

Cable's share of the prime-time audience exceeded that of the Big Four broadcast networks for the first time in 2002. Its total audience share has exceeded that of ABC, CBS, NBC, and Fox every year since. What attracts these viewers is programming, a fact highlighted by two pieces of recent industry data: cable shows annually garner the large majority of all prime-time Emmy Award nominations (HBO's *Game of Thrones alone* has 738 nominations and 269 wins), and cable viewing exceeds network viewing for every single American age demographic.

As we've seen, cable operators attract viewers through a combination of basic and premium channels, as well as with some programming of local origin. There are more than 900 national and regional cable networks. We all know national networks such as CNN, Lifetime, HBO, and the History Channel. Regional network Spectrum News North Carolina serves the area that gives it its name, and several college and regional sports-oriented channels serving different parts of the country, for example, the Big Ten Network and New England Sports Network. The financial support and targeted audiences for these program providers differ, as does their place on a system's **tiers**, groupings of channels made available to subscribers at varying prices.

BASIC CABLE PROGRAMMING In recognition of the growing dependence of the public on cable delivery of broadcast service as the spread of cable increased, Congress passed the Cable Television Consumer Protection and Competition Act of 1992. This law requires operators to offer a truly basic service composed of the broadcast stations in their area and their public access channels. Cable operators also offer another form of basic service, **expanded basic cable**, composed primarily of local broadcast stations and services with broad appeal such as TBS, TNT, the USA Network, and Comedy Central. These networks offer a wide array of programming not unlike that found on the traditional, over-the-air broadcast networks. Ad-supported cable networks such as these want to be on cable's basic tiers because sponsors covet those large potential audiences. This is the dispute, for example, at the heart of the NFL Network's frequent battles with many of the nation's cable operators. Most operators want to put the network on a premium tier to attract more subscribers, but NFL Network wants placement on basic cable where more viewers means more ad dollars.

Because of concentration, operators are increasingly choosing to carry a specific basic channel because their owners (who have a financial stake in that channel) insist that they do. **Multiple system operators (MSOs)** are companies that own several cable franchises. For example, Time Warner owns truTV, Comcast owns Syfy and Bravo, and Viacom owns BET. Naturally, these networks are

▼ HBO's *Game of Thrones* earned 738 Emmy nominations and 269 wins in its 8 seasons.

PictureLux/The Hollywood Archive/ Alamy Stock Photo

more likely to be carried by systems controlled by the MSOs that own them and are less likely to be carried by other systems.

The long-standard concept of different pricing for different packages or tiers of channels is frequently under attack by the FCC and some members of Congress. Concerns over viewers' accidental access to unwanted, offensive content and rising cable prices are leading to calls for **à la carte pricing**—that is, paying for cable on a channel-by-channel basis. System operators and programmers are split on the issue. System operators argue that à la carte means a much smaller lineup of programming. For example, if most people are unwilling to pay for CSPAN or a Lithuanian-language channel, it would be impossible for system operators to carry them. But programmers, such as ESPN, which spends over $8.8 billion a year on content (Sanchez, 2020), argue that à la carte is fairer to them because they will earn what they are actually worth as operators will not have to "waste" money on CSPAN or a Lithuanian-language channel. As you can read in the essay "Should You Cut the Cord?" this debate has recently lost some steam because of the availability of app-based, streamed skinny bundles of programs.

▲ MSOs want the NFL Network on a premium tier; the NFL is happy to stay on basic cable.
Joe Robbins/Getty Images

PREMIUM CABLE As the FCC lifted restrictions on cable's freedom to import distant signals and to show current movies, HBO grew and was joined by a host of other satellite-delivered pay networks. Today, among the most familiar and popular premium cable networks are HBO, Showtime, Sundance Channel, and Cinemax.

In addition to freedom from regulatory constraint, two important programming discoveries ensured the success of the new premium channels. After television's early experiments with over-the-air **subscription TV** failed, many experts believed people simply would not pay for television. So the first crucial discovery was that viewers would indeed pay for packages of contemporary, popular movies. These movie packages could be sold less expensively than

CULTURAL FORUM
Should You Cut the Cord?

The average cable or satellite TV bill is now over $109 a month, and as Americans' wages have been flat for some time, a situation exacerbated by difficult economic times because of the 2020 coronavirus pandemic, there is a growing affordability gap between consumer income and the cost of cable TV (Newman, 2020). At the same time, overall traditional television viewing for every age group continues to decline year-to-year, with the greatest drop off for younger viewers, as much as 50% to 60% from 2010 to today (Mandese, 2019). This perfect storm of high cable costs and low levels of TV watching has put cord-cutting squarely into the cultural forum.

Between cord-cutters and cord-nevers, cable TV is bleeding customers, and the primary reason is cost. Among today's cord-cutters, 87% said they canceled their service because of its high price, and only 34% of those who remain are happy with the value they receive from their cable subscriptions ("Key Cord," 2020).

Still, as you read earlier in the chapter, tens-of-millions of Americans remain connected to the cord, and the industry argues that cable is still a great buy for the money, claiming that it would cost a viewer $135.96 in Internet and streaming service fees to equal the number and variety that cable can deliver for $89.99 (Internet & Television Association, 2020).

Enter Your Voice

- Have you cut the cord? If so, why did you do it? If you're a cord-never, how did you reach your decision to be one?
- Do you still have cable or satellite TV? If so, what keeps you connected?
- Do you find the industry argument of greater bang for the buck persuasive? Why or why not?

could films bought one at a time, and viewers were willing to be billed on a monthly basis for the whole package rather than pay for each viewing.

The second realization boosting the fortunes of the premium networks was the discovery that viewers not only did not mind repeats (as many did with over-the-air television) but welcomed them as a benefit of paying for the provider's slate of films. Premium channel owners were delighted. Replaying content reduced their programming costs and solved the problem of how to fill all those hours of operation.

Premium services come in two forms: movie channels (HBO, Starz!, and Encore, for example) that offer packages of new and old movies along with big sports and other special events—all available for one monthly fee—and pay-per-view channels, through which viewers choose from a menu of offerings (almost always of very new movies and very big sporting events) and pay a fee for the chosen viewing.

People enjoy premium channels in the home for their ability to present unedited and uninterrupted movies and other content not usually found on broadcast channels—for example, adult fare, championship boxing, ultimate fighting, and wrestling. Increasingly, however, that "content not usually found on broadcast channels" often consists not of movies and sports but of high-quality serial programming—content unencumbered by the need to attract the largest possible audience possessing a specific set of demographics. Premium cable series such as *Game of Thrones*, *I May Destroy You*, *Outcast*, *Westworld*, *Billions*, and *I Am Chi* attract large and loyal followings.

The other dominant multichannel service, first available to the public in 1994, is direct broadcast satellite (DBS), television signals received from a satellite dish. What is on a DBS-supplied screen differs little from what is on a cable-supplied screen; only the mode of delivery is different. DBS in the United States is dominated by two companies: DirecTV (owned by AT&T) and Dish Network. Look at the list of the 10 largest pay-TV services in Figure 8.3. Note that Dish and DirecTV are among that group. But they, like other MSOs, face the troubling problem of **cord-cutting**, viewers leaving cable and DBS altogether and relying on Internet-only television viewing. In 2020 alone, cable and satellite shed 6 million subscribing households, a decline of 7.3% from 2019, dropping US pay TV penetration to mid-1990 levels (Zara, 2021). Making matters worse, 12% of Americans, 31 million people, have never subscribed to cable, which means they are **cord-nevers** (Tingley, 2019). Much of this decline is attributed to what the industry calls **over-the-top (OTT)** television, delivery of video without the involvement of an MSO, as in "over (avoiding) the set-top box." Because

▶ **Figure 8.3** Top 10 Pay-TV Services, 2020.
Source: Internet & Television Association, 2020.
(Photo): sturti/Getty Images

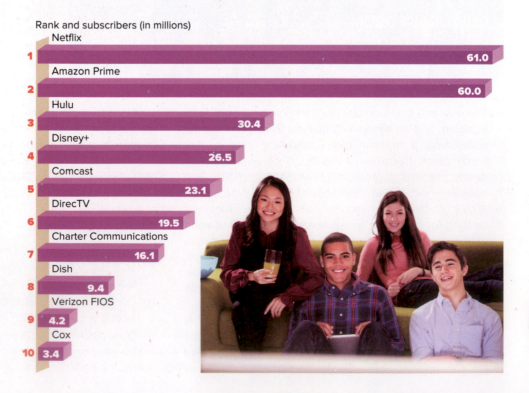

Rank and subscribers (in millions)

Rank	Service	Subscribers
1	Netflix	61.0
2	Amazon Prime	60.0
3	Hulu	30.4
4	Disney+	26.5
5	Comcast	23.1
6	DirecTV	19.5
7	Charter Communications	16.1
8	Dish	9.4
9	Verizon FIOS	4.2
10	Cox	3.4

▲ Peak TV. We have many choices among a wealth of really fine options. Here are four (clockwise from top left): *Better Call Saul*, *Insecure*, *Stranger Things*, and *This Is Us*. Can you identify the platform on which each originally appeared, network TV, basic cable, premium cable, or streaming?

(top left) Warrick Page/Sony/AMC/Kobal/Shutterstock; (top right) HBO/Kobal/Shutterstock; (bottom left) 20TH CENTURY FOX TV/Album/Alamy Stock Photo; (bottom right) Netflix/Kobal/Shutterstock

of OTT, the number of **zero-TV homes**, those that simply have no TV set, now accounts for 5% of all US homes ("Is Digital," 2020).

Look again at Figure 8.3. You'll notice that there are four non-MSO services, Netflix, Amazon, Hulu, and Disney+, among the country's top 10 providers of pay television in 2020. They tank 1 through 4, with Netflix and Amazon sitting at 1 and 2 by a very wide margin. In 2019 video streaming subscriptions surpassed cable subscriptions for the first time (Clarke, 2019).

All of these channels—streaming, cable, traditional broadcast—have ushered in the era of **peak TV**, a time of significant viewer choice and high-quality content. The average American household receives 191.8 channels (Mandese, 2020a); there are 1,534 original series offering new episodes now on network, cable, and streaming TV, compared with 882 in 2010 (Steinberg, 2020); the number of "unique program titles" available to an American TV viewer is 646,000, a 10% rise from 2018 (Mandese, 2020b); and in 2020, "acknowledging that the volume of eligible programs continues to rise," the Television Academy announced that it would expand the number of nominees for best drama and best comedy from seven to eight (Schnieder, 2020a, p. 23).

Trends and Convergence in Television and Cable

The long-standing relationship between television and its audiences is being redefined. This profound change, initially wrought by cable and satellite, has also been and is being driven by other technologies—VCR, DVD, DVR, the Internet, digitization, and even the smartphone.

VCR

Introduced commercially in 1976, videocassette recorders (VCRs) quickly became common in American homes but were declared dead in 2016 as the last manufacturer, Japan's Funai Electronics, ceased production. In its prime, this technology further eroded the audience for traditional over-the-air television, as people, for the first time, could now watch rented and purchased videos on their own schedules. VCR also introduced the public to **time-shifting**, taping a show for later viewing, and **zipping**, fast-forwarding through taped commercials. As a result, people became comfortable with, and in fact came to expect, more control over when, what, and how they watched television.

DVD

In March 1996, the **digital video disc (DVD)** went on sale in US stores. Using a DVD, viewers can stop images with no loss of fidelity; can subtitle a movie in a number of languages; can search for specific scenes from an on-screen menu; and can access bonus features that give background on the movie, its production, and its personnel. Scenes and music not used in the theatrical release of a movie are often included on the disc.

Innovations such as these made DVD at the time of its introduction the fastest-growing consumer electronic product of all time. DVD players now sit in a little over half of US homes, down from 80% just a few years ago (Kunst, 2020). Because of the many viewing options now available, DVD sales and rentals have fallen dramatically for the last several years. In 2012, the number of online movie transactions (sales and rentals) exceeded the number of DVD sales for the first time, 3.4 billion to 2.4 billion (Smith, 2012); and in 2016, video streaming subscription revenues surpassed those from physical disc sales and rentals for the first time (Richter, 2017).

Despite its looming obsolescence, DVD served to further alter the relationship between television and its audiences. Viewers became accustomed to having greater control over what they watched, when they watched, and how they watched on a platform much more satisfying than the earlier VCR. In addition, people watching DVDs were viewers that broadcasters could not sell to advertisers, helping to erode television's dominance as an advertising medium.

DVR

In March 1999, Philips Electronics unveiled the **digital video recorder (DVR)**. It contains digital software that puts a significant amount of control over content in viewers' hands. They can "rewind" and play back portions of a program while they are watching and recording it without losing any of that show. By designating their favorite shows, viewers can instruct DVR to automatically record and deliver not only those programs but all similar content over a specified period of time. This application can even be used with the name of a favorite actor. Type in Shemar Moore, and DVR will automatically record all programming in which he appears.

DVR does not deliver programming the way broadcasters, cablecasters, and DBS systems do. Rather, it is employed *in addition to* these content providers. Both DBS providers and almost every MSO now offer low-cost DVR as part of their technology platform, significantly hastening its diffusion into American homes. Today, just over 68 million households have DVR (Lukovitz, 2019). Naturally, traditional broadcast and ad-supported cable networks initially found the rapid diffusion of DVR troubling. And while it is true that DVR dramatically changed television viewing as we knew it, it has not had as negative an effect on those traditional programming sources as originally anticipated. While DVR does allow viewers to fast-forward through commercials, we saw earlier in this chapter that traditional broadcasters rely on DVR playback to boost their ratings and therefore profits.

Streaming Video

Television on the Internet was slow to take off because of copyright and piracy concerns, and because few viewers had sufficient bandwidth, space on the wires bringing content into their homes. So for several years, the most typical video fare on the Internet was a variety of short specialty transmissions such as movie trailers, music videos, and news clips. However, the development of increasingly sophisticated video compression software and the parallel rise of homes with **broadband** Internet connections (80% of all US Internet homes have broadband; Internet & Television Association, 2020) have changed that. Because broadband offers greater information-carrying capacity (that is, it increased bandwidth), watching true television on the Internet is now common. Twenty-five percent of all US TV time is spent watching streamers; 78% of Americans subscribe to at least one paid video streaming service, 55% to two or more (Lukovitz, 2020c; Lukovitz, 2020b). This viewing, as you read earlier, is accomplished OTT.

And as we saw in this chapter's opening, the distinction between Web-only and broadcast/cable programming is disappearing. Internet video sites Netflix, Hulu, Amazon, and YouTube commission original content, as do social networking sites like Facebook and Instagram. There are, as you read in Chapter 6, more than 270 streaming services operating in the United States alone (Barnes, 2019), including not only subscription streamers like Hulu, Netflix, and Apple TV+, but ad-supported streamers like Tubi and Pluto TV, and **virtual multichannel video programming distributors (VMVPD)**, services that aggregate live and on-demand television and deliver it over the Internet, for example, Sling and YouTube Live. This wealth of Internet video is altering viewing habits and is the major factor in the growing number of viewers who are fleeing cable. In fact, you can see in Figure 8.4 that of all the ways Americans can access video, they see cable and satellite as delivering the least value.

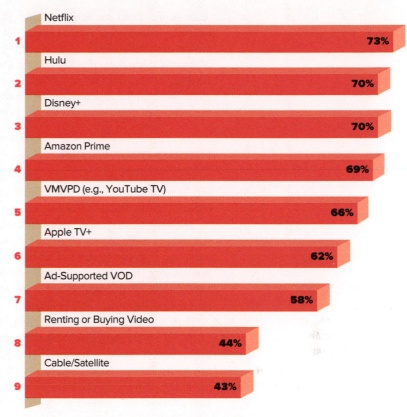

▲ **Figure 8.4** Percentage of Americans Who See Good or Excellent Value in a Specific Video Provider.
Source: "Users," 2020.

Interactive Television

The Internet is not the only technology that permits interactivity. Cable and satellite also allow viewers to "talk back" to content providers. But nearly universally available **digital cable television**, the delivery of digital images and other information to subscribers, offers the truest form of interactive television.

Cable's digital channels permit multiplexing, carrying two or more different signals over the same channel. This, in turn, is made possible by *digital compression*, which "squeezes" signals to permit multiple signals to be carried over one channel. Digital compression works by removing redundant information from the transmission of the signal. For example, the set behind two actors in a movie scene might not change for several minutes. So why transmit the information that the set is there? Simply transmit the digital data that indicate what has changed in the scene, not what has not.

This expanded capacity makes possible *interactive cable*, that is, the ability of subscribers to talk back to the system operator (extra space on the channel is used for this back talk). And *this* permits the following services, many of which you already use: one-click shopping (you see it, you click on it, you buy it), use of QR codes (Chapter 5) to connect to advertisers' websites via smartphone app, local information on demand (news, traffic, and weather), program interactivity (choose a camera angle,

▼ Streaming makes us all rulers of the video kingdom.
Whitehead, Bill/CartoonStock

learn more about an actor's career, play along with game show contestants), interactive program guides, and video games. But it is **video-on-demand (VOD)**—the ability to access pay-per-view movies and other content that can be watched at any time—that best shows the economic advantage of putting more control into viewers' hands. And VOD, as you read in Chapter 2, was the central lifeline for Hollywood in 2020 when movie theaters across the globe were closed because of the coronavirus pandemic. Studios turned to VOD to bring their features directly to the public, often with great success (Friedman, 2020).

Phone-over-Cable

Another service offered by many MSOs is phone service over cable wires. Currently, there are 30 million cable-delivered residential telephone subscribers (Internet & Television Association, 2020). Phone-over-cable offers a special benefit to MSOs. If telephone service can be delivered by the same cable that brings television into the home, so too can the Internet. And what's more, if the cable line is broadband and capable of handling digitally compressed data, that Internet service can be even faster than the service provided over traditional phone lines. Cable, in other words, can become a one-stop communications provider: television, VOD, audio, high-speed Internet access, long-distance and local phone service, multiple phone lines, and fax. This is **bundling**.

How valuable is a bundle-receiving subscriber to an MSO? Add together the bills you might be paying right now—basic or premium cable, your Internet service provider, and your phone bill. What does that total? Now speculate how much pay-per-view and VOD you might buy now that you have broadband and a superfast cable modem. And what would you pay for home delivery of real-time sports or financial data? The MSO would collect each time you accessed an interactive classified or commercial ad. That's how valuable a bundled subscriber will be.

Smartphones, Tablets, and Social Networking Sites

Smartphones and tablets (and all contemporary handheld video game consoles) have made television watching an anywhere, anytime activity. Watching streamed video on mobile devices is now quite routine. Mobile video consumption is growing at a faster rate than on a desktop or laptop, showing 100% growth year-over-year in time spent watching ("55 Video," 2020). This is likely to become even more common as social networking sites increase their commitment to video.

Snapchat, for example, streams daily episodic video programs, Snap Originals, and channels on Instagram's IGTV offer short- and long-form programming. Twitter live streams NBA basketball games. The league has also developed original programming for the site, which also live streams, among other content, NFL football games, Wimbledon tennis matches, CBS News, the NHL, major league baseball, and the Pac-12 Network. Additionally, Twitter live streams the Republican and Democratic national conventions. Facebook Live streams major league baseball, professional soccer, and the US men's and women's national basketball teams. In addition, all the major professional sports leagues offer free apps that let mobile users access their content while on the go. There is also original nonsports content on Facebook Watch—for example, horror series, *The Birch*, and mystery *Limetown*.

▼ Wisconsin member of the US House of Representatives, Republican Mike Gallagher, using Periscope, livestreamed his demand that President Trump call off his supporters as they stormed the Capitol in a violent effort to stop the certification of then-President-Elect Biden's electoral win.
Mike Gallagher

There are several apps that encourage not only mobile viewing but mobile broadcasting as well. Facebook Live and Twitter's Periscope let users connect to their social networking accounts and stream live video directly to their followers. These sites, joined by videogame-centric Twitch, were crucial to the success of the summer 2020 Black Lives Matter movement, telecasting ongoing protests from around the globe. "Over the past few weeks, we've seen creators livestreaming content from the protests and engaging their communities in open conversations around race, inequality and how to effect change," said Twitch spokeswoman Brielle Villablanca (in Browning, 2020, p. B3). Likewise, in January 2021, when insurrectionists stormed Washington, D.C.'s Capitol Building to stop the certification of Joe Biden election to President, numerous locked-down representatives and senators live streamed their reactions to the attacks to a stunned country and world (Fenwick, 2021). Others make more routine use of these technologies—for example, the NASDAQ stock exchange livestreams interviews with financial luminaries and corporate executives and broadcasts the market's opening and closing bells, and retailer Kohl's streams live workouts with its exercise experts.

DEVELOPING MEDIA LITERACY SKILLS

Watching Satirical News

Do you watch television's satirical news shows? Do you ever reflect on their value? Programs like HBO's *Last Week Tonight with John Oliver*, TBS's *Full Frontal with Samantha Bee*, Comedy Central's *The Daily Show with Trevor Noah*, and NBC's *Saturday Night Live* all play significant roles in helping people make sense of what is often a confusing political world. But should they? *The New York Times* television critic Jason Zinoman (2018) writes, "While a comedian is not going to single-handedly change the hearts and minds of the American electorate, no other art form has been more effective at changing the public debate" (p. AR11).

You are a media-literate television viewer, so you understand and respect the power of media messages, you have knowledge of television's genre conventions and recognize when they are being mixed, and above all, you enjoy television content. This is what makes televised satirical news such an interesting genre for consideration. Satirical television news, by definition, mixes genre conventions, is specifically wielded to have an impact (to reach people's consciences by poking fun at the powerful), and is designed to be enjoyed.

And if you sense that satirical TV news has a liberal bent, as opposed to the conservative orientation of most of talk radio, you are correct. Conservatives, explains communication scholar Dannagal Young (2019), "have a lower tolerance for uncertainty and ambiguity," and liberals are "more comfortable with uncertainty and ambiguity . . . They are more open to play and experimentation." Uncertainty, ambiguity, play, and experimentation are at the heart of good comedy in general and satire specifically. Put another way, satire, because it challenges the certainty of the status quo, cannot be conservative.

There is little doubt that satirical television news is an important voice in the cultural forum, but its popularity and apparent bias raise a number of questions for media-literate TV viewers. First, do these programs have an impact on people's political views? At a time when so few Americans see merit in traditional news media, is the satirists' influence magnified? Is satirical TV news a voice that adds to the conversation, or does it diminish how we talk about our world and how we talk to one another?

Does its inevitable partisan orientation contribute to our country's divisions or, as some recent research suggests, do people of different political orientations read these shows in ways consistent with their existing political leanings (Garrett, Bond, & Poulsen, 2019)? Does the fact that a number of polls conducted over the last few years (McClennan, 2018) have revealed that viewers who get their news primarily from these satire programs are more informed about current events and issues than are viewers who watch more traditional news programs change your thinking?

▼ What is the role and value of satirical television news such as that delivered by John Oliver?
Jesse Dittmar/The Washington Post/Getty Images

MEDIA LITERACY CHALLENGE
No Video for a Week

There is no better way to *become aware of the impact of the media on you and society* than to do without them. As a media-literate individual, you can test for yourself just how free you are of the power of one specific medium: video. See if you control your viewing or if your viewing controls you. To start, pick a 5-day period and simply stop watching. No television. No videos on the Internet or your smartphone. No video games. Simply put, don't watch or even look at any video screen anywhere for five entire days. If you are adventurous, enlist one or more friends, family members, or roommates.

Simply changing your routine viewing behavior will not do very much for you unless you reflect on its meaning. Ask yourself (and any others you may have enlisted) the following questions: How easy or difficult was it for you to break away from all video? Why was it easy or difficult? What did you learn about your video consumption habits? How did you use the freed-up time? Were you able to find productive activity, or did you spend your time longing for a screen? Be sure to describe how not watching affected your other life habits (eating, socializing with family and friends, news gathering, and the like). Describe your interactions with other people during this week. Did your conversations change? That is, were there alterations in duration, depth, or subject matter? If you were unable to complete the week of nonviewing, describe why. How easy or difficult was it to come to the decision to give up? Do you consider it a failure to have resumed watching before the five days were up? Why or why not? Once you resume your normal video habits, place yourself on a scale of 1 to 10, with 1 being "I Control Video" and 10 being "Video Controls Me." Explain your self-rating.

Resources for Review and Discussion

REVIEW POINTS: TYING CONTENT TO LEARNING OUTCOMES

▶ **Recognize the history and development of the television and cable television industries and television itself as a medium.**

- ☐ In 1884, Paul Nipkow developed the first device for transmitting images. John Logie Baird soon used this mechanical scanning technology to send images long distance. Vladimir Zworykin and Philo Farnsworth developed electronic scanning technology in the 1920s, leading to the public demonstration of television in 1939.
- ☐ In the 1950s, the quiz show scandal, the business acumen of Lucille Ball, McCarthyism, and the ratings system shaped the nature of broadcast television. Cable, introduced in 1948, would soon effect even more change.
- ☐ Cable, designed initially for the importation of distant signals, became a mature medium when it began offering movies and other premium content.

▶ **Describe how the organizational and economic nature of the contemporary television and cable industries shapes the content of television.**

- ☐ Cable, dominated by large MSOs, offers programming in tiers that include basic, expanded basic, and premium cable. Some favor a new pricing scheme, à la carte, but many people are abandoning cable altogether as cord-cutters and cord-nevers.
- ☐ Direct broadcast satellite is the primary multichannel competitor to cable, now joined by fiber-optic systems like FiOS.

▶ **Explain the relationship between television in all its forms and its viewers.**

- ☐ Once described as a vast wasteland, television is immensely popular, Americans' most-used medium.
- ☐ Television has the greatest reach of all ad-supported media, and consumers cite it as the medium most likely to influence their purchasing decisions.

▶ **Identify new and converging video technologies and their potential impact on the television industry and its audience.**
  □ A host of technologies influence the television–viewer relationship, including DVD, DVR, streaming video, VMVPD, and interactive television.

▶ **Describe the digital and mobile television revolution.**
  □ Mobile video on smartphones, tablets, and other portable video devices is now common, aided by the availability of

streaming and live broadcasting apps and the delivery of video via social networking sites.

▶ **Apply key television-viewing media literacy skills to satirical news.**
  □ Satirical television news makes a significant contribution to the cultural forum, but is it for the better?

KEY TERMS

bandwidth, 182
Nipkow disc, 183
pixel, 183
iconoscope tube, 183
kinescope, 183
coaxial cable, 185
microwave relay, 185
spot commercial sales, 185
community antenna television (CATV), 188
importation of distant signals, 188
Global Television Audience Metering (GTAM) meter, 188
nonlinear TV, 188
C3 and C7 ratings, 188
long-tail viewing, 188
total viewer impressions, 189

share, 189
all-channel legislation, 189
vast wasteland, 189
clear time, 191
reverse compensation, 191
retransmission fees, 191
off-network, 191
pilot, 192
first-run syndication, 193
stripped, 193
premium cable, 194
fiber optics, 194
tiers, 194
expanded basic cable, 194
multiple system operator (MSO), 194
à la carte pricing, 195

subscription TV, 195
cord-cutting, 196
cord-never, 196
over-the-top (OTT), 196
zero-TV homes, 197
peak TV, 197
time-shifting, 198
zipping, 198
digital video disc (DVD), 198
digital video recorder (DVR), 198
broadband, 199
virtual multichannel video programming distributors (VMVPD), 199
digital cable television, 199
video-on-demand (VOD), 200
bundling, 200

QUESTIONS FOR REVIEW

1. What is the importance of each of the following to the history of television: Paul Nipkow, John Logie Baird, Vladimir Zworykin, Philo Farnsworth, and Newton Minow?

2. What was the impact on television of the quiz show scandal, *I Love Lucy*, McCarthyism, and the Nielsen ratings?

3. How are the ratings taken? What are some complaints about the ratings system? What are some possible improvements in audience measurement?

4. How does a program typically (and atypically) make it to the air? How does syndication figure in this process?

5. How have cable, VCR, DVD, DVR, and DBS affected the networks?

6. What are some of the changes in television wrought by cable?

7. Explain the difference between basic cable, expanded basic cable, premium cable, pay-per-view, and à la carte pricing.

8. What are importation of distant signals, premium cable, and fiber optics? How are they related? What do they have to do with cable's maturity as a medium?

9. What is OTT, and how does it affect what we see on the screen?

10. In what ways can viewers access video on the Internet? Via mobile devices? What kinds of content are available on these platforms?

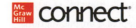

To maximize your study time, check out CONNECT to access the SmartBook study module for this chapter, watch videos, and explore other resources.

QUESTIONS FOR CRITICAL THINKING AND DISCUSSION

1. As an independent producer, what kind of program would you develop for the networks? How immune do you think you could be from the pressures that exist in this process?

2. Are you a cable subscriber? Why or why not? If so, at what level? Would you prefer à la carte pricing? Why or why not?

3. Do you ever stream video from your smartphone? If so, what types of content do you broadcast? Has there ever been a time when an impromptu situation called for such activity? Explain.

REFERENCES

1. "55 Video Marketing Statistics for 2020." (2020). *Biteable*. Retrieved from https://biteable.com/blog/video-marketing-statistics/

2. Ball, S., & Bogatz, G. A. (1970). *The first year of* Sesame Street: *An evaluation*. Princeton, NJ: Educational Testing Service.

3. Barnes, B. (2019, December 1). The streaming era has finally arrived. Everything is about to change. *New York Times*, pp. F3–F4.

4. Browning, K. (2020, June 20). Streaming marches, not video games, all night on Twitch. *New York Times*, p. B3.

5. Buckman, A. (2020, April 23). "Sesame Street" help brought to you by the letters C-O-V-I-D. *MediaPost*. Retrieved from https://www.mediapost.com/publications/article/350382/sesame-street-help-brought-to-you-by-the-letters.html

6. Chin, F. (1978). *Cable television: A comprehensive bibliography*. New York: IFI/Plenum.

7. Cisco. (2020, March 9). *Cisco annual internet report (2018–2023) white paper*. Retrieved from https://www.cisco.com/c/en/us/solutions/collateral/executive-perspectives/annual-internet-report/white-paper-c11-741490.html

8. Clarke, C. (2019, March 24). Video streaming subscriptions surpass cable customers for the first time. *The Drum*. Retrieved from https://www.thedrum.com/news/2019/03/24/video-streaming-subscriptions-surpass-cable-customers-first-time#:~:text=The%20number%20of%20video%20streaming,increase%20of%2027%25%20on%202017.

9. Cook, T. D., Appleton, H., Conner, R. F., Shaffer, A., Tamkin, G., & Weber, S. J. (1975). *Sesame Street Revisited*. New York: Russell Sage Foundation.

10. Epstein, A. (2020, February 13). Streaming still has a long way to go before it catches regular old TV. *QZ.com*. Retrieved from https://qz.com/1801623/streaming-has-a-long-way-to-go-to-catch-regular-tv/

11. Fenwick, C. (2021, January 6). 'Call it off! It's over!': Republican lawmaker loses it at Trump as his supporters assault the Capitol. *Alternet*. Retrieved from https://www.alternet.org/2021/01/mike-gallagher/?utm_source=&utm_medium=email&utm_campaign=6311

12. Friedman, W. (2021, April 20). Big streaming shows up costs: Amazon Prime video drops $465m on 'LOTR'. *MediaPost*. Retrieved from https://www.mediapost.com/publications/article/362461/big-streaming-shows-up-costs-amazon-prime-video-d.html

13. Friedman, W. (2020, May 4). Should studios, movie theaters consider new TV deals? *MediaPost*. Retrieved from https://www.mediapost.com/publications/article/350933/should-studios-movie-theaters-consider-new-tv-dea.html

14. Friedman, W. (2019, September 4). For TV networks, fewer pilots: Shows faster to market—or just more content. *MediaPost*. Retrieved from https://www.mediapost.com/publications/article/340235/for-tv-networks-fewer-pilots-shows-faster-to-mar.html?edition=115181

15. Garrett, R. K., Bond, R., & Poulsen, S. (2019, August 19). Maybe *you* know that article is satire, but a lot of people can't tell the difference. *Nieman Lab*. Retrieved from https://www.niemanlab.org/2019/08/maybe-you-know-that-article-is-satire-but-a-lot-of-people-cant-tell-the-difference/

16. Goldberg, L. (2019, August 7). "Game of Thrones" creators close $200M Netflix overall deal. *Hollywood Reporter*. Retrieved from https://www.hollywoodreporter.com/live-feed/game-thrones-creators-close-200m-netflix-deal-1230119

17. Ha, A. (2020, February 11). Streaming accounts for nearly one-fifth of total US TV watching, according to Nielsen. *TechCrunch*. Retrieved from https://techcrunch.com/2020/02/11/nielsen-streaming-wars-total-audience-report/

18. Internet & Television Association. (2020). *Industry data*. Retrieved from https://www.ncta.com/industry-data

19. "Is Digital the New Traditional." (2020). *Giant Media*. Retrieved from https://giantmedia.com/2017/03/digital-new-traditional/

20. "Key Cord-Cutting Statistics in 2020." (2020, January 12). *Cablecompare*. Retrieved from https://cablecompare.com/key-cord-cutting-statistics-is-cable-tv-dead/

21. Kunst, A. (2020, January 21). Share of Americans owning a blu-ray/DVD player 2018, by age. *Statista*. Retrieved from https://www.statista.com/statistics/369955/people-living-in-households-that-own-a-blu-ray-dvd-player-usa/

22. Kuralt, C. (1977). *When television was young* (videotape). New York: CBS News.

23. Lepore, J. (2020, May 11). When Ernie met Bert. *New Yorker*, pp. 57–62.

24. Lukovitz, K. (2020a, September 24). NBCU: CTV viewership up 95% last year; half to three-quarters of all TV viewing now time-shifted. *MediaPost*. Retrieved from https://www.mediapost.com/publications/article/356229/

25. Lukovitz, K. (2020b, September 1). 78% Of U.S. households now have one leading SVOD service; 55% have two or more. *MediaPost*. Retrieved form https://www.mediapost.com/publications/article/355322/78-of-us-households-now-have-one-leading-svod-s.html?edition=119666

26. Lukovitz, K. (2020c, August 13). Streaming now accounts for 25% of U.S. TV usage. *MediaPost*. Retrieved from https://www.mediapost.com/publications/article/354705/streaming-now-accounts-for-25-of-us-tv-usage.html

27. Lukovitz, K. (2019, July 2). OTT surpassing DVR, but growth is slowing. *MediaPost*. Retrieved from https://www.mediapost.com/publications/article/337728/ott-surpassing-dvr-but-growth-is-slowing.html

28. Malkin, M. (2020, June 30). Priyanka Chopra Jonas is on a global quest. *Variety*, p. 21.

29. Mandese, J. (2020a, February 13). Number of TV channels received by U.S. households falls dramatically. *MediaPost*. Retrieved from https://www.mediapost.com/publications/article/347034/number-of-tv-channels-received-by-us-households.html#:~:text=Detailed%20data%20analysis%20is%20available,2019%20from%20191.8%20in%202018.

30. Mandese, J. (2020b, February 11). Nielsen reveals 646,000 program universe. *MediaPost*. Retrieved from https://www.mediapost.com/publications/article/346900/nielsen-reveals-646000-program-universe.html#:~:text=In%20a%20finding%20that%20makes,a%2010%25%20increase%20from%202018.

31. Mandese, J. (2019, September 11). Analysis finds TV's 55+ viewing eroding for first time, younger demos have plunged. *MediaPost*. Retrieved from https://www.mediapost.com/publications/article/340580/analysis-finds-tvs-55-viewers-eroding-for-first.html

32. Marsh, C. (2018, June 22). Reality casting joins the social-media age. *Variety*, pp. 145–146.

33. McClennan, S. A. (2018, March 17). The science of satire and lies: Watching Colbert can fight right-wing brain rot. *Salon*. Retrieved from https://www.salon.com/2018/03/17/the-science-of-satire-and-lies-watching-colbert-can-fight-right-wing-brain-rot/

34. National Association of Broadcasters. (1961). *John F. Kennedy's new FCC chair, Newton Minow*. Retrieved from https://www.americanrhetoric.com/speeches/newtonminow.htm

35. "Netflix Projected to Spend More Than $17 Billion on Content in 2020." (2020, January 6). *Variety*. Retrieved from https://variety.com/2020/digital/news/netflix-2020-content-spending-17-billion-1203469237/

36. Newman, J. (2020, February 21). Look how far cable TV has fallen. *Fast Company*. Retrieved from https://www.fastcompany.com/90466112/look-how-far-cable-tv-has-fallen

37. Poggi, J. (2020, October 30). What it costs to advertise in TV's biggest shows in 2020-2021 season. *Ad Age*. Retrieved from https://adage.com/article/media/tvs-most-expensive-shows-advertisers-season/2281176

38. Richter, F. (2017, January 18). Netflix & co. surpass DVD & Blu-ray sales. *Statista*. Retrieved from https://www.statista.com/chart/7654/home-entertainment-spending-in-the-us/?utm_source=Infographic+Newsletter&utm_campaign=22cf6e09df-InfographicTicker_EN_Late_00026&utm_medium=email&utm_term=0_666fe64c5d-22cf6e09df-295452301

39. Sanchez, L. (2020, April 19). How Disney's ESPN makes money from sports broadcasting? *Motley Fool*. Retrieved from https://www.fool.com/investing/2020/04/19/how-disneys-espn-makes-money-sports-broadcasting.aspx#:~:text=In%20Disney's%202019%20annual%20report,expensive%20broadcasting%20rights%20have%20become.

40. Schnieder, M. (2020a, June 30). Peak TV, peak nominees. *Variety*, p. 23.

41. Schnieder, M. (2020b, February 18). "Friends" gets old-school binge. *Variety*, p. 20.

42. Sedulus. (1970, June 5). *Sesame Street. New Republic*. Retrieved from https://newrepublic.com/article/123405/sesame-street

43. Smith, S. (2012, March 23). End of an age: Netflix, Hulu, Amazon will beat physical video viewing in 2012. *MediaPost*. Retrieved from http://www.mediapost.com/publications/article/170863/end-of-an-age-netflix-hulu-amazon-will-beat-phy.html

44. Steinberg, B. (2020, December 9). A pause in peak TV. *Variety*, p. 20.

45. Sterling, C. H., & Kittross, J. M. (1990). *Stay tuned: A concise history of American broadcasting*. Belmont, CA: Wadsworth.

46. Taylor, C. (2021, January 13). Watch for even more celebrities and music in Super Bowl LV ads. *Forbes*. Retrieved from https://www.forbes.com/sites/charlesrtaylor/2021/01/13/watch-for-even-more-celebrities-and-music-in-super-bowl-lv-ads/?sh=19e99aa24260

47. Television Advertising Bureau. (2020). *Research*. Retrieved from https://www.tvb.org/Public/Research.aspx

48. Tingley, B. (2019, April 17). Forget cord cutters; 31 million Americans are cord nevers. *Soda*. Retrieved from https://www.soda.com/news/cord-nevers/#:~:text=Cord%20nevers%20are%20defined%20by,%25%2C%20or%2031%20million%20Americans.

49. "Tops of 2020: Television." (2020, December 12). *A. C. Nielsen*. Retrieved from https://www.nielsen.com/us/en/insights/article/2020/tops-of-2020-television/

50. "Total U.S. Ad Spending by Media 2017-2024." (2020, January 27). *Ad Age*, p. 23.

51. "Users: Cable, Satellite TV Have Lowest Value." (2020, June 30). *Variety*, p. 12.

52. Watson, A. (2020, July 9). Binge-viewing in the U.S.—statistics & facts. *Statista*. Retrieved from https://www.statista.com/topics/2508/binge-watching-in-the-us/

53. Young, D. G. (2019, December 5). Why liberal satire and conservative outrage are both responses to mainstream media—but with very different powers. *Nieman Lab*. Retrieved from https://www.niemanlab.org/2019/12/why-liberal-satire-and-conservative-outrage-are-both-responses-to-mainstream-media-but-with-very-different-powers/

54. Zara, C. (2021, March 2). Cord cutting was so bad last year that pay-TV penetration is down to 1994 levels. *Fast Company*. Retrieved from https://www.fastcompany.com/90609976/cord-cutting-was-so-bad-last-year-that-pay-tv-penetration-is-down-to-1994-levels

55. Zinoman, J. (2018, July 29). A backlash bedevils joke tellers. *New York Times*, pp. AR1, AR11.

Cultural Forum Blue Column icon, Media Literacy Red Torch Icon, Using Media Green Gear icon, Developing Media book in starburst icon: ©McGraw Hill

Yurii_Dr/Alamy Stock Photo

Video Games

9

◀ *Fortnite*, with more than 200 million players, is testimony to video games' popularity.

Learning Objectives

Video games are accelerating the five forces reshaping mass communication and the mass media industries. They are the product of a highly concentrated industry, they are luring people away from the more traditional media (audience fragmentation), they are used as and filled with advertising (hypercommercialization), they know no borders (globalization), and they are played on numerous technologies, from game consoles to personal computers to the Internet to smartphones and tablets (convergence). And even though worldwide game industry revenues more than triple those of the movie and music industries ("The Video," 2020), mass communication experts have only recently begun to take this medium seriously. After studying this chapter, you should be able to

▶ Recall the history and development of games and the gaming industry.

▶ Describe how the organizational and economic nature of the contemporary gaming industry shapes the content of games.

▶ Explain the relationship between games and their players.

▶ Identify changes in the game industry brought about by new and converging technologies.

▶ Apply key gameplaying media literacy skills to understanding and combating the frequent mistreatment of female gamers by some male players.

1931 ▶ *Baffle Ball,* first mass-produced arcade game · · · · ·
1933 *Contact,* first electric pinball game

1947 ▶ Flippers come to pinball · · · · · · · · · · · · · · · **1940**
1951 Japanese playing-card company Marufuku
changes its name to Nintendo

1961 Russell creates *Spacewar* **1955**
1964 Sega formed
1966 Sega exports *Periscope* to United States and
Europe; first amusement game export;
▶ 25 cents per play established as arcade
game standard ·
1968 Baer patents interactive television game

1971 ▶ *Computer Space,* first arcade computer game · · · **1970**
1972 *Odyssey* released; Atari formed, develops *Pong*
1975 *Home Pong* debuts; *Gunfight,* first game to use
a microprocessor
1976 *Channel F,* first programmable, cartridge-based
home game
1977 First handheld video game
1979 First handheld programmable game system
1980 Home *Space Invaders,* first arcade game for
home systems; *Pac-Man*
1981 *Donkey Kong*

1985 Nintendo's NES introduced **1985**
1986 *Legend of Zelda*
1987 PC games introduced
1989 ▶ Game Boy ·
1990 *Super Mario Bros. 3*
1993 *Doom* released
1994 ESRB ratings established; *Myst* released
1995 PlayStation in United States

2000 ▶ Xbox · **2000**
2001 Game Cube
2003 *Second Life* launched
2004 *Halo 2* released; PlayStation Portable introduced
2006 Nintendo Wii
2011 *Call of Duty: Modern Warfare 3* earns $1 billion
in 16 days
2012 Xbox entertainment use surpasses gaming;
GamerGate erupts
2013 Wii U, PlayStation 4, Xbox One
2014 *Destiny* earns $500 million in 24 hours
2015 Global mobile gaming revenues overtake
console revenues for the first time
2016 Virtual reality gaming
2017 Hyper-casual games
2018 Mobile gaming constitutes half of all global
video-game revenues; professional e-sports
leagues Overwatch League and NBA 2K
League debut; e-sports revenue reaches $1
billion
2019 Protecting Children From Abusive Games Act;
gaming disorder added to International
Classification of Diseases
2020 Coronavirus in the US; PlayStation 5 and Xbox
Series X and S introduced

Courtesy of Wayne Namerow
Collection

Courtesy of Wayne Namerow
Collection

Brian Hagiwara/
Stockbyte/Getty Images

Ken Hively/Los Angeles Times/
Getty Images

Rob Van Petten/Photodisc/
Getty Images

Toy Alan King/Alamy Stock Photo

"WHY ARE YOU PLAYING VIDEO GAMES? Don't you have homework or a paper due or something?"

"This is more important. And anyway, what are you, my mother?"

"Nope, I just don't want to have to dig up another roommate when you flunk out, that's all."

"Glad to know you care. And anyway, I'm playing *Foldit*."

"You mean *Fortnite*?"

"No, *Foldit*; it's an online game. Players have to fold various proteins into stable shapes. The more stable the shape, the more energy in each fold, and that means a greater likelihood that the protein will stick to the coronavirus protein, and, almost as important, more points for the player. You want to play?"

"No thanks. If I'm going to play games, I'd like to kill bad guys with a vast array of magnificent weapons and be able to leap over tall buildings in a single bound."

In this chapter, we examine games played on a variety of electronic, microprocessor-based platforms. But before we get deeper into our discussion of the sophisticated, entertaining, and often important games like the opening vignette's *Foldit*, developed by the University of Washington's Center for Game Science and employed in 2020's race to harness the wisdom of the gaming universe to find a coronavirus treatment (Brown, 2020), let's look at their roots in the convergence of pinball machines and military simulators. This is fitting because, as with other media, possibly even more so, converging technologies define video games' present and future.

A Short History of Computer and Video Games

Carnival man David Gottlieb invented the first mass-produced arcade game, *Baffle Ball*, in 1931. A small wooden cabinet, it had only one moving part, a plunger. Players would launch a ball into the playing field, a slanted surface with metal "pins" surrounding "scoring holes." The object was to get the ball into one of the holes. Gottlieb was soon manufacturing 400 cabinets a day. Just as quickly, he had many imitators.

One, Harry Williams, invented *Contact*, the first electronic pinball game. Williams was an engineer, and his 1933 gaming innovations were electronic scoring (*Baffle Ball* players had to keep their scores in their heads) and scoring holes, or pockets, that threw

Gottlieb's *Baffle Ball* and *Humpty Dumpty*.

(Both): Courtesy of Wayne Namerow Collection

the ball back into the playing field (in *Baffle Ball,* when a ball dropped into a hole it was gone).

The popularity of arcade games exploded, and players' enthusiasm was fueled even more when slot-machine makers entered the field, producing games with cash payouts. With the Depression in full force in the 1930s, however, civic leaders were not much in favor of this advance, and several locales, most notably New York City, banned the games. Pinball was considered gambling.

David Gottlieb had the answer. Games of skill were not gambling, nor were games that paid off in additional games. In 1947, he introduced *Humpty Dumpty,* a six-flipper game that rewarded high-scorers with replays. Bans were lifted, pinball returned to the arcades, even more players were attracted to the skills-based electronic games, and the stage was set for what we know today as video games.

As Steven Baxter of the *CNN Computer Connection* wrote, "You can't say that video games grew out of pinball, but you can assume that video games wouldn't have happened without it. It's like bicycles and the automobile. One industry leads to the other and then they exist side-by-side. But you had to have bicycles to one day have motor cars" (in Kent, 2001, pp. 1–2).

Today's Games Emerge

Throughout the late 1950s and 1960s, computers were hulking giants, filling entire rooms (see Chapter 10). Most displayed their output on paper in the form of teletype. But the very best, most advanced computers, those designed for military research and analysis, were a bit sleeker and had monitors for output display. Only three universities—MIT, the University of Utah, and Stanford—and a few dedicated research installations had these machines.

At MIT, a group of self-described nerds, the Tech Model Railroad Club (TMRC), began writing programs for fun for a military computer. Club members would leave their work next to the computer so that others could build on what had come before. One member, Steve Russell, decided to write the ultimate program, an interactive game. It took him 200 hours over 6 months to produce the first interactive computer game, *Spacewar,* completed in 1961. His final version, completed the next year, included remote control units with switches for every game function, the first gamepad. "We thought about trying to make money off it for two or three days but concluded that there wasn't a way that it could be done," said Russell (quoted in Kent, 2001, p. 20).

But another college student, Nolan Bushnell, thought differently (DeMaria & Wilson, 2004). For two years after the completion of Russell's game, the TMRC distributed it to other schools for free. Bushnell, who worked in an arcade to pay for his engineering studies at the University of Utah, played *Spacewar* incessantly. After graduation, he dedicated himself to developing a coin-operated version of the game that had consumed so much of his time. He knew that to make money, it would have to attract more than computer enthusiasts, so he designed a futuristic-looking fiberglass cabinet. The result, *Computer Space,* released in 1971, was a dismal failure. Yet Bushnell was undeterred. With two friends and investments of $250 each, he quit his engineering job and incorporated Atari in 1972.

Long before this, in 1951, Ralph Baer, an engineer for a military contractor charged with developing "the best TV set in the world," decided a good set should do more than receive a few channels (remember, this was before cable's rise). He suggested building games into the receivers. His bosses were unimpressed. Fifteen years later, Baer was working for another defense contractor when he drafted the complete schematics for a video-game console that would sell for about $20. He patented it in 1968 and licensed his device to Magnavox, which, in 1972, marketed the first home video-game system as *Odyssey* and sold it for $100.

Odyssey was a simple game offering two square spots to represent two players (or paddles), a ball, and a centerline. It had six plug-in cartridges and transparent, colored TV screen overlays producing 12 games, all very rudimentary. Its high cost and Magnavox's

▼ Nolan Bushnell and a few of his toys.
*Ken Hively/*Los Angeles Times/ *Getty Images*

▲ Original *Pong*.
Mike Derer/AP Images

decision to sell it through its television set dealers—leading to the incorrect perception that it could be played only on Magnavox sets—limited its success. Only 100,000 units were sold. But with *Odyssey* and Atari, "the stage was set for the introduction of a new art form, and a new industry" (DeMaria & Wilson, 2004, p. 17).

The spark that set off the game revolution was *Pong*, Atari's arcade Ping-Pong game, introduced in 1972. Bushnell had seen *Odyssey* at an electronics show and set his people to creating a coin-operated version (Atari later agreed to pay a licensing fee to Magnavox). The two-player game was an overnight hit, selling 100,000 units in its first year—and twice as many knockoffs (Burnham, 2001, p. 61). Players poured quarters into games looking remarkably like *Pong*, including Harry Williams's *Paddle-Ball*, Rally's *For-Play*, and then in an effort to head off what Nolan Bushnell called "the jackals," Atari's own *Pong Doubles*, *Super Pong*, and *Quadrapong* (Sellers, 2001).

Rapid-Fire Developments

What followed, partly as a result of the swift advance of the microchip and computer industries (and a healthy dose of technological genius from a thriving game industry in Japan), was a rapid-fire succession of innovation and development. In 1975 Atari, marketing *Home Pong* through retailer Sears, made its first steps toward bringing arcade games into the home. Its 1980 release of home *Space Invaders* cemented the trend. Also in 1975, Midway began importing *Gunfight* from Japanese manufacturer Taito. *Gunfight* was significant for two reasons. Although Sega, with *Periscope*, began importing arcade games into the United States in 1966, *Gunfight* was the first imported video game. It was also the first game to use a computer microprocessor.

In 1976, Fairchild Camera and Instrument introduced *Channel F*, the first programmable, cartridge-based home game. Mattel Toys brought true electronic games to handheld devices in 1977, with titles like *Missile Attack*, *Auto Race*, and *Football* played on handheld, calculator-size **LED (light-emitting diode)** and **LCD (liquid crystal display)** screens. In 1979, Milton Bradley released Microvision, the first programmable handheld game system.

▲ As you can see here, the character of Zelda can escape her pursuer by exiting the lake from any direction the player chooses. She can even climb trees. Prior to this game, characters could only walk in a straight line, reducing the player's ability to make choices. With Zelda, gaming became more of a game instead of watching a movie where the viewer simply has to tell the console that it's okay to continue on with the story.
Nintendo

Two Japanese arcade imports became instant classics: in 1980, Namco's *Pac-Man* (the best-selling arcade game of all time; Buchholz, 2020) and Nintendo's *Donkey Kong* in 1981. With the 1985 introduction of Nintendo's groundbreaking game console NES, these two games became home-version successes. The Japanese company further advanced gaming with its 1986 release of home console game *Legend of Zelda*, revolutionary because it introduced open structure play—that is, players could go wherever they wanted and there were multiple routes to winning, now standard in modern games.

Arcade games, handheld systems, and home game consoles were joined by personal computer games, beginning with the 1987 release of NEC's hybrid PC/console in Japan. By the early 1990s, CD-ROM-based computer games were common and successful. *Doom* and *Myst,* both released in 1993, were among the first big personal computer game hits. *Myst*, with dramatic, realistic visuals, marked games' artistic maturity, and *Doom* hinted at another development soon to come to games because it could be played over **LANs (local area networks)** of computers, typically in a single building; that is, it was an interactive game played by several people over a computer network. It also popularized the **first-person perspective game** as well as the first-person shooter game; gamers "carried" the weapon, and all action in the game was seen through their eyes.

▲ Namco's *Pac-Man* and Nintendo's *Donkey Kong*, introduced as arcade games in the early 1980s, became instant home-version classics when Nintendo introduced its NES game console in 1985.
(Left): JLangridge /Stockimo/Alamy Stock Photo; (Right): Jamaway/Alamy Stock Photo

▲ Two of the first interactive games, iD Software's *Doom (left)* and Cyan, Inc.'s *Myst (right)*. Note *Doom's* central placement of the hand and gun, designed to give players the sense that they were personally controlling the weapon even though they were simply clicking keys on a keyboard. It popularized the first-person shooter game. Looking at *Myst's* visually stunning landscape (and comparing it to *Doom's*), it's clear that it was a giant leap forward in game design.
(Left): iD Software; (Right): Cyan, Inc.

Games and Their Players

Three-quarters of all American households are home to at least one person who plays video games, and 64% of Americans, 70% of those under 18, play regularly (Entertainment Software Association, 2020). But before we look at these people a bit more closely, we need to define exactly what constitutes a video game.

What Is a Video Game?

As technologies converge, the same game can be played on an increasing number of platforms. *Myst*, for example, was originally a computer game written for Macintosh computers, then IBM PCs, then external CD-ROM drives, and then video-game consoles such as Play-Station. Now it can be played online. Versions of *Donkey Kong* can be played in arcades, on consoles, on the Internet, on Macs and PCs, and on handheld game consoles. *Q*bert* can be played on arcade machines and on collectible Nelsonic game wristwatches.

USING MEDIA TO MAKE A DIFFERENCE
Using Games for Good

The popularity and ubiquity of video games have led to the **gamification** of society, using video-game skills and conventions to solve real-world problems in medicine, health, policy, personal responsibility, and in fact, any issue that humans face, including battling a global pandemic, as you read in the chapter's opening. In this sense, gamification is the ultimate use of games for good.

Now that the video-game industry has reached a level of legitimacy and respectability equal to that of other mass media, it is being asked the same questions regarding content as the older media are: What is the impact on kids? What regulations should be imposed? How is the medium used? And just as important, how can we use the medium to make a positive difference?

Game industry professionals, social scientists, educators, and parents regularly examine this last question. Their efforts focus on the use of games for policy change, training, and learning. Their products include initiatives such as Cisco Systems's *Peter Packet Game and Challenge,* designed to confront poverty. The National Academy of Sciences funds game development by the Federation of American Scientists, designed to build enthusiasm for science as a discipline and a career. The International Red Cross uses games to "change the narrow view of heroism" from those who kill in wartime to those who show compassion and "are fighting to save innocent lives" by asking players on the massively popular online game *Fortnite* to administer to those in need (Jardine, 2020). And global press freedom organization Reporters Without Borders has embedded in *Minecraft* a library stocked with banned books and articles available to the online game's 145 million active players, many living in countries with no press freedom ("RSF Opens," 2020).

One of the most successful games-for-good efforts is Games for Health, a community of game developers, researchers, and health care and medical professionals who maintain an ongoing "best practices" conversation—online and in annual conferences—to share information about the impact existing and original games can have on health care and policy. Japanese game maker Konami's *Dance Dance Revolution*, for example, is an existing **exergame** that invites people to exercise while they play. Players follow cascading arrows on a video screen, mimicking their movements on a large footpad attached by a cable to a game console.

New games, too, are developed specifically to meet people's health needs. They are particularly effective in matters of health because of their interactivity. "One of the great strengths of video games is that automatically a player goes into a game expecting to have some agency," wrote Amy Green, one of the developers of *That Dragon, Cancer*, a game designed to aid people dealing with a family member's cancer (in Suellentrop, 2016, p. C1). For example, Nintendo's *GlucoBoy* and *Dr. Mario* help children and other patients manage their own diabetic needs.

Another games-for-good practitioner, Games for Change, joined forces with the Half the Sky Movement, a global effort to reduce oppression and build opportunity for poor women, to bring *Half the Sky Movement: The Game* to Facebook. Players take on virtual tasks such as collecting books for young girls in Kenya. Their in-game success leads to real-world payoff; for example, collecting enough books unlocks a donation of actual books to a nonprofit that brings improved literacy and gender equality to developing countries.

Thousands of games can be played on smartphones and tablets. For our purposes, then, a game is a **video game** when the action of the game takes place interactively on-screen. By this definition, an online text-based game such as a **MUD (multiuser dimension)**, which has no moving images (games such as 1977's *Zork* and 2016's *Azereth*), is a video game. The essay titled "Using Games for Good" looks at games that function as more than entertainment.

Who Is Playing?

What do we know about the 214 million regular American video-game players? For one thing, they are not necessarily the stereotypical teenage boys gaming away in their parents' basements, as you can see in Figure 9.1 and from these data (Entertainment Software Association, 2020):

- The average age range of a gameplayer is 35 to 44 years old; 64% of American gameplayers are 18 or over.
- Forty-one percent of all American gamers are female. Women 18 or older represent a greater proportion of the gaming population than boys 18 or younger.
- Seventy-three percent of American gamers own a dedicated game console.

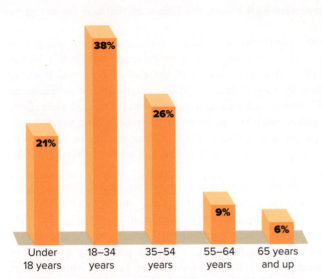

▲ **Figure 9.1** Age Breakdown of Video Game Players, 2020.
Source: Entertainment Software Association, 2020.

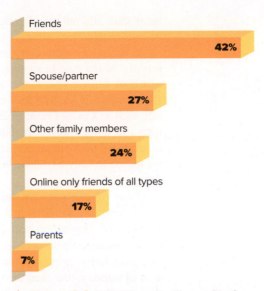

▲ **Figure 9.2** With Whom Do Players Play?
Source: Entertainment Software Association, 2020.

- Sixty-five percent of gamers play with others, either in-person or online, and the large majority plays with friends and family (Figure 9.2).

- Fifty-five percent feel video games help them connect with friends; 50% say games help them spend time with family.

- During 2020's coronavirus lock-down, almost everyone was playing; daily gameplay was up 115% over pre-quarantine levels (Waterman, 2020) and streaming and sales records were set (Sherr, 2020), as games proved to be an ideal boredom filler, loneliness palliative, and social-contact keeper (Suderman, 2020).

Scope and Nature of the Video-Game Industry

Players in the United States spend more than $35.8 billion a year on game content and another $7.5 billion on hardware (Richter, 2019b). Globally, the world's nearly 2 billion players spend $159.3 billion, an amount expected to surpass $200 billion by 2023 (Stedman, 2020). A championship video-game tournament can easily draw 70,000 live spectators, and tens-of-millions across the globe watch high-level gameplay on the Internet, an audience large enough to lead Amazon to buy Twitch, a game streaming site with 15 million daily viewers who log 43 million hours a day (Iqbal, 2020b).

Several college sports conferences (for example, the Big Ten) host intercollegiate **e-sports**, and many schools house their teams in their athletic departments, even offering e-gaming scholarships. Revenue from e-sports, including game-related media, sponsorships, merchandise, tickets, and publisher fees, reached $1.1 billion in 2019, and top prizes, as high as $3 million, exceed those of other major sports tournaments (Capps, 2020). Forty-six million people online watched the 2020 League of Legends world championship in Shanghai, China, and 3 million more tried to buy tickets to attend in person (Browning, 2021). There are several professional e-sports leagues, each specific to a popular game; both the 20-team Overwatch League and the 17-team NBA 2K League debuted in 2018.

Grand Theft Auto V made $1 billion in 3 days in 2013, 14 days faster than the amount of time it took the movie *Avatar* to make $1 billion; it earned $800 million in its first day, selling 16.5 million units, both records. Eight free-to-download, unrestricted-play online games earned their developers more than a billion dollars in 2018, and one, *Fortnite*, with

▲ The old stereotype of gamers as lonely teens doesn't fit the reality of today's game demographics.
Carter, Jon/CartoonStock

more than 200 million players, generated $2.4 billion, the biggest annual take for any game in history (Richter, 2019a).

As is the case with every media industry we've studied so far, concentration and globalization are the rule in gaming. In 2016 alone, major game-design shops bought $28 billion worth of smaller operations; in 2015, Activision, owner of the *Call of Duty* and *World of Warcraft* franchises, paid $5.9 billion for King Digital Entertainment, makers of mobile game hits such as *Candy Crush*; in 2017, global media conglomerate Vivendi acquired GameLoft, then the world's largest mobile games publisher in terms of downloads; and the industry experienced $1.6 billion in mergers and acquisitions in the first three months of 2020 alone, compared to only $1 billion for the full 6 months of the first half of 2019 (Matney, 2018; Takahashi, 2020).

Game console sales are the sole province of three companies: the United States' Microsoft, best known for Xbox and Kinect, and Japan's Nintendo (Wii) and Sony (PlayStation). Versions of PlayStation and Xbox have long dominated sales and time-of-play. But Wii, introduced in 2006 to appeal specifically to new, nontraditional gamers, has gained significant popularity, primarily because it permits full-body, interactive play using a variety of control wands rather than the typical game's button-laden controller. In 2010, Microsoft met Wii's challenge with Kinect, a motion-sensitive game that reads players' body movements without controllers or wands of any kind. Equipped with facial- and voice-recognition capabilities, Kinect remains the fastest-selling consumer electronics device in history, selling 8 million units in its first 60 days of availability (besting former champs iPhone and iPad; Kato, 2012).

Nintendo's Switch, released in 2017, is a fully Internet-capable hybrid console/handheld device that can also play cartridge games. Sony's PlayStation 4 and PlayStation 4 Pro, introduced in 2016, let players broadcast their games in real time to the Internet, encouraging friends to join in. Microsoft's Xbox One S, also released in 2016, while maintaining Kinect's features, was a home entertainment hub, integrating gaming, television, the Internet, and movie and music streaming services. 2020 saw the next big console advance, as Sony and Microsoft introduced new consoles, PlayStation 5 and Xbox Series S and Series X respectively, gaming's first consoles powerful enough to permit **ray tracing**, an advanced method of rendering light and shadows in a scene to produce more life-like images, visuals equal to those of the best computer graphics in movies and TV shows.

Three Nintendo devices dominate the handheld gaming market: the cartridge-based Game Boy Advance (released in 2001), multimedia DSi (2009), and glasses-free 3D, Internet-capable 3DS (2011). Sony countered in 2004 with PlayStation Portable, offering Internet access for multiplayer gaming, and in 2012 with Wi-Fi–capable PlayStation Vita, boasting video streaming and the power and graphics of a console.

Their dominance in hardware provides Microsoft, Nintendo, and Sony with more than sales revenue. **Third-party publishers**, companies that create games for existing systems, naturally want their best games on the most popular systems. And just as naturally, better games attract more buyers to the systems that support them. Third-party publishers produce their most popular titles for all systems. For example, Activision's *Call of Duty* is available for all consoles and Macs and PCs; the hugely popular *Madden NFL*, which has sold more than 130 million copies since its 1988 debut, and the *MVP Baseball* series come from EA Sports; *Metal Gear* is from Konami; *Tony Hawk* is from Activision; *Elder Scrolls* is from Bethesda Softworks; and *Batman* is from Warner Bros. Interactive.

Conversely, Codemaster's *MTV Music Generator* is available only for PlayStation and Xbox, and some third-party publishers produce Wii-only games, for example, EA's Headgate studios. Console makers do produce their own titles. Nintendo has the *Pokémon*, *Super Mario* (the best-selling game franchise in history; Richter, 2020), and *Pikmin* series. Sony publishes the *Gran Turismo* line, and Microsoft offers titles such as *XNS Sports* and *Halo*.

Concentration exists in the game software business just as it does on the hardware side. Atari Interactive owns several game

▼ A championship game tournament can easily draw 70,000 spectators.
Robyn Beck/AFP/Getty Images

makers, including Webfoot Technologies, and EA controls nearly 50% of all video-game sales. In mid-2011, EA further increased its dominance of the content side of the industry with its purchase of casual game developer PopCap, source of some of the most popular free online games such as *Bejeweled* and *Plants vs. Zombies.*

In an effort to counter this trend, however, a number of websites for independent game designers have sprung up. Most notable is Humble Indie Bundle. Small developers who cannot afford to distribute and market their games on the scale of the big companies upload their games to its website. Interested players can buy them free of copy- and other theft-protection so that they can be shared with other gamers. The games are designed for all platforms and, once bundled with other games, are for sale at whatever price a buyer wishes to pay, with a portion of the proceeds going to charity. In its first 2 years of operation, it earned more than $11 million for the site operators, game designers, and charities, and *PC Gamer* magazine named Humble Indie Bundle its 2011 community hero for its support of the indie game development market (Francis, 2011).

▲ One of video games' most popular titles, Activision's *360 Call of Duty* is from a third-party publisher.
Pumkinpie/Alamy Stock Photo

A serious problem faced by third-party game creators is that, as in the more traditional media, especially film, production and marketing costs are skyrocketing. Not only has the production technology itself become more sophisticated and therefore expensive, but also games, like movie franchises, build followings. With that, the creative forces behind them can demand more recognition and compensation. In 2001, the average game cost $5 million to produce and $2 million to promote. Today, the cost of development *alone* averages between $25 and $50 million, and a blockbuster such as *Destiny*, with its musical score by Paul McCartney, cost $500 million to produce (but consider that *Destiny* returned that much in sales in its first 24 hours on the market; Graser, 2014).

Again, as with film, industry insiders and fans are expressing concern over the industry's reliance on sequels of franchises and licensed content, including movie- and television-based games. For example, there are over 100 different *Mario* games, and money is increasingly diverted to pay for licensed properties such as *James Bond 007* and *Spider-Man.* And while industry research indicates that a majority of players want game makers to rely less on licensed content and sequels, those wants are in conflict with three important realities of the contemporary game industry: Production, promotion, and distribution costs are soaring; 50% of all games introduced to the market fail; and all 10 of 2020's best sellers were either a franchise sequel or a licensed title. Buffeted by difficult economic times like other media, the game industry wants to mitigate its risks, and when franchise titles such as *Call of Duty* and *Grand Theft Auto* can top half a billion dollars in sales in their first few days of availability, insiders see sequels as a reasonable, if not necessary, strategy.

Trends and Convergence in the Video-Game Industry

As with every media industry we've studied, the game industry is experiencing significant change, most of it driven by convergence and hypercommercialism.

Convergence Everywhere

Cable television giants Comcast and Cox each offer game services for their broadband customers; both direct broadcast satellite (DBS) providers also offer interactive game services. Most Internet service providers offer some form of online interactive games (see Chapter 10). AOL Games, for example, provides scores of games from designers such as EA Sports and Funkitron. Newspapers *USA Today*, the *Los Angeles Times*, and *The New York Times* maintain gaming platforms to foster loyalty, sell advertising, and connect with their readers. Many game makers, too, offer online interactive gaming. EA's Pogo.com offers board, puzzle, word, casino, sports, and card games (some for free and some for a fee) and can be linked to your Facebook account. Facebook itself, through its gaming tab, provides Instant Games which produced 20 billion gaming sessions in a 2-year span (Torbet, 2019).

All handheld game devices are Internet capable now, so, in an obvious bow to convergence, all new consoles are designed to perform a wide range of game and nongame functions. For example, iHeart Radio brings live-concert broadcasts and digital-only radio stations to Xbox users who, if they have Kinect, can control their listening through voice and body movements. Xbox users can also access Slacker's personal radio service and its tens of millions of music tracks, and if they subscribe to Microsoft's SmartGlass service, they can stream any and all content from their smartphones and tablets to their televisions through their gaming consoles.

Cable companies Verizon and Comcast and program providers such as HBO, Epix, Netflix, and Hulu stream content via game consoles. In fact, in 2012, for the first time, entertainment usage passed multiplayer game usage on the Xbox; that is, users spent more time with online video and music than playing games (Tsukayama, 2012). Home computer users, able to interact with other gamers for decades via MUDs, have been joined by console players in flocking to **massively multiplayer online roleplaying games (MMORPGs)** such as *Ultima Online*, *World of Warcraft*, *EverQuest*, and *Second Life*. Thirty million people worldwide play these **virtual worlds games**, and one, the hugely popular *World of Warcraft*, has more than 3.4 million subscribers.

This convergence of the console with other technologies, however, hides an important truth about the future of console gaming—it is coming to a close. "I think we will see another generation, but there is a good chance that step-by-step we will see less and less hardware," said Ubisoft CEO Yves Guillemot. "With time, I think streaming will become more accessible to many players and make it not necessary to have big hardware at home. There will be one more console generation and then after that, we will be streaming, all of us" (in Crecente, 2018). This stream-to-any-device capability is made possible by games' migration to *cloud computing* (see the discussion of *cloud computing* in Chapter 6). The most computer-processing-hungry **AAA games** (big-budget, sophisticated, graphics-rich games) such as *Call of Duty* and *Fortnite* can be played seamlessly, without any skip or lag in action on any device, even an older smartphone, if all the computing power necessary resides on distant computers. The console's once-necessary processing power is unnecessary. You can see the types of devices gamers own in Figure 9.3.

Games can be played not only on game consoles and handheld devices, but also on personal computers, on cable television, and online through social networking sites, game developers' websites, tablets, and smartphones. Technology and players' comfort with it are two reasons for this wave of convergence (and the likely demise of the home console).

As smaller, faster, more powerful microprocessors were developed and found their way into game consoles, the distinction between game consoles and personal computers began to disappear. A game console with high-speed microprocessors attached to a television set is, for all intents and purposes, a computer and monitor, and cloud computing makes all games on all devices equal.

▶ **Figure 9.3** What Devices Do Gamers Own?

Source: Entertainment Software Association, 2020.

(Photo): Richard Keppel-Smith/Gallo Images/Getty Images

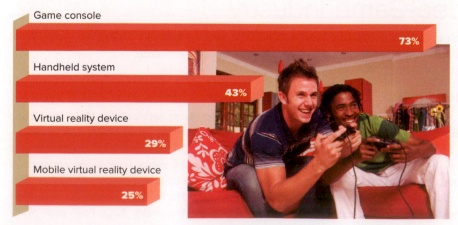

Game console — 73%

Handheld system — 43%

Virtual reality device — 29%

Mobile virtual reality device — 25%

As the distinction between the technologies on which games are played has diminished, players' willingness to play games on different platforms has grown. Demographics help account for this trend. Today's typical high school and college age players have grown up with computer, console, and handheld games as routine parts of their lives; they have a lifetime of familiarity with playing interactive games. In addition, especially since the introduction of mobile devices such as smartphones and tablets, they are largely agnostic in their choice of game platform. In fact, there may be no better evidence of people's comfort playing games across a variety of technologies than that which resides in the smartphone you most probably already use. As it is, 90% of all American gamers play on those devices (Lynkova, 2020).

Players' comfort with technology has also been a factor behind the early growth of **virtual reality (VR) games**, which through the use of a headset generate realistic images, sounds, and other sensations that replicate an actual or imaginary environment, simulate players' physical presence there, and make it possible for them to interact with the space. Sony offers PlayStation VR, and Microsoft has Oculus Quest. As you saw in Figure 9.3, 29% of American gamers already own a VR gaming device, up from 8% from the previous year, and 25% have mobile versions (Entertainment Software Association, 2020).

Smartphones, Tablets, and Social Networking Sites

Smartphones and tablets have revolutionized the video-game industry. In 2015 worldwide revenues from mobile gaming—$30 billion—overtook those from console gaming—$26 billion—for the first time (Gaudiosi, 2015), and in 2019, 60% of *all* game revenue worldwide came from mobile gaming's 1.4 billion players, a number expected to grow to 1.7 billion by 2024 (Williams, 2020). Hugely popular mobile location-based *Pokémon Go*, for example, has over 1 billion downloads since its launch in 2016 (Iqbal, 2020a).

Much, if not most, of today's mobile gaming takes the form of **casual games**—classic games such as card games (poker, cribbage, solitaire), table games (checkers, pool), matching games, and word and trivia games. Casual matching game *Candy Crush Saga*, for example, has had more than 1 trillion plays since its debut in 2012 ("Candy Crush," 2020). Globally, single-player casual games like *Candy Crush*, *Angry Birds*, and *Farmville* are gaming's most popular genre, topping, in second place, single-shooter games ("The State," 2020).

Casual games can be played in spurts and are easily accommodated by the phone's small screen. To be sure, however, casual games are a hit among Internet players as well, with more than 100 million online casual game players regularly visiting sites such as miniclip.com and pogo.com. They are joined by hundreds of millions of gamers, again primarily female, playing at social networking sites such as Facebook, whose Facebook Gaming app alone has 700 million monthly users (Forbes, 2020).

▲ Hyper-casual and casual games, for example, *Sand Balls* and *Farmville* respectively, dominate mobile gaming.
(Left): Postmodern Studio/Shutterstock; (Right): PhotoEdit/Alamy Stock Photo

Beginning in 2017, games that are even more casual, **hyper-casual games**, became available. Introduced by studios like Ketchapp and Voodoo, these are easy-to-play, typically no-cost mobile games offering minimalistic user interfaces. They can be quickly enjoyed once downloaded because they are so simple they require no tutorial or instruction. By 2019, hyper-casual games came to dominate mobile gaming, as 16 of the world's top 20 mobile game downloads, titles like *Fun Race 3D*, *Stack Balls*, and *Sand Balls*, were hyper-casual games (Dealessandri, 2020).

Hypercommercialism

Hypercommercialism has come to all media. Advertisers' desire to find new outlets for their messages and avoid the advertising clutter in traditional media has combined with gamers' attractive, segmented demographics to make video games particularly appealing vehicles for many types of commercial and other persuasive campaigns. Advertisers have come to think of games much like magazines.

Different titles attract different demographics—*Mortal Kombat* and *Grand Theft Auto* draw different players than do *Spider-Man* and *Viva Piñata*. Another reason advertisers are attracted to online games is that they are **sticky**. Players tend to stay (stick) with a game site longer than with other websites. Players don't just "visit" sites so much as they seek them out to stay and play a while. Regardless of the platform, industry research indicates the average console or online gamer spends 2 to 4 hours playing a single game in a single sitting. Sponsors—and the games they advertise on—hope to monetize this attention. Online and app-based games also provide marketers an easy opportunity to gather invaluable data while players play. This situation may benefit advertisers, but it raises serious legal issues when kids are tracked because the Children's Online Privacy Protection Act requires that without explicit, verifiable permission from parents, children's sites and apps are forbidden from collecting kids' personal details, a prohibition very frequently ignored (University of Texas, 2020). Sponsors use games to reach their targets in four ways: product placement, freemium games, advergaming, and advocacy gaming.

PRODUCT PLACEMENT   Advertisers like product placement for several reasons:

- First, a product used in a game is there forever—every time the game is played, the advertiser's brand appears.

- Second, the placement is not only permanent, but it can't be skipped like a commercial in a recorded TV show.

- Third, a brand's association with a game renders it "cool," but equally important, games' interactivity creates a stronger emotional connection and therefore a more positive association for players with brands—more so, for example, than simply viewing a TV spot.

- Fourth, players don't seem to mind the ads and even welcome them if it means a game costs less or can be played online for free (Ho, 2020).

- Fifth, they are effective, and that effectiveness can be measured for online games because the response, clicking through to the sponsor, can be precisely measured.

- Finally, where in-game ads were once static—a billboard atop a building or a logo on the side of a race car—today's online game product placements are dynamic. Sponsor can alter them remotely and on the fly, tailoring them to players' specific real-life locations and times of day.

But why, beyond the cash they earn, do game designers want product placements in their creations, a practice begun in the 1980s when Sega put Marlboro banners in its arcade racing games? First, brand names add a bit of realism to the game's virtual world, presumably enhancing the player's enjoyment. Second, advertisers and game makers frequently engage in cross-promotion. For example, retail store Target offers several mobile

▼ In-game product placement is ubiquitous.

ArcadeImages/Alamy Stock Photo

games on behalf of the brands it sells; each new edition of *Madden NFL* brings with it a new set of cross-promotions from various companies; and Adidas and Dick's Sporting Goods team with the Snapchat game *Baseball's Next Level* to allow players to buy limited edition cleats worn by the baseball stars appearing in the game's home run derby. The massively multiplayer online *EverQuest II* and Pizza Hut have a cross-promotion that lets players order a pizza in real life using an in-game command.

So mutually beneficial has game product placement become that placements, which can cost more than $1 million in a popular game, are frequently bartered for free; that is, the game maker and the brand advertiser exchange no money. The brand image is provided to the designer (for realism), and the sponsor gets placement (for exposure).

FREEMIUM GAMES Even more deeply integrating products into games are **freemium games**, in which consuming advertising or even spending actual cash allows players to progress in their play. Freemiums happen in a number of ways. In some games, in exchange for watching a commercial, players can obtain virtual goods, such as weapons or armor, rather than work to earn the credits necessary to buy them. Many games on Google's Play Games app, for example, include in-game commercials that, if viewed, "pay" gamers with "power-ups" that let them move to a higher level of play. And in some games, choosing to use a brand-name product imbues players with special in-game attributes unavailable to players content with generic products.

There is another form of freemium game in which players can spend actual money in order to advance. "Most games nowadays are not designed to be rewarding on their own, but to operate as digital cortisol drips that encourage players to spend money on 'rewards,' the 'gems' and 'coins' that, once upon a time, Mario would have discovered simply by hitting a question mark block," says tech writer Mark Wilson (2018). *Candy Crush Saga*, for example, contains *progress gates*, spots in the game where a player's progress is stymied by increasing difficulty. They can be overcome simply by paying to do so.

Some games, *Pokémon Go*, for example, require that real money be converted into in-game currency in order to mask how much cash players are actually spending. The game *World of Warriors* has energy meters; when players run out of energy-giving food or elixirs, they must recharge their depleted energy levels to continue their quest to vanquish the Skull Army. There are three primary ways to do this: wait, barter for energy with in-game earned crystals, or buy it with actual cash. And some games, such as *Fortnite*, *Overwatch*, and *Fifa 18*, contain **loot boxes**, in-game treasure chests that can be opened through gameplay or by paying real money, giving players access to some unnamed treasure inside. Belgium and the Netherlands have already deemed loot boxes a form of illegal gambling, and in late 2019, the US Senate took up the Protecting Children From Abusive Games Act that would ban the practice but it had little chance of passage given Congress's preference for industry self-regulation (Valdes, 2019).

ADVERGAMING Product placement in games has proven so successful that, in many instances, brands have become the games themselves in **advergames**. Brand-specific game websites are sometimes downloadable and sometimes played online, and many brands offer mobile app versions of their games. Their goal is to produce an enjoyable experience for players while introducing them to the product and product information. Chipotle Mexican Grill's *The Scarecrow*, a free iPhone game app designed to deliver the message that the chain uses only natural products, is a well-known award-winning effort. Mattel's *Hot Wheels: Infinite Loop* challenges players to race against other gamers around the world. Cable television's Hallmark Channel goes in even another direction, establishing its own game site, *Fun & Games*, which offers scores of games, all conveniently designed to promote its basic cable programming.

ADVOCACY GAMING Companies or organizations that want to get their noncommercial messages out turn to **advocacy games**, primarily on the Web and for mobile devices. Many national political candidates are supported by advocacy games. During the

▼ In Chipotle's *The Scarecrow* advergame, players help the Scarecrow smuggle animals away from his employer, Crow Foods, to save them from mistreatment. His farm attire of overalls and a straw hat are in stark contrast to his factory surroundings. This imagery promotes Chipotle's message that its practices are more natural than those of other fast-food companies. *Chipotle*

▶ *Fatworld*, from ITVS Interactive, is an advocacy game exploring the relationships between obesity, nutrition, and socioeconomics. Clicking on "Game," kids can learn how to improve their nutrition, letting them choose their avatar's starting weight and health conditions, how much to exercise, and what foods to prepare, eat, and avoid. Its playful characters and bright colors appeal to the game's target audience—children—and make playing feel more fun than educational.

TVS Interactive, "Online Video Game, Fatworld", Public Broadcasting Service-Independent Lens, http://www.fatworld.org. 2006 Persuasive Games, LLC.

2020 Presidential race you could travel to *Biden HQ*, an island in *Animal Crossing*, to interact with the then-candidate and his platform, or you might have preferred to fight "big money, special interests, fat cats, and mudslingers" on Vermont senator Bernie Sanders's *Bernie Arcade*. Dr. Ian Bogost, who created the genre with his 2004 release of the *Howard Dean for Iowa Game*, said, "I didn't get into games because I wanted to reach a demographic. I did it because I think games can communicate political concepts and processes better than other forums" (quoted in Erard, 2004, p. G1).

Supporters of political advocacy games see three significant strengths. First, the games are relatively inexpensive. A good political game can be created in a few weeks for about $20,000, well under the cost of television time. Second, like other advergames, they are sticky, and the message is reinforced with each play while broadcast ads are fleeting. Finally, they are interactive, making them a powerful means of communicating with potential voters, especially younger ones. More traditional forms of advocacy messaging, such as radio and television ads and campaign fliers, passively engage voters with their campaign rhetoric, but games encourage potential voters to interact with the message.

Not all advocacy games are about politics, however. There are games advocating the use of energy alternatives to oil (*Oiligarchy*), religious freedom (*Faith Fighter*), a more flexible application of copyright (*The Free Culture Game*), and improving kids' nutrition (*Fatworld*). Retired Supreme Court Justice Sandra Day O'Connor's nonprofit education group iCivics offers a series of games and accompanying lesson plans designed to introduce middle school students to the Constitution and encourage civic involvement. You can read about the gaming industry's efforts to make games a safer and more inviting environment for children in the box "Using the ESRB Ratings."

CULTURAL FORUM
Using the ESRB Ratings

The link between video games and antisocial behavior has been at issue ever since there have been video games. In fact, in 2019 the World Health Organization added *gaming disorder* to its authoritative International Classification of Diseases (Jabr, 2019). The next year then-Presidential candidate Joe Biden, in a campaign interview, called an unnamed game maker a "little creep" whose product serves as a means "to teach you how to kill people" (Gilbert, 2020).

However, despite these newsworthy events, the connection between video games and disturbing behavior is rarely far from the spotlight because of America's all-too-common deadly school shootings (for example, at Columbine High School in 1999 and the Sandy Hook Elementary School in 2013). In both instances, the teen-aged shooters' "addiction" to video games was prominently noted. The Columbine shooters had even created a custom *Doom* to represent the killing of their classmates, and the Sandy Hook gunman practiced on a game that simulates school shootings.

While critics do not argue that video games *cause* violence, there is significant scientific evidence (and agreement) that they can be a contributing factor (see, for example, Anderson et al., 2003, and Swing et al., 2010). Given this link, Congress first investigated the effects of video games in 1993, the same year that *Doom* was released for home computers. In an effort to head off government restrictions, in 1994 the industry established the Entertainment Software Ratings Board (ESRB) rating system. It has six ratings (a seventh, RP for Rating Pending, is the equivalent of "this film has not yet been rated"):

EC	Early Childhood	ages 3 and up
E	Everyone	ages 6 and up
E10+	Everyone 10 and Up	ages 10 and up
T	Teen	ages 13 and up
M	Mature	ages 17 and up
AO	Adults Only	ages 18 and up

Similar to the movie rating system, the ESRB system requires that games offer content descriptors somewhere on the front or back of the game package explaining why a particular rating was assigned. Although the Federal Trade Commission has lauded the ESRB ratings as the most comprehensive of the three rated industries (games, recordings, movies), media-literate gamers (or friends and parents of gamers) should understand the strengths and weaknesses of this system.

Depending on your perspective, this self-regulation is either a good thing because it keeps government's intrusive hand out of people's lives and protects game makers' First Amendment rights, or a bad thing because it is self-serving and rarely enforced. The value of the content descriptors, too, is in dispute. All a game maker is required to list is *any one* of the descriptors that has led to a given rating—for example, *strong lyrics*. For some, this is useful information. For others, it masks potential problems. First, according to the ESRB system, if this content is sufficient to give the game an M rating, no other content that might have contributed to that rating, such as *mature sexual themes* or *violence*, need be listed. Second, *strong lyrics* might apply to song lyrics about sex, violence, alcohol, or drug use. Only when the game is played will the player identify the reason for the rating and descriptor.

An additional concern over the rating system is that it is poorly enforced, but this concern may not be well founded. There's no doubt that some underage buying does occur, but the Federal Trade Commission's own undercover investigation of the problem revealed that video-game retailers do an effective job of enforcing age-based ratings; only 13% of underage shoppers are usually able to purchase M-rated video games (Jay, 2018). This is no doubt due in part to the fact that 87% of gamers' parents are aware of the ratings and 92% "pay attention" to the games their kids play (Entertainment Software Association, 2020).

Enter Your Voice

- How much attention do you pay to game ratings?
- Have you ever played a game with a rating that surprised you? If so, how much thought did you give that discrepancy?
- If you agree with critics that the industry-supplied ratings are little more than a public relations move to avoid regulation, can you think of a better system for informing parents and players about the games they are about to buy or play?

DEVELOPING MEDIA LITERACY SKILLS
The Treatment of Female Gamers

GamerGate thrust the issue of women in gaming into the cultural forum in 2012. It has remained there ever since because of the sexist portrayal of females in the video games themselves and the continued bullying of female players, especially in live online play (Warzel, 2019).

In 2012 feminist media critic Anita Sarkeesian began a Kickstarter campaign to raise $6,000 to produce a series of videos on female representation in games. She clearly hit a nerve among female gamers, because she attracted $158,000 from enthusiastic backers. However, she also drew relentless online harassment from many male gamers, including threats of murder and rape.

An enraged community of hardcore gamers, using the hashtag #GamerGate and supposedly in the name of fighting censorship and political correctness, unleashed brutal harassment of Sarkeesian and others, including female game developers Zoë Quinn and Briana Wu and gaming journalist Leigh Alexander, who had written in their defense. News site Reddit and messaging sites 4chan and 8chan became platforms for coordinated harassment campaigns. All these women had their social networking sites hacked and their personal information published online. Facing constant and detailed threats of harm, all were forced to leave their homes (Jeong, 2019).

Certainly the situation has improved; after all, women make up half the gaming community. "I wish I could tell you that it's gotten better," explains Ms. Wu. "It hasn't. Gamergate gave birth to a new kind of celebrity troll, men who made money and built their careers by destroying women's reputations. It poisoned our politics and our society. Attacks on journalists, disinformation campaigns, the online radicalization of young men—these are depressingly familiar symptoms of our current dysfunction" (2019, p. SR6).

Apart from the harassment, which is never remotely appropriate, is the issue of the treatment of female players much ado about nothing, just more political correctness? Does it matter that only 21% of game developers are female (Faber, 2019)? Should we care that only 24% of female gamers say they are treated "about equally" by other players (Clarke, 2019)? Keeping your answers in mind, test your commitment to gender equality in gaming by using the Video Game Sexism Scale developed by communication researchers Jesse Fox and Wai Yen Tang (2014). Answer each question on a 1 to 7 scale, with 1 being "completely disagree" and 7 being "completely agree."

Video Game Sexism Scale

1. Most women who play video games just do so with their boyfriends.
2. Most women who play video games are not very good at them.
3. Women who play video games are actually seeking special favors from men.
4. Women who play video games just do it to get attention from men.
5. Women are too easily offended by what goes on in video games.
6. Women get too offended by sexual comments in games.
7. Women are too sensitive about sex jokes and nude pictures of women that circulate in games.
8. Women who call themselves gamer girls think they deserve special treatment.
9. Having a woman play brings down the quality of the game.
10. If a woman plays with a team or guild, she is almost always the weakest link.
11. Women can't handle trash talking in games like men can.
12. Having women around makes the game less fun.
13. Video games are a man's world, and women don't belong.
14. Women are more worried about socializing than anything else in a game.
15. Women prefer spending time dressing up their character rather than playing.
16. Women don't play games to kill or achieve.

Add each number to calculate your score. A score higher than 56 suggests some discomfort with female players—the higher the number the more discomfort—and below 56 suggests otherwise. What does your score tell you about yourself and your reaction to GamerGate? Reenter your voice in the debate surrounding the treatment of women in gaming by looking at how you scored. If your results suggest even small discomfort with female gamers, what changes to your game experiences might you take or recommend to your friends to become a more inclusive player?

MEDIA LITERACY CHALLENGE
Masculinity and Femininity in Game World

Select five games that feature both male and female characters. For each of those characters, list the first three descriptors that come to mind as you look at them. Are there common traits among the men? Among the women? If so, why do you think they exist? How realistic are the portrayals of the men? Of the women? Can you explain your findings and your reactions to those findings in terms of these media literacy skills: your *ability and willingness to pay attention to and understand video-game content*, your *respect for the power of games' messages*, and your *ability to distinguish emotional from reasoned reactions when playing video games*?

Media-literate game players have *an understanding of the ethical and moral obligations of those who design the games they play.* Critics of the portrayal of gender in games agree that games are protected speech, but they argue this does not mean that developers are free of responsibility for their contribution to the culture in which we all live. Given what you've learned in this exercise about games' portrayal of men and women, can you address the question of the ethics of gender representation in video games?

Resources for Review and Discussion

REVIEW POINTS: TYING CONTENT TO LEARNING OUTCOMES

▶ **Recall the history and development of games and the gaming industry.**
- While the pinball games developed by David Gottlieb and Harry Williams are the precursors to video games, Steve Russell, Nolan Bushnell, and Ralph Baer are most responsible for what we now call electronic video games.
- A game is a video game when a player has direct involvement in some on-screen action to produce a desired outcome.

▶ **Describe how the organizational and economic nature of the contemporary gaming industry shapes the content of games.**
- Games are most frequently played on game consoles (home and portable), PC and Mac computers, and the Internet, but increasingly smartphones are serving as a popular game platform.
- Game consoles are the sole province of Microsoft, Nintendo, and Sony.

- Third-party publishers design games for the most popular systems.
- Rising costs in the production of games have led to hypercommercialism and a reliance on blockbusters, franchises, and sequels.
- Hypercommercialism in games takes the form of product placement, freemium games, advergaming, and advocacy gaming.

▶ **Explain the relationship between games and their players.**
- Three-quarters of all American households are home to at least one person who regularly plays video games.
- Game players' demographics are changing; women 18 or older represent a greater proportion of the gaming population than boys 18 or younger, primarily because of the growth of casual and hyper-casual games.

▶ **Identify changes in the game industry brought about by new and converging technologies.**
- □ Convergence, driven by more powerful technology and people's comfort with it, has overtaken gaming, as games can be played on a host of platforms including virtual reality devices.
- □ Wi-Fi–capable handheld devices, smartphones, and tablets have not only freed games from the console but have also fueled the rise of casual and hyper-casual games and swelled the ranks of female and adult players.
- □ Social networking sites like Facebook further encourage these changes.

▶ **Apply key game-playing media literacy skills to understanding and combating the frequent mistreatment of female gamers by some male players.**
- □ GamerGate, the controversy surrounding the mistreatment of female gameplayers, revealed widespread misogyny among male gamers.
- □ Not only are women gamers subject to attack and disrespect, they also make up a distressingly small proportion of the game-designer community.
- □ The misrepresentation of women in video games may well be the result of this mistreatment and exclusion.

KEY TERMS

LED (light-emitting diode), 210

LCD (liquid crystal display), 210

LAN (local area network), 210

first-person perspective game, 210

gamification, 212

exergame, 212

video game, 212

MUD (multiuser dimension), 212

e-sports, 213

ray tracing, 214

third-party publishers, 214

massively multiplayer online
    roleplaying games (MMORPGs), 216

virtual worlds games, 216

AAA games, 216

virtual reality (VR) games, 217

casual games, 217

hyper-casual games, 218

sticky, 218

freemium games, 219

loot boxes, 219

advergames, 219

advocacy games, 219

QUESTIONS FOR REVIEW

1. Who are David Gottlieb and Harry Williams? What were their contributions to the development of pinball?

2. How did *Pong* affect the development of video gaming?

3. What makes a video game a video game?

4. What are the most frequently employed platforms for gameplaying?

5. What is a third-party publisher?

6. How are movie studios and game developers similar in their efforts to reduce the financial risks involved in creating their products?

7. How does product placement occur in games?

8. What are the different forms of advergaming?

9. What is advocacy gaming?

10. What are the levels of the ESRB rating system?

To maximize your study time, check out CONNECT to access the SmartBook study module for this chapter, watch videos, and explore other resources.

QUESTIONS FOR CRITICAL THINKING AND DISCUSSION

1. What is your favorite game platform? Why? Do you think different types of players gravitate toward different platforms? Why or why not?

2. Does advergaming, especially where children are the players, bother you? Do you find advergaming inherently deceptive for these young players? Why or why not?

3. Have you ever played an advocacy game? If so, what was it? Was it from a group with which you were sympathetic? What would it take to get you to play a game from a site with which you disagree?

REFERENCES

1. Anderson, C. A., Berkowitz, L., Donnerstein, E., Huesmann, L. R., Johnson, J. D., Linz, D., et al. (2003). The influence of media violence on youth. *Psychological Science in the Public Interest, 4,* 81–110.

2. Browning, K. (2021, January 30). They're flocking to America to make a fortune playing video games. *New York Times.* Retrieved from https://www.nytimes.com/2021/01/30/technology/esports-league-of-legends-america.html?searchResultPosition=1

3. Burnham, V. (2001). *Supercade: A visual history of the videogame age 1971–1984.* Cambridge: MIT Press.

4. "Candy Crush Saga." (2020). *Sensor Tower.* Retrieved from https://sensortower.com/ios/us/king/app/candy-crush-saga/553834731/overview

5. Capps, R. (2020, February 23). Re: Play for pay. *New York Times Magazine,* pp. 46–59.

6. Clarke, L. (2019, December 24). Silencing the haters. *Washington Post*. Retrieved from https://www.washingtonpost.com/graphics/2019/sports/toxic-online-culture-women-esports/

7. Crecente, B. (2018, June 6). Ubisoft believes next gen is the last for consoles as Microsoft looks beyond platforms. *Variety*. Retrieved from https://variety.com/2018/gaming/features/death-of-the-console-1202833926/

8. Dealessandri, M. (2020, March 30). Hyper casual dominated new mobile downloads in 2019. *Gameindustrybiz*. Retrieved from https://www.gamesindustry.biz/articles/2020-03-30-hyper-casual-dominated-new-mobile-game-downloads-in-2019

9. DeMaria, R., & Wilson, J. L. (2004). *High score: The illustrated history of electronic games*. New York: McGraw-Hill.

10. Entertainment Software Association. (2020). *2020 essential facts about the video game industry*. Retrieved from https://www.theesa.com/esa-research/2020-essential-facts-about-the-video-game-industry/

11. Erard, M. (2004, July 1). In these games, the points are all political. *New York Times*, p. G1.

12. Faber, T. (2019, July 23). Does gaming have a woman problem? *Financial Times*. Retrieved from https://www.ft.com/content/8a7a4c1c-ac9b-11e9-b3e2-4fdf846f48f5

13. Forbes, T. (2020, April 20). Facebook launches gaming app to compete with Twitch, YouTube. *MediaPost*. Retrieved form https://www.mediapost.com/publications/article/350248/facebook-launches-gaming-app-to-compete-with-twitc.html

14. Fox, J., & Tang, W. Y. (2014). Sexism in online video games: The role of conformity to masculine norms and social dominance orientation. *Computers in Human Behavior, 33*, 314–320.

15. Francis, T. (2011, December 26). The Humble Bundle guys—*PC Gamer*'s community heroes of the year. *PC Gamer*. Retrieved from http://www.pcgamer.com/2011/12/26/the-humble-bundle-guys-pc-gamers-community-heroes-of-the-year/

16. Gaudiosi, J. (2015, January 15). Mobile game revenues set to overtake console games in 2015. *Fortune*. Retrieved from http://fortune.com/2015/01/15/mobile-console-game-revenues-2015/

17. Gilbert, B. (2020, January 21). Joe Biden called a "billionaire" video game maker a "little creep" who makes "games to teach you how to kill people." *Business Insider*. Retrieved from https://www.businessinsider.com/joe-biden-on-video-games-2020-1

18. Graser, M. (2014, December 2). Studios to unwrap digital viewing riches. *Variety*, pp. 14–15.

19. Ho, D. (2020, April 17). Dispelling in-game mobile advertising myths. *The Drum*. Retrieved from https://www.thedrum.com/opinion/2020/04/17/dispelling-game-mobile-advertising-myths

20. Iqbal, M. (2020a, June 23). Pokémon GO revenue and usage statistics (2020). *Business of Apps*. Retrieved from https://www.businessofapps.com/data/pokemon-go-statistics/

21. Iqbal, M. (2020b, June 23). Twitch revenue and usage statistics (2020). *Business of Apps*. Retrieved from https://www.businessofapps.com/data/twitch-statistics/#2

22. Jabr, F. (2019, October 27). Can you really be addicted to video games? *New York Times Magazine*, pp. 36–41, 54–55.

23. Jardine, A. (2020, January 23). The Red Cross infiltrates "Fortnite" to get gamers to "save" lives. *Ad Age*. Retrieved from https://adage.com/creativity/work/red-cross-infiltrates-fortnite-get-gamers-save-lives/2230071#:~:text=A%20new%20campaign%20for%20the,Red%20Cross%20(ICRC)%20workers.

24. Jay, M. (2018, July 1). FTC: ESRB has most effective ratings enforcement. *Entertainment Software Rating Board*. Retrieved from https://www.esrb.org/blog/federal-trade-commission-finds-that-esrb-has-most-effective-ratings-enforcement/

25. Jeong, S. (2019, August 18). When the online mob comes after you. *New York Times*, p. SR6.

26. Kato, M. (2012, January). Arrested development. *Game Informer*, pp. 10–12.

27. Kent, S. L. (2001). *The ultimate history of video games*. New York: Three Rivers Press.

28. Lynkova, D. (2020, May 19). Video game statistics [click the "start" button]. *Review 42*. Retrieved from https://review42.com/video-game-statistics/

29. Matney, L. (2018, June 10). Microsoft acquires a whole bunch of game studios. *TechCrunch*. Retrieved from https://techcrunch.com/2018/06/10/microsoft-acquires-a-whole-bunch-of-game-studios/

30. O'Malley, G. (2019, January 31). VR headsets forecast to reach 54M by 2023. *MediaPost*. Retrieved from https://www.mediapost.com/publications/article/331302/

31. Richter, F. (2020, March 11). Super Mario: The timeless bestseller. *Statista*. Retrieved from https://www.statista.com/chart/5764/best-selling-super-mario-games/

32. Richter, F. (2019a, January 17). Fortnite made billions in 2018 despite being free-to-play. *Statista*. Retrieved from https://www.statista.com/chart/16687/top-10-free-to-play-games/

33. Richter, F. (2019b, January 23). U.S. video game sales reach a new highscore. *Statista*. Retrieved from https://www.statista.com/chart/16754/video-game-industry-revenue/

34. "RSF Opens "The Uncensored Library"—the Digital Home of Press Freedom Within a Global Computer Game." (2020, March 11). *Reporters Without Borders*. Retrieved from https://rsf.org/en/news/rsf-opens-uncensored-library-digital-home-press-freedom-within-global-computer-game

35. Sellers, J. (2001). *Arcade fever*. Philadelphia: Running Press.

36. Sherr, I. (2020, March 30). Lots of people are playing video games during coronavirus lockdowns. *Cnet*. Retrieved from https://www.cnet.com/news/lots-of-people-are-playing-video-games-during-coronavirus-lockdowns/

37. "The State of Online Gaming." (2020). *Limelight*. Retrieved from https://www.limelight.com/resources/white-paper/state-of-online-gaming-2020/

38. Stedman, A. (2020, October 21). Video game market levels up. *Variety*, pp. 7–8.

39. Suderman, P. (2020, March 24). Why you should play videogames. *New York Times*, p. A23.

40. Suellentrop, C. (2016, February 5). This game will break your heart. *New York Times*, p. C1.

41. Swing, E. L., Gentile, D. A., Anderson, C. A., & Walsh, D. A. (2010). Television and video game exposure and the development of attention problems. *Pediatrics, 126,* 214–221.

42. Takahashi, D. (2020, April 11). Gaming acquisitions and investments continued in Q1 despite coronavirus. *Venture Beat.* Retrieved from https://venturebeat.com/2020/04/11/gaming-acquisitions-and-investments-were-strong-in-q1/

43. Torbet, G. (2019, July 26). Facebook's Instant Games are leaving Messenger. *Engadget.* Retrieved from https://www.engadget.com/2019-07-26-instant-games-facebook-gaming-tab.html

44. Tsukayama, H. (2012, March 28). Xbox adds HBO Go, MLB. TV, Xfinity, as it evolves from game console. *Washington Post.* Retrieved from https://www.washingtonpost.com/business/technology/xbox-adds-hbo-go-mlbtv-xfinity-as-it-evolves-from-game-console/2012/03/28/gIQASdAWgS_story.html?utm_term=.dfd3489a9e13

45. University of Texas at Dallas. (2020, June 23). Tool to protect children's online privacy: Tracking instrument nabs apps that violate federal law with 99% accuracy. *Science Daily.* Retrieved from https://www.sciencedaily.com/releases/2020/06/200623145354.htm

46. Valdes, G. (2019, May 13). "Zero chance" it passes: Game analysts break down senator's anti-loot box bill. *Venture Beat.* Retrieved from https://venturebeat.com/2019/05/13/zero-chance-it-passes-game-analysts-break-down-senators-anti-loot-box-bill/

47. "The Video Games Industry is Bigger than Hollywood." (2020, June 17). *Myboosting.* Retrieved from https://www.myboosting.gg/blog/esports-news/the-video-games-industry-is-bigger-than-hollywood#:~:text=The%20global%20video%20gaming%20industry,%2457%20billion%20market%20in%20value.)

48. Warzel, C. (2019, August 18). Gamergate gave us the post-truth information war. *New York Times,* SR6–7.

49. Waterman, H. (2020, April 9). 4/9 update: How Americans are spending time in the new normal. *Telecom Ramblings.* Retrieved from https://newswire.telecomramblings.com/2020/04/4-9-update-how-americans-are-spending-time-in-the-new-normal/

50. Williams, R. (2020, January 2). Mobile games sparked 60% of 2019 global game revenue, study finds. *Mobile Marketer.* Retrieved from https://www.mobilemarketer.com/news/mobile-games-sparked-60-of-2019-global-game-revenue-study-finds/569658/

51. Wilson, M. (2018, March 16). Google is turning ads into games you can play. *Fast Company.* Retrieved from https://www.fastcompany.com/90164244/google-is-turning-ads-into-games-you-can-play

52. Wu, B. (2019, August 18). Why was there no reckoning? *New York Times,* pp. SR6–7.

Cultural Forum Blue Column icon, Media Literacy Red Torch Icon, Using Media Green Gear icon, Developing Media book in starburst icon: ©McGraw Hill

The Internet and Social Media 10

◀ Are you confident that the online you is the *real* you?

Daniel M Ernst/Shutterstock

Learning Objectives

It is not an overstatement to say that the Internet and social media have changed the world, not to mention all the other mass media. In addition to being powerful communication media themselves, these technologies sit at the center of virtually all the media convergence we see around us. After studying this chapter, you should be able to

▶ Recall the history and development of the Internet and social media.

▶ Describe how the organizational and economic natures of the contemporary Internet and social media industries shape their content.

▶ Recall how and why individuals use social media.

▶ Analyze social and cultural questions posed by the Internet, social media, and related emerging technologies.

▶ Apply key Internet social media literacy skills, especially in protecting your privacy and reflecting on the Internet's double edge of (potentially) good and troublesome change.

1885 ▶ Babbage designs "computer" ············

1940s British develop Colossus and binary code 1940
1946 ▶ ENIAC ·····························
1950 UNIVAC
1951 Census Bureau makes first successful commercial use of computers

1957 ▶ *Sputnik* launched ·················· 1955
1960 Licklider's *Man–Computer Symbiosis*; IBM mainframe technology
1962 ARPA commissions Baran to develop computer network
1964 McLuhan's *Understanding Media*
1969 ARPAnet goes online

1972 E-mail 1970
1974 Internet emerges
1975 ▶ Gates develops PC operating system ·····
1977 Jobs and Wozniak develop Apple II
1979 BITNET
1981 IBM PC introduced

1990 HTTP developed 1985
1992 Internet society chartered
1994 ▶ Spam appears; first banner ad ·········
1995 Classmates.com launches
1999 Emojis appear

2000 ▶ US women pass men as users ······· 2000
2004 Facebook launched
2006 Twitter
2007 Laptops outsell desktops; Apple app store opens
2009 Internet surpasses newspapers as news source; social networking surpasses e-mail for person-to-person communication
2010 First popular tablet computer
2012 25 billionth app download from Apple app store; Facebook buys Instagram; mobile becomes top e-mail platform
2015 Search engines overtake traditional media as most trusted news source; tablets outsell laptops and desktops
2016 Fake news plague; UN declares Internet access a fundamental human right
2017 Number of Internet of Things devices surpasses world population
2018 EU's General Data Protection Regulation; Trump's tweets ruled official government communication
2019 Internet Bill of Rights introduced in Congress
2020 Coronavirus in the US; United Nations declares broadband Internet access a fundamental human right; California Consumer Privacy Act; global app spending passes $100 billion
2021 Insurrection at US Capitol; President Trump's Twitter account permanently suspended
2023 Third-party cookies banned from Chrome

Apic/Hulton Archive/Getty Images

Library of Congress Prints and Photographs Division [LC-USZ62-66023]

ZENTRALBILD PICTURE SERVICE/ TASS-MOS/AP Images

Doug Wilson/Corbis Historical/Getty Images

Y H Lim/Alamy Stock Photo

Onoky Photography/ SuperStock

▲ John Perry Barlow.
ZUMA Press, Inc./Alamy Stock Photo

JOHN PERRY BARLOW AND MARSHALL MCLUHAN HAVE BEEN TWO OF YOUR INTELLECTUAL HEROES EVER SINCE YOU STARTED COLLEGE. Cofounder of the Electronic Frontier Foundation, Barlow helped shape the world's hopes for the Internet in its earliest days. You can recite almost verbatim his vision. "We are creating a world that all may enter without privilege or prejudice accorded by race, economic power, military force, or station of birth," he said in 1996, "A world where anyone, anywhere may express his or her beliefs, no matter how singular, without fear of being coerced into silence or conformity" (in Leman, 2020).

Scholar and public intellectual McLuhan developed the concept of "the global village," the idea that as electronic media "shrink" the world, humans will become increasingly involved in one another's lives. As people come to know more about others once separated from them by distance, they will form a new, beneficial relationship, a global village.

But have electronic media brought you together? You've put yourself on a Twitter diet and dropped Facebook altogether because of the ugliness you encounter there every day. Your liberal and conservative friends seem to be living in different worlds entirely, getting their news and information from completely different news feeds off the Internet and social media. What's worse, they seem to be growing increasingly intolerant of each other's views. Far from living in a global village, it seems they're wrestling in a global mud pit.

You and your roommates aren't speaking because of an argument over a Reddit posting from the Centers for Disease Control and Prevention warning against masks during the coronavirus pandemic. On seemingly official letterhead, it was a hoax meant to politicize communal health campaigns (Reader, 2020). When you offered official evidence, they thought you were calling them dupes. Maybe not everyone should express their beliefs, and your relationship with your roomies is anything but beneficial.

But the Internet can be magnificent. Sure, sometimes it's a challenge to get past the bad stuff, but you spend hours there every, not just on social media sharing joy with your friends, but streaming entertainment, looking for jobs and job advice, doing research for school. After all, the Internet puts the accumulated knowledge of the entire world's population at your fingertips.

In this chapter, we study the history of the Internet, beginning with the development of the computer, and then we look at the Internet as it exists today. We examine its formats and its capabilities. As you well know, digital technologies are significantly reshaping the operation of traditional media; and as the media with which we interact change, the role they play in our lives and the impact they have on us and our culture will likewise be altered. We will look at the new technologies' double edge (their ability to have both good and bad effects), their ability to foster greater freedom of expression, efforts to control that expression, changes in the meaning of and threats to personal privacy, and the promise and perils of practicing democracy online. Finally, our discussion of improving our media literacy takes the form of an examination of the Internet Bill of Rights.

▲ Marshall McLuhan.
Bettmann/Getty Images

A Short History of the Internet

There are conflicting versions about the origins of the Internet. In the words of media historian Daniel J. Czitrom (2007), they involve "the military and the counterculture, the need for command and control and the impulse against hierarchy and toward decentralization" (p. 484). The more common story—the command-and-control version—is that the Internet is a product of the Cold War. In this version, the air force in 1962, wanting to maintain the military's ability to transfer information around the country even if a given area was destroyed in an enemy attack, commissioned leading computer scientists to develop the means to do so. However, many researchers and scientists dispute this "myth that [has] gone unchallenged long enough to become widely accepted as fact," that the Internet was initially "built to protect national security in the face of nuclear attack" (Hafner & Lyon, 1996, p. 10).

In the decentralization version, as early as 1956 psychologist Joseph C. R. Licklider, a devotee of Marshall McLuhan's thinking on the power of communication technology, foresaw linked computers creating a country of citizens "informed about, and interested in, and involved in, the process of government" (as quoted in Hafner & Lyon, 1996, p. 34). He foresaw "home computer consoles" and television sets connected in a nationwide network. "The political process would essentially be a giant teleconference," he wrote, "and a campaign would be a months-long series of communications among candidates, propagandists, commentators, political action groups, and voters. The key," he added, "is the self-motivating exhilaration that accompanies truly effective interaction with information through a good console and a good network to a good computer" (p. 34).

In what many technologists now consider to be the seminal essay on the potential and promise of computer networks, *Man-Computer Symbiosis*, Licklider, who had by now given up psychology and devoted himself completely to computer science, wrote in 1960, "The hope is that in not too many years, human brains and computing machines will be coupled . . . tightly, and the resulting partnership will think as no human brain has ever thought and process data in a way not approached by the information handling machines we know today" (as quoted in Hafner & Lyon, 1996, p. 35). Scores of computer experts, enthused by Licklider's vision (and many more who saw networked computers as a way to gain access to the powerful but otherwise expensive and unavailable computers just beginning to become available), joined the rush toward the development of what we know today as the **Internet**, a global network of interconnected computers that communicate freely and share and exchange information.

Development of the Computer

The title "originator of the computer" resides with Englishman Charles Babbage. Lack of money and unavailability of the necessary technology stymied his plan to build an "analytical engine," a steam-driven computer. But in the mid-1880s, aided by the insights of mathematician Lady Ada Byron Lovelace, Babbage did produce designs for a "computer" that could conduct algebraic computations using stored memory and punch cards for input and output. His work provided inspiration for those who would follow.

Over the next 100 years, a number of mechanical and electromechanical computers were attempted, some with success. But Colossus, developed by the British to break the Germans' secret codes during World War II, was the first electronic **digital computer**. It reduced information to a **binary code**—that is, a code made up of the digits 1 and 0. In this form, information could be stored and manipulated. The first "full-service" electronic computer, ENIAC (Electronic Numerical Integrator and Calculator), based on the work of Iowa State's John V. Atanasoff, was introduced by scientists John Mauchly and John Presper Eckert of the Moore School of Electrical Engineering at the University of Pennsylvania in 1946.

ENIAC hardly resembled the computers we know today: 18 feet tall, 80 feet long, and weighing 60,000 pounds, it was composed of 17,500 vacuum tubes and 500 miles of electrical wire. It could fill an auditorium and ate up 150,000 watts of electricity. Mauchly and Eckert eventually left the university to form their own computer company, later selling it to the Remington Rand Corporation in 1950. At Remington, they developed UNIVAC (Universal Automatic Computer), which, when bought for and used by the Census Bureau in 1951, became the first successful commercial computer.

The commercial computer explosion was ignited by IBM. Using its already well-entrenched organizational system of trained sales and service professionals, IBM helped businesses find their way in the early days of the computer revolution. One of its innovations was to sell rather than rent computers to customers, boosting diffusion of the new technology.

▼ Joseph C. R. Licklider envisioned a national system of interconnected home computers as early as 1956.

From the MIT Museum, ©Koby-Antupit Studio, Cambridge/Belmont, MA

▶ ENIAC.
Apic/Hulton Archive/Getty Images

▼ The Soviet Union's 23-inches-in-diameter, 184-pound *Sputnik* was not only the first human-made satellite to orbit Earth; it also sent shudders throughout the American scientific and military communities. *ZENTRALBILD PICTURE SERVICE/ TASS-MOS/AP Images*

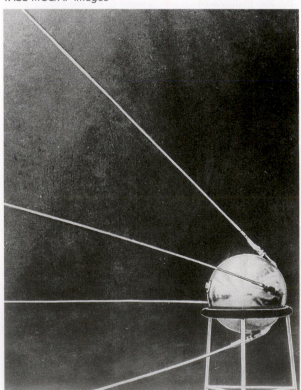

Military Applications

In 1957, the Soviet Union launched *Sputnik*, Earth's first human-constructed satellite. The once-undisputed supremacy of the United States in science and technology had been usurped, and American scientists and military officials were in shock. The Advanced Research Projects Agency (ARPA) was immediately established to sponsor and coordinate sophisticated defense-related research. In 1962, as part of a larger drive to promote the use of computers in national defense (and giving rise to one of the stories of the Internet's origins), ARPA commissioned Paul Baran of the Rand Corporation to produce a plan that would enable the US military to maintain command over its missiles and planes if a nuclear attack knocked out conventional means of communication. The military thought a decentralized communication network was necessary. In that way, no matter where the bombing occurred, other locations would be available to launch a counterattack. Among Baran's plans was one for a "packet switched network." He wrote,

> Packet switching is the breaking down of data into datagrams or packets that are labeled to indicate the origin and the destination of the information and the forwarding of these packets from one computer to another computer until the information arrives at its final destination computer. This (is) crucial to the realization of a computer network. If packets are lost at any given point, the message can be resent by the originator. (As cited in Kristula, 1997, p. 1)

The genius of the system Baran envisioned is twofold: (1) common communication rules (called **protocols**) and common computer languages would enable any type of computer, running with any operating system, to communicate with any other; and (2) destination or delivery instructions embedded in all information sent on the system would enable instantaneous "detours" or "rerouting" if a given computer on the network became unavailable.

Using Honeywell computers at Stanford University, UCLA, the University of California–Santa Barbara, and the University of Utah, the switching network, called ARPAnet, went online in 1969 and

◀ A 1960s-vintage IBM main-frame computer. The personal computer in your home probably carries more computing power than this giant machine.
Agence France Presse/Getty Images

became fully operational and reliable within one year. Other developments soon followed. In 1972, an engineer named Ray Tomlinson created the first e-mail program (and gave us the ubiquitous @ symbol). In 1974, Stanford University's Vinton Cerf and the military's Robert Kahn coined the term "the Internet." In 1979, a graduate student at the University of North Carolina, Steve Bellovin, created Usenet and, independent of Bellovin, IBM created BITNET. These two networking software systems enabled virtually anybody with access to a Unix or IBM computer to connect to others on the growing network.

By the time the Internet Society was chartered and the World Wide Web was released in 1992, there were more than 1.1 million **hosts**—computers linking individual personal computer users to the Internet. Today there is an ever-expanding number, 1.1 billion and growing (Clement, 2020).

The Personal Computer

A crucial part of the story of the Internet is the development and diffusion of personal computers. IBM was fantastically successful at exciting businesses, schools and universities, and other organizations about computers. But IBM's and other companies' **mainframe** and **minicomputers** employed **terminals**, and these stations at which users worked were connected to larger, centralized machines. As a result, the Internet at first was the province of the people who worked in those settings.

When the semiconductor (or integrated circuit, or chip) replaced the vacuum tube as the essential information processor in computers, its tiny size, absence of heat, and low cost made possible the design and production of small, affordable **microcomputers**, or **personal computers (PCs)**. This, of course, opened the Internet to anyone, anytime. Laptop computers, which outsold desktop models for the first time in 2007, extended that reach to anywhere. The tablet computer was first introduced in 2006 by Microsoft. It remained a niche computer favored by medical professionals for years. But the 2010 introduction of the iPad (operated not by mouse but by touch screen) not only continued the expansion of computing to anyone, anywhere, but it also made it even more convenient. In 2013, tablets outsold laptops for the first time and outsold both laptops and desktops in 2015 (Anthony, 2014).

The leaders of the personal computer revolution were Bill Gates and the duo of Steve Jobs and Stephen Wozniak. As a first-year college student in 1975, Gates saw a magazine story about a small, low-powered computer, the MITS Altair 8800 (developed by Micro

▲ The originators of the personal computing revolution—Bill Gates, Steve Jobs, and Stephen Wozniak.
(Left): Doug Wilson/Corbis Historical/Getty Images; (Middle): Paul Sakuma/AP Images; (Right): Mickey Pfleger/The LIFE Images Collection/Getty Images

▲ The desktop computer opened the Internet to anyone, anytime. The laptop extended that reach to anywhere. The tablet made anytime, anywhere more convenient.
(Left): Canadapanda/Shutterstock; (Right Top): sdecoret/Shutterstock; (Right Bottom): PSL Images/Alamy Stock Photo

Instrumentation and Telemetry Systems, an American electronics company), that could be built from a kit and used to play a simple game. Sensing that the future of computing was in these personal computers and that the power of computers would reside not in their size but in the software that ran them, Gates dropped out of Harvard University and, with his friend Paul Allen, founded Microsoft Corporation. They licensed their **operating system**—the software that tells the computer how to work—to MITS.

With this advance, people no longer had to know sophisticated operating languages to use computers. At nearly the same time, in 1977, Jobs and Wozniak, also college dropouts, perfected Apple II, a low-cost, easy-to-use microcomputer designed specifically for personal rather than business use. It was immediately and hugely successful, especially in its development of **multimedia** capabilities—advanced sound and image applications. IBM, stung by its failure to enter the personal computer business, contracted with Microsoft to use its operating system in its IBM PC, first introduced in 1981. All of the pieces were now in place for the home computer revolution.

The Internet Today

The Internet is most appropriately thought of as a "network of networks" that is still growing at an incredibly fast rate. These networks consist of LANs (local area networks), connecting two or more computers, usually within the same building, and **WANs (wide area networks)**, connecting several LANs in different locations. When people access the Internet from a computer in a university library, they are most likely on a LAN. But when several universities (or businesses or other organizations) link their computer systems, their users are part of a WAN.

As the popularity of the Internet has grown, so has the number of **ISPs (Internet service providers)**, companies that offer Internet connections at monthly rates depending on the kind and amount of access needed. There are hundreds of ISPs operating in the United States, including some of the better known such as Earthlink and Century Link. Americans increasingly find that their ISP and video (cable or FiOS) providers are one and the same—for example, Comcast and Verizon. A majority of all American Internet users have their cable company as their ISP. Through providers, users can avail themselves of the Internet's many services, among them the World Wide Web, search engines, and browsers.

The World Wide Web

Although we often use the terms interchangeably, the Internet and the World Wide Web aren't the same thing. The Internet is a massive network of networks, a networking infrastructure connecting billions of computers across the globe, allowing them to communicate with one another. However, the **World Wide Web** (usually referred to as "the Web") is a means of accessing information on the Internet. Think of the Internet as "composed of the machines, hardware and data, and the World Wide Web is what brings this technology to life," suggests technology writer Jessica Toothman (2017).

The Web is not a physical place, or a set of files, or even a network of computers. The heart of the Web lies in the protocols that define its use. The World Wide Web (WWW) uses hypertext transfer protocols (HTTP) to transport files from one place to another. Hypertext transfer was developed in the early 1990s by England's Tim Berners-Lee, who was working at CERN, the international particle physics laboratory near Geneva, Switzerland. Berners-Lee gave HTTP to the world for free. "The Web is more a social creation than a technical one," he wrote. "I designed it for a social effect—to help people work together—and not as a technical toy. The ultimate goal of the Web is to support and improve our web-like existence in the world" (Berners-Lee & Fischetti, 1999, p. 128).

Berners-Lee is acutely aware of the problems of the Internet that gave rise to our opening vignette, but remains optimistic. "Against the backdrop of news stories about how the web is misused, it's understandable that many people feel afraid and unsure if the web is really a force for good," he wrote on the occasion of the 30th anniversary of the release of his innovation. "But given how much the web has changed in the past 30 years, it would be defeatist and unimaginative to assume that the web as we know it can't be changed for the better in the next 30" (in Sullivan, 2019).

▶ Web inventor Tim Berners-Lee.
Catrina Genovese/WireImage/Getty Images

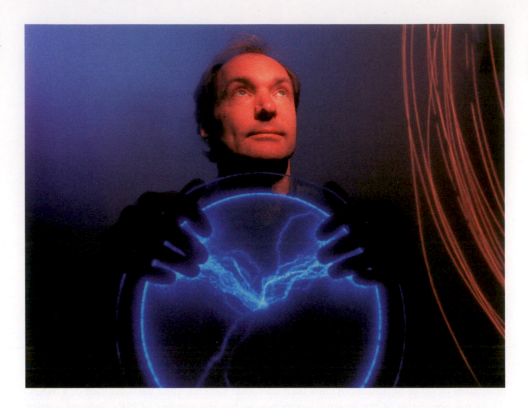

We enjoy the World Wide Web in part because of its ease of access, a function of a number of components: hosts, URLs, browsers, search engines, and home pages.

HOSTS (COMPUTERS CONNECTED TO THE INTERNET) Most Internet activity consists of users accessing files on remote computers. To reach these files, users must first gain access to the Internet through "wired-to-the-Net" hosts. These hosts are often called servers.

Once users gain access to a host computer on the Internet, they then have to find the exact location of the file they are looking for *on* the host. Each file or directory on the Internet (that is, on the host computer connected to the Internet) is designated by a **URL (uniform resource locator)**. A URL is, in effect, a site's official address. But as any user of the Web knows, sites are more commonly recognized by their **domain names**. The last part of a site's address, the *.com* or *.org*, is its top-level domain name, so we know that .com is a business and .org is a nonprofit. But in 2012 the Internet Corporation for Assigned Names and Numbers, or ICANN, authorized the use of a virtually unlimited number of generic top-level domains to include almost any word or name, for example, *.defibrillator* or *.newyorkcity.* It also permits, for the first time, the use of non-Latin language scripts, such as Arabic, Chinese, and Cyrillic. The number of individual domains, or websites, changes by the minute, but a 2017 analysis by Google counted 130 trillion unique URLs operating on the Internet, a growth of 100 million pages in the previous 4 years ("Google Search," 2017).

BROWSERS Software programs loaded onto the user's computer and used to download and view Web files are known as **browsers**. Browsers take separate files (text files, image files, and sound files) and put them all together for viewing. Google Chrome, Firefox, and Internet Explorer are three of the most popular Web browsers.

SEARCH ENGINES Finding information on the Web is simple thanks to **search engines**, software that allows users to navigate the Internet simply by entering a search word and selecting a page from the results. Among the better known are Ask and Bing, but the best known and most frequently used—with more than 90% of all searches worldwide and 92.5 billion visits a month—is Google. The Web's most-visited site, Google produces its results with technology that uses the collective intelligence of the Web itself; that is, search results are presented and ranked based primarily on how frequently a given site is linked to others (Neufield, 2021). Increasingly popular alternatives do exist; for example, DuckDuckGo and Startpage promise privacy in searching and do not profile users or sell their data to third parties.

Smartphones

Smartphones make connecting to the Internet, already an anytime, anywhere activity thanks to laptops and tablets, even more convenient. There is no need to search for a site or use a browser because an app on your smartphone will take you directly to its designated content. (Global spending on apps from the Apple Apps Store and Google Play passed the $100 billion mark in 2020; Richter, 2021.) Today, 77% of all Americans own at least one smartphone (Georgiev, 2020). And they are committed to those mobile devices; the average user spends more than 3 hours a day on a smartphone (Dolliver, 2020), and 47% say they "couldn't live" without one (Metev, 2020). Since 2017, mobile devices have accounted for half of all global Internet usage, in fact, more than 60% ("Ultimate," 2021).

Social Media

Of course, much mobile use is devoted to social media. Where e-mail was long the Internet's most common and fastest-growing use, it was surpassed in 2009 by **social networking sites (SNSs)**, websites that function as online communities of users. Today 80% of all Americans belong to at least one SNS (Edison Research, 2020); globally, SNS users average 2 hours and 25 minutes a day engaged with social media (Americans average 18 fewer minutes; Faw, 2021). And it was Facebook's specific desire to make itself even more attractive to mobile users that drove the company in 2012 to buy the 2-year-old, purely mobile photo start-up Instagram for $1 billion. Instagram now has more than a billion worldwide users, 89% outside the United States (Systrom, 2020).

Classmates.com's 1995 launch began the social networking movement, and it was soon followed by similar sites, most notably Friendster in 2002 and LinkedIn in 2003. MySpace also launched in 2003 and quickly became a favorite of young people around the world until it was unseated by Facebook, which was Harvard University–specific at birth in 2004 and became global in 2006. Worldwide, there are 2.8 billion active monthly Facebook users, 1.84 billion of whom log in daily (Moshin, 2021).

These "old line" sites were joined in 2006 by Twitter, a social media site designed for "microblogging," posts of up to 280 characters (called *tweets*) displayed on senders' profile pages and delivered to their subscribers (*followers*). Delivery can be restricted to a specific circle of followers, or, by default, it can be public. There are 353 million active monthly users globally, 187 million of whom access the site daily (Dean, 2021). While much of this activity is innocuous, such as following a celebrity (singer Justin Bieber has 114 million followers), much of it is serious.

To push back at the flood of misinformation about the coronavirus during the 2020 pandemic, dozens of celebrities gave their Twitter accounts over to health experts as part of the #PassTheMic campaign (Wanshel, 2020). And it was Twitter that helped galvanize global protests in support of the Black Lives Matter movement following the police killing of George Floyd. "Social media participation becomes a key site from which to contest mainstream media silences and the long history of state-sanctioned violence against racialized populations" explained researchers Yarimar Bonilla and Jonathan Rosa (in Warzel, 2020, p. SR2).

Twitter is also the medium of choice for many world leaders and other newsmakers. For example, President Trump regularly used it to bypass what he called the "fake news" to communicate directly with his millions of followers, though the traditional media would often report on his tweets. So central had Twitter become to the conduct of this particular president's governance that a federal judge in 2018 ruled Mr. Trump's Twitter feed "an official government account," akin to a "digital town hall," and therefore open to supporters and critics alike, free from the threat of blocking (Herman & Savage, 2018, p. B1). However, in January 2021, in the wake of the violent assault on the US Capitol by the President's supporters hoping to overturn his reelection loss, both Twitter and Facebook suspended Mr. Trump's accounts, citing his sedition- and violence-inciting postings (Perrigo, 2021). Twitter, concerned about "the risk of further incitement of violence," banned the President's account "permanently" (Conger & Isaac, 2021, p. A1). The use of SNSs for news and politics, as you can see, is a very sharp double-edged sword.

There are scores of other social networking sites. Some are general interest and growing in popularity, especially with younger users, for example, Snapchat (users post images and video that are viewable for only a short time) and Pinterest (users upload or search, save, sort, and manage images and videos into collections called *boards* that serve as personalized media platforms). Others are narrower communities built around specific interests, for example, CafeMom (for mothers), BlackPlanet (for the African American community), and Foursquare (for those who want their followers to know where they are and make recommendations of nearby services and activities). There are even audio SMS, for example, Clubhouse, which allow invited users to "drop in" for conversation.

The Debate over Social Media's Value

Just as the benefits and risks—the double edge—of the Internet as a whole continue to be debated, a number of issues specific to social media are generating their own disagreement. We'll take a brief look at some of the most common questions surrounding our use of social media: Why do we engage others on social media, and how realistically do we present ourselves when we do? Do Facebook depression and Facebook envy exist? And are we substituting social media interaction for real-world relationships?

PRESENTATION OF SELF There must be a reason that 80% of all US adults belong to at least one social networking site and that the average North American Internet user has 6.8 social media accounts (Mander, Kavanagh, & Buckle, 2020).

One answer to the *why* of our engagement with social networking sites resides in the **dual-factor model of social media use**, which claims that this engagement is motivated by two basic social needs. The first is *the need to belong*, our natural desire to associate with other people and gain their acceptance. The second, *the need for self-presentation*, is our ongoing effort to shape what others think of us. The two operate simultaneously because social media activity not only tells us we belong (that's where our friends are), but it increases our sense of acceptance and, therefore, our self-esteem (Nadkarni & Hofmann, 2012). In fact, the simple act of updating and reading our own profiles boosts our self-esteem (Gonzales & Hancock, 2011).

But once we've made the decision to use social media, we must decide *how* we present ourselves. Many people worry about their privacy when online, but in our everyday use of social media we willingly offer even the minutest details about our lives, taking pains to update those offerings, and even supporting those entries with visual evidence. When we do this we make judgments about the self we choose to reveal. We select our screen names and profile pictures to identify ourselves as we wish to be identified. But do we openly try to deceive? If you think most social media users do, you subscribe to the **idealized virtual identity hypothesis**, which argues that social media users tend to show idealized characteristics that do not reflect who they really are.

But this does not happen as much as you might think. For most users, time on social media constitutes "an extended social context in which to express [their] actual personality characteristics, thus fostering accurate interpersonal perceptions. [Social media] integrate various sources of personal information that mirror those found in personal environments, private thoughts, facial images, and social behavior, all of which are known to contain valid information about personality" (Back et al., 2010, p. 372). As a result, social media use makes it a bit difficult to hide who we actually are, and as such it's more likely that the **extended real-life hypothesis**, the idea that we use social media to communicate something close to our actual identities, holds true. The openness of social media makes it very difficult to control information about ourselves and our reputations—others can post information about us—and our friends constantly provide accountability and feedback on our profiles and other material we post. That is, those who know us keep us honest.

Nonetheless, the widespread use of **finstas**, second ("f" for fake) Instagram accounts offering less-curated, more natural versions of self to a trustworthy circle of friends, suggests that users are keenly aware that the selves they present on their primary SNS accounts are likely a bit optimistically painted (Kang & Wei, 2020).

SOCIAL MEDIA USE AND SUBJECTIVE WELL-BEING Can all this effort to present our best, truthful selves carry too much of a toll? For many young people the answer seems to be "yes." The American Academy of Pediatrics recognizes **Facebook depression**, "depression that develops when preteens and teens spend a great deal of time on social media sites, such as Facebook, and then begin to exhibit classic symptoms of depression. Acceptance by and contact with peers is an important element of adolescent life. The intensity of the online world is thought to be a factor that may trigger depression in some adolescents" (O'Keeffe & Clarke-Pearson, 2011, p. 802).

Indeed, Christina Sagioglou and Tobias Greitmeyer (2014), whose research led them to express surprise "that Facebook enjoys such great popularity," demonstrated that **affective forecasting error**—the discrepancy between the expected and actual emotions generated by Facebook activity—produces a decline in users' mood after using the social networking site (p. 361).

There is also evidence of another emotional downside to social networking: **Facebook envy**. As many as one in three Facebook users say they are sometimes resentful of the happiness others show on social media. Commentary on "travel and leisure," "social interactions," and "happiness" are the three most frequent generators of envy (Krasnova et al., 2013, p. 7). And if you use social media, you know that these are the topics your friends usually emphasize in their posts; who wants friends who report where they didn't go, who they didn't spend time with, and how unhappy they are? You can see what frustrates users about their SNS use in Figure 10.1.

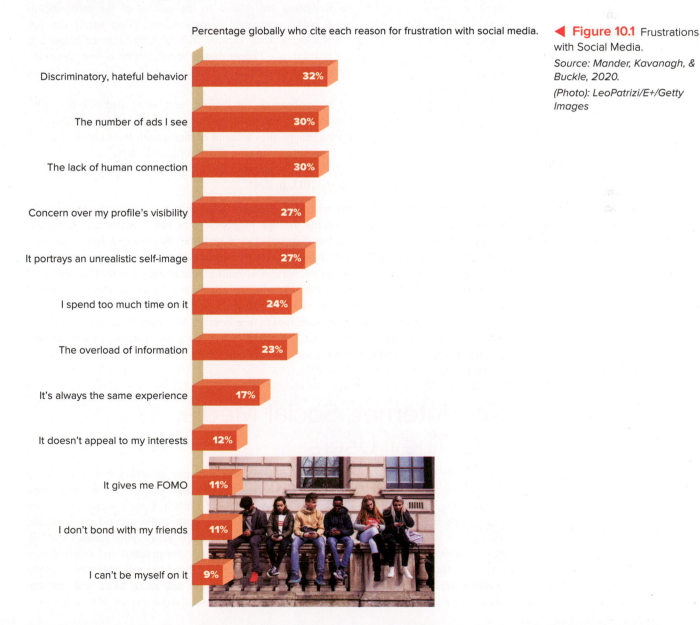

Percentage globally who cite each reason for frustration with social media.

Reason	Percentage
Discriminatory, hateful behavior	32%
The number of ads I see	30%
The lack of human connection	30%
Concern over my profile's visibility	27%
It portrays an unrealistic self-image	27%
I spend too much time on it	24%
The overload of information	23%
It's always the same experience	17%
It doesn't appeal to my interests	12%
It gives me FOMO	11%
I don't bond with my friends	11%
I can't be myself on it	9%

◀ **Figure 10.1** Frustrations with Social Media.
Source: Mander, Kavanagh, & Buckle, 2020.
(Photo): LeoPatrizi/E+/Getty Images

Findings such as these have led social scientists to test the relationship between SNSs and subjective well-being, that is, how users feel about themselves. *Subjective well-being* operates on two levels: how people feel about themselves in the moment, and how satisfied they are with their lives in general. Subjective well-being is important in how we live our lives, as it is related to such things as better health and a longer life, career success and even marital satisfaction.

Existing research suggests that SNS use diminishes our personal sense of well-being to the point that it can weaken the benefits of actual real-world friendships. Public health researchers Holly Shakya and Nicholas Christakis (2017) discovered that Facebook use is negatively associated with self-reported mental health, self-reported life satisfaction, and body mass index. This led them to conclude, "The negative associations of Facebook use were comparable to or greater in magnitude than the positive impact of offline interactions" (p. 203).

Many users recognize SNS's impact on their emotional health. Three-quarters of Americans have taken steps to distance themselves from Facebook (Tolentino, 2019), and 54% of 13 to 38 year-olds admit that being constantly on social media worsens their mental well-being (O'Malley, 2019).

So while there may be little disagreement that SNS use generally leads to declines in subjective well-being, the actual *use* of SNSs may not be the important issue. For example, research shows that effects on well-being are related to the *quality* of the relationships between SNS users: "Receiving targeted, composed communication from strong ties [is] associated with improvements in well-being while viewing friends' wide-audience broadcasts and receiving one-click feedback [is] not. . . . People derive benefits from online communication, as long it comes from people they care about and has been tailored for them" (Burke & Kraut, 2016, p. 265).

And Philippe Verduyn and his colleagues discovered, and as a media-literate SNS user you'll understand, that it is not SNS use itself, but how active people are in that use. Specifically, *passive* use (monitoring others' sites without engaging with them) leads to lower subjective well-being because it "provokes social comparisons and envy," and *active* use (directly engaging with others) boosts it "by creating social capital and stimulating feelings of social connectedness" (Verduyn, 2017, p. 274).

SOCIAL ISOLATION Finally, this raises the question of what is a "friend" on social media. What does *friendship* mean when the average Facebook user has 338 friends (K. Smith, 2019)? Are we connected online but disconnected in real life? Psychologist John Cacioppo has indeed demonstrated that "the greater the proportion of face-to-face interactions, the less lonely you are. The greater the proportion of online interactions, the lonelier you are." However, recognizing social media's double edge, he concluded that social media are not at the root of social isolation; they are merely tools, good or bad, depending on how they are used. "If you use Facebook to increase face-to-face contact, it increases social capital," he said. "Facebook can be terrific, if we use it properly. It's like a car. You can drive it to pick up your friends. Or you can drive alone" (in Marche, 2012).

The Internet, Social Media, and Their Users

We typically think of people who access a medium as audience members, but social media and the Internet have *users*, not audience members. At any time—or even at the same time— a person may be both *reading* online content and *creating* content. E-mail, social media, and chat rooms are obvious examples of online users being both audience and creators, but others exist as well. For example, massively multiplayer online roleplaying games (MMORPGs) enable entire alternative realities to be simultaneously constructed and engaged (see Chapter 9 for more on MMORPGs), and computer screens that have multiple open windows enable users to read one site while writing on another and uploading audio and video to even another. With ease, we can access the Web, link from site to site and page to page, and even build our own sites. The Internet makes us all journalists, broadcasters, commentators, critics, filmmakers, and advice columnists.

It is almost impossible to tell exactly how many users there are on the Internet. People who own computers are not necessarily linked to the Internet, and people need not own computers to use the Internet, as many users access the Internet through devices at school, a library, or work. Current best estimates indicate that there are at least 4.9 billion users worldwide—63% of Earth's population and a 1,271% increase since 2000. Ninety percent of North Americans use the Internet, a 208% increase since 2000, a rapid rate of growth due in large part to the spread of smartphones ("World Internet Users," 2021). The Internet's demographics have undergone some dramatic shifts since its early years. In 1996, for example, 62% of American Internet users were men. In 2000, women became the Internet's majority gender for the first time (Hamilton, 2000). Today, women in every age group use the Internet more than men do. And not surprisingly, the younger a person, the greater the likelihood is that he or she has access to the Internet. And for better or worse, 63% of global Internet users say they are "constantly online" (Mander, Kavanagh, & Buckle, 2020).

Reconceptualizing Life in an Interconnected World

What happens to people as they are increasingly interconnected? What becomes of audiences and users as their roles are electronically intertwined? How free are we to express ourselves? Does greater connectivity with others mean a loss of privacy? These are only a few of the questions confronting us as we attempt to find the right balance between the benefits and drawbacks that come from the new communication technologies.

The Double Edge of Technology

The root of the frustration with the Internet highlighted in the opening vignette is one of perspective. McLuhan was theorizing in the relative youth of the electronic media. When *Understanding Media* was published in 1964, television had just recently become a mass medium, the personal computer was years away, and Paul Baran was still envisioning ARPAnet. Barlow began writing about the Internet in the 1990s, the Internet's wide-open early days. The Web was brand new; there was no Facebook, Twitter, Instagram, or TikTok; no Google, no apps, not even Wikipedia.

Still, neither visionary was completely right or wrong in their optimism. Technology alone, even the powerful electronic media that fascinated both, cannot create new worlds or new ways of seeing them. *We* use technology to do these things. This is why technology is a double-edged sword. Its power—for good and for bad—resides in us. The same aviation technology that we use to visit relatives halfway around the world can also be used to drop bombs in a war zone. The same communication technologies used to create a truly global village can be used to dehumanize and demean the people who live in it. For better or worse, ongoing misuse of the Internet's great power has even its developers and once-staunch supporters calling for dramatic change in the Internet itself and how it's used, as you can read in the essay "From Those on the Inside: It's Time to Fix the Internet."

▼ Technologies, even those with as much potential as the Internet and social media, are only as good as the uses we make of them.
Bacall, Aaron/CartoonStock

"I'm making sure that my self-inflated Wikipedia entry corresponds to my self-inflated Facebook profile."

USING MEDIA TO MAKE A DIFFERENCE
From Those on the Inside: It's Time to Fix the Internet

In 1969, computer interconnectivity visionary J. C. R. Licklider predicted, "Life will be happier for the on-line individual" (in Lepore, 2021, p. 56). But is it? Massive data breaches reveal the personal data of billions of users to identity thieves and other criminals (Gontovnikas, 2020). When Facebook's own employees presented evidence that their platform was being used to sow divisiveness and hate, management buried the report rather than take steps to address the problem (Horwitz & Seetharaman, 2020). Because of their failure to control the spread of lies about the integrity of the 2020 presidential election, much of the blame for the violent invasion of the US Capitol by angry Trump-supporting insurrectionists in January 2021 fell directly at the feet of Facebook, Twitter, and YouTube (Ghosh, 2021).

Reddit is a major platform in the **manosphere**, the on-line home to self-proclaimed men's rights activists who harbor, express, and occasionally act on their ill will toward women (Basu, 2020). Users worry about their privacy (Reicin, 2021) and kids are illegally tracked by the online games they play (University of Texas, 2020). In April 2020, as the global COVID-19 pandemic was escalating, a group of 82 websites spreading COVID misinformation gathered half a billion Facebook's views. The 10 most popular alone drew 300 million views; the 10 leading legitimate health institutions, 70 million. The National Center for Disaster Preparedness estimated that of the 217,000 COVID deaths by October, 130,000 could have been avoided but for a "mislead public" and, not unrelated, lack of a mask mandate (Zuboff, 2021, p. SR4).

Critics contend that social media feed **surveillance capitalism**, an economic system dependent on the buying and selling of people's personal data, the capture and production of which relies on mass surveillance of the Internet. Under surveillance capitalism, our personal human experiences become free source material for tech giants, "one-way-mirror operations engineered for our ignorance and wrapped in a fog of misdirection, euphemism, and mendacity," in the words of Harvard University business scholar Shoshana Zuboff (2020, p. SR1). And as you read in Chapter 4, the Internet decimated the newspaper industry's financial foundation in particular, and that of democracy-sustaining journalism in general.

It's no surprise, then, that the number of Internet users who see the Web as "good for society" is declining (Smith & Olmstead, 2018). But what is surprising is the growing demand for change coming from those who built the Internet's great power. Inventor of the World Wide Web Tim Berners-Lee is "devastated" by the failure of the Web to serve humanity (Brooker, 2018). Apple CEO Tim Cook warns, "We see vividly, painfully how technology can harm, rather than help. [The platforms can] magnify our worst human tendencies . . . deepen divisions, incite violence and even undermine our shared sense or what is true or false. This crisis is real. Those of us who believe in technology's potential for good must not shrink from this moment" (in Grothaus, 2018).

Chamath Palihapitiya, an early Facebook executive, feels "tremendous guilt" about his role in building that SNS. "The short term, dopamine-driven feedback loops that we have created are destroying how society works," he wrote. "No civil discourse, no cooperation, misinformation, mistruth" (in Gelles, 2018, p. B1). Former Google executive Tristan Harris (2018) laments, "Religions and governments don't have that much influence over people's lives. But we have three technology companies [Facebook, Google, and Amazon] who have this system that frankly they don't even have control over. . . . Right now, 2 billion people's minds are already jacked in to this automated system, and it's steering people's thoughts toward either personalized paid advertising or misinformation or conspiracy theories."

These insiders are clearly not satisfied with the difference their medium is making. But what about you? Must we accept the Internet's bad to benefit from its good? Yes, 53% of Americans say the Internet has been an essential source of information during the 2020 coronavirus pandemic (Vogels, Perrin, Rainie, & Anderson, 2020), but the flood of online misinformation and outright deception is so great that the United Nations Secretary-General warned of "a pandemic of misinformation," and the head of the World Health Organization said we are suffering an "infodemic" (Rogers, 2020). Is this a reasonable trade-off?

Why is so much of the criticism of this seemingly marvelous technology coming from those on the inside? Is it that they feel a heightened sense of responsibility for what they have built and promoted? If that's the case, what is *our* responsibility to ensure that the Internet is used for good? Consider tech writer Joanne McNeil's admonition. The Internet's "infrastructure is power," she said, "but it is not the law, which means there is still an opportunity for users—as individuals and collectives, and working with government bodies—to hold platforms accountable" (in Borst, 2020, p. 33).

Changes in the Mass Communication Process

Concentration of ownership, globalization, audience fragmentation, hypercommercialism, and convergence are all influencing the nature of the mass communication process (see Chapter 2). Each redefines the relationship between audiences and media industries. For example, elsewhere in this text, we have discussed the impacts of concentration on newspaper readership, of globalization on the type and quality of films available to moviegoers, of audience fragmentation on the variety of channel choices for television viewers, of convergence on the music industry's reinvention, and of hypercommercialism on all media.

The Internet is different from these more traditional media. Rather than changing the relationship between audiences and industries, the Internet changes the *definition* of the different components of the process and, as a result, changes their relationship. We are the people formerly known as the audience, and many of us are **digital natives**, people who have never known a world without the Internet. On the Internet, a single individual can communicate with as large an audience as can the giant, multinational corporation that produces a network television program. That corporation fits our earlier definition of a mass communication source—a large, hierarchically structured organization—but the Internet user does not. Feedback in mass communication is traditionally described as inferential and delayed, but online feedback can be, and very often is, immediate and direct. It is more similar to feedback in interpersonal communication than to feedback in mass communication.

This Internet-induced redefinition of the elements of the mass communication process is refocusing attention on issues such as freedom of expression, privacy, responsibility, and democracy.

The Internet and Freedom of Expression

By their very nature, the Internet and social media raise a number of important issues of freedom of expression. There is no central location, no on-and-off button for these technologies, making it difficult for those who want to control them. For free expression advocates, this freedom from control is these media's primary strength. The anonymity of their users provides their expression—even the most radical, profane, and vulgar—great protection, giving voice to those who would otherwise be silenced. However, advocates of strengthened Internet control believe this anonymity is a breeding ground for abuse. Opponents of control counter that the Internet and social media's affordability and ease of use make them our most democratic media. Internet freedom-of-expression issues, then, fall into two broad categories. The first is the potential of the Internet and social media to make the First Amendment's freedom-of-the-press guarantee a reality for greater numbers of people. The second is the problem of setting boundaries of control.

Freedom of the Press for Whom?

The late veteran *New Yorker* columnist A. J. Liebling, author of that magazine's "Wayward Press" feature and often called the "conscience of journalism," frequently argued that freedom of the press is guaranteed only to those who own one. Theoretically, anyone can own a broadcast outlet or cable television operation. However, the number of outlets in any community is limited, and they are unavailable to all but the richest people and corporations. Theoretically, anyone can own a newspaper or magazine, but again the expense involved makes this an impossibility for most people. Newsletters, similar to soap-box speakers on a street corner, are limited in reach, typically of interest to those who already agree with the message, and relatively unsophisticated when compared with the larger commercial media.

The Internet, however, turns every user into a potential mass communicator. Equally important, on the Internet every "publisher" is equal. The websites of the biggest government agency, the most powerful broadcast network, the newspaper with the highest circulation, the richest ad agencies and public relations firms, the most far-flung religion, and the lone user with an idea or cause figuratively sit side by side. Each is only as powerful as its ideas.

In other words, the Internet can give voice to those typically denied expression. Because the Internet is fast, far-reaching, personal, and easy to use, *connective action* can produce effective *collective action* (you can read more about the Internet's political power in Chapter 15). Movement researchers Lance Bennett and Alexandra Segerberg (2012) explain, "In this connective logic, taking public action or contributing to a common good becomes an act of personal expression and recognition or self-validation achieved by sharing ideas and actions in trusted relationships. Sometimes the people in these exchanges may be on the other side of the world, but they do not require a club, a party, or a shared ideological frame to make the connection" (pp. 752–753).

But not all online activism is collective. There is much individually inspired social involvement, sometimes derogatorily called **slacktivism** because it seems to require little real effort. Social movement scholar Jennifer Earl (2016) argues that "slacktivists" have no need to apologize for their work, because slacktivism can effect significant social good given that the Web provides slacktivists with two important benefits: It greatly reduces the costs for creating, organizing, and participating in protests, and it erases the need for activists to be physically together in order to act collectively.

For example, slacktivists publicly embarrassed white supremacists, tricking them into rallying against an imaginary Gettysburg National Military Park flag burning (Boburg & Bennett, 2020); spawned scores of individual actions demanding justice for Breonna Taylor after her killing by Louisville, Kentucky police (de la Cretaz, 2020); and as you read earlier, fueled the #MeToo movement against sexual assault and led *Seventeen* to commit to a "Body Peace Treaty" in which it promised to stop changing models' body and face shapes (see Chapter 5). Thirty-two percent of American social media users have used their accounts to encourage others to take action on issues they deem important (Auxier, 2020).

The Internet also offers expanded expression through weblogs, or blogs. Before September 11, 2001, blogs were typically personal online diaries. But after that tragic day, possibly because millions of people felt that the traditional press had left them unprepared and clueless about what was really going on in the world, blogs changed. *Blogs* now refers to regularly updated online journals of commentary, often containing links to the material on which they are commenting. There are more than 600 million active blogs worldwide ("27 Important," 2020).

Blogs can also be more agile than the traditional media. More so than these older, more cumbersome media, they encourage citizen action in a newly *see-through society*. For example, millions of bloggers constantly and in real time fact-check political candidates. Some track the flow of money to politicians, connecting it to how they vote on important public

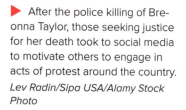

▶ After the police killing of Breonna Taylor, those seeking justice for her death took to social media to motivate others to engage in acts of protest around the country.
Lev Radin/Sipa USA/Alamy Stock Photo

◀ In 2020, slacktivists used social media to dupe white supremacists into rallying against an imaginary flag burning at the Gettysburg National Military Park. *Andrew Lichtenstein/Corbis/Getty Images*

issues. They remind the powerful that "little brother" is watching. Images caught by chance on a smartphone, arcane public data that go otherwise unexamined, and citizen video taken at official events all make their way to the Internet and social media and to the people. This is no small matter, as the Internet has surpassed newspapers as Americans' primary news source (Mindlin, 2009) and, in 2015, search engines, primarily Google, overtook the traditional media as Americans' most trusted way to find news (Sterling, 2015).

Fake News

Of course, the very same technologies that can empower users who wish to challenge those more powerful than themselves can also be used to lie and cheat. The Internet and social media do not distinguish between true and false, biased and objective, trivial and important. Once misinformation has been loosed online, it is almost impossible to catch and correct it.

The *smear forward* has plagued countless people and organizations. Procter & Gamble was victimized by stories that its cleaners killed pets. The life of US Army reservist Maatje Benassi, mother of two, was endangered after she was "identified" online as the source of the coronavirus by bringing the disease to China (O'Sullivan, 2020). Other Internet-sustained falsehoods can have far more damaging real-world effects, such as the scientifically discredited belief that vaccines cause autism, leading many parents to deny their children potentially life-saving vaccinations. "Science has become just another voice in the room," explains infectious disease expert Dr. Paul Offit, "It has lost its platform. Now, you simply declare your own truth" (in Hoffman, 2019, p. A1). The result? Reduced vaccination rates have led to a "skyrocketing" recurrence of measles outbreaks, once completely eradicated in the United States (Stinchombe, 2020).

Lies and rumors have always been part of human interaction; the Internet only gives them greater reach. However, there is little the government can do to control this abuse. Legal remedies already exist in the form of libel laws and prosecution for fraud. Users can help by teaching themselves to be more attentive to unfamiliar Web addresses and by ignoring messages that are sent anonymously or that have suspicious origins. There are e-based solutions as well. FactCheck.org maintains an exhaustive, alphabetically organized list of debunkings of the Internet's biggest lies. Also of value is Snopes.com, the self-proclaimed "definitive Internet reference source for urban legends, folklore, myths, rumors, and misinformation." Individual sites, too, have taken up the cause of precision and fact. Wikipedia's tens of thousands of editors, for example, review new and altered entries in search of erroneous material or public-relations-written material.

The prevalence—and power—of Internet lies is most obvious in the spread of **fake news**—inaccurate news stories intentionally designed to deceive and be spread online, specifically on social media. Fake news played a pivotal role in the 2016 American presidential election (Jamieson, 2018) and worked its way into the 2020 contest as well (Barnes, 2020). It was central to genocide in Myanmar (Smith, 2020), antirefugee violence in Germany (Taub & Fisher, 2018), and the "Brexit" vote leading to Britain's departure from the European Union (Pegg & Duncan, 2018), among other events. Fake news, generated by agents of the Russian government and designed to undermine Americans' faith in their system of government, spread lies such as the coronavirus was originally an American biological weapon (Barnes & Sanger, 2020). Researchers at Carnegie Mellon University identified more than 100 false narratives about COVID-19 aimed at sowing division in America (Allyn, 2020).

Fake news prospers online because of the Internet's business model—sites make advertising money by maximizing user engagement; they get paid by the number of clicks a story generates, and the most outrageous, most negative, most anger-generating stories, unfortunately, generate the greatest number of clicks. (For more on click bait, see Chapter 4.) As such, fake and biased stories flourish on SNSs, news sites, and YouTube. According to Guillaume Chaslot, an ex-YouTube employee, although "there are many ways YouTube can change its algorithms to suppress fake news and improve the quality and diversity of videos people see," his research "suggests YouTube systematically amplifies videos that are divisive, sensational and conspiratorial" (in Lewis, 2018).

Fake news is not news you don't like or disagree with; it is an intentional, pernicious attempt to debase public discourse and thwart the public's will. It is not **misinformation**, mere falsehoods; it is **disinformation**, falsehoods designed to achieve a political goal, in the words of social critic Andrew Sullivan, the "dismemberment of a public discourse centered on objective truth" (2018, p. 1), leading to **truth decay**, the diminishing role of facts and analysis in public life (Kavanaugh & Rich, 2020). Philosophy professor Michael Lynch explains, "Fake news has the effect of getting people not to believe real things." People think, "There's no way for me to know what is objectively true, so we'll stick to our guns and our own evidence. We'll ignore the facts because nobody knows what's really true anyway" (in Tavernise, 2016, p. A1).

David Becker, founder of the Center for Election Innovation, elaborates, "Changing elections in the United States is very, very difficult to do. But getting Americans to doubt their own machinery of democracy? And to start wondering whether their own vote matters? That's very low risk and very high reward" (in Dumenco, 2018, p. 35). Dramatic evidence of this troubling dynamic was on vivid display in January 2021, as thousands of violent

▶ Despite the objective reality that the results of the 2020 presidential election were clearly legitimate, a pernicious disinformation campaign, carried out in large part online, convinced millions of Americans that their votes had been "stolen." One result was the insurrectionist attack on the US Capitol as Congress was certifying the electoral results.

lev radin/Alamy Stock Photo

insurrectionists, believing the lie that their votes had been "stolen," attacked the US Capitol in an effort to overturn the results of a presidential election that, in objective reality, had been easily won by their disfavored candidate (Cummings, Garrison, & Sergent, 2021).

As it stands, exposure to fake news lowers Americans' trust in *all* media (Ognyanova et al., 2020), but matters may become even worse because of the development and diffusion of **deep fakes**, artificial intelligence-enhanced video and audio designed to present people saying or doing things that they never actually said or did, for example, President Obama uttering an expletive to describe President Trump, Mark Zuckerberg admitting that Facebook's true goal is manipulating and exploiting its users, a drunken Speaker of the House Nancy Pelosi slurring her speech. (The *deep* refers to deep AI learning.) Designed to be spread online, some are quite convincing, so much so that the *Wall Street Journal* alone has dedicated a team of 21 staff from across its newsroom to detect and navigate deep fakes (Southern, 2019).

Pornography on the Internet

Many efforts at controlling the Internet are aimed at indecent or pornographic Web content. You can read more about how indecent and pornographic expression is protected in Chapter 14. The particular concern with the Internet, therefore, is shielding children.

The Child Pornography Prevention Act of 1996 forbade online transmission of any image that "appears to be of a minor engaging in sexually explicit conduct." Proponents argued that the impact of child porn on the children involved, as well as on society, warranted this legislation. Opponents argued that child pornography per se was already illegal, regardless of the medium. Therefore they saw this law as an unnecessary and overly broad intrusion into freedom of expression on the Internet.

In April 2002, the Supreme Court sided with the act's opponents. Its effect would be too damaging to freedom of expression. "Few legitimate movie producers or book publishers, or few other speakers in any capacity, would risk distributing images in or near the uncertain reach of this law," wrote Justice Anthony Kennedy. "The Constitution gives significant protection from over-broad laws that chill speech within the First Amendment's vast and privileged sphere" (in "Justices Scrap," 2002, p. A3). Kennedy cited the antidrug film *Traffic,* Academy Award–winning *American Beauty,* and Shakespeare's *Romeo and Juliet,* all works containing scenes of minors engaged in sexual activity, as examples of expression that would disappear from the Internet.

The primary battleground, then, became protecting children from otherwise legal content. The Internet, by virtue of its openness and accessibility, raises particular concerns. Children's viewing of sexually explicit material on cable or streaming television can theoretically be controlled by parents. Moreover, viewers must specifically order this content and typically pay an additional fee for it. The purchase of sexually explicit videos, books, and magazines is controlled by laws regulating vendors. But computers sit in homes, schools, and libraries. Children are encouraged to explore their possibilities. A search for a seemingly innocent term may have multiple meanings and might turn up any number of pornographic sites.

Proponents of stricter control of the Internet liken the availability of smut online to a bookstore or library that allows porn to sit side by side with books that children *should* be reading. In actual, real-world bookstores and libraries, professionals, whether book retailers or librarians, apply their judgment in selecting and locating material, ideally striving for appropriateness and balance. Children are the beneficiaries of this professional judgment. No such selection or evaluation is applied to the Internet. Opponents of control accept the bookstore/library analogy but argue that, as troubling as the online proximity of all types of content may be, it is a true example of the freedom guaranteed by the First Amendment.

The solution seems to be in technology. Filtering software, such as Net Nanny, can be set to block access to websites by title and by the presence of specific words and images. Few free speech advocates are troubled by filters on home computers, but they do see them as problematic when used on more public machines—for example, in schools and libraries. They argue that software that can filter sexual content can also be set to screen out birth control information, religious sites, and discussions of racism. Virtually any content can be blocked. This, they claim, denies other users—adults and mature teenagers, for example—their freedoms.

Congress weighed in on the filtering debate, passing the Children's Internet Protection Act in 2000, requiring schools and libraries to install filtering software. However, First Amendment concerns invalidated this act, as well. A federal appeals court ruled in June 2002 that requiring these institutions to install filters changes their nature from places that provide information to places that unconstitutionally restrict it. Nonetheless, in June 2003, a sharply divided Supreme Court upheld the Children's Internet Protection Act, declaring that Congress did indeed have the power to require libraries to install filters.

Copyright (Intellectual Property Ownership)

Another freedom-of-expression issue that takes on a special nature on the Internet is copyright. Copyright protection is designed to ensure that those who create content are financially compensated for their work. The assumption is that more "authors" will create more content if assured of monetary compensation from those who use it. When the content is tangible (books, movies, magazines, CDs), authorship and use are relatively easy to identify. But in the cyberworld, things become a bit more complex. John Perry Barlow (1996), whom you met in the chapter's opening vignette, explained the situation relatively early in the life of the Internet:

> The riddle is this: If our property can be infinitely reproduced and instantaneously distributed all over the planet without cost, without our knowledge, without its even leaving our possession, how can we protect it? How are we going to get paid for the work we do with our minds? And, if we can't get paid, what will assure the continued creation and distribution of such work? (p. 148)

Technically, copyright rules apply to the Internet as they do to other media. Material on the Internet belongs to the author, so its use, other than fair use, requires permission and possibly payment. However, because material on the Internet is not tangible, it is easily, freely, and privately copied. This renders it difficult, if not impossible, to police those who do copy.

Another confounding issue is that new and existing material is often combined with other existing material to create even "newer" content. This makes it difficult to assign authorship. If a user borrows some text from one source, combines it with images from a second, surrounds both with a background graphic from a third, and adds music sampled from many others, where does authorship reside?

To deal with these thorny issues, in 1998, the US Congress passed the Digital Millennium Copyright Act. Its primary goal was to bring American copyright law into compliance with that of the World Intellectual Property Organization (WIPO), headquartered in Geneva, Switzerland. The act does the following:

- Makes it a crime to circumvent antipiracy measures built into commercial software
- Outlaws the manufacture, sale, or distribution of code-breaking devices used to illegally copy software
- Permits breaking of copyright protection devices to conduct encryption research and to test computer security systems
- Provides copyright exemptions for nonprofit libraries, archives, and educational institutions under certain circumstances
- Limits the copyright infringement liability of Internet service providers for simply transmitting information over the Internet, but ISPs are required to remove material from users' websites that appears to constitute copyright infringement
- Requires webcasters (those who broadcast music over the Internet) to pay licensing fees to record companies
- States explicitly that **fair use**—instances in which copyrighted material may be used without permission or payment, such as taking brief quotes from a book—applies to the Internet

What the debate over Internet copyright represents—such as concern about controlling content that children can access and efforts to limit troublesome or challenging expression—is a clash of fundamental values that has taken on added nuance with the coming of computer networks. Copyright on the Internet is discussed more fully in Chapter 14.

Privacy

The issue of privacy in mass communication has traditionally been concerned with individuals' rights to protect their privacy from invasive, intrusive media. For example, should newspapers publish the names of rape survivors and juvenile offenders? When does a person become a public figure and forfeit some degree of privacy? In the global village, however, the issue takes on a new character. Whereas Supreme Court Justice Louis Brandeis could once argue that privacy is "the right to be left alone," today privacy is just as likely to mean "the right to maintain control over our own data." Privacy in the global village has two facets. The first is protecting the privacy of communication we wish to keep private. The second is the use (and misuse) of private, personal information willingly given away online. Refer to Chapter 14 for more on privacy.

PROTECTING PRIVACY IN COMMUNICATION The 1986 Electronic Communications Privacy Act guarantees the privacy of our e-mail. It is a criminal offense to either "intentionally [access] without authorization a facility through which an electronic communication service is provided; or intentionally [exceed] an authorization to access that facility." In addition, the law "prohibits an electronic communications service provider from knowingly divulging the contents of any stored electronic communication." The goal of this legislation is to protect private citizens from official abuse; it gives e-mail "conversations" the same protection that phone conversations enjoy. If a government agency wants to listen in, it must secure permission, just as it must get a court order for a telephone wiretap.

And while the 1986 act is still the law, whistle-blower Edward Snowden's 2013 revelation that the National Security Agency, in its efforts to thwart terrorism, was collecting virtually every piece of data that traveled the Internet made it clear that privacy of communication on the Internet is, at best, a hoped-for ideal. Debate has raged over whether Snowden is a hero or traitor, but no one disputes the fact that US government agencies constantly and ubiquitously track our online activity.

You may argue that this benign surveillance—computers recording what other computers are doing to look for suspicious patterns—is more beneficial than harmful; it's keeping us safe. Or you might argue, as does reporter Chris Hedges (2014), that "the relationship between those who are constantly watched and tracked and those who watch and track them is the relationship between masters and slaves." In either case, as a media-literate Internet user, you should be aware of what national security reporter Robert Sheer (2015) calls "the great contradiction of our time: the unprecedented liberating power of the supercomputer combined with the worldwide Internet . . . also contain[s] the seeds of freedom's destruction because of the awesome power of this new technology to support a surveillance state that exceeds the wildest dream of the most ingenious dictator." This tension between ensuring our national security and protecting our personal privacy is, in the words of Amazon founder Jeff Bezos, the "issue of our age" (in Tsukayama, 2016).

PROTECTING PRIVACY OF PERSONAL INFORMATION Every online act leaves a "digital trail," making possible easy **dataveillance**—the massive collection and distillation of consumer data. Ironically, we willingly participate in this intrusion into our privacy. Online marketer Shelly Palmer (2017) explains, "Most of us are willing to give up our data—location, viewing, purchasing, or search history—for our online enjoyment. We can call this the 'willing suspension of our privacy' because if you spent a moment to consider what your data was actually being used for, you would refuse to let it happen" (p. 18). She wants us to understand that because of computer storage, networking, and cross-referencing power, the information we willingly give to one entity is easily and cheaply given to countless unknown others.

One form of dataveillance is distributing and sharing personal, private information among organizations other than the one for whom it was originally intended. Information from every credit card transaction (online or at a store), credit application, phone call, supermarket or other purchase made without cash (for example, with a check, debit card, or "club" card), and newspaper, magazine, and cable television subscription is digitally recorded, stored, and most likely sold to others.

The increased computerization of medical files, banking information, job applications, and school records produces even more salable data. Eventually, anyone who wants to know something about a person can simply buy the necessary information—without that person's permission or even knowledge. These data can then be used to further invade people's privacy. For example, employers can withhold jobs for reasons unknown to applicants.

Recognizing the scope of data collection and the potential problems that it raises, Congress passed the 1974 Federal Privacy Act, restricting *government's* ability to collect and distribute information about citizens. The act, however, expressly exempted businesses and other nongovernmental organizations from control. As a result, Americans have become increasingly concerned about privacy and security concerns, so much so that more than half of all Americans, 52%, have decided against using a product or service because of worries about the collection and use of their personal information (Perrin, 2020).

The Internet industry and the federal government responded in 2012 with a "Consumer Privacy Bill of Rights," voluntary guidelines suggesting sites place a "do not track" button on their Web pages. Critics contend that these guidelines are insufficient protection, as not all sites comply, and even those with the button may still collect and hold users' personal data for their own market research. They object to the idea that websites should provide us that security only if we specifically ask for it, called **opt-out**. "When did privacy become a choice rather than the default?" they ask. Instead, sites should have to get our permission before they collect and disseminate our personal data; that is, we should be able to **opt-in**, as is the case with the European Union's General Data Protection Regulation. Privacy advocates ask the question, "If we have legislation to bring our copyright laws into compliance with those of other nations, why shouldn't we do the same with our privacy laws?"

The state of California instituted a sweeping data privacy law on January 1, 2020. The California Consumer Privacy Act was designed to mimic the privacy protections long enjoyed by Internet users in the European Union. It mandated that businesses earning at least 50% of their annual revenue from selling consumer information must:

- Post a consent banner on their website informing consumers that their data are being collected and they have the right to opt-out;
- Give consumers the right to know what personal information is being collected from them;
- Offer users the right to ask companies to delete that information or opt-out of its collection altogether; and,
- Create a process allowing users to request all the data a company has collected on them and provide instructions on how to delete all that data.

Because of the size of the California economy and the universality of the Internet, the hope was that in an effort to comply with the state's rules, businesses would make these requirements universal (Ray, 2020).

Another form of dataveillance is the electronic tracking of the choices we make when we are online, called our **click stream**. Despite the anonymity online users think they enjoy, every click of a link can be, and often is, recorded and stored. This happens whether or not the user actually enters information—for example, a credit card number to make a purchase or a Social Security number to verify identity. This tracking is made possible by **cookies**, an identifying code added to a computer's hard drive by a visited website.

Normally, only the site that has sent the cookie can read it—the next time you visit that site it "remembers" you. However, some sites bring "third-party" cookies to your computer. Maintained by big Internet advertising networks such as DoubleClick and Engage, these cookies can be read by any of the thousands of websites also belonging to that network, whether you've visited them or not, and without your knowledge. As a result, this software is more commonly referred to as **spyware**, identifying code placed on a computer by a website without permission or notification. Spyware not only facilitates tracking by unknown sites and/or people (those "third parties") but opens a computer to unwanted pop-up ads and other commercial messages.

At any given time, a regular Web user will have dozens of cookies on his or her hard drive, but commercial browsers like Chrome, Firefox, and Safari come equipped with the capacity to block or erase them. The Anti-Spyware Coalition offers information and assistance on how to deal with cookies and spyware. In addition, users can purchase cookie-scrubbing software. But with Google's announcement that starting in 2023 it would no longer allow cookies in its Chrome browser (joining Safari which had already banned them), such software may no longer be necessary. Commercial firms such as Anonymizer sell programs that not only block and erase spyware but also allow users to surf the Web anonymously.

ADDITIONAL PRIVACY THREATS Four relatively new technological advances pose additional privacy problems: the **radio frequency identification (RFID) chip**; cloud computing; the **Internet of Things (IoT)** in which everyday objects have built-in network connectivity, allowing them to send and receive data, and **facial recognition technology**, technology capable of identifying or verifying the identity of an individual from a digital image or video source.

The first, RFID, already used by many retailers, is a grain-of-sand-size microchip and antenna embedded in consumer products that transmits a radio signal. The advantage to retailers is greater inventory control and lower labor costs. The retailer has an absolute, up-to-the-minute accounting of how many boxes of widgets are on the shelf, and consumers simply walk out the door with their boxes while the RFID sends a signal charging the correct amount to the proper credit card; no checkout personnel is needed. Privacy advocates' concern should be clear. That signal keeps on sending.

Now marketers, the government, and others will know where you and your box of widgets are at all times, how quickly you go through your box of widgets, and where you are when you run out of widgets. How soon until your e-mail's inbox fills up with offers of widgets on sale? What if a burglar could use an RFID reader from outside your house to preview its contents? What happens when these data are networked with all your other personal information? What if you buy a case of beer rather than a box of widgets? Will your employer know?

A second advance worrying privacy advocates is the growing use of cloud computing and its storage of data, including personal information, on third-party environments. Google, Microsoft, and numerous independent providers offer cloud computing, and advocates tout the increased power and memory of the cloud, arguing that even if your laptop is lost or destroyed, you lose nothing. However, privacy advocates counter that data stored online have less privacy protection both in practice and under the law.

Cloud services claim data are protected by **encryption**, the electronic coding or masking of information that can be deciphered only by a recipient with the proper decrypting key. Yet there are no guarantees, argue online privacy advocates, given repeated revelations that not only does the federal government tap into the files of Internet search engines and e-mail and cloud service providers, but many of these companies willingly provide people's data to the authorities (e.g., Whittaker, 2020). Privacy experts say there's simply no way to ever be completely sure your data will remain secure once you've moved them to the cloud.

Almost any everyday device we use today—consumer electronics, cars, utility meters, refrigerators, automatic coffeemakers, vending machines, thermostats, lights, clothes, and wearable devices (Pampers sells a smart baby diaper), vacuum cleaners—can be connected to the Internet. In 2017, the number of IoT devices surpassed the number of people living on Earth (Martin, 2017), and by 2022 businesses and consumers annually will spend $1.1 trillion on those devices ("Prognosis," 2020).

If everything that exists on the Internet is linkable, IoT means that others will have access to an ever-greater array of the most personal and intimate aspects of our lives. "Think of a world where the physical location of every single item is logged and known at every single moment," suggests tech writer Jason Rhode (2018). "A fully realized IoT [50–100 trillion code-bearing devices] will know more about you than you know about yourself. . . . Every single action point in your physical existence has a river of data streaming from it."

Your refrigerator can alert you when you need more mustard, but it can also tell your boss that you stayed home and had a few beers while watching football rather than attending your aunt's funeral as you claimed. Your fitness tracker can measure your burned calories, but it can also tell your insurance provider that your blood pressure is rising. Your retailer's chip-bearing price tag can better track store inventory, but it can also raise the price of the shoes you want as you approach the register because it reads your up-scale zip code from the thousands of websites where you willingly provided it. Revelations such as Samsung smart TVs secretly recording private home conversations, voice assistants Alexa and Siri making recordings of everything they hear after users say their names, and reports that domestic abusers use smart-home IoT to track, monitor, and trap their victims (Riley, 2020) seem to confirm privacy advocates' worst IoT fears.

Finally, facial recognition technologies employ computer algorithms to identify specific, distinctive details about a person's face, such as the distance between the eyes or shape of the lips. These are then converted into a mathematical representation and compared to data on other faces collected and stored in huge facial recognition databases. A great way to catch those bad guys and a good way to shorten lines at the airport say its advocates. A very obvious risk to our right to privacy, say its opponents, not to mention to our First Amendment rights of speech and assembly (as the authorities can employ the technology at protests). Moreover, facial recognition technology is notoriously unreliable, especially with older folks and people of color, leading several localities, including Portland, Oregon, San Francisco and Oakland, California, and the state of Massachusetts to ban its use (Hill, 2021). Vermont Senator Bernie Sanders has called for a complete prohibition of facial recognition technology by the federal government (Read, 2020).

Worries over this technology are such that even tech giant Microsoft has asked for government regulation to ensure independent oversight of police and government use and to require those who employ it to post notices that facial-recognition technology is being employed in public spaces (Harwell, 2018).

Virtual Democracy

The Internet and social media are characterized by freedom and self-governance, which are also the hallmarks of true democracy. It is no surprise, then, that these technologies are often trumpeted as the newest and best tools for increased democratic involvement and participation. You saw in this chapter's opening pages that there was once great optimism that this would be the case: electronic technology would unite distant peoples; the Internet would give equal voice to all; America would become a country of informed citizens engaged in a political process akin to a giant teleconference.

Yet you've also seen that the Internet and social media can be used to spread hate and division, to deny people fundamental rights like privacy, to misinform and erode trust in a common good. Critics argue that the Internet will be no more of an asset to democracy than have been radio and television because the same economic and commercial forces that have shaped the content and operation of those more traditional media will constrain the Internet just as rigidly.

They point to the endless battles to keep the Internet open and free. There are frequent fights over **network neutrality** (often just called net neutrality), the requirement that all ISPs, including cable MSOs, allow free and equal flow of all Web traffic. For example, if all sites

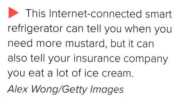

▶ This Internet-connected smart refrigerator can tell you when you need more mustard, but it can also tell your insurance company you eat a lot of ice cream.
Alex Wong/Getty Images

were not equal, one that was willing (and able) to pay would have its content transmitted to people's devices more quickly. Another, a political activist site for example, that was unwilling (or unable) to pay would have its content slowed down.

Their pessimism also resides in part in concentration and conglomeration of the Internet—Google's acquisition of massively popular YouTube; Microsoft's purchase of Internet video phone company Skype and social networking sites LinkedIn and Yammer; Facebook's purchase of Instagram and WhatsApp; Yahoo!'s purchase of blogging service Tumblr and its later acquisition by Verizon; and AT&T's merger with DirecTV and its efforts to acquire Time Warner, to list a few.

Still, optimism for the Internet, especially social media, persists. For example, while granting that each of his seven "things that social media can do for democracy" has a dark side, Ethan Zuckerman (2018) of the Center for Civic Media argues that, on the whole, they can serve democracy well. You'll no doubt recognize evidence of these benefits in what you've already read in this chapter. Social media, he argues, inform us; amplify important voices and issues; serve as tools for connection and solidarity; are spaces for mobilization; are forums for deliberation and debate; show us a diversity of views and perspectives; and can serve as models for democratically governed spaces.

THE TECHNOLOGY GAP If the civic promise of the Internet is to be fulfilled, the basic tenet of democracy—one person, one vote—must be met. But if democracy is increasingly practiced online, those lacking the necessary technology and skill will be denied their vote. This is the **technology gap**—the widening disparity between the communication technology haves and have-nots. The "democratization" of the Internet still favors those who have the money to buy the equipment needed to access the Internet as well as to pay for that connection. This leaves out many US citizens—those on the wrong side of the **digital divide**, the lack of technological access among specific groups of Americans. To be offline means exclusion from opportunities to learn, earn a living, access important services, and participate fully in democracy.

Although the vast majority of Americans regularly access the Internet, 7% do not (Perrin & Atske, 2021). Making matters worse, nearly a quarter of the population does not have access to broadband or other high-speed Internet at home (Perrin, 2021). These deficiencies fall heaviest on those less educated, people with disabilities, those with lower incomes, those in rural areas, Hispanic and African American households, and less affluent elderly people.

The digital divide was never more clear than during the 2020 coronavirus pandemic as "schooling, jobs, government services, medical care, and child care that once were performed in person have been turned over to the web, exposing a deep rift between the broadband haves and have-nots," explained the *New York Times* ("The Limits," 2020, p. SR10). You can see how the divide played out with children from different demographic groups in Figure 10.2, and you can weigh in on the debate surrounding the necessity of access to broadband in the box, "Is High-Speed Internet a Human Right?"

▼ **Figure 10.2** Percentage of K-12 Students Without Adequate Internet or Devices to Sustain Effective Distance Learning at Home.
Source: Chandra et al., 2020.

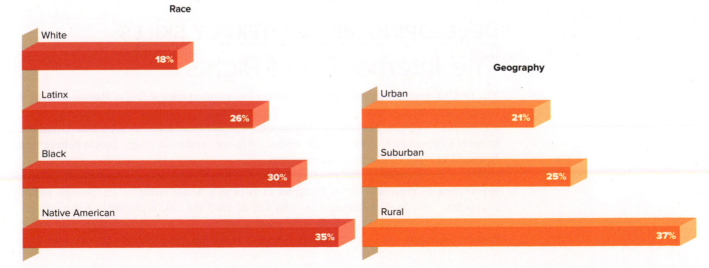

Race

White — 18%
Latinx — 26%
Black — 30%
Native American — 35%

Geography

Urban — 21%
Suburban — 25%
Rural — 37%

CULTURAL FORUM
Is High-Speed Internet a Human Right?

In 2016 the United Nations declared Internet access a fundamental human right; it went even further in 2020, declaring *broadband* Internet access a fundamental human right (Salway, 2020), putting the issues of who should have high-speed Internet and who should ensure its availability squarely into the cultural forum.

Long-time advocate for universal access, Vermont Senator Bernie Sanders, argues that high-speed Internet is essential to the basic functioning of families, students, and businesses. "High-speed Internet service must be treated as the new electricity—a public utility that everyone deserves as a basic human right. The Internet as we know it was developed by taxpayer-funded research, using taxpayer-funded grants in taxpayer-funded labs. Our tax dollars built the internet and access to it should be a public good for all" (2020).

The American government has not completely ignored the need for broadband. For example, the FCC, through its E-Rate program, invests about $1 billion a year to provide, expand, and upgrade broadband Internet access to American schools and libraries with money raised from the universal service fee you see on your phone bill. Additionally, more than 300 cities and towns across America provide their citizens low-cost broadband. But local MSOs, antagonistic to any competition and with little incentive to provide broadband to poorer or rural areas themselves, use their lobbying might to slow the spread of these **municipal broadband** programs. In 2015, the Obama administration attempted to forbid state legislatures from outlawing these efforts, but that effort was defeated by a 2016 court decision, so restrictions remain on the books in 22 states.

Still, municipal broadband continues to expand, and states such as Vermont are investigating universal broadband to bring affordable, modern connections to every home and business in the state (Trombly, 2020). Other than the fundamental fairness of granting all people equal access to information, these efforts are encouraged by evidence that there is economic benefit to the municipalities and regions that provide expanded broadband access beyond faster Internet speed at lower cost, for example, lower unemployment, greater economic vitality, and increased population stability (Chamberlain, 2020; Lindzon, 2020).

Enter Your Voice

- Should access to high-speed Internet be a fundamental human right, like the right to an education or the right to free speech? Why or why not?

- Do you accept Senator Sanders's argument that because "the people" paid for the development of the Internet it should be a public good available to all? Why or why not?

- If it is the case that for-profit companies are actively impeding the diffusion of a valuable resource (in this case, broadband), what argument, if any, can you make that the government (municipal, state, or federal) has a right to provide that resource to its citizens?

DEVELOPING MEDIA LITERACY SKILLS
The Internet Bill of Rights

The first 10 Amendments to the United States Constitution are the Bill of Rights, so named because they spell out the Founders' belief that people, by simple virtue of their humanity, are entitled to certain guaranteed, "unalienable" (unable to be taken away) rights. Given the Internet's importance to virtually all aspects of human endeavor, many people believe that it should be treated as a basic human right.

This is the philosophy that moved US House of Representatives member from California Ro Khanna to present a bill to Congress in 2019 that would enshrine an Internet Bill of Rights into law. As Tim Berners-Lee, who helped craft the bill, explained, "If the internet is to live up to its potential as a force for good in the world, we need safeguards that ensure fairness, openness, and human dignity. This Bill of Rights provides a set of principles that are about giving users more control of their online lives while creating a healthier internet economy" (in Swisher, 2018, p. SR9). It reads, *You should have the right*:

1. *to have access to and knowledge of all collection and uses of personal data by companies;*
2. *to opt-in consent to the collection of personal data by any party and to the sharing of personal data with a third party;*
3. *where context is appropriate and with a fair process, to obtain, correct or delete personal data controlled by any company and to have those requests honored by third parties;*
4. *to have personal data secured and to be notified in a timely manner when a security breach or unauthorized access of personal data is discovered;*
5. *to move all personal data from one network to the next;*
6. *to access and use the Internet without Internet service providers blocking, throttling, engaging in paid prioritization or otherwise unfairly favoring content, applications, services or devices;*
7. *to Internet service without the collection of data that is unnecessary for providing the requested service absent opt-in consent;*
8. *to have access to multiple viable, affordable Internet platforms, services and providers with clear and transparent pricing;*
9. *not to be unfairly discriminated against or exploited based on your personal data; and*
10. *to have an entity that collects your personal data have reasonable business practices and accountability to protect your privacy.*

As the Internet, the World Wide Web, and social media increasingly become necessities and even life-sustaining utilities, media-literate users have an obligation to know and defend these fundamental communication freedoms.

It is important to remember that culture is neither innate nor inviolate. *We* construct culture—both dominant and bounded. Increasingly, we do so through mass communication, and the Internet has given us voice once unimaginable. So before we can enter the forum in which those cultures are constructed and maintained, we must understand where we stand and what we believe. We must be able to defend our positions. The hallmarks of a media-literate individual are analysis and self-reflection. Reread the Internet Bill of Rights. After having read this chapter's discussion of privacy, freedom of expression, fake news and deep fakes, the digital divide, net neutrality, and municipal broadband, how well do you think they are being met?

MEDIA LITERACY CHALLENGE
Internet Addiction Self-Diagnosis

The American Psychiatric Association lists "Internet Addiction Disorder" as a recognized mental illness in its *Diagnostic and Statistical Manual of Mental Disorders*. And while you no doubt have tried to unplug for a while, somehow you just can't seem to do it. But you're a media-literate Internet user, so you should be able to explain why it's so hard to ditch your technology. After all, you certainly are *aware of the impact of the Internet on your life*. Possibly you are addicted. No, you say? Then take the Internet Addiction Test, developed by Kimberly S. Young (2004) of the Center for Online Addiction.

Before answering its eight questions, keep in mind that this is a measure of *Internet* addiction, not *computer* addiction. So consider your Internet usage on all devices—computers, smartphones, tablets, and game consoles—when replying. Be sure to count only recreational usage over the last six months; Internet time for school or work doesn't count.

1. Do you feel preoccupied with the Internet (think about previous online activity or anticipate next online session)?
2. Do you feel the need to use the Internet for increasing amounts of time to achieve satisfaction?
3. Have you repeatedly made unsuccessful efforts to control, cut back, or stop Internet use?
4. Do you feel restless, moody, depressed, or irritable when attempting to cut down or stop Internet use?
5. Do you stay online longer than originally intended?
6. Have you jeopardized or risked the loss of a significant relationship, job, or educational or career opportunity because of the Internet?
7. Have you lied to family members, therapists, or others to conceal the extent of your involvement with the Internet?
8. Do you use the Internet as a way of escaping from problems or of relieving feelings of helplessness, guilt, anxiety, or depression?

Interpreting your answers is simple: Addiction is present if you answered "yes" to at least five of the questions. If that is your situation, consider why that is the case. Why are you so dependent on the Internet? What can you do to shed your addiction? Do you even want to? If not, why not? As a media-literate Internet, Web, and social media user, you understand that any medium is only as beneficial as you make it; therefore, these are questions, regardless of any level or absence of addiction, that you should ask and re-ask yourself. Doing so will improve your media literacy and increase the benefits you derive from these technologies.

Resources for Review and Discussion

REVIEW POINTS: TYING CONTENT TO LEARNING OUTCOMES

▶ **Recall the history and development of the Internet and social media.**
- The idea for the Internet came either from technological optimists such as Joseph C. R. Licklider or from the military, hoping to maintain communication networks in time of enemy attack—or from both.
- Paul Baran devised a packet-switching network, the technological basis for the Internet, to be used on powerful computers developed by John V. Atanasoff, John Mauchly, and John Presper Eckert.
- The personal computer was developed by Bill Gates and the team of Steve Jobs and Stephen Wozniak.
- Classmates.com started the social media revolution in 1995; Facebook made social media mainstream in 2004.

▶ **Describe how the organizational and economic natures of the contemporary Internet and social media industries shape their content.**
- The Internet facilitates e-mail, VoIP, social networking, and the World Wide Web, all greatly facilitated by the rapid diffusion of smartphones and tablets.
- The Web relies on a system of hosts, browsers, and search engines to bring users to websites, characterized by URLs and home pages.

- Many of us are digital natives; we've never known a world without the Internet and social media.
- Our messages on the Internet and social media sit side by side with those of the largest and most powerful organizations in the world.
- Feedback on the Internet and social media is instant and direct, more like that in interpersonal rather than mass communication.

▶ **Recall how and why individuals use social media.**
- We use social media for self-presentation and because of our need to belong.
- We tend to present a realistic version of ourselves when on social media.
- Some users may suffer from Facebook depression or Facebook envy, raising questions of the relationship between SNSs and subjective well-being.
- Social media use can lead to social isolation, or it may not; the outcome is dependent on how we choose to participate in social media.

▶ **Analyze social and cultural questions posed by the Internet, social media, and related emerging technologies.**

  ☐ The Internet and social media make freedom of expression a reality for anyone linked to them, but abuse of that freedom has led to calls for greater control.

  ☐ Restrictions on access to pornography, protection of copyright, and threats to identity are primary battlegrounds for opponents and proponents of control.

  ☐ The Internet and social media's potential contributions to participatory democracy are also in debate, as problems such as the technology gap and the digital divide have yet to be resolved.

▶ **Apply key Internet and social media literacy skills, especially in protecting your privacy and reflecting on the Internet's double edge of (potentially) good and troublesome change.**

  ☐ The Internet and social media, especially with their power to reshape all the mass media, raise multiple issues for media-literate users hoping to effectively make their way in an interconnected world, guidance for which can be found in the Internet Bill of Rights.

KEY TERMS

Internet, 231

digital computer, 231

binary code, 231

protocols, 232

hosts, 233

mainframe computer, 233

minicomputer, 233

terminals, 233

microcomputer (or personal computer or PC), 233

operating system, 235

multimedia, 235

WAN (wide area network), 235

ISP (Internet service provider), 235

World Wide Web, 235

URL (uniform resource locator), 236

domain name, 236

browsers, 236

search engines, 236

social networking sites (SNSs), 237

dual-factor model of social media use, 238

idealized virtual identity hypothesis, 238

extended real-life hypothesis, 238

finstas, 238

Facebook depression, 239

affective forecasting error, 239

Facebook envy, 239

manosphere, 242

surveillance capitalism, 242

digital natives, 243

slacktivism, 244

fake news, 246

misinformation, 246

disinformation, 246

truth decay, 246

deep fake, 247

fair use, 248

dataveillance, 249

opt-out, 250

opt-in, 250

click stream, 250

cookies, 250

spyware, 250

radio frequency identification (RFID) chip, 251

Internet of Things (IoT), 251

facial recognition technology, 251

encryption, 251

network neutrality, 252

technology gap, 253

digital divide, 253

municipal broadband, 254

QUESTIONS FOR REVIEW

1. What is the importance of each of these people to the development of the computer: Charles Babbage, John Atanasoff, John Mauchly, and John Presper Eckert?

2. What were the contributions of Joseph C. R. Licklider, Paul Baran, Bill Gates, Steve Jobs, and Stephen Wozniak to the development and popularization of the Internet?

3. What are digital computers, microcomputers, and mainframe computers?

4. What is the dual-factor model of social media use? How does it explain our affinity for social media?

5. Differentiate between the idealized virtual identity and the extended real-life hypotheses of social media use. Why do finstas exist?

6. What are Facebook depression and Facebook envy? What is subjective well-being and what is its relationship with SNS use?

7. What are the primary privacy issues for online communication? What are some of the new technological threats?

8. What is a blog? How might blogs influence journalism?

9. What are some of the arguments supporting the idea that the Internet will be a boost to participatory democracy? What are some of the counterarguments?

10. What are the technology gap and digital divide? What do they have to do with the Internet's ability to aid or impede democracy?

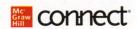

To maximize your study time, check out CONNECT to access the SmartBook study module for this chapter, watch videos, and explore other resources.

QUESTIONS FOR CRITICAL THINKING AND DISCUSSION

1. Are you an active social media user? If so, how accurate a representation of yourself do you tend to present? Do you show the "real you" because that's what you want to do, or do you feel restricted in your presentation of yourself by the presence of your online friends?

2. Do you ever make personal information available online? If so, how confident are you of its security? Do you take steps to protect your privacy?

3. Do you believe online communication technologies will improve or damage participatory democracy? Why? Can you relate a personal experience of how the Internet or social media increased or limited your involvement in the political process?

REFERENCES

1. "27 Important Blogging Statistics Every Blogger Should Know in 2020." (2020, June 15). *TechJury*. Retrieved from https://techjury.net/blog/blogging-statistics/

2. Allyn, B. (2020, May 20). Researchers: Nearly half of accounts tweeting about coronavirus are likely bots. *NPR*. Retrieved from https://www.npr.org/sections/coronavirus-live-updates/2020/05/20/859814085/researchers-nearly-half-of-accounts-tweeting-about-coronavirus-are-likely-bots

3. Anthony, S. (2014, July 8). In 2015 tablet sales will finally surpass PCs, fulfilling Steve Jobs' post-PC prophecy. *Extreme Tech*. Retrieved from http://www.extremetech.com/computing/185937-in-2015-tablet-sales-will-finally-surpass-pcs-fulfilling-steve-jobs-post-pc-prophecy

4. Auxier, B. (2020, July 13). Activism on social media varies by race and ethnicity, age, political party. *Pew Research Center*. Retrieved from https://www.pewresearch.org/fact-tank/2020/07/13/activism-on-social-media-varies-by-race-and-ethnicity-age-political-party/

5. Back, M. D., Stopfer, J. M., Vazire, S., Gaddis, S., Schmukle, S. C., Egloff, B., & Gosling, S. D. (2010). Facebook profiles reflect actual personality, not self-idealization. *Psychological Science, 21*, 372–374.

6. Barlow, J. P. (1996). Selling wine without bottles: The economy of mind on the global Net. In L. H. Leeson (Ed.), *Clicking in: Hot links to a digital culture*. Seattle, WA: Bay Press.

7. Barnes, J. E. (2020, August 8). Russia is trying to assist Trump in race, U.S. says. *New York Times*, p. A1.

8. Barnes, J. E., & Sanger, D. E. (2020, July 29). To influence Americans in election year, Russia spreads fake virus data. *New York Times*, p. A11.

9. Basu, T. (2020, February 7). The "manosphere" is getting more toxic as angry men join the incels. *MIT Technology Review*. Retrieved from https://www.technologyreview.com/2020/02/07/349052/the-manosphere-is-getting-more-toxic-as-angry-men-join-the-incels/

10. Bennett, L. W., & Segerberg, A. (2012). The logic of connective action. *Information, Communication & Society, 15*, 739–768.

11. Berners-Lee, T., & Fischetti, M. (1999). *Weaving the Web: The original design and ultimate destiny of the World Wide Web by its inventor*. New York: HarperCollins.

12. Boburg, S., & Bennett, D. (2020, July 4). Militias flocked to Gettysburg to foil a supposed antifa flag burning, an apparent hoax created on social media. *Washington Post*. Retrieved from https://www.washingtonpost.com/investigations/hundreds-of-armed-men-went-to-gettysburg-to-defend-it-from-a-phantom-antifa-flag-burner-created-on-social-media/2020/07/04/206ee4da-bb05-11ea-86d5-3b9b3863273b_story.html

13. Borst, L. (2020, August 24/31). The user always loses. *Nation*, pp. 33–36.

14. Brooker, K. (2018, July 1). "I was devastated." *Vanity Fair*. Retrieved from https://archive.vanityfair.com/article/2018/8/i-was-devastated

15. Burke, M., & Kraut, R. E. (2016). The relationship between Facebook use and well-being depends on communication type and tie strength. *Journal of Computer-Mediated Communication, 21*, 265–281.

16. Chamberlain, K. (2020, May 13). Municipal broadband is roadblocked or outlawed in 22 states. *Broadband Now*. Retrieved from https://broadbandnow.com/report/municipal-broadband-roadblocks/

17. Chandra, S., Chang, A., Day, L., Fazlullah, A., Liu, J., McBride, L., Mudalige, T., Weiss, D. (2020). *Closing the K–12 digital divide in the age of distance learning*. San Francisco, CA: Common Sense Media.

18. *The Child Pornography Prevention Act of 1996*.

19. Clement, J. (2020, May 15). Number of worldwide internet hosts in the domain name system (DNS) from 1993 to 2019. *Statista*. Retrieved from https://www.statista.com/statistics/264473/number-of-internet-hosts-in-the-domain-name-system/#:~:text=The%20statistic%20shows%20the%20trend,were%20available%20on%20the%20DNS.

20. Conger, K., & Isaac, M. (2021, January 9). Citing risk of violence, Twitter permanently suspends Trump. *New York Times*, p. A1.

21. Cummings, W., Garrison, J., & Sergent, J. (2021, January 6). By the numbers: President Donald Trump's failed efforts to overturn the election. *USA Today*. Retrieved from https://www.usatoday.com/in-depth/news/politics/elections/2021/01/06/trumps-failed-efforts-overturn-election-numbers/4130307001/

22. Czitrom, D. J. (2007). Twenty-five years later. *Critical Studies in Media Communication, 24*, 481–485.

23. Dean, B. (2021, February 10). How many people use Twitter in 2021. *Backlinko*. Retrieved from https://backlinko.com/twitter-users

24. de la Cretaz. (2020, June 5). Breonna Taylor should be turning 27 today. Here's how to demand justice for her death. *Refinery29*. Retrieved from https://www.refinery29.com/en-us/2020/06/9852492/breonna-taylor-birthday-petition-justice-fund

25. Dolliver, M. (2020, April). US time spent with media 2020. *eMarketer*. Retrieved from https://www.emarketer.com/content/us-time-spent-with-media-2020

26. Dumenco, S. (2018, April 30). From Russia with fear. *Advertising Age*, p. 35.

27. Earl, J. (2016, December 24). Slacktivism for everyone: How keyboard activism is affecting social movements. *Salon*. Retrieved from http://www.salon.com/2016/12/24/slacktivism-how-online-activism-is-affecting-social-movements_partner/

28. Edison Research. (2020). *The infinite dial 2020*. Retrieved from https://www.rab.com/whyradio/wrnew/wr-research/pdf/Infinite%20Dial%202020.pdf

29. Electronic Communications Privacy Act of 1986 (ECPA), 18 U.S.C. § 2510–22.

30. Faw, L. (2021, February 17). People spend nearly 2 1/2 hours daily on social media. *MediaPost*. Retrieved from https://www.mediapost.com/publications/article/360626/

31. Gelles, D. (2018, January 9). Prodding Apple on addiction. *New York Times*, p. B1.

32. Georgiev, D. (2020, July 3). 67+ revealing smartphone statistics for 2020. *Techjury*. Retrieved from https://techjury.net/blog/smartphone-usage-statistics/

33. Ghosh, D. (2021, January 7). Blame Facebook, Twitter and YouTube for the mob at the Capitol. *Washington Post*. Retrieved from https://www.washingtonpost.com/outlook/2021/01/07/social-media-facebook-capitol-mob/

34. Gontovnikas, M. (2020, July 1). The 11 biggest data breaches of 2020 (so far). *Auth0*. Retrieved from https://auth0.com/blog/the-11-biggest-data-breaches-of-2020-so-far/

35. Gonzales, A. L., & Hancock, J. T. (2011). Mirror, mirror on my Facebook wall: Effects of exposure to Facebook on self-esteem. *Cyberpsychology, Behavior, and Social Networking, 14*, 79–83.

36. Grothaus, T. (2018, October 24). Apple's Tim Cook warns of threat from the growing "data industrial complex." *Fast Company*. Retrieved from https://www.fastcompany.com/90256013/apples-tim-cook-warns-of-threat-from-growing-data-industrial-complex

37. Hafner, K., & Lyon, M. (1996). *Where wizards stay up late: The origins of the Internet*. New York: Simon & Schuster.

38. Hamilton, A. (2000, August 21). Meet the new surfer girls. *Time*, p. 67.

39. Harris, J. (2018, January 1). Take it from the insiders: Silicon Valley is eating your soul. *Guardian*. Retrieved from https://www.theguardian.com/commentisfree/2018/jan/01/silicon-valley-eating-soul-google-facebook-tech

40. Harwell, D. (2018, July 13). Microsoft calls for regulation of facial recognition, saying it's too risky to leave to tech industry alone. *Washington Post*. Retrieved from https://www.washingtonpost.com/technology/2018/07/13/microsoft-calls-regulation-facial-recognition-saying-its-too-risky-leave-tech-industry-alone/?utm_term=.0048a16c3c2a

41. Hedges, C. (2014, February 24). Edward Snowden's moral courage. *Truthout.org*. Retrieved from http://www.truthdig.com/report/item/edward_snowdens_moral_courage_20140223

42. Herman, J., & Savage, C. (2018, May 24). Judge rules president can't block Twitter foes. *New York Times*, p. B1.

43. Hill, K. (2021, February 21). How one state wrote rules on facial recognition. *New York Times*, p. BU5.

44. Hoffman, J. (2019, September 24). How anti-vaccine sentiment took hold in U.S. *New York Times*, p. A1.

45. Horwitz, J., & Seetharaman, D. (2020, May 26). Facebook executives shut down efforts to make the site less divisive. *Washington Post*. Retrieved from https://www.wsj.com/articles/facebook-knows-it-encourages-division-top-executives-nixed-solutions-11590507499

46. Jamieson, K. H. (2018). *Cyberwar: How Russian hackers and trolls helped elect a president*. New York: Oxford University Press.

47. "Justices scrap Internet child porn law." (2002, April 17). *Providence Journal*, p. A3.

48. Kang, J., & Wei, L. (2020). Let me be at my funniest: Instagram users' motivations for using Finsta (a.k.a., fake Instagram). *Social Science Journal, 57*, 58–71.

49. Kavanaugh, J., & Rich, M. D. (2020). Countering truth decay. *Rand Corporation*. Retrieved from https://www.rand.org/research/projects/truth-decay.html

50. Krasnova, H., Wenninger, H., Widjaja, T., & Buxmann, P. (2013, March). *Envy on Facebook: A hidden threat to users' life satisfaction?* Paper presented to the 11th International Conference on Wirtschaftsinformatik, Leipzig, Germany.

51. Kristula, D. (1997, March). *The history of the Internet*. Retrieved from http://www.davesite.com/webstation/net-history.shtml

52. Leman, N. (2020, February 27). Can journalism be saved? *New York Review of Books*. Retrieved from https://www.nybooks.com/articles/2020/02/27/can-journalism-be-saved/

53. Lepore, J. (2021, February 8). Zero day. *New Yorker*, pp. 55–58.

54. Lewis, P. (2018, February 2). "Fiction is outperforming reality": How YouTube's algorithm distorts truth. *Guardian*. Retrieved from https://www.theguardian.com/technology/2018/feb/02/how-youtubes-algorithm-distorts-truth

55. Lindzon, J. (2020, November 30). Remote work can't change everything until we fix this $80 billion problem. *Fast Company*. Retrieved from https://www.fastcompany.com/90578964/rural-internet-broadband-access

56. Mander, J., Kavanagh, D., & Buckle, C. (2020). *Global Web Index*. Retrieved from https://www.globalwebindex.com/reports/social

57. Marche, S. (2012, May). Is Facebook making us lonely? *Atlantic*. Retrieved from http://www.theatlantic.com/magazine/archive/2012/05/is-facebook-making-us-lonely/308930/

58. Martin, C. (2017, February 7). IoT devices to surpass world population this year; consumer segment leads. *MediaPost*. Retrieved from https://www.mediapost.com/publications/article/294645/iot-devices-to-surpass-world-population-this-year.html

59. Metev, D. (2020, June 5). 39+ smartphone statistics you should know in 2020. *Review 42*. Retrieved from https://review42.com/smartphone-statistics/

60. Mindlin, A. (2009, January 5). Web passes papers as news source. *New York Times*, p. B3.

61. Moshin, M. (2021, February 16). 10 Facebook statistics every marketer should know in 2021. *Oberlo*. Retrieved from https://www.oberlo.com/blog/facebook-statistics#:~:text=Get%20Started%20Free-,1.,site%20on%20a%20daily%20basis.

62. Nadkarni, A., & Hofmann, S. G. (2012). Why do people use Facebook? *Personality and Individual Differences, 52*, 243–249.

63. Neufield, D. (2021, January 27). The 50 most visited websites in the world. *Visual Capitalist*. Retrieved from https://www.visualcapitalist.com/the-50-most-visited-websites-in-the-world/

64. Ognyanova, K., Lazer, D., Robertson, R. E., & Wilson, C. (2020, June 2). Misinformation in action: fake news exposure is linked to lower trust in media, higher trust in government when your side is in power. *Misinformation Review*. Retrieved from https://misinforeview.hks.harvard.edu/article/misinformation-in-action-fake-news-exposure-is-linked-to-lower-trust-in-media-higher-trust-in-government-when-your-side-is-in-power/

65. O'Keeffe, G. S., & Clarke-Pearson, K. (2011). Clinical report—the impact of social media on children, adolescents, and families. *Pediatrics, 127*, 800–804.

66. O'Malley, G. (2019, July 24). Report: Gen Z, Millennials unhappy with social media's impact on their lives. *MediaPost*. Retrieved from https://www.mediapost.com/publications/article/338497/report-gen-z-millennials-unhappy-with-social-med.html

67. O'Sullivan, D. (2020, April 27). Exclusive: She's been falsely accused of starting the pandemic. Her life has been turned upside down. *CNN*. Retrieved from https://www.cnn.com/2020/04/27/tech/coronavirus-conspiracy-theory/index.html

68. Palmer, S. (2017, January 9). Just how dangerous is Alexa? *Advertising Age*, p. 18.

69. Pegg, D., & Duncan, P. (2018, April 16). Fake news inquiry raises concerns over targeting of voters in Brexit referendum. *Guardian*. Retrieved form https://www.theguardian.com/politics/2018/apr/16/fake-news-inquiry-raises-concerns-over-targeting-of-voters-in-brexit-referendum

70. Perrigo, B. (2021, January 7). Facebook and Twitter finally locked Donald Trump's accounts. Will they ban him permanently? *Time*. Retrieved from https://time.com/5927398/facebook-twitter-trump-suspension-capitol/

71. Perrin, A. (2021, June 3). Mobile technology and home broadband 2021. *Pew Research Center*. Retrieved from https://www.pewresearch.org/internet/2021/06/03/mobile-technology-and-home-broadband-2021/

72. Perrin, A. (2020, April 14). Half of Americans have decided not to use a product or service because of privacy concerns. *Pew Research Center*. Retrieved from https://www.pewresearch.org/fact-tank/2020/04/14/half-of-americans-have-decided-not-to-use-a-product-or-service-because-of-privacy-concerns/

73. Perrin, A., & Atske, S. (2021, April 2). 7% of Americans don't use the internet. Who are they? *Pew Research Center*. Retrieved from https://www.pewresearch.org/fact-tank/2021/04/02/7-of-americans-dont-use-the-internet-who-are-they/

74. "Prognosis of worldwide spending on the Internet of Things (IoT) from 2018 to 2023." (2020, April 23). *Statista*. Retrieved from https://www.statista.com/statistics/668996/worldwide-expenditures-for-the-internet-of-things/

75. Ray, S. (2020, July 1). California begins enforcing broad data privacy law—here's what you should know. *Forbes*. Retrieved from https://www.forbes.com/sites/siladityaray/2020/07/01/california-begins-enforcing-broad-data-privacy-law—heres-what-you-should-know/#10bbcbac3de5

76. Read, M. (2020, January 30). Why we should ban facial recognition. *New York Magazine*. Retrieved from https://nymag.com/intelligencer/2020/01/why-we-should-ban-facial-recognition-technology.html

77. Reader, R. (2020, July 25). The latest pandemic hoax: a fake CDC notice advising against masks. *Fast Company*. Retrieved from https://www.fastcompany.com/90532354/the-latest-pandemic-hoax-a-fake-cdc-notice-advising-against-masks

78. Reicin, E. (2021, January 19). In 2021, consumer and stakeholder privacy is about defining trust. *Forbes*. Retrieved from https://www.forbes.com/sites/forbesnonprofitcouncil/2021/01/19/in-2021-consumer-and-stakeholder-privacy-is-about-defining-trust/?sh=2d1cf71d1b55

79. Rhode, J. (2018, February 19). Why the Internet of Things is designed for corporations, not consumers. *Salon*. Retrieved from https://www.salon.com/2018/02/19/why-the-internet-of-things-is-designed-for-corporations-not-consumers/

80. Richter, F. (2021, January 7). Global app spending passed $100 billion in 2020. *Statista*. Retrieved from https://www.statista.com/chart/22377/global-consumer-spending-on-leading-app-stores/

81. Riley, A. (2020, May 11). How your smart home devices can be turned against you. *BBC*. Retrieved from https://www.bbc.com/future/article/20200511-how-smart-home-devices-are-being-used-for-domestic-abuse

82. Rogers, K. (2020, May 21). How bad is the COVID-19 misinformation epidemic? *FiveThirtyEight*. Retrieved from https://fivethirtyeight.com/features/how-bad-is-the-covid-19-misinformation-epidemic/

83. Sagioglou, C., & Greitmeyer, T. (2014). Facebook's emotional consequences: Why Facebook causes a decrease in mood and why people still use it. *Computers in Human Behavior, 35*, 359–363.

84. Salway, D. (2020, March 6). United Nations: Broadband access is a basic human right. *Lifewire*. Retrieved from https://www.lifewire.com/united-nations-broadband-access-is-a-basic-human-right-436784

85. Shakya, H. B., & Christakis, N. A. (2017). Association of Facebook use with compromised well-being: A longitudinal study. *American Journal of Epidemiology, 185*, 203–211.

86. Sanders, B. (2020). High-speed internet for all. *BernieSanders.com*. Retrieved from https://berniesanders.com/issues/high-speed-internet-all/

87. Sheer, R. (2015, March 7). The Internet killed privacy: Our liberation, and our capture, are within the same tool. *Salon*. Retrieved from http://www.salon.com/2015/03/07/the_internet_killed_privacy_our_liberation_and_our_capture_are_within_the_same_tool/

88. Smith, K. (2019, June 1). 53 incredible Facebook statistics and facts. *Brandwatch*. Retrieved from https://www.brand-watch.com/blog/facebook-statistics/

89. Smith, M. (2020, August 18). Facebook wanted to be a force for good in Myanmar. Now it is rejecting a request to help with a genocide investigation. *Time*. Retrieved from https://time.com/5880118/myanmar-rohingya-genocide-facebook-gambia/

90. Southern, L. (2019, July 1). "A perfect storm": The Wall Street Journal has 21 people detecting "deepfakes." *Digiday*. Retrieved from https://digiday.com/media/the-wall-street-journal-has-21-people-detecting-deepfakes/

91. Sterling, G. (2015, January 20). Google overtakes traditional media to become most trusted news source. *Searchengine-land.com*. Retrieved from http://searchengineland.com/google-over-takes-traditonal-media-become-trusted-source-news-online-213176

92. Stinchombe, C. (2020, November 13). Measles infections are skyrocketing because of low vaccination rates. *Self*. Retrieved from https://www.self.com/story/measles-infections-increase

93. Sullivan, A. (2018, March 18). Can Donald Trump be impeached? *New York Times Book Review*, p. 1.

94. Sullivan, M. (2019, March 11). Tim Berners-Lee: Happy 30th birthday, Web! You're a mess. *Fast Company*. Retrieved form https://www.fastcompany.com/90318541/the-web-3-biggest-cancers-according-to-tim-berners-lee

95. Swisher, K. (2018, October 7). Introducing the Internet Bill of Rights. *New York Times*. Retrieved from https://www.nytimes.com/2018/10/04/opinion/ro-khanna-internet-bill-of-rights.html

96. Systrom, K. (2020, February 10). Instagram by the numbers: stats, demographics & fun facts. *Omnicore*. Retrieved from https://www.omnicoreagency.com/instagram-statistics/

97. Taub, A., & Fisher, M. (2018, August 23). As attacks on refugees rise, a link is uncovered: Facebook. *New York Times*, p. A1.

98. Tavernise, S. (2016, December 7). As fake news spreads lies, more readers shrug at truth. *New York Times*. Retrieved from https://www.nytimes.com/2016/12/06/us/fake-news-partisan-republican-democrat.html

99. Tolentino, J. (2019, April 29). Eye candy. *New Yorker*, pp. 71–75.

100. Toothman, J. (2017). What's the difference between the Internet and the World Wide Web? *HowStuffWorks*. Retrieved from http://computer.howstuffworks.com/internet/basics/internet-versus-world-wide-web1.htm

101. Trombly, J. (2020, May 12). State stepping up broadband efforts as feds mull the same. *VTDigger*. Retrieved from https://vtdigger.org/2020/05/12/state-stepping-up-broadband-efforts-as-feds-mull-the-same/

102. Tsukayama, H. (2016, May 18). Amazon CEO Jeffrey Bezos: Debate between privacy and security is "issue of our age." *Washington Post*. Retrieved from https://www.washingtonpost.com/news/the-switch/wp/2016/05/18/amazon-ceo-jeffrey-bezos-debate-between-privacy-and-security-is-issue-of-our-age/?utm_term=.e6da8beafefc

103. Uberti, D., & Vernon, P. (2017, January 19). The coming storm for journalism under Trump. *Columbia Journalism Review*. Retrieved from http://www.cjr.org/special_report/trump_media_journalism_washington_press.php

104. "The Ultimate List of Marketing Statistics for 2021." (2021). *Hubspot*. Retrieved from https://www.hubspot.com/marketing-statistics

105. University of Texas at Dallas. (2020, June 23). Tool to protect children's online privacy: Tracking instrument nabs apps that violate federal law with 99% accuracy. *Science Daily*. Retrieved from https://www.sciencedaily.com/releases/2020/06/200623145354.htm

106. Verduyn, P., Ybarra, O., Résibois, M., Jonides, J., & Kross, E. (2017). Do social network sites enhance or undermine subjective well-being? A critical review. *Social Issues and Policy Review, 11*, 274–302.

107. Vogels, E. A., Perrin, A., Rainie, L., & Anderson, M. (2020, April 30). 53% of Americans say the Internet has been essential during the COVID-19 outbreak. *Pew Research Center*. Retrieved from https://www.pewresearch.org/internet/2020/04/30/53-of-americans-say-the-internet-has-been-essential-during-the-covid-19-outbreak/

108. Wanshel, E. (2020, May 20). Dr. Fauci's #PassThe Mic campaign will take over Julia Roberts' social media accounts. *Huffington Post*. Retrieved from https://www.huffpost.com/entry/coronavirus-julia-roberts-celebrities-passthemic-fauci-experts_n_5ec56fcbc5b689d9f14be4c9

109. Warzel, C. (2020, June 14). The protests show that Twitter is real life. *New York Times*, p. SR2.

110. Whittaker, Z. (2020, July 30). Amazon says police demands for customer data have gone up. *Tech Crunch*. Retrieved from https://techcrunch.com/2020/07/30/amazon-police-data-demands/

111. "World Internet Users and 2021 Population Stats." (2021, January). *Internet World Stats*. Retrieved from https://www.internetworldstats.com/stats.htm

112. Young, K. S. (2004). Internet addiction: A new clinical phenomenon and its consequences. *American Behavioral Scientist, 48*, 402–415.

113. Zuboff, S. (2021, January 31). The knowledge coup. *New York Times*, pp. SR4–SR5.

114. Zuboff, S. (2020, January 26). The known unknown. *New York Times*, pp. SR1, SR7.

115. Zuckerman, E. (2018, May 30). Six or seven things social media can do for democracy. *Medium*. Retrieved from https://medium.com/trust-media-and-democracy/six-or-seven-things-social-media-can-do-for-democracy-66cee083b91a

Cultural Forum Blue Column icon, Media Literacy Red Torch Icon, Using Media Green Gear icon, Developing Media book in starburst icon: ©McGraw Hill

Public
Relations

11

◄ Corporate social responsibility at its best. Budweiser converted parts of its manufacturing and distribution operations to manufacture hand sanitizer during the coronavirus pandemic.

Bill Greenblatt/UPI/Alamy Stock Photo

Learning Objectives

It is no small irony that public relations (PR) has such poor PR. We criticize the flacks who try to spin the truth because PR is most obvious when used to reclaim the reputation of someone or some organization in need of such help. But public relations is essential for maintaining relationships between organizations and their publics. In fact, much PR is used for good. After studying this chapter, you should be able to

▶ Recall the history and development of the public relations industry.

▶ Describe how the organizational and economic nature of the contemporary public relations industry shapes the messages with which publics interact, especially in an increasingly converged media environment.

▶ Identify different types of public relations and the different publics each is designed to serve.

▶ Explain the relationship between public relations and its various publics.

▶ Apply key media literacy skills when consuming public relations messages, especially fake online reviews.

1773 ▶ Boston Tea Party ·

1833 ▶ Andrew Jackson hires Amos Kendall, first
presidential press secretary · · · · · · · · · ·

1800

*Library of Congress,
[LC-DIG-ds-03379]*

1896 ▶ William Jennings Bryan and William
McKinley launch first national political
campaigns ·

1850

1889 Westinghouse establishes first corporate
public relations department

*Library of Congress,
[LC-USZC2-2402]*

1906 The Publicity Bureau, first publicity
company

1900

1913 Lee's *Declaration of Principles*

1915 Cadillac's Penalty of Leadership

1917 ▶ President Wilson establishes Committee
on Public Information ·

1929 Torches of Liberty

1938 Foreign Agents Registration Act

1941 Office of War Information

1946 Federal Regulation of Lobbying Act

1947 Public Relations Society of America (PRSA);
The Hucksters

*Library of Congress,
[LC-DIG-ppmsca-28850]*

*Library of Congress,
[LC-USZC4-10221]*

1954 PRSA Code of Ethics

1950

1962 PRSA accreditation program

1980 ▶ MADD ·

Tony Freeman/PhotoEdit

2006 TOMS begins buy-one-give-one program

2000

2007 Rise of the transparentists

2013 Lobbyists become government relations
professionals

2014 Coalition of PR firms rules out work for
climate-change deniers

2019 New Principles of Corporate Governance;
the Helsinki Declaration; FTC says fake
reviews are illegal

2020 Coronavirus in the US; Clean Creatives
campaign

"DRINKING ON A SCHOOL NIGHT? THAT'S NOT LIKE YOU."

"First, you know that I don't drink, school night, weekends, I don't drink. Second, what makes you think I'm drinking?"

"The evidence in plain sight. That's a bottle of Budweiser."

"Yes, it is, but no it isn't. It's not beer. Bud repurposed some of its production and distribution operations to produce and ship hand sanitizer during the coronavirus pandemic. I needed disinfectant, and because I don't drink, buying some from Bud just seemed like a good way to pay them back for good citizenship. You want a shot? This Bud's for you."

"Not on a school night!"

These two friends were joking about one company's public service campaign, an effort mirrored by thousands of other businesses: to do good while burnishing their corporate images, not unimportant at a time when confidence in many of the country's institutions was bit shaky. Nike developed a process to manufacture clear-plastic face shields out of used sneakers; New Balance shoes and clothier Brooks Brothers manufactured masks and gowns; Panera launched Panera Grocery, allowing customers to order essential items such as milk, bread, and fresh produce directly from its vendors; educational materials publisher Scholastic created a free online education hub providing materials for stay at home learning. Restaurants Chipotle, Popeyes, and KFC waived delivery fees for people under stay-at-home orders, and jeans manufacturer Levi's hosted an online concert series featuring artists like Questlove and Jaden Smith to spread a bit of joy.

But it did not take a global pandemic to demonstrate the good that meaningful public relations campaigns could accomplish. Since 2006 TOMS's buy-one-give-one program has delivered tens of millions of pairs of shoes to kids in need, with footwear based on the terrain and weather where they live. Similarly, diaper maker Pampers partners with UNICEF for "1 pack = 1 vaccine," a program to donate one tetanus vaccine for every package it sells. Car maker Subaru and the National Forest Foundation restore lost forests by teaming up to replant 500,000 trees.

In this chapter, we investigate the public relations industry and its relationship with mass media and their audiences. We first define public relations. Then we study its history and development as the profession matured from its beginnings in hucksterism to a full-fledged, communication-based industry. We see how the needs and interests of the profession's various publics became part of the public relations process, and we also define exactly who those publics are. We then detail the scope and nature of the industry and describe the types of public relations activities and the organization of a typical public relations operation. We study trends such as globalization and specialization, as well as the impact of new, converging communication technologies on the industry. Finally, we discuss trust in public relations. As our media literacy skill, we learn how to recognize fake online reviews.

Defining Public Relations

UNICEF and the National Forest Foundation, like Mothers Against Drunk Driving, Save Venice, Inc., Handgun Control Incorporated, the National Environmental Trust, and countless other nonprofit organizations, are interest groups that use a variety of public relations tools and strategies to serve a variety of publics. They want to use public relations to do good. The companies that sponsor their activities also want to do good—for their communities *and* for themselves. Even the most cynical person must applaud their efforts on behalf of helping people in need.

However, for many people, efforts such as these serve to demonstrate one of the ironies of public relations, both as an activity and as an industry: Public relations has terrible public relations. We dismiss some information as "just PR." Public relations professionals are frequently equated with snake oil salespeople, hucksters, and other willful deceivers. They are sometimes referred to both inside and outside the media industries as **flacks**. They are often accused of engaging in **spin**, outright lying or obfuscation. Yet virtually every organization and institution—big and small, public and private, for-profit and volunteer—uses public relations as a regular part of its operation. Many have their own public relations departments; Facebook, for example, has more than 500 full-time employees in its PR department (Marantz, 2020). The term *public relations* often carries such a negative connotation that most independent companies and company PR departments now go by the name "public affairs," "corporate affairs," or "public communications."

The problem rests, in part, on confusion over what public relations actually is. As public relations scholar Lee Edwards (2016) explains, most definitions of PR stress its potentially positive influence: a "means of exchanging ideas" and "creating and sustaining connections between individuals and groups." However, she writes, "In practice, public relations is most widely used as a strategic tool for corporates and governments to realise [sic] self-interest and advantage in competitive environments—contexts that do not necessarily lend themselves to democratic engagement" (p. 60).

In fact, there is no universally accepted definition of public relations because it can be and is many things—publicity, research, public affairs, media relations, promotion, merchandising, and more. Much of the observable contact media consumers have with public relations occurs when the industry defends people, companies, even countries that have somehow run afoul of the public.

For example, in 2019, investigative reporters revealed that flattering profiles of wealthy and well-connected financier Jeffrey Epstein that appeared in several national publications after his 2009 conviction for soliciting a minor for prostitution were, in fact, written by his PR operation. In these stories, appearing under the names of various publications' own staff, the convicted pedophile was described as a "selfless and forward-thinking philanthropist with an interest in science," never mentioning his legal woes (Hsu, 2019b, p. B1).

Buffeted by bad publicity involving its involvement in the 9/11 terror attacks and frequent reports of abuse of women, gay men, lesbians, and businesspeople unfriendly to the throne, Saudi Arabia enlisted a quartet of Western PR firms—the Podesta Group, Qorvis, APCO World, and the Sonoran Policy Group—to burnish its image and that of its leader, Crown Prince Mohammed bin Salman (Maguire, 2018). Their efforts produced a wealth of glowing media coverage, including a glossy, 100-page magazine, *The New Kingdom*, on American newsstands.

Some PR takes the form of **astroturf** (fake grassroots organizations); their true mission is to thwart government efforts that threaten their funders' profits. For example, Texans for Natural Gas, Alaska's Arctic Energy Center, which advocated increased oil drilling in the Arctic wildlife refuge, and the Main Street Investors Coalition, which warned that climate activism hurts small stock market investors, present themselves as local grassroots organizations. They are actually creations of Washington, D.C., PR firm FTI Consulting, hired by several of the world's largest oil and gas companies to help them promote fossil fuels (Tabuchi, 2020).

Beyond the obvious problem of intentional deception, an additional issue for the PR industry as a whole is that such groups sometimes employ **mercenary science**, science-for-hire, contracted out to consulting firms like Exponent and Gradient "to prove that their harmful products aren't harmful" by giving them the quantitative cover of seemingly objective scientific research. "Sometimes you will be working for evildoers and trying to make it seem like they did nothing wrong," explained one Exponent scientist (Spencer, 2020).

But PR, sometimes without drawing attention to itself, often serves the public good. For example, when General Motors was rocked by a 1.6-million-car recall and 13 deaths linked to a faulty ignition switch in 2014, the company took not only to traditional media—letters to customers, blogs, call centers, and news media—in its efforts to better serve its customers and save its reputation, but it also mounted a massive social media public relations campaign—connecting with owners, getting them loaner cars, and even paying for public transit. With the number of suicides spiking among New York city police, the NYPD mounted an internal communication campaign to save officers' lives by reducing the stigma associated with seeking help (Joffe, 2019). The public relations campaign by Mothers Against Drunk Driving (MADD)

▲ *The New Kingdom*, a glossy, 100-page magazine about Saudi Arabia and its new crown prince, was only one of many products of that country's extensive PR efforts to sway Western public opinion.
J. David Ake/AP Images

▼ Save Venice, Inc. is just one of countless nonprofit organizations that use a variety of public relations tools and strategies to do good.
Jordan Dowd

led directly to passage of tougher standards in virtually every state to remove drunk drivers from the road and to provide stiffer sentences for those convicted of driving under the influence. Dramatic reductions in the number of alcohol-related traffic accidents resulted from this effort. (See the essay "The MADD Campaign.")

"P.R. has a P.R. problem," says Syracuse University public relations professor Brenda Wrigley. "We have to get our own house in order. . . . We are advocates and there's no shame in that as long as it's grounded in ethics and values" (in O'Brien, 2005, p. 31). PR ethicist Shannon Bowen (2017) adds, "To be ethical communicators and leaders, the power of public relations should be used to empower others—to facilitate wise decisions through providing information, by making a range of options possible and actionable, and by serving the interests of society—as well as those of clients." And in a post-pandemic world, "firms will be held to a higher standard," explains industry strategist Alex Slater, "It won't be enough to do the job—the PR industry will join the rest of corporate America in a new era of ethical business practices, philanthropy, pro-bono work, and above-and-beyond community engagement" (2020).

Accepting, therefore, that public relations should be honest, ethical, and employed in the service of others, our definition of public relations is drawn from the Public Relations Society of America's widely accepted definition: "Public relations is a strategic communication process that builds mutually beneficial relationships between organizations and their publics" (PRSA, 2020).

USING MEDIA TO MAKE A DIFFERENCE
The MADD Campaign

After her child was killed in a drunk-driving accident in 1980, Candy Lightner sought out others like herself, mothers who had lost children to the volatile mix of cars and alcohol. She hoped they could provide one another with emotional support and campaign to ensure that other parents would never know their grief. Thus, Mothers Against Drunk Driving (MADD) was born.

Among MADD's publics are teenagers. With its parallel organization, Students Against Destructive Decisions (SADD), MADD targets this high-risk group through various educational campaigns and in the media that attract teen audiences. The organization also conducts public information campaigns aimed at adult drivers and repeat drunk drivers, often in conjunction with state and other authorities. It also assists legislators in their efforts to pass drunk-driving legislation. Two more of MADD's publics are public servants such as police and paramedics who must deal with the effects of drunk driving, as well as the families and friends who have lost loved ones in alcohol- or drug-related driving accidents.

Has MADD made a difference? Since 1988, numerous prime-time television programs have featured episodes about the dangers of drunk driving. MADD's professional staff has served as script advisers to these programs. MADD was instrumental in the passage of the federal Drunk Driving Prevention Act of 1988, offering states financial incentives to set up programs that would reduce alcohol- and drug-related automobile fatalities. This legislation also made 21 the national minimum legal drinking age. MADD successfully campaigned for the Victim's Crime Act of 1984, making compensation from drunk drivers to victims and their families federal law.

There are three even more dramatic examples of how successful Lightner's group has been. According to the National Highway Traffic Safety Administration, since the 1980s, drunk-driving fatalities on American roads have decreased by a third ("Drunk Driving," 2020). MADD's cultural impact also shows in the way people treat drunk drivers. It is no longer cool to talk about how smashed we got at the party, or how we can't believe we made it home. Almost every evening out with a group of friends includes a designated driver. Drunk drivers today are considered nearly as despicable as child molesters. Many in public relations, traffic safety, and law enforcement credit MADD's public relations efforts with this change.

A third impact is its service as a model for effective, truly grassroots activism. After the 2012 shootings at the Sandy Hook Elementary School that took the lives of 20 young children and 6 adults, distraught PR professional Shannon Watts took to the Internet to get involved, hoping to find something similar to MADD for gun safety. When she could not, she founded what is now known as Moms Demand Action, a growing activist organization with chapters in every state. After the 2018 high school shooting in Parkland, Florida, more than 170,000 additional moms signed on. Moms Demand Action and Mayors Against Illegal Guns joined forces in 2014 to form Everytown for Gun Safety, becoming the largest gun-violence-prevention group in the country (Karlis, 2018).

A Short History of Public Relations

The history of this complex industry can be divided into four stages: early public relations, the propaganda–publicity stage, early two-way communication, and advanced two-way communication. These stages have combined to shape the character of this industry.

Early Public Relations

Archaeologists in Iraq have uncovered a tablet dating from 1800 B.C.E. that today we would call a public information bulletin. It provided farmers with information on sowing, irrigating, and harvesting their crops. Julius Caesar fed the people of the Roman Empire constant reports of his achievements to maintain morale and to solidify his reputation and position of power. Genghis Khan would send "advance men" to tell stories of his might, hoping to frighten his enemies into surrendering.

Public relations campaigns abounded in pre-Revolutionary War America and helped create the colonies. Merchants, farmers, and others who saw advantage in a growing colonial population used overstatement, half-truths, and lies to entice settlers to the New World; *A Brief and True Report of the New Found Land of Virginia* by Thomas Hariot and John White was published in 1588 to lure European settlers. The Boston Tea Party was a well-planned media event organized to attract public attention for a vital cause. Today we'd call it a **pseudo-event**, an event staged specifically to attract public attention. Benjamin Franklin organized a sophisticated campaign to thwart the Stamp Act, the Crown's attempt to limit colonial press freedom, using his publications and the oratory skills of criers (see Chapter 3). The *Federalist Papers* of John Jay, James Madison, and Alexander Hamilton were originally a series of 85 letters published between 1787 and 1789, which were designed to sway public opinion in the newly independent United States toward support and passage of the new Constitution, an early effort at issue management. In all these examples, people or organizations were using communication to inform, to build an image, and to influence public opinion.

The Propaganda–Publicity Stage

Mass circulation newspapers and the first successful consumer magazines appeared in the 1830s, expanding the ability of people and organizations to communicate with the public. In 1833, for example, Andrew Jackson hired former newspaper journalist Amos Kendall as

THE DESTRUCTION OF TEA AT BOSTON HARBOR.

◀ The December 16, 1773, Boston Tea Party was one of the first successful pseudo-events in the new land. Had cameras been around at the time, it would also have been a fine photo op. *Library of Congress, [LC-DIG-ds-03379]*

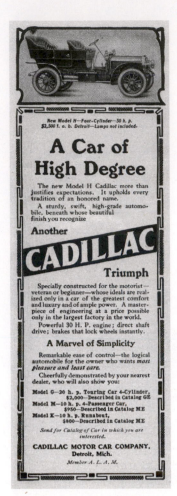

New Model H—Four-Cylinder—30 h. p.
$2,500 f. o. b. Detroit—Lamps not included.

A Car of High Degree

The new Model H Cadillac more than justifies expectations. It upholds every tradition of an honored name.

A sturdy, swift, high-grade automobile, beneath whose beautiful finish you recognize

Another

CADILLAC

Triumph

Specially constructed for the motorist—veteran or beginner—whose ideals are realized only in a car of the greatest comfort and luxury and of ample power. A masterpiece of engineering at a price possible only in the largest factory in the world.

Powerful 30 H. P. engine; direct shaft drive; brakes that lock wheels instantly.

A Marvel of Simplicity

Remarkable ease of control—the logical automobile for the owner who wants *most pleasure and least care.*

Cheerfully demonstrated by your nearest dealer, who will also show you:

Model G—20 h. p. Touring Car 4-Cylinder, $2,000—Described in Catalog GE
Model M—10 h. p. 4-Passenger Car, $950—Described in Catalog ME
Model K—10 h. p. Runabout, $800—Described in Catalog ME

Send for Catalog of Car in which you are interested.

CADILLAC MOTOR CAR COMPANY, Detroit, Mich.

Member A. L. A. M.

▲ The 1906 Car of High Degree Cadillac campaign was an early but quite successful example of image advertising—using paid ads to build goodwill for a product.

Jay Paull/Archive Photos/Getty Images

his publicist and the country's first presidential press secretary in an effort to combat the aristocrats who saw Jackson as too common to be president.

Abolitionists sought an end to slavery; industrialists needed to attract workers, entice customers, and enthuse investors; and P. T. Barnum, allegedly convinced that there's a sucker born every minute, worked to lure those suckers into his shows. All of these used the newspaper and the magazine to serve their causes.

Politicians recognized that the expanding press meant that a new way of campaigning was necessary. In 1896, presidential contenders William Jennings Bryan and William McKinley both established campaign headquarters in Chicago from which they issued news releases, position papers, and pamphlets. As a result, the modern national political campaign was born.

It was during this era that public relations began to acquire its deceitful, huckster image. PR was associated more with propaganda than with useful information. A disregard for the public and the willingness of public relations experts to serve the powerful fueled this view, and public relations began to establish itself as a profession during this time. The burgeoning press was its outlet, but westward expansion and rapid urbanization and industrialization in the United States were its driving forces. As the railroad expanded to unite the new nation, cities exploded with new people and new life. Markets, once small and local, became large and national.

As the political and financial stakes grew, business and government became increasingly corrupt and selfish: "The public be damned" was William Vanderbilt's official comment when asked in 1882 about the effects of changing the schedule of his New York Central Railroad (Gordon, 1989). The muckrakers' revelations badly tarnished the images of industry and politics. Massive and lengthy coal strikes led to violence and more antibusiness feeling. In the heyday of the journalistic exposé and the muckraking era, government, and business both required some good public relations.

In 1889, Westinghouse Electric established the first corporate public relations department, hiring a former newspaper writer to engage the press and ensure that company positions were always clear and in the public eye. Advertising agencies, including N. W. Ayer & Sons and Lord and Thomas, began to offer public relations services to their clients. The first publicity company, The Publicity Bureau, opened in Boston in 1906 and later expanded to New York, Chicago, Washington, St. Louis, and Topeka to help the railroad industry challenge federal regulations that it opposed.

The railroads also had other problems, and they turned to *New York World* reporter Ivy Lee for help. Beset by accidents and strikes, the Pennsylvania Railroad usually responded by suppressing information. Lee recognized, however, that this was dangerous and counterproductive in a time when the public was already suspicious of big business, including the railroads. Lee escorted reporters to the scene of trouble, established press centers, distributed press releases, and assisted reporters in obtaining additional information and photographs.

When a Colorado coal mine strike erupted in violence in 1913, the press attacked the mine's principal stockholder, New York's John D. Rockefeller Jr., blaming him for the shooting deaths of several miners and their wives and children. Lee handled press relations and convinced Rockefeller to visit the scene to talk (and be photographed) with the strikers. The strike ended, and Rockefeller was soon being praised for his sensitive intervention. Eventually, Lee issued his *Declaration of Principles*, arguing that public relations practitioners should be providers of information, not purveyors of publicity.

Not all public relations at this time was damage control. Henry Ford began using staged events such as auto races to build interest in his cars, started the in-house employee publication *Ford Times*, and made heavy use of image advertising.

Public relations in this stage was typically one-way, from organization to public. Still, by the outbreak of World War I, most of the elements of today's large-scale, multifunction public relations agency were in place.

Early Two-Way Communication

Because the American public was not particularly enthusiastic about the nation's entry into World War I, President Woodrow Wilson recognized the need for public relations in support of the war effort (Zinn, 1995, pp. 355–357). In 1917, he placed former newspaper journalist George Creel at the head of the newly formed Committee on Public Information (CPI). Creel assembled opinion leaders from around the country to advise the government on its public relations efforts and to help shape public opinion. The committee sold Liberty Bonds and helped increase membership in the Red Cross. It engaged in public relations on a scale never before seen, using movies, public speakers, articles in newspapers and magazines, and posters.

It was about this time that public relations pioneer Edward Bernays began emphasizing the value of assessing the public's feelings toward an organization. He would then use this knowledge as the basis for the development of the public relations effort. Together with Creel's committee, Bernays's work was the beginning of two-way communication in public relations—that is, public relations practitioners talking to people and, in return, listening to them when they talked back. Public relations professionals began representing their various publics to their clients, just as they represented their clients to those publics.

There were other advances in public relations during this stage. During the 1930s, President Franklin D. Roosevelt, guided by adviser Louis McHenry Howe, embarked on a sophisticated public relations campaign to win support for his then-radical New Deal policies. Central to Roosevelt's effort was the new medium of radio. The Great Depression plaguing the country throughout this decade once again turned public opinion against business and industry. To counter people's distrust, many more corporations established in-house public relations departments; for example, General Motors opened its PR operation in 1931. Public relations professionals turned increasingly to the newly emerging polling industry, founded by George Gallup and Elmo Roper, to better gauge public opinion as they constructed public relations campaigns and to gather feedback on the effectiveness of those campaigns. Gallup and Roper successfully applied newly refined social science research methods—advances in sampling, questionnaire design, and interviewing—to meet the business needs of clients and their publics.

The growth of the industry was significant enough and its reputation so sufficiently fragile that the National Association of Accredited Publicity Directors was founded in 1936. The American Council on Public Relations was established three years later. They merged in 1947, creating the Public Relations Society of America (PRSA), the principal professional group for today's public relations professionals.

World War II saw the government undertake another massive campaign to bolster support for the war effort, this time through the Office of War Information (OWI). Employing techniques that had proven successful during World War I, the OWI had the additional advantage of public opinion polling, fully established and powerful radio networks and their stars, and a Hollywood eager to help. Singer Kate Smith's war-bond radio fundraiser brought in millions, and director Frank Capra produced the *Why We Fight* film series for the OWI.

During this era, both public relations and Ivy Lee suffered a serious blow to their reputations. Lee was the American public relations spokesman for Germany and its leader, Adolf Hitler. In 1934, Lee was required to testify before Congress to defend himself against charges that he was a Nazi sympathizer. He was successful, but the damage had been done. As a result of Lee's ties with Germany, Congress passed the Foreign Agents Registration Act in 1938, requiring anyone who engages in political activities in the United States on behalf of a foreign power to register as an agent of that power with the Justice Department.

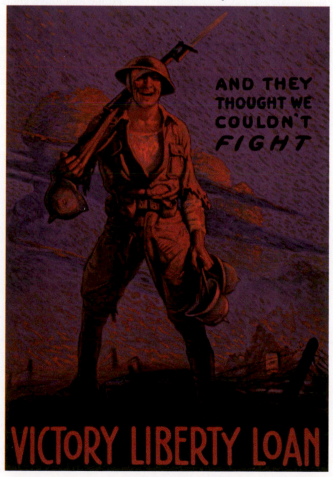

▼ World War I brought government into large-scale public relations. Even today, the CPI's posters—like this one encouraging citizens to support the war effort through war bonds—are recognized.
Library of Congress, [LC-USZC4-10221]

AND THEY THOUGHT WE COULDN'T FIGHT

VICTORY LIBERTY LOAN

▲ Better known for hits such as *Mr. Smith Goes to Washington* and *It's a Wonderful Life*, director Frank Capra brought his moviemaking talents to the government's efforts to explain US involvement in World War II and to overcome Americans' isolationism. His *Why We Fight* documentary series still stands as a classic of the form.
Courtesy Everett Collection

▶ Criticism of public relations found its way into the cultural forum through a number of popular films and books. This scene is from the movie *The Hucksters.*
Courtesy Everett Collection

Advanced Two-Way Communication

Post–World War II US society was confronted by profound social change and expansion of the consumer culture. It became increasingly important for organizations to know what their clients were thinking, what they liked and disliked, and what concerned and satisfied them. As a result, public relations turned even more decidedly toward integrated two-way communication, employing research, advertising, and promotion.

As the public relations industry became more visible, it opened itself to closer scrutiny. Best-selling novels such as *The Hucksters* and *The Man in the Gray Flannel Suit* (and the hit movies made from them) painted a disturbingly negative picture of the industry and those who worked in it. Vance Packard's best-selling book *The Hidden Persuaders*, dealing with both public relations and advertising, further eroded PR esteem. As a result of public distrust of the profession, Congress passed the Federal Regulation of Lobbying Act in 1946, requiring, among other things, that those who deal with federal employees on behalf of private clients disclose those relationships. And as the industry's conduct and ethics came under increasing attack, the PRSA responded with a code of ethics in 1954 and an accreditation program in 1962. Both, with modification and improvement, stand today.

Public relations's contemporary era is characterized by other events as well. More people buying more products meant that greater numbers of people were coming into contact with a growing number of businesses. As consumer markets grew in size, the basis of competition changed. Texaco, for example, used advertising to sell its gasoline. But because its gasoline was not all that different from that of other oil companies, it also sold its fuel using its good name and reputation. Increasingly, then, advertising agencies began to add public relations divisions. This change served to blur the distinction between advertising and PR.

Women, who had proved their capabilities in all professional settings during World War II, became prominent in the industry. Anne Williams Wheaton was associate press secretary

to President Eisenhower, and Leone Baxter was president of the powerful public relations firm Whitaker and Baxter. Companies and their executives and politicians increasingly turned to television to polish their images and shape public opinion. Nonprofit, charitable, and social activist groups also mastered the art of public relations. The latter used public relations especially effectively to counter the PR power of targeted businesses. Environmentalist, civil rights and women's rights groups, and safety and consumer advocate organizations were successful in moving the public toward their positions and, in many cases, toward action.

Shaping the Character of Public Relations

Throughout these four stages in the development of public relations, several factors combined to shape the identity of public relations, influence the way the industry does its job, and clarify the necessity for PR in the business and political world.

Advances in technology. Advances in industrial technology made possible the mass production, distribution, and marketing of goods. Advances in communication technology (and their proliferation) made it possible to communicate more efficiently and effectively with ever larger and more specific audiences.

Growth of the middle class. A growing middle class, better educated and more aware of the world around it, required more and better information about people and organizations.

Growth of organizations. As business, organized labor, and government grew bigger after World War II, the public saw them as more powerful and more remote. As a result, people were naturally curious and suspicious about these forces that seemed to be influencing all aspects of their lives.

Better research tools. The development of sophisticated research methodologies and statistical techniques allowed the industry to know its audiences better and to better judge the effectiveness of its campaigns.

Professionalization. Numerous national and international public relations organizations helped professionalize the industry and burnish its reputation.

Public Relations and Its Audiences

Virtually all of us consume public relations messages on a daily basis. Increasingly, the video clips we see on the local evening news are provided by a public relations firm or the PR department of some company or organization. The content of many of the stories we read online or hear on local radio news comes directly from PR-provided press releases. As one media relations firm explained in a promotional piece sent to prospective clients, "The media are separated into two categories. One is content and the other is advertising. They're both for sale. Advertising can be purchased directly from the publication or through an ad agency, and the content space you purchase from PR firms" (quoted in Jackson & Hart, 2002, p. 24). In addition, the feed-the-hungry campaign we support, the poster encouraging us toward safer sex, and the corporation-sponsored art exhibit we attend are all someone's public relations effort.

Public relations professionals interact with seven categories of publics, and a **public** is any group of people with a stake in an organization, issue, or idea. Who are those publics?

Employees. An organization's employees are its lifeblood, its family. Good public relations begins at home with company newsletters, social events, and internal and external recognition of superior performance.

Stockholders. Stockholders own the organization (if it is a public corporation). They are "family" as well, and their goodwill is necessary for the business to operate. Annual reports and stockholder meetings provide a sense of belonging as well as information.

Communities. An organization has neighbors where it operates. Courtesy, as well as good business sense, requires that an organization's neighbors are treated with consideration and support. Information meetings, company-sponsored safety and food drives, and open houses strengthen ties between organizations and their neighbors.

Media. Very little communication with an organization's various publics can occur without the trust and goodwill of professionals in the mass media. Press packets, briefings, and the facilitation of access to an organization's newsmakers build that trust and goodwill.

Government. Government is "the voice of the people" and, as such, deserves the attention of any organization that deals with the public. From a practical perspective, governments have the power to tax, regulate, and zone. Organizations must earn and maintain the goodwill and trust of the government. The providing of information and access through reports, position papers, and meetings with official personnel keeps the government informed and builds trust in an organization. The government is also the target of many PR efforts, as organizations and their lobbyists seek favorable legislation and other action.

Investment community. Corporations are under the constant scrutiny of those who invest their own or others' money or make recommendations on investment. The value of a business and its ability to grow are functions of the investment community's respect for and trust in it. As a result, all PR efforts that build an organization's good image speak to that community.

Customers. Consumers pay the bills for companies through their purchase of products or services. Their goodwill is invaluable. That makes good PR, in all its forms, invaluable.

Scope and Structure of the Public Relations Industry

Today some 275,000 people in the United States identify themselves as working in public relations (Bureau of Labor Statistics, 2021), and virtually every major American company or organization has a public relations department, some housing as many as 400 employees. There are over 45,364 public relations firms in the United States, the largest employing as many as 2,000 people. Most, however, have fewer employees, some employing only a few people. American PR firms had $14.5 billion in revenue in 2020 ("Public Relations Firms," 2020). Figure 11.1 shows the 10 largest public relations firms globally.

 **Figure 11.1** The 10 Largest PR Firms Globally, 2019.
Source: "Top 10 Global," 2020.

Net fees in millions of dollars by firm rank

Rank	Firm	Net fees
1	Edelman (USA)	$888.4
2	Weber Shandwick (USA)	$840.0
3	BCW (USA)	$723.0
4	FleishmanHillard (USA)	$605.0
5	Ketchum (USA)	$545.0
6	MSL (France)	$450.0
7	Hill+Knowlton Strategies (USA)	$400.0
8	Ogilvy (USA)	$388.0
9	BlueFocus (China)	$363.4
10	Brunswick (UK)	$280.0

There are full-service public relations firms and those that provide only special services. Media specialists for company CEOs, Web commentary monitoring services, and makers of **video news releases (VNRs)**, preproduced reports about a client or its product that are distributed free of charge to television stations, are special service providers. Public relations firms bill for their services in a number of ways. They may charge an hourly rate for services rendered, or they may be on call, charging clients a monthly fee to act as their public relations counsel. Hill+Knowlton, for example, charges a minimum fee of several thousand dollars a month. Another way to bill is through **fixed-fee arrangements**, wherein the firm performs a specific set of services for a client for a specific and prearranged fee. Finally, many firms bill for **collateral materials**, adding a surcharge as high as 17.65% for handling printing, research, and photographs. For example, if it costs $3,000 to have a poster printed, the firm charges the client $3,529.50 to cover the cost of the poster plus 17.65% of that cost.

Public Relations Activities

Regardless of the way public relations firms bill their clients, they earn their fees by offering all or some of these 14 interrelated services.

1. *Community relations.* This type of public affairs work focuses on the communities in which the organization exists. If a city wants to build a new airport, for example, those whose property will be taken or devalued must be satisfied. If they are not, widespread community opposition to the project may develop.

2. *Counseling.* Public relations professionals routinely offer advice to an organization's management concerning policies, relationships, and communication with its various publics. Management must tell its publics "what we do." Public relations helps in the creation, refinement, and presentation of that messaging.

3. *Development/fundraising.* All organizations, commercial and nonprofit, survive through the voluntary contributions in time and money of their members, friends, employees, supporters, and others. Public relations helps demonstrate the need for those contributions.

    This **corporate social responsibility** (CSR), the integration of business operations and organizational values, sometimes takes the form of **cause marketing**—work in support of social issues and causes. The importance of CSR to clients is evidenced by the fact that 63% of consumers view brands more favorably if they stand up for social causes and 64% do so if those brands donate to those causes ("Year End Report," 2021). But does CSR represent a sincere effort to serve a company's publics or is it mere window dressing? You can enter the debate after reading the essay "Expression of a Company's Values or 'Just More PR'."

4. *Employee/member relations.* This form of public relations responds specifically to the concerns of an organization's employees or members and its retirees and their families. The goal is maintenance of high morale and motivation, and as we saw earlier in the case of the NYPD, even to save lives.

5. *Financial relations.* Practiced primarily by corporate organizations, financial PR is the enhancement of communication between investor-owned companies and their shareholders, the financial community (for example, banks, annuity groups, and investment firms), and the public. Much corporate strategy, such as expansion into new markets and acquisition of other companies, is dependent upon good financial public relations.

6. *Government affairs.* This type of public affairs work focuses on government agencies. **Lobbying**—directly interacting to influence elected officials or government regulators and agents—is often a central activity. The term *lobbyist*, however, has developed a bit of a negative connotation. As such, in 2013 the American League of Lobbyists changed its name to the Association of Government Relations Professionals, and its members, no longer *lobbyists*, became *government relations professionals* (Clines, 2013).

7. *Industry relations.* Companies must interact not only with their own customers and stockholders but also with other companies in their line of business, both competitors

and suppliers. In addition, they must also stand as a single voice in dealing with various state and federal regulators. For example, groups as disparate as the Texas Restaurant Association, the American Petroleum Institute, and the National Association of Manufacturers all require public relations in dealing with their various publics. The goal is the maintenance and prosperity of the industry as a whole.

8. *Issues management.* Often an organization is as interested in influencing public opinion about some larger issue that will eventually influence its operation as it is in the improvement of its own image. Issues management typically uses a large-scale public relations campaign designed to move or shape opinion on a specific issue. Usually the issue is an important one that generates deep feelings. Anti-death-penalty activists, for example, employ a full range of communication techniques to sway people to their side. Exxon-Mobil frequently secures paid media placements that address environmentalism and public transportation—important issues in and of themselves, but also important to the future of a leading manufacturer of fossil fuels.

9. *Media relations.* As the number of media outlets grows and as advances in technology increase the complexity of dealing with them, clients require help in understanding the various media, in preparing and organizing materials for them, and in placing those materials. In addition, media relations requires that the public relations practitioner maintain good relationships with professionals in the media, understand their deadlines and other constraints, and earn their trust.

10. *Marketing communication.* This is a combination of activities designed to promote a product, service, or idea. It can include the creation of advertising; generation of publicity and promotion; design of packaging, point-of-sale displays, and trade show presentations; and design and execution of special events. Advertising becomes a public relations function when its goal is to build an image or to motivate action, as opposed to its usual function of selling products. The Ad Council's seat-belt safety campaign featuring the Crash Test Dummies is a well-known, successful public relations advertising campaign.

It is important to note that PR professionals often use advertising but that the two are not the same. The difference is one of control. Advertising is controlled communication—advertisers pay for ads to appear in specific media exactly as they want; it is *paid* media. PR tends to be less controlled; it is *earned* media. A PR firm, for example, cannot control how or when its client's announcement of a new minority outreach effort is reported by the local paper. It cannot control how the media report Nike's ongoing insistence that it has rectified reported worker abuses in its overseas shops. But that does not mean that the success of earned media cannot be assessed, given AI-driven measurement technologies, such as PRophet, which sample millions of reporters' stories across tens of thousands of outlets for evidence of a piece of earned media's reach (Faw, 2020).

Advertising and public relations obviously overlap for manufacturers of consumer products. Chevrolet must sell cars, but it must communicate with its various publics as well. General Motors, too, must sell cars, but in the wake of the ignition switch recall, it needed serious public relations help.

One result of the overlap of advertising and public relations is that most big advertising agencies house their own public relations divisions and most big PR agencies now produce paid media. For example, nearly a third of Edelman's business is brand marketing; the ratio is 50% at Weber

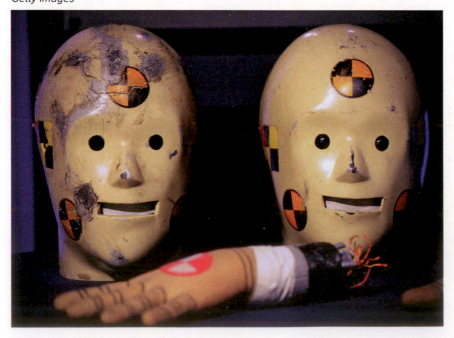

▼ You might recognize the Crash Test Dummies, seen here at their introduction into the Smithsonian National Museum of American History, from their long-running seat-belt safety public relations advertising campaign.
Bill O'Leary/The Washington Post/ Getty Images

Shandwick. "The industry has moved beyond an ecosystem of neatly defined channel or specialist providers" explains industry analyst Jay Pattisall. "Strategically, marketers are asking for more integrated and holistic marketing solutions that bring together the content and the context" (in Rittenhouse, 2019, p. 18).

Another way that advertising and public relations differ is that advertising people typically do not set policy for an organization. Advertising people *execute* policy after organization leaders set it. In contrast, public relations professionals usually are part of the policy-making process because they are the liaison between the organization and its publics. Effective organizations have come to understand that even in routine decisions the impact on public opinion and subsequent consequences can be of tremendous importance. As a result, public relations has become a management function, and a public relations professional typically sits as a member of a company's highest level of management. You'll soon read more about this.

11. *Minority relations/multicultural affairs.* Public affairs activities are directed toward specific racial and ethnic minorities in this type of work. For example, in the summer of 2020, as ongoing protests in the wake of the murder of George Floyd were building public support for the Black Lives Matter movement, Starbucks drew global criticism by forbidding its employees from wearing Black Lives Matter t-shirts, buttons, and other supporting paraphernalia while at work. A move designed to limit potential conflict in its coffee shops was seen as hypocritical given the company's social media support of the protestors. With its much-valued progressive image in jeopardy, its response had to be quick and effective. Its PR operation made sure it was. The ban was quickly rescinded; it issued a very public statement of support: "We see you. We hear you. Black Lives Matter. That is a fact and will never change. This movement is a catalyst for change, and right now, it's telling us a lot of things need to be addressed so we can make space to heal"; and the company even introduced its own line of Black Lives Matter-themed apparel (Adams, 2020).

12. *Public affairs.* The public affairs function includes interacting with officials and leaders of the various power centers with whom a client must deal. Community and government officials and leaders of pressure groups are likely targets of this form of public relations. Public affairs emphasizes social responsibility and building goodwill, such as when a company donates money for a computer lab at the local high school.

13. *Special events and public participation.* Public relations can be used to stimulate interest in an organization, person, or product through a well-planned, focused "happening," an activity designed to facilitate interaction between an organization and its publics. The ubiquitous 5K and 10K charity fun runs are only one example.

14. *Research.* Organizations often must determine the attitudes and behaviors of their various publics in order to plan and implement the activities necessary to influence or change those attitudes and behaviors.

◀ Special events are an important public relations activity.

Steve Kelley Editorial Cartoon used with the permission of Steve Kelley and Creators Syndicate. All rights reserved.

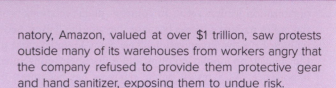

CULTURAL FORUM
Expression of a Company's Values
or "Just More PR?"

The CSR movement reached its zenith with the August 2019 agreement by 181 American companies belonging to the Business Roundtable to accept new Principles of Corporate Governance. Their CEO's agreed "to lead their companies for the benefit of all stakeholders—customers, employees, suppliers, communities, and shareholders." Observers called this explicit articulation of CSR "a historical milestone" (Goodman, 2020, p. B1), the moment when corporate executives "explicitly rebuked the notion that the role of the corporation is to maximize profits at all costs" (Forbes, 2019).

There were, however, skeptics. They argued that CSR serves primarily as a distraction from corporations' more egregious practices; companies can do all the cause marketing they want, but their lobbying efforts and political donations are a truer expression of their real values; CSR is designed primarily to ward off government regulation; it offers little more than convenient opportunities for good PR with small costs to companies' bottom lines. Critics pointed to Facebook, whose stated corporate purpose is to "give people the power to build community and bring the world together." Media literate Internet users are more than aware that this social media site, along with others, is a source of much cultural and political divisiveness, in fact, prospering precisely by defying its expressed values (see Chapter 10).

Already in the cultural forum, the temperature on this debate was raised by COVID-19. We've seen elsewhere in this chapter that scores of companies stepped up during the coronavirus pandemic, putting profit second to social responsibility. Yet new-Principles-of-Corporate-Governance signatory Marriott International Hotels, which earned $1.2 billion in 2019, furloughed most of its US workers, leaving them without access to health care, while paying out more than $160 million in quarterly dividends and pursuing a raise for its CEO. Another sig-

natory, Amazon, valued at over $1 trillion, saw protests outside many of its warehouses from workers angry that the company refused to provide them protective gear and hand sanitizer, exposing them to undue risk.

But other signers did stay true to their word. Bank of America and Wells Fargo vowed to avoid layoffs; JP Morgan Chase paid cash bonuses to its lower-paid employees; Apple paid employees and contract workers even though its stores were closed; Pepsi boosted employees' sick pay while continuing to pay workers forced to stay home to tend to children (all in Goodman, 2020).

Enter Your Voice

- CSR, cause marketing, new Principles of Corporate Governance—are they expressions of a company's true values or "just more PR"?

- If some companies that practice CSR meet their social responsibilities but others do not, should that call into question the entire practice?

- Consumers want the companies with whom they interact to practice CSR and reward those that do, but there is also evidence that it positively impacts employee morale, leading to higher levels of worker productivity and retention; that it helps attract better job applicants; and that it builds up a stock of goodwill with the media and the public that can help a company weather a later PR crisis (Hill, 2019). So with all these demonstrated benefits, why would a company that has made a public CSR commitment not follow through?

Organization of a Public Relations Operation

Public relations operations come in all sizes. Regardless of size, however, the typical PR firm or department will have these types of positions (but not necessarily these titles):

Executive. This is the chief executive officer who, sometimes with a staff, sometimes alone, sets policy and serves as the spokesperson for the operation.

Account executives. Each account has its own executive who provides advice to the client, defines problems and situations, assesses the needs and demands of the client's publics, recommends a communication plan or campaign, and gathers the PR firm's resources in support of the client.

Creative specialists. These are the writers, graphic designers, artists, video and audio producers, Web designers, and photographers—anybody necessary to meet the communication needs of the client. Increasingly important in the creation and execution of paid media for brand marketing.

Media specialists. Media specialists are aware of the requirements, preferences, limitations, and strengths of the various media used to serve the client. They find the right media for clients' messages.

Larger public relations operations may also have these positions as need demands:

Researcher. The key to two-way public relations communication rests in research—assessing the needs of a client's various publics and the effectiveness of the efforts aimed at them. Polling, one-on-one interviews, and **focus groups**, in which small groups of a targeted public are interviewed, provide the PR operation and its client with feedback.

Government relations specialist. Depending on the client's needs, lobbying or other direct communication with government officials may be necessary.

Financial services specialist. Very specific and sophisticated knowledge of economics, finance, and business or corporate law is required to provide clients with dependable financial public relations.

Trends and Convergence in Public Relations

As you've read throughout this text, digital technologies—the Internet, the Web, and social media—are altering the relationship between media and their audiences. In those instances, what was once primarily one-way communication—content producer to audience member—is increasingly becoming a conversation. Modern public relations, although already a conversation based on the two-way flow of communication, is equally susceptible to digital technologies' transformative influence.

Globalization, Concentration, and Specialization

As they have in the media industries themselves, globalization and concentration have come to public relations in the form of foreign ownership, reach of PR firms' operations into foreign countries, and the collection of several different companies into giant marketing organizations. Dentsu Aegis Network alone has 38,000 employees serving clients in more than 145 countries. New York–based independent Edelman PR has 6,000 employees in 60 offices around the world. Marketing giant Omnicom Group operates in 100 countries, has over 70,000 employees, and serves more than 5,000 clients through the more than 1,500 agencies it controls. It accomplishes this with 3 of the world's top-7-earning PR firms and several specialty PR shops (for example, Brodeur Worldwide, Clark & Weinstock, Gavin Anderson & Company, and Cone). Omnicon is also parent to several national and international advertising agencies, including several of the industry's top global earners (for example, BBDO Worldwide, DDB Worldwide, and Rapp); several media planning and buying companies; event branding and planning companies; outdoor, direct marketing, and online advertising specialty shops; and the global marketing company Diversified Agency Services, which itself is home to more than 200 companies offering services through its 700 offices in 71 countries. Four of the world's 10 largest marketing organizations have ownership outside the United States, as you can see in Figure 11.2.

Another trend in public relations is specialization. We've seen the 14 activities of public relations professionals, but specialization can expand that list. This specialization takes two forms. The first is defined by issue. Environmental public relations is attracting ever-larger numbers of people, both environmentalists and industrialists. E. Bruce Harrison Consulting attracts corporate clients in part because of its reputation as a firm with superior **greenwashing** skills. That is, Harrison is particularly adept at countering the public relations efforts aimed at its clients by environmentalists. Health care and pharmaceuticals has also recently emerged as a significant public relations specialty.

Another, unfortunate in label as well as specialization, are companies that practice **black PR**, firms that "use every tool and take every advantage available in order to

▼ **Figure 11.2** World's 10 Largest Marketing Companies, 2019. *Source: "Agency Companies," (2020).*

Net fees in millions of dollars by rank and company headquarters

WPP (London)
1 — $16.9

Omnicom Group (New York)
2 — $15.0

Publicis Groupe (Paris)
3 — $12.3

Accenture Interactive (New York)
4 — $10.3

Interpublic Group (New York)
5 — $10.2

Dentsu Group (Tokyo)
6 — $9.6

Deloitte Digital (New York)
7 — $7.9

PwC Digital Services (New York)
8 — $6.7

IBM iX (Armonk, NY)
9 — $5.6

Bluefocus Communication (Beijing)
10 — $4.1

change reality according to [their] client's wishes" (Silverman, Lytvynenko, & Kung, 2020). It is the unethical use of mass communication to misinform. Operating worldwide, these firms traffic in fake social media accounts, false narratives, fake fact-checking pages, and counterfeit local news websites (referred to as *pink slime journalism*; Bengani, 2020), all for the right price. Some noted practitioners are the Archimedes Group in Israel, Pragmatico in the Ukraine, KOI in Puerto Rico, and Smaat in Saudi Arabia. Their existence has generated a reckoning in the PR industry as you'll soon read.

Convergence

The second impetus driving specialization has to do with the increasing number of media outlets used in public relations campaigns that rely on new and converging technologies. Online information and advertising and a social media presence are major parts of the total public relations media mix, as are video news releases. In addition, Web publishing has greatly expanded the number and type of available media outlets. All require professionals with specific skills.

The public relations industry has responded to the convergence of traditional media with the Internet in other ways as well. One is the development of **integrated marketing communications (IMC)**. We saw earlier how advertising and PR often overlap, but in IMC, firms actively combine public relations, marketing, advertising, and promotion functions into a more or less seamless communication campaign that is as at home on the Web as it is on the television screen and magazine page. The goal of this integration is to provide the client and agency with greater control over communication (and its interpretation) in an increasingly fragmented but synergized media environment. For example, a common IMC tactic is to employ **viral marketing**, a strategy that relies on targeting specific Internet users with a given communication and relying on them to spread the word through the communication channels with which they are most comfortable. This is IMC, and it is inexpensive and effective.

But the Internet also provides various publics with the means to challenge even the best public relations effort. Tony Juniper of the British environmental group Friends of the Earth calls the Internet "the most potent weapon in the toolbox of resistance." As Peter Verhille of PR giant Entente International explains, "One of the major strengths of pressure groups—in fact the leveling factor in their confrontation with powerful companies—is their ability to exploit the instruments of the telecommunication revolution. Their agile use of global tools such as the Internet reduces the advantages that corporate budgets once provided" (both quotes from Klein, 1999, pp. 395–396).

For example, the Internet is central to United Students Against Sweatshops's ongoing efforts to monitor the child labor, safety, and working conditions of US apparel and shoe manufacturers' overseas operations. USAS used the Internet to build a nationwide network of students that organized protests and boycotts, resulting in several victories—for example, forcing Nike and Reebok to allow workers at one of its Mexican factories to unionize. Public relations agencies and in-house PR departments have responded in a number of ways. One is IMC. Another is the hiring of in-house Web monitors; a third way is the growth of specialty firms such as eWatch, whose function is to alert clients to negative references on the Web and suggest effective countermeasures.

Smartphones, Tablets, and Social Networking Sites

Public relations has "arrived at the moment the 'Empowered Consumer' takes control," announced *Forbes*'s Steven Rosenbaum (2015). This "global citizen" is mobile, hands-on, smart, and committed. Mobile technology and social networking combine to grant publics "free megaphones that carry a customer's complaint around the world," writes *New York Times* technology writer Randall Stross (2011, p. BU3). Yelp, for example, is a website and mobile app for smartphones and tablets that allows the instantaneous posting of complaint or praise to a business's Yelp review page, as well as to the poster's Facebook friends and Twitter followers. In addition, it provides data about local businesses, including health inspection scores, and to foster better relationships between customers and businesses, hosts social events for reviewers, serves as a reservations and food-delivery app, and trains businesses on how to respond to reviewers.

Smartphones and tablets give PR's publics instant, on-the-spot opportunities to pan or praise its clients; that's obvious. But just as important, they give people, especially young people, a greater sense of involvement with a company or organization. "Millennials demand fairness, transparency and clear, consistent rules in every aspect of life," writes Nick Shore, vice president of MTV's research group. He continues, "As consumers they feel comfortable leveraging their power (individually and collectively) to 'level the playing field'" (in Goetzl, 2011).

Trust in Public Relations

We began our discussion of public relations with the industry's self-admission that the profession sometimes bears a negative reputation. Edward Bernays's call for greater sensitivity to the wants and needs of the various publics and Ivy Lee's insistence that public relations be open and honest were the industry's first steps away from its huckster roots. The post–World War II code of ethics and accreditation programs were a second and more important step. Yet Bernays himself was dissatisfied with the profession's progress. The father of public relations died in 1995 at the age of 103. He spent the greater part of his last years demanding that the industry, especially the PRSA, police itself. For example, in 1986, Bernays wrote that in professions such as the law and medicine, unethical practice can result in "disbarment." But PR has no formal standards, making "it possible for anyone, regardless of education or ethics, to use the term 'public relations' to describe his or her function" (p. 11).

Many people in the profession share Bernays's concern, especially because the public's ambivalence toward PR—only 12% of the public trusts public relations and 69% do not—may not be completely misplaced. The industry's own research shows that 28% of PR professionals would "manufacture news" to benefit a client and 54% are willing to "tell white lies" (Loechner, 2018). As a result, Laurence Evans, chief executive of PR firm Reputation Leaders, is adamant about restoring trust in PR, declaring that "distrust is bad for business. High levels of public distrust affect PR businesses, from recruitment to the regulatory environment they inhabit. In addition, PR professionals depend on public credibility to get their clients' message across" (Griggs, 2015).

The industry has responded in a number of ways. One is in its choice of clients. For example, a coalition of several of the world's top 25 PR firms mutually agreed in 2014 to no longer work for clients who would use their services to deny climate change (Goldenberg & Karim, 2014). In 2020, a group of activist executives launched the Clean Creatives campaign to encourage PR professionals to force their companies to drop fossil fuel clients and their industry front groups (Peters, 2020), resulting in firms like global giant Forsman & Bodenfors ceasing work for oil and gas producers, as well as utility companies and their lobbyists (Hsu, 2021). Additionally, many agencies have faced internal revolts over working with anti-immigration organizations, with Edelman going as far as to drop its work for the GEO Group, operators of the migrant children detention centers for the federal government (Hsu, 2019a).

The trust issue has also given greater voice to the **transparentists**. In reaction to industry embarrassment at the discovery that Walmart's and Sony's PR operations were paying authors of fake blogs (**flogs**) to promote their brands (and attack competitors'), the transparentists demanded that the profession "adopt a position of full and total disclosure, driven by the innate openness and accessibility to information available on the Internet." If public relations is to hold consumer (and client) trust, PR executive Eric Webber (2007) argued, its practitioners must recognize that "it's too easy now for journalists, pro and amateur alike, to figure out when companies and their PR people lie, so we'd better tell the truth" (p. 8). As such, this second response to building renewed trust is the call for an industry-wide commitment to the Three Ts: transparency, truthfulness, and timeliness (Bashe, 2020)

A third response, especially as the industry as a whole is diminished by unethical practices like black PR, is to publicly reaffirm, with specifics, the industry's commitment to ethical operation. This was the impetus behind the 2019 establishment of the Helsinki Declaration by the International Communications Consultancy Organisation [sic], an umbrella organization representing PR trade groups around the world. It established 10 principles:

1. To work ethically and in accordance with applicable laws;
2. To observe the highest professional standards in the practice of public relations and communications;

▲ The father of public relations, Edward Bernays, used the last years of his long career and life to campaign for improved industry ethics.

Bettmann/Getty Images

3. To respect the truth, dealing honestly and transparently with employees, colleagues, clients, the media, government, and the public;

4. To protect the privacy rights of clients, organizations, and individuals by safeguarding confidential information;

5. To be mindful of their duty to uphold the reputation of the industry;

6. To be forthcoming about sponsors of causes and interests and never engage in misleading practices such as "astroturfing";

7. To be aware of the power of social media, and use it responsibly;

8. To never engage in the creation of or knowingly circulate fake news;

9. To adhere to their Association's Code of Conduct, be mindful of the Codes of Conduct of other countries, and show professional respect at all times;

10. To take care that their professional duties are conducted without causing offence [sic] on the grounds of gender, ethnicity, origin, religion, disability, or any other form of discrimination (ICCO, 2020).

Still, today in the United States, PR professionals outnumber journalists six to one (Walley-Wiegert, 2021), and because of the economic stress on the traditional press that you've read about throughout this text, they are better paid, better financed, and better equipped. Estimates are that 75% of the news we receive begins as PR (Jansen, 2017). "The widening employment and income disparities have left journalists underpaid, overworked, and increasingly unable to undertake independent, in-depth reporting," write the Center for Public Integrity's Erin Quinn and Chris Young (2015). As a result, many news organizations that once engaged in serious coverage of important topics, such as science and health, no longer have the resources to do so adequately, "and special interests have filled the void." This puts a particularly heavy burden on public trust because, as many PR professionals argue, the only bad public relations effort is one that people recognize as PR. Therefore, the "best" PR is invisible.

Nonetheless, if people *are* lied to by public relations, the cultural implications could not be more profound, especially if the lying is invisible. What becomes of the negotiation function of culture, wherein we debate and discuss our values and interests in the cultural forum, if public relations gives some voices advantages not available to others? One remedy for this potential problem is that consumers must make themselves aware of the sources of information and the process by which it is produced. As we've seen throughout this book, nothing less would be expected of a media-literate person.

DEVELOPING MEDIA LITERACY SKILLS
Recognizing Fake Online Reviews

During the first 7 months of the 2020 coronavirus pandemic lockdown, when people were particularly dependent on online commerce, more than 4 in 10, 42%, of 720 million Amazon reviews were fakes ("Amazon Fake," 2020). Overall, there are more fake online reviews than real ones (Djordjevic, 2020). The problem has grown so bad, that in 2019 the Federal Trade Commission made posting fake review, as well as selling followers and likes, illegal (Hutchinson, 2019).

Although the Internet and social media have empowered customers and clients, that empowerment is only as good as the information on which it is based, especially as industry research indicates that 97% of consumers say that customer reviews influence their purchasing decisions and 84% trust them as much as they trust personal recommendations (Djordjevic, 2020).

So how can media-literate consumers know when a review is authentic or not? There are a number of strategies:

1. *Find more than one source.* There are quite a few review sites, including user forums, product evaluation sites, paid membership sites such as Angie's List, and Amazon's product reviews. If you find only positive reviews, look again somewhere else, and the more reviews the better.

2. *Look for copycat reviews.* Too much common phrasing and too many nearly identical adjectives and adverbs suggest complaint or praise mills.

3. *Avoid all caps reviews.* IF THEY HAVE TO SCREAM THEIR OPINION, IT'S PROBABLY NOT WORTH MUCH.

4. *Look for links.* A reviewer has no need to link you to a product or service. A faker or a plant does.

5. *Look for balanced comments.* Too positive, too good to be true. Too negative, too bad to be true. Reviews that discuss both pros and cons tend to be authentic.

6. *Look for experts.* A review that demonstrates technical knowledge probably comes from someone with some expertise as opposed to a plant.

7. *Look for verifiable information.* Does the review contain data, facts, or details that you can check against other, possibly more objective, sources?

8. *Read professional reviews.* The Internet abounds with interest-specific sites for everything from consumer electronics to kitchen appliances to photography. There is also always *Consumer Reports* if you're willing to pay for a subscription.

9. *Ask questions.* Many review sites, such as Amazon, permit conversations between reviewers and their readers. There are also user forums set up explicitly to foster question asking.

10. *Seek consensus.* Find agreement from professional and nonprofessional reviews alike.

11. If all else fails and you are still unsure, *paste a review link into ReviewMeta or Fakespot* that estimate the percentage of fake reviews there and calculate an adjusted rating.

MEDIA LITERACY CHALLENGE
Ferreting Out Fake Online Reviews

An important component of media literacy is *possessing critical thinking skills that enable a person to develop independent judgments about media content.* Naturally, this encompasses *the ability to recognize when genre conventions are mixed,* in this case, public relations promotional material and authentic online reviews. Challenge your media literacy skills by choosing a product (a juicer or vacuum cleaner, for example) or service (possibly a restaurant or comedy club) and finding as many online reviews as you can. Begin with the target's own website and go from there. What sites did you visit? Were there Yelp reviews? Does your local newspaper, alternative weekly, or area-based magazine offer reviews? Did you visit established review sites such as Amazon or product-specific sites such as CNET for consumer electronics and appliances, Edmunds for cars, or Steve's Digicams for photography equipment?

Having amassed your collection of review sites, apply the various techniques you learned in this chapter to ferret out fake reviews. You can take this challenge as either an opportunity for personal reflection by committing your thoughts to paper, or you can duel with classmates to see who can find the greatest number of fake reviews or possibly the most egregious example of deception for the chosen product or service. Honorable mention goes to the classmate with the greatest number and greatest variety of review sites.

Resources for Review and Discussion

REVIEW POINTS: TYING CONTENT TO LEARNING OUTCOMES

▶ **Recall the history and development of the public relations industry.**
- ☐ The history of public relations can be divided into four stages: early public relations, the propaganda–publicity stage, early two-way communication, and advanced two-way communication.
- ☐ The evolution of public relations has been shaped by advances in technology, the growth of the middle class, growth of organizations, better research tools, and professionalization.

▶ **Describe how the organizational and economic nature of the contemporary public relations industry shapes the messages with which publics interact, especially in an increasingly converged media environment.**
- ☐ Public relations tells an organization's "story" to its publics (communication) and helps shape the organization and the way it performs (management).
- ☐ Advertising executes an organization's communication strategy; public relations provides several important management functions.
- ☐ Firms typically are organized around an executive, account executives, creative specialists, and media specialists. Larger firms typically include research, government relations, and financial service professionals.

▶ **Identify different types of public relations and the different publics each is designed to serve.**
- ☐ The publics served by the industry include employees, stockholders, communities, media, government, investment communities, and customers.
- ☐ Public relations firms provide all or some of these 14 services: community relations, counseling, development and fundraising, employee/member relations, financial relations, government affairs, industry relations, issues management, media relations, marketing communication, minority relations and multicultural affairs, public affairs, special events and public participation, and research.

▶ **Explain the relationship between public relations and its various publics.**
- ☐ Globalization, specialization, and convergence—in the form of video news releases, integrated marketing communications, and viral marketing—are reshaping contemporary PR's relationships with its clients and its publics.
- ☐ Trust in public relations is essential if the industry is to perform its role for its clients and publics.

▶ **Apply key media literacy skills when consuming public relations messages, especially fake online reviews.**
- ☐ Recognizing fake online reviews is difficult, but media-literate viewers look for a variety of clues and seek multiple evaluations from professionals and customers alike.

KEY TERMS

flack, 264

spin, 264

astroturf, 265

mercenary science, 265

pseudo-event, 267

public, 271

video news release (VNR), 273

fixed-fee arrangement, 273

collateral materials, 273

corporate social
    responsibility, 273

cause marketing, 273

lobbying, 273

focus groups, 277

greenwashing, 277

black PR, 277

integrated marketing
    communications (IMC), 278

viral marketing, 278

transparentists, 279

flog, 279

QUESTIONS FOR REVIEW

1. What elements are essential to a good definition of public relations?
2. What are the four stages in the development of the public relations industry?
3. Who were Ivy Lee, George Creel, and Edward Bernays?
4. What is the difference between public relations and advertising?
5. Who are public relations's publics? What are their characteristics?
6. What are the 14 services that public relations firms typically offer?
7. What positions typically exist in a public relations operation?
8. How have new communication technologies influenced the public relations industry?
9. What is integrated marketing communications? What is its goal?
10. What is viral marketing? How does it work?

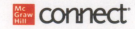

To maximize your study time, check out CONNECT to access the SmartBook study module for this chapter, watch videos, and explore other resources.

QUESTIONS FOR CRITICAL THINKING AND DISCUSSION

1. Are you familiar with Budweiser beer, the brewer/hand sanitizer manufacturer mentioned in the chapter opener? What was your opinion of it before you read of its efforts to help people in need? What is your opinion now? Does corporate social responsibility such as this really work, or do most people see it as self-serving? Do you agree or disagree that a company's pre-crisis reputation can help it weather a crisis should one occur? Why or why not?

2. Have you ever been part of an Internet-fueled movement against the activities of an organization or in support of some good cause? If so, you were engaged in public relations. Measure your experience against the lessons in this chapter. What kinds of public relations activities did you undertake? Who were your publics? Were you successful? Why or why not?

3. Knowing that many of the online reviews you read might be fake or planted, how likely are you to accept without question their veracity or accuracy? If you too readily accept others' evaluations, they are essentially useless. If you too readily reject them, again they hold little value. Online information is only as good and useful as *you* make it. Why or why not might you subject the online reviews you read to the kinds of scrutiny you most likely apply to your everyday interactions with the "real" world?

REFERENCES

1. Adams, P. (2020, June 22). Starbucks' stumble on Black Lives Matter shows rising stakes for brands in addressing race. *Marketing Dive*. Retrieved from https://www.marketingdive.com/news/starbucks-stumble-black-lives-matter-rising-stakes-race/580131/

2. "Agency Companies." (2020, May 11). *Ad Age*, p. 11.

3. "Amazon Fake Reviews Reach Holiday-Season Levels During Pandemic." (2020, October 19). *Ad Age*. Retrieved from https://adage.com/article/digital/amazon-fake-reviews-reach-holiday-season-levels-during-pandemic/2288521

4. Bashe, G. (2020, March 24). Why we need to communicate from the heart now. *PR News*. Retrieved from https://www.prnewsonline.com/heart-emotion-coronavirus-Bashe

5. Bengani, P. (2020, August 4). As election looms, a network of mysterious 'pink slime' local news outlets nearly triples in size. *Columbia Journalism Review*. Retrieved from https://www.cjr.org/analysis/as-election-looms-a-network-of-mysterious-pink-slime-local-news-outlets-nearly-triples-in-size.php

6. Bernays, E. L. (1986). *The later years: Public relations insights, 1956–1988.* Rhinebeck, NY: H&M.

7. Bowen, S. (2017, June 24). Is PR ethical? Only when its practitioners are. *PRWeek*. Retrieved from https://www.prweek.com/article/1400160/pr-ethical-when-its-practitioners

8. Bureau of Labor Statistics. (2021, April 9). *Public relations specialists*. Retrieved from https://www.bls.gov/ooh/media-and-communication/public-relations-specialists.htm

9. Clines, F. X. (2013, September 22). Lobbyists look for a euphemism. *New York Times*, p. SR10.

10. Djordjevic, N. (2020, January 17). 26 mind-boggling online review statistics & facts for 2020. *Website Builder*. Retrieved from https://websitebuilder.org/online-review-statistics/

11. "Drunk Driving." (2020). *National Highway Traffic Safety Administration*. Retrieved from https://www.nhtsa.gov/risky-driving/drunk-driving

12. Edwards, L. (2016). The role of public relations in deliberative systems. *Journal of Communication*, 66, 60–81.

13. Faw, L. (2020, October 6). MDC partners launches earned media analytics platform. *MediaPost*. Retrieved from https://www.mediapost.com/publications/article/356554/mdc-partners-launches-earned-media-analytics-platf.html

14. Forbes, T. (2019, August 20). 181 major companies declare shareholders no longer come first. *MediaPost*. Retrieved from https://www.mediapost.com/publications/article/339486/181-major-companies-declare-shareholders-no-longer.html

15. Goetzl, D. (2011, December 23). MTV Research: It's (video) game time for marketers. *MediaPost*. Retrieved from http://www.mediapost.com/publications/article/164789/mtv-research-its-video-game-time-for-marketers.html

16. Goldenberg, S., & Karim, N. (2014, August 4). World's top PR companies rule out working with climate deniers. *Guardian*. Retrieved from http://www.theguardian.com/environment/2014/aug/04/worlds-top-pr-companies-rule-out-working-with-climate-deniers,

17. Goodman, P. S. (2020, April 14). A vow by big business proves too hard to keep. *New York Times*, p. B1.

18. Gordon, J. S. (1989, October). The public be damned. *American Heritage*. Retrieved from http://www.americanheritage.com/content/%E2%80%9C-public-be-damned%E2%80%9D

19. Griggs, I. (2015, March 19). PR in the dock: Nearly 70 percent of the general public does not trust the industry. *PRWeek*. Retrieved from http://www.prweek.com/article/1339167/pr-dock-nearly-70-per-cent-general-public-does-not-trust-industry

20. Hill, S. (2019, November 27). Business have been practicing social responsibility for decades, but is that really a good thing? *Newsweek*. Retrieved from https://www.newsweek.com/2019/11/29/corporate-social-responsibility-good-bad-1473934.html

21. Hsu, T. (2021, March 30). Ad agencies reassess promoting oil and gas. *New York Times*, p. B1.

22. Hsu, T. (2019a, July 31). Publicity firm drops client tied to migrant detention. *New York Times*, p. B1.

23. Hsu, T. (2019b, July 22). Goal was image rehab, Epstein had media help. *New York Times*, p. B1.

24. Hutchinson, A. (2019, October 23). FTC rules that selling followers and likes is illegal, along with posting fake reviews. *Social Media Today*. Retrieved from https://www.socialmediatoday.com/news/ftc-rules-that-selling-followers-and-likes-is-illegal-along-with-posting-f/565598/

25. International Communications Consultancy Organisation (2020). *The Helsinki Declaration*. Retrieved from https://iccopr.com/helsinki-declaration/

26. Jackson, J., & Hart, P. (2002, March/April). Fear and favor 2001. *Extra!*, pp. 20–27.

27. Jansen, S. C. (2017, July 1). How Putin and Russia use powerful U.S. PR firms to shape American opinion. *Fast Company*. Retrieved from https://www.fastcompany.com/40437170/russia-quiet-public-relations-war

28. Joffe, J. (2019, July 29). NYPD's response to officer suicide crisis sets standard for employee comms. *PR News*. Retrieved from https://www.prnewsonline.com/nypd-response-officer-suicides-employee-comms/

29. Karlis, N. (2018, April 22). How Shannon Watts became the NRA's number one enemy. *Salon*. Retrieved from https://www.salon.com/2018/04/22/how-shannon-watts-became-the-nras-number-one-enemy/

30. Klein, N. (1999). *No logo: Taking aim at the brand bullies*. New York: Picador.

31. Loechner, J. (2018, July 26). Fake news OK for some. *MediaPost*. Retrieved from https://www.mediapost.com/publications/article/322551/fake-news-ok-for-some.html

32. Maguire, C. (2018, April 1). Inside the vast web of PR firms popularizing the Saudi crown prince. *RT.com*. Retrieved from https://www.rt.com/news/422858-saudi-pr-firms-yemen-terrorism/

33. Marantz, A. (2020, October 19). Explicit content. *New Yorker*, pp. 20–27.

34. O'Brien, T. L. (2005, February 13). Spinning frenzy: P.R.'s bad press. *New York Times*, p. B1.

35. Peters, A. (2020, November 25). Inside the campaign to push PR firms to fire fossil fuel clients. *Fast Company*. Retrieved from https://www.fastcompany.com/90579261/inside-the-campaign-to-push-pr-firms-to-fire-fossil-fuel-clients

36. PRSA. (2020). About public relations. *Public Relations Society of America*. Retrieved from https://www.prsa.org/about/all-about-pr

37. "Public Relations Firms Industry in the US—Market Research Report." (2020, June). *IBIS World*. Retrieved from https://www.ibisworld.com/united-states/market-research-reports/public-relations-firms-industry/

38. Quinn, E., & Young, C. (2015, January 15). Who needs lobbyists? See what big business spends to win American minds. *Huffington Post*. Retrieved from http://www.huffingtonpost.com/2015/01/15/big-business-lobbying_n_6476600.html

39. Rittenhouse, L. (2019, October 28). Blurred lines. *Ad Age*, pp. 16–18.

40. Silverman, C., Lytvynenko, J., & Kung, W. (2020, January 6). Disinformation for hire: How a new breed of PR firms is selling lies online. *BuzzFeed*. Retrieved from https://www.buzzfeednews.com/article/craigsilverman/disinformation-for-hire-black-pr-firms

41. Slater, A. (2020, May 27). The pandemic will hasten changes in PR and PR agencies. *PR News*. Retrieved from https://www.prnewsonline.com/changes-coronavirus-pr/

42. Spencer, K. A. (2020, February 2). The art of scientific deception: How corporations use "mercenary science" to evade regulation. *Salon*. Retrieved from https://www.salon.com/2020/02/02/the-art-of-scientific-deception-how-corporations-use-mercenary-science-to-evade-regulation/

43. Stross, R. (2011, May 29). Consumer complaints made easy. Maybe too easy. *New York Times*, p. BU3.

44. Tabuchi, H. (2020, November 12). Global firm casts big oil's messages as grass-roots campaigns. *New York Times*, p. A1.

45. "Top 10 Global PR Agency Ranking 2019." (2020). *PRovoke*. Retrieved from https://www.provokemedia.com/ranking-and-data/global-pr-agency-rankings/2019-pr-agency-rankings/top-10

46. Walley-Wiegert, K. (2021, January 13). How we stop hating PR. *PR Week*. Retrieved from https://www.prweek.com/article/1704403/stop-hating-pr

47. Webber, E. (2007, April 30). No need to bare all: PR should strive for translucence. *Advertising Age*, p. 8.

48. "Year End Report: U.S. 2020." (2021, January). *MRC Data*. Retrieved from https://www.musicbusinessworldwide.com/files/2021/01/MRC_Billboard_YEAR_END_2020_US-Final.pdf

49. Zinn, H. (1995). *A People's History of the United States: 1492–Present*. New York: Harper Perennial.

Cultural Forum Blue Column icon, Media Literacy Red Torch Icon, Using Media Green Gear icon, Developing Media book in starburst icon: ©McGraw Hill

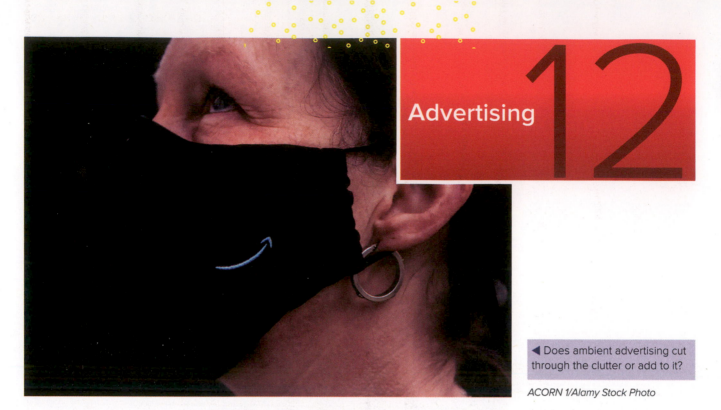

Advertising 12

◀ Does ambient advertising cut through the clutter or add to it?

ACORN 1/Alamy Stock Photo

Learning Objectives

Advertising is everywhere. As it becomes more ubiquitous, we tend to ignore it. But as we tend to ignore it, advertisers find new ways to make it more ubiquitous. As a result, no one is neutral about advertising. We love it or we hate it. Many of us do both. After studying this chapter, you should be able to

▶ Recall the history and development of the advertising industry.

▶ Evaluate contemporary criticisms and defenses of advertising.

▶ Describe how the organizational and economic nature of the contemporary advertising industry shapes the content of advertising, especially in an increasingly converged media environment.

▶ Identify different types of advertising and their goals.

▶ Explain the relationship between advertising content and its consumers.

▶ Apply key media literacy skills when consuming advertising, especially when interpreting intentional imprecision.

1625 ▶ First newsbooks with ads ·······

1735 Ben Franklin sells ad space in *Pennsylvania Gazette*

Hulton Archive/Getty Images

1841 ▶ Palmer begins first ad agency ······ 1800

1869 Ayer begins first full-service ad agency 1850

1880s ▶ Brands appear ·······

Library of Congress

1914 Federal Trade Commission established 1900

1922 First radio commercial

1923 *The Eveready Hour,* first regularly broadcast sponsored series

1936 Consumers Union established

1938 Wheeler-Lea Act

1941 ▶ War Advertising Council (Ad Council) founded·······

1948 Television to the public

Science History Images/Alamy Stock Photo

1957 Packard's *The Hidden Persuaders* 1950

1959 Quiz show scandal

1971 National Advertising Review Board established; TV cigarette commercial ban

1994 First banner ad; spam appears

Fotosearch/Archive Photos/ Getty Images

2008 Internet ad spending exceeds radio's 2000

2009 Internet ad spending exceeds magazines'

2012 ▶ Internet ad spending exceeds all print advertising; tobacco companies ordered to run corrective ads·······

2013 Pay-for-performance deals now in majority of agency–client contracts

2016 Internet ad spending exceeds TV's; online purchases exceed in-store purchases; Trustworthy Accountability Group

2017 Coalition for Better Ads formed

2018 Advertising Protection Bureau established; Facebook and Twitter unveil ad verification protocols

2019 Advertising Research Foundation's Member Code of Conduct

2020 Coronavirus in the US; digital accounts for more than half of US ad spending; global out-of-home ad spending exceeds newspaper ad spending

2021 Ad Council's *It's Up to You* campaign

Scott Dunlap/iStock/Getty Images

Creative Crop/Digital Vision/Getty Images

▲ Even in death, it's difficult to avoid advertising.

Susan Baran

YOUR ROOMMATES, BOTH ADVERTISING MAJORS, CHALLENGE YOU: "We bet you $20 that you can't go all of tomorrow without seeing an ad." You think, "I'll just stay away from radio and television—no problem, considering I stream music and I have tons of homework to do." That leaves newspapers and magazines, but you can avoid their ads simply by not reading either for 24 hours. Online ads? You'll simply stay offline. Facebook and Twitter? You can survive a day friendless and unfollowed. "What about billboards?" you counter.

"We won't count them," your roomies graciously concede, "but everything else is in."

You shake hands and go to bed planning your strategy. This means no cereal in the morning—the Cheerios box has a Chiquita Banana ad on it. There'll be no bus to school. Not only are the insides packed with ads, but a lot of buses are now covered in vinyl wraps that turn them into gigantic rolling commercials. Can't walk either. There are at least two ad kiosks on the way. It'll cost you close to $20 to get an Uber, but this is about winning the bet, not about money. Uber it will be! You sleep well, confident victory will be yours.

The next evening, over pizza, you hand over your $20.

"What was it?," asks one of your friends. "Sneak a peek at TV?"

"No," you say, and then you begin the list: The Uber driver was listening to a country music station that ran near-nonstop commercials for McDonald's breakfast sandwiches. Escaping that, you stepped out of the car onto the sidewalk near campus, which had the stenciled message "From here it looks like you could use some new underwear—Bamboo Lingerie" in water-soluble iridescent red paint. The restrooms on campus have Volkswagen ads pasted on their walls. Your ATM receipt carried an ad for a brokerage firm. You encountered a Domino's Pizza ad on the back of the receipt you got at the grocery store, the kiwi you bought there had a sticker on it reminding you to buy Snapple, and the shopping basket had a realtor's pitch pasted to the side—even the little rubber bar you used to separate your kiwi and mineral water from the groceries of the shopper in front of you had an ad on each of its four sides.

"Easiest $20 we ever made," your roommates gloat.

In this chapter we examine the history of advertising, focusing on its maturation with the coming of industrialization and the Civil War. The development of the advertising agency and the rise of professionalism within its ranks are detailed, as is the impact of magazines, radio, World War II, and television.

We discuss the relationship between consumers and contemporary advertising in terms of how advertising agencies are structured, how various types of advertising are aimed at different audiences, and the trends—converging technologies, audience segmentation, and globalization—that promise to alter those relationships.

We study the controversies that surround the industry. Critics charge that advertising is intrusive (3 out of 4 of us consciously try to avoid advertising; Bretous, 2021), deceptive, inherently unethical when aimed at children, and corrupting of the culture. We look at industry defenses, too.

Finally, in the media literacy skills section, we discuss advertisers' use of intentional imprecision and how to identify and interpret it.

A Short History of Advertising

Your roommates had the advantage. They know that American advertisers and marketers spend hundreds of billions of dollars a year trying to get your attention and influence your decisions. They also know that you typically encounter between 6,000 and 10,000 ads a day (Carr, 2021), unless they're considering marketing messages in general (across all media on all platforms, including when you open the refrigerator and see all those brand labels and when you're passed by all those cars with their manufacturers' logos), in which case you have closer to 4 million daily interactions with brands (Kivijarv, 2018).

There are a lot of ads and a lot of advertisers. Almost everyone in the ad business complains about commercial **clutter**, yet, in the words of *Advertising Age* writer Matthew Creamer (2007), "Like a fly repeatedly bouncing off a closed window, the ad industry is trying to fix the problem by doing more of the same. That is, by creating more ads" (p. 1). Sometimes "more ads" literally means "more ads," for example television networks' increased use of **blinks**, 1- or 2-second commercials interspersed between more traditional commercials (Deighton, 2020). Often "more ads" takes the form of **ambient advertising**, sometimes referred to as **360 marketing**, and by whatever name, they are showing up in some fairly nontraditional settings. This is because advertisers know that "we, the public, are so good at avoiding or ignoring traditional advertising. We are fickle fish, cynical creatures who have already been hooked so many times that the simpler lures no longer work" (Wu, 2016).

▲ Unwilling to waste a good pandemic, Walmart and several of its brand partners teamed up to offer branded COVID-19 vaccine sites. Advertising is indeed everywhere.

David J. Griffin/Icon Sportswire/ Getty Images

There seems to be no limit to how and where we find ads. The rPlate looks like a traditional automobile license plate when a vehicle is moving, but it becomes a digital billboard when it is parked, its message targeted to its location. Google offers technology that lets advertisers subsidize self-driving car passengers' rides in exchange for watching their ads en route, and there is tech that lets those advertisers suggest detours to their businesses midride. During the pandemic, people who made their Burger King orders online received a custom-printed version of that order written on a face mask. When they arrived at the restaurant, no need to talk; and of course they then sported a new mask with a prominent Burger King logo. We find ads in outer space, as NASA astronauts aboard the International Space Station record themselves using Estée Lauder skincare products for use in the company's ad campaigns.

Radio, concert promotion, and outdoor ad company Clear Channel Outdoor maintains a separate Branded Cities division in the business of turning locations—parks, city centers, specific streets—into destinations where people can go for all kinds of activities into which brands can be integrated, a practice called **experiential marketing**, the melding of brands and experiences. Other examples include Busch Beer's pop-up bars in the middle of national forests, Universal Music's chain of music-based experiential destinations, UMUSIC Hotels, and Taco Bell's 4-day takeover of a Palm Springs hotel, transforming it into The Bell: A Taco Bell Hotel & Resort. And of course, folks at these "branded experiences" become commercial creators themselves, brand marketers capturing the goings-on with their phones and sharing them across social media, making even more clutter. We see ads on door hangers, on urinal deodorant cakes, in the mail, behind the batter at a baseball game, and on basketball backboards in city parks. We use digital ad-screen hand driers in public restrooms. It wasn't always like this, but advertising itself has been with us for a long time.

Early Advertising

Babylonian merchants hired barkers to shout out goods and prices at passersby in 3000 B.C.E. The Romans wrote announcements on city walls. This ad was discovered in the ruins of Pompeii:

> The Troop of Gladiators of the Aedil
> Will fight on the 31st of May
> There will be fights with wild animals
> And an Awning to keep off the sun. (Berkman & Gilson, 1987, p. 32)

By the 15th century, ads as we know them now were abundant in Europe. **Siquis**—pinup want ads for all sorts of products and services—were common. Tradespeople promoted themselves with **shopbills**—attractive, artful business cards. Taverners and other merchants were hanging eye-catching signs above their businesses. In 1625 the first **newsbook** containing ads, *The Weekly News*, was printed in England. From the beginning, those who had products and services to offer used advertising.

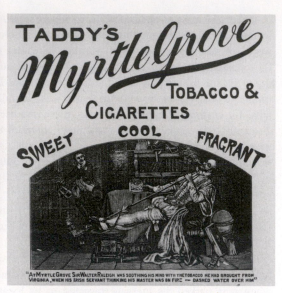

▲ This narrow street in Salzburg, Austria, still exhibits evidence of early European advertising, which often took the form of artistically designed signs announcing the nature of the business below.
Siepmann/imageBROKER/age fotostock

▲ This early-18th-century tobacco label shows that the British had already mastered the use of celebrities in their advertising.
Hulton Archive/Getty Images

Advertising came to the colonies via England. British advertising was already leaning toward exaggeration and hyperbole, but colonial advertising was more straightforward. Ben Franklin sold advertising space in his *Pennsylvania Gazette*, and this 1735 ad is a typical example for the time:

> A Plantation containing 300 acres of good Land, 30 cleared, 10 or 12 Meadow and in good English Grass, a house and barn & c. [creek] lying in Nantmel Township, upon French-Creek, about 30 miles from Philadelphia. Inquire of Simon Meredith now living on the said place. (Sandage, Fryburger, & Rotzoll, 1989, p. 21)

Advertising, however, was a small business before the Civil War. The United States was primarily an agricultural country at that time, with 90% of the population living in self-sufficiency on farms. Advertising was used by local retailers primarily to encourage area residents to come to their businesses. The local newspaper was the major advertising medium.

Industrialization and the Civil War

The Industrial Revolution and the Civil War altered the social and cultural landscape and brought about the expansion of advertising. By the 1840s, the telegraph made communication over long distances possible. Railroads linked cities and states. Huge numbers of immigrants were welcomed to the United States to provide labor for the expanding factories. Manufacturers wanted access to larger markets for their goods. Advertising copywriter Volney B. Palmer recognized in 1841 that merchants needed to reach consumers beyond their local newspaper readership. He contacted several Philadelphia newspapers and agreed to broker the sale of space between them and interested advertisers. Within 4 years Palmer had expanded his business to Boston, and in 1849, he opened a branch in New York. The advertising agency had been invented.

The Civil War sped industrialization. More factories were needed to produce war material, and roads and railroads were expanded to move that material, as well as the troops. As farmworkers went to war or to work in the new factories, more farm machinery was needed to compensate for their departure. That meant that more factories were needed to make more machinery, and the cycle repeated.

By the early 1880s, the telephone and the electric light had been invented. That decade saw numerous innovations in manufacturing as well as an explosion in the type and availability of products. In the year 1880 alone, there were applications for more than 13,000 US copyrights and patents. Over 70,000 miles of new railroad track were laid in the 1880s, linking cities and towns of all sizes. With more producers chasing the growing purchasing power of more consumers, manufacturers were forced to differentiate their products—to literally and figuratively take the pickle out of the barrel and put it in its own recognizable package. And so brands were born: Quaker Oats, Ivory Soap, Royal Baking Powder, and many more. What advertisers now needed was a medium in which to tell people about these brands.

Magazine Advertising

The expansion of the railroads, the rise in literacy, and advantageous postal rates fueled the explosive growth of the popular magazine just before the end of the 19th century. The marriage of magazines and advertising was natural. Cyrus H. K. Curtis, who founded the *Ladies' Home Journal* in 1883, told a group of manufacturers:

> The editor of the *Ladies' Home Journal* thinks we publish it for the benefit of American women. This is an illusion, but a very proper one for him to have. The real reason, the publisher's reason, is to give you who manufacture things American women want, a chance to tell them about your product. (in Sandage et al., 1989, p. 32)

By the turn of the century, magazines were financially supported primarily by their advertisers rather than by their readers, and aspects of advertising we find common today—creativity in look and language, mail-order ads, seasonal ads, and placement of ads in proximity to content of related interest—were already in use (see Chapter 5 for more on magazines).

▲ Magazines provided the first national medium for advertisers. Here is an imaginative ad for the still popular Pears' soap.
Library of Congress, (LC-USZ62-84425)

The Advertising Agency and Professionalism

In the years between the Civil War and World War I, advertising had rapidly become more complex, more creative, and more expensive, and it was conducted on a larger scale. Advertising agencies had to expand their operations to keep up with demand. Where Palmer offered merely to broker the sale of newspaper space, F. Wayland Ayer began his "full service" advertising agency in 1869, N. W. Ayer and Sons. He provided clients with ad campaign planning, created and produced ads with his staff of artists and writers, and placed them in the most appropriate media. At a time when women wanted their future husbands to buy them a washing machine rather than an engagement ring ("money down the drain"), Ayer's work for the De Beers mining company upended that priority, giving the world "A diamond is forever," an ad slogan still used today (Caesar, 2020, p. 34). Several big agencies still operating today started at this time, including J. Walter Thompson, William Esty, and Lord & Thomas.

During this period, three factors combined to motivate the advertising industry to establish professional standards and to regulate itself. First was the reaction of the public and the medical profession to the abuses of patent medicine advertisers. These charlatans used fake claims and medical data in their ads to sell tonics that at best were useless and, at worst, deadly. The second was the critical examination of most of the country's important institutions, led by the muckrakers (see Chapter 5). The third factor was the establishment in 1914 of the Federal Trade Commission (FTC), which had among its duties monitoring and regulating advertising. As a result, a number of leading advertising agencies and publishers mounted a crusade against gross exaggeration, false testimonials, and other misleading forms of advertising. The Audit Bureau of Circulations was established to verify circulation

▲ Reaction to the deception and outright lies of patent medicine advertising—such as this 1880 piece for Pratts Healing Ointment—led to important efforts to professionalize the industry.

Science History Images/Alamy Stock Photo

▲ A 1930s hard-sell ad from Quaker Oats oatmeal. The hard sell made its debut during the Great Depression as advertisers worked to attract the little consumer money that was available.

f8 archive/Alamy Stock Photo

claims. The Advertising Federation of America (now the American Advertising Federation), the American Association of Advertising Agencies, the Association of National Advertisers, and the Outdoor Advertising Association all began operation at this time.

Advertising and Radio

The first radio ad was broadcast on WEAF in 1922 (the cost was $50 for a 10-minute spot). Radio was important to advertising in three major ways. First, although many people both inside and outside government were opposed to commercial support for the new medium, the general public had no great opposition to radio ads. In fact, in the prosperous Roaring Twenties, many welcomed them; advertising seemed a natural way to keep radio "free." Second, advertising agencies virtually took over broadcasting, producing the shows in which their commercials appeared. The ad business became show business. The 1923 variety show *The Eveready Hour*, sponsored by a battery maker, was the first regularly broadcast sponsored series. Ad agency Blackett-Sample-Hummert even developed a new genre for its client Procter & Gamble—the soap opera. Third, money now poured into the industry. That income was used to expand research and marketing on a national scale, allowing advertisers access to sophisticated nationwide consumer and market information for the first time. The wealth that the advertising industry accrued from radio permitted it to survive during the Depression.

The Depression did have its effect on advertising, however. The stock market crashed in 1929, and by 1933 advertising had lost nearly two-thirds of its revenues. Among the responses were the hard sell—making direct claims about why a consumer *needed* a product—and a tendency away from honesty. At the same time, widespread unemployment and poverty bred a powerful consumer movement. The Consumers Union, which still publishes *Consumer Reports*, was founded in 1936 to protect people from unscrupulous manufacturers and advertisers. And in 1938 Congress passed the Wheeler–Lea Act, granting the FTC extended powers to regulate advertising.

World War II

The Second World War, so important in the development of all the mass media, had its impact on advertising, as well. Production of consumer products came to a near halt during the war (1941–1945), and traditional advertising was limited. The advertising industry turned its collective skills toward the war effort, and what product advertising that there was typically adopted a patriotic theme.

In 1941, several national advertising and media associations joined to develop the War Advertising Council. The council used its expertise to promote numerous government programs. Its best-known campaign, however, was on behalf of the sale of war bonds. The largest campaign to date for a single item, the war bond program helped sell 800 million bonds, totaling $45 billion. When the war ended, the group, now called the Advertising Council, directed its efforts toward a host of public service campaigns on behalf of countless nonprofit organizations (see the essay "Effecting Positive Social Change"). Most of us have read or heard, "This message is brought to you by the Ad Council."

The impact of World War II on the size and structure of the advertising industry was significant. A high excess-profits tax was levied on manufacturers' wartime profits that exceeded prewar levels. The goal was to limit war profiteering and ensure that companies did not benefit too greatly from the death and destruction of war. Rather than pay the heavy tariff, manufacturers reduced their profit levels by putting income back into their businesses. Because the lack of raw materials made expansion or recapitalization difficult, many companies invested in corporate image advertising. They may not have had products to sell to the public, but they knew that the war would end someday and that stored-up goodwill would be important. One result, therefore, was an expansion in the number and size of manufacturers' advertising departments and of advertising agencies. A second result was a public primed by that advertising for the return of consumer goods.

◄ Consumer products go to war. Advertisers and manufacturers joined the war effort. This magazine-ad GI is enjoying the comforts of a holiday home—wife, child, and a cold Coke or two. *Fotosearch/Archive Photos/Getty Images*

Advertising and Television

There was no shortage of consumer products when the war ended. The nation's manufacturing capacity had been greatly expanded to meet the needs of war, but afterward, that manufacturing capability was turned toward the production of consumer products for people who found themselves with more leisure time and more money. People were also having more children and, thanks to the GI Bill, were able to think realistically about owning homes. They wanted products to enhance their leisure, please their children, and fill their houses.

Advertising was well positioned to put products and people together, not only because agencies had expanded during the war but also because of television. Radio's formats, stars, and network structure had moved wholesale to the new medium. Television soon became the primary national advertising medium. Advertisers bought $12 million in television time in 1949; two years later they spent $128 million.

USING MEDIA TO MAKE A DIFFERENCE
Effecting Positive Social Change

Advertising can often lead people to do good, and there is no better example of this than the work of the Ad Council, whose mission since 1942 has been to use advertising to bring about beneficial social change. Has it succeeded in making a difference? Who are Smokey Bear, Rosie the Riveter, McGruff the Crime Dog, the Crash Test Dummies, and the Crying Indian (Chief Iron Eyes Cody)? All are creations of the Ad Council. And of course, you are aware that friends don't let friends drive drunk and that love has no labels. You certainly understand when to just say no and that a mind is a terrible thing to waste. You know these things because of Ad Council campaigns.

Can the ability of the Ad Council to make a difference be quantified? Consider the following:

- Applications for mentors rose from 90,000 a year to 620,000 in the first nine months after the start of its campaign for Big Brothers Big Sisters.
- The number of parents willing to talk to a doctor about their child's autism doubled with the introduction in 2019 of the Autism Awareness campaign.
- Thirty thousand American kids eight years old and over have been adopted since the 2004 start of the "AdoptUSKids" campaign. ("A Focus," 2021)

The Ad Council typically has 35 to 40 active public service campaigns running at one time, and it is able to secure about $2 billion a year in donated time and space from 28,000 different media outlets. The Ad Council does not shy away from controversial issues. In the 1970s it took on sexually transmitted infections with its "VD Is for Everyone" campaign, an effort attacked by many religious groups, and many broadcasters refused to air its "Help Stop AIDS. Use a Condom" spots in 1987. Its 2015 "Love Has No Labels" campaign challenged racism, homophobia, and intolerance.

And although wearing face masks during the coronavirus pandemic should never have been controversial, it was. Nonetheless, the Ad Council released its "You Will See Me" campaign to encourage people of color, disproportionately affected by the virus, to wear the potentially life-saving protection. Then, with a full third of Americans saying that they were unwilling to receive the COVID19 vaccine, the Ad Council assembled more than 300 major brands, media companies, community-based organizations, and other organizations into its "It's Up to You" campaign, the largest single public service campaigns in history (Faw, 2021).

The Ad Council is able to make a difference because dozens of ad agencies, big and small, donate their time, energy, and creativity. One ad executive reportedly claimed that he never sees a pitch reel that doesn't contain at least one Ad Council campaign (Crain, 2016, p. 38).

▲ Among the earliest demonstration ads, Timex took many a licking but kept on ticking.
Courtesy of The Advertising Archives

Television commercials, by virtue of the fact that consumers could see and hear the product in action, were different from the advertising of all other media. The ability to demonstrate the product—to do the torture test for Timex watches, to smoothly shave sandpaper with Rapid Shave—led to the **unique selling proposition (USP)**. Once an advertiser discovered a product's USP, it could drive it home in repeated demonstration commercials. Inasmuch as most brands in a given product category are essentially the same—that is, they are **parity products**—advertisers were often forced to create a product's USP. Candy is candy, for example, but M&M's are unique: They melt in your mouth, not in your hand.

Some observers were troubled by this development. Increasingly, products were being sold not by touting their value or quality but by emphasizing their unique selling propositions. Ads were offering little information about the product, yet people were increasing their spending. This led to growing criticism of advertising and its contribution to the consumer culture (more on this controversy later in the chapter). The immediate impact was the creation of an important vehicle of industry self-regulation. In response to mounting criticism in books such as *The Hidden Persuaders* (Packard, 1957) and concern over increasing scrutiny from the FTC, the industry in 1971 established the National Advertising Review Board (NARB) to monitor potentially deceptive advertising. The NARB, the industry's most important self-regulatory body, investigates consumer complaints as well as complaints made by an advertiser's competitors.

Advertising and Its Audiences

The typical individual living in the United States will spend more than 1 year of his or her life just watching television commercials. It is a rare moment when we are not in the audience of some ad or commercial. This is one of the many reasons advertisers have begun to place their messages in many venues beyond the traditional commercial media, as we saw earlier, hoping to draw our attention. We confront so many ads every day that we overlook them, and they become invisible. As a result, many people become aware of advertising only when it somehow offends them.

Criticisms and Defenses of Advertising

Advertising does sometimes offend, and it is often the focus of criticism. However, industry defenders argue the following:

- Advertising supports our economic system; without it, new products could not be introduced and developments in others could not be announced. Competitive advertising of new products and businesses powers the engine of our economy, fostering economic growth and creating jobs in many industries.
- People use advertising to gather information before making buying decisions.
- Ad revenues make possible the "free" mass media we use not only for entertainment but also for the maintenance of our democracy.
- By showing us the bounty of our capitalistic, free enterprise society, advertising increases national productivity (as people work harder to acquire more of these products) and improves the standard of living (as people actually acquire more of these products).

The first defense is a given. Ours is a capitalistic society whose economy depends on the exchange of goods and services. Complaints, then, have less to do with the existence of advertising than with its conduct and content, and they are not new. At the 1941 founding meeting of the Advertising Council, J. Walter Thompson executive James Webb Young argued that such a public service commitment would go far toward improving the public's negative attitude toward his industry. He described it as "a sort of repugnance for the manifestations of advertising—or its banality, its bad taste, its moronic appeals, and its clamor" (quoted in "Story of the Ad Council," 2001).

The second defense assumes that advertising provides information, but much—critics would say most—advertising is devoid of useful information. Rarely does consumer advertising tout the functional benefits of a product or service (**demonstrative advertising**) because marketers know well that rather than products, people buy the lifestyles, experiences, and emotions associated with those products; so **associative advertising**—this product is associated with these lifestyle ideals—dominates.

The third defense assumes that the only way media can exist is through commercial support, but many nations around the world have built fine media systems without heavy advertiser support (see Chapter 15). To critics of advertising, the fourth defense—that people work hard only to acquire more things and that our standard of living is measured by the material things we have—draws an unflattering picture of human nature.

Specific Complaints

Specific complaints about advertising are that it is often intrusive, deceptive, and, in the case of children's advertising, inherently unethical. Advertising is also said to demean or corrupt the culture.

ADVERTISING IS INTRUSIVE Many critics fault advertising for its intrusiveness. Advertising is everywhere; it interferes with and alters our experience. Giant wall advertisements change the look of cities. Ads beamed by laser light onto night skies destroy evening stargazing. School learning aids provided by candy makers asking students to "count the Tootsie Rolls" alter education. Constant commercials diminish the television-viewing experience, so much

Too many ads	48%
Ads are annoying or irrelevant	47%
Ads are too intrusive	44%
Ads contain viruses or bugs	38%
Ads take up too much screen space	38%
Ads slow down page-load times	33%
Ads compromise online privacy	26%
To stop using up data	23%
To stop battery drain	23%
To avoid ad personalization	22%

▲ **Figure 12.1** Top Motivations for Ad Blocking.
Source: Baum, 2019.

so that *fewer* commercials actually produce greater program popularity and advertising effectiveness (Friedman, 2020).

Many Internet users once believed that "targeted advertising would be a blessing for consumers. That vision has soured and even seems like a bad joke given how plagued we are by the rise of stealth advertising, the invasions of privacy, the proliferation of click bait and stalking advertising, and the general degradation of much of the web" (Wu, 2016, p. 21). Today, 90% of people online believe that Internet advertising is obtrusive (Bukhari, 2020). That's why more than 527 million people globally block ads on their mobile devices and 236 million block on their desktops (Slefo, 2020). You can see what prompts people to block ads in Figure 12.1.

Hoping to protect the Internet as an otherwise valuable advertising medium, a collection of the Internet's biggest companies and biggest advertisers formed the Coalition for Better Ads in 2017 to promote industry-wide, self-imposed ad blocking for digital ads considered the most annoying by users—for example, pop-up ads, auto-play ads with sound, flashing animation, and countdown ads that force users to wait to access sites. Many sites also practice **frequency capping**, limiting the number of times a user sees the same commercial message in a given period of time.

ADVERTISING IS DECEPTIVE   Many critics say that much advertising is inherently deceptive in that it implicitly and sometimes explicitly promises to improve people's lives through the consumption or purchase of a sponsor's products. Communication researchers Kathleen Hall Jamieson and Karlyn Campbell (1997) described this as the "If . . . then" strategy: "A beautiful woman uses a certain brand of lipstick in the ad, and men follow her everywhere. Without making the argument explicit, the ad implies that if you use this product you will be beautiful, and if you are beautiful (or use this product), you will be more attractive to men" (p. 242). They called the opposite strategy "If not . . . then not." When Hallmark says, "When you care enough to send the very best," the implication is that when you do not send Hallmark, you simply do not care.

Advertising promises health, long life, sexual success, wealth, companionship, popularity, and acceptance. Industry defenders argue that people understand and accept these as allowable exaggerations, not as deception, yet 84% of Millennials say they do not like traditional advertising, nor do they trust it (Metev, 2020).

ADVERTISING EXPLOITS CHILDREN   Because they now spend more time on video games and streaming television (which, as you've already read, have their own means of advertising to kids), contemporary American children are seeing fewer TV commercials for unhealthy food and soft drinks as well as those for gambling and alcohol than they were just a few years ago. But that new number still exceeds more than 161 a week (Watson, 2019). Countries such as Norway and Sweden, on the other hand, completely ban television ads aimed at kids, as does Chile and the Canadian province of Quebec. Ads and commercialism are increasingly invading schools—90% of American high school students and 70% of American elementary school students attend schools that allow on-campus food advertising, 90% of which is for soda, sports drinks, and other beverages (Morrison, 2014). Companies spend nearly $20 billion a year targeting children, with a quarter of that amount spent touting "mostly unhealthy products." Not only can a typical first grader recognize 200 logos, but kids aged 3 to 5 show recognition rates as high as 92% for 50 different brands in 16 product categories—McDonald's was most recognizable—demonstrating that children as young as 3 can readily recognize the brands they see advertised (Andronikidis & Lambrianidou, 2010; Rettner, 2013).

Critics contend that children are simply not intellectually capable of interpreting the intent of these ads, nor are they able before the age of 7 or 8 to rationally judge the worth of the advertising claims. This makes children's advertising inherently unethical. Television advertising to kids is especially questionable because children consume it in the home—with implicit parental approval, and most often without parental supervision. Ad critics ask the following question: "If parents would never allow living salespeople to enter their homes to sell their children products, why do they allow the most sophisticated salespeople of all to do it every day on home screens they, the parents themselves, provided?"

According to the Campaign for a Commercial-Free Childhood (2021), this early and constant exposure to advertising "designed first-and-foremost to build brand loyalty, sell licensed products, and capture [their] attention for advertisers," produces kids who "interact with peers and adults mostly via commercial technology or screen-based play" and that "play is driven by branded toys, media, and storylines." They cease to be children, but rather "a mass market. . .valued for what they can spend (or nag their parents to spend)" on "toys, clothes, and other products [that] are hypergendered and gender-segregated, because more products means more profits." Inevitably, their "values are shaped by marketing messages."

The particular issue of fast-food and snack advertising to children is the subject of the essay "Kids' Advertising: Is Self-Regulation Enough?"

ADVERTISING DEMEANS AND CORRUPTS CULTURE In our culture, we value beauty, kindness, prestige, family, love, and success. As human beings, we need food, shelter, and the maintenance of the species—in other words, sex. Advertising succeeds by appealing to these values and needs. The basis for this persuasive strategy is the **AIDA approach**—to persuade consumers, advertising must attract *attention*, create *interest*, stimulate *desire*, and promote *action* (Medhora, 2020). According to industry critics, however, problems arise

▲ Advertising in schools and on educational material is now common—and quite controversial. Ads adorn school buses, gymnasiums, report cards, and more.

RJ Sangosti/The Denver Post/Getty Images

CULTURAL FORUM
Kids' Advertising: Is Self-Regulation Enough?

There is no shortage of critics of advertising to children, especially advertising that promotes unhealthy diets. In 1983, companies spent $100 million on child-focused advertising; today they annually spend close to $20 billion, and much of that money is for fast food, cereal, and snacks. Opponents of advertising to kids point to social science evidence demonstrating a strong correlation between exposure to advertising and childhood obesity. One in five children and teens is obese, continuing a generation-long upward trend (Stobbe, 2020), leading the Federal Trade Commission to call childhood obesity the "most serious health crisis facing today's youth." The 65,000-member American Academy of Pediatrics has called for a ban on fast-food commercials on kids' television shows (which the Disney Company agreed in 2012 to do). The US Government Accountability Office has demanded greater FCC oversight of kids' television advertising.

The advertising and fast-food industries have responded with a number of plans that they hope will help protect kids while maintaining their own freedom of expression. Television sponsors have promised to strictly adhere to commercial time limits set by the 1990 Children's Television Act, and the Better Business Bureau's Children's Food and Beverage Advertising Initiative said it would enforce voluntary nutritional standards among its member companies. The National Restaurant Association launched an initiative among its members, including companies such as Burger King and Denny's, to offer and promote healthful kids' meals, a move mirrored by several companies such as Coca-Cola and a number of kid-oriented media outlets, including Cartoon Network. The question in the cultural forum, however, is how to find the correct balance between freedom of commercial speech and the protection of children.

Enter Your Voice

- Should children be considered a special class of people in need of extra protection? Or does the First Amendment outweigh critics' concerns about children's intellectual ability to understand ads?

- Why is the government involved at all? Aren't parents responsible for their children's well-being?

- Why do other developed countries regulate advertising to children and the United States relies primarily on industry self-regulation? What cultural, political, and economic factors might explain the difference?

when important aspects of human existence are reduced to the consumption of brand-name consumer products. Freedom is choosing between a Big Gulp and a canned soda at 7-Eleven. Being a good spouse is as simple as buying your partner a Peloton bike. Success is drinking Cristal. Love is giving your husband a shirt without ring-around-the-collar or your fiancée a diamond worth three months' salary.

Critics argue that ours has become a **consumer culture**—a culture in which personal worth and identity reside not in ourselves but in the products with which we surround ourselves. The consumer culture is corrupting because it imposes new definitions that serve the advertiser and not the culture on traditionally important aspects of our lives. If love, for example, can be bought rather than being something that has to be nurtured, how important can it be? If success is not something an individual values for the personal sense of accomplishment but rather is something chased for the material things associated with it, how does the culture evaluate success? Name the five most successful people you know. How many teachers did you name? How many social workers? How many wealthy or famous people did you name?

Critics further contend that the consumer culture also demeans the individuals who live in it. A common advertising strategy for stimulating desire and suggesting action is to imply that we are inadequate and should not be satisfied with ourselves as we are. We are too fat or too thin, our hair is in need of improvement, our clothes are all wrong, and our spouses don't respect us. Personal improvement is only a purchase away. "To keep their markets growing, companies must keep persuading us that we have unmet needs," explains social critic George Monbiot (2011). "In other words, they must encourage us to become dissatisfied with what we have. To be sexy, beautiful, happy, relaxed, we must buy their products. They shove us on to the hedonic treadmill, on which we must run ever faster to escape a growing sense of inadequacy."

This ad-created consumer culture, according to former Wieden+Kennedy and Martin Agency executive Jelly Helm (2002) (his clients included Nike, Coke, and Microsoft), has produced an America that is "sick. . . . We work too hard so that we can buy things we don't need, made by factory workers who are paid too little, and produced in ways that threaten the very survival of the earth." It has produced an America that "will be remembered as the greatest wealth-producer ever. It will be a culture remembered for its promise and might and its tremendous achievements in technology and health. It also will be remembered as a culture of hedonism to rival any culture that has ever existed." And ranking only 19th in the United Nations's World Happiness Report, it is a culture that increasingly finds little joy in everyday life (Yardney, 2021).

Scope and Nature of the Advertising Industry

The proliferation of the different types of sales pitches described in the opening vignette is the product of an avalanche of advertising. Advertisers are exploring new ways to be seen and heard, to stand out, to be remembered, and to be effective. With so many kinds of commercial messages, the definition of advertising must be very broad. For our purposes, advertising is mediated messages paid for by and identified with a business or institution seeking to increase the likelihood that those who consume those messages will act or think as the advertiser wishes.

The American advertising industry annually spends more than $254 billion to place commercial messages before the public; globally the number is $628 billion ("The Big List," 2019). This amount does not include the billions of dollars spent in the planning, production, and distribution of those ads. An overwhelming proportion of all this activity is conducted through and by advertising agencies.

The Advertising Agency

There are approximately 13,000 ad agencies operating in the United States, employing roughly 189,000 people (Guttmann, 2020a). However, for the first time in history, ad agency employment has declined at the same time ad spending is increasing, primarily because of **programmatic buying**—automated, data-driven buying of online advertising—and the migration of much advertising to companies' in-house agencies. Fewer than 500 agencies annually earn more than $1 million, and while the giant agencies garner most of our attention, there is significant growth among **boutique agencies**, smaller, more personalized, and task-specific ad agencies (for example, dealing primarily with social media marketing) or product-specific agencies (for example, handling only pet supply accounts). Many agencies produce the ads they develop, and virtually all buy time and space in various media for their clients. Production is billed at an agreed-upon price called a **retainer**; placement of advertising in media is compensated through **commissions**, typically 15% of the cost of the time or space. Commissions account for as much as 75% of the income of larger agencies. You can see the ad revenues of the world's top-earning agencies in Figure 12.2.

Ad agencies are usually divided into departments, the number determined by the size and services of the operation. Smaller agencies might contract with outside companies for the services of these typical ad agency departments:

- *Administration* is the agency's management and accounting operations.
- *Account management* is typically handled by an account executive who serves as liaison between agency and client, keeping communication flowing between the two and heading the team of specialists assigned by the agency to the client.
- The *creative department* is where the advertising is developed from idea to ad. It involves copywriting, graphic design, and often the actual production of the piece—for example, radio, television, and Web spots.
- The *media department* makes the decisions about where and when to place ads and then buys the appropriate time or space. (See Figure 12.3 for a projected breakdown of ad spending by major medium in the United States.) The effectiveness of a given placement is judged by its **cost per thousand (CPM)**, the cost of reaching 1,000 audience members. For example, an ad that costs $20,000 to place in a major magazine and is read by 1 million people has a CPM of $20.

Global revenues in billions of dollars by agency rank, parent company, and headquarters

◄ **Figure 12.2** World's Largest Ad Agency Networks, 2018.
Source: "Consolidated Networks," 2019.

1. Accenture Interactive*, Accenture, New York — $8.5
2. PwC Digital Services, PwC, New York — $5.4
3. Deloitte Digital*, Deloitte, New York — $5.3
4. IBM iX, IBM Corp., Armonk, NY — $5.0
5. Cognizant Interactive, Cognizant, New York — $4.9
6. BlueFocus*, BlueFocus Communication Group, Beijing — $3.3
7. McCann Worldgroup, Interpublic, New York — $3.0
8. Wonderman Thompson*, WPP, New York — $2.8
9. Dentsu Aegis Network*, Dentsu, London — $2.7
10. DDB Worldwide, Omnicom, New York — $2.4

*Denotes non-U.S. ownership

▶ **Figure 12.3** Share of US Ad Spending by Medium, 2024 Projection.
Source: "Share," 2020.

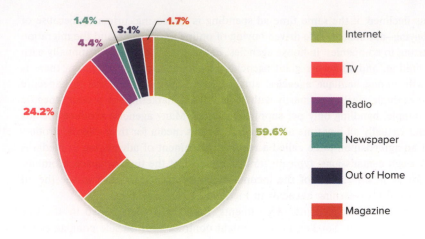

- Internet — 59.6%
- TV — 24.2%
- Radio — 4.4%
- Newspaper — 1.4%
- Out of Home — 3.1%
- Magazine — 1.7%

▼ Through this magazine industrial ad, Spain's Canary Islands hope to entice movie makers from around the world to bring their productions to their shores.

Jordan Dowd

- *Market research* tests product viability in the market, the best venues for commercial messages, the nature and characteristics of potential buyers, and sometimes the effectiveness of the ads.
- Many larger agencies have *public relations departments* as well.

Types of Advertising

The advertising produced and placed by ad agencies can be classified according to the purpose of the advertising and the target market. You may be familiar with the following types of advertising:

Institutional or corporate advertising. Companies do more than just sell products; companies also promote their names and reputations. If a company name inspires confidence, selling its products is easier. Some institutional or corporate advertising promotes only the organization's image, such as "FTD Florists support the US Olympic Team." But some advertising sells the image at the same time it sells the product: "You can be sure if it's Westinghouse."

Trade or professional advertising. Typically found in trade and professional publications, messages aimed at retailers do not necessarily push the product or brand but rather promote product issues of importance to the retailer—volume, marketing support, profit potential, distribution plans, and promotional opportunities.

Retail advertising. A large part of the advertising we see every day focuses on products sold by retailers such as Macy's. Ads are typically local, reaching consumers where they live and shop.

Promotional retail advertising. Typically placed by retailers, promotional advertising focuses not on a product but on a promotion, a special event held by a retailer. "Midnight Madness Sale" and "Back to School Sale" are two promotions that often benefit from heavy advertising, particularly in newspapers and local television.

Industrial advertising. Advertising of products and services directed toward a particular industry is usually found in industry trade publications. For example, *Broadcasting & Cable*, the primary trade magazine for the television industry, runs ads from program syndicators hoping to sell their shows to stations. It also runs ads from transmitter and camera manufacturers.

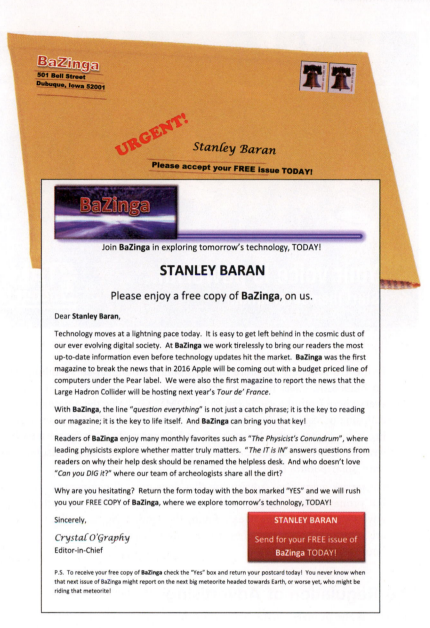

In this direct marketing piece, the advertiser has not only personalized the pitch—Dear Stanley Baran—but has also targeted this consumer's particular interests in the environment and technology based on its knowledge of his magazine subscriptions and Web usage.

(Envelope): Ingram Publishing/SuperStock; (Exploding Star): Brand X/ Superstock; (postage stamps): Mark Steinmetz/McGraw Hill

National consumer advertising. National consumer advertising constitutes the majority of what we see in the media we routinely consume. It is usually product advertising, commissioned by the manufacturer—McDonald's, Honda, Cheerios, Sony, Nike—aimed at potential buyers.

Direct market advertising. Product or service advertising aimed at likely buyers rather than at all consumers is called direct market advertising. These targeted consumers are reached through direct mail, catalogs, and telemarketing (the original addressable technologies). This advertising can be personalized—"Yes, BILL CAMPBELL, you can drive a Jeep Grand Cherokee for less than you think"—and customized. Computer data from credit card and other purchases, zip codes, telephone numbers, and organizational memberships are a few of the ways consumers are identified.

Often thought of as old-fashioned, direct mail generates more response—as much as 10 times more—than digital efforts such as e-mail, social media advertising, and paid search, especially for high-consideration and high-value purchases such as life insurance and real estate (Brooks, 2020).

Out-of-home advertising. As we saw in the opening vignette, advertising is inescapable. One reason is that we are exposed to advertising even when away from home and otherwise not actually engaged in media consumption. Out-of-home advertising, which

▶ Public service advertising
allows advertisers to use their
skills to serve society. Here is a
still from a spot for the National
Sexual Violence Resource Center.

*From "Public Service Announcement
Posters" by the National Sexual
Violence Resource Center, 2012.
Available from http://www.nsvrc.
org. Copyright 2012 by the National
Sexual Violence Resource Center.
Reprinted with permission.*

Your voice is powerful.
Start the conversation.

Sexual violence
thrives in silence
Let's TALK
about it

in the US accounts for more than $8 billion in annual ad spending, can include ads on billboards, street furniture, transit vehicles, and the digital screens we encounter everywhere from the gas pump to the DMV. Globally, the amount is over $40 billion, eclipsing newspaper advertising for the first time in 2020. Much out-of-home ad spending is on digital technologies, such as billboards that can be tailored by time of day, weather, traffic conditions, and even proximity of individual consumers as revealed by their smartphones (Queiroz, 2020).

Public service advertising. Advertising that does not sell commercial products or services but promotes organizations and themes of importance to the public is public service advertising. Ads for the Heart Fund, the United Negro College Fund, and MADD are typical of this form. They are usually carried free of charge by the medium that houses them.

The Regulation of Advertising

The FTC is the primary federal agency for the regulation of advertising. The FCC regulates the commercial practices of the broadcasting industry, and individual states can police deceptive advertising through their own regulatory and criminal bureaucracies. In the deregulation movement of 1980, oversight by the FTC changed from regulating unfair and deceptive advertising to regulating and enforcing *complaints* against deceptive advertising, typically from a brand's competitor.

The FTC has several options for enforcement when it determines that a false-claim complaint against an advertiser is justified. It can issue a **cease-and-desist order** demanding that the practice be stopped. It can impose fines. It can order the creation and distribution of **corrective advertising**—that is, a new set of ads must be produced by the offender that corrects the original misleading effort. For example, in 2012, American tobacco companies were ordered to run corrective ads containing wording such as "Cigarettes cause cancer, lung disease, heart attacks, and premature death."

One of the greatest difficulties for the FTC is finding the line between false or deceptive advertising and **puffery**—that little lie that makes advertising more entertaining than it might otherwise be. "Whiter than white" and "stronger than dirt" are just two examples of puffery. On the assumption that the public does not read commercials literally—we know that Red Bull won't give us wings—the courts and the FTC allow a certain amount of exaggeration. Puffery may be allowed, but many in the ad industry dislike its slippery slope; puffery, says Keller & Heckman's Richard Leighton, means "never having to say you're sorry for untruths or exaggerated claims" (in Greenberg, 2009).

The FTC and courts, however, do recognize that an advertisement can be false in a number of ways. An advertisement is false if it does any one of the following:

- *Lies outright.* During the COVID-19 pandemic, when restaurants were especially dependent on take-out orders, food-delivery company Grubhub was sued for using its advertising "to steer patrons to its partner restaurants by falsely declaring that its competitors are closed or not accepting online orders when they are in fact open for business." In other words, the ads lied. Grubhub agreed to settle out of court (Ellwanger, 2021).

- *Does not tell the whole truth.* Miller Lite's "new taste protector cap" does indeed better preserve the taste of the beer. However, ads touting this feature do not tell the whole truth because Miller Lite's bottle caps are exactly the same as all other bottled beers' and have no taste-protecting characteristics beyond those of ordinary cans and bottles.

- *Lies by implication, using words, design, production device, sound, or a combination of these.* Television commercials for children's toys end with the product shown in actual size against a neutral background (a shot called an **island**). This is required because production techniques such as low camera angles and close-ups can make these toys seem larger or better than they actually are.

  Likewise, a University of Phoenix ad campaign featuring corporations such as Microsoft, AT&T, and the American Red Cross resulted in the online university forgiving $141 million in student debt and refunding another $50 million to students. The implication was that these companies partnered with the school for special job opportunities or to design curriculum. None of the identified companies had any official relationship with the university (Forbes, 2019).

Measuring the Effectiveness of Advertising

It might seem reasonable to judge the effectiveness of an ad campaign by a subsequent increase in sales, but many factors other than advertising influence how well a product fares, including changes in the economy, product quality, breadth of distribution, and competitors' pricing and promotion strategies. Department store magnate John Wanamaker is said to have complained in the late 1880s, "I know that fifty percent of my advertising is wasted. I just don't know which fifty percent." Today's advertisers feel much the same way, and, as you might imagine, they find this a less-than-comforting situation. Agencies, therefore, turn to research to provide greater certainty.

A number of techniques may be used before an ad or ad campaign is released. **Copy testing**—measuring the effectiveness of advertising messages by showing them to consumers—is used for all forms of advertising. It is sometimes conducted with focus groups, collections of people brought together to see the advertising and discuss it with agency and client personnel. Sometimes copy testing employs **consumer juries**. These people, considered to be representative of the target market, review a number of approaches or variations of a campaign or ad. **Forced exposure**, used primarily for television advertising, requires advertisers to bring consumers to a theater or other facility (typically with the promise of a gift or other payment), where they see a television program, complete with the new commercials. People are asked their brand preferences before the show and then after. In this way, the effectiveness of the commercials can be gauged.

Once the campaign or ad is before the public, a number of different tests can be employed to evaluate the effectiveness of the ad. In **recognition tests** people who have seen a given publication are asked, in person or by phone, whether they remember seeing specific ads. In **recall testing,** consumers are asked, again in person or by phone, to identify which print or broadcast ads they most easily remember. This recall can be unaided—that is, the researcher offers no hints ("Have you seen any interesting commercials or ads lately?")—or aided—that is, the researcher identifies a specific class of products ("Have you seen any interesting pizza commercials lately?"). In recall testing, the advertisers assume that an easily recalled ad is an effective ad. **Awareness tests** make this same assumption, but they are not aimed at specific ads. Their goal is to measure the cumulative effect of a campaign in terms of "consumer consciousness" of a product. A likely question in an awareness test, usually made by telephone, is "What brands of laundry detergent can you name?"

What these research techniques lack is the ability to demonstrate the link that is of most interest to the client—did the ad move the consumer to buy the product? The industry hopes that all-important connection can be better discovered using **neuromarketing research**—biometric measures such as brainwaves, facial expressions, eye tracking, sweating, and heart rate monitoring. Neuromarketing research employs electroencephalogram (EEG; measuring electrical activity in the brain in response to ads); functional magnetic resonance imaging (fMRI; tracking blood flow to see what parts of the brain are activated by ads); eye tracking (monitoring the eye's movement across an ad); facial coding (monitoring how expressions change in response to ads); and galvanic skin response (measuring changes in electrical resistance across the skin caused by an emotional reaction to an ad). Because the unconscious accounts for the vast majority of the way peoples' brains process information, these methods tap consumers' unconscious reactions to marketing and advertising.

This research is not without critics, however, who argue that because neuromarketing appeals to the base level of human consciousness, it exploits consumers' nonreasoned, instinctual responses. Such concerns were central to the creation in 2019 of the Advertising Research Foundation's Member Code of Conduct. Still, industry dissatisfaction with more traditional research methods continues to fuel work on neuromarketing research.

Trends and Convergence in Advertising

Today, the advertising industry is facing, as media writer Bob Garfield calls it, "a jarring media universe in which traditional forms of mass entertainment swiftly disappear and advertisers are left in the lurch" (in Klosterman, 2005, p. 63). In fact, although time spent with media is at an all-time high, as you read in Chapter 1, time spent with *ad-supported* media, both in the US and globally, is at an all-time low (Mandese, 2021). As a result, marketers are responding with constant reinvention of the industry's *economics*, *creativity*, and *relationship with consumers*.

New and Converging Technologies

The production of advertising has obviously been altered by computers. Computer graphics, morphing (digitally combining and transforming images), and other special effects are now common in national retail television advertising. And the same technology used to change the ads behind the batter in a televised baseball game is now employed to insert product placements into programs where no placement originally existed.

But it is digital advertising, the convergence of all traditional forms of advertising with new digital technologies, that now attracts the most industry interest. Digital accounted for more than half of all US ad spending for the first time in 2020 (Vranica, 2020). Over the past decade, Internet advertising has surpassed one-by-one traditional media outlets, starting with radio, then magazines and newspapers (Ives, 2012), and then television (Mandese, 2016). You can see the biggest digital ad revenue earners, as well as the dominance of the top two, Google and Facebook, in Figure 12.4.

Web advertising has matured since the first display advertising, or **banners**, static online billboards placed conspicuously somewhere on a Web page, appeared in May 1994 (D'Angelo, 2009). Other forms are **search marketing**, advertising sold next to or in search results produced by users' keyword searches; **rich media**, sophisticated, interactive Web advertising, usually employing sound and video; **lead generation** directing users who've expressed an interest to a brand's sales website; and online classified advertising.

▼ **Figure 12.4** Top 5 US Digital Ad Revenue Earners by Share of Market.
Source: Wagner, 2019.

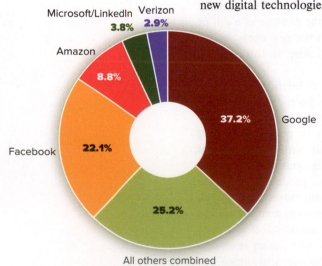

Smartphones, Tablets, and Social Networking Sites

Boosting all forms of digital advertising is their movement to mobile technologies, such as smartphones and tablets, and the expansion of social networking sites. US Internet ad spending may have exceeded $100 billion in 2018, but in 2020, mobile Internet ad spending alone exceeded that amount, accounting for a majority of all online ad spending (Zote, 2020).

Industry data indicate that smartphone and tablet advertising encourages **e-commerce**, the buying of products and services online. In 2016, for the first time, people made more of their purchases online than they did in stores. As online shopping accelerated, so did the use of mobile devices to make purchases. That's the good news for advertisers. The bad news, according to tech writer Sam Biddle (2018), is that research indicates that because our mobile devices know quite a bit about us, including where we are at the moment, who we communicate with, and what we like, "when the data mining curtain is pulled back, we really don't like what we see. There's something unnatural about the kind of targeting that's become routine in the ad world . . . something taboo, a violation of norms we consider inviolable—it's just harder to tell they're being violated online than off." Highly targeted mobile marketing, therefore, walks an even finer personalization versus privacy line than do other forms of online commercial interaction, so much so that 40% of ad professionals personally feel uneasy about their company's use of the data they collect (Mandese, 2020a).

Social networking sites are clearly a boon to advertisers, as they can direct very specific messages to very specific users based on their freely provided information, a fact, as you just read, that does not make everyone happy. Advertisers also take advantage of sites' interactivity, and virtually every company of any size has at the very least a Facebook and Twitter presence. Social media sites take in more than $100 billion in advertising a year in the United States, with Facebook and Twitter commanding most of that revenue. Social media ad spending is expected to grow at an annual rate of over 8% (Zote, 2020).

This promised growth, however, is challenged by the explosion of the Internet's **toxic content**—racist, misogynistic, threatening, or otherwise hateful online content—particularly on social media. The issue is brand safety; companies worry that their ads will show up in or adjacent to content that they would prefer not to be associated with. In 2017, Procter & Gamble slashed its digital ad budget specifically to avoid "spending money on ads that are placed in inappropriate places," according to chief financial officer John Moeller (in Neff, 2017, p. 4). A year later, another major global advertiser, Unilever, promised to do the same. "Fake news, racism, sexism, terrorists spreading messages of hate, toxic content directed at children—parts of the Internet we have ended up with is a million miles from where we thought it would take us," explained chief marketing officer Keith Weed. "It is in the digital media industry's interest to listen and act on this" (in Shaban, 2018).

And the industry did just that. In 2018, Facebook, with a tab labeled "Info and Ads," and Twitter, with its Ads Transparency Center, unveiled protocols designed to verify the legitimacy of advertisers on their sites (Frenkel, 2018). In that same year, the American Association of Advertising Agencies established the Advertiser Protection Bureau to develop a safety metric to rate sites from "most safe" to "least safe," to commit agencies and brands to alerting one another when their ads appeared in unsafe environments, and to flag and investigate risky sites (Faw, 2018).

Still, digital advertising in all its forms sits firmly at the center of the change buffeting today's ad industry because of its low cost (relative to traditional media), great reach, and, most important, interactivity, which gives it an accountability unparalleled in the traditional media.

NEW ECONOMICS Consumers are increasingly dissatisfied with hypercommercialism in other media and the lack of relevancy that much advertising has for them. They are becoming resistant to and resentful of much of the marketing they encounter, as you saw earlier in this chapter. As a result, many advertisers are now less interested in CPM, focusing instead on **return on investment (ROI)**. After all, who cares how many thousands you are reaching if they reject your message? Industry professionals who look at Internet advertising and see that it is ideally suited for increased ROI have begun asking why all media can't offer some of that benefit. "As technology increasingly enables fine targeting and interaction between marketer and consumer," Bob Garfield (2005) argued, "the old measurement and deployment standards are primitive almost to the point of absurdity" (p. 58).

Rather than simple brand exposure, measured by CPM, advertisers have begun to demand accountability. As such, the Web's **performance-based advertising**, for example, provides the ideal. The website carrying the ad gets paid only when the consumer takes some specific action, making a purchase or linking to the sponsor's site. This Web-inspired demand for accountability led to calls for the development of a new measure of the *effectiveness of all advertising*—engagement. Beyond moving advertising dollars to platforms promising greater engagement, demands for accountability can be seen in a number of innovations that threaten the traditional agency–brand relationship described earlier in this chapter: Clients are increasingly demanding from agencies—and receiving—agreements on campaign-specific outcomes and consensus on **accountability metrics**—that is, how the effectiveness of a specific ad or campaign will be judged. Some agencies now offer money-back guarantees if they cannot improve a brand's ROI or **value-compensation programs** in which all or part of the payment of an agency's fees is based on meeting preestablished goals. A majority of all agency–client contracts now contain these pay-for-performance incentives.

One reason there is increased demand for accountability, especially for online advertising, is the growth of programmatic buying. Programmatic buying now accounts for 85% of all digital ad spending, and is expected to grow at a rate of 15% a year (Mandese, 2020b). Because most online advertising is targeted to some degree to specific user demographics (if not specific users), the data used for programmatic buying can be manipulated by the creation of fake impressions or views. These false positives are created primarily by *bots*, in effect "robot" users. Sophisticated bots can take over any computer that's online. They can then simulate human Internet activity (for example, commandeering the mouse and moving the cursor over ads to create exposures). They can even fake search histories and cookies to become demographically appealing to programmatic buying algorithms. This **programmatic ad fraud** costs advertisers more than $44 billion annually, up from $19 billion a year in 2018 ("Estimated Cost," 2021). In response, in 2016 a consortium of advertising industry professional groups created the Trustworthy Accountability Group to identify and eliminate ad fraud, in part through the implementation of an antifraud certification program, TrustX, intended to serve as the industry standard.

Nonetheless, estimates are that half of all online ad clicks are fraudulent, resulting in serious strains on the agency–brand relationship, to the point that 28% of companies say they have lost trust in their ad agencies over the last few years (Mandese, 2019). The solution for many advertisers, then, is to trust themselves; while 90% of brands continue to retain outside ad agencies, 78% of the Association of National Advertisers' 1,100 member companies representing 25,000 brands have established in-house agencies, primarily to handle sponsored content (see Chapter 4), social media advertising, and data/marketing analytics (Whitman, 2019).

NEW CREATIVITY Virtually all advertisers understand that the Internet-fueled fragmentation and democratization of media require a new type of appeal to consumers. If people are increasingly rejecting traditional *mass* media and the commercial messages they carry, the industry must become more creative in its messages and how it gets them to desired consumers. We've already seen many examples—product placement in all media, specially designed and targeted commercials delivered through cable or called up by DVR, online advergames, and the examples of ambient advertising and branded experiences that opened this chapter.

Much of advertising's creative community has learned to distinguish between typical, often unappreciated contextual advertising on the Internet and imaginative video advertising delivered mobile technologies, portable game devices, and online. For example, traditional big-time television advertisers such as BMW, IKEA, Lincoln-Mercury, Hidden Valley Ranch, and Burger King have moved significant amounts of their advertising dollars to the creation and distribution of short online films, sometimes episodic and often featuring well-known actors, to tout their products. Among the best received have been YouTube's thousands of brand channels. The LEGO channel, for example, features reimagining of famous movie plots played out by LEGO characters. A new release of one of these webisodes, available in several different languages, can attract as many as a million views in a single week. The

◀ Moving beyond the TV commercial. A-list Hollywood talent now bring greater creativity to marketing brands. *The Journey*, a mini-movie featuring actor Sylvia Hoeks chasing through the streets of Istanbul and running on Turkish Airlines' website, is directed by Ridley Scott.

Photo 12/Universal Studios/Alamy Stock Photo

GoPro channel offers professionally produced webisodes shot on that video technology, as well as compilations of user-generated videos.

However, not all online brand video lives on YouTube. Fans can find director Ridley Scott's (*Alien, Blade Runner*) *The Journey*, a mini-movie featuring actor Sylvia Hoeks (*The Girl in the Spider's Web*) chasing through the streets of Istanbul, on the website of Turkish Airlines. Cable TV viewers can enjoy *A Recipe for Seduction* on the Lifetime Channel. Starring Mario Lopez as a young Col. Sanders, the 15-minute original movie offers "mystery, suspense, deception, 'fowl' play and—at the heart of it all—love and fried chicken," Kentucky Fried Chicken, of course (Adams, 2020). "You can create content that is compelling, and you don't have to spend money [on TV commercials]. We think this is the direction advertising is headed," says commercial producer Steve Golin. "There is a lot of resistance to watching bread-and-butter advertising" (in Tugend, 2016, p. B3).

NEW RELATIONSHIP WITH CONSUMERS The Internet, as we've seen throughout this text, makes mass communication less of a monologue and more of a conversation. Today's consumers are no longer passive media *receivers*, taking whatever the television networks and movie studios insist they should. Instead, they are empowered media *users*, increasingly free to control and shape the content they receive. In the relative youth of Internet advertising, Ogilvy & Mather's vice chair Steve Hayden predicted that "as all media becomes addressable, all media becomes refusable." He argued that because the consumer now has the power to accept or reject content, an advertiser has to enter into a transaction with him or her, saying, "'I'll give you this content in exchange for your attention,' which has always been the model of mass advertising. But now, I've got to make that deal on a person-to-person basis" (in Kirsner, 2005).

This new **permission marketing**, of necessity, has led to a rethinking of the relationship between advertiser and consumer, one in which they act as partners, sharing information for mutual benefit. The new model of advertising is, as Hayden predicted, a conversation between marketers and **prosumers**, proactive consumers who reject most traditional advertising and use multiple sources—traditional media, the Internet, product-rating magazines, recommendations from friends in the know—not only to research a product but also to negotiate price and other benefits. Economists call this *expressing disapproval*. Consumers now have two choices: *exit* (they simply do not buy the product) or *voice* (they explain exactly why they are dissatisfied and what they'd like instead). Active media users, who are at the same time skilled prosumers who have access to interactive technologies, ensure that voice will, indeed, replace exit as the measure of advertisers' success.

"Me da toda la protección que necesito y además, mi piel se siente increíble".
Natasha Lawson

Dove
advanced care

Dove Advanced Care es más que protección.
9 de cada 10 mujeres coincidieron en que hizo sus axilas suaves y tersas.

▲ The growing American Hispanic population is increasingly targeted by advertisers in both English and Spanish. Here is an example from Dove made by Unilever.
Spencer Grant/PhotoEdit

Increased Audience Segmentation

Advertisers face other challenges as well. As the number of media outlets for advertising grows, and as audiences for traditional media are increasingly fragmented, advertisers have been forced to refine their ability to reach and speak to ever-narrower audience segments. Digital technology facilitates this practice, but segmentation exists apart from the new technologies.

The ethnic composition of the United States is changing, and advertising is keeping pace. African Americans constitute approximately 13% of the total US population; Hispanics, now the nation's largest minority, make up approximately 18% (more than half of both populations is younger than 35); and Asian Americans make up roughly 6% of the population. **Demographic segmentation**—the practice of appealing to audiences defined by varying personal and social characteristics such as race/ethnicity, gender, and economic level—is the ad industry's dominant form of targeting. This is no surprise as African Americans spend $1.4 trillion annually on consumer products. US Hispanics wield $1.7 trillion in purchasing power, and Asian Americans have $1.2 trillion ("Buying Power," 2020).

Obviously, advertisers would be foolish to ignore these consumers, just as they have belatedly come to realize the need to appeal to an oft-neglected group, older Americans, 77% of whom feel they are ignored by advertisers. Despite the fact that many industry insiders consider the 18- to 34-year-old demographic to be their Holy Grail, Americans 50 and older not only represent a third of the population and control $3.2 trillion in consumer spending (Topken, 2019), but they spend more, have greater household income, have amassed more accumulated wealth, and are more likely to own their own homes than those under 50 (Bradbury, 2019).

Psychographics

In addition to demographic segmentation, advertisers are making increased use of **psychographic segmentation**—that is, appealing to consumer groups with similar lifestyles, attitudes, values, and behavior patterns.

Psychographics entered advertising in the 1970s and has received considerable attention as advertisers work to reach increasingly disparate consumers in increasingly segmented media. **VALS**, a psychographic segmentation strategy that classifies consumers according to values and lifestyles, is indicative of this lifestyle segmentation. Developed by SRI Consulting, a California consulting company, VALS II divides consumers into eight VALS segments (Bhasin, 2020). Each segment is characterized by specific values and lifestyles, demographics, and, of greatest importance to advertisers, buying patterns. The segments, including some of their key demographic identifiers, are listed here:

Innovators: Successful, sophisticated, high self-esteem; have abundant resources; are change leaders and receptive to new ideas and technologies.

Thinkers: Motivated by ideas; mature, satisfied, comfortable, reflective; value order, knowledge, and responsibility; well educated, actively seek out information.

Achievers: Have goal-oriented lifestyles and deep commitment to career and family; social lives structured around family, place of worship, and work.

Experiencers: Motivated by self-expression; young and impulsive consumers; quickly become enthusiastic about new possibilities but equally quick to cool; seek variety and excitement.

Believers: Motivated by ideals; conservative, conventional, with concrete beliefs based on traditional, established codes: family, religion, community, and nation.

Strivers: Trendy, fun loving; motivated by achievement; concerned about opinions and approval of others; money defines success, but don't have enough to meet their desires; favor stylish products.

Makers: Motivated by self-expression; express themselves through work/projects; practical; have constructive skills; and value self-sufficiency.

Survivors: Live narrowly focused lives; have few resources; comfortable with the familiar; primarily concerned with safety and security; focus on meeting needs rather than fulfilling desires.

Globalization

As media and national economies have globalized, advertising has adapted. US agencies are increasingly merging with, acquiring, or affiliating with agencies from other parts of the world. Revisit Figure 12.2. You'll see that five of the top 10 global agencies are owned by foreign companies. In addition to the globalization of media and economies, a second force driving this trend is the demographic fact that today 80% of the world's population lives in developing countries, and nearly two-thirds of all the people in the world live in Asia alone. The industry is already putting its clients in touch with these consumers. Foreign ad spending first exceeded US totals in 1980, and ad spending in *developing* nations is growing at a faster rate than it is in the developed world. In fact, the Asia-Pacific region surpassed North America as the world's largest advertising market in 2015, and emerging markets such as the "BRIC" countries (Brazil, Russia, India, and China) routinely post year-to-year rates of growth in advertising that exceed that of the United States. Figure 12.5 shows the growth of global ad spending from 2010 to 2019.

Global ad spending in billions of dollars.

Year	Spending
2010	$399.3
2011	$418.3
2012	$434.0
2013	$451.1
2014	$467.6
2015	$486.2
2016	$503.7
2017	$521.4
2018	$543.7
2019	$563.0

◀ **Figure 12.5** Global Advertising Spending, 2010–2019. *Source: Guttmann, 2020b. Brand X Pictures/PunchStock/Getty Images*

DEVELOPING MEDIA LITERACY SKILLS

Interpreting Intentional Imprecision

Advertisers often use intentional imprecision in words and phrases to say something other than the precise truth, and they do so in all forms of advertising—profit and nonprofit, scrupulously honest and less so. There are three categories of intentional imprecision: unfinished statements, qualifiers, and connotatively loaded words and expressions.

We are all familiar with *unfinished statements*, such as the one for the battery that "lasts twice as long." Others include "You can be sure if it's Westinghouse," "Magnavox gives you more," and "Easy-Off makes oven cleaning easier." A literate advertising consumer should ask, "Twice as long as *what*?" "Of *what* can I be sure?" "Gives me more of *what*?" "Easier than *what*?" *Better, more, stronger, whiter, faster*—all are comparative adjectives whose true purpose is to create a comparison between two or more things. When the other half of the comparison is not identified, intentional imprecision is being used to create the illusion of comparison.

Qualifiers are words that limit a claim. A product "helps" relieve stress, for instance. It may not relieve stress as well as rest and better planning and organization, but once the qualifier "helps" appears, an advertiser is free to make just about any claim for the product because all the ad really says is that it helps, not that it does anything in and of itself. It's the consumer's fault for misreading. A product may "fight" grime, but there is no promise that it will win. In the statement "Texaco's coal gasification process could mean you won't have to worry about how it affects the environment," "could" relieves the advertiser of all responsibility. "Could" does not mean "will." Moreover, the fact that you *could stop worrying about the environment* does not mean the product does not harm the environment—only that you could stop worrying about it.

Some qualifiers are more apparent. "Taxes not included," "limited time only," "only at participating locations," "prices may vary," "some assembly required," "additional charges may apply," and "batteries not included" are qualifiers presented after the primary claims have been made. Often these words are spoken quickly at the end of radio and television commercials, or they appear in small print on the screen or at the bottom of a newspaper or magazine ad.

Other qualifiers are part of the product's advertising slogan. Boodles gin is "the ultra-refined British gin that only the world's costliest methods could produce. Boodles. The world's costliest British gin." After intimating that the costliest methods are somehow necessary to make the best gin, this advertiser qualifies its product as the costliest "British" gin. There may be costlier, and possibly better, Irish, US, Russian, and Canadian gins. Many sugared children's cereals employ the tactic of displaying the cereal on a table with fruit, milk, and toast. The announcer says or the copy reads, "Coco Yummies are *a part of* this complete breakfast"—so is the tablecloth. But the cereal, in and of itself, adds little to the nutritional completeness of the meal. It is "a part of" it.

Advertising is full of words that are *connotatively loaded*. "Best-selling" may say more about a product's advertising and distribution system than its quality. "More of the pain-relieving medicine doctors prescribe most" means aspirin. Cherry-*flavored* products have no cherries in them. On the ecolabeling front, "no additives" and "clean" are meaningless; the manufacturer decides what is and is not an additive and what is or is not clean. "Cruelty free"—again, the company decides. Other connotatively loaded ecolabels are "hypoallergenic" (advertiser-created, scientific-sounding, and meaningless), "fragrance free" (you can't smell the scent because of the chemicals used to hide it), "nontoxic" (won't kill you, but could cause other health problems), and "natural," "science-based," "earth smart," "green," and "nature's friend"—all meaningless. Advertisers want consumers to focus on the connotation, not the actual meaning of these words.

"Yes, it IS a powerful message...
but we're selling dental floss."

◀ We regularly encounter advertising text that is less than informative, although maybe not as bad as that offered by this advertiser.
Wildt, Chris/CartoonStock

Intentional imprecision is puffery. It is not illegal; neither is it sufficiently troubling to the advertising industry to warrant self-regulatory limits. But puffery is neither true nor accurate, and its purpose is to deceive. This means that the responsibility for correctly and accurately reading advertising that is intentionally imprecise rests with the media-literate consumer.

MEDIA LITERACY CHALLENGE
Finding Those Little White Lies

Finding intentional imprecision—those little white lies—in contemporary advertising can be a challenge, but one that a media-literate consumer should welcome. So, record all the commercials during one hour of either TV watching or radio listening. Then go through them carefully and identify ways in which they might have been intentionally imprecise. Did you find any *unfinished statements* such as "It lasts twice as long"? List them and the questions you were left to ponder (Twice as long as what?). How many *qualifiers* such as "helps relieve stress" or "this could be the last car you'll ever own" did you find? Were there examples of *connotatively loaded* words such as "Coco Yummies are part of a complete breakfast"? How easy were these imprecisions to identify? Do you consider them deceptive or harmless? Why? Can you explain your results and your reaction to those results in terms of media literacy skills, such as your *willingness to make an effort to understand ad content and filter out noise* and your *understanding of and respect for the power of commercial messages?*

Resources for Review and Discussion

REVIEW POINTS: TYING CONTENT TO LEARNING OUTCOMES

▶ **Recall the history and development of the advertising industry.**
- Advertising has been a part of commerce for centuries, but it became an industry in its own right with the coming of industrialization and the American Civil War.

▶ **Evaluate contemporary criticisms and defenses of advertising.**
- Advertising suffers from a number of criticisms—it is intrusive, it is deceptive, it exploits children, and it demeans and corrupts culture.
- Advertising is also considered beneficial—it supports our economic system, it provides information to assist buying decisions, it supports our media system, and it improves our standard of living.

▶ **Describe how the organizational and economic nature of the contemporary advertising industry shapes the content of advertising, especially in an increasingly converged media environment.**
- Advertising agencies typically have these departments: administration, account management, creative, media, market research, and public relations.
- There are several ways to measure an ad's effectiveness: copy testing, consumer juries, forced exposure, recognition tests, recall testing, awareness tests, and neuromarketing research.
- The interaction of converging technologies and the changes they drive in how, when, and why people consume them (and the ads they contain) is reshaping the economics and creativity of the advertising industry as well as its relationship with consumers.

- Reshaping of the industry has led to calls for better measures of effectiveness, such as engagement, return on investment (ROI), and performance-based advertising.

▶ **Identify different types of advertising and their goals.**
- There are different types of advertising: institutional or corporate, trade or professional, retail, promotional retail, industrial, national consumer, direct market, out-of-home, and public service.
- Advertisers must deal with consumers increasingly segmented not only by their media choices but also along demographic and psychographic lines.
- As with the media it supports, the advertising industry is increasingly globalized.

▶ **Explain the relationship between advertising content and its consumers.**
- Regulation of advertising content is the responsibility of the Federal Trade Commission, which recognizes that an ad can be false if it lies outright, does not tell the whole truth, or lies by implication. Puffery, the entertaining "little lie," is permissible.
- Largely because of the Internet, people have become proactive consumers who now have two options when dealing with marketers: exit and voice.

▶ **Apply key media literacy skills when consuming advertising, especially when interpreting intentional imprecision.**
- Interpreting advertisers' intentional imprecision—unfinished statements, qualifiers, and connotatively loaded words—tests consumers' media literacy skills.

KEY TERMS

clutter, 289
blinks, 289
ambient advertising, 289
360 marketing, 289
experiential marketing, 289
siquis, 289
shopbills, 289
newsbook, 289
unique selling proposition (USP), 294
parity products, 294
demonstrative advertising, 295
associative advertising, 295
frequency capping, 296
AIDA approach, 297
consumer culture, 298
programmatic buying, 299

boutique agencies, 299
retainer, 299
commissions, 299
cost per thousand (CPM), 299
cease-and-desist order, 302
corrective advertising, 302
puffery, 302
island, 303
copy testing, 303
consumer juries, 303
forced exposure, 303
recognition tests, 303
recall testing, 303
awareness tests, 303
neuromarketing research, 304
banners, 304

search marketing, 304
rich media, 304
lead generation, 304
e-commerce, 305
toxic content, 305
return on investment (ROI), 305
performance-based advertising, 306
engagement, 306
accountability metrics, 306
value-compensation program, 306
programmatic ad fraud, 306
permission marketing, 307
prosumer, 307
demographic segmentation, 308
psychographic segmentation, 308
VALS, 308

QUESTIONS FOR REVIEW

1. Why are we seeing so many ads in so many new and different places?

2. Why do some people consider advertising to children unethical and immoral?

3. In what ways can an ad be false?

4. What are the departments in a typical advertising agency? What does each do?

5. What are the different categories of advertising and the goal of each?

6. What is a cease-and-desist order? Corrective advertising? Puffery?

7. What are copy testing, consumer juries, forced exposure, recognition tests, recall testing, and awareness tests? How do they differ?

8. What is a prosumer? How do prosumers change the relationship between advertisers and their audience?

9. In what two ways do consumers express dissatisfaction? How does this affect contemporary advertising?

10. What are demographic and psychographic segmentation?

To maximize your study time, check out CONNECT to access the SmartBook study module for this chapter, watch videos, and explore other resources.

QUESTIONS FOR CRITICAL THINKING AND DISCUSSION

1. If you owned an advertising agency, would you produce advertising aimed at children? Why or why not?

2. If you were an FTC regulator, to what extent would you allow puffery? Where would you draw the line between deception and puffery? Give examples.

3. What do you think of the exit–voice dichotomy of consumer behavior? Can you relate it to your own use of advertising? If so, how?

REFERENCES

1. Adams, P. (2020, December 7). KFC gets steamy with Lifetime movie starring Mario Lopez as Col. Sanders. *Marketing Dive*. Retrieved from https://www.marketingdive.com/news/kfc-gets-steamy-with-lifetime-movie-starring-mario-lopez-as-col-sanders/591732/

2. Andronikidis, A. I., & Lambrianidou, M. (2010). Children's understanding of television advertising: A grounded theory approach. *Psychology and Marketing, 27*, 299–332.

3. Baum, D. (2019, November 14). Ad blocker trends for 2020. *iMpact*. Retrieved from https://www.impactbnd.com/blog/ad-blocker-trends-for-2019

4. Berkman, H. W., & Gilson, C. (1987). *Advertising: Concepts and strategies*. New York: Random House.

5. Bhasin, H. (2020, January 30). Vals—Values attitude lifestyle. *Marketing91*. Retrieved from https://www.marketing91.com/vals-values-attitude-lifestyle/

6. Biddle, S. (2018, May 9). You can't handle the truth about Facebook ads, new Harvard study shows. *The Intercept*. Retrieved from https://theintercept.com/2018/05/09/facebook-ads-tracking-algorithm/

7. "The Big List." (2019, December 23). *Ad Age market fact pack 2020*, p. 4.

8. Bradbury, M. (2019, July 15). The increasing insanity of marketers' indifference toward older customers. *MediaPost*. Retrieved from https://www.mediapost.com/publications/article/338155/the-increasing-insanity-of-marketers-indifference.html

9. Bretous, M. (2021, April 16). The most annoying types of ads & what to do instead [new data]. *HubSpot*. Retrieved from https://blog.hubspot.com/marketing/worst-ads-poll-survey

10. Brooks, R. (2020, May 21). As purchase habits change, impact of direct mail remains. *MediaPost*. Retrieved from https://www.mediapost.com/publications/article/351712/as-purchase-habits-change-impact-of-direct-mail-r.html

11. Bukhari, T. (2020, January 7). The future of media quality in digital advertising. *The Drum*. Retrieved from https://www.thedrum.com/industryinsights/2020/01/07/the-future-media-quality-digital-advertising

12. "Buying Power: Quick Take." (2020, April 27). *Catalyst*. Retrieved from https://www.catalyst.org/research/buying-power/

13. Caesar, E. (2020, February 3). The rock. *New Yorker*, pp. 32–45.

14. Campaign for a Commercial-Free Childhood. (2021). *Imagine a world where kids can be kids*. Retrieved from https://commercialfreechildhood.org/commercialfree/

15. Carr, S. (2021, February 15). How many ads do we see a day in 2021? *PPC Protect*. Retrieved from https://ppcprotect.com/how-many-ads-do-we-see-a-day/#:~:text=Fast%20forward%20to%202021%2C%20and,10%2C000%20ads%20every%20single%20day.

16. "Consolidated networks." (2019, April 29). *Advertising Age*, p. 24.

17. Crain, R. (2016, November 14). Peggy Conlon on using advertising to shape culture. *Advertising Age*, p. 38.

18. Creamer, M. (2007, April 2). Caught in the clutter crossfire: Your brand. *Advertising Age*, pp. 1, 35.

19. D'Angelo, F. (2009, October 26). Happy birthday, digital advertising! *Advertising Age*. Retrieved from http://adage.com/digitalnext/article?article_id=139964

20. Deighton, K. (2020, March 4). How short can you go? Inside the quest for the two-second ad. *The Drum*. Retrieved from https://www.thedrum.com/news/2020/03/04/how-short-can-you-go-inside-the-quest-the-two-second-ad

21. Ellwanger, S. (2021, April 23). Grubhub agrees to settle false-advertising claims involving non-partners. *MediaPost*. Retrieved from https://www.mediapost.com/publications/article/362627/grubhub-agrees-to-settle-false-advertising-claims.html

22. "Estimated Cost of Digital Ad Fraud Worldwide in 2018 and 2022." (2021, January 14). *Statista*. Retrieved from https://www.statista.com/statistics/677466/digital-ad-fraud-cost/

23. Faw, L. (2021, February 25). Ad Council unites 300+ participants for largest PSA campaign in U.S. history. *MediaPost*. Retrieved from https://www.mediapost.com/publications/article/360892/ad-council-unites-300-participants-for-largest-ps.html

24. Faw, L. (2018, April 10). 4As, agencies form protection bureau. *MediaPost*. Retrieved from https://www.mediapost.com/publications/article/317386/4as-agencies-form-protection-bureau.html

25. "A Focus on Impact." (2021). *Ad Council*. Retrieved from https://www.adcouncil.org/our-impact

26. Forbes, T. (2019, December 11). FTC reaches record deceptive ads settlement with University of Phoenix. *MediaPost*. Retrieved from https://www.mediapost.com/publications/article/344426/ftc-reaches-record-deceptive-ads-settlement-with-u.html

27. Frenkel, S. (2018, June 29). Facebook and Twitter unveil new systems to verify advertisers. *New York Times*, p. B2.

28. Friedman, W. (2020, January 20). Fewer TV ads correlates with program, commercial success. *MediaPost*. Retrieved from https://www.mediapost.com/publications/article/345936/fewer-tv-ads-correlates-with-program-commercial-s.html

29. Garfield, B. (2005, April 4). The chaos scenario. *Advertising Age*, pp. 1, 57–59.

30. Greenberg, K. (2009, March 10). ANA discusses line between falsehood, puffery. *MediaPost*. Retrieved from http://www.mediapost.com/publications/article/101890/

31. Guttmann, A. (2020a, July 22). Advertising agencies in the U.S.—statistics & facts. *Statista*. Retrieved from https://www.statista.com/topics/3945/advertising-agencies/

32. Guttman, A. (2020b, January 8). Global advertising spending from 2010 to 2019. *Statista*. Retrieved from https://www.statista.com/statistics/236943/global-advertising-spending/

33. Helm, J. (2002, March/April). When history looks back. *Adbusters* [no page number].

34. Ives, N. (2012, January 19). Online ad spending to pass print for the first time, forecast says. *Advertising Age*. Retrieved from http://adage.com/article/mediaworks/emarketer-online-ad-spending-pass-print-time/232221/

35. Jamieson, K. H., & Campbell, K. K. (1997). *The interplay of influence: News, advertising, politics, and the mass media*. Belmont, CA: Wadsworth.

36. Kirsner, S. (2005, April). Interview: Steve Hayden, Ogilvy & Mather Worldwide. *Magnosticism*. Retrieved from https://magnostic.wordpress.com/best-of-cmo/interview-steve-hayden-ogilvy-mather-worldwide/

37. Kivijarv, L. (2018, April 2). Time spent with advertising daily. *MediaPost*. Retrieved from https://www.mediapost.com/publications/article/316932/time-spent-with-advertising-daily.html

38. Klosterman, C. (2005, August). What we have here is a failure to communicate. *Esquire*, pp. 62–64.

39. Mandese, J. (2021, January 19). Time spent with ad-supported media hits all-time low, despite gains in total media use. *MediaPost*. Retrieved from https://www.mediapost.com/publications/article/359711/time-spent-with-ad-supported-media-hits-all-time-l.html

40. Mandese, J. (2020a, June 1). Got ethics? *MediaPost*. Retrieved from https://www.mediapost.com/publications/article/352025/got-ethics.html

41. Mandese, J. (2020b, February 24). IAB: Programmatic now 85% of all U.S. digital advertising. *MediaPost*. Retrieved from https://www.mediapost.com/publications/article/347524/iab-programmatic-now-85-of-all-us-digital-adve.html

42. Mandese, J. (2019, March 19). Client-agency trust erodes, ANA unveils new consortium to address it. *MediaPost*. Retrieved from https://www.mediapost.com/publications/article/333380/client-agency-trust-erodes-ana-unveils-new-consor.html

43. Mandese, J. (2016, September 13). "Digital" poised to overtake TV ad spending earlier than expected. *MediaPost*. Retrieved from http://www.mediapost.com/publications/article/284577/digital-poised-to-overtake-tv-ad-spending-earlie.html

44. Medhora, N. (2020, March 6). The AIDA model in marketing. *Kopywriting Kourse*. Retrieved from https://kopywritingkourse.com/aida-formula/

45. Metev, D. (2020, May 19). 37+ stats to be divine at millennial marketing in 2020. *Review42*. Retrieved from https://review42.com/millennial-marketing/

46. Monbiot, G. (2011, October 24). Advertising is a poison that demeans even love—and we're hooked on it. *Guardian*. Retrieved from https://www.theguardian.com/commentisfree/2011/oct/24/advertising-poison-hooked

47. Morrison, M. (2014, February 26). Why proposal to limit school marketing does not worry food and beverage companies. *Advertising Age*. Retrieved from http://adage.com/article/news/regulation-groups-applaud-school-marketing-proposal/291888/

48. Neff, J. (2017). P&G slashes digital—and sales get a boost. *Advertising Age*, p. 4.

49. Packard, V. O. (1957). *The hidden persuaders*. New York: David McKay.

50. Queiroz, R. (2020, January 3). 2020 shocker: outdoor advertising spend will surpass print. *Dash Two*. Retrieved from https://dashtwo.com/blog/outdoor-advertising-shocker-2020/

51. Rettner, R. (2013, November 5). Fast food ads: Kids seeing less on TV, more on social media. *Live Science*. Retrieved from http://www.livescience.com/40969-fast-food-advertising-kids.html

52. Sandage, C. H., Fryburger, V., & Rotzoll, K. (1989). *Advertising theory and practice.* New York: Longman.

53. Shaban, H. (2018, February 12). One of the world's largest advertisers threatens to pull its ads from Facebook and Google over toxic content. *Washington Post.* Retrieved from https://www.washingtonpost.com/news/the-switch/wp/2018/02/12/one-of-the-worlds-largest-advertisers-threatens-to-pull-its-ads-from-facebook-and-google-over-toxic-content/?utm_term=.93b21b24077e

54. "Share of U.S. Ad Spending by Medium, 2012-2024." (2020, July 13). *Ad Age Leading National Advertisers 2020 Fact Pack*, p. 19.

55. Slefo, G. P. (2020, February 6). Mobile blocking in U.S. sees significant growth: Pagefare. *Ad Age.* Retrieved from https://adage.com/article/digital/mobile-ad-blocking-us-sees-significant-growth-pagefair/2234011

56. Stobbe, M. (2020, May 8). Nearly 1 in 5 US kids are obese, according to latest data. *Medical Xpress.* Retrieved from https://medicalxpress.com/news/2020-05-kids-obese-latest.html

57. "The story of the Ad Council." (2001, October 29). *Broadcasting & Cable,* pp. 4–11.

58. Topken, M. (2019, October 1). Not dead yet: Boomers still wield significant buying power. *MediaPost.* Retrieved from https://www.mediapost.com/publications/article/341436/not-dead-yet-boomers-still-wield-significant-buyi.html

59. Tugend, A. (2016, August 15). An action-packed 30-minute commercial. *New York Times*, p. B3.

60. Vranica, S. (2020, December 1). Google, Facebook and Amazon gain as coronavirus reshapes ad spending. *Wall Street Journal.* Retrieved from https://www.wsj.com/articles/google-facebook-and-amazon-gain-as-coronavirus-reshapes-ad-spending-11606831201

61. Wagner, K. (2019, February 20). Digital advertising in the US is finally bigger than print and television. *Recode.* Retrieved from https://www.vox.com/2019/2/20/18232433/digital-advertising-facebook-google-growth-tv-print-emarketer-2019

62. Watson, I. (2019, February 1). The number of harmful ads that kids are exposed to has declined, says ASA. *The Drum.* Retrieved from https://www.thedrum.com/news/2019/02/01/the-number-harmful-ads-kids-are-exposed-has-declined-says-asa

63. Whitman, R. (2019, July 16). ANA highlights in-house agency growth, concerns. *MediaPost.* Retrieved from https://www.mediapost.com/publications/article/338216/ana-highlights-in-house-agency-growth-concerns.html

64. Wu, T. (2016, November 7). Content confusion. *New York Times Review of Books*, p. 21.

65. Yardney, M. (2021, April 19). Revealed: The 20 happiest countries in the world for 2021. *Yahoo!Finance.* Retrieved from https://au.finance.yahoo.com/news/revealed-the-20-happiest-countries-in-the-world-for-2021-210035590.html

66. Zote, J. (2020, January 7). 55 critical social media statistics to fuel your 2020 strategy. *Sprout Social.* Retrieved from https://sproutsocial.com/insights/social-media-statistics/

Cultural Forum Blue Column icon, Media Literacy Red Torch Icon, Using Media Green Gear icon, Developing Media book in starburst icon: ©McGraw Hill

Theories and Effects of Mass Communication 13

◀ There's much more than good comedy happening on *Black-ish*. The potential for powerful—and positive—media effects provides a strong argument for increased media literacy.

ABC/Photofest

Learning Objectives

Media have effects. People may disagree about the extent of that influence, but advertisers would not spend billions of dollars a year to place their messages in the media nor would our Constitution, in the form of the First Amendment, seek to protect the freedoms of the media if media use did not have important consequences. We attempt to understand and explain these effects through mass communication theory. After studying this chapter, you should be able to

▶ Recall the history and development of mass communication theory.

▶ Explain what is meant by theory, why it is important, and how it is used.

▶ Describe influential traditional and contemporary mass communication theories.

▶ Analyze controversial effects issues, such as violence, media's impact on drug and alcohol consumption, and media's contribution to racial and gender stereotyping.

▶ Apply mass communication theory to your own use of media.

~1900–1938 ▶ Common entertainment seen as corrupting influence that undermines the social order ·····

~1930s The Frankfurt School ·····

~1900–1938 Era of mass society theory

Ronald Grant Archive/Alamy Stock Photo

1938 ▶ Welles's *War of the Worlds* ·····

1941 ▶ Office of War Information ·····

1945 Allport and Postman rumor study

1955 Two-step flow ·····

1960 Klapper's *The Effects of Mass Communication*/reinforcement theory

~1938–1960 Era of limited effects theories

Office of War Information Photograph Collection/ Library of Congress

CBS Radio/Photofest

~1960s ▶ Social cognitive theory; symbolic interaction; social construction of reality; British cultural studies ·····

~1970s ▶ Media content seen as having significant cultural influence; cultivation analysis ·····

1972 Agenda setting; Surgeon General's Report on Television and Social Behavior

1975 Uses and gratifications; dependency theory

1988 Hollywood undertakes prime-time activism

~1960–1975 Era of cultural theory

Andrey_Popov/Shutterstock

Ernst Haas/Hulton Archive/Getty Images

2000 National medical and psychological groups' joint report on long-lasting effects of media violence

2002 National Institute of Alcohol Abuse and Alcoholism report on youthful alcohol abuse

2015 ▶ Evidence of a *Will & Grace* effect emerges ·····

~2000s Mediatization theory

2020 Coronavirus in the US; Attorney General Barr warns that media threaten traditional values

1975–today Era of the meaning-making perspective

Allstar Picture Library/NBC/Alamy Stock Photo

"**I KNOW THIS ISN'T LISTED ON THE SYLLABUS.** But let's call it a pop quiz." Your instructor has surprised you.

"Will this count in our final grade?," you ask. You are seared by the professor's stare.

"Put everything away except a piece of paper and a pen."

You do as instructed.

"Number your paper from 1 to 5. Items 1 through 3 are true or false. One. Most people are just looking out for themselves. Two. You can't be too careful in dealing with people. Three. Most people would take advantage of you if they got the chance. Now, number four. How much television do you watch each week?"

Not too tough, you think. You can handle this.

"Finally, number 5. Draw the outline of a dime as close to actual size as possible."

You think you get the point about watching TV and trusting people, but what's with the dime? What does that have to do with mass communication theory?

In this chapter, we examine mass communication theory (and we explain the significance of the dime and the other questions from the quiz). After we define theory and discuss why it is important, we see how the various theories of mass communication that are prevalent today developed. We then study several of the most influential contemporary theories before we discuss the relationship between media literacy and mass communication theory. These theories and their application form the basis of our understanding of how media and culture affect one another.

The Effects Debate

Whether the issue is online hate groups, media violence, junk food advertising and childhood obesity, or a decline in the quality of political discourse, the topic of the effects of mass communication is—and has always been—hotly debated. Later in this chapter, we will take detailed looks at issues surrounding these effects, such as the media's impact on violence, the use of drugs and alcohol, and stereotyping. But before we can examine specific effects issues, we must understand that fundamental disagreement exists about the presence, strength, and operation of these effects. Many people still hold to the position that media have limited or minimal effects. Here are their arguments, accompanied by often-made counterarguments.

1. *Media content has limited impact on audiences because it's only make-believe; people know it isn't real.* The counterarguments: (a) News is not make-believe (at least it's not supposed to be), and we are supposed to take it seriously. (b) Many film and television dramas (for example, *NCIS* and *Fleabag*) are intentionally produced to seem real to viewers, with documentary-like production techniques such as handheld cameras and uneven lighting. (c) Much contemporary television is expressly *real*—reality shows such as *Below Deck* and *Unsolved Mysteries* and talk shows such as *The Steve Wilkos Show* purport to present real people. (d) Advertising is supposed to tell the truth. (e) Before they develop the intellectual and critical capacity to know what is not real, children confront the world in all its splendor and vulgarity through television, what television effects researchers call the **early window**. To kids, what they see is real. (f) To enjoy what we consume, we engage the **willing suspension of disbelief**; that is, we willingly accept as real what is put before us.

2. *Media content has limited impact on audiences because it is only play or just entertainment.* The counterarguments: (a) News is not play or entertainment (at least it's not supposed to be). (b) Even if media content is only play, play is very important to the way we develop our knowledge of ourselves and our world. When we play organized sports, we learn teamwork, cooperation, the value of hard work, obedience to authority, and respect for the rules. Why should play be any less influential if we do it on the Internet or at the movies?

3. *If media have any effects at all, they are not the media's fault; media simply hold a mirror to society and reflect the status quo, showing us and our world as they already are.* The counterargument: Media hold a very selective mirror. The whole world, in all its vastness and complexity, cannot possibly be represented, so media practitioners must make choices. For example, when was the last time you saw a car explode in an accident or

police shoot it out with the bad guys on a city street? The vast majority of police officers will go their entire careers without ever firing their guns on duty and most will make only one felony arrest a year, but our screens are filled with raging gun battles between police and evil-doers and all kinds of criminals routinely thrown into jail (Kaba, 2020). At best, media hold a fun-house mirror to society, distorting what they reflect. Some things are overrepresented, others underrepresented, and still others disappear altogether.

4. *If media have any effect at all, it is only to reinforce preexisting values and beliefs. Family, church, school, and other socializing agents have much more influence.* The counterarguments: (a) The traditional socializing agents have lost much of their power to influence in our complicated and fast-paced world. (b) And *whose* values and beliefs are being reinforced? Not all families, religions, and schools share the same beliefs. (c) Moreover, *reinforcement* is not the same as having no effects. If media can reinforce the good in our culture, media can just as easily reinforce the bad. Is racism eradicated yet? Sexism? Disrespect for others? If our media are doing no more than reinforcing the values and beliefs that already exist, then they are as empty as many critics contend. As former FCC commissioner Nicholas Johnson long argued of television, the real crime is not what the medium is doing *to* us but what it could be doing *for* us, but isn't.

5. *If media have any effects at all, they are only on the unimportant things in our lives, such as fads and fashions.* The counterarguments: (a) Fads and fashions are not unimportant to us. The cars we drive, the clothes we wear, and the way we look help define us; they characterize us to others. In fact, it is media that have helped make fads and fashions central to our self-definition and happiness. Kids don't kill other kids for their $300 basketball shoes because their mothers told them that Air Jordans were cool (Collier, 2020). (b) If media influence only the unimportant things in our lives, why are billions of dollars spent on media efforts to vote for particular political candidates or sway opinion about social issues such as universal health care, nuclear power, and climate change (see Chapter 11)?

▲ The mirror that media hold up to culture is like a fun-house mirror—some things appear bigger than they truly are, some things appear smaller, and some disappear altogether.
Susan Baran

One reason these arguments about media power and effects continue to rage is that people often come to the issues from completely different perspectives. In their most general form, the debates over media influence have been shaped by three closely related dichotomies: micro- versus macro-level effects, administrative versus critical research, and transmissional versus ritual perspective.

Micro- versus Macro-Level Effects

People are concerned about the effects of media. Does television cause violence? Do beer ads cause increased alcohol consumption? Does pornography cause rape? The difficulty here is with the word *cause*. Although there is much scientific evidence that media cause many behaviors, there is also much evidence that they do not.

As long as we debate the effects of media only on individuals, we risk remaining blind to what many believe is media's more powerful influence (both positive and negative) on the way we live. For example, when the shootings at the Littleton, Colorado, Columbine High School in 1999 once again brought public debate on the issue of media effects, USA Network copresident Steve Brenner was forced to defend his industry. "Every American has seen hundreds of films, hundreds of news stories, hundreds of depictions, thousands of cartoons," he said. "Millions don't go out and shoot people" (as quoted in Albiniak, 1999, p. 8).

Who can argue with this? For most people, media have relatively few *direct* effects at the personal or **micro level**. But we live in a culture in which people *have* shot people or are quick to use violence to settle disputes, at least in part because of the cultural messages

► What are the effects of tele-vised violence? The debate swirls as different people mean different things by "effects." This scene is from *S.W.A.T.*
Bill Inoshita/CBS/Getty Images

embedded in our media fare. The less visible, but much more important, impact of media operates at the cultural or **macro level**. Violence on television contributes to the cultural climate in which real-world violence becomes more acceptable. Sure, perhaps none of us have gone out and shot people. But do you have bars on the windows of your home? Are there parts of town where you would rather not walk alone? Do you vote for the "tough on crime" candidate over the "education" candidate?

The micro-level view is that media violence has little impact because although some people may be directly affected, most people are not. The macro-level view is that media violence has a great impact because it influences the cultural climate. Communication researcher Sut Jhally (2013), speaking specifically about violent video games, highlighted the distinction. Violent games, he said, "don't create violent people; what they do is glorify a violent culture and shut down our capacity as a society to imagine anything different. They short-circuit our ability to think in more productive ways about the real violence in our lives. That is their real tragedy."

Administrative versus Critical Research

Administrative research asks questions about the immediate, observable influence of mass communication. Does a commercial campaign sell more cereal? Does a heavy dose of celebrity gossip bring more clicks to an online news site? Did video games inspire the killings of the 20 children and six adults at Sandy Hook Elementary School? For decades the only proof of media effects that science (and therefore the media industries, regulators, and audiences) would accept were those with direct, observable, immediate effects. More than 80 years ago, however, Paul Lazarsfeld (1941), the father of social science research and possibly the most important mass communication researcher of all time, warned of the danger of this narrow view. He believed **critical research**—asking larger questions about what kind of nation we are building, what kind of people we are becoming—would serve our culture better. Writing long before the influence of television and information access through the Internet, he stated:

Today we live in an environment where skyscrapers shoot up and elevateds [commuter trains] disappear overnight; where news comes like shock every few hours; where continually new news programs keep us from ever finding out details of previous news; and where nature is something we drive past in our cars, perceiving a few quickly changing flashes which turn the majesty of a mountain range into the impression of a motion picture. Might it not be that we do not build up experiences the way it was possible decades ago. . . ? (p. 12)

Administrative research concerns itself with direct causes and effects; critical research looks at larger, possibly more significant cultural questions.

Transmissional versus Ritual Perspective

Last is the debate that led Professor James W. Carey to articulate his cultural definition of communication (see Chapter 1). The **transmissional perspective** sees media as senders of information for the purpose of control; that is, media either have effects on our behavior or they do not. The **ritual perspective**, Carey (1975) wrote, views media not as a means of transmitting "messages in space" but as central to "the maintenance of society in time." Mass communication is "not the act of imparting information but the representation of shared beliefs" (p. 6). In other words, the ritual perspective is necessary to understand the *cultural* importance of mass communication.

▲ The transmissional message in this billboard ad is obvious— buy Sea and Ski sun tan lotion. The ritual message communicates many more interesting ideas about the culture.
Ernst Haas/Hulton Archive/Getty Images

Consider an ad for Sea and Ski sun tan lotion. What message is being transmitted? Buy the product, of course. So people either do or do not buy Sea and Ski. The message either controls or does not control people's lotion-buying behavior. That is the transmissional perspective. But what is happening culturally in that ad? What reality about men and women is shared? Can young people really interact without foregrounding sex? Is a woman to be admired only for her looks? What constitutes a good-looking woman? A good-looking man? The ritual perspective illuminates these messages—the culturally important content of the ad.

Defining Mass Communication Theory

Whether you accept the limited effects arguments or their counterarguments, all the positions you just read are based on one or more **mass communication theories**, explanations and predictions of social phenomena that attempt to relate mass communication to various aspects of our personal and cultural lives or social systems. Your responses to the five quiz questions that opened the chapter, for example, can be explained (possibly even predicted) by different mass communication theories.

The first four items are a reflection of **cultivation analysis**—the idea that people's ideas of themselves, their world, and their place in it are shaped and maintained primarily through television. People's responses to the three true or false items can be fairly accurately predicted by the amount of viewing they do (question 4). The more people watch, the more likely they are to respond "true" to these unflattering statements that others are generally selfish, untrustworthy, and out to get you.

The solution to the dime-drawing task is predicted by **attitude change theory**, which explains how people's attitudes are formed, shaped, and changed and how those attitudes influence behavior. Almost everyone draws the dime too small. Because a dime is an inconsequential coin (it won't even buy you a piece of penny candy!), we perceive it as smaller than it really is, and our perceptions guide our behavior. Even though every one of us has held a real-world dime in our hands, our attitudes toward that coin shape our behavior regarding it. Mass communication theorists study media's contribution to the formation of our attitudes on a wide array of issues of far greater importance than the size of a dime.

To understand mass communication theory, you should recognize these important ideas:

1. *There is no one mass communication theory.* There is a theory, for example, that describes something as grand as how we give meaning to cultural symbols and how these symbols influence our behavior (symbolic interaction), and there is a theory that explains something as individual as what a person chooses to do with media (the uses and gratifications approach). Mass communication theorists have produced a number of **middle-range theories** that explain or predict specific, limited aspects of the mass communication process (Merton, 1967). You can see an overview of some historically important mass communication theories later on in Table 13.1.

2. *Mass communication theories are often borrowed from other fields of social science.* Attitude change theory (the dime question), for example, comes from psychology. Mass communication theorists adapt these borrowed theories to questions and issues in communication. People's behavior with regard to issues more important than the size of a dime—democracy, ethnicity, government, and gender roles, for example—is influenced by the attitudes and perceptions presented by our mass media.

3. *Mass communication theories are human constructions.* People create them, and therefore their creation is influenced by human biases—the times in which we live, the position we occupy in the mass communication process, and a host of other factors. Broadcast industry researchers, for example, have developed somewhat different theories to explain how violence is learned from television than have university researchers.

4. *Mass communication theories are dynamic* because theories are human constructions and the environments in which they are created constantly change; they undergo frequent recasting, acceptance, and rejection. For example, theories that were developed before television and social networking sites became commonplace have to be reexamined and sometimes discarded in the face of these new technologies.

A Short History of Mass Communication Theory

The dynamic nature of mass communication theory can be seen in its history. All disciplines' bodies of knowledge pass through various stages of development. Hypotheses are put forth, tested, and supported or rejected. Eventually a consensus develops that shapes a discipline's central ideas and, as such, the kinds of questions it asks and the answers it seeks—and expects. However, over time some answers come to challenge those expectations. So new questions have to be asked, new answers are produced, and, eventually, a new consensus emerges. Mass communication theory is particularly open to evolving ideas for three reasons:

- *Advances in technology or the introduction of new media* fundamentally alter the nature of mass communication. The coming of radio and movies, for example, forced rethinking of theories based on a print-oriented mass communication system.

- *Calls for control or regulation* of these new technologies require, especially in a democracy such as ours, an objective, science-based justification.

- As a country committed to protecting *democracy and cultural pluralism*, we ask how each new technology or medium can foster our pursuit of that goal.

The evolution in thinking that resulted from these factors has produced four major eras of mass communication theory: the era of mass society theory, the era of the limited effects perspective, the cultural theory era, and the era of the meaning-making perspective. The first two may be considered early eras; the latter two best represent contemporary thinking.

The Era of Mass Society Theory

As we've seen throughout this text, several important mass media appeared or flourished during the second half of the 19th century and the first decades of the 20th century. Mass circulation newspapers and magazines, movies, talkies, and radio all came to prominence at this time. This was also a time of profound change in the nature of US society. Industrialization and urbanization spread, African Americans and poor southern whites streamed northward, and immigrants landed on both coasts in search of opportunity and dignity. People in traditional seats of power—the clergy, politicians, and educators—feared a disruption in the status quo. The country's peaceful rural nature was beginning to slip further into history.

In its place was a cauldron of new and different people with new and different habits, all crammed into rapidly expanding cities. Crime grew, as did social and political unrest. Many cultural, political, educational, and religious leaders thought the United States was becoming too pluralistic. They charged that the mass media catered to the low tastes and limited reading and language abilities of these newcomers by featuring simple and sensation-alistic content. Media, they proclaimed, needed to be controlled to protect traditional values.

The successful use of propaganda by totalitarian governments in Europe, especially Germany's National Socialist Party (the Nazis), provided further evidence of the overwhelming power of media. Social and cultural elites therefore called for greater control of the media to prevent similar abuses at home.

The resulting theory was **mass society theory**—the idea that the media are corrupting influences that undermine the social order and that "average" people are defenseless against their influence. To mass society theorists, "average" people were all those who did not hold their (the theorists') superior tastes and values.

Walter Lippmann, a nationally syndicated columnist for *The New York Times* and one of the country's most important social commentators, was indicatively skeptical of average people's ability to make sense of the confusing world around them. Political essayist Eric Alterman explained and summarized Lippmann's thinking as expressed in the legendary social critic's influential 1922 book *Public Opinion*. He said that Lippman saw the average American as akin to a spectator at an event, sitting in the back row: "He lives in a world he cannot see, does not understand and is unable to direct." American journalism, with its devotion to profit and sensationalism, only compounded the problem; therefore, politics and governing were best left to a "specialized class of men," those sitting closer to the action. Alterman (2008) summarized Lippmann's argument: "No one expects a steel-worker to understand physics, so why should he be expected to understand politics?" (p. 10).

The fundamental assumption of this thinking is sometimes expressed in the **hypodermic needle theory** or the **magic bullet theory**. The symbolism of both is apparent—media are a dangerous drug or a killing force against which "average" people are defenseless.

Mass society theory is an example of a **grand theory**, one designed to describe and explain all aspects of a given phenomenon. But clearly not all average people were mindlessly influenced by the evil mass media. People made consumption choices. They interpreted media content, often in personally important ways. Media did have effects, often good ones. No single theory could encompass the wide variety of media effects claimed by mass society theorists, and the theory eventually collapsed under its own weight.

◄ Agnes Ayers recoils in Rudolph Valentino's arms in the 1921 movie *The Sheik.* Mass society theorists saw such common entertainment fare as debasing the culture through its direct and negative effects on helpless audience members.
Ronald Grant Archive/Alamy Stock Photo

The Emergence of the Limited Effects Perspective

Shifts in a discipline's dominant thinking usually happen over a period of time, and this is true of the move away from mass society theory. However, media researchers often mark the emergence of the limited effects perspective on mass communication as occurring on the eve of Halloween 1938. On that night, actor and director Orson Welles broadcast his dramatized version of the H. G. Wells science fiction classic *The War of the Worlds* on the CBS radio network. Produced in what we would now call docudrama style, the realistic radio play in which Earth came under deadly Martian attack frightened thousands. People fled their homes in panic. Elite media critics argued this was proof of mass society theory, pointing to a radio play with the power to send people into the hills to hide from aliens.

Research by scientists from Princeton University demonstrated that, in fact, 1 million people had been frightened enough by the broadcast to take some action, but the other 5 million people who heard the show had not, mass society theory notwithstanding. More important, however, these scientists determined that different factors led some people to be influenced and others not (Lowery & DeFleur, 1995).

The researchers had the benefit of advances in survey research, polling, and other social scientific methods developed and championed by Austrian immigrant Paul Lazarsfeld. They were, in fact, his students and colleagues. Lazarsfeld (1941) argued that mere speculation about the impact of media was insufficient to explain the complex interactions that mass communication comprised. Instead, well-designed, sophisticated studies of media and audiences would produce more valuable knowledge.

Using Lazarsfeld's work, researchers identified those individual and social characteristics that led audience members to be influenced (or not) by media. What emerged was the view that media influence was limited by *individual differences* (for example, in intelligence and education), *social categories* (such as religious and political affiliation), and *personal relationships* (such as friends and family). The theories that emerged from this era of the first systematic and scientific study of media effects, taken together, are now called the **limited effects theory**.

TWO-STEP FLOW THEORY Lazarsfeld's own **two-step flow theory** of mass media and personal influence is a well-known product of this era and an example of a limited effects theory (Katz & Lazarsfeld, 1955). His research on the 1940 presidential election indicated that media influence on people's voting behavior was limited by **opinion leaders**—people who

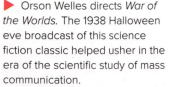

▶ Orson Welles directs *War of the Worlds.* The 1938 Halloween eve broadcast of this science fiction classic helped usher in the era of the scientific study of mass communication.

CBS Radio/Photofest

Step 1

Step 2

Books
Magazines
Newspapers
Books
Magazines
Radio
Movies
MASS
MEDIA
Movies
Newspapers
Radio

Media
messages
to opinion
leaders

Messages passed on to opinion followers

◀ **Figure 13.1** Model of Lazarsfeld's Two-Step Flow of Media Influence. Media influence passes from the mass media through opinion leaders to opinion followers. Because leaders and followers share common personal and social characteristics, the potential influence of media is limited by their shared assumptions, beliefs, and attitudes.

Source: Free Press

initially consumed media content on topics of particular interest to them, interpreted it in light of their own values and beliefs, and then passed it on to **opinion followers**, people like them who had less frequent contact with media (Figure 13.1).

Two-step flow theory, naturally, has been rethought since Lazarsfeld's time. For example, television and the Internet have given everyone a more or less equal opportunity to consume media content firsthand. There is no doubt that opinion leaders still exist—we often ask friends what they've read or heard about a certain movie, video game, or band for example—but because we now have ubiquitous and universal access to information on our own if we wish, their centrality to the mass communication process has diminished.

ATTITUDE CHANGE THEORY During and after World War II, the limited effects perspective and several theories it supported became more fully entrenched, controlling research and thinking about media until well into the 1960s. As was the case with virtually all the media and support industries we've studied, the war itself was crucial to the development of mass communication theory during this era.

Memories of World War I were still very much alive, and not all Americans were enthused about entering another seemingly remote world conflict. Those who joined or were drafted into the armed forces apparently knew very little about their comrades-in-arms from different regions of the country and from different backgrounds. German propaganda seemed to prove the view of mass society theorists who claimed that mass media wielded remarkable power. The Office of War Information (OWI), therefore, set out to change public opinion about the wisdom of entering the war, to educate those in the military about their fellow soldiers and sailors, and to counter Nazi propaganda. Speeches and lectures failed. So, too, did informational pamphlets. The OWI then turned to filmmakers such as Frank Capra and radio personalities such as Kate Smith for their audience appeal and looked to social scientists to measure the effectiveness of these new media campaigns.

The army established the Experimental Section inside its Information and Education Division, staffing it with psychologists who were experts on issues of attitude change. Led by Carl Hovland, these researchers tested the effectiveness of the government's mass communication campaigns. Continuing its work at Yale University after the war, this group produced some of our most influential communication research. Their work led to development of *attitude change theory*, which explains how people's attitudes are formed, shaped, and changed through communication and how those attitudes influence behavior (Hovland, Lumsdaine, & Sheffield, 1949).

Among the most important attitude change theories are the related ideas of dissonance and selective processes. **Dissonance theory** argues that when confronted by new or conflicting information, people experience a kind of mental discomfort, a dissonance. As a result, they consciously and subconsciously work to limit or reduce that discomfort through three interrelated **selective processes**. These processes help us "select" what information we consume, remember, and interpret in personally important and idiosyncratic ways:

- **Selective exposure** (or **selective attention**) is the process by which people expose themselves to or attend to only those messages consistent with their preexisting attitudes and beliefs. How often do you read the work of an online pundit who occupies a different place on the political spectrum from you? You're more likely to read those pieces that confirm what you already believe. It's quite common for someone who buys a new car, electronic device, or other expensive item to suddenly start to see more of that product's advertising. You've spent a lot of money; that creates dissonance. The ads confirm the wisdom of your decision, reducing dissonance.

- **Selective retention** assumes that people remember best and longest those messages that are consistent with their preexisting attitudes and beliefs. Television viewers, for example, remember much more detail from the convention broadcasts of the political party to which they are philosophically closer than they do the broadcasts of competing parties.

- **Selective perception** predicts that people will interpret messages in a manner consistent with their preexisting attitudes and beliefs. When your favorite politicians change positions on an issue, they're evolving and heeding the public's will. When those you don't like do so, they're flip-flopping and have no convictions. Selective perception explains why, even though they view the same Fox News, 77% of American liberals *distrust* that cable channel and 65% of the country's conservatives *trust* that very same outlet (Jurkowitz, Mitchell, Shearer, & Walker, 2020).

The dominant thinking at the time of the development of dissonance theory was limited effects theory; thus, the selective processes were seen as limiting media impact because content is selectively filtered to produce as little attitude change as possible. Contemporary mass communication theorists accept the power of the selective processes to limit the influence of media content when it is primarily informational. However, because so much content is symbolic rather than informational, other theorists see the selective processes as relatively unimportant when it comes to explaining media's contribution to some important cultural effects. You will recognize these differing perspectives on media's power in the distinction made earlier in this chapter between the transmissional and ritual views of mass communication.

Here is an example of the distinction between informational and symbolic content and the way they relate to the selective processes. Few television stations would broadcast lecture programs by people who openly espouse the racist opinion that people of color are genetically more prone to commit crime. If we were to see such a show, however, the selective processes would likely kick in. We would change to another channel (selective exposure). If we did watch, we would interpret the ideas as racist or sick (selective perception); later we would quickly forget the speaker's arguments (selective retention).

Fortunately, the media rarely offer such overtly racist messages. Unfortunately, the more likely situation in contemporary television is that the production conventions and economic and time demands of television news production lead to the common portrayal of certain people as more likely to be involved in violence and crime. It is easier and cheaper, for example, for stations to cover downtown violent crime—it's handy, it's visual, and it needs no significant research or writing—than to cover nonviolent crime, even though the vast majority of all felonies in the United States are nonviolent. As a result of these largely symbolic portrayals of crime, our selective processes do not have an opportunity to reshape the "information" in these news reports. There is little information, only a variety of interesting images, which themselves interfere with the intake of any factual information that may have been included in the report (Lull & Bushman, 2015).

Cultural theorists (we'll meet them later in this chapter) point to official government statistics as proof of the power of the media to shape attitudes toward race. Crime in the United States is committed by all races in near proportion to their presence in the population, yet young African Americans are incarcerated at more than four times the rate of young white people, and African Americans overall are imprisoned at more than five times that rate (Owens, 2020). African American drivers are 20% more likely to be pulled over by police than are white drivers, and once stopped, they are nearly twice as likely to have their cars searched (McHarris, 2020).

An example of this bias in the perception of criminals can be found in a 1947 study on rumor that demonstrated the operation of the selective processes. In this famous experiment, psychologists Gordon Allport and John Postman asked people to whisper from one to another the subject of a drawing in which an African American man is clearly being menaced by a razor-wielding white man. Only the first participant saw the image; more often than not, as the story was passed from person to person, the razor shifted from the left hand of the white aggressor to that of the African American. If our criminal laws and our justice system are supposed to be racially neutral, cultural theorists ask, why do these disparities continue to exist? Why does the razor still change hands? Why are unarmed young Black men 13 times more likely to be shot by police than are their white peers (Schimmack & Carlsson, 2020)?

▲ The race of this driver will determine to a large degree the likelihood that his car will be pulled over by police and searched.
Hill Street Studios/Blend Images/ Getty Images

REINFORCEMENT THEORY The selective processes formed the core of what is arguably the most influential book ever published on the impact of mass communication. In *The Effects of Mass Communication*, written in 1960 by the eminent scientist and eventual head of social research for CBS Broadcasting Joseph Klapper, the core of the limited effects perspective is articulated firmly and clearly. Klapper's theory is based on social science evidence developed prior to 1960 and is often called **reinforcement theory**. It was very persuasive at a time when the nation's social fabric had yet to feel the full impact of the cultural change brought about by the war in Vietnam. In addition, flush with enthusiasm and optimism for the technology and science that had helped the United States defeat the Axis powers, the public could see little but good coming from the media technologies, and they trusted the work of Klapper and other scientists.

In retrospect, the value of reinforcement theory may have passed with the book's 1960 publication date. With rapid postwar urbanization, industrialization, and the increase of women in the workplace, Klapper's "nexus of mediating factors and influences" (church, family, and school) began to lose its traditional socializing role for many people. During the 1960s, a decade both revered and reviled for the social and cultural changes it fostered, it became increasingly difficult to ignore the impact of media. Most important, however, is that all the research Klapper had studied in preparation for his book was conducted before 1960, the year in which it is generally accepted that television became a truly mass medium, present in 90% of American homes. Almost none of the science he examined in developing his reinforcement theory considered television.

THE USES AND GRATIFICATIONS APPROACH Academic disciplines do not change easily. Limited effects researchers were unable to ignore obvious media effects such as the impact of advertising, the media's role in sustaining sentiment against the war in Vietnam and in spreading support for civil rights and the feminist movement, and increases in real-world crime that appeared to parallel increases in televised violence. Therefore, they turned their focus to media consumers to explain how influence is limited. The new body of thought that resulted, called the **uses and gratifications approach**, claimed that media do not do things *to* people; rather, people do things *with* media. In other words, the influence of media is limited to what people allow it to be.

Because the uses and gratifications approach emphasizes *audience members'* motives for making specific consumption choices and the consequences of that intentional media use, it is sometimes seen as being too apologetic for the media industries. In other words, when negative media effects are seen as the product of audience members' media choices and use, the media industries are absolved of responsibility for the content they produce or carry. Media simply give people what they want.

This approach is also criticized because it assumes not only that people know why they make the media content choices they do but also that they can clearly articulate those reasons to uses-and-gratifications researchers. A third criticism is that the approach ignores the fact that much media consumption is unintentional—when we go online for election news, we can't help but see ads. When we go to an action movie, we are presented with various representations of gender and ethnicity that have nothing to do with our reasons for choosing that film. A fourth criticism is that the approach ignores media's cultural role in shaping people's media choices and use.

Despite these criticisms, the uses and gratifications approach served an important function in the development of mass communication theory by stressing the reciprocal nature of the mass communication process. That is, scientists began to take seriously the idea that people are important in the process—they choose content, they make meaning, they act on that meaning.

AGENDA SETTING During the era of limited effects, several important ideas were developed that began to cast some doubt on the assumption that media influence on people and cultures was minimal. These ideas are still respected and examined even today. Among the most influential is **agenda setting**, a theory that argues that media may not tell us what to think, but media certainly tell us what to think *about*. In 1972, based on their study of the media's role in the 1968 presidential election, Maxwell McCombs and Donald Shaw (1972) wrote:

> In choosing and displaying news, editors, newsroom staff, and broadcasters play an important part in shaping political reality. Readers learn not only about a given issue, but how much importance to attach to that issue from the amount of information in a news story and its position. . . . The mass media may well determine the important issues—that is, the media may set the "agenda" of the campaign. (p. 176)

The agenda-setting power of the media resides in more than the amount of space or time devoted to a story and its placement in the broadcast or on the page. Also important is the fact that there is great consistency between media sources across all media in the choice and type of coverage they give an issue or event. This consistency and repetition signal to people the importance of the issue or event.

Researchers Shanto Iyengar and Donald Kinder (1987) tested the application of agenda-setting theory to the network evening news shows in a series of experiments. Their conclusions supported McCombs and Shaw. "Americans' views of their society and nation," they wrote, "are powerfully shaped by the stories that appear on the evening news" (p. 112). But Iyengar and Kinder took agenda setting a step or two further. They discovered that the position of a story affected the agenda-setting power of television news. As you might expect, the lead story on the nightly newscast had the greatest agenda-setting effect, in part because first stories tend to have viewers' full attention—they come before interruptions and other distractions can occur. The second reason, said the researchers, is that viewers accept the broadcasters' implicit categorization of the lead story as the most important.

Agenda-setting theory has evolved since its inception to argue that media *do* tell us what to think as they tell us what to think about. Media *frame* or otherwise set the context for our judgments in what McCombs called **second-order agenda setting** (McCombs & Ghanem, 2001). Agenda setting actually operates at two levels: the *object level* (how media coverage influences the priority people give to objects—for example, issues, candidates, events, and problems) and the *attribute level* (how media coverage influences what attributes of those objects people consider important). For example, heavy news coverage may lead us to think about immigration (object) as an important issue, but the nature of that coverage may cause us to consider different aspects (attributes) of immigration—jobs, national security, human decency, legal arguments—in making our judgments of that complex issue.

SOCIAL COGNITIVE THEORY While mass communication researchers were challenging the limited effects perspective with ideas such as agenda setting and dependency theory, psychologists were expanding **social cognitive theory**—the idea that people learn through observation—and applying it to mass media, especially television (Bandura, 2001).

Social cognitive theory argues that people model (copy) the behaviors they see and that **modeling** happens in two ways. The first is **imitation**, the direct replication of an observed behavior. For example, after seeing cartoon mouse Jerry hit cartoon cat Tom with a stick, a child might then hit his sister with a stick. The second form of modeling is **identification**, a special form of imitation in which observers do not copy exactly what they have seen but make a more generalized but related response. For example, the child might still be aggressive toward his sister but dump a pail of water on her head rather than hit her with a stick.

The idea of identification was of particular value to mass communication theorists who studied television's impact on behavior. Everyone admits that people can imitate what they see on television. But not all do, and when this imitation does occur in dramatic instances—for example, when a Washington State man strangled his girlfriend and attempted to dissolve her body in a tub of acid as he had seen in an episode of *Breaking Bad* (the police discovered a DVD in his home cued up to that very scene; Terle, 2016)—it is so outrageous that it is considered an aberration. Identification, although obviously harder to see and study, is the more likely way that television influences behavior.

Social cognitive theorists demonstrated that imitation and identification are products of three processes:

Observational learning. Observers can acquire (learn) new behaviors simply by seeing those behaviors performed. Many of us who have never fired a handgun could do so because we've seen it done.

Inhibitory effects. Seeing a model, a movie character, for example, punished for a behavior reduces the likelihood that the observer will perform that behavior. In the media we see Good Samaritans sued for trying to help someone, and it reduces our willingness to help in similar situations. That behavior is inhibited by what we've seen.

Disinhibitory effects. Seeing a model rewarded for prohibited or threatening behavior increases the likelihood that the observer will perform that behavior. This, for example, is the basis for complaints against the glorification of crime and drugs in movies. Behaviors that people might not otherwise make, those that are inhibited, now become more likely to occur. The behaviors are disinhibited.

Cultural Theory—A Return to the Idea of Powerful Effects

The questions asked and the answers produced by the agenda-setting and social cognitive theorists were no surprise to their contemporaries, the cultural theorists. These observers were primarily European social theorists and North American humanities scholars such as Marshall McLuhan and James Carey, both of whom we met earlier in this text.

As America entered the 1960s, no one could remain unaware of the obvious and observable impact television was having on the culture; the increased sophistication of media industries and media consumers; entrenched social problems such as racial strife and gender inequality; the apparent cheapening of the political process; and the emergence of calls for controls on new technologies such as cable, satellite, and computer networks. Mass communication theorists were forced to rethink media's influence. Clearly, the limited effects idea was inadequate to explain the media impact they saw around themselves every day. But just as clearly, mass society theory explained very little.

It's important to remember that prominent theories never totally disappear. Joseph McCarthy's efforts to purge Hollywood of communists in the 1950s, for example, were based on mass society notions of evil media and malleable audiences, as was William Barr's public assertion, while serving as Attorney General in the Trump administration, that "secularists . . . have marshaled all the force of mass communications, popular culture, the entertainment industry, and academia in an unremitting assault on religion and traditional values" (in Ford, 2020, p. 32). Mass society theory was also at the heart of one-time White House adviser Sebastian Gorka's insistence that the Teletubbies started "that whole trans

▲ Did the Teletubbies start "that whole trans thing"?
MARKA/Alamy Stock Photo

thing" (Langum, 2019), although some observers felt that soda maker Sprite and its "Pride-Sprite" ad campaign should share the "shame" of "transgender indoctrination"; after all, they warned, "the word 'Sprite' denotes an enchanter, goblin, or demon" (Lane, 2019). Social cognitive theory, limited effects, and uses and gratifications are regularly raised in today's debates over the regulation of video games and fast-food advertising aimed at kids (see Chapters 9 and 12).

However, the theories that have gained the most support among today's media researchers and theorists are those that accept the potential for powerful media effects, a potential that is *either* enhanced or thwarted by audience members' involvement in the mass communication process. Important to this perspective on audience–media interaction are **cultural theories**. Stanley Baran and Dennis Davis (2021) wrote that these theories share "an underlying assumption that our experience of reality is an ongoing, social construction in which we have some responsibility, not something that is only sent, delivered, or otherwise transmitted by some authority or elite" (p. 341). This book's focus on media literacy is based in large part on cultural theories, which say that meaning and, therefore, effects are negotiated by media and audiences as they interact in the culture.

CRITICAL CULTURAL THEORY A major influence on mass communication theory came from European scholarship on media effects. **Critical cultural theory**—the idea that media operate primarily to justify and support the status quo at the expense of ordinary people—is openly political and is rooted in **neo-Marxist theory**. "Old-fashioned" Marxists believed that people were oppressed by those who owned the factories and the land (the means of production). They called the factories and land the *base*. Modern neo-Marxist theorists believe that people are oppressed by those who control the culture, the *superstructure*—religion, politics, art, literature, and of course the mass media.

Modern critical cultural theory encompasses a number of different conceptions of the relationship between media and culture, but all share these identifying characteristics:

- *They tend to be macroscopic in scope.* They examine broad, culturewide media effects.
- *They are openly and avowedly political.* Based on neo-Marxism, their orientation is from the political left.
- *Their goal is at the least to instigate change in government media policies, and at the most to effect wholesale change in media and cultural systems.* Critical cultural theories logically assume that the superstructure, which favors those in power, must be altered.
- *They investigate and explain how elites use media to maintain their positions of privilege and power.* Issues such as media ownership, government–media relations, and corporate media representations of labor and disenfranchised groups are typical topics of study for critical cultural theory because they center on the exercise of power. You can read a critical cultural theory critique of the common charge that the media have a progressive slant in the box titled "Are the News Media Really Liberal?"

▲ Former US Attorney General William Barr lamented the "unremitting assault on religion and traditional values" unleashed by "mass communication, popular culture, the entertainment industry, and academia."
Bill Greenblatt/UPI/Alamy Stock Photo

THE FRANKFURT SCHOOL The critical cultural perspective actually came to the United States in the 1930s when two prominent media scholars from the University of Frankfurt escaped Hitler's Germany. Theodor Adorno and Max Horkheimer were at the heart of what became known as the **Frankfurt School** of media theory (Arato & Gebhardt, 1978). Their approach, centered in neo-Marxism, valued serious art (literature, symphonic music, and theater) and saw consumption of art as

CULTURAL FORUM
Are the News Media Really Liberal?

During his two campaigns for office and throughout his time in the White House, President Trump regularly called the news media "highly slanted," "fake news," and "the liberal media." His accusations resonated with millions of Americans in part because the claim that "the media are liberal" had long been unquestioned. For many conservatives, "the existence of a liberal media bias is an established fact, like the temperature at which water freezes," explains *Columbia Journalism Review*'s Larry Light. "Scores of opinion polls show that Republicans think journalists favor Democrats and oppose the GOP. A [recent] survey found that 63% of Republicans believe that journalists are the 'enemy of the people'" (2018).

This conventional wisdom, that the media are liberal, is so much a part of the cultural forum, critical theorists had little choice but to respond; in fact, they argue that the traditional news media are actually quite conservative. Yes, there are more Democrats than Republicans among the nation's reporters and editors, but they have little control over what makes it into "the news" (Hassell, Holbein, & Miles, 2020). Therefore, the "salient questions around bias" writes journalist Lisa Graves (2018), "have little to do with staffer headcounts, and more with the allegiances and affiliations of owners. They also, in this increasingly polarized news environment, have to do with the sources where Americans get their news. The answers there point, overwhelmingly, to conservative control."

For example, the country's largest owner of local TV stations, Americans' most trusted source of news, is highly conservative Sinclair Media Group. Proudly conservative Fox News has been cable television's top-rated network for two decades, and offline and online combined, the news outlet with the largest weekly reach in the country (Bazelon, 2020). Conservative-leaning pages lead *all* sources with the most engaged-with posts on Facebook (Zakrzewski, 2021). The conservative *Wall Street Journal* has been ranked the most believable and credible newspaper in every Pew Research newspaper study since 1985 and has a paid daily circulation, print and digital, of nearly 3 million readers.

These media outlets are extremely popular, but they are hardly liberal. Even *The New York Times*, often accused of a liberal slant, is not very liberal, charge critical theorists. The nation's "paper of record" led public opinion in support of the 2003 invasion of Iraq, a conflict loathed by liberals, and its coverage of the 2016 presidential election favored the conservative Mr. Trump over the liberal Hillary Clinton, especially in its heavier focus on her alleged scandals as opposed to his (Boehlert, 2020). The liberal NPR? Conservative "experts" appear twice as often as their liberal counterparts on public radio's flagship morning show, *Morning Edition* (Soundbites, 2018), and in its coverage of immigration, the network's programming consistently quotes organizations designated as "hate groups" by the Southern Poverty Law Center (Hagle, 2021).

Beyond pointing out the "non-liberalness" of these powerful American journalistic institutions, critical theorists also argue that it is impossible for profit-motivated companies to be anything other than conservative. They see, according to media critic Anya Schiffrin, an American media "system dominated by powerful elites who have limited the range of political points of view, narrowed the field of reporting, and starved local news of funds" (2020, p. 60). Veteran reporter Jim Naureckas explains the inevitability of this situation: "It's a bad idea to have journalism mainly carried out by large corporations whose chief interest in news is how to make the maximum amount of money from it. And it's a bad idea to have as these corporations' main or sole source of revenue advertising from other large corporations" (2009, p. 5).

Enter Your Voice

- If you believed the claim that the news media are liberal, have the critical theorists' arguments swayed your thinking? If not, why not?

- Is it possible for a media industry enriched by the status quo to effectively challenge the way things are? What would cause it to do so?

- Recent social science research may help resolve the debate. Yes, reporters tend to be more liberal than the general population. But because most legitimate journalists adhere to strong governing professional standards, "the media exhibits no bias against conservatives (or liberals for that matter) in what news that they choose to cover" (Hassell, Holbein, & Miles, 2020, p. 1). Convinced? Can the hostile media effect (Chapter 1) explain your response?

a means to elevate all people toward a better life. Typical media fare—popular music, slapstick radio and movie comedies, the soft news dominant in newspapers—pacified ordinary people while assisting in their repression.

Adorno and Horkheimer's influence on US media theory was small during their lifetimes. The limited effects perspective was about to blossom, neo-Marxism was not well received, and their ideas sounded a bit too much like mass society theory claims of a corrupting and debasing popular media. More recently, though, the Frankfurt School has been "rediscovered," and its influence can be seen in three final examples of contemporary critical theory, British cultural theory, news production research, and mediatization.

BRITISH CULTURAL THEORY There was significant class tension in England after World War II. During the 1950s and 1960s, working-class people who had fought for their country were unwilling to return to England's traditional notions of nobility and privilege. Many saw the British media—with broadcasting dominated by graduates of the best upper-crust schools, and newspapers and magazines owned by the wealthy—as supporting long-standing class distinctions and divisions. This environment of class conflict produced theorists such as Stuart Hall (1980), who first developed the idea of media as a public forum in which various forces fight to shape perceptions of everyday reality (see Chapter 1). Hall and others in British cultural studies trusted that the media *could* serve all people. However, because of ownership patterns, the commercial orientation of the media, and sympathetic government policies toward media, the forum was dominated by the reigning elite. In other words, the loudest voice in the give-and-take of the cultural forum belonged to those already well entrenched in the power structure. **British cultural theory** today provides a home for much feminist research and research on popular culture both in Europe and in the United States.

NEWS PRODUCTION RESEARCH Another interesting strand of critical cultural theory is **news production research**—the study of how economic and other influences on the way news is produced distort and bias news coverage toward those in power. W. Lance Bennett (1988) identified four common news production conventions used by US media that bolster the position of those in power:

1. *Personalized news.* Most news stories revolve around people. If a newspaper wants to do a report on homelessness, for example, it will typically focus on one person or family as the center of its story. This makes for interesting journalism (and more clicks, higher ratings, or bigger circulation), but it reduces important social and political problems to soap opera levels. The two likely results are that these problems are dismissed by the public as specific to the characters in the story and that the public is not provided with the social and political contexts of the problem that might suggest avenues of public action.

2. *Dramatized news.* News, like other forms of media content, must be attractively packaged. Especially on television, this packaging takes the form of dramatization. Stories must have a hero and a villain, a conflict must be identified, and there has to be a showdown. "The idea that politics is sport is undeniable, and we understood that and approached it that way," explains CNN president Jeff Zucker (in Magary, 2017). Again, one problem is that important public issues take on the character of a soap opera or a Western movie. But a larger concern is that political debate is trivialized. Fundamental alterations in tax law or defense spending or any of a number of important issues are reduced to environmental extremists versus greedy corporations or the White House versus Congress. This complaint is often raised about media coverage of campaigns. The issues that should be at the center of the campaign become lost in a sea of stories about the "horse race"—who's ahead; how will a good showing in Iowa help Candidate X in her battle to unseat Candidate Y as the front-runner?

3. *Fragmented news.* The daily time and cost demands of US journalism result in newspapers and broadcasts composed of a large number of brief, capsulated stories. There is little room in a given report for perspective and context. Another contributor to fragmented news, according to Bennett (1988), is journalists' obsession with objectivity. Putting any given day's story in context—connecting it to other events of the time or the past—would require the reporter to make decisions about which links are most important. Of course, these choices would be subjective, and so they are avoided. Reporters typically get one comment

from somebody on one side of the issue and a second comment from the other side, juxtapose them as if they were equally valid, and then move on to tomorrow's assignment.

4. *Normalized news.* The US newswriting convention typically employed when reporting on natural or human-made disasters is to seek out and report the opinions and perspectives of the authorities. When an airplane crashes, for example, the report invariably concludes with these words: "The FAA was quickly on the scene. The cockpit recorder has been retrieved, and the reason for this tragedy will be determined soon." In other words, what happened here is bad, but the authorities will sort it out. Journalists give little independent attention to investigating any of a number of angles that a plane crash or flood might suggest, perspectives that might produce information different from that of officials. The same normalization occurs in times of civil unrest. News accounts and editorials are filled with politicians, think-tank experts, academics, and other authorities, those with the answers. Rarely are the people making demands allowed their independent voices. All will be fine, said many of the top print and network television news outlets who, in the three weeks after the 2020 George Floyd killing at the hands of the police set off massive protests, included almost no activists among their scores of authors, guests, and interviewees weighing in on the subject (Graceffo, 2020).

The cultural effect of news produced according to these conventions is daily reassurance by the media that the system works if those in power are allowed to do their jobs. Any suggestions about opportunities for meaningful social action are suppressed as reporters serve the powerful as "stenographers with amnesia" (Gitlin, 2004, p. 31).

MEDIATIZATION THEORY A wide-ranging macro-level perspective, **mediatization theory**, has recently emerged from Europe. It asserts that media have become so central and essential to modern societies that those societies are forced to change in important ways to accommodate them. The institutions that people have come to rely on, for example, politics, religion, business, and education, "have been 'mediatized'—their structures and their routine social practices have been altered and continue to be altered to accommodate media. . .These institutions don't just use media—they are used by media and made to fit within constraints set by media" (Baran & Davis, 2021, p. 372). If you are a sports fan, for example, you no doubt have seen how the games you follow have changed—games and seasons are longer and more reliant on spectacle and there are constant rule changes—all to accommodate television.

The political system offers another example. Its traditional role is to enlighten voters and engage citizens. But it does not, according to researchers Silvia Knobloch-Westerwick and Axel Westerwick, because it has become mediatized. "Given that politics in a democracy

◀ Normalized news: No media account of a plane crash is complete without assurance that the flight recorder will help officials pinpoint the cause of the crash.
Mehdi Fedouach/AFP/Getty Images

depend on acceptance and voters' support," they wrote, "actors in the political system will frequently act to accommodate media logic" (2020, p. 119). Former President Trump, for example, instructed his White House advisers to "think of every day of his administration as an episode of a reality [TV] show" (Poniewozik, 2020, p. A4).

An inevitable result of mediatization, **media logic** means that institutions and the people in them must respond to the demands of the medium in which they wish to express themselves. Andrew Yang, candidate for the 2020 Democratic Presidential nomination, decried media logic from the stage of one of that contest's debates: "Instead of talking about automation [of the workforce] and our future. . .we're up here with makeup on our faces and our rehearsed attack lines, playing roles in this reality TV show" (in Nichols, 2019, p. 3).

According to mediatization theory, even our everyday lives have been mediatized. There was no such thing as a gender-reveal party until social media made knowing the sex of a fetus a "big reveal" on Instagram. And are you really married if your ceremony has no well-choreographed wedding party YouTube dance entrance? Or simply point your smartphone camera at a group of friends and watch their behavior immediately change; their interactions have become mediatized.

The Meaning-Making Perspective

A more micro-level-centered view of media influence, one paralleling cultural theories in its belief in the power of mass communication, is the **meaning-making perspective**, the idea that active audience members use media content to create meaning, and meaningful experiences, for themselves. Naturally, this use can produce important macro-level, or cultural, effects as well. Cultural and meaning-making theories, taken together, make a most powerful case for becoming media literate. They argue that who we are and the world in which we live are in large part of our own making.

SYMBOLIC INTERACTION Mass communication theorists borrowed **symbolic interaction** from psychology. It is the idea that cultural symbols are learned through interaction and then mediate that interaction. In other words, people give things meaning, and that meaning controls their behavior. The flag is a perfect example. We have decided that an array of red, white, and blue cloth, assembled in a particular way, represents not only our nation but its values and beliefs. The flag has meaning because we have given it meaning, and that meaning now governs certain behavior toward the flag. We know to stand when a color guard carries the flag into a room. Failing to do so is considered a mark of disrespect, an insult. This is symbolic interaction.

Communication scholars Don Faules and Dennis Alexander (1978) define communication as "symbolic behavior which results in various degrees of shared meaning and values between participants" (p. 23). In their view, symbolic interaction is an excellent way to explain how mass communication shapes our behaviors. Accepting that these symbolic meanings are negotiated by participants in the culture, mass communication scholars are left with these questions: What do the media contribute to these negotiations, and how powerful are they?

Symbolic interaction theory is frequently used in the study of the influence of advertising because marketers often succeed by encouraging the audience to perceive their products as symbols that have meaning beyond the products' actual function. This is called **product positioning**. For example, what does a Cadillac mean? Success. A Porsche? Virility. General Foods International Coffees? Togetherness and intimacy.

SOCIAL CONSTRUCTION OF REALITY If we keep in mind James Carey's cultural definition of communication—a symbolic process whereby reality is produced, maintained, repaired, and transformed—we cannot be surprised that mass communication theorists have been drawn to the ideas of sociologists Peter Berger and Thomas Luckmann. In their 1966 book, *The Social Construction of Reality*, they don't directly discuss mass communication, but they offer a compelling theory to explain how cultures use signs and symbols to construct and maintain a uniform reality.

Social construction of reality theory argues that people who share a culture also share "an ongoing correspondence" of meaning. Things generally mean the same to me as they do to you. A stop sign, for example, has just about the same meaning for everyone. Berger and Luckmann call these things that have "objective" meaning **symbols**—we routinely interpret them in the usual way. But there are other things in the environment to which we assign "subjective" meaning. These things they call **signs**. In social construction of reality, then, a car is a symbol of mobility, but a Cadillac or Mercedes-Benz is a sign of wealth or success. In either case, the meaning is negotiated, but for signs, the negotiation is a bit more complex.

Through interaction in and with the culture over time, people bring together what they have learned about these signs and symbols to form **typification schemes**—collections of meanings assigned to some phenomenon or situation. These typification schemes form a natural backdrop for people's interpretation of and behavior in "the major routines of everyday life, not only the typification of others . . . but typifications of all sorts of events and experiences" (Berger & Luckmann, 1966, p. 43). When you enter a classroom, you automatically recall the cultural meaning of its various elements: desks in rows, chalkboard or whiteboard, lectern. You recognize this as a classroom and impose your "classroom typification scheme." You know how to behave: address the person standing at the front of the room with courtesy, raise your hand when you have a question, talk to your neighbors in whispers. These "rules of behavior" were not published on the classroom door. You applied them because they were appropriate to the "reality" of the setting in your culture. In other cultures, behaviors in this setting may be quite different.

Social construction of reality is important to researchers who study the effects of advertising for the same reasons that symbolic interaction has proven valuable. But it is also widely applied when looking at how media, especially news, shape our political realities.

Crime offers one example. What do politicians mean when they say they are "tough on crime"? What is their (and your) reality of crime? It is likely that "crime" signifies (is a sign for) gangs, drugs, and violence. However, the statistical (rather than the socially constructed) reality is that there is 10 times more white-collar crime in the United States than there is violent crime. And why, when violent crime is at a 30-year low, do 6 in 10 Americans believe that crime is at an all-time high (Gramlich, 2020)? Now think of welfare. What reality is signified? Is it big corporations, failing to pay their fair share of taxes, seeking subsidies and tax breaks from the government? Or is it unwed, unemployed mothers, unwilling to work, looking for a handout? Social construction theorists argue that the "building blocks" for the construction of these "realities" come primarily from the mass media.

CULTIVATION ANALYSIS Symbolic interaction and social construction of reality provide a strong foundation for *cultivation analysis*, which says that television "cultivates" or constructs a reality of the world that, although possibly inaccurate, becomes meaningful to us simply because we believe it to be true. We then base our judgments about and our actions in the world on this cultivated reality provided by television.

Although cultivation analysis was developed by media researcher George Gerbner and his colleagues out of concern over the effects of television violence, it has been applied to countless other television-cultivated realities such as beauty, sex roles, religion, the judicial process, and marriage. In all cases the assumptions are the same—television cultivates realities, especially for heavy viewers.

Cultivation analysis is based on five assumptions:

1. *Television is essentially and fundamentally different from other mass media.* Unlike books, newspapers, and magazines, television requires no reading ability. Unlike the movies, television requires no mobility or cash; it is in the home, and it is free. Unlike radio, television combines pictures and sound. It can be consumed from people's very earliest to their last years of life.

2. *Television is the "central cultural arm" of US society.* Gerbner and his colleagues (1978) wrote that television, as our culture's primary storyteller, is "the chief creator of synthetic cultural patterns (entertainment and information) for the most heterogeneous mass publics in history, including large groups that have never shared in any common public message systems" (p. 178). The product of this sharing of messages is the **mainstreaming** of reality, moving individual and different people toward a shared, television-created understanding of how things are.

3. *The realities cultivated by television are not necessarily specific attitudes and opinions but rather more basic assumptions about the "facts" of life.* Television does not teach facts and figures; it builds general frames of reference. Return to our earlier discussion of the portrayal of crime on television. Television newscasters never say, "Most crime is violent, most violent crime is committed by people of color, and you should be wary of those people." But by the choices news producers make, television news presents a broad picture of "reality" with little regard for how its "reality" matches that of its audience.

4. *The major cultural function of television is to stabilize social patterns.* That is, the existing power relationships of the culture are reinforced and maintained through the meaning-making television images encourage. Gerbner and his colleagues (1978) made this argument:

> The repetitive pattern of television's mass-produced messages and images forms the main-stream of the common symbolic environment that cultivates the most widely shared conceptions of reality. We live in terms of the stories we tell—stories about what things exist, stories about how things work, and stories about what to do—and television tells them all through news, drama, and advertising to almost everybody most of the time. (p. 178)

Because the media industries have a stake in the political, social, and economic structures as they exist, their stories rarely challenge the system that has enriched them.

5. *The observable, measurable, independent contributions of television to the culture are relatively small.* This is not a restatement of limited effects theory. Instead, Gerbner and his colleagues (1980) explained its meaning with an "ice-age analogy":

> Just as an average temperature shift of a few degrees can lead to an ice age . . . so too can a relatively small but pervasive influence make a crucial difference. The "size" of an effect is far less critical than the direction of its steady contribution. (p. 14)

In other words, even though we cannot always see media effects on ourselves and others, they do occur and eventually will change the culture, possibly in profound ways.

▶ **Table 13.1** Mass Communication Theories

MASS COMMUNICATION THEORY	DESCRIPTION
Mass Society Theory	Idea, propagated by cultural and societal elites, that the media are corrupting influences that undermine the social order; "average" people are defenseless against the influence.
Limited Effects Theory	Media's influence is limited by people's individual differences, social categories, and personal relationships. These factors "limit" media's influence.
Two-Step Flow Theory	Idea that media's influence on people's behavior is limited by opinion leaders, who consume content, interpret it in light of their own values and beliefs, and pass it on to opinion followers. Therefore the source of effects is interpersonal rather than mass communication.
Attitude Change Theory	Collection of theories explaining how people's attitudes are formed, shaped, and changed through communication and how those attitudes influence behavior.
Dissonance Theory	Argument that people, when confronted by new information, experience mental discomfort (dissonance), so they consciously and subconsciously work to limit or reduce that discomfort through the selective processes.

Reinforcement Theory	Joseph Klapper's idea that if media have any impact at all, it is in the direction of reinforcement, especially as important social factors—school, parents, religion—also reinforce cultural norms.
Uses and Gratifications Approach	Idea that media don't do things to people; people do things *with* media. Audience members are powerful agents in either limiting or allowing effects.
Agenda Setting	Theory that media may not tell us what to think, but do tell us what to think about, meaning media can have important effects for individuals and society.
Social Cognitive Theory	Idea that people learn through observation, either as imitation or identification; actual exhibition of these behaviors is dependent on the reinforcement we associate with them.
Cultural Theory	Idea that meaning and effects are negotiated by media and audiences as they interact in the culture; debate exists over who has the upper hand.
Critical Cultural Theory	Idea that media operate primarily to justify and support the status quo at the expense of ordinary people. Media and other elites have the upper hand in the negotiation of meaning.
The Frankfurt School	Theory that values serious art, viewing its consumption as a means to elevate people toward a better life; but common media content pacifies and represses ordinary people.
British Cultural Theory	Theory of elites' domination over the larger culture, primarily through mass communication, and its influence on bounded cultures, limiting the expression of their values.
News Production Research	Study of how economic and other influences on the way news is produced distort and bias news coverage toward those in power, especially through news practices such as personalized, dramatized, fragmented, and normalized news.
Mediatization Theory	Argues that media have become so central and essential for modern social orders that those social orders are continually changing in important ways to accommodate the ever-changing media; modern societies are locked into a process of constant change centered around media.
The Meaning-Making Perspective	Idea that active audience members use media content to create meaning and meaningful experiences for themselves. Media-literate consumers can have greater control over the meanings that are made.
Symbolic Interaction	Idea that people give meaning to symbols, which then control people's behavior in their presence.
Social Construction of Reality	Theory that cultures construct and maintain realities by using signs and symbols; people learn to behave in their social world through interaction with them, as those mutually negotiated meanings allow members of a culture to better know one another and predict interactions and behaviors.
Cultivation Analysis	Idea that television "cultivates" or constructs a reality of the world that, although possibly inaccurate, becomes the accepted reality simply because we as a culture believe it to be; we then base our judgments about and our actions in the world on this cultivated reality.

The Effects of Mass Communication—Four Questions

Scientists and scholars use these theories, the earliest and the most recent, to form conclusions about the effects of mass communication. You are of course familiar with the long-standing debate over the effects of television violence. However, there are many other fascinating and important media effects questions that occupy researchers' interest beyond that and the others highlighted here.

Does Media Violence Lead to Aggression?

No media effects issue has captured public, legislative, and industry attention as has the relationship between media portrayals of violence and subsequent aggressive behavior. Among the reasons for this focus are the facts that violence is a staple of television and movies and that the United States experienced an upsurge in real violence in the 1960s, just about the time television entrenched itself as the country's dominant mass medium and movies turned to increasingly graphic violence to differentiate themselves from and to compete with television.

The prevailing view during the 1960s was that *some* media violence affected *some* people in *some* ways *some* of the time. Given the dominance of the transmissional perspective of communication and the limited effects theories, researchers believed that for "normal" people—that is, those who were not predisposed to violence—*little* media violence affected *few* people in *few* ways *little* of the time. However, increases in youth violence, the assassinations of Robert F. Kennedy and the Reverend Martin Luther King Jr., and the violent eruption of cities during the civil rights, women's rights, and anti–Vietnam War movements led to the creation of the Surgeon General's Scientific Advisory Committee on Television and Social Behavior in 1969. After 2 years and $1 million worth of research, the committee

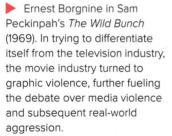

▶ Ernest Borgnine in Sam Peckinpah's *The Wild Bunch* (1969). In trying to differentiate itself from the television industry, the movie industry turned to graphic violence, further fueling the debate over media violence and subsequent real-world aggression.

Warner Brothers/Photofest

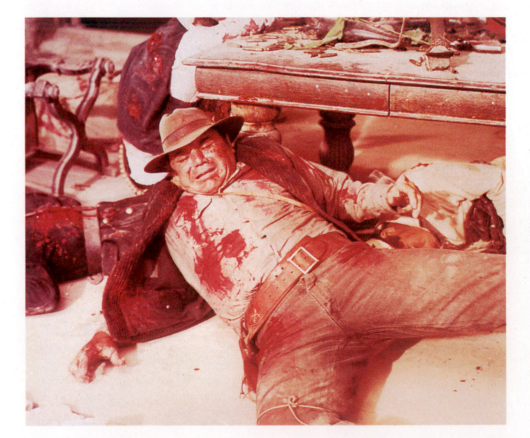

(whose members had to be approved by the television networks) produced findings that led Surgeon General Jesse L. Steinfield to report to the US Senate:

> While the . . . report is carefully phrased and qualified in language acceptable to social scientists, it is clear to me that the causal relationship between televised violence and antisocial behavior is sufficient to warrant appropriate and immediate remedial action. The data on social phenomena such as television and violence and/or aggressive behavior will never be clear enough for all social scientists to agree on the formulation of a succinct statement of causality. But there comes a time when the data are sufficient to justify action. That time has come. (Ninety-Second Congress, 1972, p. 26)

Despite the apparent certainty of this statement, disagreement persists over the existence and extent of the media's contribution to aggressive behavior. Few would argue that media violence *never* leads to aggressive behavior. The disagreement is about what circumstances are needed for such effects to occur, and to whom.

UNDER WHAT CIRCUMSTANCES? A direct causal relationship between violent content and aggressive behavior—the **stimulation model**—has been scientifically demonstrated in scores of laboratory experiments. So has the **aggressive cues model**—the idea that media portrayals can suggest that certain classes of people, such as women or foreigners, are acceptable targets for real-world aggression, thereby increasing the likelihood that some people will act violently toward people in these groups.

Both the stimulation and aggressive cues models are based on social cognitive theory. Fueled by the research of psychologists such as Albert Bandura, social cognitive theory has made several additional contributions to the violence debate.

Social cognitive theory deflated the notion of **catharsis**, the idea that watching violence in the media reduces people's innate aggressive drive. Social scientists were already skeptical: viewing people eating does not reduce hunger; watching pornography does not decrease sex drive. But social cognitive theory provided a scientific explanation for the research that did show a reduction in aggression after viewing violence. This phenomenon was better explained not by some cathartic power of the media but by inhibitory effects. That is, as we saw in our discussion of social cognitive theory, if media aggression is portrayed as punished or prohibited, it can indeed lead to the reduced likelihood that the behavior will be modeled.

Some people, typically media industry practitioners, to this day defend catharsis theory. However, about 50 years ago, respected media researcher and theorist Joseph Klapper, who at the time was the head of social research for CBS television, told the US Senate, "I myself am unaware of any, shall we say, hard evidence that seeing violence on television or any other medium acts in a cathartic . . . manner. There have been some studies to that effect; they are grossly, greatly outweighed by studies as to the opposite effect" (Ninety-Second Congress, 1972, p. 60).

Social cognitive theory introduced the concept of **vicarious reinforcement**—the idea that observed reinforcement operates in the same manner as actual reinforcement. This helped direct researchers' attention to the context in which media violence is presented. Theoretically, inhibitory and disinhibitory effects operate because of the presence of vicarious reinforcement. That is, seeing the bad guy punished is sufficient to inhibit subsequent aggression on the part of the viewer. Unfortunately, what researchers discovered is that in contemporary film and television, when the bad guys are punished, they are punished by good guys who out-aggress them. The implication is that even when media portray punishment for aggressive behavior, they may in fact be reinforcing that very same behavior.

Social cognitive theory also introduced the concept of **environmental incentives**—the notion that real-world incentives can lead observers to ignore the negative vicarious reinforcement they have learned to associate with a given behavior.

In 1965, Bandura conducted a now-classic experiment in which nursery school children saw a video aggressor, a character named Rocky, punished for his behavior. The children subsequently showed lower levels of aggressive play than did those who had seen Rocky rewarded. This is what social cognitive theory would have predicted. Yet Bandura later offered "sticker-pictures" to the children who had seen Rocky punished if they could perform

▶ Only the most ardent media industry defenders reject the link between media violence and real-world aggression.

Andrey_Popov/Shutterstock

the same actions they had seen him perform. They all could. Vicarious negative reinforcement may reduce the likelihood that the punished behavior will be performed, but that behavior is still observationally learned. It's just that, at the same time it is observed and learned, observers also learn not to repeat it. When the real world offers sufficient reward, the originally learned behavior can be demonstrated.

FOR WHOM? The compelling evidence of cognitive learning researchers aside, it's clear that most people do not exhibit aggression after viewing film or video violence. There is also little doubt that those predisposed to violence are more likely to be influenced by media aggression. Yet viewers need not necessarily be predisposed for this link to occur because at any time anyone can become predisposed. For example, experimental research indicates that frustrating people before they view media violence can increase the likelihood of subsequent aggressive behavior.

However, the question remains: Who exactly is affected by mediated violence? If a direct causal link is necessary to establish effects, then it can indeed be argued that some media violence affects some people in some ways some of the time. But if the larger, macro-level ritual view is applied, then we all are affected because we live in a world in which there is more violence than there might be without mass media. We live in a world, according to cultivation analysis, in which we are less trusting of our neighbors and more accepting of violence in our midst. This need not be the case. As researcher Ellen Wartella (1997) said, "Today, we find wide consensus among experts that, of all the factors contributing to violence in our society, violence on television may be the easiest to control" (p. 4). And in a clear sign of that wide consensus, the American Medical Association, the American Academy of Pediatrics, the American Psychological Association, and the American Academy of Child & Adolescent Psychiatry issued a joint report in summer 2000 offering their combined view that the effects of violent media are "measurable and long lasting" and that "prolonged viewing of media violence can lead to emotional **desensitization** toward violence in real life" (as quoted in Wronge, 2000, p. 1E).

Do Portrayals of Drugs and Alcohol Increase Consumption?

Concern about media effects reaches beyond the issue of violence. The claims and counterclaims surrounding media portrayals of drugs and alcohol parallel those of the violence debate.

The wealth of scientific data linking media portrayals of alcohol consumption, especially in ads, to increases in youthful drinking and alcohol abuse led the US Department of Health and Human Services's National Institute of Alcohol Abuse and Alcoholism to report in 1995 that "the preponderance of the evidence indicates that alcohol advertising stimulates higher consumption of alcohol by both adults and adolescents" (Martin & Mail, 1995), a conclusion repeatedly reaffirmed. For example, researchers writing in 2016 in the *Journal of Studies on Alcohol and Drugs* demonstrated that "among underage youth, the quantity of brand-specific advertising exposure is positively associated with the total quantity of consumption of those advertised brands" (Naimi et al., 2016). The National Institute on Alcohol Abuse and Alcoholism (2021) also reports the following:

- Research clearly indicates that, in addition to parents and peers, alcohol advertising and marketing have a significant impact on youth decisions to drink.
- Underage youth who drink alcohol are more likely to experience consequences related to risky sexual behavior.
- The gender gap in drinking has closed. Young girls are drinking more than underage boys.
- More youth in the United States drink alcohol than smoke tobacco or marijuana, making it the drug most used by American young people.

Yet there is a good deal of scientific research—typically from alcohol industry scientists—that discounts the causal link between media portrayals and real-world drinking. Again, researchers who insist on the demonstration of this direct causal relationship will rarely agree on media's influence on individuals' behavior. The larger cultural perspective, however, suggests that media portrayals of alcohol, both in ads and in entertainment fare, tell stories of alcohol consumption that predominantly present it as safe, healthy, youthful, sexy, necessary for a good time, effective for dealing with stress, and essential to ceremonies and other rites of passage.

The same scenario exists in the debate over the relationship between media portrayals of nonalcohol drug use and behavior. Relatively little contemporary media content presents the use of illegal drugs in a glorifying manner. In fact, the destructive power of illegal drugs is often the focus of television shows such as *Law and Order: SVU* and *Euphoria* and is a central theme in movies such as *The Wolf of Wall Street* (2013) and *American Made* (2017). Much scientific concern has centered therefore on the impact of commercials and other media portrayals of legal over-the-counter drugs. Again, impressive amounts of experimental research suggest a causal link between this content and subsequent abuse of both legal and illegal drugs; however, there also exists research that discounts the causal link between media portrayals and the subsequent abuse of drugs. It cannot be denied, however, that media often present legal drugs as a cure-all for dealing with that pesky mother-in-law, those screaming kids, that abusive boss, and other daily annoyances. Prescription drug advertising is enough of a public health issue that the Food and Drug Administration on several occasions has considered banning it. Nonetheless, it is illegal in every country in the world except the United States and New Zealand.

▲ What does this magazine ad say about drinking? About attractiveness? About having fun? About women? Are you satisfied with these representations of important aspects of your life? *Courtesy of The Advertising Archives*

What Is Media's Contribution to Gender and Racial/Ethnic Stereotyping?

Stereotyping is the application of a standardized image or concept to members of certain groups, usually based on limited information. Because media cannot show all realities of all things, the choices media practitioners make when presenting specific people and groups may well facilitate or encourage stereotyping.

Numerous studies conducted over the past 75 years have demonstrated that women, people of color, older people, gays, and lesbians—in fact, all of our nation's "outgroups"—are consistently underrepresented or misrepresented in our mass media. For example, a 2020 A. C. Nielsen study of the top 100 programs each on broadcast, cable, and streaming television demonstrated that women in general, and especially women over 50, were dramatically underrepresented relative to their numbers in the actual American population. Latinos and non-white Hispanics were among the most underrepresented racial groups, as were Native Americans (Deggans, 2020). Media effects research over those same seven-and-a-half decades has consistently demonstrated the impact of this underrepresentation and misrepresentation. Bryant, Thompson, and Finklea (2013) summarized, "Media images of minorities have been shown to have considerable impact. . . . The portrayal of lazy, incompetent, rebellious, or violent persons of color can be an enduring mental image." The result, they conclude, is the creation of harmful stereotypes (p. 261).

Any of a number of theories, especially cultivation analysis, symbolic interaction, and social construction of reality, can explain these effects. This underrepresentation and misrepresentation influence people's perceptions, and people's perceptions influence their behaviors. Examine your own perceptions not only of women and people of color but of older people, lawyers, college athletes, and people sophisticated in the use of computers. What images or stereotypes immediately come to mind?

Sure, maybe you were a bit surprised at the data on race and traffic stops described earlier; still, you're skeptical. You're a smart, modern, college-educated individual. Use the following quiz to test yourself on your stereotypes of people from different parts of the country, drug use, and the poor:

1. Among America's 50 states, which of the following is *not* among the top-10 "most sinful" (angry and hateful, jealous, and showing excesses of vice, greed, lust, vanity and laziness): Georgia, Tennessee, Michigan, or Louisiana?

2. Which group of Americans—white, Hispanic, or African American—has the highest rate of drug overdose death?

3. What percentage of women receiving welfare (Aid to Families with Dependent Children) is also employed: under 10%; about 25%; nearly 40%?

Are you surprised to learn that urban, industrial Michigan was number 15, much less "sinful" than heartland states Georgia, Tennessee, and Louisiana (numbers 5, 6, and 7; McCann, 2020)? Drug deaths? The rate of overdose death for Caucasians is a third higher than it is for African Americans and 159% higher than for Hispanics ("Opioid Crisis," 2020). Welfare? Thirty-nine percent of mothers receiving welfare also work outside the home ("Important Welfare," 2020). How did you develop your stereotypes of these people and places? Where did you find the building blocks to construct your realities of their lives?

Can other building blocks, that is, realistic portrayals of outgroups that challenge typical cultural stereotypes, produce beneficial effects? In the case of homosexuality, researchers believe that repeated and frequent exposure to a wide range of realistic media representations can positively influence people's perceptions of gays and lesbians and issues relating to homosexuality. Some call this the *Will & Grace* effect, where "the single most important indicator of one's support for gay rights is whether one knows someone who is gay, [and a gay person] on TV will do" (Lithwick, 2012, p. 77).

Today, having "met" many gay people in real and media life, a majority of Americans (67%) favor same-sex marriage (Weber, 2021). Mass communication researchers explain this prosocial effect using the **parasocial contact hypothesis**: viewers who "meet" people different from themselves in the media increase their understanding of those people and develop improved attitudes toward them (Schiappa, Gregg, & Hewes, 2005). So powerful is this mediated contact that its impact can be extended to explain the **mediated intergroup contact hypothesis**, which argues that seeing media characters like themselves *interacting* with characters unlike themselves can move viewers to become more open toward those other people (Ortiz & Harwood, 2007).

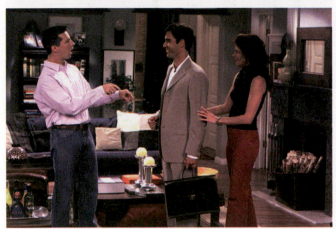

▲ These images (clockwise from top left) from *Grey's Anatomy*, *Schitt's Creek, Pose,* and *Will & Grace* offer samples of contemporary, nonstereotypical television portrayals of gay people and homosexuality.

(Clockwise from top left): ABC/ Photofest; Pop TV Network/ Photofest; FX Network/Photofest; Allstar Picture Library/NBC/Alamy Stock Photo

Do Media Have Prosocial Effects?

Virtually every argument that can be made for the harmful or negative effects of media can also be applied to the ability of media to do good. A sizable body of science clearly demonstrates that people can and will model the good or prosocial behaviors they see in the media, often to a greater extent than they will the negative behaviors. For example, research on the positive impact of media portrayals of cooperation and constructive problem solving (Baran, Chase, & Courtright, 1979) and on prosocial video-game play's ability to reduce the propensity for distracted driving (Downs et al., 2018) indicate that much more than negative behavior can be socially learned from the media.

There is also a large body of research demonstrating that entertainment media can be instrumental in improving people's health. Recalling *willing suspension of disbelief* from earlier in this chapter, it's easy to understand **narrative persuasion theory**, the idea that being "absorbed" into a narrative is one way that media stories can influence people's real-world beliefs and behaviors (Kim et al., 2012, p. 473). When people are transported into media content, they focus their attention and thinking on what's on the screen in front of them, see similarity between themselves and the characters, and empathize with them as a result. They are then less likely to become aware of—and resist—any possible persuasion or "lessons" embedded in the story.

Emily Moyer-Gusé (2008) combined this idea with social cognitive theory to develop her **entertainment overcoming resistance model**, which argues that there are "features of entertainment media" that produce involvement with characters or the stories themselves that lead to "story-consistent attitudes and behaviors by overcoming various forms of resistance" to health advice, such as reluctance to see a physician or ignoring exercise and dietary information (p. 420). Does narrative persuasion work? Shelia Murphy and her colleagues showed they do, using a lymphoma storyline from the television drama *Desperate Housewives*

USING MEDIA TO MAKE A DIFFERENCE
Television and the Designated Driver

Television's ability to serve prosocial ends is obvious in the public service messages we see sprinkled throughout the shows we watch. For example, NBC's *The More You Know* series has been running short, clever PSAs mixed among its regular commercials for more than 30 years. They feature the network's biggest stars, cover issues such as quitting smoking, good parenting, remembering to take prescriptions, and exercising, but you probably remember them from their iconic shooting star and rainbow tail.

However, television writers and producers also more aggressively use their medium to produce prosocial effects by embedding important cultural messages in the entertainment they create. The relationship between the Centers for Disease Control and Prevention (CDC) and several popular programs is indicative. Aware that most Americans say they learn about health issues from television, experts at the CDC have worked with the writers of series such as *Black-ish*, *Grey's Anatomy*, *ER*, *Army Wives*, *Law & Order*, and *Madam Secretary* to include important health information in their scripts.

If you watched the "Maggie's Mom" storyline on *Grey's Anatomy* you learned about inflammatory breast cancer; its episode on rape kits created a massive increase in Internet searches about rape and sexual assault and calls to the National Sexual Assault Hotline; *This Is Us* tackles mental health throughout its seasons; *Black-ish*'s "Sprinkles" episode revolves around pre-eclampsia; and *Sesame Street*'s "Meet Julia" episode offered understanding of autism. The CDC even offers "Resources for Writers" so that they can better represent the many different health issues that will inevitably make their way into movie and TV scripts.

This "prime-time activism" can be traced to Harvard professor Jay Winsten and his 1988 campaign to get Hollywood to push his novel "designated driver" idea. You know what a designated driver is—he or she is the person among a group of friends who is selected to remain alcohol-free during a get-together and then drive everyone else home. The concept, much less the term, did not even exist until Professor Winsten, through the intervention of CBS executive Frank Stanton, contacted Stanton's friend Grant Tinker, then chair of NBC, to ask for help. Intrigued by Winsten's plan to develop a new social norm, Tinker put his considerable clout behind the effort, writing letters to the heads of the 13 production companies that did the most business with the networks. Tinker personally escorted Professor Winsten, director of Harvard's Center for Health Communication, to meetings with all 13 producers.

In the four network television seasons that followed these meetings, designated drivers were part of the story lines of 160 different prime-time shows seen by hundreds of millions of viewers. Professor Winsten was successful in placing his message in entertainment programming, but did his message make a difference? Absolutely. Within three years, among Americans under the age of 30, 52% had actually served as a designated driver; among frequent drinkers, 54% had been driven home by a designated driver. When the campaign began, annual alcohol-related traffic fatalities stood at 23,626. By 1994, fatalities had declined by 30 (Center for Health Communication, 2021).

(Murphy et. al., 2011). They demonstrated that involvement with the show's characters improved not only knowledge of cancer but also produced life-saving changes in behavior, for example getting checkups and searching the Web for information on the disease and related public health organizations. You can read about another valuable use of entertainment fare in the essay "Television and the Designated Driver."

DEVELOPING MEDIA LITERACY SKILLS
Applying Mass Communication Theory

There are many more theories of mass communication and effects issues than we've covered here. Some apply to the operation of media as part of specific social systems. Some examine mass communication at the most micro level; for example, how do viewers process individual television scenes? This chapter has focused on a relatively small number of theories and effects that might prove useful to people trying to develop their media literacy skills. Among media scholar Art Silverblatt's (2008) elements of media literacy are understanding the process of mass communication and accepting media content as a "text" providing insight into ourselves and our culture. Additionally, one of the most important media literacy skills is to have an understanding of and respect for the power of media messages. See Chapter 1 for the full list of Silverblatt's elements of media literacy and the full list of necessary media literacy skills. Good mass communication theory speaks to these elements and skills. Good mass communication theorists understand media effects. Media-literate people, then, are actually good mass communication theorists. They apply the available conceptions of media use and impact to their own content consumption and the way they live their lives.

MEDIA LITERACY CHALLENGE
Be a News Production Researcher

An awareness of the impact of media on individuals and society is an important component of media literacy, and as you've read, news production research suggests that media do indeed have a powerful effect on people and culture. This body of thought examines economic and other influences on the way news is produced and how these influences distort coverage in favor of society's elites. Like much of critical cultural theory, this is a controversial perspective, but your challenge is to test its validity for yourself. First, choose one of the following media outlets (or if you want to compete against your classmates, divide them between yourselves): a daily newspaper, a local television news broadcast, a national news magazine, a network television news broadcast, and a cable TV news show. Then, identify as many examples of the four common news production conventions as you can find—personalized, dramatized, fragmented, and normalized news—and discuss their "slant." Once you've completed this exercise, explain why you are more or less likely to accept the arguments of the news production research perspective.

Resources for Review and Discussion

REVIEW POINTS: TYING CONTENT TO LEARNING OUTCOMES

▶ **Recall the history and development of mass communication theory.**
- Developments in mass communication theory are driven by advances in technology or the introduction of new media, calls for their control, and questions about their democratic and pluralistic use.

▶ **Explain what is meant by theory, why it is important, and how it is used.**
- To understand mass communication theory we must recognize the following:
  - There is no one mass communication theory.
  - Theories are often borrowed from other fields of science.
  - Theories are human constructions and are dynamic.

- Three dichotomies characterize the different sides in the effects debate:
  - Micro- versus macro-level effects.
  - Administrative versus critical research.
  - Transmissional versus ritual perspective on communication.
- In the media effects debate, these arguments for limited media influence have logical counters:
  - Media content is make-believe; people know it's not real.
  - Media content is only play or entertainment.
  - Media simply hold a mirror to society.
  - If media have any influence, it is only in reinforcing preexisting values and beliefs.
  - Media influence only the unimportant things like fads and fashions.

▶ **Describe influential traditional and contemporary mass communication theories.**

    □ The four major eras of mass communication theory are mass society theory, limited effects theory, cultural theory, and the meaning-making perspective. The latter two mark a return to the idea of powerful media effects.

▶ **Analyze controversial effects issues, such as violence, media's impact on drug and alcohol consumption, and media's contribution to racial and gender stereotyping.**

    □ Despite lingering debate, the media violence–viewer aggression link is scientifically well established.

□ The same holds true for the relationship between media portrayals of drug and alcohol use and their real-world consumption.

□ The stories carried in the media can and do contribute to stereotyping of a wide array of people and phenomena.

□ The same scientific evidence demonstrating that media can have negative effects shows that they can produce prosocial effects as well.

▶ **Apply mass communication theory to your own use of media.**

    □ Media-literate individuals are themselves good mass communication theorists because they understand media effects and how and when they occur.

KEY TERMS

early window, 318

willing suspension of disbelief, 318

micro-level effects, 319

macro-level effects, 320

administrative research, 320

critical research, 320

transmissional perspective, 321

ritual perspective, 321

mass communication
   theories, 321

cultivation analysis, 321

attitude change theory, 321

middle-range theories, 321

mass society theory, 323

hypodermic needle theory, 323

magic bullet theory, 323

grand theory, 323

limited effects theory, 324

two-step flow theory, 324

opinion leaders, 324

opinion followers, 325

dissonance theory, 326

selective processes, 326

selective exposure
   (selective attention), 326

selective retention, 326

selective perception, 326

reinforcement theory, 327

uses and gratifications approach, 327

agenda setting, 328

second-order agenda setting, 328

social cognitive theory, 329

modeling, 329

imitation, 329

identification, 329

observational learning, 329

inhibitory effects, 329

disinhibitory effects, 329

cultural theory, 330

critical cultural theory, 330

neo-Marxist theory, 330

Frankfurt School, 330

British cultural theory, 332

news production research, 332

mediatization theory, 333

media logic, 334

meaning-making perspective, 334

symbolic interaction, 334

product positioning, 334

social construction of reality theory, 334

symbols, 335

signs, 335

typification schemes, 335

mainstreaming, 335

stimulation model, 339

aggressive cues model, 339

catharsis, 339

vicarious reinforcement, 339

environmental incentives, 339

desensitization, 340

stereotyping, 341

parasocial contact hypothesis, 342

mediated intergroup contact hypothesis, 342

narrative persuasion theory, 343

entertainment overcoming
   resistance model, 343

QUESTIONS FOR REVIEW

1. What are the four eras of mass communication theory?

2. What are dissonance theory and the selective processes?

3. What is agenda setting? Second-order agenda setting?

4. What is the distinction between imitation and identification in social cognitive theory?

5. What assumptions about people and media are shared by symbolic interaction and social construction of reality?

6. What are the five assumptions of cultivation analysis?

7. What four common news production conventions shape the news to suit the interests of the elite?

8. What are the characteristics of critical cultural studies?

9. What are the early window and willing suspension of disbelief?

10. What are the stimulation and aggressive cues models of media violence? What is catharsis?

To maximize your study time, check out CONNECT to access the SmartBook study module for this chapter, watch videos, and explore other resources.

QUESTIONS FOR CRITICAL THINKING AND DISCUSSION

1. Do media set the agenda for you? If not, why not? If they do, can you cite examples from your own experience?

2. Can you find examples of magazine or television advertising that use ideas from symbolic interaction or social construction of reality to sell their products? How do they do so?

3. Do you pay attention to alcohol advertising? Do you think it influences your level of alcohol consumption?

REFERENCES

1. Albiniak, P. (1999, May 3). Media: Littleton's latest suspect. *Broadcasting & Cable*, pp. 6-15.

2. Allport, G. W., & Postman, L. J. (1945). The basic psychology of rumor. *Transactions of the New York Academy of Sciences, 8,* 61-81.

3. Alterman, E. (2008, February 24). The news from Quinn-Broderville. *Nation*, pp. 11-14.

4. Arato, A., & Gebhardt, E. (1978). *The essential Frankfurt School reader.* New York: Urizen Books.

5. Bandura, A. (1965). Influence of models' reinforcement contingencies on the acquisition of imitative responses. *Journal of Personality and Social Psychology, 1,* 589-595.

6. Bandura, A. (2001). Social cognitive theory of mass communication. *Media Psychology, 3,* 265-299.

7. Baran, S. J., Chase, L. J., & Courtright, J. A. (1979). *The Waltons:* Television as a facilitator of prosocial behavior. *Journal of Broadcasting, 23,* 277-284.

8. Baran, S. J., & Davis, D. K. (2021). *Mass communication theory: Foundations, ferment and future* (8th ed.). New York: Oxford University Press.

9. Bazelon, E. (2020, October 18). Freedom of speech will preserve our democracy. *New York Times Magazine*, pp. 26-31, 41-45.

10. Bennett, W. L. (1988). *News: The politics of illusion.* New York: Longman.

11. Berger, P. L., & Luckmann, T. (1966). *The social construction of reality: A treatise in the sociology of knowledge.* Garden City, NY: Doubleday.

12. Boehlert, E. (2020, August 19). Trump, Putin, and the emails—Hillary deserves media apology. *Press Run.* Retrieved from https://pressrun.media/p/trump-putin-and-the-emails-hillary

13. Bryant, J., Thompson, S., & Finklea, B. W. (2013). *Fundamentals of media effects.* Long Grove, IL: Waveland Press.

14. Carey, J. W. (1975). A cultural approach to communication. *Communication, 2,* 1-22.

15. Center for Health Communication. (2021). Harvard alcohol project: Designated driver. *Harvard School of Public Health.* Retrieved from https://www.hsph.harvard.edu/chc/harvard-alcohol-project/

16. Collier, G. (2020, April 19). Gene Collier: 35 years after Air Jordans, we're still killing each other over sneakers. *Pittsburgh Post-Gazette.* Retrieved from https://www.post-gazette.com/sports/gene-collier/2020/04/19/Kanye-West-Yeezys-Jordan-Dr-J-shoes-violence-gene-collier/stories/202004190048

17. Deggans, E. (2020, December 4). More evidence TV doesn't reflect real life diversity. *National Public Radio.* Retrieved from https://www.npr.org/2020/12/04/942574850/more-evidence-tv-doesnt-reflect-real-life-diversity

18. Downs, E., et al. (2018). Fair game: Using simulators to change likelihood of distracted driving at the Minnesota State Fair. *Communication Research Reports, 35,* 121-130.

19. Ford, M. (2020, July-August). Bill Barr's invisible crusade. *New Republic*, pp. 30-34, 37.

20. Faules, D. F., & Alexander, D. C. (1978). *Communication and social behavior: A symbolic interaction perspective.* Reading, MA: Addison-Wesley.

21. Gerbner, G., Gross, L., Jackson-Beeck, M., Jeffries-Fox, S., & Signorielli, N. (1978). Cultural indicators: Violence profile no. 9. *Journal of Communication, 28,* 176-206.

22. Gerbner, G., Gross, L., Morgan, M., & Signorielli, N. (1980). The "mainstreaming" of America: Violence profile no. 11. *Journal of Communication, 30,* 10-29.

23. Gitlin, T. (2004, July). It was a very bad year. *American Prospect,* pp. 31-34.

24. Graceffo, L. (2020, August 12). Activist voices missing from corporate coverage of uprisings. *FAIR.* Retrieved from https://fair.org/home/activist-voices-missing-from-corporate-coverage-of-uprisings/

25. Gramlich, J. (2019, November 20). What the data says (and doesn't say) about crime in the United States. *Pew Research Center.* Retrieved from https://www.pewresearch.org/fact-tank/2020/11/20/facts-about-crime-in-the-u-s/

26. Graves, L. (2018, January 2). Trump's attacks against a biased liberal media obscure one fact: It doesn't exist. *Guardian.* Retrieved from https://www.theguardian.com/commentisfree/2018/jan/02/trump-biased-liberal-media-television

27. Hagle, C. (2021, January 22). Local and national media outlets are citing anti-immigrant extremist groups to discuss Biden's immigration plan. *Media Matters.* Retrieved from https://www.mediamatters.org/immigration/local-and-national-media-outlets-are-citing-anti-immigrant-extremist-groups-discuss

28. Hall, S. (1980). Cultural studies: Two paradigms. *Media, Culture and Society, 2,* 57-72.

29. Hassell, G., Holbein, J. B., & Miles, R. M. (2020). There is no liberal media bias in which news stories political journalists choose to cover. *Science Advances, 6:* 9344.

30. Hovland, C. I., Lumsdaine, A. A., & Sheffield, F. D. (1949). *Experiments on mass communication.* Princeton, NJ: Princeton University Press.

31. "Important Welfare Statistics for 2020." (2020, January 3). *Lexington Law*. Retrieved from https://www.lexingtonlaw.com/blog/finance/welfare-statistics.html

32. Iyengar, S., & Kinder, D. R. (1987). *News that matters: Television and American opinion*. Chicago: University of Chicago Press.

33. Jurkowitz, M., Mitchell, A., Shearer, E., & Walker, M. (2020, January 24). U.S. media polarization and the 2020 election: a nation divided. *Pew Research Center*. Retrieved from https://www.journalism.org/2020/01/24/u-s-media-polarization-and-the-2020-election-a-nation-divided/

34. Jhally, S. (2013). *Joystick warriors*. Retrieved from http://www.mediaed.org/transcripts/Joystick-Warriors-Transcript.pdf

35. Kaba, M. (2020, June 14). Yes, we mean literally abolish the police. *New York Times*, p. SR2.

36. Katz, E., & Lazarsfeld, P. F. (1955). *Personal influence: The part played by people in the flow of communications*. New York: Free Press.

37. Kim, H. S., Bigman, C. A., Leader, A. E., Lerman, C., & Cappella, J. N. (2012). Narrative health communication and behavior change: The influence of exemplars in the news on intention to quit smoking. *Journal of Communication, 62*, 473–492.

38. Klapper, J. T. (1960). *The effects of mass communication*. New York: Free Press.

39. Knobloch-Westerwick, S., & Westerwick, A. (2020). *Mediated communication dynamics: Shaping you and your society*. New York: Oxford University Press.

40. Lane, D. (2019, November 19). Shame on Sprite for partnering with destructive transgender indoctrination. *Charisma News*. Retrieved from https://www.charismanews.com/opinion/renewing-america/78848-shame-on-sprite-for-partnering-with-destructive-transgender-indoctrination

41. Langum, F. (2019, July 23). Gorka blames Teletubbies for "that whole trans thing." *Crooks & Liars*. Retrieved from https://crooksandliars.com/2019/07/seb-gorka-says-teletubbies-started-whole

42. Lazarsfeld, P. F. (1941). Remarks on administrative and critical communications research. *Studies in Philosophy and Social Science, 9*, 2–16.

43. Light, L. (2018, November 14). How did Republicans learn to hate the news media? *Columbia Journalism Review*. Retrieved from https://www.cjr.org/first_person/republicans-media.php

44. Lithwick, D. (2012, March 12). Extreme makeover. *New Yorker*, pp. 76–79.

45. Lowery, S. A., & DeFleur, M. L. (1995). *Milestones in mass communication research*. White Plains, NY: Longman.

46. Lull, R. B., & Bushman, B. J. (2015). Do sex and violence sell? A meta-analytic review of the effects of sexual and violent media and ad content on memory, attitudes, and buying intentions. *Psychological Bulletin, 141*, 1022–1048.

47. Magary, D. (2017, April 5). CNN's Jeff Zucker thinks this is all just a game. *GQ*. Retrieved from https://www.gq.com/story/cnn-jeff-zucker-thinks-this-is-a-game

48. Martin, S. E., & Mail, P. D. (1995). *The effects of the mass media on the use and abuse of alcohol*. Washington, DC: U.S. Department of Health and Human Services.

49. McCann, A. (2020, February 18). Most sinful states in America. *Wallethub*. Retrieved from https://wallethub.com/edu/most-sinful-states/46852/

50. McCombs, M., & Ghanem, S. I. (2001). The convergence of agenda setting and framing. In S. D. Reese, O. H. Gandy, and A. E. Grant (Eds.), *Framing public life: Perspectives on media and our understanding of the social world* (pp. 67–82). Mahwah, NJ: Erlbaum.

51. McCombs, M. E., & Shaw, D. L. (1972). The agenda-setting function of mass media. *Public Opinion Quarterly, 36*, 176–187.

52. McHarris, P. V. (2020, November 30). When police traffic in racism. *Nation*, pp. 24–27.

53. Merton, R. K. (1967). *On theoretical sociology*. New York: Free Press.

54. Moyer-Gusé, E. (2008). Toward a theory of entertainment persuasion: Explaining the persuasive effects of entertainment-education messages. *Communication Theory, 18*, 407–425.

55. Murphy, S. T., Frank, L. B., Moran, M. B., & Patnoe-Woodley, P. (2011). Involved, transported, or emotional? Exploring the determinants of change in knowledge, attitudes, and behavior in entertainment-education. *Journal of Communication, 61*, 407–431.

56. Naimi, T. S., Ross, C. S., Siegel, M. B., DeJong, W., & Jernigan, D. H. (2016). Amount of televised alcohol advertising exposure and the quantity of alcohol consumed by youth. *Journal of Studies on Alcohol and Drugs, 77*, 723–729.

57. National Institute on Alcohol Abuse and Alcoholism. (2021, March). Underage drinking. *U.S. Department of Health and Human Services*. Retrieved from https://www.niaaa.nih.gov/publications/brochures-and-fact-sheets/underage-drinking

58. Naureckas, J. (2009, July). Before we "save" journalism. *Extra!*, p. 5.

59. Nichols, J. (2019, August 26/September 2). News you can lose. *Nation*, pp. 3–4.

60. Ninety-Second Congress. (1972). *Hearings before the Subcommittee on Communications on the Surgeon General's Report by the Scientific Advisory Committee on Television and Social Behavior*. Washington, DC: U.S. Government Printing Office.

61. "The Opioid Crisis and the Black/African American Population: An Urgent Issue." (2020, May 2). *U.S. Department of Health and Human Services*. Retrieved from https://store.samhsa.gov/sites/default/files/SAMHSA_Digital_Download/PEP20-05-02-001_508%20Final.pdf

62. Owens, E. (2020, April 6). Justice on the streets of Philadelphia. *Nation*, pp. 22–25.

63. Ortiz, M., & Harwood, J. (2007). A social cognitive theory approach to the effects of mediated intergroup contact on intergroup attitudes. *Journal of Broadcasting and Electronic Media, 51*, 615–631.

64. Poniewozik, J. (2020, November 22). This show has been canceled. *New York Times*, pp. AR1, AR4.

65. Schiappa, E., Gregg, P. B., & Hewes, D. E. (2005). The parasocial contact hypothesis. *Communication Monographs*, *72*, 92–115.

66. Schimmack, U., & Carlsson, R. (2020). Young unarmed nonsuicidal male victims of fatal use of force are 13 times more likely to be Black than White. *Proceedings of the National Academy of Sciences*, 117: 1263.

67. Schiffrin, A. (2020, October 19/26). The infodemic. *Nation*, pp. 58–62.

68. Silverblatt, A. (2008). *Media literacy* (3rd ed.). Westport, CT: Praeger.

69. Soundbites. (2018, November). Morning Edition's think tank guests skew right. *Extra!*, p. 2.

70. Terle, R. (2016, August 23). The 15 most horrific crimes inspired by the media. *The Richest*. Retrieved from http://www.therichest.com/rich-list/most-shocking/the-15-most-horrific-crimes-inspired-by-the-media/

71. Wartella, E. A. (1997). *The context of television violence.* Boston: Allyn & Bacon.

72. Weber, P. (2021, March 24). Majority of Republicans now support same-sex marriage, poll finds. *Yahoo News*. Retrieved from https://www.yahoo.com/now/majority-republicans-now-support-same-111614413.html

73. Wronge, Y. S. (2000, August 17). New report fuels TV-violence debate. *San Jose Mercury News,* pp. 1 E, 3 E.

74. Zakrzewski, C. (2021, February 1). The Technology 202: New report calls conservative claims of social media censorship "a form of disinformation." *Washington Post*. Retrieved from https://www.washingtonpost.com/politics/2021/02/01/technology-202-new-report-calls-conservative-claims-social-media-censorship-a-form-disinformation/

Cultural Forum Blue Column icon, Media Literacy Red Torch Icon, Using Media Green Gear icon, Developing Media book in starburst icon: ©McGraw Hill

◀ Whether or not to publish images of protesters who can be easily identified and punished by authorities or harassed by extremists is one of many ethical dilemmas facing media professionals.

Jelani Photography/Shutterstock

Learning Objectives

Free and responsible mass media are essential to our democracy because access to a wide array of information from a wide array of sources is the foundation of our self-governance. But media, because of their power and the conflicting demands of profit and service under which they operate, are (and should be) open to some control. The level and sources of that control, however, are controversial issues for the media, in the government, and in the public forum. After studying this chapter, you should be able to

▶ Recall the history and development of our contemporary understanding of the First Amendment.

▶ Explain the justification for and exercise of media regulation.

▶ Compare a media system that operates under a libertarian philosophy with one that operates under a social responsibility philosophy.

▶ Recall how media ethics are applied.

▶ Describe the operation and pros and cons of self-regulation.

▶ Apply skills to better judge the value of news reports using ethical values.

1644 Milton's *Areopagitica*

1791 ▶ Bill of Rights ratified

National Archives and Records Administration

1900

1919 ▶ "Clear and present danger" ruling

Mel Curtis/Photodisc/Getty Images

1925

1931 *Near v. Minnesota* prior restraint ruling

1935 ▶ Hauptmann/Lindbergh trial

1943 NBC "traffic cop" decision

1947 Social responsibility theory of the press

1950

1964 *New York Times v. Sullivan* public figure ruling

1969 *Red Lion* decision

1971 ▶ Pentagon Papers

1973 *Miller* decision defines obscenity

Bettmann/Getty Images

1975

1980 Deregulation of media begins in earnest

1984 *Betamax* decision

1988 Extensive rewriting of copyright law

Bettmann/Getty Images

2000

2001 Creative Commons founded

2005 *MGM v. Grokster P2P* ruling; Judith Miller jailed

2009 Pirate Bay founders jailed; Supreme Court upholds FCC indecency rules

2011 *Brown v. Entertainment Merchants Assn.*

2012 *FCC v. Fox*

2013 Edward Snowden revelations

2014 SPJ revised Code of Ethics; California anti-paparazzi law

2016 *The New York Times* overhauls confidentiality rules

2017 *The New York Times* eliminates public editor position

2018 Press critic Gillmor calls for activist journalism

2020 Coronavirus in the US; calls for movement journalism

2021 Insurrection at US Capitol; Parler de-platformed; AP limits use of mugshots

UP UNTIL NOW, EVERYTHING HAD BEEN RIGHT ABOUT THE JOB. Editor of a major college daily newspaper makes a great résumé entry; you are treated like royalty at school events; and you get to do something good for your campus and, if you do your job well, even for the larger world out there. But as the tension around you grows, you start to wonder if it's all worth it.

First, there was issue of the paper's coverage of hate on campus and in the country. The FBI had announced that hate-based violence had reached a 16-year high (Shattuck & Risse, 2021), so you thought this difficult issue should not be ignored. The staff was on board but balked at using terms in their reporting such as *white supremacists*, *racists*, *bigots*, and *Nazis*. They wanted to use the labels many of those people had given themselves, *alt-right* or *militias*. You're the editor, you reminded them, and you want clear language in your stories. "Those who spew hate and racism aren't alt-anything; the so-called militias are more vigilantes than patriots," you argued, maybe a bit too angrily.

"But we want to be fair," was the counter. "If that's what they want to be called, is it our place to say otherwise?"

"Yes, it is" you explained. "A militia, is supposed to be well-regulated, formed to supplement a legitimate army in an emergency, not to create chaos. And *alt-right* is a meaningless euphemism; *alternative* to what? Murders don't get to call themselves *alternative population managers*.

"We don't have to be neutral in our rejection of bigotry," argued your assistant editor, "just neutral in our choice of words."

You snap at him, "We are journalists! We are truthful, not neutral. It isn't our job to tidy up who these people are, what they say, and what they stand for. Our job as journalists is to tell the truth, right?"

Hearing no answer, you waded into the issue of a change in the AP Stylebook, your paper's writer's guide. The news service had recently amended its advice on how to report on incidents of police use of firearms. "Avoid the vague 'officer-involved' for shootings and other cases involving police," it stated. "Be specific about what happened."

"But what if the police use the term. They're the authorities; shouldn't we quote them?" asked one staffer.

The AP is clear on this as well, you responded, "If police use the term, ask: How was the officer or officers involved? Who did the shooting? If the information is not available or not provided, spell that out" (Associated Press, 2020).

This, too, did not sit well with many of your colleagues, who rejected your argument that the passive construction of "officer-involved shooting" hides who the shooter is and who was shot. Although the phrase has been in journalistic use since the early 1970s (Frazier, 2020), you explained, again maybe a little too vehemently, journalists don't need the AP stylebook to tell them that a straightforward declarative sentence—subject, transitive verb, object—is not only good grammar but good reporting.

In these instances, you've argued in favor of more, rather than less clarity, more straightforward reporting and less obfuscation. This is America; who can have a problem with that? The first article on your series on racism in America is headlined, "Racists and Bigots Demean a Great Country." And before you even have the opportunity to edit away even one "officer-involved shooting," you get 37 angry phone calls and e-mails, 4 longtime advertisers pull their regular weekly ads, and your assistant editor and two other staffers quit the paper.

These conflicts, routinely faced by real college and professional editors, highlight two important lessons offered in this chapter. First, what is legal and permissible may not always be what is right; even seemingly routine choices, such as word style, carry important implications. Second, when media practitioners do try to do the right thing, they have to consider the interests, needs, and values of others besides themselves.

In this chapter, we look at how the First Amendment has been defined and applied over time. We study how the logic of a free and unfettered press has come into play in the area of broadcast deregulation. We also detail the shift in the underlying philosophy of media freedom from libertarianism to social responsibility theory. This provides the background for our examination of the ethical environment in which media professionals must work as they strive to fulfill their socially responsible obligations.

A Short History of the First Amendment

The US Constitution mentions only one industry by name as deserving special protection— the press. Therefore, our examination of media regulation, self-regulation, and ethics must begin with a discussion of this "First Freedom."

The first Congress of the United States was committed to freedom of the press. The First Amendment to the new Constitution expressly stated that "Congress shall make no law . . . abridging the freedom of speech, or of the press." As a result, government regulation of the media must be not only unobtrusive but also sufficiently justified to meet the limits of the First Amendment. Media industry self-regulation must be sufficiently effective to render official restraint unnecessary, and media practitioners' conduct should be ethical in order to warrant this special protection.

Early Sentiment for a Free Press

Democracy—government by the people—requires a free press. The framers of the Bill of Rights understood this because of their experience with the European monarchies from which they and their forebears had fled. They based their guarantee of this privileged position to the press on **libertarianism**, the philosophy of the press asserting that good and rational people can tell right from wrong if presented with full and free access to information; therefore, censorship is unnecessary. Libertarianism is based on the **self-righting principle**, originally stated in 1644 by English author and poet John Milton in his book *Areopagitica*. His argument was simple: The free flow or trade of ideas, even bad or uncomfortable ones, will inevitably produce the truth because a rational and good public will correct, or right, any errors.

However, even the First Amendment and libertarian philosophy did not guarantee freedom of the press. The Alien and Sedition Acts were passed a scant eight years after the Constitution was ratified, making it illegal to print criticism of government or its leaders. And Milton himself was to become the chief censor of Catholic writing in Oliver Cromwell's English government. How committed are you to free expression? You can decide after reading the essay "Who Decides Who Has an Online Voice?"

◀ The 1787 Philadelphia Constitutional Convention. Because they knew democracy could not survive otherwise, the framers of the Constitution wrote the First Amendment to guarantee that the new nation would enjoy freedom of speech and press.
MPI/Archive Photos/Getty Images

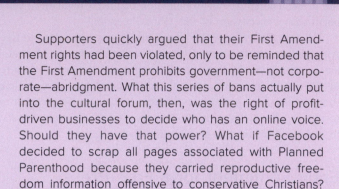

Over the last few years, as America's political divide has grown increasingly toxic and the country has suffered violence, protests, and fracture along political lines so severe that, in the words of historian Sophia Rosenfeld, "Common ground—the low-level shared realm of common sense necessary to start a meaningful conversation in the public sphere with a random interlocutor—[became] impossible to locate" (in Luo, 2020), a number of Internet companies moved to distance themselves from what they deemed the worst offenders.

Web hosting company GoDaddy stopped hosting neo-Nazi website *The Daily Stormer*. Google and Cloudflare also refused it a home. PayPal and Apple Pay refused to transact its business. GoFundMe and Kickstarter declined to host fundraising campaigns for it and other bigoted projects. Following suit, Spotify pulled several white supremacist bands from its platform and OkCupid banned racist relationship seekers. Facebook, YouTube, and Apple eliminated conspiracy theorist Alex Jones's *Infowars* pages. America's fourth most visited website, Reddit, banned several "communities," including r/Coontown and r/KillAllJews.

Troubled by the cult-like insistence of conspiracy group QAnon and its millions of online followers that there exists a cabal of liberal political, business, and Hollywood elites who worship Satan and abuse, murder, and cannibalize children, Twitter banned 7,000 of its accounts for violating its rules against manipulation, misinformation, and harassment (Sen & Zadronzy, 2020). In the face of evidence that moderator-free social network Parler had been a hub for instigation of and planning for the deadly insurrectionist attack on the US Capitol in January 2021, Apple and Google removed its app from their stores and Amazon dropped it from its web hosting service, effectively **deplatforming** it; that is, denying it an audience by eradicating followers' access (Bazelon, 2021).

Supporters quickly argued that their First Amendment rights had been violated, only to be reminded that the First Amendment prohibits government—not corporate—abridgment. What this series of bans actually put into the cultural forum, then, was the right of profit-driven businesses to decide who has an online voice. Should they have that power? What if Facebook decided to scrap all pages associated with Planned Parenthood because they carried reproductive freedom information offensive to conservative Christians? What if Twitter closed the accounts of groups pushing for national single-payer health insurance because some thought it smacked of socialism?

But surely, you say, there's a big difference between expressions of hate and fomenting sedition and advocating for what might be unpopular or controversial policy or political positions. However, to those denied their voice there may be no difference. What has become of the argument that the best remedy for bad speech is more speech?

Enter Your Voice

- You can't falsely shout "fire" in a crowded theater, so should online speakers be able to freely shout ideas that lead to violence and threats of bodily harm?
- Is there any place in civil society for expression that diminishes the humanity of others?
- If you reject the idea that the government should determine whose ideas are given voice, why would you be comfortable granting that power to big corporations such as Facebook, Twitter, and Google?

Defining and Refining the First Amendment

Clearly, the idea of freedom of the press needed some clarification. One view is housed in the **absolutist position**, which is expressed succinctly by Supreme Court Justice Hugo Black:

> No law means no law. . . . My view is, without deviation, without exception, without any ifs, buts, or whereases, that freedom of speech means that government shall not do anything to people, either for the views they have or the views they express, or the words they speak or write. (*New York Times v. United States,* 1971)

Yet the absolutist position is more complex than this would suggest. Although absolutists accept that the First Amendment provides a central and fundamental wall of protection for the press and free expression, several questions about its true meaning remained to be answered over time.

WHAT DOES "NO LAW" MEAN? The First Amendment said that the US Congress could "make no law," but could state legislatures? City councils? Mayors? Courts? Who has the power to proscribe the press? This issue was settled in 1925 in a case involving the right of a state to limit the publication of a socialist newsletter. The Supreme Court, in *Gitlow v. New York,* stated that the First Amendment is "among the fundamental personal rights and 'liberties' protected by the due process clause of the Fourteenth Amendment from impairment by the states" (Gillmor & Barron, 1974, p. 1). Given this, "Congress shall make no law" should be interpreted as "government agencies shall make no law." Today, "no law" includes statutes, laws, administrative regulations, executive and court orders, and ordinances from government, regardless of locale.

WHAT IS "THE PRESS"? Just what "press" enjoys First Amendment protection? The Supreme Court, in its 1952 *Joseph Burstyn, Inc. v. Wilson* decision, declared that movies are protected expression. In 1973, Justice William O. Douglas wrote in *CBS v. Democratic National Committee* (1973),

> What kind of First Amendment would best serve our needs as we approach the 21st century may be an open question. But the old fashioned First Amendment that we have is the Court's only guideline; and one hard and fast principle has served us through days of calm and eras of strife, and I would abide by it until a new First Amendment is adopted. That means, as I view it, that TV and radio . . . are all included in the concept of "press" as used in the First Amendment and therefore are entitled to live under the laissez faire regime which the First Amendment sanctions.

Advertising, or commercial speech, enjoys First Amendment protection. This was established by the Supreme Court in 1942. Despite the fact that the decision in *Valentine v. Christensen* went against the advertiser, the Court wrote that just because expression was commercial did not necessarily mean that it was unprotected. Some justices argued for a "two-tiered" level of protection, with commercial expression being somewhat less worthy of protection than noncommercial expression. But others argued that this was illogical because almost all media are, in fact, commercial, even when they perform a primarily journalistic function. Newspapers, for example, print the news to make a profit, as do podcasts and websites.

In its 1967 *Time, Inc. v. Hill* decision, the Supreme Court applied similar logic to argue that the First Amendment grants the same protection to entertainment content as it does to nonentertainment content. Is an entertainingly written news report less worthy of protection than one that is dully written? Rather than allow the government to make these kinds of narrow and ultimately subjective judgments, the Supreme Court has consistently preferred expanding its definition of protected expression to limiting it.

WHAT IS "ABRIDGMENT"? **Abridgment** is the curtailing of rights, and even absolutists accept the idea that some curtailment or limits can be placed on the time, place, and manner of expression—as long as the restrictions do not interfere with the substance of the expression. Few, for example, would find it unreasonable to limit the use of a sound truck to broadcast political messages at 4:00 a.m. But the Supreme Court did find unconstitutional an ordinance that forbade all use of sound amplification except with the permission of the chief of police in its 1948 decision in *Saia v. New York*. The permissibility of other restrictions, however, is less clear-cut.

CLEAR AND PRESENT DANGER Can freedom of the press be limited if the likely result is damaging? The Supreme Court answered this question in 1919 in *Schenck v. United States*. In this case involving the distribution of a pamphlet urging illegal resistance to the military draft during World War I, Justice Oliver Wendell Holmes wrote that expression could be limited when "the words used are used in such circumstances and are of such a nature as to create a clear and present danger that they will bring about the substantive evils that Congress has a right to prevent." Justice Holmes added, "Free speech would not protect a man in falsely shouting fire in a theater and causing panic." This decision is especially important because it firmly established the legal philosophy that there is no absolute freedom of expression; the level of protection is one of degree.

BALANCING OF INTERESTS This less-than-absolutist approach is called the **ad hoc balancing of interests**. That is, in individual First Amendment cases several factors should be weighed in determining how much freedom the press is granted. In his dissent to the Court's 1941 decision in *Bridges v. California*, a case involving a *Los Angeles Times* editorial, Justice Felix Frankfurter wrote that freedom of speech and press is "not so absolute or irrational a conception as to imply paralysis of the means for effective protection of all the freedoms secured by the Bill of Rights. . . . In the cases before us, the claims on behalf of freedom of speech and of the press encounter claims on behalf of liberties no less precious."

FREE PRESS VERSUS FAIR TRIAL One example of the clash of competing liberties is the conflict between free press (First Amendment) and fair trial (Sixth Amendment). This debate typically takes two forms: (1) Can pretrial publicity deny citizens judgment by 12 impartial peers, thereby denying them a fair trial? (2) Should cameras be allowed in the courtroom, supporting the public's right to know, or do they so alter the workings of the court that a fair trial is impossible?

Courts have consistently decided in favor of fair trial in conflicts between the First and Sixth Amendments, but it was not until 1961 that a conviction was overturned because of pretrial publicity. In *Irvin v. Dowd* the Court reversed the death sentence conviction of accused killer Leslie Irvin because his right to a fair trial had been hampered by extremely prejudicial press coverage. As a result of this negative reporting, of 430 potential jurors screened before the trial by attorneys, 370 said they were already convinced Irvin was guilty. Although "tainted" by pretrial publicity, four of the 370 were seated as jurors. The Court determined that Irvin's trial was therefore unfair.

Print reporters have long enjoyed access to trials, but broadcast journalists have been less fortunate. In 1937, after serious intrusion by newspaper photographers during the 1935 trial of Bruno Hauptmann, accused of kidnapping the baby of transatlantic aviation hero Charles Lindbergh, the American Bar Association (ABA) adopted Canon 35 as part of its Code of Judicial Ethics. This rule forbade cameras and radio broadcasting of trials. In 1963 the ABA amended the canon to include a prohibition on television cameras. Nine years later the ABA replaced Canon 35 with Canon 3A(7), allowing some videotaping of trials for specific purposes but reaffirming its opposition to the broadcast of trial proceedings.

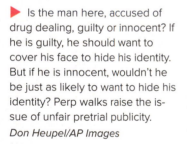

▶ Is the man here, accused of drug dealing, guilty or innocent? If he is guilty, he should want to cover his face to hide his identity. But if he is innocent, wouldn't he be just as likely to want to hide his identity? Perp walks raise the issue of unfair pretrial publicity.
Don Heupel/AP Images

But in 1981 the Supreme Court, in *Chandler v. Florida*, determined that television cameras in the courtroom were not inherently damaging to fairness. Today, all 50 states allow cameras in some courts—47 permit them in trial courts—and the US Congress periodically debates opening federal courts, including the Supreme Court, to cameras. For now, photography and broadcast of federal trials is banned by Federal Rule of Criminal Procedure 53. These limits persist despite the fact that two-thirds of Americans favor cameras in the Supreme Court, whose proceedings are otherwise released in transcripts and audio recordings (Bonazzo, 2018).

A related conflict between free press and fair trial involves seemingly routine images of the accused, typically in handcuffs, being escorted by law officers. These so-called perp walks often suggest guilt, but in our judicial system, no one is guilty until convicted at trial.

An extension of this issue is the growing use of mugshot galleries, especially online. These police photos are powerful click magnets, but they suffer from multiple problems beyond their suggestion of guilt. One is the implied seriousness of the crime; the mugshot of a murderer and that of a parent arrested protesting cuts in school funding not only look the same, but also often appear in the same gallery. Another is the lack of follow-up reporting. If the accused is acquitted and the posting site bothers to publish that fact, which most do not, it is far too late to undo any damage—for example, lost careers, friendships, and reputation. In 2021 the AP announced it would cease publishing accounts of minor crimes "driven" by embarrassing or odd-looking mugshots (Daniszewski, 2021).

LIBEL AND SLANDER **Libel**, the false or malicious publication of material that damages a person's reputation, and **slander**, the oral or spoken defamation of a person's character, are not protected by the First Amendment. The distinction between libel and slander, however, is sufficiently narrow so that "published defamation, whether it is in a newspaper, on radio or television, in the movies, or whatever, is regarded since the 1990s as libel. And libel rules apply" (Pember, 1999, p. 134). Therefore, if a report (1) defames a person, (2) identifies that person, and (3) is published or broadcast, it loses its First Amendment protection.

A report accused of being libelous or slanderous, however, is protected if it meets any one of three tests. The first test is *truth*. Even if a report damages someone's reputation, if it is true, it is protected. The second test is *privilege*. Coverage of legislative, court, or other public activities may contain information that is not true or that is damaging to someone's reputation. The press cannot be deterred from covering these important news events for fear that a speaker's or witness's comments will open it to claims of libel or slander. The third test is *fair comment*; that is, the press has the right to express opinions or comment on public issues. For example, theater and film reviews, however severe, are protected, as is commentary on other matters in the public eye.

For public figures, however, a different set of rules applies. Because they are in the public eye, public figures are fair game for fair comment. But does that leave them open to reports that are false and damaging to their reputations? The Supreme Court faced this issue in 1964 in *New York Times v. Sullivan*. In 1960, the Committee to Defend Martin Luther King bought a full-page ad in *The New York Times* asking people to contribute to Dr. King's defense fund. The ad detailed abuse of Dr. King and other civil rights workers at the hands of the Montgomery, Alabama, police. L. B. Sullivan, one of three elected commissioners in that city, sued the *Times* for libel. The ad copy was not true in some of its claims, he said, and because he was in charge of the police, he had been "identified."

The Supreme Court ruled in favor of the newspaper. Even though some of the specific facts in the ad were not true, the *Times* had not acted with **actual malice**. The Court defined the standard of actual malice for reporting on public figures as *knowledge of its falsity or reckless disregard* for whether or not it is true.

PRIOR RESTRAINT There is much less confusion about another important aspect of press freedom, **prior restraint**. This is the power of the government to *prevent* the publication or broadcast of expression. US law and tradition make the use of prior restraint relatively rare, but there have been a number of important efforts by government to squelch content before dissemination.

In 1931, the Supreme Court ruled in *Near v. Minnesota* that freedom from prior restraint was a general, not an absolute, principle. Two of the four exceptions it listed were in times of war when national security was involved and when the public order would be endangered by the incitement to violence and overthrow by force of orderly government. These exceptions were to become the basis of two landmark prior restraint decisions. The first, involving *The New York Times*, dealt with national security in times of war; the second, focusing on protecting the public order, involved publishing instructions for building an atomic bomb.

On June 13, 1971, at the height of the Vietnam War, *The New York Times* began publication of what became known as the Pentagon Papers. The papers included detailed discussion and analysis of the conduct of that unpopular war during the administrations of presidents Kennedy and Johnson. President Nixon's National Security Council (NSC) had stamped them top secret. Believing that this was an improper restriction of the public's right to know, NSC staff member Daniel Ellsberg gave copies to the *Times*. After the first three installments had been published, the Justice Department, citing national security, was able to secure a court order stopping further publication. Other newspapers, notably *The Washington Post* and *The Boston Globe*, began running excerpts while the *Times* was silenced until they, too, were enjoined to cease.

On June 30, 1971, the Supreme Court ordered the government to halt its restraint of the *Times*'s and other papers' right to publish the Pentagon Papers. Among the stirring attacks on prior restraint written throughout its decision was Justice Hugo Black's:

> In the First Amendment the Founding Fathers gave the free press the protection it must have to fulfill its essential role in our democracy. The press was to serve the governed, not the governors. The Government's power to censor the press was abolished so that the press would remain forever free to censure the Government. The press was protected so that it could bare the secrets of government and inform the people. Only a free and unrestrained press can effectively expose deception in government. (*New York Times v. United States,* 1971)

OBSCENITY AND PORNOGRAPHY Another form of media expression that is not protected is **obscenity**. Two landmark Supreme Court cases established the definition and illegality of obscenity. The first is the 1957 *Roth v. United States* decision. The Court determined that sex and obscenity were not synonymous, a significant advance for freedom of expression. It did, however, legally affirm for the first time that obscenity was unprotected expression. The definition or test for obscenity that holds even today was expressed in the

► Daniel Ellsberg, who gave the Pentagon Papers to *The New York Times*, celebrates that paper's Supreme Court victory.
Bettmann/Getty Images

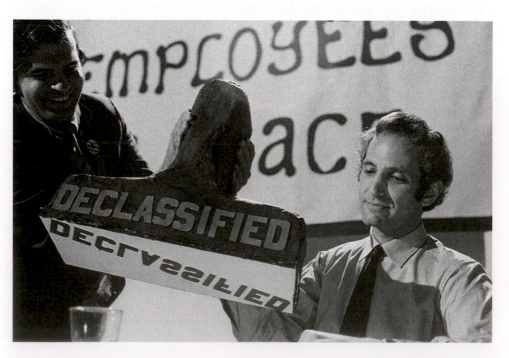

1973 *Miller v. State of California* decision. Chief Justice Warren Burger wrote that the basic guidelines must be

(a) whether the average person, applying contemporary community standards, would find that the work, taken as a whole, appeals to the prurient interest, (b) whether the work depicts or describes, in a patently offensive way, sexual conduct specifically defined by the applicable state law, and (c) whether the work, taken as a whole, lacks serious literary, artistic, political, or scientific value.

The problem for the courts, the media, and the public, of course, is judging content against this standard. For example, what is patently offensive to one person may be quite acceptable to others. What is serious art to one may be serious exploitation to another. And what of an erotic short story written by an author in New York City for a website hosted by a company in Memphis and accessed and read by people in Peoria? Whose community standards would apply?

An additional definitional problem resides in **pornography**. Pornography is protected expression. The distinction between obscenity and pornography may, however, be a legal one. Sexually explicit content is pornography (and protected) until a court rules it illegal; then it is obscene (and unprotected). The difficulty of making such distinctions can be seen in Justice Potter Stewart's famous declaration in *Jacobellis v. Ohio* (1964), "I may not be able to come up with a definition of pornography, but I certainly know it when I see it," and his dissent two years later in *Ginzburg v. United States* (1966), "If the First Amendment means anything, it means that a man cannot be sent to prison merely for distributing publications which offend a judge's sensibilities, mine or any others." Clearly, the issues of the definition and protection of obscenity and pornography may never be clarified to everyone's satisfaction.

Ongoing Issues of Freedom and Responsibility

The First Amendment has application to a number of specific issues of media responsibility and freedom, including indecency, deregulation, and copyright laws. Though all Americans typically say they support the First Amendment and the guaranteed freedom of speech and press, these three issues continue to bedevil even the amendment's staunchest supporters.

INDECENCY Obscenity and pornography are rarely issues for broadcasters. Their commercial base and wide audience make the airing of such potentially troublesome programming unwise. However, broadcasters frequently do confront the issue of **indecency**. According to the FCC, indecent language or material is that which depicts sexual or excretory activities in a way that is offensive to contemporary community standards.

The FCC recently modified, much to broadcasters' dissatisfaction, its way of handling indecency complaints, making it easier for listeners and viewers to challenge questionable content. Stations must now prove they are innocent; in other words, a complaint has validity by virtue of having been made. To broadcasters, this "guilty until proven innocent" approach is an infringement of their First Amendment rights, as it requires them to keep tapes of all their content in the event they are challenged, even in the absence of evidence that a complaint has merit.

The debate over indecency, however, has been confounded by a number of events. First, a huge surge in complaints (from 111 in the year 2000 to more than a million in 2004) followed two specific broadcast events: the split-second baring of Janet Jackson's breast at the 2004 Super Bowl football game and rocker Bono's spontaneous award-show utterance of an expletive later that year. Even though the FCC's own data revealed that 99.9% of the complaints, most with identical wording, originated with one group, the conservative Christian Parents Television Council, it still boosted indecency fines by 100% (Rich, 2005; Soundbites, 2005).

Then, faced with penalties of up to $325,000, there was a series of high-profile incidents of broadcaster self-censorship, among them CBS affiliates' refusal to air *9/11 Camera at Ground Zero* honoring the New York City police, firefighters, and other rescue personnel who lived and died on that tragic day because some on-screen rescuers uttered curses as they

▶ In 2006, worried about heavy FCC indecency fines, several CBS affiliates chose not to run a documentary honoring the 9/11 rescue effort because several of the first responders in it cursed as they fought smoke, debris, and fear. The award-winning movie had aired four years earlier without complaint.
Anthony Correia/Getty Images News/Getty Images

fought through the inferno. The award-winning documentary had aired four years earlier without a single complaint. Citing examples such as this, lawsuits by NBC and Fox eventually made their way in 2012 to the Supreme Court which, in its unanimous *FCC v. Fox* decision, overturned the commission's indecency rulings, not because the FCC had no right to make such judgments but because it did not give broadcasters "fair notice" as to what was and was not permissible; that is, the rules were too vague to be constitutional (Barnes, 2012).

Today, the commission regulates language that is so "grossly offensive" to "members of the public" that it becomes a "nuisance." However, language found "grossly offensive" just a few years ago is quite common in our everyday conversations today. As such, the FCC acts in only the most egregious cases.

DEREGULATION The difficulty of balancing the public interest and broadcasters' freedom is at the heart of the debate over deregulation and the relaxation of ownership and other rules for radio and television. Changes in ownership rules have always been controversial, but relaxation of the regulation of broadcasters' public service obligations and other content controls have provided just as much debate.

The courts have consistently supported the FCC's right to evaluate broadcasters' performance in serving the public interest. Naturally, that evaluation must include some judgment of the content broadcasters air. Broadcasters long argued that such "judgment" amounted to unconstitutional infringement of their First Amendment freedom. Many listeners and viewers saw it as a reasonable and quite small price to pay for the use of their (the public's) airwaves (see Chapter 7's discussion of this once industry-welcomed trade off).

The Supreme Court resolved the issue in 1943 in *National Broadcasting Co. v. United States*. NBC argued that the FCC was no more than a traffic cop, limited to controlling the "flow of traffic." In this view, the regulation of broadcasters' frequency, power, times of operation, and other technical matters was all that was constitutionally allowable. Yet the Court turned what is now known as the **traffic cop analogy** against NBC. Yes, the justices agreed, the commission is a traffic cop. But even traffic cops have the right to control not only the flow of traffic but its composition as well. For example, drunk drivers can be removed from the road. Potentially dangerous "content," such as cars with faulty brakes, can also be restricted. It was precisely this traffic cop function that required the FCC to judge content. The commission was thus free to promulgate rules such as the **Fairness Doctrine**, which required broadcasters to cover issues of public importance and to be fair in that coverage, and **ascertainment**, which required broadcasters to ascertain or actively and affirmatively determine the nature of their audiences' interest, convenience, and necessity.

However, the Fairness Doctrine, ascertainment, and numerous other regulations, such as rules on children's programming and overcommercialization, disappeared with the coming of deregulation during the Reagan and Clinton administrations. License renewal, for example, was once a long and detailed process for stations, which had to generate thousands of pages of documents to demonstrate that they not only knew what their audiences wanted and needed but had met those wants and needs. The burden of proof in their efforts to keep their licenses rested with them. Had they been fair? Had they kept commercial time to acceptable levels? What was their commitment to news and public affairs?

Now deregulated, renewal is conducted through a much less onerous process that satisfies broadcasters but angers advocates of greater media responsibility. Broadcasters simply file brief quarterly reports with the commission indicating compliance with technical and other FCC rules. Then, when their licenses are up for renewal (every eight years), they file a short, postcard-like renewal application. This may be convenient for broadcasters, but former FCC commissioner Michael Copps (2014) calls this an "automatic, no-questions-asked eight-year extension . . . nothing more than conferring monopoly power with no public oversight" (p. 38).

The deregulation drive began in earnest with President Reagan's FCC chair, Mark Fowler, in the 1980s. Fowler rejected the trustee model of broadcast regulation, believing that "the market" was the audience's best protector. He said that special rules for the control of broadcasting were unnecessary, likening television to just another home appliance. He called television no more than "a toaster with pictures."

This view of deregulation is not without its critics. Republican and Democratic congressional leaders, liberal and conservative columnists, and numerous public interest groups from across the political spectrum continue to campaign against such fruits of deregulation as concentration, conglomeration, overcommercialization, the abandonment of regulation of children's television, the lowering of decency standards, and the debasement of news. Their argument for rolling back the deregulation of broadcasting rests in the philosophy of noted First Amendment scholar Alexander Meiklejohn (1960), who argued more than half a century ago that what is forbidden is regulation limiting the media's freedom, "but not legislation to enlarge and enrich it." He continued:

> The freedom of mind which benefits members of a self-governing society is not a given and fixed part of human nature. It can be increased and established by learning, by teaching, by the unhindered flow of accurate information, by giving men health and vigor and security, by bringing them together in activities of communication and mutual understanding. And the federal legislature is not forbidden to engage in that positive enterprise of cultivating the general intelligence upon which the success of self-government so obviously depends. On the contrary, in that positive field the Congress of the United States has a heavy and basic responsibility to promote the freedom of speech. (pp. 19–20)

◀ Broadcast deregulation produced a rush of toy-based children's television shows such as *Pokémon*, which critics contend are inherently unfair to children who cannot recognize them as program-length commercials. *Warner Bros./Courtesy of Everett Collection*

COPYRIGHT The First Amendment protects expression. *Copyright*—identifying and granting ownership of a given piece of expression—is designed to protect the creator's financial interest in that expression. Recognizing that the flow of art, science, and other expression would be enhanced by authors' financial interest in their creation, the framers of the Constitution wrote Article I, Section 8 (8), granting authors exclusive rights to their "writings and discoveries." A long and consistent history of Supreme Court decisions has ensured that this protection would be extended to the content of the mass media that have emerged since that time.

The years 1978 and 1998 saw extensive rewritings of US copyright law. Copyright now remains with creators (in all media) for the span of their lives, plus 70 years. During this time, permission for the use of the material must be obtained from the copyright holder, and if financial compensation (a fee or royalty) is requested, it must be paid. Once the copyright expires, the material passes into the **public domain**, meaning it can be used without permission.

The exception to copyright is *fair use*, instances in which material can be used without permission or payment. Fair use includes (1) limited noncommercial use, such as photocopying a passage from a novel for classroom use; (2) use of limited portions of a work, such as excerpting a few lines or a paragraph or two from a book for use in a magazine article; (3) use that does not decrease the commercial value of the original, such as videotaping a daytime football game for private, at-home evening viewing; and (4) use in the public interest, such as *Consumer Reports*'s use of pieces of drug company television commercials to highlight its media literacy efforts.

Two specific applications of copyright law pertain to recorded music and cable television. Imagine the difficulty cable companies would have in obtaining permission from all the copyright holders of all the material they import and deliver to their subscribers. Yet the cable operators do make money from others' works—they collect material from original sources and sell it to subscribers. The solution to the problem of compensating the creators of the material carried by cable systems was the creation of the Copyright Royalty Tribunal, to which cable companies paid a fee based primarily on the size of their operations. These moneys were then distributed to the appropriate producers, syndicators, and broadcasters. Congress abolished the Copyright Royalty Tribunal in 1993, leaving cable copyright issues in the hands of several different arbitration panels under the auspices of the Library of Congress.

Now imagine the difficulty songwriters would have in collecting royalties from all who use their music—not only film producers and radio and television stations, but also bowling alleys, supermarkets, and restaurants. Here the solution is the **music licensing company**. The two biggest are the American Society of Composers, Authors and Publishers (ASCAP) and Broadcast Music Inc. (BMI). Both collect fees based on the users' gross receipts and distribute the money to songwriters and artists.

THE INTERNET AND EXPANDING COPYRIGHT The Internet has forced a significant rethinking of copyright, one that disturbs many advocates of free expression. They fear that efforts to protect the intellectual property rights of copyright holders are going too far. The expansion of copyright, argues technology writer Dan Gillmor (2000), gives "the owners of intellectual property vast new authority, simultaneously shredding users' rights" (p. 1C). The American Civil Liberty Union agrees, "Any system to enable easier enforcement of copyrights runs the risk of creating a chilling effect with respect to speech online" (in Kelly, 2019).

For example, in January 2000, a California superior court, citing the Digital Millennium Copyright Act, ruled the posting of DVD decryption software to be illegal (see Chapter 10). The defendants argued that they did not violate copyright. The court ruled against them because they posted "tools" on the Web that might allow others to violate copyright. Tech writer Gillmor (2000) scoffed, "Let's ban cars next. Were you aware that bank robbers use them for getaways?" (p. 6C). In August of that same year, a New York court reaffirmed the ban on posting decryption software, adding that even posting links to sites offering the software is a violation of copyright.

Copyright exists, say critics of its expansion, to encourage the flow of art, science, and expression, and it grants a financial stake to creators, not to enrich those creators but to ensure that there is sufficient incentive to keep the content flowing. "It's always important to remember that copyright is a restriction on free speech, and it's a constitutionally granted restriction on free speech," argued copyright expert Siva Vaidhyanathan (in Anderson, 2000, p. 25). In other words, tightening copyright restrictions can have the effect of inhibiting the flow of art, science, and expression.

The **digital rights management (DRM)** debate escalated with the Supreme Court's 2005 *MGM v. Grokster* decision. The entertainment industries were heartened by the ruling that a technology was illegal if it "encouraged" copyright infringement; digital rights activists and technologists were appalled. The Court had rejected Hollywood's 1984 challenge to video-tape (*Sony Corp. v. Universal City Studios*, the so-called *Betamax* decision) precisely because VCR, even if some people used it to violate copyright, had "substantial non-infringing uses." But *Grokster*, argued its critics, changed that standard from a technology's primary, legal use to the question of whether innovators "created their wares with the 'intent' of inducing consumers to infringe" (Gibbs, 2005, p. 50).

As we've seen at several junctures of this text, a reassessment of DRM and copyright is under way, as the involved parties seem to be seeking accommodation. One effort is Creative Commons, a nonprofit corporation founded in 2001 as an easy way for people to share and build on the work of others, consistent with the rules of copyright. Creative Commons provides users with free licenses and other legal tools to mark (copyright) their creative work with the level of freedom they wish it to carry, granting to others specific rights to share, remix, or even use it commercially.

As for the traditional media companies, all the major record labels now sell their catalogs with no DRM. Low-cost streaming of virtually all movie and television content is ubiquitous. Most of the world's books will soon find themselves living online with quite robust reader access. Most big media companies are embracing websites such as YouTube, TikTok, and Facebook, willing to forfeit a bit of DRM control in exchange for exposure of their content.

The future of copyright and DRM, then, is being negotiated in the culture right now. You and other media consumers sit on one side of the table; the media industries are on the other. You will be in a stronger position in these cultural negotiations if you approach these developments as a media-literate person.

Social Responsibility Theory

As we saw at the beginning of this chapter, the First Amendment is based on the libertarian philosophy that assumes a fully free press and a rational, good, and informed public. However, we have also seen in this chapter that the media are not necessarily fully free. Government control is sometimes allowed. Corporate control is assumed and accepted.

During the 1930s and 1940s, serious doubts were also raised concerning the public's rationality and goodness. As World War II spread across Europe at the end of the 1930s, libertarians were hard-pressed to explain how Nazi propaganda could succeed if people could in fact tell right from wrong. As the United States was drawn closer to the European conflict, calls for greater government control of press and speech at home were justified by less-than-optimistic views of the "average American's" ability to handle difficult information. As a result, libertarianism came under attack for being too idealistic.

Time magazine owner and publisher Henry Luce then provided money to establish an independent commission of scholars, politicians, legal experts, and social activists (but no journalists) who would study the role of the press in American society and make recommendations on how it should best operate in support of democracy. The Hutchins Commission on Freedom of the Press, named after its chairperson, University of Chicago chancellor Robert Maynard Hutchins, began its work in 1942 and, in 1947, produced its report "The Social Responsibility Theory of the Press."

Social responsibility theory is a **normative theory**—that is, it explains how media should *ideally* operate in a given system of social values—and it is even today the standard against which the public should judge the performance of the US media (Luo, 2020). Other social and political systems adhere to different normative theories, and these will be detailed in Chapter 15.

Social responsibility theory asserts that media must remain free of government control but, in exchange, media must serve the public. The core assumptions of this theory are a cross between libertarian principles of freedom and practical admissions of the need for some form of control on the media (McQuail, 1987):

- Media should accept and fulfill certain obligations to society.
- Media can meet these obligations by setting high standards of professionalism, truth, accuracy, and objectivity.
- Media should be self-regulating within the framework of the law.
- Media should avoid disseminating material that might lead to crime, violence, or civil disorder or that might offend minority groups.
- The media as a whole should be pluralistic, reflect the diversity of the culture in which they operate, and give access to various points of view and rights of reply.
- The public has a right to expect high standards of performance, and official intervention can be justified to ensure the public good.
- Media professionals should be accountable to society as well as to their employers and the market.

In rejecting government control of media, social responsibility theory calls for responsible, ethical industry operation; it is practitioners, through the conduct of their duties, who are charged with operating in a manner that obviates the need for official intrusion. But social responsibility theory does not free audiences from *their* responsibility. We must be sufficiently media literate to develop firm yet reasonable expectations and judgments to better guide the media in meeting their obligations to us.

Media Industry Ethics

A number of formal and informal controls, both external and internal to the industry, are aimed at ensuring that media professionals operate in an ethical manner consistent with social responsibility theory. Among the external formal controls are laws and regulations, codified statements of what can and can't be done and what content is permissible and not permissible, and industry codes of practice. Among the external informal controls are pressure groups, consumers, and advertisers. We have seen how these informal controls operate throughout this text. Our interest here is in examining media's internal controls, or ethics.

Defining Ethics

Ethics are rules of behavior or moral principles that guide our actions in given situations. The word comes from the Greek *ethos*, which means the customs, traditions, or character that guide a particular group or culture. In our discussion, ethics specifically refer to the application of rational thought by media professionals when they are deciding between two or more competing moral choices. "Unlike rules of law," explains media ethicist Patrick Plaisance (2014), "which generally set forth boundaries of our behavior and guide us on what we cannot or should not do, the focus of ethics . . . is more active, or positive: It deals with what we ought to do as moral agents with personal and social obligations" (p. 83).

For example, it is not against the law to publish the name of someone who was raped. But is it ethical? It is not illegal to stick a microphone in a crying father's face as he cradles the broken body of his child at an accident scene. But is it ethical?

The application of media ethics almost always involves finding the *most morally defensible* answer to a problem for which there is no single correct or even best answer. Let's return to the grieving father. The reporter's job is to get the story; the public has a right to know. The man's sorrow is part of that story, but the man has a right to privacy. As a human being, he deserves to be treated with respect and to be allowed to maintain his dignity. The reporter has to decide whether to get the interview or leave the grief-stricken man in peace. That decision is guided by the reporter's ethics.

Three Levels of Ethics

Because ethics reflect a culture's ideas about right and wrong, they exist at all levels of that culture's operation. **Metaethics** are fundamental cultural values. What is justice? What does it mean to be good? Is fairness possible? We need to examine these questions to know ourselves, but, as valuable as they are for self-knowledge, metaethics provide only the broadest foundation for the sorts of ethical decisions people make daily. They define the basic starting points for moral reasoning.

Normative ethics are more or less generalized theories, rules, and principles of ethical or moral behavior. The various media industry codes of ethics or standards of good practice are examples of normative ethics. They serve as real-world frameworks within which people can begin to weigh competing alternatives of behavior. Fairness is a metaethic, but journalists' codes of practice, for example, define what is meant by fairness in the world of reporting, how far a reporter must go to ensure fairness, and how fairness must be applied when being fair to one person means being unfair to another.

Ultimately, media practitioners must apply both the big rules and the general guidelines to very specific situations. This is the use of **applied ethics**, and applying ethics invariably involves balancing conflicting interests.

Balancing Conflicting Interests

In applying ethics, the person making the decisions is the **moral agent**; this person, as ethicist Plaisance explained, has specific personal and social obligations that invariably bring together conflicting interests—for example, those of the editor, readers, advertisers, those being reported on in this chapter's opening vignette.

Media ethicist Louis Day (2006) identified six sets of individual or group interests that often conflict:

- The interests of the moral agent's *individual conscience:* media professionals must live with their decisions.
- The interests of *the object of the act:* a particular person or group is likely to be affected by media practitioners' actions.
- The interests of *financial supporters:* someone pays the bills that allow the station to broadcast or the newspaper, magazine, or website to publish.
- The interests of *the institution:* media professionals have company loyalty, pride in the organization for which they work.
- The interests of *the profession:* media practitioners work to meet the expectations of their colleagues; they have respect for the profession that sustains them.
- The interests of *society:* media professionals, like all of us, have a social responsibility. Because of the influence their work can have, they may even have greater responsibilities than do many other professionals.

In mass communication, these conflicting interests play themselves out in a variety of ways. Some of the most common, yet thorniest, require us to examine such basic issues as truth and honesty, privacy, confidentiality, personal conflict of interest, profit and social responsibility, and protection from offensive content.

TRUTH AND HONESTY Can the media ever be completely honest? As soon as a camera is pointed at one thing, it is ignoring another. As soon as a video editor combines two different images, that editor has imposed his or her definition of the truth. Truth and honesty are overriding concerns for media professionals. But what is truth? Can something be true but not honest? Take two examples from the 2020 Presidential election. First, Fox News anchor Martha MacCallum, in an effort to discredit the security of mail-in voting, truthfully informed her viewers that in the just-held Michigan primary elections, "they had 864 dead people vote." Yes, 864 "dead people" voted by mail in that election. But an honest account would have noted that those people died *after* they mailed in their ballots, and their votes were subsequently invalidated by Michigan's secretary of state (Baragona, 2020).

▶ It is the truth that at the 2020 Democratic National Convention Rep. Alexandria Ocasio-Cortez placed the name of Senator Bernie Sanders in nomination for her party's Presidential candidacy. But some media outlets were less than honest in reporting that truth.
Brian Snyder/UPI/Alamy Stock Photo

Then there was NBC News's reporting on Rep. Alexandria Ocasio-Cortez placing the name of Senator Bernie Sanders into nomination for her party's Presidential candidacy. NBC truthfully reported, "In one of the shortest speeches of the [Democratic National Convention], Rep. Ocasio-Cortez did not endorse Joe Biden." True, Representative Ocasio-Cortez did not endorse the eventual Democratic nominee at the convention; she had done that weeks before. But an honest account of her appearance would have acknowledged that her sole assigned convention task was to second the nomination of Mr. Sanders, a formality required by convention rules because the senator had earned enough delegates throughout the primaries to be on the convention ballot (Sullivan, 2020a).

PRIVACY Do public figures forfeit their right to privacy? In what circumstances? Are the president's marital problems newsworthy if they do not get in the way of the job? Who is a public figure? When are people's long-ago stints in drug rehab newsworthy? Do you report the names juvenile offenders? What about sex offenders? How far do you go to interview grieving parents? When is secret taping permissible?

Our culture values privacy. We have the right to maintain the privacy of our personal information. We use privacy to control the extent and nature of the interactions we have with others. Privacy protects us from unwanted government intrusion. The media, however, by their very nature, are intrusive. Privacy proves to be particularly sensitive because it is a metaethic, a fundamental value. Yet the applied ethics of the various media industries allow, in fact sometimes demand, that privacy be denied.

The media have faced a number of very important tests regarding privacy in recent years. Media pursuit of celebrities is one. Celebrities are public figures. They therefore lose some right to privacy. But what about their children? People surely want to know about them. How much privacy are they entitled to? In 2014, the California legislature passed anti-paparazzi legislation designed to make illegal the photography of celebrities' children in a manner that "seriously alarms, annoys, torments, or terrorizes" them. Despite complaints that this law infringed on photographers' First Amendment rights, most objective observers would say that the protection of children is more important than selling a few more magazines.

However, other privacy issues aren't as clear. For example, in the wake of protests across the summer of 2020 following the police killing of George Floyd and shooting of Jacob Blake, video and photojournalists were confronted by the question of demonstrators' privacy. There is no legal question about shielding the identity of people involved in a news event; they are part of the story. Imagine attempting to secure **informed consent**, explaining to a subject why her or his image is being used and what the potential consequences might be,

◀ There's little disagreement that the children of celebrities should be protected from intrusion into their private lives. Many other privacy issues, however, aren't as clear.
Paul Bradbury/Getty Images

to people fleeing a fuselage of rubber bullets or clouds of tear gas. But what if those images are used, not to further the public interest, but by police to track people down and charge them with crimes or by extremist groups to find them and harass them at home?

"It's not always practical to stop in the middle of a tense situation and chat with a demonstrator," writes journalist Ari Paul (2020), "In crisis journalism, photographers are often making split-second decisions, and are also working to protect themselves. If it is not feasible to get consent from everyone pictured, if media can't fully show the faces and bodies in the streets against the police, how else are people to know how historic, enormous, and urgent these protests are? Isn't it in the protesters' interest to visually show their 'people power'?"

Whose interests are served by publishing protesters' images? The photojournalists who need to make a living? The demonstrators putting themselves in harm's way to make a statement? The police charged with maintaining order? The public who has a right to know? As you can imagine, there is more disagreement among media professionals on this issue than there is on photographing celebrities' kids.

CONFIDENTIALITY An important tool in contemporary news gathering and reporting is **confidentiality**, the ability of media professionals to keep secret the names of people who provide them with information. Without confidentiality, employees could not report the misdeeds of their employers for fear of being fired; people would not tell what they know of a crime for fear of retribution from the offenders or unwanted police attention. The anonymous informant nicknamed "Deep Throat" would never have felt free to divulge the Nixon White House involvement in the Republican break-in of the Democratic Party's Watergate campaign offices were it not for the promise of confidentiality from *Washington Post* reporters Carl Bernstein and Bob Woodward.

But how far should reporters go to protect a source's confidentiality? Should reporters go to jail rather than divulge a name? Every state in the Union, except Wyoming, and the District of Columbia has either a **shield law**, legislation that expressly protects reporters' rights to maintain sources' confidentiality in courts of law, or court precedent upholding that right. There is no shield law in federal courts, and many journalists want it that way. Their fear is that once Congress makes one "media law" it may want to make another. For example, media professionals do not want the government to legislate the definition of "reporter" or "journalist."

The ethics of confidentiality are regularly tested by reporters' frequent use of quotes and information from "unnamed sources," "sources who wish to remain anonymous," and "inside

▲ *The Washington Post*'s Carl Bernstein and Bob Woodward (*left, from left to right*) never would have broken the story of the Nixon White House's involvement in the Watergate break-in if it had not been for an anonymous source. The reporters honored their promise of confidentiality for 35 years until "Deep Throat," then-FBI Assistant Director Mark Felt (right), revealed himself in 2005. *(Left): AP Images; (Right): Justin Sullivan/Getty Images News/Getty Images*

sources." Often the guarantee of anonymity is necessary to get the information, and a large majority of Americans, 82%, agree that there are times when it is appropriate for journalists to use anonymous sources (Gottfried & Walker, 2020). But is this fair to those who are commented on by these nameless, faceless newsmakers? Don't these people—even if they are highly placed and powerful themselves—have a right to know their accusers? In 2016 *The New York Times* hoped to provide its reporters with safeguards for the use of anonymous sources that serve as an industry model:

- Special rules apply when the lead of a story—that is, the primary news element—is based entirely on one or more anonymous sources. All such stories must be presented by the department head to one of the paper's top three editors.

- Every other use of anonymous sourcing anywhere in any story must be personally approved in advance by the department head or deputy.

- Direct quotes from anonymous sources will be allowed only in rare instances and with the approval of the department head or deputy.

- At least one top editor must know the specific identity of any anonymous source before publication. (Sullivan, 2016)

CONFLICTS OF INTEREST As we've seen, ethical decision making requires a balancing of interests. But what of a media professional's own conflicts of interest? Should they accept speaking fees, consulting contracts, or other compensation from groups that may have a vested interest in issues they may someday have to cover? Consider this situation. In 2020, it was discovered that the *Virginian-Pilot*, having published several unsigned editorials supportive of Dominion Energy, praising the company's projects and attacking its critics, had failed to inform its readers that many of those editorials were authored by a long-time columnist who was a paid speech writer for the energy giant (Pavior, 2020).

Likewise, must media organizations disclose any and all possible conflicts of the commentators who appear in their news shows? Consider this situation. When, in 2020, an American drone attack near Iraq's Baghdad airport killed Major General Qassim Suleimani, a powerful Iranian military commander, tensions between Iran and the United States were raised to the point where war was a distinct possibility. Despite national and international debate over the legality of what critics called the general's "assassination," American news outlets featured numerous defenders such as retired Army general Jack Keane, a partner at a venture capital firm that invests in defense contractors, and John Negroponte, vice chair of defense and aerospace lobbying firm McLarty Associates. Neither was identified as having financial ties to the arms industry, masking the conflict of interest in advocating actions that would benefit their paymasters (Fang, 2020).

And remember reading about video-news releases in Chapter 11? These preproduced reports distributed free of charge to television stations certainly benefit the subject of the report, and the stations using them are well-served, as VNRs provide a convenient source of sometimes interesting information. But as is often the case, broadcasters use them without attribution.

For example, during the COVID-19 pandemic Amazon provided video and a script mimicking a journalistic investigation offering "a glimpse inside Amazon's fulfillment centers to see just how the company is keeping its employees safe and healthy." But only one of the scores of stations across the country that aired the segment informed viewers that the footage had been produced and provided by Amazon (Soundbites, 2020, p. 2). Free promotion for Amazon in exchange for free content for the station; the broadcasters' obvious conflict of interest goes unacknowledged.

Other conflict-of-interest issues bedevil media professionals. The ongoing military actions across the globe raise the problem of **embedding**, reporters accepting military control over their reporting in exchange for close contact with the troops. The interests in conflict here are objectivity and access—do reporters pay too high a price for their exciting video or touching personal interest stories? Typically more subtle, this **access journalism**—reporters acting deferentially toward news sources in order to ensure continued access—inevitably produces compliant reporters, explains press critic Eric Boehlet, who are "nervous about having their access cut off—about not being called on at briefings, being shut out of press gaggles, having no chance at landing a [subsequent] interview, or landing lucrative book deals" (Boehlet, 2021).

Access journalism offers much more power over journalists than is warranted because, according to *Columbia Journalism Review*'s Ross Barkan (2016), "The best reporting is done on the margins, away from the siren charms of power and prestige." The box titled "Should Journalists Be Activists?" offers a deeper look at the relationship between journalists and those they cover.

PROFIT AND SOCIAL RESPONSIBILITY The media industries are just that—industries. They exist not only to entertain and inform their audiences but also to make a profit for their owners and shareholders. What happens when serving profit conflicts with serving the public?

In 2017, for example, the Walt Disney Company, an important advertiser, barred reporters from the *Los Angeles Times* from press screenings of its movies after the paper published a two-part series on tax breaks Disney had extracted from the city of Anaheim and the company's influence in local elections. Several publications, including *The New York Times*, said that until the *L.A. Times* was reinstated, they would boycott the screenings, denying Disney films prerelease publicity. Journalists belonging to the Los Angeles Film Critics Association, the New York Film Critics Circle, the Boston Society of Film Critics, and the National Society of Film Critics voted to disqualify Disney's movies from year-end award consideration. In the face of this media solidarity, Disney quickly lifted the ban (Ember & Barnes, 2018).

The *Times* was at the center of another profit/social responsibility conflict, but this time on the wrong side of the issue. According to a staff member, the Pac-12 collegiate sports conference, seeking ways to "identify positive voices," was looking for a news outlet it could "pay to write positive stories." To accomplish this ethically dubious goal, the Pac-12 found the *Times*, promising to "steer $100,000 in advertising to the newspaper in exchange for an expansion in conference coverage." An internal revolt by the paper's journalists, coupled with public revelation of the arrangement, led the paper to cancel the deal 4 months into the arrangement (Canzano, 2020).

Balancing profit and social responsibility is a concern not just for journalists. Practitioners in entertainment, advertising, and public relations often face this dilemma. Does an ad

USING MEDIA TO MAKE A DIFFERENCE
Should Journalists Be Activists?

The conventional argument is that if journalists are to make a difference, they should never be activists in service of a social or political goal. Who could disagree with that? We want our journalists to simply report, don't we? The answer to those questions rests in what we mean by "activists" and "make a difference."

Journalist Dan Gillmor (2018) wrote in an open letter to his colleagues, "Your job is not to uncritically 'report'—that is, do stenography and call it journalism—when the people you're covering are deceiving the public. Your job is, in part, to help the public be informed about what powerful people and institutions are doing with our money and in our names." Isn't that activism in service of making a difference?

Wesley Lowery of *The Washington Post* thinks it is. "Even beyond big, long investigations, journalists perform acts of activism every day. Any good journalist is an activist for truth, in favor of transparency, on the behalf of accountability. It is our literal job to *pressure* powerful people and institutions via our questions." His *Post* colleague, media writer Margaret Sullivan, thinks so, too. "The role of journalism in democratic society: to dig out and present the information that helps citizens hold their elected officials accountable," she wrote, "What if we framed coverage with this question at the forefront: What journalism best serves the real interests of American citizens?. . . I don't like to see mainstream reporters acting like partisans—for example, by working on political campaigns. But it's more than acceptable that they should stand up for civil rights—for press rights, for racial justice, for gender equity and against economic inequality" (2020b).

Do you agree? Should journalists be activists? At a time of unprecedented national debate over racial, gender, and economic inequality, is it time for **movement journalism**, journalism that meets the needs of communities directly affected by injustice (Vasquez, 2020)?

Perhaps journalists make their greatest difference when they move others to activism. Was it activism when Thomas Paine's *Common Sense* helped ignite the American Revolution? What about when muckraking journalists wrote magazine exposés that afflicted the comfortable and comforted the afflicted? Was Frederick Douglass's *North Star,* advocating equality for all, an activist newspaper? Was *The New York Times*'s publication of the *Pentagon Papers* the work of activism? Before you consider your answers, keep in mind the bedrock belief among good journalists that no one ever became a journalist not to make a difference.

agency accept as a client the manufacturer of sugared children's cereals even though doctors and dentists consider these products unhealthy? Does a public relations firm accept as a client the trade office of a country that forces prison inmates to manufacture products in violation of international law? Does a syndication company distribute the 1950s television series *The Amos 'n' Andy Show* knowing that it embodies many offensive stereotypes of African Americans?

Moreover, balancing profit and the public interest does not always involve big companies and millions of dollars. Often, a media practitioner will face an ethical dilemma at a very personal level. What would you do in this situation? The editor at the magazine where you work has ordered you to write an article about the 14-year-old daughter of your city's mayor. The girl's addiction to amphetamines is a closely guarded family secret, but it has been leaked to your publication. You believe that this child is not a public figure. Your boss disagrees, and the boss *is* the boss. By the way, you've just put a down payment on a lovely condo, and you need to make only two more installments to pay off your car. Do you write the story?

OFFENSIVE CONTENT   Entertainment, news, and advertising professionals must often make decisions about the offensive nature of content. Other than the particular situation of broadcasters discussed earlier in this chapter, this is an ethical rather than a legal issue.

Offensive content is protected. Logically, we do not need the First Amendment to protect sweet and pretty expression. Freedom of speech and freedom of the press exist expressly to allow the dissemination of material that *will* offend. But what is offensive? Clearly, what is offensive to one person may be quite satisfactory to another. Religious leaders on the political right have attacked the cartoon show *SpongeBob SquarePants* for supposedly promoting homosexuality, and critics from the political left have attacked just about every classic

◀ To some, the friendship between SpongeBob and Patrick is offensive, crossing a moral line. Others might disagree. Where you draw the line on offensive content is an ethical, not a legal, issue. *Paramount/Courtesy of Everett Collection*

Disney cartoon for racial and gender stereotyping. Television stations and networks regularly bleep cusswords that are common on cable television and in the schoolyard but leave untouched images of stabbings, beatings, and shootings. Where do we draw the line? Do we consider the tastes of the audience? Which members of the audience—the most easily offended? These are ethical, not legal, determinations.

Codes of Ethics and Self-Regulation

To aid practitioners in their moral reasoning, all major groups of media professionals have established formal codes or standards of ethical behavior. Among these are the Society of Professional Journalists's *Code of Ethics*, the American Society of News Editors's *Statement of Principles*, the Radio–Television Digital News Association's *Code of Broadcast News Ethics*, the American Advertising Federation's *Advertising Principles of American Business*, and the Public Relations Society of America's *Code of Professional Standards for the Practice of Public Relations*.

These are prescriptive codes that tell media practitioners what they should do. For example, the Society of Professional Journalists in 2014 approved a new *Code of Ethics*. Its preamble reads, "Members of the Society of Professional Journalists believe that public enlightenment is the forerunner of justice and the foundation of democracy. Ethical journalism strives to ensure the free exchange of information that is accurate, fair, and thorough. An ethical journalist acts with integrity."

To some, these codes are a necessary part of a true profession. They offer at least two important benefits to ethical media practitioners: They are an additional source of information to be considered when making moral judgments, and they represent a particular media industry's best expression of its shared wisdom. To others, they are unenforceable collections of clichés that do little more than ward off more meaningful oversight. Ethicists Jay Black and Ralph Barney (1985) argue, "It is indeed not difficult to find examples of codified professional ethics that ultimately become self-serving. That is, they tend to protect the industry, or elements of the industry, at the expense of individuals and other institutions, even of the full society" (pp. 28–29).

In addition to industry professional codes, many media organizations have formulated their own institutional policies for conduct. In the case of the broadcast networks, these are enforced by **Standards and Practices Departments**. Local broadcasters have what are called **policy books**. Newspapers and magazines standardize behavior in two ways: through **operating policies** (which spell out standards for everyday operations) and **editorial policies** (which identify company positions on specific issues).

A declining number of media organizations also utilize an **ombudsperson**, practitioners internal to the company who serve as "judges" in disputes between the public and the organization. Sometimes they have titles such as public editor or reader advocate. *The Washington Post*, which eliminated its ombudsperson in 2013, now uses a **readers' representative**, who regularly responds to outside criticism. Despite data indicating that having an ombudsperson fosters increased credibility among readers and audiences, as of 2017, after *The New York Times* eliminated its public editor, the only major US media outlet with such a full-time position is NPR, although government-owned but independent US military newspaper *Stars and Stripes* also maintains the position.

Determined to rectify the situation, in 2019 the *Columbia Journalism Review* appointed its own "public editors" for *The New York Times, The Washington Post,* CNN, and MSNBC. "As watchdogs for the biggest news organizations in the country," its editor wrote, these veteran journalists selected from across the news media, will "be ready to call out mistakes, observe bad habits, and give praise where it's due. Most importantly, these public editors will engage with readers and viewers, bridging a critical gap" (Pope, 2019). Their reporting appears in scores of news outlets.

These mechanisms of normative ethics are a form of self-regulation, designed in part to forestall more rigorous or intrusive government regulation. In a democracy dependent on mass communication, they serve an important function. We are suspicious of excessive government involvement in media. Self-regulation, however, has certain limitations:

- *Media professionals are reluctant to identify and censure colleagues who transgress.* To do so might appear to be admitting that problems exist; whistle-blowers in the profession are often met with hostility from their peers.

- *The standards for conduct and codes of behavior are abstract and ambiguous.* Many media professionals see this flexibility as a necessary evil; freedom and autonomy are essential. Others believe the lack of rigorous standards renders the codes useless.

- *As opposed to those in other professions, media practitioners are not subject to standards of professional training and licensing.* Again, some practitioners view standards of training and licensing as limiting media freedom and inviting government control. Others argue that licensing has not had these effects on doctors and lawyers.

- *Media practitioners often have limited independent control over their work.* Media professionals are not autonomous, individual professionals. They are part of large, hierarchically structured organizations. Therefore, it is often difficult to punish violations of standards because of the difficulty in assigning responsibility.

Critics of self-regulation argue that these limitations are often accepted willingly by media practitioners because their "true" function is "to cause the least commotion" for those working in the media industries (Black & Whitney, 1983, p. 432). True or not, the decision to perform his or her duties in an ethical manner ultimately rests with the individual media professional. As Black and Barney (1985) explain, an ethical media professional "must rationally overcome the status quo tendencies . . . to become the social catalyst who identifies the topics and expedites the negotiations societies need in order to remain dynamic" (p. 36).

But even for the most dedicated media practitioner, this is not always as simple a professional task as may appear. As media law expert Charles Tillinghast lamented, "One need not be a devotee of conspiracy theories to understand that journalists, like other human beings, can judge where their interests lie, and what risks are and are not prudent, given the desire to continue to eat and feed the family. . . . It takes no great brain to understand one does not bite the hand that feeds—or that one incurs great risk by doing so" (2000, pp. 145–146).

DEVELOPING MEDIA LITERACY SKILLS
Judging News Using Ethical Values

Earlier in this chapter you read about social responsibility theory, a set of norms against which people inside and outside the industry can judge the performance of a media outlet or the media system itself.

But what of our ability to judge the work of individual journalists? After all, as media ethicist Patrick Lee Plaisance (2016) explains, "Notwithstanding the realities of norms derived from organizational structures or societal and community interconnectedness, the self (or group of selves) is the locus of morality and of ethical deliberation" (p. 456). How do we, as media-literate individuals who must make judgments of worth every time we interact with a news account, make those judgments? Journalism ethicists Philip Patterson, Lee Wilkins, and Chad Painter (2019) propose evaluating journalists' work according to nine ethical news values:

Accuracy: Are the account's facts correct and its words accurate, and are they placed in the proper context? Is the journalist independent and aware of her or his own biases?

Confirmation: Can the report withstand scrutiny in the newsroom that produced it and in the world in which it is consumed?

Tenacity: Has the story been given the fullest individual and institutional effort? Have no stones been left unturned?

Dignity: Are the subjects of a report afforded as much self-respect as possible?

Reciprocity: Does the story demonstrate an awareness that journalists and their readers, listeners, and viewers are partners in meaning making? Does it avoid talking down to those consumers?

Sufficiency: Have adequate journalistic resources been allocated to all important aspects of an issue?

Equity: Recognizing a complicated world with multiple points of view, has justice been sought for everyone involved in a controversial issue and have all sources and subjects been treated fairly? Are all points of view considered but not necessarily presented as equally compelling?

Community: Does the account value social cohesion? Does the story suggest that the journalist has the goal of doing good and the outlet that he or she works for has a higher motive than profit?

Diversity: Are all segments of the report's audience fairly and adequately covered? Does it suggest that the journalist considered gender, racial, ethnic, and economic diversity in the story's preparation?

How easily do you think even the most media-literate news consumer can apply these ethical tests to a given piece of journalism? Are there any of these ethical news values that you think are more easily met than others? Remember that ethics, the values and norms that guide practice where there is no clear legal line, are the dilemmas that challenge media professionals and media-literate consumers the greatest. If that is indeed the case, where do you think the greater responsibility rests—with journalists to meet ethical standards or with news consumers to identify and call out violations?

MEDIA LITERACY CHALLENGE
Talk to the FCC

The primary telecommunications regulatory agency in the United States is the Federal Communications Commission (FCC). Its website (www.fcc.gov) offers a true bounty of information, including the FCC's efforts to make better use of the Internet to interact with industry and audiences. Inasmuch as *an understanding of the ethical and moral obligations of media practitioners* is an important component of media literacy, your challenge is to access this site and find the links to topics of particular interest to you. Then answer these questions: What links did you identify as of particular interest to audience members? Why? Did any of these links offer you an opportunity to "talk" to the commission's staff? If yes, which ones? Contact the commission's staff and ask a question (or two or three) that is of interest to you. Detail that question and the FCC's response. Offer a retort. That is, ask another question raised by the commission's initial response. Detail your question and its answer. Did the commission offer to provide you with documents or other material to help you with your queries? If so, what were they? Do you think it is important that the FCC stays in touch with audience members? Why or why not? Describe your general reaction to your "conversation" with this federal regulatory agency.

Resources for Review and Discussion

REVIEW POINTS: TYING CONTENT TO LEARNING OUTCOMES

▶ **Recall the history and development of our contemporary understanding of the First Amendment.**
- ☐ The First Amendment is based on libertarianism's self-righting principle.
- ☐ The absolutist position—no law means no law—is not as straightforward as it may seem. Questions have arisen over the definition of the press, what constitutes abridgment, balancing of interests, the definition of libel and slander, the permissibility of prior restraint, and control of obscenity and pornography.

▶ **Explain the justification for and exercise of media regulation.**
- ☐ Media professionals face other legal issues, such as how to define and handle indecent content, the impact of deregulation, and the limits of copyright.

▶ **Compare a media system that operates under a libertarian philosophy with one that operates under a social responsibility philosophy.**
- ☐ Libertarianism assumes a good and rational public with full access to all ideas; social responsibility theory, favoring responsible self-interest over government regulation, is the norm against which the operation of the American media system should be judged.

▶ **Recall how media ethics are applied.**
- ☐ Ethics, rules of behavior or moral principles that guide our actions, are not regulations, but they are every bit as important in guiding media professionals' behavior.
- ☐ There are three levels of ethics—metaethics, normative ethics, and applied ethics.
- ☐ Ethics require the balancing of several interests—the moral agent's individual conscience, the object of the act, financial supporters, the institution itself, the profession, and society.
- ☐ Ethics, rather than regulation, influence judgments about matters such as truth and honesty, privacy, confidentiality, personal conflict of interest, the balancing of profit and social responsibility, and the decision to publish or air potentially offensive content.

▶ **Describe the operation and pros and cons of self-regulation.**
- ☐ There is divergent opinion about the value and true purpose of much industry self-regulation.

▶ **Apply skills to better judge the value of news reports using ethical values.**
- ☐ The work of individual journalists should demonstrate accuracy, confirmation, tenacity, dignity, reciprocity, sufficiency, equity, community, and diversity.

KEY TERMS

QUESTIONS FOR REVIEW

1. What are the basic tenets of libertarianism? How do they support the First Amendment?

2. What is the absolutist position on the First Amendment?

3. Name important court cases involving the definition of "no law," "the press," "abridgment," "clear and present danger," "balancing of interests," and "prior restraint."

4. Define obscenity, pornography, and indecency.

5. What is the traffic cop analogy? Why is it important in the regulation of broadcasting?

6. What is copyright? What are the exceptions to copyright? What is DRM?

7. What are the basic assumptions of social responsibility theory?

8. What are ethics? What are the three levels of ethics?

9. What is confidentiality? Why is confidentiality important to media professionals and to democracy?

10. What are some forms of media self-regulation? What are the strengths and limitations of self-regulation?

To maximize your study time, check out CONNECT to access the SmartBook study module for this chapter, watch videos, and explore other resources.

QUESTIONS FOR CRITICAL THINKING AND DISCUSSION

1. How much regulation or, if you prefer, deregulation do you think broadcasters should accept?

2. Of the six individual and group interests that must be balanced by media professionals, which ones do you think would have the most influence over you if you were an investigative reporter for a big-city television station? Explain your answer.

3. In general, and from your own interaction with the mass media, how ethical do you believe media professionals to be—specifically, print journalists? Television journalists? Advertising professionals? Public relations professionals? Television and film writers? Direct mail marketers? Explain your answers.

REFERENCES

1. Anderson, M. K. (2000, May/June). When copyright goes wrong. *Extra!*, p. 25.

2. Associated Press. (2020, August 25). *AP stylebook*. Retrieved from https://twitter.com/APStylebook/status/1298283084631150592

3. Baragona, J. (2020, August 17). Fox News pushes debunked myth about dead Michigan voters. *Daily Beast*. Retrieved from https://www.msn.com/en-us/news/politics/fox-news-anchor-pushes-debunked-myth-about-dead-michigan-voters/ar-BB184dn2

4. Barkan, R. (2016, November 4). Journalists too easily charmed by power, access, and creamy risotto. *Columbia Journalism Review*. Retrieved from http://www.cjr.org/first_person/podesta_emails_journalists_dinner.php

5. Barnes, R. (2012, June 21). Supreme Court overturns FCC sanctions on networks, sidestepslarger issue. *Washington Post*. Retrieved from https://www.washingtonpost.com/politics/supreme-court-overturns-fcc-sanctions-on-networks-sidesteps-larger-issue/2012/06/21/gJQAwffxsV_story.html?utm_term=.dae984d52514

6. Bazelon, E. (2021, January 31). Unspeakable. *New York Times Magazine*, pp. 34–37.

7. Black, J., & Barney, R. D. (1985). The case against mass media codes of ethics. *Journal of Mass Media Ethics, 1,* 27–36.

8. Black, J., & Whitney, F. C. (1983). *Introduction to mass communications.* Dubuque, IA: William C. Brown.

9. Boehlet, E. (2021, January 21). Bullied—How Trump beat the press for four years. *Press Run.* Retrieved from https://pressrun. media/p/bullied-how-trump-beat-the-press?token=eyJ1c2VyX2l kIjo0OTQzMjUzLCJwb3N0X2lkIjozMTcyMjg4OCwiXyI6 ImdTU2hDIiwiaWF0IjoxNjExMjM0MjIwLCJleHAiOjE2 MTEyMzc4MjAsImlzcyI6InB1Yi0zMzE4Iiwic3ViIjoicG9 zdC1yZWFjdGlvbiJ9.ONLWXmXdnHjiLSnukHq8e_7AtLzu DPX7Vn4LxLa8aEQ

10. Bonazzo, J. (2018, August 28). Voters want Supreme Court arguments televised, but justices think mystery should stay. *Observer.* Retrieved from https://observer.com/2018/08/ supreme-court-television-cspan-brett-kavanaugh/

11. *Bridges v. California,* 314 U.S. 252 (1941).

12. *Burstyn, Inc. v. Wilson,* 343 U.S. 495 (1952).

13. Canzano, J. (2020, July 30). Canzano: Amid crisis, Pac-12 signed agreement to fund news coverage from Los Angeles Times. *Oregonian.* Retrieved from https://www.oregonlive.com/ sports/john_canzano/2020/07/canzano-amid-crisis-pac-12-signed-agreement-to-fund-news-coverage-from-los-angeles-times.html

14. *CBS v. Democratic National Committee,* 412 U.S. 94 (1973).

15. *Chandler v. Florida,* 449 U.S. 560 (1981).

16. Copps, M. J. (2014, March/April). From the desk of a former FCC commissioner. *Columbia Journalism Review,* pp. 35–38.

17. Daniszewski, J. (2021, June 15). Why we're no longer naming suspects in minor crime stories. *Associated Press.* Retrieved from https://blog.ap.org/behind-the-news/why-were-no-longer-naming-suspects-in-minor-crime-stories

18. Day, L. A. (2006). *Ethics in media communications: Cases and controversies* (6th ed.). Belmont, CA: Wadsworth.

19. Ember, S., & Barnes, B. (2017, November 8). Disney ends ban on Los Angeles Times after fierce backlash by news outlets. *New York Times,* p. B3.

20. Fang, L. (2020, January 6). TV pundits praising Suleimani assassination neglect to disclose ties to arms industry. *The Intercept.* Retrieved from https://theintercept.com/2020/01/06/ iran-suleimani-tv-pundits-weapons-industry/

21. *Federal Communications Commission v. Fox Television Stations, Inc.,* 556 U.S. 502 (2009).

22. Frazier, M. (2020, August 7). Stop using "officer-involved shooting." *Columbia Journalism Review.* Retrieved from https:// www.cjr.org/analysis/officer-involved-shooting.php

23. Gibbs, M. (2005, July 18). A new theory with consequences. *Network World,* p. 50.

24. Gillmor, D. (2000, August 18). Digital Copyright Act comes back to haunt consumers. *San Jose Mercury News,* pp. 1C, 6C.

25. Gillmor, D. (2018, June 15). Dear journalists: Stop being loud-speakers for liars. *Medium.* Retrieved from https://medium. com/@dangillmor/dear-journalists-stop-letting-liars-use-your-platforms-as-loudspeakers-cc64c4024eeb

26. Gillmor, D. M., & Barron, J. A. (1974). *Mass communication law: Cases and comments.* St. Paul, MN: West.

27. *Ginzburg v. United States,* 383 U.S. 463 (1966).

28. *Gitlow v. New York,* 268 U.S. 652 (1925).

29. Gottfried, J., & Walker, M. (2020, October 9). Most Americans see a place for anonymous sources in news stories, but not all the time. *Pew Research Center.* Retrieved from https://www. pewresearch.org/fact-tank/2020/10/09/most-americans-see-a-place-for-anonymous-sources-in-news-stories-but-not-all-the-time/

30. *Irvin v. Dowd,* 366 U.S. 717 (1961).

31. *Jacobellis v. Ohio,* 378 U.S. 184, 197 (1964).

32. *Joseph Burstyn, Inc. v. Wilson,* 343 U.S. 495 (1952).

33. Kelly, M. (2019, October 22). House overwhelmingly approves contentious new copyright bill. *The Verge.* Retrieved from https://www.theverge.com/2019/10/22/20927545/copyright-bill-house-congress-hakeem-jeffries-case-act-dmca

34. Luo, M. (2020, July 11). How can the press best serve a democratic society? *New Yorker.* Retrieved from https:// www.newyorker.com/news/the-future-of-democracy/how-can-the-press-best-serve-democracy

35. McQuail, D. (1987). *Mass communication theory: An introduction.* Beverly Hills, CA: Sage.

36. Meiklejohn, A. (1960). *Political freedom.* New York: Harper.

37. *MGM Studios, Inc. v. Grokster, Ltd.,* 545 U.S. 913 (2005).

38. *Miller v. State of California,* 413 U.S. 15 (1973).

39. *National Broadcasting Co. v. United States,* 319 U.S. 190 (1943).

40. *Near v. Minnesota,* 283 U.S. 697 (1931).

41. *New York Times v. Sullivan,* 376 U.S. 254 (1964).

42. *New York Times v. United States,* 403 U.S. 713 (1971).

43. Patterson, P., Wilkins, L., & Painter, C. (2019). *Media ethics: Issues and cases.* Lanham, MD: Rowman & Littlefield.

44. Paul, A. (2020, July 1). Photographers grapple with "informed consent" in uprising. *FAIR.* Retrieved from https:// fair.org/home/photographers-grapple-with-informed-consent-in-uprising/

45. Pavior, B. (2020, December 14). Behind unsigned editorials, a columnist with ties to Dominion. *VPM.* Retrieved from https:// vpm.org/news/articles/18780/behind-unsigned-editorials-a-columnist-with-ties-to-dominion

46. Pember, D. (1999). *Mass media law.* New York: McGraw-Hill.

47. Plaisance, P. L. (2016). Media ethics theorizing, reoriented: A shift in focus for individual-level analysis. *Journal of Communication, 66,* 454–474.

48. Plaisance, P. L. (2014). *Media ethics.* Los Angeles: Sage.

49. Pope, K. (2019, June 11). Meet your new public editors. *Columbia Journalism Review.* Retrieved from https://www.cjr.org/ public_editor/meet-your-new-public-editors.php

50. Rich, F. (2005, February 6). The year of living indecently. *New York Times,* p. B.1.

51. *Roth v. United States,* 354 U.S. 476 (1957).

52. *Saia v. New York,* 334 U.S. 558 (1948).

53. *Schenck v. United States,* 249 U.S. 47 (1919).

54. Sen, A., & Zadronzy, B. (2020, August 10). QAnon groups have millions of members on Facebook, documents show. *NBC News*. Retrieved from https://www.nbcnews.com/tech/tech-news/qanon-groups-have-millions-members-facebook-documents-show-n1236317

55. Shattuck, J., & Risse, M. (2021, February 22). Reimagining rights & responsibilities in the United States: Hate crimes. *Carr Center for Human Rights Policy*. Retrieved from https://carrcenter.hks.harvard.edu/files/cchr/files/hate_crimes.pdf

56. Society of Professional Journalists. (2014, September 6). *SPJ code of ethics*. Retrieved from https://www.spj.org/ethicscode.asp

57. *Sony Corp. v. Universal City Studios*, 464 U.S. 417 (1984).

58. Soundbites. (2020, July). Relying on Amazon—to do reporter's work for them. *Extra!*, p. 2.

59. Soundbites. (2005, December). A better mousetrap. *Extra! Update*, p. 2.

60. Sullivan, M. (2020a, August 19). How not to apologize when your publication makes a mistake. *Washington Post*. Retrieved from https://www.washingtonpost.com/lifestyle/media/how-not-to-apologize-when-your-publication-makes-a-mistake/2020/08/19/35fa9870-e234-11ea-8dd2-d07812bf00f7_story.html

61. Sullivan, M. (2020b, June 7). What's a journalist supposed to be now—an activist? A stenographer? You're asking the wrong question. *Washington Post*. Retrieved from https://www.washingtonpost.com/lifestyle/media/whats-a-journalist-supposed-to-be-now-an-activist-a-stenographer-youre-asking-the-wrong-question/2020/06/06/60fdfb86-a73b-11ea-b619-3f9133bbb482_story.html

62. Sullivan, M. (2016, March 15). Tightening the screws on anonymous sources. *New York Times*. Retrieved from http://publiceditor.blogs.nytimes.com/2016/03/15/new-york-times-anoymous-sources-policy-public-editor/

63. Tillinghast, C. H. (2000). *American broadcast regulation and the First Amendment: Another look.* Ames: Iowa State University Press.

64. *Time, Inc. v. Hill*, 385 U.S. 374 (1967).

65. *Valentine v. Christensen*, 316 U.S. 52 (1942).

66. Vasquez, T. (2020, August 25). Is movement journalism what's needed during this reckoning over race and inequality? *Nieman Reports*. Retrieved from https://niemanreports.org/articles/158195/

Cultural Forum Blue Column icon, Media Literacy Red Torch Icon, Using Media Green Gear icon, Developing Media book in starburst icon: ©McGraw Hill

Muhammad Hamed/REUTERS/
Alamy Stock Photo

◀ Mass communication transcends national borders. Arabic-language *Ahlan Simsim* (*Welcome Sesame*) is produced specifically for displaced kids in the war-torn Middle East. This is its 5-year-old main character, Basma.

Learning Objectives

Satellites and the Internet have made mass media truly global. Earth has become a global village. But not all countries use mass media in the same ways. Moreover, many people around the world resent the "Americanization" of their indigenous media systems. After studying this chapter, you should be able to

▶ Recall the development of global media.

▶ Explain the practice of comparative analysis.

▶ Identify different media systems from around the world.

▶ Describe the debate surrounding cultural imperialism and other controversies raised by the globalization of media.

1901 ▶ Marconi sends wireless signal transatlantic

1900

Bildagentur-online/Universal Images Group/Getty Images

mid-1920s European colonial powers use shortwave radio to connect holdings

1923 Radio comes to China

1928 ▶ Baird sends television image from London to New York

1925

1940 Voice of America goes on air

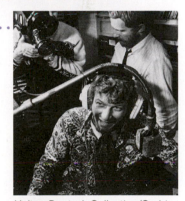

PA Images/Alamy Stock Photo

1960s ▶ British pirate broadcasters go on air

1950

1962 McLuhan's *The Gutenberg Galaxy*

1967 McLuhan's *Understanding Media: The Extensions of Man*

1980 MacBride Report calls for New World Information Order

1975

1984 German RTL goes on air

1985 Radio Martí goes on air

1989 Fall of European communism

1990 TV Martí goes on air

1997 China begins crackdown on the Internet

Hulton-Deutsch Collection/Corbis Historical/Getty Images

2002 Reporters Without Borders initiates annual press freedom reports

2000

2009 UK okays/limits product placement

2010 Sweden says TV movie commercial breaks may be finable offense; Spain limits TV beauty ads

2011 ▶ Arab Spring

2013 Swedish movies must have gender ratings

2014 French government declares books an "essential good," also puts restrictions on after-work e-mailing

Nacerdine ZEBAR/Gamma-Rapho/Getty Images

2015 Call for Universal Charter of Media Freedoms

2016 Chinese media must serve the Party proclamation

2017 China becomes world's biggest movie market

2018 United States Agency for Global Media

2019 Canada supports journalism with $600 million in tax money; UK calls for establishment of tax-funded Institute of Public Interest News to support local journalism; Loyalty test imposed on Chinese journalists

2020 Global COVID-19 pandemic

2021 Reporters Without Borders ranks US press 44th freest in the world; US ranks last among 46 global democracies in citizens' trust

HENRI AND YOU HAVE BEEN PEN PALS SINCE SEVENTH GRADE. He's visited you here in the United States, and you've been to his house in the small, walled village of Alet, near Carcassonne in southern France. You treat each other like family, which means you sometimes fight. But unlike siblings living under the same roof, you have to carry on your dispute by e-mail.

Dear Henri,

What's with you guys and your language police? For everyone else it's e-mail. For you it's *courriel.* People around the world are innovating with Internet start-ups. You have *jeunepousses.* My French isn't as good as yours, but doesn't that mean "little flower" or something? You guys aren't keeping up with the rest of the world. The world's air traffic control systems all use English for their communication, but your airports refuse to comply.

English is the world's most-spoken language and 60% of the world's websites are in English. English is the primary language for the publication of scientific and scholarly reports and for many international organizations such as the European Union and the Association of Southeast Asian Nations. In fact, 97% of French students study English in school, as do 91% of other European kids.

Mon ami,

Your translations are close, mais pas de cigare (but no cigar, my linguistically challenged friend). I admit that we may seem a little foolish to the rest of you, but the Académie Française (what you called the language police) is simply trying to protect our language because it represents the deepest expression of our national identity. We're sick and tired of *le weekend* and *le self-made man.* And we do keep up with the rest of the world! In fact, we are the globe's cultural leader. Surely you've heard of the French avant-garde.

Dear Henri,

Say what you will, my friend, but every one of world's 100 all-time box office hit movies is American. Want one more? Nine of your country's top-10 TV show last year were English-language imports!

It's true; English is the world's—and the Internet's—most-spoken language (Ghosh, 2020; Bhutada, 2021) and more than 9 out of 10 kids in Europe are learning English (Devlin, 2020). And not only is it true that American movies dominate everywhere ("All Time," 2021) and American TV shows are global (as well as French) favorites ("TV Series," 2020), but American TV formats are also widely popular material for translation into local productions. Foreign-language *Hollywood Reporter, Dr. Oz, Wheel of Fortune, Law & Order,* and *The Good Wife* clones exist all over the world. Local versions of foreign shows also travel the other way: *Power Rangers* and *Shark Tank* originated in Japan; *Shameless, House of Cards,* and *The Office* came to the United States via England; *The Masked Singer* came to America from Korea, as did *The Good Doctor; The Voice* is from the Netherlands, *Survivor* is from Sweden, and *Euphoria* is from Israel. And every video streaming service that produces original content created by native talent for their home markets streams that programming back home in North America. HBO Max's *30 Coins* (in Spanish) and Netflix's *Lupin* (in French) are two examples.

Throughout this text, we have seen how globalization is altering the operation of the various mass media industries, as well as the process of mass communication itself. In this chapter, we focus specifically on this globalization and its impact.

In doing so, we will look at the beginnings of international media and their development into a truly global mass media system. To study today's global media we will use comparative analyses to see how different countries establish media systems consistent with their specific people, cultures, and political systems. Naturally, we will discuss the programming available in other countries. And because global media influence the cultures that use them both positively and negatively, we visit the debate over cultural imperialism. Finally, our media literacy discussion deals with contrasting the way other countries interact with different media with the way we do things here in America.

A Short History of Global Media

It is fair to argue that radio and television were, in effect, international in their earliest days. Guglielmo Marconi was the British son of an Italian diplomat, and among his earliest successes was the 1901 transmission of a wireless signal from England to Newfoundland. American inventors Philo Farnsworth and Russian immigrant Vladimir Zworykin improved on the mechanical television design of Scotland's John Logie Baird, among whose greatest achievements was the successful transmission of a television picture from London to New York in 1928. It was not much later in the development of radio and television that these media did indeed become, if not truly global, at least international as they quickly attracted audiences from around the world.

The Beginning of International Mass Media

Almost from the very start, radio signals were broadcast internationally. Beginning in the mid-1920s, the major European colonial powers—the Netherlands, Great Britain, and Germany—were using **shortwave radio** to connect with their various colonies in Africa, Asia, and the Middle East, as well as, in the case of the British, North America (Canada) and the South Pacific (Australia). Shortwave was (and still is) well suited for transmission over very long distances because its low frequencies easily and efficiently reflect—or **skip**—off the ionosphere, producing **sky waves** that can travel vast distances.

CLANDESTINE STATIONS It was not only colonial powers that made use of international radio. Antigovernment or antiregime radio also constituted an important segment of international broadcasting, as illegal or unlicensed broadcast operations were used for political purposes. These **clandestine stations** typically emerged "from the darkest shadows of political conflict. They [were] frequently operated by revolutionary groups or intelligence agencies" (Soley & Nichols, 1987, p. vii). In World War II, for example, Allies operating German-language stations in Britain and other Allied nations pretended to be German and encouraged German soldiers and sailors to sabotage their vehicles and vessels rather than be killed in battle. Allied stations, such as the Atlantic Station and Soldiers' Radio Calais, also intentionally broadcast misleading reports. Posing as two of the many official stations operated by the German army, they frequently transmitted false reports to confuse the enemy or to force official Nazi radio to counter with rebuttals, thus providing the Allies with exactly the information they sought.

However, it was during the Cold War that clandestine broadcasting truly flowered. In the years between the end of World War II and the fall of European communism in 1989, thousands of radio, and sometimes television, pirates took up the cause of either revolutionary (procommunist) or counterrevolutionary (anticommunist) movements. In addition, other governments tangentially related to this global struggle—especially the growing anticolonial movements in South and Central America and in Africa—made use of clandestine broadcasting.

During the Cold War, unauthorized, clandestine opposition stations typically operated outside the nations or regions to which they broadcast to avoid discovery, capture, and imprisonment or death. Today the relatively few clandestine operations functioning inside the regions to which they transmit can be classified as **indigenous stations**, and they can make use of technologies other than radio. For example, Radio Amiltzinko is one of several "community" stations operating without official sanction in Mexico to push for human rights and report on organized crime and abuse of power by government officials. Its staff lives under constant threat and several members have been murdered. Therefore, the Internet and satellites are increasingly employed by in-country operators because they offer more anonymity and, therefore, safety.

Opposition stations transmitting into the regions they hope to influence from outside those areas are **exogenous stations**. Free North Korea Radio, operated primarily by North Korean defectors and refugees, is an example of an exogenous (or international) station. It broadcasts from near Seoul, South Korea, in opposition to the despotic rule of North Korea's Kim Jong Un. However, because radios sold in North Korea are pretuned to receive

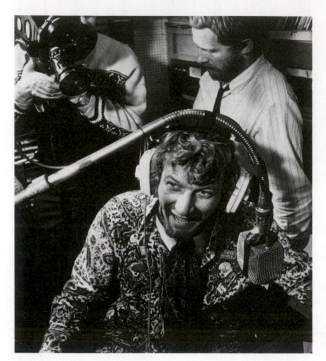

▲ Disc jockey Robby Dale broadcasts from pirate station Radio Caroline aboard the MV *Frederika*, anchored off Great Britain's Isle of Man.

Hulton-Deutsch Collection/Corbis Historical/Getty Images

nothing but official government stations and cannot be changed, only radios smuggled into the country can deliver FreeNK. FreeNK's response, therefore, is heavier reliance on the Internet, although access to that medium in North Korea is also quite limited.

Naturally, many other clandestine operations have also migrated to the Internet. For example, Iran International, a Persian-language television channel operated by Iranian exiles in London since 2017, receives Internet video pirated out of Iran, repackages it as part of modern-looking news broadcasts, and using multiple satellites with signals set at different frequencies and angles to defeat the country's network of jamming stations, transmits news and information back into Iran. Most of its Iranian audience, however, is on the Web.

PIRATE BROADCASTERS Another type of broadcast operation transmitting from outside its desired audience's geographic location involved something a bit more benign than war and revolution. These were stations that began broadcasting into Great Britain in the 1960s. Called **pirate broadcasters**, they were illegally operated stations broadcasting to British audiences from offshore or foreign facilities. Among the more notable were Radio Caroline, which reached a daily audience of a million listeners with its signal broadcast from the MV *Frederika* anchored 3½ miles off the Isle of Man, and Radio Veronica, broadcasting from a ship off the coast of the Netherlands.

These pirates, unlike their politically motivated clandestine cousins, were powerful and well subsidized by advertisers and record companies. Moreover, much like the commercial radio stations with which we are now familiar, they broadcast 24 hours a day, every day of the year. These pirates offered listeners an alternative to the controlled and low-key programming of the British Broadcasting Corporation's (BBC) stations. Because the BBC was noncommercial, pirate stations represented the only opportunity for advertisers who wanted to reach British consumers. Record companies intent on introducing Britain's youth to their artists and to rock 'n' roll also saw the pirates as the only way to reach their audience, which the staid BBC all but ignored.

Enterprising broadcasters also made use of foreign locales to bring commercial television to audiences otherwise denied. The top-rated network in Germany today, for example, is RTL. Now broadcasting from the German city of Cologne, it began operations in January 1984 in Luxembourg, transmitting an American-style mix of children's programming, sports, talk shows, and action–adventure programming into Germany to compete with that country's two dominant public broadcasters, ARD and ZDF.

THE UNITED STATES AS INTERNATIONAL BROADCASTER World War II brought the United States into the business of international broadcasting. Following the lead of Britain, which had just augmented its colonial broadcast system with an **external service** called the BBC World Service, the United States established in 1940 what would eventually be known as the Voice of America (VOA) to counter enemy propaganda and disseminate information about America. The VOA originally targeted countries in Central and South America friendly to Germany, but as the war became global, it quickly began broadcasting to scores of other nations, attracting, along with Britain's World Service, a large and admiring listenership, first in countries occupied by the Axis powers, and later by those in the Soviet sphere of influence.

It was this Cold War with the Soviets that moved the United States into the forefront of international broadcasting, a position it still holds today. To counter the efforts of what was then the Soviet Union's external service, Radio Moscow, the United States established three additional services. Radio in the American Sector (RIAS), broadcasting in German, served people inside East Berlin and East Germany; Radio Free Europe (RFE) broadcast to all of the other communist-bloc Eastern European countries in their native languages; and Radio Liberty (RL) was aimed at listeners in the Soviet Union itself. When these services were initiated, people both in the United States and abroad were told that they were funded by contributions from American citizens. However, as a result of the furor that arose when it was revealed in 1971 that they were in fact paid for by the Central Intelligence Agency, they were brought openly under government control and funded and administered first by the International Broadcasting Bureau, and in 2018 by the United States Agency for Global Media, whose members are appointed by the president.

The communist nations targeted by these services attempted to jam their signals by broadcasting on the same frequencies at higher powers, but they were only minimally successful in keeping their people from listening to these Western broadcasts. It was the success of these **surrogate services**—broadcast operations established by one country to substitute for another's own domestic service—that prompted President Ronald Reagan in 1985 to establish a special division of the VOA, Radio Martí, to broadcast into communist Cuba. Radio Martí, still in operation, was joined by TV Martí in 1990.

A final US external service established during World War II and the Cold War is the Armed Forces Radio and Television Service (AFRTS), which remains active today under its new name, American Forces Radio and Television Service, and maintains the American Forces Network. The American military, navy personnel at sea, the Department of Defense, and other government civilians and their families stationed overseas receive popular radio and television network fare delivered by shortwave radio, Earth-orbiting satellites, and Internet technology, all commercial-free.

THE VOA TODAY Today, VOA broadcasts in more than 40 languages across a wide variety of platforms draw 280 million people a week. Most of that audience is for the VOA itself, but millions of people in 23 developing countries access VOA programming on its surrogate operations, for example, Radio Free Europe and Radio Liberty, serving eastern Europe and central Asia; Radio y Televisión Martí; Radio Free Asia; Arabic-language Radio Sawa; and Awera24, a 24-hour-a-day satellite channel beamed into Nigeria to counter propaganda from radical groups such as schoolgirl kidnappers Boko Haram.

Throughout its history, the VOA has frequently vacillated between two roles in response to world events and political pressures at home: (1) disseminating Western propaganda and (2) providing objective information. With the threat of communist world domination now nonexistent, it attempts to meet the far less contradictory goals of spreading American culture and disseminating health and social information.

The VOA's legally mandated independence it expressed in the VOA Firewall, which "prohibits interference by any US government official in the objective, independent reporting of news, thereby safeguarding the ability of our journalists to develop content that reflects the highest professional standards of journalism, free of political interference" (2020). But critics inside and out of the organization recognize the tenuousness of the firewall, as partisan politics have sometimes come into play in the its operation. The VOA's commitment to independence, they say, is only as strong as the existing Presidential administration's willingness to grant it ("Voice of America Staff," 2020).

Nonetheless, the VOA's focus on transmitting health and other practical information can be seen in the increased effort it devotes to programs aimed at developing nations on AIDS prevention, nutrition, and vaccination. In pursuit of this humanitarian goal, the VOA now frequently strikes agreements with local stations in these countries to broadcast its programs over their AM and FM stations, making them accessible to people who listen outside the shortwave band.

Even in the United States, people may access other countries' surrogate services. Of course, these are more complements than substitutes for domestic media, but their goal is indeed to offer other nations' perspectives on the world. Television's *BBC America* has aired in the United States since 1998, is commercially funded, and is available to a majority of American homes. Iran operates *Press TV* and, like Russia's state-funded and operated *RT* and China's *Today China*, tends to echo official government talking points. France's *France 24* is more independent.

Global Media Today

HBO simultaneously aired new episodes of *Game of Thrones* in 170 countries around the globe. Nickelodeon is the world's most distributed kids' channel, viewable in more than 320 million households worldwide. Britain's BBC is America's most trusted news brand

(Egan, 2020). American cable giant Altice USA is actually former cable giant Cablevision under its new French ownership. *The New York Times* publishes a hard-copy magazine, *Chinese Monthly*, written in simplified Chinese for readers in Hong Kong and Macau and sells its *New York Times Travel Magazine* 新视线 in bookstores, boutiques, luxury hotels, and airport VIP lounges in Beijing, Shanghai, Xi'an, and Shenzhen. British newspaper *The Independent* offers a online Spanish-language edition targeted at Hispanic readers in the United States.

More than 50% of Netflix's streaming revenue comes from outside the United States, where the majority of its subscribers live (Iqbal, 2020). American media giants own British production houses Carnival (*Downton Abbey, Jamestown*), Left Bank Pictures (*The Crown, Outlander*), Shed (*Man on Wire, The Real Housewives of New York City*), and All3Media (*Master Chef, Penny Dreadful*), among others. American cable company Liberty Global owns part of British TV network ITV, and Comcast owns controlling interest in Great Britain's leading pay-TV service, Sky TV.

The New York Times may be the world's most popular newspaper website, but second is the *India Times*. American Spanish-language network Telemundo, owned by NBC, has programming offices in Tokyo; Mexican media conglomerate Televisa has offices in China and coproduction deals with state-run China Central Television, as does Venezuela's Venevision; and Brazilian media company Globo produces content for a number of India's television networks. TV France International, that country's umbrella distribution organization, has partnerships with Fox, Warner Bros., Discovery Channel, Sundance TV, and Bravo. Hundreds of millions of Internet users spread throughout scores of countries can tune in to thousands of Web radio stations originating from every continent except Antarctica. Media know few national borders.

However, the global flow of expression and entertainment is not welcomed by everyone. In response to the American ownership of British media companies, Colin Browne of the British grassroots group Voice of the Listener & Viewer cautioned, "It is a key part of society that we do have our own cultural broadcasting coming from a U.K. cultural point of view. That's not to say there isn't a great role for international stuff as well, but it's that prime focus on producing U.K. material for a U.K. audience that it is important not to lose" (in Clarke, 2018, p. 19).

French law requires that 40% of all music broadcast by its radio stations be in French. Iran bans "Western music" altogether from radio and television, going so far as to sentence the members of Iranian heavy metal band Arsames to 15 years in prison, forcing its three members into exile (Smith, 2020). Jamaica's Broadcasting Commission bans American hip-hop music in order to, it says, guard against underage sex and juvenile delinquency.

▶ Netflix's worldwide hit series *The Crown* is the story of a British queen, shot on location in Great Britain by British production company Left Bank Pictures, which is owned by America's Sony Pictures Television, which itself is owned by Japan's Sony Corporation.

Netflix/Photofest

You can enjoy *The Simpsons* just about everywhere in the Middle East, but if you do catch it there, you'll never see Homer drink a beer or visit Moe's Bar. *Fox/Photofest*

America's northern neighbor mandates that all television programming contains at least 15% "Canadian-made content," while the European Union sets its minimum at 20%.

Though *The Simpsons* is widely distributed across the Middle East by Saudi Arabian DBS provider MBC, all references to Duff Beer have been changed to soda, and Moe's Bar does not appear at all. The Germans and Austrians are wary of *The Simpsons* as well, refusing to air episodes that include the topic of a nuclear accident at the plant where Homer works. To ensure that its people do not access "foreign" or otherwise "counterrevolutionary" Internet content, the Chinese government requires that all Internet accounts be registered with the police. It employs 40,000 "e-police" to enforce its dozens of Internet-related laws (dissidents call it the Great Firewall). Media may know few national borders, but there is growing concern that they at least respect the cultures within them.

One traditional way to understand the workings of the contemporary global media scene is to examine the individual media systems of the different countries around the world. In doing so, we can not only become familiar with how different folks in different places use media but also better evaluate the workings of our own system. Naturally, not every media system resembles that of the United States. As a result, such concepts as audience expectations, economic foundations, and the regulation of mass media differ across nations. The study of different countries' mass media systems is called **comparative analysis** or **comparative studies**.

Comparing Media Systems Around the World: Comparative Analyses

Different countries' mass media systems reflect the diversity of their levels of development and prosperity, values, and political systems. That a country's political system will be reflected in the nature of its media system is only logical. Authoritarian governments need to control the mass media to maintain power. Therefore, they will institute a media system very different from that of a democratic country with a capitalistic, free economy. The overriding philosophy of how media ideally operate in any given system of social values is called a normative theory (see Chapter 14). You can see where the media systems of different countries rank in their degree of press freedom in the box titled "We're Number 44! Media Freedom Rankings around the Globe."

Reporters Without Borders, or *Reporters Sans Frontières* as it is known outside the United States, is an international nonprofit, nongovernmental organization that promotes press freedom around the world. Since 2002 the Paris-based group has issued an annual index ranking the level of press freedom in 180 countries. It takes into account factors such as media independence, self-censorship, media transparency, and the quality of the media's physical infrastructure. It looks at official government regulations, official penalties, and the level of independence of public media. It evaluates impediments to the free flow of information on the Internet and violence against journalists.

Its 2021 report found that journalism, "the best vaccine against the virus of disinformation, is totally blocked or seriously impeded in 73 countries and constrained in 59 others, which together represent 73% of the countries evaluated." It identified "a dramatic deterioration in people's access to information and an increase in obstacles to news coverage," as governments used the coronavirus pandemic "as grounds to block journalists' access to information sources and reporting in the field." Ominously, the report's authors wondered whether "this access will be restored when the pandemic is over" (Reporters Without Borders, 2021).

But of course that's the rest of the world; the situation in the greatest democracy on Earth, even with the coronavirus, must be better than that, right? Maybe not. The United States ranked 44th. Here are some representative rankings:

1	Norway
2	Finland
3	Sweden
4	Denmark
5	Costa Rica
10	Switzerland
13	Germany
14	Canada
24	Namibia
33	United Kingdom
37	Burkina Faso
43	Taiwan
44	United States
45	Organization of Eastern Caribbean States
177	China
179	North Korea
180	Eritrea

How surprised are you, if at all, by the idea that the United States enjoys only the 44th freest media system in the world? In rating American press freedom so poorly, Reporters Without Borders cited the disappearance of local news, the unchecked spread of online conspiracy theories, and the widespread distrust of mainstream media fed by President Donald Trump's vilification of "bona fide news outfits as 'fake news' and qualified award-winning journalists as the 'enemy of the people.'" They argued that these problems demand correction to ensure that "press freedom in the US runs more than just skin deep" ("The United States," 2021).

Enter Your Voice

• There is evidence that the countries that have the freest media systems are those that spend most heavily on public media (Pan, 2020). Top rankings for Scandinavian countries would seem to bear this out. So why do you think the United States, which ranks 25th out of 27 representative democracies in public financing of media (Pickard & Neff, 2021), does not invest more heavily in its journalism to ensure a free press? Would you advocate for this kind of spending? Why or why not?

• One of the identified problems is distrust of the media. Today, fewer than half of Americans have any trust in their media (Meek, 2021) and, among the world's leading 46 democracies, the US news media are the least trusted by their citizens (Edmonds, 2021). Why do you think people are so distrustful of the media system on which their self-governance depends? What would you do to remedy the situation?

• Much of this distrust of traditional media is driven by political polarization. In the United States, there are stark partisan differences of opinion on how well the media perform their role as government and corporate watchdog. Among Democrats, 84% believe journalists either get it about right or don't go far enough; among Republicans, 59% believe journalists go too far and only 16% think they get it right (Jurkowitz, 2020). Why such completely different perspectives? What kind of media system might produce a more unified assessment?

William Hachten (1992) offered five concepts that guide the world's many media systems: Western, development, revolutionary, authoritarianism, and communism. We'll examine each and provide a look at places that exemplify them.

THE WESTERN CONCEPT: GREAT BRITAIN The **Western concept** is an amalgamation of the original libertarian and social responsibility models (see Chapter 14). It recognizes two realities: There is no completely free (libertarian) media system on Earth, and even the most commercially driven systems include the expectation not only of public service and responsibility but also of meaningful government oversight of mass communication to ensure that media professionals meet those responsibilities.

Great Britain offers a good example of a media system operating under the Western concept. The BBC was originally built on the premise that broadcasting was a public trust (the social responsibility model). Long before television, BBC radio offered several services—one designed to provide news and information, another designed to support high or elite culture such as symphony music and plays, and a third designed to provide popular music and entertainment. To limit government and advertiser control, the BBC was funded by license fees levied on receivers (currently about $238 a year), and its governance was given over to a nonprofit corporation. Many observers point to this goal-oriented, noncommercial structure as the reason that the BBC developed, and still maintains, the most respected news operation in the world.

Eventually, Britain, like all of western Europe, was forced by public demand to institute more American-style broadcasting. Fueled by that demand and advances in digital broadcasting, there are now hundreds of radio stations in the United Kingdom. Most prominent are the 10 domestic BBC networks. The BBC also maintains 40 local stations that program a combination of local news and music, primarily for older listeners. There are also three national commercial radio networks (Virgin Radio, Classic FM, and talkSPORT) and a growing number of local commercial stations. As in the United States, most belong to larger chains.

The BBC also maintains 14 television networks, all digital, each having its own character; for example, BBC One carries more popular fare, while BBC Two airs somewhat more serious content. Several of those networks serve quite specific audiences, for example, BBC Hindi TV. Commercial television exists, too. Independent Television (ITV), and Channel 5 together maintain about a dozen digital networks. These commercial operations accept limits on the amount of advertising they air and agree to specified amounts of public affairs and documentary news programming in exchange for their licenses to broadcast. This is referred to as their **public service remit**.

In terms of other regulation, the media in Great Britain do not enjoy a First Amendment-like guarantee of freedom. Prior restraint does occur, but only when a committee of government officials and representatives of the media industry can agree on the issuance of what is called a **D-notice**. Strong self-regulation does exist, however, in the form of the Independent Press Standards Organisation, a voluntary (more than 2,000 outlets agree to its monitoring) body that accepts complaints from the public and investigates them with the involved outlet, primarily print and online. Its power resides in publication of its findings to embarrass offenders into corrective reporting and hopefully improved performance.

However, don't mistake the absence of First Amendment-like protection for a lack of commitment to good journalism. In 2019, facing a loss of local reporting much like that in the United States, the British government called for public tax support for local newspapers through the establishment of an Institute of Public Interest News (Waterson, 2019).

THE DEVELOPMENT CONCEPT: HONDURAS The media systems of many developing African, Asian, Latin and South American, and eastern European nations formerly part of the Soviet bloc best exemplify the **development concept**. Here government and media work in partnership to ensure that media assist in the planned, beneficial development of the country. Content is designed to meet specific cultural and societal needs—for example, teaching new farming techniques, disseminating information on methods of disease control, and improving literacy. This isn't the same as authoritarian control. There is less censorship and other official control of content, but often only marginally so.

Honduras offers one example. This small Central American country of approximately 9.6 million people is one of the poorest in the Western Hemisphere; half its

▼ Unlike American media, British media do not enjoy First Amendment protections. Nonetheless, as their notorious daily tabloids demonstrate, they operate with a great deal of freedom.

Amer ghazzal/Alamy Stock Photo

population lives in poverty. As a result, ownership of radio and television sets is quite low, and only 30% of Hondurans have Internet access (Enamorado Perez, 2020). All of Honduras's 19 television stations are commercial, but hundreds of TV channels remain unused because of the cost of setting up broadcast operations and radio's overwhelming popularity with the country's rural and poor citizens. There are 432 commercial radio stations, and the government network, Radio Honduras, operates about 20. Radio and printed leaflets have been particularly successful in reducing the number of infant deaths in Honduras caused by diarrheal dehydration and helping people with issues of family planning.

The 1982 Honduras Constitution guarantees freedom of the press, but there is significant control of media content. All the major newspapers are owned by powerful business executives or politicians with allegiances to different elites. Because the media in Honduras are constitutionally mandated to "cooperate with the state in the fulfillment of its public functions," journalists must be licensed and adhere to the Organic Law of the College of Journalists of Honduras. As such, they are forbidden to produce reports that "preach or disseminate doctrines that undermine the foundation of the State or of the family." Nor can journalists produce content that "threatens, libels, slanders, insults, or in any other way attacks the character of a public official in the exercise of his or her function."

These were the "decrees" invoked by the Honduran military government when it ordered the National Commission of Telecommunications (Conatel), the official body that regulates the country's media, to close down television station Canal 36 and Radio Globo after they broadcast messages from ousted president Manuel Zelaya during a 2009 coup.

A recent analysis of media freedom in Honduras by Reporters Without Borders rated the country's media system only the 151st freest, noting that "those working for opposition media or community media are often subjected to harassment, intimidation campaigns, and death threats, and some are forced to flee abroad. The security forces, especially the military police and army, are responsible for most of the abuses and violence against the media . . . Journalists are also often the targets of abusive judicial proceedings, and prison sentences for defamation are common, sometimes accompanied by bans on working as a journalist after release" ("Honduras," 2021).

THE REVOLUTIONARY CONCEPT: POLAND AND THE ARAB SPRING No country "officially" embraces the **revolutionary concept** as a normative theory, but this does not mean that a nation's media will never serve the goals of revolution. International media scholar Robert Stevenson (1994) identified four aims of revolutionary media: ending government monopoly over information, facilitating the organization of opposition to the incumbent powers, destroying the legitimacy of a standing government, and bringing down a standing government. The experience of the Polish democracy movement Solidarity is a well-known example of the use of media as a tool of revolution, as is the Arab Spring, despite its mixed success.

By the first years of the 1980s, the Polish people had grown dissatisfied with the domination of almost all aspects of their lives by a national Communist Party perceived to be a puppet of the Soviet Union. This frustration was fueled by the ability of just about all Poles to receive radio and television signals from neighboring democratic lands (Poland's location in central Europe made it impossible for the authorities to block what the people saw and heard).

In addition, Radio Free Europe, the VOA, and the BBC all targeted Poland with their mix of Western news, entertainment, and propaganda. Its people's taste for freedom thus whetted, Solidarity established an extensive network of clandestine revolutionary media. Much of it was composed of technologies traditionally associated with revolution—pamphlets, newsletters, audiotapes, and videocassettes—but much of it was also sophisticated radio and television technology used to disrupt official broadcasts and disseminate information. Despite government efforts to shut the system down, which went as far as suspending official broadcasting and mail services in order to deny Solidarity these communication channels, the revolution was a success, making Poland the first of the Eastern-bloc nations to defy the party apparatus and install a democratically elected government, setting off the ultimate demise of the Soviet bloc.

More recently, the Internet and social media proved to be powerful tools of revolution in what has become known as the Arab Spring. From 2011 to 2014 people in the Middle Eastern countries of Iran, Tunisia, Egypt, Yemen, Libya, Bahrain, Algeria, Morocco, Jordan, Oman, Iraq, Syria, and Saudi Arabia took to Facebook, Twitter, and YouTube to organize protests, monitor abuse, and demand the freedoms enjoyed by most other nations. Many of the movements were met with government brutality, but others produced "voluntary" reform on the part of once-powerful rulers who saw that new media were growing, uncontrollable checks on their authority.

It is impossible to isolate the influence of social media from all the other factors—unemployment, lack of opportunity, and anger at corruption, repression, and torture, for example—that led to the Arab Spring, but, wrote *New York Times* reporter Jennifer Preston (2011), there is no doubt that these technologies "offered a way for the discontented to organize and mobilize. . . . Far more decentralized than political parties, the strength and agility of the networks clearly caught [Middle Eastern] authorities . . . by surprise" (p. A10).

Unfortunately, those authorities overcame their surprise and learned how to employ those very same revolutionary technologies to destroy the freedom movements they helped spawn. They used social media to spread false information to discredit movement leaders, tracked down users, shut down social networking sites, and jailed and tortured site administrators. Now, understanding the revolutionary power of social media even better, those repressive regimes will even go so far as to deny their people access to the Internet altogether.

In fact, 33 different governments shut down their nations' Internet more than 213 times in 2019 alone, led by India's 121 interruptions that totaled just over 16,000 hours of national digital downtime. Those interruptions cost those 33 economies more than $8 billion (Griffith, 2020; McCarthy, 2020). You can read how, despite these governments' efforts, the Internet, and social media in particular, continue to make a difference in those places where people are willing to challenge power in the essay "The Logic of Connective Action."

Many observers believe that several factors, primarily authoritarian governments' need to control communication within their borders, many nations' worry over American tech companies' "digital colonization" of their cultures and economies, and general government and business fear of cybersecurity threats from outside, will inevitably produce an Internet fragmented and divided along national lines, the **splinternet**. Rather than one global Internet, the splinternet promises several isolated, nation-specific Internets where governments can better control information and their populations (Ovide, 2021).

◄ Arab Spring protesters face off against Algerian police. Social media helped ignite the democracy movements that swept the Middle East.
Nacerdine ZEBAR/Gamma-Rapho/ Getty Images

USING MEDIA TO MAKE A DIFFERENCE
The Logic of Connective Action

Repressive governments around the world work tirelessly to control the Internet because it gives voice to the people. That's why, for example, Turkey blocks tens of thousands of websites, social media accounts, and blogs (Human Rights Watch, 2020) and why Russia's Center for Combating Extremism, a special police department in that country's powerful Interior Ministry, monitors social media activity, harassing and jailing "offenders" (Bennetts, 2018). One important reason the Internet threatens authoritarian governments is that it helps overcome traditional impediments to collective action (see Chapter 10). This is especially true in developing countries where social media use continues to grow (Koetsier, 2020) and in regions such as the Middle East, where 9 out of 10 young people use social media every day and half get their daily news on Facebook ("Social Media Use," 2020).

Traditional collective action—large-scale protests and demonstrations—is often difficult to initiate and sustain for two reasons. First, people are unwilling to participate until they are certain their efforts will bear fruit. They become *free riders*, hoping to benefit from the work of others. They make a rational, cost–benefit decision to not participate because they can enjoy any positive outcome without contributing to it. The second hurdle is the level of resources traditionally necessary to identify, reach out to, and mobilize people potentially committed to the sought social good. That's why collective action has typically been initiated by resource-rich organizations such as labor unions, political parties, and interest groups such as Planned Parenthood or the National Action Network.

The mobilization of resources necessary to overcome free riding is not only costly, but it suffers from an additional problem: many people seeking a specific social good often have no commitment to the organization making that effort, further diminishing the returns of that effort. For example, an Arab couple may be in favor of greater educational opportunity for their daughter, but they may not identify with the trade union or political party mobilizing protests to secure that social good.

Researchers Lance Bennett and Alexandra Segerberg's (2012) theory of the **logic of connective action** explains how ubiquitous, low-cost digital technologies erase both problems: "In place of the initial collective action problem of getting the individual to contribute, the starting point of connective action is the self-motivated . . . sharing of already internalized or personalized ideas [via social media]" (p. 753). Not only do those digital networks reduce the "cost" of involvement, dissuading free-riding, but they also make possible quick and efficient "coordinated adjustments and rapid action aimed at often shifting political targets, even crossing geographic and temporal boundaries in the process," once collective action is underway.

This connective logic gave the world the ongoing global Black Lives Matter protests; the American student-led school shooting protests and multiple Women's Marches during the Donald Trump presidency; Spain's anti-austerity movement; the protests that greet every G8, G20, and World Bank meeting of the world's leading economic powers wherever they are held; and massive protests in Iraq demanding basic human survival needs and in Iran challenging a faltering economy and strict religious rule. In these and many other open expressions of the people's will, the Internet made a difference by harnessing connective action in the service of collective action.

THE AUTHORITARIANISM AND COMMUNISM CONCEPTS: CHINA Because only five communist nations remain and because the actual operation of the media in these and other **authoritarian systems** is quite similar, we can discuss authoritarianism and communism as a single concept. Both call for the subjugation of media for the purpose of serving the government. China is not only a good example of a country that operates its media according to the authoritarian/communist concepts, but it also demonstrates how difficult it is becoming for authoritarian governments to maintain strict control over media and audiences.

The Chinese media system is based on that of its old ideological partner, the now-dissolved Soviet Union. For a variety of reasons, however, it has developed its own peculiar nature. China has approximately 1.4 billion people living in more than a million hamlets, villages, and cities. As a result, in the early 2000s, the government undertook an extensive program called *Cuncun Tong*, designed to bring at least radio, but preferably radio and television, to every one of those locales.

At the same time, it closed down hundreds of local newspapers and broadcast stations to solidify its control over content through its central and provincial government operations, primarily China Central Television. In fact, all of the country's more than 2,400 radio and 1,200 television stations are owned by or affiliated with the Communist Party of China or a government agency. There is no privately owned television or radio, and state-run Chinese Central TV and the provincial and municipal stations offer more than 2,000 channels. The country's Central Propaganda Department lists subjects that are forbidden to appear on those channels, and the government maintains the authority to approve all programming.

Only relatively recently has the newspaper become an important medium. Widespread rural illiteracy and the lack of good pulpwood restricted the newspaper to the larger cities. Towns and cities were dotted with hundreds of thousands of reading walls where people could catch up on the official news. However, when China embarked on its Open Door Policy in the late 1970s, it committed itself to developing the newspaper as a national medium. As a result, most reading walls are now gone, with the few remaining used primarily by older people.

The media exist in China to serve the government. Chairman Mao Zedong, founder of the Chinese Communist Party, clarified the role of the media very soon after coming to power in 1949: The media exist to propagandize the policies of the Party and to educate, organize, and mobilize the masses. In 2016, to counter what he saw as a drift away from that mission, Chinese president Xi Jinping announced that the mission of the news media is to "love the party, protect the party, and serve the party" (Hernández, 2019, p. A11). In 2019 the party instituted an app-based test of loyalty to the Chinese president, *Study Xi, Strong Nation*, that journalists must pass; two failures means their press credentials will be pulled (Mosbergen, 2019). As it stands, China is among the world's leading jailer of journalists (Allsop, 2021).

Radio came to China via American reporter E. C. Osborn, who established an experimental radio station in China in 1923. Official Chinese broadcasting began three years later. Television went on the air in 1958, and from the outset it was owned and controlled by the Party in the form of Central China Television (CCTV), which in turn answers to the Ministry of Radio and Television. Radio, now regulated by China People's Broadcasting Station (CPBS), and television stations and networks develop their own content, but it must conform to the requirements of the Propaganda Bureau of the Chinese Communist Party Central Committee.

Historically, Chinese broadcasting has operated under direct government subsidy. However, in 1979 the government approved commercial advertising for broadcasting, and it has evolved into an important means of financial support. Coupled with the Chinese government's desire to become a more active participant in the international economy, this commercialization has led to increased diversity in broadcast content.

For several decades, only the state's China TV Programming Agency could buy foreign content, and it was limited to purchasing no more than 500 hours a year. Rules also restricted stations to programming no more than 25% of their time with imported fare. Restrictions on *foreign* content still exist, but there is now an emphasis on *domestic* coproduction with foreign programmers. In 2005, the central government began to allow foreign investment in and coproduction of media content for Chinese audiences, with the condition that all content be at least 51% government-owned. This is why producers from across the globe have set up shop in China and why local versions of Western fare such as *The Good Wife* now flourish there.

Basic government control over major media and the Internet remains, however. For example, only 34 foreign movies are permitted exhibition in China each year. These films must pass a prerelease censorship screening. For example, in *Top Gun: Maverick,* the Taiwanese and Japanese flags were removed from the back of Tom Cruise's flight jacket in response to Chinese demands. Nonetheless, and although a foreign studio can take home no more than 25% of a film's box-office income, those studios are still eager for a crack at what is the largest movie market in the world in terms of number of moviegoers and screens, more than 60,000.

In December 1997, anticipating the explosive growth of the Internet, the Party began enforcing criminal sanctions against those who would use the Internet to "split the country," "injure the reputation of state organs," "defame government agencies," "promote feudal superstitions," or otherwise pose a threat to "social stability." Now with more than 900 million users, 90% of whom are mobile, China has the world's largest and fastest-growing online population (Thomala, 2020). The state has established a 24-hour Internet task force to find

 China boasts the world's largest and fastest-growing population of Internet users, 90% of whom are mobile.
StreetVJ/Shutterstock

and arrest senders of "counterrevolutionary" commentary. Popular bulletin boards are shut down when their chat becomes a bit too free. Websites such as Human Rights Watch, *The New York Times*, YouTube, Wikipedia, and publications about China that are independent of government control are officially blocked by the government's Cyberspace Administration, but not very successfully, as skilled Internet users can traverse the Web by routing themselves through VPNs (virtual private networks) and distant servers such as DynaWeb and FreeGate. Nonetheless, China maintains the "world's most extensive and sophisticated online censorship system," abetted by private company self-censorship and commercial "censorship factories" (Yuan, 2019, p. B1).

The effects of this Internet censorship have rippled back to the United States as its tech giants, eager to enter and stay in that massive consumer market, willingly accept government demands that they tailor their technologies to aid control and surveillance of its online population. Apple's 2017 decision to halt the sale of VPN apps in China (Guangcheng, 2018), its removal of news site *Quartz* from its Chinese app store after complaints from the government (Williams, 2019), and Google's 2018 plans to build a censored version of its search engine (Swisher, 2018) brought global condemnation and revolt by those companies' employees.

▶ Only 34 foreign movies a year can be exhibited in China. *Mulan* made the cut in 2020.
GREG BAKER/AFP/Getty Images

Programming Around the Globe

Regardless of the particular concept guiding media systems in other countries, those systems produce and distribute content, in other words, programming. In most respects, radio and television programming throughout the world looks and sounds much like that found in the United States. There are two main reasons for this situation: (1) The United States is a world leader in international distribution of video fare, and (2) very early in the life of television, American producers flooded the world with their programming at very low prices. Foreign operators of emerging television systems were delighted to have access to this low-cost content because they typically could not afford to produce their own high-quality domestic material. For American producers, this strategy served the dual purpose of building markets for their programming and ensuring that foreign audiences would develop tastes and expectations similar to those in the United States, further encouraging future sales of programs originally produced for American audiences (Barnouw, 1990).

Naturally, programming varies somewhat from one country to another. The commercial television systems of most South American and European countries are far less sensitive about sex and nudity than are their counterparts in the United States. In Brazil, for example, despite a constitutional requirement that broadcasters respect society's social and ethical values, television networks such as SBT, TV Record, and TV Globo compete in what critics call the *guerra da baixaria*, the war of the lowest common denominator. Guests on variety shows wrestle with buxom models dressed only in bikinis and eat sushi off women's naked bodies. On game shows, male contestants who give wrong answers can be punished by having patches of leg hair ripped out, while those who answer correctly are rewarded by having a nearly naked model sit on their laps. European commercial operations regularly air shows

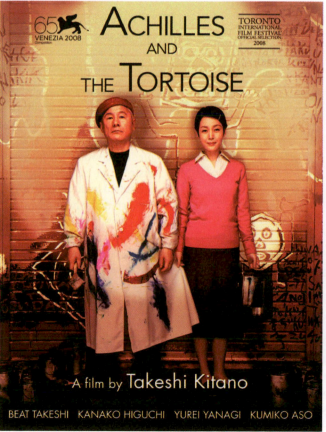

▲ Many countries hope their fare will find a worldwide audience, especially an American one. Here are two posters from Japanese films hoping to make their way to American screens.

(Left): Tokyo Theatres K.K./Courtesy of Everett Collection; (Right): Fever Dreams/Courtesy of Everett Collection

featuring both male and female nudity, sometimes because it is integral to the plot and sometimes simply for titillation.

Another difference between American programming and that of its global neighbors is how that content is utilized in different places. Naturally, broadcasting systems relying on the sale of commercial time find most value in programming that attracts the greatest number of viewers or a large number of viewers with the desired demographics. Commercial channels are just that, commercial. However, many broadcast systems, those relying on license fees or other public support, frequently offer publicly funded programming and channels specifically designed to have educational, social, or political value. Many nations, even those with commercially supported systems, use the soap opera genre for educational and social purposes.

The Global Village and the Debate over Cultural Imperialism

The most famous and oft-considered of communication theorist Marshall McLuhan's many groundbreaking ideas is the concept of the **global village**, introduced in his books *The Gutenberg Galaxy* (1962) and discussed again in *Understanding Media: The Extensions of Man* (1964). As you read earlier, McLuhan predicted that new communication technologies would permit people to become increasingly involved in one another's lives. And as you might imagine, with the subsequent development of the Internet and social media, debates over the global village's double edge have become quite intense. Although McLuhan's critics accuse him of having an unrealistic, utopian infatuation with technology, the theorist himself never said all would be tranquil in the global village. Yes, he did believe electronic media would permit "the human tribe" to become "one family," but he also realized that families fight:

> There is more diversity, less conformity under a single roof in any family than there is with the thousands of families in the same city. The more you create village conditions, the more discontinuity and division and diversity. The global village absolutely insures maximal disagreement on all points. (McLuhan & Stearn, 1967, p. 279)

Involvement does not mean harmony, but it does mean an exchange of ideas. As McLuhan said, the global village is "a world in which people encounter each other in depth all the time" (McLuhan & Stearn, 1967, p. 280). And how does that in-depth-all-the-time interaction play out now that there are few physical borders between countries in a globally mediated world? Governments that could once physically prohibit the introduction and distribution of unwanted newspapers, magazines, and books had to work harder at jamming unwanted radio and television broadcasts. But they could do it until satellite came along. Governments have much more difficulty disrupting satellite signals, but to some degree they can. Now, with the Internet, a new receiving technology is cheap, easy to use, and available to more and more millions of people in every corner of the world—and because of the universal availability of free translation software such as Google Translate, its content is readable, often in spite of government efforts at control, by those millions of people wherever they live. As a result, difficult questions of national sovereignty and cultural diversity are being raised anew.

The MacBride Report and the NWICO

The debate over the global village reached its height with the 1980 release of the MacBride Report by the United Nations Educational, Scientific, and Cultural Organization (UNESCO). It was named after the chair of the commission set up to study the question of how to maintain national and cultural sovereignty in the face of rapid globalization of mass media. At the time, many developing and communist countries were concerned that international news coverage was dominated by the West, especially the United States, and that Western-produced content was overwhelming the media of developing countries, which lacked sufficient resources to create their own quality fare. The fear was that Western cultural

▲ The book that helped introduce the world to the concept of the global village.

McLuhan, Marshall. Introduction by Lewis H. Lapham, Understanding Media, cover image, © 1994 Massachusetts Institute of Technology, by permission of The MIT Press.

values, especially those of the United States, would overshadow and displace those of other countries. These countries saw this as a form of colonialization, a **cultural imperialism**—the invasion of an indigenous people's culture by powerful foreign countries' cultures.

Fears of cultural imperialism are based in **electronic colonialism theory**, the belief "that cultural products produced, created, or manufactured in another country have the ability to influence, or possibly displace, indigenous cultural productions, artifacts, and media to the detriment of the receiving nations" (McPhail, 2014, p. 291). The MacBride Report was designed to calm these concerns. But it called for the establishment of a New World Information and Communication Order (NWICO) that contained several elements problematic to Western democracies. In arguing that individual nations should be free to control the news and entertainment that entered their lands, it called for monitoring of all such content, monitoring and licensing of foreign journalists, and requiring that prior government permission be obtained for direct radio, television, and satellite transmissions into foreign countries. Western nations rejected these rules as a direct infringement on the freedom of the press.

Western allies of the United States may have agreed that the restrictions of the NWICO were a threat to the free flow of information, yet virtually every one had rules (in the form of quotas) in place that limited American media content in their own countries. Canada, the US's closest cultural neighbor, requires that specific proportions of all content—print and broadcast—either be produced in Canada or reflect Canadian cultural identity. Canadian law forbids foreign (read: American) ownership in its commercial broadcasting channels. The French made illegal the printing of certain American words, including *hamburger* and *cartoon* (France maintains an official office to prosecute those who would "debase" its language, the Académie Française in our opening vignette). The European Union's Television Without Frontiers Directive requires member countries' broadcasters to dedicate a majority of their airtime to European-produced programming and to commission at least 10% of all their shows from local, independent producers, and in 2018 the European Parliament ruled that at least 30% of all streaming content from companies such as Netflix and Amazon must be produced in Europe. South Korean law mandates that movie theaters show native films at least 146 days out of each year.

In October 2005, UNESCO approved the *Convention on the Protection and Promotion of the Diversity of Cultural Expressions* by a vote of 148 to 2. The only two dissenters were the United States and Israel. The convention permits countries to treat "cultural products" such as movies, books, music, and television shows differently than they do other, more durable commodities. That is, countries can legally establish quotas and subsidies to protect their local media industries. And while the convention's text argued that the defense of every country's cultural heritage is "an ethical imperative, inseparable from respect for human dignity," it was clear from the debate preceding its passage that its true goal was protecting other countries' "cultural heritage" specifically from American media (UNESCO, 2005).

The resistance to US media would not exist among our international friends if they did not worry about the integrity of their own cultures. It is folly, then, to argue that non-native media content will have no effect on local culture—as do some American media content producers. The question today is, how much influence will countries accept in exchange for fuller membership in the global community? In light of instant, inexpensive, and open computer network communication, a parallel question is, have notions such as national sovereignty and cultural integrity lost their meaning?

For example, American hit TV shows *The Simpsons, Bob's Burgers, The Boondocks*, and *Family Guy* are animated in South Korea. Three of the United States' most influential satirical television news shows are hosted by people from different cultures: *The Daily Show with Trevor Noah* (South Africa), *Last Week Tonight with John Oliver* (Great Britain), and *Full Frontal with Samantha Bee* (Canada). BBC Radio broadcasts daily to a worldwide audience in 40 languages, as does Radio Beijing from China. CNN uses its satellites to transmit to a billion viewers in almost 200 countries. Two of the three largest US record companies have international ownership. America's largest movie chain AMC is owned by Chinese conglomerate Dalian Wanda Group, and the number two chain, Regal Cinemas, is owned by Britain's Cineworld. Hollywood's Columbia Pictures is owned by Japanese Sony. Bertelsmann, a German company that controls a large proportion of the US book publishing market, earns more money from the United States than from any other nation, including its homeland.

▶ American satirical TV news program *Full Frontal* is hosted by Samantha Bee, now an American citizen but originally from Canada.
Dimitrios Kambouris/ Staff/TBS/ Getty Images

The Case for the Global Village

There are differing opinions about the benefits of this trend away from nation-specific cultures. Global village proponents see the world community coming closer together as a common culture is negotiated and, not incidentally, as we become more economically interconnected. There should be little fear that individual cultures and national identities will disappear, because the world's great diversity will ensure that culture-specific, special-interest fare remains in demand. Modern media technology makes the delivery of this varied content not only possible but profitable.

Not only do native-language versions of American television shows such as *Jeopardy* exist in virtually every western European country, but other "translations" are also taking place. For example, with the worldwide success of the *Spider-Man* movies, Marvel Comics and India's Gotham Entertainment Group announced the birth of *Spider-Man India*, in which a young Bombay lad, Pavitr Prabhakar, inherits powers from a sacred yogi and accessorizes his Spidey suit with a traditional dhoti. There also exist 120 "translations" of *Sesame Street* across the globe, including *Jalan Sesama* in Indonesia and the Arabic *Ahlan Simsim* produced specifically for displaced children in Iraq, Syria, Jordan, and Lebanon.

As a result of these cultural exchanges, argue proponents of globalization, "a global culture is created, piece by piece, but it grows more variegated and complex along the way. And even as geographically based identities blur and fade, new subcultures, based on shared tastes in music or literature or obscure hobbies, grow up" (Bennett, 2004, p. 62). The resulting world culture, in "which the local is the global and the global is in the local," they argue, confirms the **hybridization hypothesis**, the idea that globalization inevitably and beneficially "entails the existence of traces of other cultures in every culture" (Roy & Speck, 2008, p. 1213).

▼ Proponents of the global flow of communication find value in the local adoption of varied cultures. In Indonesia, *Sesame Street* becomes *Jalan Sesama* and counts among its residents the book-reading orangutan Tantan.
Bay Ismoyo/AFP/Getty Images

The Case against the Global Village

The global village is here, say those with a less optimistic view, and the problem is what it looks like. *Time* media writer James Poniewozik (2001) calls it "the new cold war—between the Hollywood/Mickey D's axis and every other world culture" (p. 69). When, for example, American coffee giant Starbucks opened a luxurious outlet in Milan, famous for its coffee bars, local coffee seller Maurizio Stocchetto said of the company's first foray into Italy, "I must admit I do feel a bit invaded by Starbucks' arrival."

◀ Not all Italians welcomed Starbucks to Milan, a city famous for its coffee bars.
Fotogramma/Ropi/ZUMA Press/ Newscom

Italian journalist Silvia Marchetti concurred, "It's as if Pizza Hut opened a restaurant in Naples, or Baskin-Robbins an ice-cream parlor in Sicily—where pizza and gelato were first made and then exported to the rest of the world" (both in Marchetti, 2018). A Facebook poll by the magazine *Local Italy* revealed that 87% of its readers refused to "welcome Starbucks into Italy." Reader commentary such as "If anybody buys Starbucks in Italy they should be immediately deported" and "The Italians know how to make decent coffee not like the overpriced buckets of brown water that Starbucks charge a fortune for. Stop trying to turn every country into the worse type of America" were typical (Filloon, 2018).

There is no simple answer to the debate over protecting the integrity of local cultures. As we've just seen, there is even disagreement over the wisdom of doing so. Media-literate people should at least be aware of the debate and its issues, and they may also want to consider the paradox of what Josef Joffe (2006), editor of Germany's weekly *Die Zeit*, calls the "soft power" of America's exported culture. It "does not bend hearts" as cultural imperialism's critics contend. Rather, "it twists minds in resentment and rage." He points to data collected by the Pew Global Attitudes Project. When asked if they "like American music, movies, and television," large percentages, all over 60%, of citizens in England, France, Germany, and Italy said "yes."

◀ These Malaysian students are encouraged to "makan" (eat) at their local Kuala Lumpur McDonald's. Although critics of cultural imperialism see this as an intrusion of Western culture into the lives of these people, defenders of globalization of culture see the expansion of opportunity for both the "sending" and the "receiving" cultures.
Vincent Thian/AP Images

But when asked if "it's good that American ideas and customs are spreading," other large percentages of people in England (33%), France (27%), Germany (24%), and Italy (43%) said "no" (p. 15). This may be because, as British journalist Justin Webb (2015) explains, the "cultural seduction" of American movies, music, and literature makes Europeans "feel weak," producing a self-loathing that leads them to hate "the seducer" as well as themselves. Like most debates over mass communication, the simple answers aren't always the correct answers.

DEVELOPING MEDIA LITERACY SKILLS

Making the Invisible Visible: Comparative Analysis

While comparative analysis offers us a glimpse into other countries' media systems, it also helps us understand our own. This is because we tend to think that the characteristics of our own media system are "natural." Those aspects of media become so familiar that we don't see or perceive them at all. However, comparative analysis, comparing the way our media operate to the workings of another country's media, can help us identify aspects of our own system that might require a little more thought. Comparative analysis has the "capacity to render the invisible visible," to draw attention to aspects of any media system, including our own, "that may be taken for granted and difficult to detect when the focus is on only one national case" (Blumler & Gurevitch, 1975, p. 76).

We've seen elsewhere in this text that, with the exception of New Zealand, the United States is the only country in the world that permits advertising of prescription drugs, that America is alone among industrialized nations in permitting largely unregulated advertising in children's television programming, and that as opposed to here in the United States, European nations require Internet users to opt in before their personal data can be shared. Here are a number of other aspects of foreign media systems that differ from our own:

- In a "collective realisation [sic] and reflection of the power of advertising to shift culture," the United Kingdom's Advertising Standards Authority bans gender stereotyping in advertising (Kemp, 2019).

- Germany's NetzDG law grants government authorities the ability to levy fines of up to $60 million per infraction against any online service with more than 2 million users if it fails to remove illegal or offensive content within 24 hours of being notified about it. British authorities have similar powers, even if the content isn't actually illegal but might be seen as "damaging to children or other vulnerable users" (Ingram, 2020).

- Sweden's Supreme Court ruled that inserting commercial breaks into televised movies at particularly dramatic moments "violates the integrity and value of the film" and is punishable by fine (Rehlin, 2010). Movies in Sweden must also carry a gender rating. To earn an A, a film must have at least two women in it who talk to one another about something other than a man (McDonough, 2013).

- The French government has declared books an "essential good," outlawing deep discounts (no more than 5%) and subjecting books to low taxes, just like food. As a result, big chain bookstores such as Amazon struggle, Paris averages two bookstores per block, and the average French person reads 25% more books than his or her American counterpart (Mendelsohn & Hamid, 2014).

- The French government, to shore up its nation's "suffering" public affairs newspapers and magazines, gives tax credits to new subscribers (Henley, 2020).

- The Canadian government committed $600 million in public money to support commercial and nonprofit journalism (Bessonov, 2019) and gives citizens tax credits for digital news subscriptions (Schiffrin, 2020); in Great Britain, the government sets aside more than $10 million in BBC license fees to hire reporters specifically for struggling local news outlets (Tsang, 2018).

- To combat video game addiction, South Korea's Shutdown Law makes it illegal for anyone under 16 years old to play online games between midnight and 6 a.m. (Jabr, 2019).

Can you explain why these differences might exist? Would any of these rules or practices seem "natural" in our American media system? Why or why not? Are there any that you would like to see adopted by our homegrown system? Why or why not? The hallmarks of a media-literate individual are critical thinking, analysis, and reflection. As such, you should have ready answers to these questions. Do you?

MEDIA LITERACY CHALLENGE
See the World Through Others' News

As a media-literate individual, you have *developed strategies for analyzing and discussing media messages*, especially because you know that *media content is a text providing insight into contemporary culture*. Use your media-analyzing skills challenge your assumptions about the world by examining how others view it. You can accomplish this by looking at the news you rely on to explain the world and compare its messages with those of a news source that just might have a different perspective.

To start, take an American online news outlet with a global audience, for example *CNN World* (https://www.cnn.com/world) or the *New York Times* (https://www.nytimes.com/). Then choose a similar news site from a different country, for example Britain's BBC (https://www.bbc.com/news), Qatar's *al Jazeera* (https://www.aljazeera.com/), Russia's *RT* (https://www.rt.com/), *China Daily* (http://global.chinadaily.com.cn/), or *France24* (https://www.france24.com/en/). Pick a single day and approximately the same time, for example morning, early evening, or late night.

Compare the US-based outlet's homepage with that of one from another country you've chosen. Keep in mind the lessons from Chapter 3 about the placement of stories on a page as these are some obvious things to look for: top, middle, or bottom of the page; left-hand side or right-hand side of the page; length of account; with or without images, video, or links, and so on.

But there should also be differences that are more telling. What stories or types of stories dominate? What is the balance between hard and soft news? How inward or outward looking does each site's account of the day seem to be? As all these sites are in English, it should be obvious that their goal is to communicate (and influence) the English-speaking world. What image of the home nation's culture does each of your chosen sites hope to communicate to this global audience? What do they hope to communicate about how they view the world outside their own borders?

Take this challenge either by offering your responses in a brief essay or in discussion with one or more classmates.

Resources for Review and Discussion

REVIEW POINTS: TYING CONTENT TO LEARNING OUTCOMES

▶ **Recall the development of global media.**
- ☐ For decades, international mass media took the form of shortwave radio broadcasts, especially in the form of clandestine stations, both exogenous and indigenous.
- ☐ Other exogenous operations are pirate broadcasters and many countries' external services such as the BBC and VOA.

▶ **Explain the practice of comparative analysis.**
- ☐ Different countries rely on different media systems to meet their national needs. The study of these varying models is called comparative analysis.
- ☐ Naturally, different systems make varying use of different programming as their nations' needs demand.

▶ **Identify different media systems from around the world.**
  □ There are five main models or concepts: Western, development, revolutionary, authoritarianism, and communism.

▶ **Describe the debate surrounding cultural imperialism and other controversies raised by the globalization of media.**
  □ There is serious debate about the free and not-so-free flow of mass communication across borders. The conflict is between those who want the free flow of information and those who worry about the erosion of local culture, a conflict resulting from a technology-created global village.
  □ Much of this controversy, however, has more to do with protecting countries' media systems from American influence than it does with protecting all countries' cultural integrity.

KEY TERMS

shortwave radio, 381

skip, 381

sky waves, 381

clandestine stations, 381

indigenous stations, 381

exogenous stations, 381

pirate broadcasters, 382

external service, 382

surrogate service, 383

comparative analysis
    (comparative studies), 385

Western concept, 387

public service remit, 387

D-notice, 387

development concept, 387

revolutionary concept, 388

splinternet, 389

logic of connective action, 390

authoritarian system, 390

global village, 394

cultural imperialism, 395

electronic colonialism theory, 395

hybridization hypothesis, 396

QUESTIONS FOR REVIEW

1. What are clandestine broadcast stations? Differentiate between indigenous and exogenous stations.

2. What are pirate broadcasters? What differentiates them from traditional clandestine operators?

3. How did World War II and the Cold War shape the efforts of the United States in terms of its external and surrogate services?

4. What is comparative analysis?

5. What are the main characteristics of media systems operating under Hachten's Western concept?

6. What are the main characteristics of media systems operating under Hachten's development concept?

7. What are the main characteristics of media systems operating under Hachten's revolutionary concept? Authoritarianism and communism concepts?

8. What is the logic of connective action? How does it facilitate collective action?

9. What is cultural imperialism? What arguments suggest it is a problem? What is the argument that it is not?

10. What was the MacBride Report? Why did most Western nations reject it? How does it relate to McLuhan's concept of the global village?

To maximize your study time, check out CONNECT to access the SmartBook study module for this chapter, watch videos, and explore other resources.

QUESTIONS FOR CRITICAL THINKING AND DISCUSSION

1. Britain's external service, the BBC, is available on shortwave radio, the Internet, and American public broadcasting and cable and satellite television. Listen to or watch the BBC. How does its content compare to the homegrown radio and television with which you are familiar? Think especially of news. How does its reporting differ from that of cable networks such as CNN and from broadcast networks such as ABC, CBS, and NBC? Why do you think differences exist? Similarities?

2. Do you have experience with another country's media? If so, which one? Can you place that system's operation within one of the concepts listed in this chapter? Describe how that system's content is similar to and different from that with which you are familiar in the United States. Do you favor one system's fare over another's? Why or why not?

3. Do you think countries, especially developing nations, should worry about cultural imperialism? Would you argue that they should use low-cost Western fare to help their developing system get "off the ground," or do you agree with critics that this approach unduly influences their system's ultimate content?

REFERENCES

1. "All Time Worldwide Box Office." (2021). The Numbers. Retrieved from https://www.the-numbers.com/box-office-records/worldwide/all-movies/cumulative/all-time

2. Allsop, J. (2021, January 12). In China, journalists are targets and collateral. *Columbia Journalism Review*. Retrieved from https://www.cjr.org/the_media_today/china_press_freedom_bbc.php

3. Barnouw, E. (1990). *Tube of plenty: The evolution of American television.* New York: Oxford University Press.

4. Bennett, D. (2004, February). Our mongrel planet. *American Prospect*, pp. 62–63.

5. Bennett, L. W., & Segerberg, A. (2012). The logic of connective action. *Information, Communication & Society, 15*, 739–768.

6. Bennetts, M. (2018, October 9). How a social media post in Russia can land you in jail and on a list with neo-Nazis and ISIS supporters. *Newsweek*. Retrieved from https://www.newsweek.com/2018/10/19/how-social-media-post-russia-can-land-you-jail-1157822.html

7. Bessonov, A. (2019, January 18). Who's weighing in on the proposed federal tax package? *J-Source*. Retrieved from http://j-source.ca/article/journalism-fund-tracker/

8. Bhutada, G. (2021, March 26). Visualizing the most used languages on the Internet. *Visual Capitalist*. Retrieved from https://www.visualcapitalist.com/the-most-used-languages-on-the-internet/

9. Blumler, J. G., & Gurevitch, M. (1975). Towards a comparative framework for political communication research. In S. H. Chaffee (Ed.), *Political communication: Issues and strategies for research.* Beverly Hills, CA: Sage.

10. Clarke, S. (2018, September 4). U.S. invasion of U.K. reaches the next level. *Variety*, pp. 18–19.

11. Devlin, K. (2020, April 9). Most European students learn English in school. *Pew Research Center*. Retrieved from https://www.pewresearch.org/fact-tank/2020/04/09/most-european-students-learn-english-in-school/

12. Edmonds, R. (2021, June 22). US ranks last among 46 countries in trust in media, Reuters Institute report finds. *Poynter Institute*. Retrieved from https://www.poynter.org/ethics-trust/2021/us-ranks-last-among-46-countries-in-trust-in-media-reuters-institute-report-finds/

13. Egan, J. (2020, June 17). Reuters Institute study finds BBC News is America's most trusted news brand. *BBC*. Retrieved from https://www.bbc.co.uk/mediacentre/worldnews/2020/reuters-institute-study-finds-bbc-news-is-americas-most-trusted-news-brand

14. Enamorado Perez, C. B. (2020). Honduras. *Media Landscapes*. Retrieved from https://medialandscapes.org/country/honduras

15. Filloon, W. (2018, May 10). Starbucks is heading to Milan, and Italians are pissed. *Eater*. Retrieved from https://www.eater.com/2018/5/10/17338990/starbucks-milan-backlash-italians-mad

16. Ghosh, I. (2020, February 15). Ranked: The 100 most spoken languages around the world. *Visual Capitalist*. Retrieved from https://www.visualcapitalist.com/100-most-spoken-languages/

17. Griffith, E. (2020, May 4). In 2019, governments shut down their countries' Internet 213 times. *PC Magazine*. Retrieved from https://www.pcmag.com/news/in-2019-governments-shut-down-their-countries-internet-213-times

18. Guangcheng, C. (2018, January 24). Apple caves to China. *The New York Times*, p. A23.

19. Hachten, W. A. (1992). *The world news prism* (3rd ed.). Ames: Iowa State University Press.

20. Henley, J. (2020, July 1). France gives tax credits to news subscribers in effort to rescue sector. *Guardian*. Retrieved from https://www.theguardian.com/world/2020/jul/01/france-gives-tax-credits-to-news-subscribers-in-effort-to-rescue-sector

21. Hernández, J. C. (2019, July 14). "We're almost extinct": Journalists in the Xi era. *New York Times*, p. A11.

22. "Honduras." (2021). Ever-changing threats. *Reporters Without Borders*. Retrieved from https://rsf.org/en/honduras

23. Human Rights Watch. (2020, July 27). Turkey: Social media law will increase censorship. Retrieved from https://www.hrw.org/news/2020/07/27/turkey-social-media-law-will-increase-censorship

24. Ingram, M. (2020, February 13). Britain to give regulator power over social media. *Columbia Journalism Review*. Retrieved from https://www.cjr.org/the_media_today/britain-social-media.php

25. Iqbal, M. (2020, June 23). Netflix revenue and usage statistics (2020). *Business of Apps*. Retrieved from https://www.businessofapps.com/data/netflix-statistics/#3

26. Jabr, F. (2019, October 27). Can you really be addicted to video games? *New York Times Magazine*, pp. 36–41, 54–55.

27. Jurkowitz, M. (2020, February 26). Most say journalists should be watchdogs, but views of how well they fill this role vary by party, media diet. *Pew Research Center*. Retrieved from https://www.journalism.org/2020/02/26/most-say-journalists-should-be-watchdogs-but-views-of-how-well-they-fill-this-role-vary-by-party-media-diet/

28. Joffe, J. (2006, May 14). The perils of soft power. *The New York Times Magazine*, pp. 15–17.

29. Kemp, N. (2019, June 14). Out of the kitchen: Why the ASA clamping down on gender stereotyping is just the start. *The Drum*. Retrieved from https://www.thedrum.com/opin-ion/2019/06/14/out-the-kitchen-why-the-asa-clamping-down-gender-stereotyping-just-the-start

30. Koetsier, J. (2020, February 18). Why 2020 Is a critical global tipping point for social media. *Forbes*. Retrieved from https://www.forbes.com/sites/johnkoetsier/2020/02/18/why-2020-is-a-critical-global-tipping-point-for-social-media/#4a4a2c212fa5

31. Marchetti, S. (2018, September 7). Starbucks in Milan: Is this the end for Italian coffee? *CNN*. Retrieved from https://www.cnn.com/travel/article/starbucks-milan-italy/index.html

32. McCarthy, N. (2020, January 22). The countries shutting down the Internet the most. *Statista*. Retrieved from https://www.statista.com/chart/15250/the-number-of-internet-shutdowns-by-country/

33. McDonough, K. (2013, November 7). Sweden launches gender ratings for movies. *Salon*. Retrieved from http://www.salon.com/2013/11/07/sweden_introduces_a_gender_rating_system_for_films/

34. McLuhan, M. (1962). *The Gutenberg galaxy: The making of typographic man*. London: Routledge.

35. McLuhan, M. (1964). *Understanding media: The extensions of man*. New York: McGraw-Hill.

36. McLuhan, M., & Stearn, G. E. (1967). A dialogue: Q & A. In M. McLuhan & G. E. Stearn (Eds.), *McLuhan: Hot and cool: A primer for the understanding of McLuhan and a critical symposium with a rebuttal by McLuhan*. New York: Dial Press.

37. McPhail, T. L. (2014). *Global communication*. Malden, MA: Wiley.

38. Meek, A. (2021, February 20). Fewer Americans than ever before trust the mainstream media. *Forbes*. Retrieved from https://www.forbes.com/sites/andymeek/2021/02/20/fewer-americans-than-ever-before-trust-the-mainstream-media/?sh=6fb05b14282a

39. Mendelsohn, D., & Hamid, M. (2014, November 11). Should the United States declare books an "essential good"? *The New York Times*, p. BR31.

40. Mosbergen, D. (2019, September 22). Chinese journalists will soon be tested on their "loyalty" to Xi Jinping. *Huffington Post*. Retrieved from https://www.huffpost.com/entry/chinese-journalists-xi-jinping-loyalty-test_n_5d8726b1e4b070d468cdf2b8

41. Ovide, S. (2021, February 22). The 'splinternet' is here. Is this good? *New York Times*, p. B5.

42. Pan, J. C. (2020, August 13). America needs its own BBC to restore public trust in the press. *National Review*. Retrieved from https://newrepublic.com/article/158913/america-needs-bbc-restore-public-trust-press?utm_source=newsletter&utm_medium=email&utm_campaign=tnr_daily

43. Pickard, V., & Neff, T. (2021, June 2). Op-ed: Strengthen our democracy by funding public media. *Columbia Journalism Review*. Retrieved from https://www.cjr.org/opinion/public-funding-media-democracy.php

44. Poniewozik, J. (2001, September 15). Get up, stand up. *Time*, pp. 68–70.

45. Preston, J. (2011, February 6). Movement began with outrage and a Facebook page that gave it an outlet. *The New York Times*, p. A10.

46. Rehlin, G. (2010, March 1–7). Swedish court takes uncommercial break. *Variety*, p. 4.

47. Reporters Without Borders. (2021). 2021 world press freedom index. Retrieved from https://rsf.org/en/2021-world-press-freedom-index-journalism-vaccine-against-disinformation-blocked-more-130-countries

48. Roy, A., & Speck, S. K. S. (2008). The interrelationships between television viewing, values and perceived well-being: A global perspective. *Journal of International Business Studies*, *39*, 1197–1219.

49. Schiffrin, A. (2020, October 19/26). The infodemic. *Nation*, pp. 58–62.

50. Smith, D. (2020, August 21). Band flees Iran after receiving 15-year prison sentence for playing heavy metal. *Digital Music News*. Retrieved from https://www.digitalmusicnews.com/2020/08/21/arsames-flees-iran/

51. "Social Media Use by Youth Is Rising Across the Middle East." (2020, January 26). *Arab Weekly*. Retrieved from https://thearabweekly.com/social-media-use-youth-rising-across-middle-east

52. Soley, L. C., & Nichols, J. S. (1987). *Clandestine radio broadcasting: A study of revolutionary and counterrevolutionary electronic communication*. New York: Praeger.

53. Stevenson, R. L. (1994). *Global communication in the twenty-first century*. New York: Longman.

54. Swisher, K. (2018, September 13). Google's censorship scandal. *The New York Times*, p. A31.

55. Thomala, L. L. (2020, August 14). Number of internet users in China 2015-2025. *Statista*. Retrieved from https://www.statista.com/statistics/278417/number-of-internet-users-in-china/#:~:text=China%20is%20home%20to%20the,around%20281%20million%20in%202019.

56. Tsang, A. (2018, December 12). Local news gets lifeline in Britain. *The New York Times*, p. B1.

57. "TV Series, France." (2020). *IMDb*. Retrieved from https://www.imdb.com/search/title/?countries=fr&sort=moviemeter&title_type=tv_series

58. "The United States." (2021). Despite improvements, troubling vital signs for press freedom persist. *Reporters Without Borders*. Retrieved from https://rsf.org/en/united-states

59. UNESCO. (2005, October 20). General Conference adopts Convention on the Protection and Promotion of the Diversity of Cultural Expressions. Retrieved from http://portal.unesco.org/en/ev.php-URL_ID=30298&URL_DO=DO_TOPIC&URL_SECTION=201.html

60. "VOA Firewall." (2020). *Voice of America*. Retrieved from https://www.insidevoa.com/p/5831.html

61. "Voice of America staff rebel over new CEO's comments." (2020, September 1). *Columbia Journalism Review*. Retrieved from https://www.cjr.org/the_media_today/voice-of-america-staff-rebel-over-new-ceos-comments.php

62. Waterson, J. (2019, February 11). Public funds should be used to rescue local journalism, says report. *The Guardian*. Retrieved from https://www.theguardian.com/media/2019/feb/11/public-funds-should-be-used-to-rescue-local-journalism-says-report

63. Webb, J. (2015, October 30). Those who hate the US actually hate themselves. *The Times of London*. Retrieved from http://www.thetimes.co.uk/tto/opinion/columnists/article4599959.ece

64. Williams, R. (2019, October 11). Apple's removal of "Quartz" app in China marks defeat for press freedom. *MediaPost*. Retrieved from https://www.mediapost.com/publications/article/341887/apples-removal-of-quartz-app-in-china-marks-def.html

65. Yuan, L. (2019, January 3). China turns censorship into lucrative factory work. *The New York Times*, p. B1.

Cultural Forum Blue Column icon, Media Literacy Red Torch Icon, Using Media Green Gear icon, Developing Media book in starburst icon: ©McGraw Hill

Glossary

AAA games big-budget, sophisticated, graphics-rich video games

abridgment the curtailing of rights

absolutist position regarding the First Amendment, the idea that no law against free speech means no law

access journalism reporters acting deferentially toward news sources in order to ensure continued access

accountability metrics agreement between ad agency and client on how the effectiveness of a specific ad or campaign will be judged

Acta Diurna written on a tablet, an account of the deliberations of the Roman senate; an early "newspaper"

actual malice the standard for libel in coverage of public figures consisting of "knowledge of its falsity" or "reckless disregard" for whether or not it is true

ad hoc balancing of interests in individual First Amendment cases, several factors should be weighed in determining how much freedom the press is granted

addressable technology technology permitting the transmission of very specific content to equally specific audience members

administrative research studies of the immediate, observable influence of mass communication

advergames video games produced expressly to serve as brand commercials

advocacy games primarily online games supporting an idea rather than a product

affective forecasting error discrepancy between the expected and actual emotions generated by Facebook activity

affiliate a broadcasting station that aligns itself with a network

affinity how much readers enjoy magazine advertising

agenda setting the theory that media may not tell us what to think but do tell us what to think about

aggressive cues model of media violence; media portrayals can indicate that certain classes of people are acceptable targets for real-world aggression

AI (artificial intelligence) songwriting composition of music and lyrics by computers

AIDA approach the idea that to persuade consumers, advertising must attract *attention*, create *interest*, stimulate *desire*, and promote *action*

à la carte pricing charging cable subscribers by the channel, not for tiers

album equivalent measurement of consumption of music that equals the purchase of one album, including streaming, downloads, and traditional album sales

Alien and Sedition Acts series of four laws passed by the 1798 U.S. Congress making illegal the writing, publishing, or printing of "any false scandalous and malicious writing" about the president, Congress, or the U.S. government

aliteracy possessing the ability to read but being unwilling to do so

all-channel legislation 1962 law requiring all television sets imported into or manufactured in the United States to be equipped with both VHF and UHF receivers

alternative press typically weekly, free papers emphasizing events listings, local arts advertising, and "eccentric" personal classified ads

ambient advertising advertising content appearing in nontraditional venues; also known as **360 marketing**

applied ethics the application of metaethics and normative ethics to very specific situations

appointment consumption audiences consume content at a time predetermined by the producer and distributor

artificial intelligence (AI) the use of machine learning to produce human activity

ascertainment requires broadcasters to ascertain or actively and affirmatively determine the nature of their audiences' interest, convenience, and necessity; no longer enforced

associative advertising consumer advertising that connects products and services with lifestyle ideals

astroturf fake grassroots organization

attitude change theory theory that explains how people's attitudes are formed, shaped, and changed and how those attitudes influence behavior

audience fragmentation audiences for specific media content becoming smaller and increasingly homogeneous

audiobook the presentation, in sound, of a book's text, typically on tape, CD, or digital download

audion tube vacuum tube developed by DeForest that became the basic invention for all radio and television

augmented reality (AR) permits users to point phones at things in the real world and be instantly linked to websites containing information about those things superimposed over the screen image

authoritarian/communism system a national media system characterized by authoritarian control

awareness tests ad research technique that measures the cumulative effect of a campaign in terms of a product's "consumer consciousness"

B-movie the second, typically less expensive, movie in a double feature

bandwidth a communication channel's information-carrying capacity

banners online advertising messages akin to billboards

bibliotherapy using reading for therapeutic effect

Bill of Rights the first 10 amendments to the U.S. Constitution

billings total sale of broadcast airtime

binary code information transformed into a series of digits 1 and 0 for storage and manipulation in computers

binge watching watching five or more episodes of a TV series in one sitting

bitcasters "radio stations" that can be accessed only over the World Wide Web

BitTorrent file-sharing software that allows users to create "swarms" of data as they simultaneously download and upload "bits" of a given piece of content

black PR using every tool and taking every advantage available in order to change reality according to clients' wishes; unethical use of mass communication to misinform

blinks 1- or 2-second television commercials

block booking the practice of requiring exhibitors to rent groups of movies (often inferior) to secure a better one

blockbuster mentality filmmaking characterized by reduced risk taking and more formulaic movies; business concerns are said to dominate artistic considerations

blogs regularly updated online journal

bounded culture groups with specific but not dominant cultures; also called **co-cultures**

boutique agencies smaller, more personalized, and task-specific ad agencies

brand entertainment when commercials are part of and essential to a piece of media content

brand magazine a consumer magazine published by a retail business for readers having demographic characteristics similar to those consumers with whom it typically does business

branding films sponsor financing of movies to advance a manufacturer's product

British cultural theory theory of elites' domination over culture and its influence on bounded cultures

broadband a channel with broad information-carrying capacity

broadsheets see **broadsides**

broadsides (broadsheets) early colonial newspapers imported from England, single-sheet announcements or accounts of events; also called **broadsheets**

browsers software programs loaded on personal computers and used to download and view Web files

bundling delivering television, VOD, audio, high-speed Internet access, long-distance and local phone service, multiple phone lines, and fax via cable

C3 and C7 ratings measures of viewing of commercials that appear in a specific program within 3 or 7 days of its premiere telecast

calotype early system of photography using translucent paper from which multiple prints could be made

casual games classic games most often played in spurts and accommodated by small-screen devices

catalog albums in record retailing, albums more than 18 months old

catharsis the theory that watching mediated violence reduces people's inclination to behave aggressively

cause marketing PR in support of social issues and causes

cease-and-desist order demand made by a regulatory agency that a given illegal practice be stopped

censorship when someone in authority limits publication or access to it

cinématographe Lumière brothers' device that both photographed and projected action

circulation the number of issues of a magazine or newspaper that are sold

clandestine stations illegal or unlicensed broadcast operations frequently operated by revolutionary groups or intelligence agencies for political purposes

clear time when local affiliates carry a network's program

click bait Web content designed to attract ad impressions

click stream the series of choices made by a user on the Web

cloud computing storage of all computer data, including personal information and system-operating software, on remote servers hosted on the Internet

clutter overabundance of commercial messages

co-cultures groups with specific but not dominant cultures; also called **co-cultures**

coaxial cable copper-clad aluminum wire encased in plastic foam insulation, covered by an aluminum outer conductor and then sheathed in plastic

collateral materials printing, research, and photographs that PR firms handle for clients, charging as much as 17.65% for this service

commissions in advertising, method of compensation for the placement of advertising in media, typically 15% of the cost of the time or space

communication the process of creating shared meaning

community antenna television (CATV) outmoded name for early cable television

community information district (CiD) special service district paid for by taxes or annual fees assessed in a geographic area to support local journalism

comparative analysis the study of different countries' mass media systems; also called **comparative studies**

comparative studies the study of different countries' mass media systems; also called **comparative studies**

complementary copy newspaper and magazine content that reinforces the advertiser's message, or at least does not negate it

concentration of ownership ownership of different and numerous media companies concentrated in fewer and fewer hands

concept films movies that can be described in one line

confidentiality the ability of media professionals to keep secret the names of people who provide them with information

confirmation bias the tendency to accept information that confirms one's beliefs and dismiss information that does not

conglomeration the increase in the ownership of media outlets by nonmedia companies

consumer culture a culture in which personal worth and identity reside not in the people themselves but in the products with which they surround themselves

consumer juries ad research technique in which people considered representative of a target market review a number of approaches or variations of a campaign or ad

consumption on demand the ability to access any content, anytime, anywhere

controlled circulation a magazine provided at no cost to readers who meet some specific set of advertiser-attractive criteria

conventions in media content, certain distinctive, standardized style elements of individual genres

convergence the erosion of traditional distinctions among media

cookie an identifying code added to a computer's hard drive by a visited website

copy testing measuring the effectiveness of advertising messages by showing them to consumers; used for all forms of advertising

copyright identifying and granting ownership of a given piece of expression to protect the creators' financial interest in it

corantos one-page news sheets on specific events, printed in English but published in Holland and imported into England by British booksellers; an early "newspaper"

cord-cutting viewers leaving cable and DBS altogether and relying on Internet-only television

cord-never viewer who never had cable TV

corporate independent studio specialty or niche division of a major studio designed to produce more sophisticated—but less costly—movies

corporate social responsibility the integration of business operations and organizational values

corrective advertising a new set of ads required by a regulatory body and produced by the offender that correct the original misleading effort

cost of entry amount of money necessary to begin media content production

cost per thousand (CPM) in advertising, the cost of reaching 1,000 audience members, computed by the cost of an ad's placement divided by the number of thousands of consumers it reaches

cottage industry an industry characterized by small operations closely identified with their personnel

cover rerecording of one artist's music by another

critical cultural theory idea that media operate primarily to justify and support the status quo at the expense of ordinary people

critical research studies of media's contribution to the larger issues of what kind of nation we are building, what kind of people we are becoming

cultivation analysis idea that television "cultivates" or constructs a reality of the world that, although possibly inaccurate, becomes the accepted reality simply because we as a culture believe it to be reality

cultural definition of communication communication is a symbolic process whereby reality is produced, maintained, repaired, and transformed; from James Carey

cultural imperialism the invasion of an indigenous people's culture by the cultures of outside, powerful countries

cultural theory the idea that meaning and therefore effects are negotiated by media and audiences as they interact in the culture

culture the world made meaningful; socially constructed and maintained through communication, it limits as well as liberates us, differentiates as well as unites us, defines our realities and thereby shapes the ways we think, feel, and act

custom publishing publications specifically designed for an individual company seeking to reach a narrowly defined audience

D-notice in Great Britain, an officially issued notice of prior restraint

daguerreotype process of recording images on polished metal plates, usually copper, covered with a thin layer of silver iodide emulsion

dataveillance the massive electronic collection and distillation of consumer data

day-and-date release simultaneously releasing a movie to the public in some combination of theater, cable, DVD, and download

decoding interpreting sign/symbol systems

deep catalog albums albums more than 3 years old

deep fake artificial intelligence-enhanced video and audio designed to present people saying or doing things that they never actually said or did

democracy government by the people

demographic segmentation advertisers' appeal to audiences composed of varying personal and social characteristics such as race, gender, and economic level

demonstrative advertising consumer advertising touting the functional benefits of a product or service

deplatforming denying a digital destination an audience by eradicating access to it

deregulation relaxation of ownership and other rules for radio and television

desensitization the idea that viewers become more accepting of real-world violence because of its constant presence in television fare

development concept of media systems; government and media work in partnership to ensure that media assist in the planned, beneficial development of the country

digital audio radio service (DARS) direct home or automobile delivery of audio by satellite

digital cable television delivery of digital video images and other information to subscribers' homes

digital computer a computer that processes data reduced to a binary code

digital divide the lack of technological access among people of color, people who are poor or disabled, and those in rural communities

digital natives people who have never known a world without the Internet

digital recording recording based on conversion of sound into 1s and 0s logged in millisecond intervals in a computerized translation process

digital rights management (DRM) protection of digitally distributed intellectual property

digital video disc (DVD) digital recording and playback player and disc, fastest-growing consumer electronic product in history

digital video recorder (DVR) video recording device attached to a television, which gives viewers significant control over content

dime novels inexpensive late 19th- and early 20th-century books that concentrated on frontier and adventure stories; sometimes called **pulp novels**

disinformation falsehoods designed to achieve a political goal

disinhibitory effects in social cognitive theory, seeing a model rewarded for prohibited or threatening behavior increases the likelihood that the observer will perform that behavior

disintermediation eliminating gatekeepers between artists and audiences

disruptive transition radical change in an industry brought about by the introduction of some new technology or product

dissonance theory argues that people, when confronted by new information, experience a kind of mental discomfort, a dissonance; as a result, they consciously and subconsciously work to limit or reduce that discomfort through the selective processes

diurnals daily accounts of local news printed in 1620s England; forerunners of our daily newspaper

domain name on the World Wide Web, an identifying name, rather than a site's formal URL, that gives some indication of the nature of a site's content or owner

dominant culture the culture that seems to hold sway with the large majority of people; that which is normative; also called **mainstream culture**

double feature two films on the same bill

dual-factor model of social media use social media use is motivated by the need for acceptance and the need to belong

duopoly single ownership and management of multiple radio stations in one market

dynamic pricing selling movie seats at varying prices depending on demand and availability

e-book a book that is downloaded in electronic form from the Internet to a computer or handheld device

e-commerce the buying of products and services online

e-publishing the publication and distribution of books initially or exclusively in a digital format

e-reader digital book having the appearance of a traditional book but with content that is digitally stored and accessed

e-replica edition an online version of a newspaper that mimics its print version in look and format

e-sports streamed online game competition

early window the idea that media give children a window on the world before they have the critical and intellectual ability to judge what they see

economies of scale concept that relative cost declines as the size of the endeavor grows

editorial policy newspapers' and magazines' positions on certain specific issues

electronic colonialism theory belief that cultural products from one country will overwhelm those of another

electronic sell-through (EST) buying of digital download movies

embedding war correspondents exchanging control of their output for access to the front

encoding transforming ideas into an understandable sign/symbol system

encryption electronic coding or masking of information on the Web that can be deciphered only by a recipient with the decrypting key

engagement (in advertising) psychological and behavioral measure of ad effectiveness designed to replace CPM

engagement (in magazines) depth of the relationship between readers and the magazine advertising they see

engagement reporting calling on citizens to solicit tips, find sources, and identify under-reported stories

enterprise reporting stories written not from press releases, but those journalists discover on their own

entertainment overcoming resistance model idea that there are features of entertainment media that facilitate involvement with characters and/or narrative involvement that lead to story-consistent attitudes and behaviors by overcoming various forms of resistance to health advice

environmental incentives in social cognitive theory, the notion that real-world incentives can lead observers to ignore negative vicarious reinforcement

ethics rules of behavior or moral principles that guide actions in given situations

ethnic press papers, often in a foreign language, aimed at minority, immigrant, and non-English readers

exergame video game designed to encourage beneficial physical activity

exogenous stations clandestine broadcast operations functioning from outside the regions to which they transmit

expanded basic cable in cable television, a second, somewhat more expensive level of subscription

experiential marketing melding of brands and experiences

extended real-life hypothesis predicts that we use social media to communicate our actual identities

external service in international broadcasting, a service designed by one country to counter enemy propaganda and disseminate information about itself

Facebook depression depression resulting from intensity of social media activity

Facebook envy resentfulness of others' social media expressions of happiness

facial recognition technology technology capable of identifying or verifying the identity of an individual from a digital image or video source

factory studios the first film production companies

fair use in copyright law, instances in which material may be used without permission or payment

Fairness Doctrine requires broadcasters to cover issues of public importance and to be fair in that coverage; abolished in 1987

fake news intentionally and verifiably false Internet news stories designed to be spread and to deceive

feature syndicates clearinghouses for the work of columnists, cartoonists, and other creative individuals, providing their work to newspapers and other media outlets

feedback the response to a given communication

fiber optics signals carried by light beams over glass fibers

finstas second ("f" for fake) Instagram accounts offering less-curated, more natural versions of self to a trustworthy circle of friends

First Amendment "Congress shall make no law respecting an establishment of religion, or prohibiting the free exercise thereof; or abridging the freedom of speech, or of the press; or the right of the people peacefully to assemble, and to petition the Government for a redress of grievances."

first-person perspective game video game in which all action is through the eyes of the player

first-run syndication original programming produced specifically for the syndicated television market

fixed-fee arrangement the arrangement whereby a PR firm performs a specific set of services for a client for a specific and prearranged fee

flack a derogatory name sometimes applied to public relations professionals

flog fake blog; typically sponsored by a company to anonymously boost itself or attack a competitor

focus groups small groups of people who are interviewed, typically to provide advertising or public relations professionals with detailed information

forced exposure ad research technique used primarily for television commercials, requiring advertisers to bring consumers to a theater or other facility where they see a television program, complete with the new ads

format a radio station's particular sound or programming content

franchise films movies produced with full intention of producing several sequels

Frankfurt School media theory, centered in neo-Marxism, that valued serious art, viewing its consumption as a means to elevate all people toward a better life; typical media fare was seen as pacifying ordinary people while repressing them

freemium games video games in which consuming advertising or even spending actual cash allows players to progress in their play

frequency capping limiting the number of times an online user sees the same commercial message in a given period of time

gamification use of video-game skills and conventions to solve real-world problems

genre a form of media content with a standardized, distinctive style and conventions

ghost papers once-prospering newspapers cut to bare bones in an effort to maximize profits

Global Television Audience Metering (GTAM) meter video ratings technology that will actively and passively measure viewing across all platforms

global village Marshall McLuhan's theory that new communication technologies permit people to become increasingly involved in one another's lives

globalization ownership of media companies by multinational corporations

grand theory a theory designed to describe and explain all aspects of a given phenomenon

green light process the process of deciding to make a movie

greenwashing public relations practice of countering the public relations efforts aimed at clients by environmentalists

hard news news stories that help readers make intelligent decisions and keep up with important issues

hostile media effect the idea that people see media coverage of important topics of interest as less sympathetic to their position, more sympathetic to the opposing position, and generally hostile to their point of view regardless of the quality of the coverage

hosts computers linking individual personal computer users to the Internet

hybridization hypothesis idea that globalization inevitably and beneficially entails the existence of traces of other cultures in every culture

hyper-casual games easy-to-play, typically free mobile games offering minimalistic user interfaces

hypercommercialism increasing the amount of advertising and mixing commercial and noncommercial media content

hyperlocal free weeklies no-cost news and information outlets serving discrete locales within larger cities and towns

hypodermic needle theory idea that media are a dangerous drug that can directly enter a person's system

iconoscope tube first practical television camera tube, developed in 1923

idealized virtual identity hypothesis social media users tend to show idealized characteristics not reflective of who they really are

identification in social cognitive theory, a special form of imitation by which observers do not exactly copy what they have seen but make a more generalized but related response

illiteracy the inability to read or write

imitation in social cognitive theory, the direct replication of an observed behavior

importation of distant signals delivery of distant television signals by cable television for the purpose of improving reception

impressions the number of times an online ad is seen

imprint book publishing company

in-band-on-channel (IBOC) digital radio technology that uses digital compression to "shrink" digital and analog signals, allowing both to occupy the same frequency

indecency in broadcasting, language or material that depicts sexual or excretory activities in a way offensive to contemporary community standards

indigenous stations clandestine broadcast operations functioning from inside the regions to which they transmit

inferential feedback in the mass communication process, feedback is typically indirect rather than direct; that is, it is inferential

informed consent journalists explaining to a subject's why her or his image is being used and what the potential consequences might be

inhibitory effects in social cognitive theory, seeing a model punished for a behavior reduces the likelihood that the observer will perform that behavior

integrated audience reach total numbers of the print edition of a newspaper plus unduplicated Web readers

integrated marketing communications (IMC) combining public relations, marketing, advertising, and promotion into a seamless communication campaign

Internet a global network of interconnected computers that communicate freely and share and exchange information

Internet of Things (IoT) everyday objects having built-in network connectivity, allowing them to send and receive data

interpersonal communication communication between two or a few people

IP-based movie movies based on already existing intellectual property (IP), such as stories, products, imaginary worlds, or characters that have a built-in fan base

island in children's television commercials, the product is shown simply, in actual size against a neutral background

ISP (Internet service provider) company that offers Internet connections at monthly rates depending on the kind and amount of access needed

kinescope improved picture tube developed by Zworykin for RCA

kinetograph William Dickson's early motion picture camera

kinetoscope peep show devices for the exhibition of kinetographs

LAN (local area network) network connecting two or more computers, usually within the same building

LCD (liquid crystal display) display surface in which electric currents of varying voltage are passed through liquid crystal, altering the passage of light through that crystal

lead generation directing users who've expressed an interest into a brand's sales pipeline

LED (light-emitting diode) light-emitting semiconductor manipulated under a display screen

libel the false and malicious publication of material that damages a person's reputation (typically applied to print media)

libertarianism philosophy of the press asserting that good and rational people can tell right from wrong if presented with full and free access to information; therefore, censorship is unnecessary

limited effects theory media's influence is limited by people's individual differences, social categories, and personal relationships

linotype technology that allowed the mechanical rather than manual setting of print type

liquid barretter first audio device permitting the reception of wireless voices; developed by Fessenden

literacy the ability to effectively and efficiently comprehend and use written symbols

lobbying in public relations, directly interacting with elected officials or government regulators and agents

location-based mobile advertising technology allowing marketers to send targeted ads to people where they are in the moment

logic of connected action large-scale social actions such as protests and demonstrations are best organized through social media as they allow self-motivation for involvement and ease of coordination

long-tail viewing true measure of a TV program's viewership over time, across multiple platforms, and on-demand

loot boxes in-game treasure chests that can be opened through gameplay or by paying real money, giving players access to some unnamed treasure inside

low power FM (LPFM) 10- to 100-watt nonprofit community radio stations with a reach of only a few miles

macro-level effects media's widescale social and cultural impact

magalogue a designer catalog produced to look like a consumer magazine

magic bullet theory the idea from mass society theory that media are a powerful "killing force" that directly penetrates a person's system

mainframe computer a large central computer to which users are connected by terminals

mainstream culture the culture that seems to hold sway with the large majority of people; that which is normative; also called **mainstream culture**

mainstreaming in cultivation analysis, television's ability to move people toward a common understanding of how things are

manosphere online home to men who harbor and express ill will toward women

mass communication the process of creating shared meaning between the mass media and their audiences

mass communication theories explanations and predictions of social phenomena relating mass communication to various aspects of our personal and cultural lives or social systems

mass medium (pl. mass media) a medium that carries messages to a large number of people

mass society theory the idea that media are corrupting influences; they undermine the social order, and "average" people are defenseless against their influence

massively multiplayer online roleplaying games (MMORPGs) interactive online games where characters and actions are controlled by other players, not the computer; also called **virtual worlds games**

mathematical songwriting songs written specifically to be commercial hits

meaning-making perspective idea that active audience members use media content to create meaning, and meaningful experiences, for themselves

media literacy the ability to effectively and efficiently comprehend and utilize mass communication

media logic Social institutions and the people in them must respond to the demands of the medium in which they wish to express themselves

media multitasking simultaneously consuming many different kinds of media

mediated intergroup contact hypothesis seeing media characters like themselves interacting with characters from different groups can move viewers to become more open toward members of those groups

mediatization theory societal structures and their routine social practices are continually altered to accommodate media

medium (pl. media) vehicle by which messages are conveyed

meme an online idea or image that is repeatedly copied, manipulated, and shared

meme wars the use of images, slogans, and video for political purposes, typically employing disinformation and half-truths

mercenary science science-for-hire, contracted out by corporations to prove that their harmful products aren't harmful by giving them the quantitative cover of seemingly objective scientific research

metaethics a culture's fundamental values

micro-level effects effects of media on individuals

microcinema filmmaking using digital video cameras and desktop digital editing programs

microcomputer a very small computer that uses a microprocessor to handle information (also called a **personal computer** or **PC**)

micropayments small payments for individual stories provided by an aggregator

microwave relay audio and video transmitting system in which super-high-frequency signals are sent from land-based point to land-based point

middle-range theories ideas that explain or predict only limited aspects of the mass communication process

minicomputer a relatively large central computer to which users are connected by terminals; not as large as a mainframe computer

misinformation mere falsehoods

modeling in social cognitive theory, learning through imitation and identification

montage tying together two separate but related shots in such a way that they take on a new, unified meaning

moral agent in an ethical dilemma, the person making the decision

movement journalism journalism that meets the needs of communities directly affected by injustice

movie palaces elaborately decorated, opulent, architecturally stunning theaters

MP3 file compression software that permits streaming of digital audio and video data

muckraking a form of crusading journalism that primarily used magazines to agitate for change

MUD (multiuser dimension) online text-based interactive game

multimedia advanced sound and image capabilities for microcomputers

multiple points of access ability of a media-literate consumer to access or approach media content from a variety of personally satisfying directions

multiple system operator (MSO) a company owning several different cable television operations

municipal broadband publically provided low-cost, high-speed Internet access

music licensing company an organization that collects fees based on recorded music users' gross receipts and distributes the money to songwriters and artists

narrative persuasion theory idea that being absorbed into a narrative is one way that media stories can influence people's real-world beliefs and behaviors

narrowcasting aiming broadcast programming at smaller, more demographically homogeneous audiences

near-field communication (NFC) chip tag embedded in a magazine page that connects readers to advertisers' digital content

neo-Marxist theory the theory that people are oppressed by those who control the culture, the superstructure, as opposed to the base

network neutrality granting equal carriage over phone and cable lines to all websites

networks centralized production, distribution, decision-making organizations that link affiliates for the purpose of delivering their audiences to advertisers

neuromarketing research biometric measures (brain waves, facial expressions, eye tracking, sweating, and heart rate monitoring) used in advertising research

news desert communities starved for news vital to their existences due to a lack of journalistic resources

news production research the study of how economic and other influences on the way news is produced distort and bias news coverage toward those in power

newsbook early weekly British publication that carried ads

newshole the amount of space in a newspaper given to news

newspaper chains businesses that own two or more newspapers

niche marketing aiming media content or consumer products at smaller, more demographically homogeneous audiences

nickelodeons the first movie houses; admission was one nickel

Nipkow disc first workable device for generating electrical signals suitable for the transmission of a scene

noise anything that interferes with successful communication

nonlinear TV watching television on our own schedules, not the programmer's

normative ethics generalized theories, rules, and principles of ethical or moral behavior

normative theory an idea that explains how media should ideally operate in a given system of social values

O&O a broadcasting station that is owned and operated by a network

obscenity unprotected expression determined by (1) whether the average person, applying contemporary community standards, would find that the work, taken as a whole, appeals to the prurient interest; (2) whether the work depicts or describes, in a patently offensive way, sexual conduct specifically defined by the applicable state law; and (3) whether the work, taken as a whole, lacks serious literary, artistic, political, or scientific value

observational learning in social cognitive theory, observers can acquire (learn) new behaviors simply by seeing those behaviors performed

off-network broadcast industry term for syndicated content that originally aired on a network

offset lithography late 19th-century advance making possible printing from photographic plates rather than from metal casts

oligopoly a media system whose operation is dominated by a few large companies

ombudsperson internal arbiter of performance for media organizations

operating policy standards for everyday operations for newspapers and magazines

operating system the software that tells the computer how to work

opinion followers people who receive opinion leaders' interpretations of media content; from **two-step flow theory**

opinion leaders people who initially consume media content, interpret it in light of their own values and beliefs, and then pass it on to opinion followers; from **two-step flow theory**

opt-in consumers giving permission to companies to sell personal data

opt-out consumers requesting that companies do not sell personal data

over-the-top (OTT) television delivery without the involvement of an MSO

P2P peer-to-peer software that permits direct Internet-based communication or collaboration between two or more personal computers while bypassing centralized servers

parasocial contact hypothesis "meeting" people different from themselves in the media increases viewers' understanding of those people and improves their attitudes toward them

parity products products generally perceived as alike by consumers no matter who makes them

pass-along readership measurement of publication readers who neither subscribe nor buy single copies but who borrow a copy or read one in a doctor's office or library

payola payment made by recording companies to DJs to air their records

paywall making online content available only to those visitors willing to pay

peak TV a time of significant viewer choice and high-quality video content

penny press newspapers in the 1830s selling for one penny

performance-based advertising Web advertising where the site is paid only when the consumer takes some specific action

permission marketing advertising that the consumer actively accepts

persistence of vision images our eyes gather are retained by our brains for about 1/24 of a second, producing the appearance of constant motion

personal computer (PC) see **microcomputer**

pilot a sample episode of a proposed television program

piracy the illegal recording and sale of copyrighted material

pirate broadcasters unlicensed or otherwise illegally operated broadcast stations

pixel the smallest picture element in an electronic imaging system such as a television or computer screen

platform agnostic having no preference where media content is accessed

platform agnostic publishing digital and hard-copy books available for any and all reading devices

platform rollout opening a movie on only a few screens in the hope that favorable reviews and word-of-mouth publicity will boost interest

playlist predetermined sequence of selected records to be played by a disc jockey

podcasting streaming or downloading of audio files recorded and stored on distant servers

policy book delineates standards of operation for local broadcasters

pornography expression calculated solely to supply sexual excitement

premium cable cable television channels offered to viewers for a fee above the cost of their basic subscription

print on demand (POD) publishing method whereby publishers store books digitally for instant printing, binding, and delivery once ordered

prior restraint power of the government to *prevent* publication or broadcast of expression

product placement the integration, for a fee, of specific branded products into media content

product positioning the practice in advertising of assigning meaning to a product based on who buys the product rather than on the product itself

production values media content's internal language and grammar; its style and quality

programmatic ad fraud technological simulation of online activity designed to create billable ad impressions

programmatic buying automated, data-driven buying of online advertising

prosumer a proactive consumer

protocols common communication rules and languages for computers linked to the Internet

pseudo-event event that has no real informational or issue meaning; it exists merely to attract media attention

psychographic segmentation advertisers' appeal to consumer groups of varying lifestyles, attitudes, values, and behavior patterns

public in public relations, any group of people with a stake in an organization, issue, or idea

public domain in copyright law, the use of material without permission once the copyright expires

public service remit limits on advertising and other public service requirements imposed on Britain's commercial broadcasters in exchange for the right to broadcast

puffery the little lie or exaggeration that makes advertising more entertaining than it might otherwise be

pulp novels inexpensive late 19th- and early 20th-century books that concentrated on frontier and adventure stories; sometimes called **dime novels**

quick response (QR) code small barcode with squares that appear on many media surfaces that direct mobile device users to a specific website

radio frequency identification (RFID) chip grain-of-sand-size microchip and antenna embedded in consumer products that transmit a radio signal

rating percentage of a market's total population that is reached by a piece of broadcast programming

ray tracing in video game imaging, advanced method of rendering light and shadows to render scenes more life-like

readers' representative media outlet employee who regularly responds to outside criticism

recall testing ad research technique in which consumers are asked to identify which ads are most easily remembered

recognition tests ad research technique in which people who have seen a given publication are asked whether they remember seeing a given ad

reinforcement theory Joseph Klapper's idea that if media have any impact at all, it is in the direction of reinforcement

remainders unsold copies of books returned to the publisher by bookstores to be sold at great discount

retainer in advertising, an agreed-upon amount of money a client pays an ad agency for a specific series of services

retransmission fee money a local cable operation pays to a broadcast station to carry its signal

return on investment (ROI) an accountability-based measure of advertising success

reverse compensation fee paid by a local broadcast station for the right to be a network's affiliate

revolutionary concept normative theory describing a system where media are used in the service of revolution

rich media sophisticated, interactive Web advertising, usually employing sound and video

ritual perspective the view of media as central to the representation of shared beliefs and culture

RSS (really simple syndication) aggregators allowing Web users to create their own content assembled from the Internet's limitless supply of material

search engines Web-search software providing on-screen menus

search marketing advertising sold next to or in search results produced by users' keyword searches

second-order agenda setting idea that media set the public's agenda at a second level or order—the attribute level ("how to think about it")

secondary service a radio station's second, or nonprimary, format

selective attention the idea that people expose themselves to or attend to those messages that are consistent with their preexisting attitudes and beliefs; also called **selective exposure**

selective exposure the idea that people expose themselves to or attend to those messages that are consistent with their preexisting attitudes and beliefs; also called **selective attention**

selective perception the idea that people interpret messages in a manner consistent with their preexisting attitudes and beliefs

selective processes people expose themselves to, remember best and longest, and reinterpret messages that are consistent with their preexisting attitudes and beliefs

selective retention assumes that people remember best and longest those messages that are consistent with their existing attitudes and beliefs

self-righting principle the free flow or trade of ideas, even bad or uncomfortable ones, will inevitably produce the truth because a rational and good public will correct, or right, any errors

share the percentage of people listening to radio or of homes using television tuned in to a given piece of programming

shield laws legislation that expressly protects reporters' rights to maintain sources' confidentiality in courts of law

shopbills attractive, artful business cards used by early British tradespeople to promote themselves

shopfiction the embedding of links into traditional and e-books taking readers directly to paid sponsors' websites

shortwave radio radio signals transmitted at low frequencies that can travel great distances by skipping off the ionosphere

signs in social construction of reality, things that have subjective meaning

siquis pinup want ads common in Europe before and in early days of newspapers

skip ability of radio waves to reflect off the ionosphere

sky waves radio waves that are skipped off the ionosphere

slacktivism derogatory name of online activism

slander oral or spoken defamation of a person's character (typically applied to broadcasting)

social cognitive theory idea that people learn through observation

social construction of reality theory explains how cultures construct and maintain their realities using signs and symbols; argues that people learn to behave in their social world through interaction with it

social infrastructure physical spaces that shape the way people interact

social networking sites (SNSs) websites that function as online communities of users

social responsibility theory normative theory asserting that media must remain free of government control but, in exchange, must serve the public

soft news sensational stories that do not serve the democratic function of journalism

spectrum scarcity broadcast spectrum space is limited, so not everyone who wants to broadcast can; those who are granted licenses must accept regulation

spin in PR, outright lying to hide what really happened

splinternet an Internet fragmented and divided along national lines

split runs special versions of a given issue of a magazine in which editorial content and ads vary according to some specific demographic or regional grouping

sponsored content content that matches the form and function of an editorial but is, in fact, paid for by an advertiser

spot commercial sales in broadcasting, selling individual advertising spots on a given program to a wide variety of advertisers

spyware identifying code placed on a computer by a website without permission or notification

Standards and Practices Department the internal content review operation of a television network

stereotyping application of a standardized image or conception applied to members of certain groups, usually based on limited information

sticky an attribute of a website; indicates its ability to hold the attention of a user

stimulation model of media violence; viewing mediated violence can increase the likelihood of subsequent aggressive behavior

stream ripping saving streaming media to a file on a personal device to be accessed locally

streaming the simultaneous downloading and accessing (playing) of digital audio or video data

streaming ad insertion insertion into streamed content of individually tailored commercials based on user data

stripping broadcasting a syndicated television show at the same time five nights a week

subscription TV early experiments with over-the-air pay television

subsidiary rights the sale of a book, its contents, even its characters to outside interests, such as filmmakers

surrogate service in international broadcasting, an operation established by one country to substitute for another's own domestic service

surveillance capitalism an economic system dependent on the buying and selling of people's personal data, the capture and production of which relies on mass surveillance of the Internet

symbolic interaction the idea that people give meaning to symbols, and then those symbols control people's behavior in their presence

symbols in social construction of reality, things that have objective meaning

syndication sale of radio or television content to stations on a market-by-market basis

synergy the use by media conglomerates of as many channels of delivery as possible for similar content

targeting aiming media content or consumer products at smaller, more specific audiences

taste publics groups of people or audiences bound by little more than their interest in a given form of media content

technological determinism the idea that machines and their development drive economic and cultural change

technology gap the widening disparity between communication technology haves and have-nots

tentpole an expensive blockbuster around which a studio plans its other releases

terminals user workstations that are connected to larger centralized computers

terrestrial digital radio land-based digital radio relying on digital compression technology to simultaneously transmit analog and one or more digital signals using existing spectrum space

theatrical films movies produced primarily for initial exhibition on theater screens

theatrical window the time from when a movie is first released to theaters until it can be sold directly to retailers and the public

third-party publishers companies that create video games for existing systems

third-person effect the common attitude that others are influenced by media messages, but we are not

360 marketing see **ambient advertising**

tie-in novels books based on popular television shows and movies

tiers groupings of channels made available by a cable or satellite provider to subscribers at varying prices

time-shifting taping a show on a VCR for later viewing

total viewer impressions TV audience measurement using the actual number of people watching rather than a percentage of possible viewers who tune in

toxic content racist, misogynistic, threatening, or otherwise hateful online content

trade books hardcover or softcover book including fiction and most nonfiction and cookbooks, biographies, art books, coffee-table books, and how-to books

traffic cop analogy in broadcast regulation, the idea that the FCC, as a traffic cop, has the right to control not only the flow of broadcast traffic but its composition as well

transmissional perspective the view of media as senders of information for the purpose of control

transparentists PR professionals calling for full disclosure of their practices—transparency

trustee model in broadcast regulation, the idea that broadcasters serve as the public's trustees or fiduciaries

truth decay the diminishing role of facts and analysis in public life

two-step flow theory the idea that media's influence on people's behavior is limited by those who initially consume media content, interpret it in light of their own values and beliefs, and then pass it on to others who have less frequent contact with media

typification schemes in social construction of reality, collections of meanings people have assigned to some phenomenon or situation

unique selling proposition (USP) the aspect of an advertised product that sets it apart from other brands in the same product category

URL (uniform resource locator) the designation of each file or directory on the host computer connected to the Internet

user-generated content content created by users of a brand and made available for commercial or other promotional use

uses and gratifications approach the idea that media don't do things *to* people; people do things *with* media

VALS advertisers' psychographic segmentation strategy that classifies consumers according to values and lifestyles

value-compensation program ad agency–brand agreement that payment of the agency's fees is predicated on meeting preestablished goals

vast wasteland expression coined by FCC chair Newton Minow in 1961 to describe television content

vertical integration a system in which studios produced their own films, distributed them through their own outlets, and exhibited them in their own theaters

vicarious reinforcement in social cognitive theory, the observation of reinforcement operates in the same manner as actual reinforcement

video game a game involving action taking place interactively on-screen

video news release (VNR) preproduced report about a client or its product that is distributed free of charge to television stations

video-on-demand (VOD) service allowing television viewers to access pay-per-view movies and other content that can be watched whenever they want

viral marketing PR strategy that relies on targeting specific Internet users with a given communication and relying on them to spread the word

virtual multichannel video programming distributors (VMVPD) services that aggregate live and on-demand television and deliver it over the Internet

virtual reality games through the use of a headset, games that generate an imaginary environment, simulating players' physical presence there

virtual worlds games see **massively multiplayer online roleplaying games**

WAN (wide area network) network that connects several LANs in different locations

Web radio the delivery of "radio" over the Internet directly to individual listeners

webisode Web-only television show

Western concept of media systems; normative theory that combines libertarianism's freedom with social responsibility's demand for public service and, where necessary, regulation

Wi-Fi wireless Internet

willing suspension of disbelief audience practice of willingly accepting the content before them as real

wire services news-gathering organizations that provide content to members

World Wide Web a tool that serves as a means of accessing files on computers connected via the Internet

yellow journalism early 20th-century journalism emphasizing sensational sex, crime, and disaster news

zero-TV homes homes that have sets but receive neither over-the-air nor cable/satellite television

zipping fast-forwarding through taped commercials on a VCR

zonecasting technology allowing radio stations to deliver different commercials to specific neighborhoods

zoned editions suburban or regional versions of metropolitan newspapers

zoopraxiscope early machine for projecting slides onto a distant surface

Index

Boldfaced locators signify definitions in the text of glossary terms. *Italic* locators signify illustrations.